Communication Yearbook 34

Communication Yearbook 34

**Edited by
Charles T. Salmon**

Published Annually for the
International Communication Association

Routledge
Taylor & Francis Group

NEW YORK AND LONDON

First published 2010
by Routledge
270 Madison Avenue, New York, NY 10016

Simultaneously published in the UK
by Routledge
2 Park Square, Milton Park, Abingdon, Oxon OX14 4RN

Routledge is an imprint of the Taylor & Francis Group, an informa business

Typeset in Times by EvS Communication Networx, Inc.
Printed and bound in the United States of America on acid-free paper by Sheridan Books, Inc

ISSN: 0147-4642

ISBN10: 0-415-87857-8 (hbk)
ISBN10: 0-203-84627-3 (ebk)
ISBN13: 978-0-415-87857-9 (hbk)
ISBN13: 978-0-203-84627-8 (ebk)

Contents

The International Communication Association

The International Communication Association (ICA) was formed in 1950, bringing together academics and other professionals whose interests focus on human communication. The Association maintains an active membership of more than 4,000 individuals, of whom some two-thirds teach and conduct research in colleges, universities, and schools around the world. Other members are in government, law, medicine, and other professions. The wide professional and geographic distribution of the membership provides the basic strength of the ICA. The Association serves as a meeting ground for sharing research and useful dialogue about communication interests.

Through its divisions and interest groups, publications, annual conferences, and relations with other associations around the world, ICA promotes the systemic study of communication theories, processes, and skills. In addition to *Communication Yearbook*, ICA publishes the *Journal of Communication*, *Human Communication Research*, *Communication Theory*, *Journal of Computer-Mediated Communication*, *Communication, Culture & Critique*, *A Guide to Publishing in Scholarly Communication Journals*, and the *ICA Newsletter*.

For additional information about the ICA and its activities, visit online at www.icahdq.org or contact Michael L. Haley, Executive Director, International Communication Association, 1500 21st Ave. NW, Washington, DC 20036 USA; phone (202) 202-955-1444; fax 202-955-1448; email ica@icahdq.org.

Editors of the *Communication Yearbook* series:

INTERNATIONAL COMMUNICATION ASSOCIATION
EXECUTIVE COMMITTEE

President and Chair
Barbie Zelizer
University of Pennsylvania

Executive Director
Michael L. Haley (ex-officio)
ICA Headquarters

President-Elect
Francois Cooren
University of Montreal

Past President
Sonia Livingstone
London School of Economics

Immediate Past President
Patrice M. Buzzanell
Purdue University

Finance Chair
Ronald E. Rice
University of California, Santa Barbara

BOARD OF DIRECTORS

Members-at-Large

Aldo Vasquez Rios, *University de San Martin Porres, Peru*

Eun-Ju Lee, *Seoul National University*

Rohan Samarajiva, *LIRNEasia*

Gianpetro Mazzoleni, *University of Milan*

Juliet Roper, *University of Waikato*

Student Members

Michele Khoo, *Nanyang Technology University*

Malte Hinrichsen, *University of Amsterdam*

DIVISION CHAIRS

Communication & Technology
S. Shyam Sundar, *Pennsylvania State University*

Ethnicity and Race in Communication
Myria Georgiou, *Leeds University*

Communication Law & Policy
Stephen McDowell, *Florida State University*

Feminist Scholarship
Diana Rios, *University of Connecticut*

Global Communication and Social Change
Robert Huesca, *Trinity University*

Health Communication
Dave Buller, *Klein Buendel*

Information Systems
Robert F. Potter, *Indiana University*

Instructional & Developmental Communication
Kristen Harrison, *University of Illinois*

Intercultural Communication
Ling Chen, *Hong Kong Baptist University*

Interpersonal Communication
Walid Afifi, *University of California, Santa Barbara*

Journalism Studies
Maria Elizabeth Grabe, *Indiana University*

Language & Social Interaction
Richard Buttny, *Syracuse University*

Mass Communication
David R. Ewoldsen, *Ohio State University*

Organizational Communication
Dennis Mumby, *University of North Carolina*

Philosophy of Communication
Nick Couldry, *Goldsmiths College, London University*

Political Communication
Kevin Barnhurst, *University of Illinois, Chicago*

Popular Communication
Cornel Sandvoss, *University of Surrey*

Public Relations
Craig Carroll, *University of North Carolina*

Visual Communication
Luc Pauwels, *University of Antwerp*

SPECIAL INTEREST GROUP CHAIRS

Children, Adolescents and the Media
J. Alison Bryant, *Smartypants.com*

Communication History
David Park, *Lake Forest College*

Game Studies
John Sherry, *Michigan State University*

Gay, Lesbian, Bisexual, & Transgender Studies
Lynn Comella, *University of Nevada - Las Vegas*
Vincent Doyle, *IE University*

Intergroup Communication
Margaret J. Pitt, *Old Dominion University*

Reviewers

Editor's Introduction

Charles T. Salmon

To prepare for this Editor's Introduction, I read a wide assortment of prefaces, forewords, and introductions published throughout history, and considered a variety of starting points from which to launch this volume. By far, the most impressive yet daunting essay that I encountered was Dr. Samuel Johnson's preface to the *Dictionary of the English Language*, published in 1755. The inspiration that I gleaned from his ruminations was that my role as editor was not unlike that of a lexicographer, i.e., to "...remove rubbish and clear obstructions from the paths through which Learning and Genius press forward to conquest and glory..." (Project Gutenberg, 2004). Fortunately, it is a role with which I have had some considerable familiarity as a former academic dean.

Dr. Johnson's preface totaled more than 9,600 words, making it longer than some of the chapters in this volume. It is perhaps significant to note that the entire number of words that Dr. Johnson catalogued in his dictionary of the English language was 42,773.

Soon after visiting this impressive tome, by sheer coincidence I happened to encounter The Global Language Monitor's (2009) bold pronouncement that the English language gained its one-millionth word on June 10, 2009, at 10:22 a.m. GMT. Presumably, individuals frustrated by the inadequacy and limitations of a 999,999-word language at 10:21 a.m. became glib one minute later when The Global Language Monitor officially sanctioned the word "web 2.0" for use in scholarly conversations and Scrabble games throughout the world.

To the extent that the Global Language Monitor's claim has merit (which certainly is not beyond dispute),[1] this milestone of 1,000,000 words can be put in context by noting that it implies that the English language has grown by 957,227 words in 254 years, an average rate of a little more than 10 new words per day, since the work of Dr. Johnson in 1755. Yet this arithmetic average inadequately reflects the dynamic growth of the language, for it fails to account for the greater rate of increase in neologisms in contemporary society than in the 1700s. Twentieth and twenty-first century advances in science, technology, and medicine have created a seemingly unquenchable thirst for new jargon and specialized terminology. As well, the language has expanded through the absorption and integration of literally thousands of words from other languages. One veteran observer of dictionaries (Kister, 1992) estimates that, in the modern era, the English language actually has been growing at a rate of approximately 68 new words per day. Meanwhile, to put this seemingly robust figure in context, the number of new Internet domains being registered is growing at the staggering rate of more than 20,000 per day (Domaintools. com, 2009).[2]

By any metric, the building blocks and raw materials of communication are growing at an almost unmanageable pace, while the tools and applications of communication technologies are expanding at an almost incomprehensible rate. It is in this context that it is fitting to revisit another introductory essay that I consulted when preparing these remarks. Thirty-three years ago, the editor of *Communication Yearbook 1*, Brent Ruben (1977, pp. 3–4), introduced the rationale and purpose of this new series by observing that:

> Communication at present seems quite clearly in the major growth stage.... At a stage in the evolution of the field where diversification of topic and refinement of methodology are unparalleled, the need for overview, synthesis, and integration—for defining what it is that is common and generic to the field—seems especially great.

What was true in 1977, when the field of communication was experiencing growth at an arithmetic, or perhaps even geometric rate of change, is truer still in 2010 when our field is experiencing change at a hyperbolic rate. What may have appeared to be increasingly diaphanous boundaries of our field 33 years ago are far more porous and permeable in a digital era in which new communication technologies are now integral to every academic discipline on a typical university campus. A single volume of *Communication Yearbook* can no longer be expected to define what is common and generic to the field because the terrain simply has become too expansive. Nevertheless, it can offer all-important synthesis and integration of research on a range of communication issues, help to define and articulate some of the important research questions and programs of the day, and provide a measure of the vitality of the field through its scope and breadth.

In my call for papers as a new editor of this series, I sought manuscripts that were interdisciplinary, international, and oriented to the future in their creative reconfiguration of the past. My goal was for this volume of *Communication Yearbook* to truly embody the global mission and ideals of its sponsoring organization, the International Communication Association. For assistance, I recruited distinguished scholars representing six continents to serve as associate editors, and asked them to encourage authors and reviewers in their respective regions to participate in this project. Next, I recruited editorial board members from 20 countries in an attempt to further internationalize all aspects of the editorial process. In order to provide context and perspective, I invited several outstanding scholars to serve as discussants and offer commentary on the chapters in this volume.

The chapters are organized in terms of three main themes. In the first, "Communication and the Social Sciences: Contributions to Interdisciplinary Theory," the authors review several emerging and established research programs camped at the borders of our discipline, characterized by a blend of exogenous and indigenous theory and research and fulsome communication applications. In the second section, "Communication Processes, Normative Ideals, and Political Realities," the authors examine various political processes and implicitly or explicitly grapple with the discrepancy between the ideal and the actual role of communication in facilitating the development of an enlightened and empowered citizenry. The third section, "Communication and Societies in Transition," reflects the sweeping breadth of our field through its focus on challenges of communication systems in societies concomitantly undergoing massive infrastructural changes.

Looking across sections, this volume contains chapters that deal with a number of urgent public policy issues of the day, all high priorities for NGOs and government agencies throughout the world: mobile communication, deception detection, terror management, nanotechnology, and the political aftermath of genocide. It includes chapters that address questions about emerging communication systems in the Arab world, media research in the post-Soviet era, and agenda building in African democracies. And it reveals the field's enduing interest in such fundamental questions as these: How do we explain the behavior of others? How can we nurture greater citizen participation in governance? Are political campaigns becoming more superficial than substantive?

All of these topics constitute socially and politically important directions for communication scholarship, and reflect a healthy and vibrant academic discipline capable of making significant contributions at the highest levels of decision making and of leading efforts to promote the betterment of society.

Acknowledgments

No project such as this can reach a successful conclusion without the dedication, inspiration, and cooperation of a capable team of individuals.

Associate Editors Cindy Gallois, Christina Holtz-Bacha, Guillermo Mastrini, Onuora Nwuneli, Joseph B. Walther, and Xinshu Zhao identified potential reviewers, offered advice, broke ties, provided excellent commentary, and worked to make this volume more international in its reach and emphasis.

The discussants, Cindy Gallois, Matthew Hornsey, Robin Mansell, and Barbie Zelizer, generously agreed to participate in this experiment to give *Communication Yearbook 34* a new scholarly dimension, strengthening its coherence with their insightful commentary in the process.

The 58 members of the editorial board and 44 ad hoc reviewers willingly donated their time for the benefit of authors, the International Communication Association, and our academic discipline.

The authors and co-authors accepted feedback with grace and uniformly exhibited great professionalism in meeting deadlines along the way.

My very capable editorial assistant, Laleah Fernandez, deserves special thanks for countless hours spent writing emails, processing manuscripts, updating records, discussing options, checking references, and providing support to authors and editors alike.

Joseph Walther, Rebecca Chory, Rajiv Rimal, Nurit Guttman, Ronald Rice, Dietram Scheufele, and Sandi Smith deserve special acknowledgement for volunteering extra time and effort to help authors work through various conundrums during the editorial process.

ICA stalwarts Michael Haley and Sam Luna, ICA Publications Committee Chair Krishnamurthy Sriramesh, and Taylor & Francis Senior Editor Linda Bathgate provided much-appreciated support throughout the editorial process.

And finally, my colleagues at Michigan State University, in the United States, and the Interdisciplinary Center—Herzliya, Israel, offered intellectual insights, useful suggestions, occasional comic relief, and unwavering collegiality throughout the entirety of this very rewarding editorial experience.

Notes

1. This claim was met with a great deal of skepticism, given different schools of thought regarding whether all protologisms, scientific jargon, slang, plural forms, and terms appropriated from other languages should count equally—or, in some case, at all—as words in the English language. Similar claims and debates occur about the number of words in languages other than English, as well.
2. This figure refers to the net increase in Internet domains registered within the past 24 hours, taking into account 94,591 new domains and 73,137 domains that expired during the same period of time.

References

Domaintools.com (2009). Retrieved November 17, 2009, from http://www.domain tools.com/internet-statistics/

Global Language Monitor. (2009). Retrieved November 8, 2009, from http://www.lan guagemonitor.com/

Johnson, S. (1755). Preface to a Dictionary of the English Language. *The Project Gutenberg EBook of Preface to a Dictionary of the English Language by Samuel Johnson*, April, 2004. Retrieved November 8, 2009, from http://www.gutenberg. org/dirs/etext04/pengl10.txt

Kister, K. (1992). Dictionaries defined. *Library Journal, 117*(11), 43–46.

Ruben, B. (1977). Overview. In B. Ruben (Ed.), *Communication yearbook 1* (pp. 3–7). New Brunswick, NJ: Transaction Press.

Part I

Communication and the Social Sciences

Contributions to Interdisciplinary Theory

CHAPTER CONTENTS

1 Young Adults' Perpetual Contact, Social Connectivity, and Social Control through the Internet and Mobile Phones

Ronald E. Rice

University of California, Santa Barbara

Ingunn Hagen

Norwegian University of Science and Technology (NTNU)

Each new communication medium provides different combinations and levels of way to facilitate and/or constrain social connections. These different patterns of connectivity in turn both represent and influence forms of social control. In particular, the Internet and mobile phones are fostering a sense of perpetual contact, the potential for pervasive, personal, and portable communication. This chapter considers how these aspects of perpetual contact moderate the influence of Internet and mobile phone usage on aspects of social connectivity (constructing identity, fostering and changing group and network relations, and displaying social relations—both membership and sharing) and in turn on aspects of social control (dependency, balancing self and group, managing coordination and multitasking, navigating family relations, blurring public and private space, and engaging privacy and surveillance). These issues are particularly fluid and salient to young users, so the chapter reviews relevant research from around the world on use of these new media by teenagers and young adults.

Introduction

New communication media, in both wired and email forms, are becoming embedded in young people's everyday lives at home, in their bedroom, at school, in malls, and in transit (Goggin, 2006; Ito et al., 2008; Livingstone & Bovill, 2001; Rideout, Roberts, & Foehr, 2005). Grounded in the concept of *perpetual contact*, this chapter synthesizes research on two general social implications—*social connectivity* and *social control*—of teenagers' and college students' use of two sets of new media: *Internet,* including email, Instant Messaging (IM), and chat; and *mobile phones,* including voice, Short Message Service (SMS, or texting), and wireless email.

Each new medium removes more and/or different constraints on communication among people. Depending on the physical recording material, writing (tablets, letters, books) allowed communication across space and time (i.e., into the future and the past), though not between people in different places at the same time. Electronic media, beginning with the telegraph and the telephone, then with the radio and television, removed more limits of space and audience (depending on signal power, and still connected people through specific, fixed-location terminals that were not technologically associated with any particular user) and time (except still required synchronous reading/listening/viewing). Transistor radios removed the limitation of location and introduced portable electronic media (enabling the user to take the medium with them, overcoming some constraints on location and contexts of use, including becoming more public as well as more private). With email, the constraints of synchronous interaction and fixed physical location were removed, but, before wireless laptops, still required users to go to a fixed terminal (a telephone with a specific number, an office desktop computer or Internet café, or data port) locations. Now, with Internet email, instant messaging (IM), and chat (and especially through wireless laptops), and mobile phone voice and Short Messaging System (SMS, or texting, and wireless Internet), many of the remaining space and time constraints, in different combinations, have been lifted. (Other constraints, such as addressability, number of communicators, cues, storage, etc., also change; see Rice, 1987.) More and more people are learning to live with very different social relations related to distance and time, largely due to these changes in communication media (Gyorgy, 2003).[1]

Thus communication is becoming more *pervasive, personal,* and *portable* (Ito, Okabe, & Matsuda, 2005). Katz and Aakhus (2002b, p. 315) call this potential state of being *perpetual contact.* Perpetual contact is the uninterrupted potential for synchronous or asynchronous communication with others at any place or time, through an increasing array of both divergent and convergent modes (text, audio, video) in personal communication technologies (Katz & Aakhus, 2002a). "Perpetual" is probably not the best term, with its connotation of extension into the infinite future, but is more justified in the colloquial sense of seemingly non-stop potentials for interaction or symbolic displays of connectedness, both in accessing and being accessed by others, whether wanted or not.

Similar concepts reflect this concern. Licoppe (2004) argues that people can now maintain relationships through a complex web of co-present and mediated communication, where the distinction between presence and absence of a salient other is blurred because he or she is always available through some means, creating a *connected presence.* People can manage multiple encounters at the same time and across time, from most any preferred or convenient place or time, and where simply maintaining contact, or even the easy potentiality of contact, is the primary message. Gergen (2008, p. 302) also refers to *continuous contact* or *floating worlds of communication,* whereby individuals are tethered to groups through mobile phones, *increasing* dense, localized, reciprocal, bounded social interaction, which may, however, lead to *decreased* involvement in the public sphere, avoiding larger social problems and issues. Being able to communicate with different others, while "cycling-through" different communication devices, fosters a "multiplicity of digital selves." This constant, rapid cycling through creates a sense of *continual co-presence* and even *continuous partial attention* (Turkle, 2008, pp. 122, 129). Brown and Cantor (2000) use the related term *perpetual linkage*.

Factors fostering perpetual contact are motivated by both *manifest* and *latent reasoning* or premises, about both *technology* and *social relationships*. Manifest reasoning about technology includes the qualities or attributes of mobile technologies (from more places in which to use the phone, to balancing access and control). Manifest reasoning about social relationships focuses on the qualities and processes of the user's local social context (ranging from social roles to network externalities). Latent reasoning about technology considers the qualities of technology uses affecting performance and personal relationships (such as sharing digital photos or maintaining an ongoing but distant conversation through texting), while latent reasoning about social relationships emphasizes social dimensions influencing adoption and usage (from communication networks to changes in cultural values) (Katz & Aakhus, 2002b, p. 311). Indeed, this four-fold typology provides many of the types of uses and consequences—both positive and negative—that we review in this chapter. Many other studies and reviews underscore many of these social implications (e.g., Katz & Rice, 2002; Katz, Rice, Acord, Dasgupta, & David, 2004). For example, a Delphi survey about possible social consequences of mobile phones (Glotz & Bertschi, 2005), involving 150 experts from 23 countries in two waves, identified a similar set of issues: overall, the most positive effects noted as of that time included connectivity and connectedness (15%), flexibility, efficiency, and convenience (15%), and security, safety, and emergency (14%), while the most negative effects identified were accessibility and the balance of work and life (25%), privacy, stress, and distraction (23%), and inappropriate usage (17%).

The uses of new media, moderated by the extent of perpetual contact, blur or overcome or create new constraints on social relations, fostering at least two general but central sets of social implications. As Katz and Aakhus note, "whenever the mobile phone chirps, it alters the traditional nature of public space and the traditional dynamics of private relationships" (2000b, p. 301). The first is changes in *social connectivity*, or the form and extent of interactions in one's social network. The social connectivity issues considered here include constructing identity, fostering and changing group and network relations, and displaying social relations via membership and sharing. The second is changes in *social control*, or different social constraints and boundaries and the kinds, participants, and uses of social control. While media in general alter the relationship between individuals and their temporal and spatial contexts, these changes in time and space also involve power relations, as the increase in possibilities for movement and communication also entail aspects

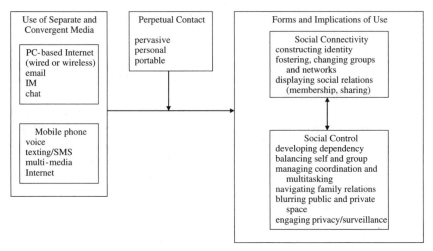

Figure 1.1 Relations among Internet and mobile phone usage and two categories of social implications of use, moderated by perpetual contact.

of control, initiation and access (Green, 2002, p. 285). The social control issues considered here include developing dependency, balancing self and group, managing coordination (including multitasking), negotiating family relations, blurring public and private space, and engaging privacy/surveillance.

Thus this review applies the concept of perpetual contact to provide a useful frame for each of the social connectivity and social control issues (Figure 1.1). The following sections first summarize general Internet and mobile phone usage, and then justify the particular focus on usage by young adults. Then, using selected research from around the world (see Wei & Kolko's call for such an approach, 2005), the subsequent sections provide a conceptual and research overview of each of the two areas of social implications and their subareas, and then specifically summarize relevant studies of teenagers and college students, generally considering Internet use first and mobile phone second.[2]

Usage of Internet and Mobile Phones

International statistics indicate the growing access to and use of the new communication media of the Internet and mobile phones, through space (across regions of the world) and time (over the past decades) (see Table 1.1). More detailed usage data for the United States and worldwide are available in a wide array of sources (Howard, Anderson, Busch, & Nafus, 2009; International Telecommunications Union, 2009a, b; Internet World Stats, 2007; Kalba, 2008; Kennedy, Smith, Wells, & Wellman, 2008; Pew Internet & American Life Project, 2007; Rice & Katz, 2008).

In spite of this growth, looming over much of these usage statistics is the

Table 1.1   Internet and Mobile Phone Users per 100 Inhabitants (and related indices)

Region	Internet (a)	Internet (b)	Mobile (b)
Africa	5.6%	6.93%	38.54%
Americas	North America: 74.4 Latin America/ Caribbean: 29.9	43.78 U.S.: 71.2	81.71 U.S.: 87.6
Asia	17.4	17.04	47.56
Middle East	23.3	—	—
Europe	48.9	47.10	118.74
Oceania	60.4	45.01	82.69
Worldwide	23.8	23.05	59.69
Highest	South Korea: 76.1	Greenland: 90.8	United Arab Emirates: 207.8

Note: Howard, Anderson, Busch, and Nafus (2009) created a "relative digital divide index" to take into account country usage relative to worldwide use and country GDP related to total world GDP (both GDPs valued at constant price to control for varying inflation rates). The index represents how far above or below a country is, relatively, from the global norm of technology diffusion and economic productivity in a given year. For 2006, the U.S. Internet user index was –.19 and the mobile phone index –.94—a bit lower than expected Internet users and considerably lower than expected mobile phone users. Average worldwide values were –.25 for Internet users (the range was –3.46 to 2.90) and .04 for mobile phone users (–3.39 to 1.65).

According to the World Economic Forum Global Competitiveness Report (2008–2009), in 2008, out of 131 countries, the U.S. ranked #9 in Internet users and #51 in mobile phone subscribers.

Sources: (a) Internet World Stats (2009). (b) International Telecommunications Union (2009a, b).

fundamental reality of digital divides, of different kinds, within and across countries and regions (van Dijk, 2005; Hargittai, 2002; Katz & Rice, 2002; Norris, 2001). The simplest conceptualization of the digital divide is differences in access and usage associated with socio-economic and demographic factors, especially income, education, race, gender, rural-urban, and developed-developing regions, with a range of consequences such as economic status and knowledge gaps (Rogers, 2003; Tichenor, Donohue, & Olien, 1970). Second-generation and more subtle aspects include differences in knowledge and technical skills needed to make sense of, and apply, online resources. Internationally, North American usage constitutes only 15.6% of total world users; Internet use grew worldwide 338.1% from 2000 to 2008 (Internetworldstats.com, 2009). In the United States, the demographic digital divide factors tend to be more influential for Internet use than mobile phone use, and, while a large percent of people use both, some use only one, and some use neither (Katz & Rice, 2002; Rice & Katz, 2003a, 2008). Although many studies analyze the factors influencing the adoption and diffusion of Internet and mobile phones (see Grinter & Eldridge, 2001; Jenson, 2005; and

Kalba, 2008, for economic and policy influences on mobile phone diffusion), this chapter primarily considers users, uses, and the two categories of social implications.

Why Young Adults' Usage of Internet and Mobile Phones?

Earlier and More Frequent Use

Most research finds significantly higher rates of Internet and mobile phone usage by teenagers and young adults than by older people. More generally, youth are increasingly "always on," engaged in perpetual contact (Ito et al., 2008). (This greater usage of new media does not necessarily mean, however, that younger users have comprehensive expertise or understanding of the technology and its features—see Lenhart et al., 2008—implying other aspects of the digital divide than age and education.)

Across the nine countries in the 2003 World Internet Project study, younger people (16 to 24 years old) were more likely to be Internet users (Korea, 95.1%; Germany, 59.6%), and spent more hours per week online (Korea 16.0; although in Hungary and Japan, they spent less time than 35- to 49-year-olds, at 5.3 hours per week). In 2008, younger people (18–24) were also greater users of the Internet around the world, from 82% in Hungary to 95% in the United States and 97% in Macao (World Internet Project, 2009). In Britain in 2008, 92% of those under 18 used the Internet, from 76% to 86% for those in ranges from 18 to 54, and much lower percentages for older ranges; students were also much more likely to report meeting people online they did not know before (66% compared to 37% for employed and 19% for retired people) (Dutton, Helsper, & Gerber, 2009). *College students* are often early adopters (not necessarily the very first innovators, but those willing to try out an innovation before the early majority; Rogers, 2003) of new media (Henke, 1985; Vincent & Basil, 1997). Almost 100% of the U.S. college class of 2001 was connected to the Internet (Miller, 2001).

In U.S. married-with-children households, 89% owned multiple mobile phones, and in 57% of those, children (7–17 years old) had their own (Kennedy et al., 2008). According to a Nielsen Company study conducted at the end of 2008, U.S. teenagers exchanged an average of 2,272 text messages per month, or about 80 messages a day (Hafner, 2009). In Canada at the end of 2008, while 8% of households overall had only mobile phones, just over a third of younger households (those with only 19- to 34-year-olds) did (CBC News, 2009). Among mobile users in Europe, the highest rate of usage (77%) comes from those aged 15–25 years. Young Europeans also were the early adopters of the mobile telephone and played a primary role in creating functions for it that were unanticipated by the original technological designers—such as texting for social maintenance purposes (Castells, Fernández-Ardèvol, Qiu, & Sey, 2006).

A Time of Change in Social Connectivity and Social Control

The teenage years, and especially college, may be the time in life most suffused with creating and maintaining multiple and extensive friendships, surpassing all other types of relationships (Lee, 2009; Ling & Yttri, 2002). "Throughout our lives, transitions ... provide new impetus for rethinking identity...." and communication devices "are even more intense and compelling for adolescents, at that point in development when identity play is at the center of life" (Turkle, 2008, pp. 125–126). Keeping connected to peers is especially important for teenagers as they make the transition from childhood to adulthood, from parent-defined to peer-defined self, dealing with insecurity and changing contexts (Boneva, Quinn, Kraut, Kiesler, & Shklovski, 2006, p. 202). During this time, teenagers tend to maintain their friendships through more media than their family relationships (Ling & Yttri, 2005). Peer communication provides both support and social construction of life experiences and relations with society. Peer groups are "midwives" to the transition and liberation from parents to one's own identity (Ling & Yttri, 2005, p. 220). Teenagers are especially susceptible to social influence (by peers and parents) on their media use (Nathanson, 2001). One challenge for young adults is to figure out how to both increase and regulate their availability at the same time (Liestøl & Rasmussen, 2007). Beginning college represents another significant transition for young adults, requiring both separating from, as well as attempting to stay in touch with and obtain support from, close friends and family, in addition to integrating into a new social context and demands (Quan-Haase, 2007). This is less an issue for those who do not go to college, however; but, as Quan-Haase, notes, even those will likely have friends who move away and, as they go to work after high school, there may be fewer occasions for face-to-face interactions with as many others.

Social Connectivity

Concepts and General Results

This section briefly reviews how the Internet and mobile phones play a role in social connectivity, from a more individual perspective (constructing one's identity) through a more group and network perspective (both fostering or changing relations, and displaying them, either as a sign of membership or through sharing).

Constructing Identity

Receiving online or mobile phone and SMS messages can be an affirmation of one's identity, status, and membership in salient groups (Ling & Haddon, 2008; Ling & Yttri, 2002, p. 149). Katz and Sugiyama (2006) emphasized the role of mobile phones, especially as a fashion object, in identity creation and maintenance.

Fostering and Changing Group and Network Relations

New media can both reinforce as well as change the form and boundaries of personal communication networks. They foster "the development of a 'connected' management of relationships, in which the (physically) absent party gains presence through the multiplication of mediated communication gestures on both sides, up to the point where co-present interactions and mediated distant exchanges seem woven into a single, seamless web" (Licoppe, 2004, p. 135).

Across the 10 countries surveyed in the 2003 World Internet Project, Internet users reported that their use had increased contact with those who: share their hobbies or recreation interests (highest for China, with 47.2% reporting an increase; lowest for Germany at 1.2%); political interests (China, 21.1%; Sweden, 3.1%); religion (China, with 11.2%; Sweden, 1.3%); profession (Spain, 32.4%; Singapore, 13.8%); family and friends (U.S., 44.4%; China 8.1%). They have also developed friendships with people they have met online but not met in person (China average of 2.3%; Japan, 1.1%). They have met some of those in person (highest Spain, average of 2.3%; lowest Japan, .6%), and the highest average numbers of people they have met online but not in person are for young users (China, 10.1%; Japan, 1.3%). Also, across the countries, Internet users reported slightly greater socializing with friends than non-users (highest for Taiwan, 23.0% reporting increased socializing; lowest for U.S., 8.4%).

The mobile phone provides different ways for different people to reinforce or reduce different sets of relationships (e.g., youth, their friends, and their parents) (Harper, 2010; Harper & Hamill, 2005). In one study nearly half of cell phone calls by family members were made from work, implying its use as a device coordinating work and social/family life (Ling & Haddon, 2003). A comparison of social network patterns through five communication channels also found interconnections between work and family through face-to-face and mobile phone, and somewhat with email, but not IM or SMS (Kim, Kim, Park, & Rice, 2007). While the cell phone seems to be used for both work, social relations, and family members, the reasons may differ (Leung & Wei, 2000).

Ling (2008b) argues that the mobile phone is one of the few technologies that increase social cohesion. The extent to which communicants attempt to maintain relations across space and time—approximating perpetual contact—is a sort of test of the level of their mutual sociability. Among Danish mobile phone users, for example, this constant availability is linked to the significance of friendship, and thus to being available for friends all the time, even at night, if they are in need of support, comfort, or someone to talk to or laugh with (Stald, 2008). Ling (2008b, p. 43) agrees with Durkheim's (1912/1995) argument that rituals expose and connect the individual to collective ideas, affirming the social. Through mutual awareness of each others' participation in and shared mood from a ritual, within a clearly bounded group, members develop a mutual sense of solidarity. Cohesion develops and exists through shared conviction, group traditions, and culture. Thus perpetual contact is a new, even replacement, ritual totem (a durable object, image or symbol strengthening memory of the group and the group's self-awareness), able to be renewed through time, instead of only at specific, formal ritual times (Ling, 2008b, p. 51). In particular, mobile phones enable the more daily, mundane rituals of social interaction as analyzed by Goffman (1967)—situations involving micro-signals, deference, and demeanor, frontstage and backstage behaviors, greetings and exits. A mobile phone call now generally trumps co-present interaction, or becomes another component of it (such as texting while navigating the sidewalk; Ling, 2008a, p. 168). Further, mediated interaction may provide a motivation or context for, and then later an opportunity for reflection about, in-person ritual interaction.

Text messaging also supports ritual engagement, through specialized jargon and spelling, group-based forms of interaction, marking group membership and boundaries, reinforcing the group's ideology, acceptable phone accessories and style, humor, communication repair, and gossip (Ling, 2008b, chapter 8). Sharing text messages, even sending them to each other while jointly observing their mobile phone screens, is a form of "doing friendship" that not only creates some mutual dependence, but also requires commitment and action (relational "work") (Harper, 2010, p. 102). Bonding is also strengthened through time spent sharing or discussing mobile phone address entries and jointly reading and discussing messages (Green, 2002).

However, mobile phones also create new challenges for the successful management of these rituals, such as talking with someone while also co-present with others (see below, under coordination). Ling notes how this requires communicators to now present themselves and maintain somewhat different identities simultaneously to two groups. Thus mobile phone users must navigate multiple connections, identities, forms of control, and tasks, without threatening the solidarity of either group. In addition, the increased group solidarity associated with ritual use of mobile phones may also reinforce current knowledge and ideologies, exclude outsiders, lower norms, and inhibit individual initiative (2008b, p. 181).

Other research from around the world reinforces the proposition that mobile phone usage is associated with, and increases, group cohesion and social networks (Castells et al., 2006). In Norway, there were positive associations between mobile phone use and peer social inclusion, being more popular, having more friends and greater sociability, though negatively with time at home (Ling, 2008b, p. 164). European studies have found greater mobile phone usage associated with several kinds of informal social interaction (Ling & Haddon, 2003) and strongly associated with friendship networks (Smoreda & Thomas, 2001). In France, mobile phone use tightened the network of close friends (de Gournay, 2002). Among Korean users, mobile phone use strongly complemented face-to-face ties, though SMS not as much (Kim et al., 2007). In Taiwan, it was associated with strengthened family bonds, and expanded social range (Wei & Lo, 2006). A Japanese study found that the mobile phone was used most frequently for communicating with one's partner and somewhat less frequently with friends, and lead to more face-to-face meetings (Matsuda, 2005). In sub-Saharan Africa, it strengthened communication with one's family and group, including for organizing and attending funerals (Donner, 2007).

More specific evidence of the relationship between mobile phone use and close personal networks is that in many cases, while people may have many addresses in their database, they typically regularly contact only a few of them (in both Norway and Japan, from 2 to 10; Ling, 2008b, p. 165), who are primarily close friends (Igarashi, Takai, & Yoshida, 2005; Ito & Okabe, 2005). These frequent communication partners represent a very bounded, close in-group, and most of these are physically nearby (Norway, half less than 10 kms.; U.S., 70% less than 25 miles), especially so for texting compared to voice mobile phone (Castells et al., 2006; Reid & Reid, 2005). And that text messaging often involved simultaneous, interconnected communication within those small groups (Igarashi et al., 2005; Reid & Reid, 2005, referring to "text circles").

Displaying Social Relations

Displaying Social Relations—Membership.   Having a large list of "buddies" and having frequent communication may help fill the need for a sense of belonging to a wide community (Grinter & Palen, 2002; cited by Boneva et al., 2006, p. 204). Having one's mobile address book filled up is a sign of one's social standing, even if most of those numbers are never actually called (Ling & Yttri, 2002, p. 161). As leaving and entering the displayed group list is indicated in IM, others are "present" whether actively IMing, or even by providing automatic messages indicating their status. Keeping one's IM buddy list open on the computer screen is a silent reminder of the group that one belongs to, even communicating to others that you belong, without having to actually communicate (Licoppe & Smoreda, 2005).

One succinct form of communication signaling close membership in a relationship or network is the "bomb call," where the caller lets the phone ring only a few times and then hangs up (Oksman & Turtianen, 2004). The receiver can view the caller's number stored in memory, so this represents the simple but significant message that the caller is thinking of the receiver. It can also be used as short codes, to convey information without incurring charges. This technique is only meaningful for those already socially connected—both because of the need to be familiar with the caller's number and with the code—and represents a subtle form of perpetual contact. Simply owning and displaying various new media, including specific models or brands, play significant symbolic roles, such as peer group identification, fashion sense, identity-shaping, status, etc. (Katz & Aakhus, 2002b; Wirth, von Pape, & Karnowski, 2008).

Holding, handling, and fiddling with the mobile phone even when not using it to converse with someone else can also provide a reminder that one is not alone, that one could interact with, or even just be aware of, members of their close network at any time (Cooley, 2004). Donath and boyd (2004) interpret displaying one's connections or being included as part of others' connections "signaling"—providing cues and indicators of underlying beliefs, values and resources, on the basis of which others can make more or less informed decisions (such as trusting someone).

The digital divide concept briefly noted early on emphasizes that non-use of the Internet or mobile phones is not a matter of preference or selection for the majority of the world's population, but still may have a wide range of social and psychological implications concerning inclusion and exclusion of social groups.

Displaying Social Relations—Sharing.   Mobile camera phones especially give people a means to interpret and share their lives visually, elaborate their experiences together, and engage in a bond maintenance ritual (Hagen & Wold, 2009; Haddon, 2004; Koskinen, 2007). Mobile phone messages, photos, and music are primarily used for sharing affective content within already close small groups, typically involving co-present showing and distribution, but also sending and redistributing, creating chains of content and comments (Koskinen, 2008, pp. 247–248). Shared texts or photos or videos are not only gifts, but part of social rituals and thus even obligations (such as calling or texting "good night"), as well as attempts at repair and maintenance of fragile relationships (Harper, 2010). Users share a range of artifacts through their mobile phones, such as documents, photos, greetings, chain messages, etc., for at least five general purposes: documentation of work-related objects, visualization of details and project status, snap shots, postcards/greetings, and "chain-messages" (Ling & Julsrud, 2005).

Teenagers and College Students

Teenagers

Internet—Identity.   In a 2004 Pew study, IM allowed users to personalize their communication, through buddy icons, personal profiles, and "away" messages, and include additional information such as links to websites, send photos or documents, or music or video files (Lenhart, Madden, & Hitlin, 2005).

Internet—Group Relations.   One of the most rigorous and comprehensive tests of various theories about social outcomes of adolescent online communication comes from Lee's (2009) analysis of 1,312 U.S. adolescents aged 12–18, using survey data from 1997 and 2003 and time diary data from 2003. Online use for communication and recreation, but not for study or computer games, displaced time spent with parents, while use for study and recreation displaced time spent with friends. Higher quality relationships were significantly related to online communication, which in turn lead to more cohesive friendships, which then influenced greater connectedness to school. So adolescent online communication fostered both decreased connectivity (in terms of time spent communicating with family and friends), as well as, especially for those who were already sociable and had high quality social relations, increased cohesiveness of their friendships. Lee did not find support for a social compensation hypothesis, but others have. That is, adolescent users may turn to the Internet to try to compensate for lower psychological well-being, a sense of isolation, or stressful life events (Gross, Juvonen, & Gable, 2002; Seepersad, 2004) through entertainment or relationship maintenance (Leung, 2007).

The Pew report stated that by 2004 87% of those between the ages of 12 and 17 were online, half went online every day, and 45% owned a cell phone They were using a wide range of communication technologies (with 44% indicating they had two or more devices such as desktop or laptop computer, cell phone, or PDA). They tended to use email for communicating with "adults" and institutions and when transmitting lengthy and detailed information to many others, while using IM for day-to-day conversations with a range of friends. Similarly, young adult Danish respondents used email more, and more for studying or work-related contacts, than did teenagers (Østergaard Madsen & Stald, 2005).

IM communication among teenagers includes content such as informal talk, socializing, event planning, and schoolwork communication (Grinter & Palen, 2002), while Flanagin and Metzger's survey (2001) found that students used IM mostly for social entertainment, social attention, task accomplishment, and meeting new people. Boneva et al.'s (2006) study of 106 communication sessions (visit, phone, chat/IM) from 26 interviews of U.S. 13- to 18-year-olds reported that much IM content is about mundane events, planning, chatting; young people may simply need numerous and frequent communication, apart from substantive content. However, in the middle of this, they often shared personal information or support or advice, so the mundane initial motivation provided a context for exchanging more emotional content. IM conversations were more likely social or personal (87.8%) than was communication during face-to-face visits (58.1%) or phone conversations (54.5%).

Mobile Phones—Identity and Display.   Young people use the mobile phone as one way to create, explore, and shape their social identity through their networked communication partners and visible, oral and aural mobile phone behaviors (Ling, 2008a, b). SMS can further facilitate the management of young people's social life through overcoming shyness, facilitating appropriate behavior, and exploiting the conciseness of messages. For young Koreans, the primary goal of mobile phone use is individualization (Yoon, 2006). Teenagers in general engage in their "identity project" by "creating" their mobile phones through their choice of model and features as well as downloadable ring tones and applications, and in projecting images and social status to peers through these choices (Caronia & Caron, 2004; Skog, 2002, p. 255).

Mobile Phones—Group Relations. Buddy/friend programs like MSN (messenger) (which can be private) and SMS (which can be public or private) have taken over from chat programs (public) as communication channels for young people in Sweden (Dunkels, 2009). Today's youth are mainly interacting based on common interests, friendships and acquaintances, school class, family or identity, thus preferring the more private and closed media forms. The youngest interviewees in Østergaard et al.'s (2005) study of teenage and young adult mobile phone users were the most eager senders and receivers of SMS. Around the world, youth perceive texting as making them easily accessible to each other nearly 100% of the time, without decreasing their independence (Castells et al., 2006). SMS/texting, compared to PC-based email, is preferred more and more in Japan and other Asian countries and by young people (Bell, 2005; Ishii, 2006; Kim et al., 2007).

Mobile phones are "used to define who belongs to important social communities and how self-presentation is constructed on a social stage in relation to others" (Oksman & Turtianen, 2004, p. 335), and to have access to a young person's entire social community wherever they go, at home or outdoors (Tønnessen, 2007), especially relevant in the long winters of Finland and Norway, respectively. Swedish children and young people use electronic communication both for maintaining existing contacts and for getting new ones (Hernwall, 2003). Some do this because they lack friends, while others felt they developed more interesting contacts through digital arenas, because it was easier to meet with people with whom one shares common interests. However, most often digital channels were used to negotiate face-to-face meetings with existing friends. Danish teenagers and young adults (15–24) emphasized that one of the major advantages of the mobile phone is that it creates reciprocal availability, especially through being able to write and receive text messages/SMS, regardless of location (Østergaard et al., 2005).

Mobile Phones—Sharing. Taylor and Harper's (2003) ethnographic study of UK teenagers described how teens use phones to participate in social practices which resembled ritualized gift-giving. Text messages, call-credit, and mobile phones themselves were treated as gifts, which carry symbolic meaning through the exchange ritual. Further, the value of that gift may vary by the content and style of the message. Young Koreans find text messaging useful in developing friendships after initial face-to-face interaction (Yoon, 2006), and perceive SMS as a strongly reciprocal form of gift-giving (Yoon, 2003).

College Students

Internet—Group Relations.   A crucial role of mediated communication is to manage the transition from high school to college, maintaining social connectivity with old friends while developing new relations. Cummings, Lee, and Kraut (2006) tracked high school students over three years as they moved to college (spring of senior year in high school through the end of their junior year in college), collecting a wide range of data on activities as well as their network of high school and college friends, involving 585 respondents and 2,526 communication partners. Email and IM seemed to guard better against declines in closeness to high school friends after one moved to college— possibly because communication frequency was least affected by distance and cost—even though phone communication was the strongest predictor of closeness. However, concerning their new college friends, the students communicated much more via in-person and phone interactions than through email and IM.

Primary uses of the Internet by U.S. college students include social communication, entertainment, easily keeping in touch with their friends, and communicating with friends and family; 42% of college student Internet users socialized online (Pew Internet & American Life Project, 2002). Based upon an analysis of U.S. college students' communication diaries, Baym, Zhang, and Lin (2004) found that the Internet was clearly integrated into college student's lives, and used as much as the telephone. Social interactions on the Internet were mostly through email (73%), but also chat (20%) and IM (7%). Still, most interactions were face-to-face (ftf; 64%), although most respondents (64%) socialized through all three media, and 24% through ftf and phone only. Canadian first-year university students also integrated the Internet (email and IM), mobile (phones and texting), and offline (ftf and telephone) to support both their local (within 30 miles) and distant social ties (Quan-Haase, 2007). Email and IM were especially valuable for integrating distant and local ties into their daily lives. Quan-Haase particularly emphasized how students used this array of media in combination, and with multiple others, sometimes at the same time, both local and distant.

Mobile Phones—Group Relations.   A majority of the college students in a four-state U.S. survey reported using their mobile phones for "the purpose of social stimulation, to remain continually available, for domestic reasons, to leave themselves memos and reminders, for time-keeping, for emergency purposes, and to use the phone's phonebook function" (Totten, Lipscomb, Cook, & Lesch, 2005, p. 13).

Mobile Phones—Display.   More recent adopters (i.e., those further along on the adoption curve, and thus less likely to be early adopters) and those with lower social skills in the Baym et al. study (2004), were more likely to indicate fashion ("the symbolic display of the cell phone"; Leung & Wei, 2000, p. 68) as a significant influence on mobile phone use.

Social Control

Concepts and General Results

As new media, and ways of using those media, decrease more and more constraints, social relations that had formerly been either separate, or clearly structured, are now blurring or expanding their domain, sometimes creating new constraints (Ishii, 2006). Thus, Internet and mobile phone use has implications for social control, ranging again from a more individual perspective such as control of one's own usage (dependency), controlling communication access to and from one's group, and iteratively coordinating plans, social activities, and multiple tasks, through negotiating changes in parental-youth relations, and the increasing dissolution of private-public space boundaries, to understanding the interplay between control over privacy by individuals, groups, corporations, government, and society (Green, 2002).

Developing Dependency

Ironically, precisely because it is now so much easier to foster a sense of perpetual contact through frequent even if short contacts, lapses of that web of contacts may generate heightened concern about belonging and relations, a panic, a sense of being disconnected and isolated from the organic network of ongoing relations (Licoppe & Smoreda, 2005). For example, perpetual contact involves constant disruptions of social situations when the mobile phone interrupts and demands attention, especially since many feel that they "have to" respond immediately to text messages (Stald, 2008). Eighty percent of Danish informants said that they never turned off their mobile phone. Many seemed afraid to miss out on something even if they only turned off their mobile for a short time. The other 20% turned it off for between 4 and 12 hours, mainly at night to get undisturbed sleep, at work when necessary, at the movies, at school, at a restaurant or in the quiet zone in trains. Even then, they may check their display for incoming messages when the mobile is vibrating (Stald, 2008). Turkle's (2008) version of the perpetual contact concept—*the tethered self*— reflects some of this dependency, as users become reliant on the gratifications, identity, and support they derive through these media. This dependency may lead to *mobile phone addiction*, found to be higher among Hong Kong adolescents who were female, experienced leisure boredom, had higher sensation seeking and lower self-esteem, and spent more time with friends/classmates (Leung, 2008).

Balancing Self and Group

Internet communication and especially mobile phone communication can allow more control over one's self-presentation as well as the actual content than face-to-face interaction (Oksman & Turtianen, 2004; Walther, 1996). Licoppe and Smoreda argue that new media "allow people to re-negotiate the constraints of individual time rhythms, and of who one communicates with," leading to changes in "roles, hierarchies and forms of power in relational economies" (2005, p. 317). Mobile phone use can be strongly connected with human perceptions of influence, power, and status (Ling & Yttri, 2005, p. 221; Ozcan & Kocak, 2003 in a study of Turkish users). New media offer communicants some similar and some different ways to control others' access to the user through what Baron (2008) called *volume control*—such as to increase, avoid, or manipulate conversation, and allow multitasking while engaged in a conversation. For example, email can reduce the influence of differential personal status and hierarchy, reduce the need to answer immediately or lose the communication, and allow broadcasting or forwarding to third parties, some of whom may be unknown to both caller and forwarder. Mobile phones allow personal ring tones for specific callers, and even offer "camouflage" services that provide false background noises and false ring tones to activate during another conversation.

Managing Coordination and Multitasking

Coordination through new media represents "deeper issues of openness, availability and access" (Katz & Aakhus, 2002a, p. 9). Themes found in Norwegian SMS messages included *coordination, praise, answers, questions, information, commands/requests*, and *personal news* (Ling, 2005b), some of which reflect issues of control.

Text messaging increases ad-hoc coordination and is a tool for keeping up socially and maintaining relationships (Brown, 2001; Grinter & Eldridge, 2001; Jenson, 2005; Ling, 2004). Mobile communication supports the management of interaction, especially when the participants are distributed through *micro-coordination* and *hyper-coordination* (Ling & Yttri, 2002). Micro-coordination bypasses centralized, large or fixed decision-making groups or structures, in three ways: (a) *basic logistics*, or adapting a trip or plan already in progress; (b) *time softening*, letting others know if your schedule has been changed; and (c) *progressively exact arrangement* of some kind of meeting or get-together. The instrumental micro-coordination of everyday life is closely related to the pervasiveness, personalization, and portability of the mobile phone. Green (2002) similarly emphasizes the micro-coordination of everyday life through mobile devices, as the potential for perpetual contact affects task sequencing and deadlines. Users can take advantage of short temporal gaps in activities to communicate with others, maintain personal relationships throughout otherwise public and other social rhythms, embed their private activities in public spaces and time, and organize activities around time instead of around space and place. However, others' access to users at any time also produce new controls and constraints, reducing temporal and spatial flexibility. Hypercoordination, on the other hand, involves (a) *expressive, or emotional and social communication*, as part of the rite of passage from adolescent to adult, learning social and technical skills not from adults but from peers; and (b) *in-group discussion about appropriate forms of self-presentation through the mobile phone* (fashion, display, location), including jargon that identifies their membership and excludes others (such as parents, but also unwanted peers) (Ling & Yttri, 2002).

Another aspect of coordination is the increased extent of *multitasking* associated with new media use, involving coordinating multiple activities (including communicating through other media) while communicating with both distant and co-present others (Ling, 2008b; Rideout et al., 2005). Multitasking as an *activity* is working on more than one task at a time (concurrent) or switching between them quickly (sequential) (Spink, Cole, & Waller, 2008). However, multitasking may also be conceptualized as an *ability* to engage in multiple tasks at the same time. People also vary in *polychronicity*—the preference for, and belief in the superiority of, engagement in two or more tasks or events (Bluedorn, 2002). Holmes, Papper, Popovich, and Bloxham (2005) found that 96% of their respondents engaged in concurrent media exposure, involving 30.7% of their total daily media exposure. In particular, 80% of the Internet use involved at least one other medium, but only 28.5% when TV was the primary task. The merging of mobile phone use with other communication—and non-communication—activities (receiving calls while watching TV, or texting while walking) (Ling, 2008a) is another form of multitasking. IM use frequently involves communicating with multiple others at the same time (Boneva et al., 2006), and SMS/texting allows for parallel communication environments, where the various multitasking activities are not seen by the different groups (Ling & Yttri, 2002, p. 165).

Navigating Family Relations

The perpetual contact afforded by the phone can create *symbolic proximity* (Wei & Lo, 2006) between children and their parents, suggesting that they are virtually together. This symbolic proximity provides reassurance and support to children and young adults. Using media to manage family relations and activities "includes elements of both control and care" (Christensen, 2009, p. 436), as well as security and safety (Mante-Meijer & Haddon, 2001), often in the same communication. Christensen's qualitative analyses found that parental-child mobile calls or texts reflected attentiveness to children, developing mutual accountability, sharing unusual experiences, personal problems, asking for permission, parental control, and micro-coordination (2009). Any call, of course, may involve more than one of these issues. A study of

Danish families showed how parents used the mobile phone to mediate a sense of closeness between each other and with their children while apart, through frequent calls and text messages (Christensen, 2009). While useful in managing, maintaining and reaffirming family relations (as well as in providing "micro-coordination" of family activities; see Ling & Yttri, 2002), these media simultaneously supported greater family dispersion through time and space, enabling the "distributed family" (p. 432). Green's (2002) ethnographic analysis of mobile temporality concluded that mobile devices facilitated shorter and more fragmented conversations requiring less time to read and respond, but also opportunities for more conversations with more people and of types not previously available, resulting in greater overall duration of communication. "The long durations act to consolidate their peer relationships, differentiate them from family or household relations, and contribute to a growing sense of both independence (from family) and collectivity (among peers)" (p. 286).

The increasing mobility, specialization, spatial individuation (such as media-rich bedrooms and mobile phones with headsets) and membership in multiple groups require coordination of the family through and around such media (Livingstone, 2002). In an early 2008 Pew survey, households, especially those with children, used their mobile phones to coordinate and connect family members during the day, while just over half used the Internet to share online browsing and entertainment when at home at least a few times a week (Kennedy et al., 2008). A quarter of adults felt their family was now closer than when they were growing up, while 11% felt they were not as close. Respondents also felt that using the Internet and mobile phones increased the quality of their communication with family members who did not live with them (53%), friends (47%), and co-workers (40%).

Certainly, social control over the timing, location, and uses of new media is a site of ongoing tension and negotiation between youth and their parents (Hagen, 2007). In a 2008 British survey, 81% of households reported having rules (such as not giving out personal information, contacting strangers, visiting some sites, time spent, etc.) on Internet use in the home for children between the ages of 14 and 17 (Dutton et al., 2009). According to a 2006 Pew survey, U.S. parental control of teenagers' Internet use tends to focus more on content (68% have rules) than time spent online (55%). Further, 65% of parents reported that they checked what their teenager had been viewing online, and 74% knew whether their teenager had ever created their own social networking profile, both indicating both control and engagement (Macgill, 2007). The mobile phone can also be used by parents as a tool for monitoring and control; they call to check up on the activities of their children, or inspect monthly calling logs (Wei & Lo, 2006). However, youth have developed media strategies to avoid their parents' control (Wei & Lo, 2006). But freedom from parental control also involves constraints and repression from new social structures and contexts, such as one's peers, as noted above.

Donner, Rangaswamy, Steenson, and Wei's (2008) three case studies in India within families concerning family finance, courtship, and domestic space highlighted how the purchase and use of mobile phones were still couched in, and reflected, ongoing discussions about traditional behaviors and values, especially as middle-class families move from traditional to modern practices. For example, tensions arose as to how to allocate a limited household budget between parents and children, sometimes requiring the children to explain and participate in making choices among features and calling plans. Mesch and Talmud (2008) discussed four dimensions generating tension with families concerning the adoption and use of ICTs by Israeli Jewish and Arab teenagers: (a) a patriarchy that fosters female inequities, whereas ICTs may break down some of the gender boundaries; (b) social behavior is based on tradition, which is somewhat resistant to ICTs, because they allow exposure to external, competing ideas; (c) thus a typically strict hierarchy in more traditional communities may enforce tradition by censorship, which may be bypassed by mobile phones; and (d) collective identity and explicit boundaries are emphasized in traditional communities, while ICTs foster not only anonymity and individual freedoms, but also interactions across these boundaries.

Blurring Public and Private Space

Pervasive, personal, and portable media are shifting boundaries—physical, temporal, and social—between what were formerly more or less explicit boundaries between public space and private space (Humphreys, 2005; Katz, Rice, Acord, Dasgupta, & David, 2004). Wellman (2001) also noted how mobile phone users become disassociated with their physical space as they turn their attention to the physically absent but communicatively present other. In a way, blurring the boundaries between public and private space can be a form of coordination and even multitasking—that is, interacting with both co-present and absent others at the same time, or engaging in what would otherwise be considered private or even intimate conversation while passing through or occupying public space.

Indeed, Rule (2002, p. 253) remarks how public use of mobile phones breaks down boundaries of a space as "distinct and protected milieu," where, potentially, "all sorts of relationships, milieus and institutions will lose their distinctive character." Baron (2008) mentions a survey by Sprint (2004) concluding that 50% of their study respondents felt unimportant when a face-to-face communication partner answered a mobile phone. Rice and Katz's analysis of a U.S. nationally representative survey found that two-thirds (of 1,094 respondents) had seen someone be thoughtless of others while using a cell phone (2003b). Two-thirds of those provided an example: driving and talking (47.0%), talking to someone [on the phone] while with someone else (17.0%), using a phone in a public place (10.7%), talking in a restaurant (9.8%), talking too loud (6.4%), or having a cell phone go off at the movies (4.7%).

Engaging Privacy and Surveillance

Applying the more familiar concern about social control in mediated environments, people are increasingly concerned about online privacy and surveillance (Fox & Lewis, 2001; Klosek, 2000; Yao, Rice, & Wallis, 2007). Many have proposed that ICTs can be a form of Bentham's proposed Panopticon, where all prisoners can be observed at once by an unseen guard, no prisoner can see or hear each other, and prisoners do not know the extent or purpose of any information collected. (In truth, however, Steadman (2007) shows that Bentham's prison design was highly impractical and even counter-productive from a surveillance perspective, and few were ever actually built.) Crucial to the original point of the Panopticon is that, because the physical and social structure provides the *potential* of *unobserved* observation, the knowledge that one *might* be gazed upon creates self-generated control and discipline. Foucault (1977) argued that technologies also can be used as disciplinary devices through regulation and observation, and others have noted that users are profiled or sorted by commercial entities into more or less valuable sets of consumers, which may be used for marketing to, redlining out, or controlling of those users (Fernback, 2007; Gandy, 1993; Huberman, 2001; Lessig, 1999).

Panoptic surveillance includes much more pervasive, subtle, inter-related, and continuous aspects than "just" recording and obtaining personal information and location. Elmer (2003), for example, argues that precisely because of the "decentered and networked aspects of information technologies" (p. 231), even the concept of consumer "choice" is highly shaped and monitored, and often consists of appearing to provide rewards for participating in having one's data and behaviors monitored, packaged, and resold. Computer-based ICTs are complex and multi-layered, so most users are unaware of the potential for monitoring and observation through collection of personal data and usage patterns, and the sharing or sale of this information to subsequent organizations (Dunkels, 2009; Lyon, 2001). Castells (2001) claims that users are unknowing prisoners of ICT architectures.

Yet more and more people are providing information about their social connectedness in ways that foster greater social control over them by others. Users, especially of IM buddy lists and mobile phone address books, each *want* to be in the center of the network, *want* others to be observing them, and *want* others to know which others are observing the self as well as the others. As discussed in the sections on identity and display, this self-display seems fundamental to the human condition. Indeed, one of the main goals in maintaining connectivity is to *increase* others' surveillance of both one's individual communication as well as one's network of communication—that is, display one's membership. Yet people post and share photographs and text revealing drug use, sexual behaviors, and anti-social attitudes. This may be attractive to one's cohesive social network, but sends quite negative signals to others in the world, especially potential employers, employees, and clients, who may find such postings by accident, through unknown forwarding, or intentionally through Google or Facebook searches or more sophisticated data mining tools. In this way, the intersection of maintaining and improving one's social connectivity, with the various forms of social control available through new media, inverts the Panopticon. We call this inversion the *Peropticon*—promoting, whether proactively or passively, the exposure of self or observation of self by others *through* the system. Users driven to manage their ritualized social connectivity are now held prisoner to, develop a dependency on, the need to maintain an interconnected network, and both constantly observe others, promote being constantly observed by others, and observe how everyone observes everyone.

One clear distinction from the original conceptualization of the Panopticon is that bounded physical space is no longer a necessary context. Rather than being constrained by the designed observable space, participants choose where, when, and in what form to locate themselves, and how they indicate their presence and behaviors, in various communication spaces. The social connectivity and social control fostered by mobile phone usage accomplishes some of the same processes as the Panopticon, but now largely (but not necessarily) intentionally by users who desire and are rewarded by this projection. The Peropticon can be seen as even more of a generalization of the original Panopticon than Mathiesen's (1997) *synopticism, reverse Panopticon*, or *spectatorship*, or Cascio's (2005) *sousveillance*, where many can observe the few or those in charge, such as through mediated public events. It is similar to Cascio's (2005) concept of the *participatory Panopticon*, inspired by the growing uses of the mobile phone camera. He argues that participatory Panopticon is not really "transparency," because this pervasive exposure is primarily passive engagement, not completely under the control, attention, or intention of the user.

The Peropticon concept in no way diminishes or repudiates the ongoing processes of surveillance, exclusion, digital fraud, commercialization of personal information, and even self-regulation associated with communication and information technologies, including mobile phones (Elmer, 2003; Fernback, 2007; Gandy, 1993; Lyon, 2001; Mansell & Collins, 2007). That is, both now occur simultaneously and interdependently.

Teenagers and College Students

Teenagers

Internet—Privacy.   Nearly half (46%) of a UK survey of a national sample aged 9–19 said that they had given out personal information to someone that they met online (Livingstone & Bober, 2005).

Mobile Phones—Dependency.   Norwegian youth have said that they would not know what was happening if they did not have a mobile (Haddon, 2004, p. 45), and that they would not have managed a day or even an hour without their mobile phone (Hagen & Wold, 2009). Seventy percent of Danish adolescents rated the mobile between 8 and 10 points out of 10 on how important they felt their mobile was for them (Stald, 2008). Despite the fact that the mobile allows for asynchronous communication, young people have come to depend on an immediate response when they send an SMS (Haddon, 2004).

Mobile Phones—Balancing Self and Group.   Teenagers like the Internet, but especially mobile phones, because they provide both control over access to and from one's group (such as by individualized private access at any time) as well as a means for shaping the nature of the communication within one's group and family. Ling (2005a) argues that for adolescents in particular, mobile phones both lower the threshold for social interaction and allow for greater control.

Mobile Phones—Navigating Family Relations.   Just under two-thirds of 12- to 19-year-old home Internet users in the UK have taken some action to hide their online activities from their parents (Livingstone & Bober, 2005). Strategies of adolescents for reducing parental control and monitoring through mobile phones include saying that the battery was flat or that they did not hear the sound of the call (Ling & Haddon, 2008), or to program the mobile phone to automatically direct a call from one's parents to voice mail (Ling & Yttri, 2002, p. 156). In addition to avoiding control through the landline phone by parents taking messages and knowing who's calling, using a mobile phone connection may also be a sign of consideration, a way to not bother others in the house during a conversation. SMS supports children's ability to communication with one's friends silently and slightly illicitly in class or at night in bed, and to share group-specific slang and abbreviations (Ling & Yttri, 2005). Interestingly though not surprisingly, while children (decreasingly so as they become older) send text messages and mobile phone calls to their parents, at the same time they tend to feel that calls and texts from their parents are intrusive and monitoring (Christensen, 2009).

Internet and Mobile Phones—Coordination through Multitasking.   As a way to coordinate demands on their time and attention, young people use several media simultaneously, seemingly without much effort (Holm Sørensen, 2001). A Kaiser foundation reported that 65% of students also do something else while they are studying (Rideout et al., 2005). In a recent large-sample newspaper poll, among those who had homework, 53% of those between ages 12 and 17, and 25% between 18 and 24, did at least one other thing while studying; of the 12- to 17-year-old respondents, 21% said they did at least three other things (Gaither, 2006). The additional activities included music listening (84%), television watching (47%), and movie watching (22%). But the respondents were also engaged in other media activities requiring involvement and interaction, such as phone (32%), Internet (21%), instant messaging (15%), email (13%), text messaging (13%), and video games (6%). A survey of 1,800 web users ages 13–17 asked about their use of Internet outside of school (BurstMedia, 2006). About half (48.9%) said they were doing offline homework while online (significantly higher for females). Other offline activities included television or movies (33.8%), radio (21.4%), music videos on TV (21.2%), sending mobile phone text messages (20.1%), talking on cell phone (19.0%), talking on landline phone (16.3%), and watching sports on TV (18.%).

College Students

Internet-Dependency.   When asked about the impact of not having access to the Internet outside of school, over one-quarter (28.9%) of U.S. student survey respondents indicated their day would be ruined (slightly higher for males), 39.8% said their day would not be ruined but would be not as good, and 31.2% said the day would be just fine (BurstMedia, 2006). Katz (2006) conducted a small experiment that asked 82 U.S. college students to not use their cell phones for 48 hours, and report on their life during that time. Only 25 lasted 36 hours, and only 12 were able to last the full time period. Reasons for not lasting the full 48 hours included "because it was too hard, urgent issues arose, people got angry with them, and responsibilities required them to use their phone" (p. 92). Only three said that their life was happier without the mobile phone.

An analysis of college communication majors' autobiographical essays (from 1998 through 2000) revealed that their Internet use had implications for four main social spheres, each with a primary duality: self (active/passive personal development and management of information), family (different abilities and support from old/young members, and staying in touch with members), real communities (participating in and planning for work/school or play even if distant), and virtual communities (expanding one's world view and social memberships, and fostering concerns about utopian/dystopian implications) (McMillan & Morrison, 2006). The respondents indicated various dependencies throughout, but more intensely in the more personal spheres. These included expectations of being continuously connected in order to participate in the community, family or friendships; concerns about addiction; and importance for future careers. U.S. college students use their mobile phones both to manage their own privacy as well as keep in touch with their parents (Aoki & Downes, 2003).

Internet and Mobile Phones—Coordination through Multitasking.   Baym et al.'s (2004) survey study of U.S. college students also found evidence of multitasking: 56% of face-to-face interactions, 42% of phone interactions, and 27% of online interactions occurred while interacting with at least one other person. The most frequently combined activities were face-to-face (74%), Internet (64%), and phone (61%). In several related studies of American college students' use of new media, Baron (2008) found increased multitasking, through phones, email, IM and mobile phones. Nearly all of students using IM were involved in at least one other activity, including an average of 2.7 ongoing IM conversations (synchronous and asynchronous). Online, the other activities included web-based activities, 70.3%; computer-based media player, 47.5%;

word processing, 38.6%. Offline, they included ftf conversation, 41.1%; eating/drinking, 36.7%; television, 28.5%; telephone, 21.5%. Reasons for multitasking included: the task may require multiple activities to complete; accommodate time demands, allowing more activities to be completed in a given day; resolve psychological condition (e.g., boredom, impatience); unintentional (such as someone calling while the first person is doing some other activity). None of Baron's respondents perceived IM as a stand-alone activity—rather, it was a "background" or "under the radar" activity, used if bored (while waiting for some other person to respond to an IM), if one has a short attention span, simply wants the ability to be in control of the nature of the IM conversation, or wants to maintain a sense of ongoing connection without actual interaction (perpetual contact or connected presence). Nearly three-quarters of a 2008 British national survey (71%) reported multitasking while online, about equal for men and women, and much higher for university students (93%) (Dutton et al., 2009).

Mobile Phones—Blurring Public and Private Space.   Of Baron's (2008) U.S. college student respondents, a majority of females, but fewer males, were bothered by people using their cell phones in public, mostly due to volume, and also because the places were inappropriate, or private communication could be heard. Some said it was inappropriate if the other person could see or tell you were doing it, and others said it made paying attention to and processing information difficult.

Conclusion

Overall, then, current and developing features and capabilities of the Internet and mobile phones, culminating in the concept of perpetual contact, shape the influence of forms and nature of usage by young adults, in different contexts ranging from intimate relationships to peer groups to families to universities to countries and cultures, on domains of social connectivity and social control. Table 1.2 summarizes positive and negative implications of the main concepts (perpetual contact, social connectivity, and social control) for Internet and mobile phone use.[3]

Additional new media, such as social networking sites, blogs, microblogs (e.g., twitter), social bookmarking, wikis, virtual reality communities, and online gaming, to the extent that they involve communicating, may well be relevant to the conceptual framework, but are beyond the scope of this chapter. Especially timely would be the implications for connectivity and control of the increasing convergence of media, especially in the form of multimedia and mobile (wireless, phone-based) Internet, allowing for more interdependencies and varieties of media experience (Akiyoshi & Ono, 2008; Anckar & D'Incau, 2002; Bates, Albright, & Washington, 2002; Brown, 2001; Chae & Kim, 2003; Haddon & Vincent, 2009; Kleinman, 2007; Koskinen, 2007; Koskinen, 2008;

Table 1.2 Summary of Main Concepts—Perpetual Contact, Positive and Negative Aspects of Social Connectivity and Social Control—by Internet and Mobile Phone

	PC Internet (email, IM, chat)	Mobile Phone (voice, SMS/text, multimedia)
Perpetual Contact	Pervasive (anywhere with connection) Personal (one or several individual accounts; though can post to and receive from lists with unknown others) Portable (physically located if desktop or Internet café; only if wireless, but laptop or email not always on) Asynchronous (email) and Synchronous (IM, chat) Longer email, short IM	Pervasive (anywhere with connection; easy to share) Personal (one or more individual phone number; individualized ringtones and accessories; typically must know addressee for SMS and multimedia sharing) Portable (carried with person, may be hands-free, with headset) Synchronous and Asynchronous (voice and text) Longer synchronous voice conversations, short asynchronous voice and text messages
Social Connectivity	Supports both wider as well as more focused social interaction	Tends to emphasize close relations, esp. SMS; enables constant potentiality of connection
Constructing Identity	More for older users, work-related, except IM	More for younger users, social-related; part of fashioning personal and social identity; personalizing profiles, ringtones, messages and phone accessories; technology as fashion
Fostering/ changing group and network relations	Exposes users to diverse and broad sets of others; maintains distant relations, including high school friends after going to college; vastly increased access to diverse other people and information; displaces time with family; promotes sharing advice	Reinforces social groupings and cohesion, especially small number of family and friends, even from work; constant awareness and maintenance of membership; ritual engagement
Displaying social relations (membership, sharing)	Distribution lists remind one of membership; IM buddy lists reflect popularity and membership; overload and increasing obligations to respond	Addresses and SMS names reflect popularity and membership; easy to share "gifts" of messages, photos, private signals; mobile phone cost, style, accessories indicates status and membership; increased sense of connectedness and belonging; perpetual obligations to be accessible, and respond

(*continued*)

Table 1.2 Continued

	PC Internet (email, IM, chat)	Mobile Phone (voice, SMS/text, multimedia)
Social Control	Changes constraints of time and space, challenging traditional controls	Changes social boundaries of presence and contact, providing more of both individual and social control
Developing dependency	Wide range of sources to keep up with; expectations of response timeliness; addiction and abuse; loss of access would ruin or harm day	Need to be constantly interacting with group; easy to integrate with, but also disrupt, daily activities; drawn away from focus on present others; cannot manage without phone
Balancing self and group	Reducing status differentials through bypassing structures, informal writing	Ring tones to identify and prioritize callers; tensions between access vs. exposure; texting makes one more available while maintaining independence
Managing coordination and multi-tasking	Asynchroneity allows response prioritization and timing; distribution lists spread awareness; multiple IM conversations; multitasking with TV, music	Iterative convergent micro- and hyper-coordination of schedules, interactions; portability allows more multitasking; tensions between co-present and remote others
Navigating family relations	Checking in on family from work via email; isolating as well as joint use	Allows freedom as well as attempts at parental control; develop excuses for not answering calls from parents; crossing traditional local, gender, and ethnic boundaries through SMS
Blurring public and private space	Wireless laptops, Internet cafes, create personalized spaces	Private communications heard and seen in public space; shifting of interactions between public and private space
Engaging privacy/ surveillance	Online monitoring and surveillance, re-use of personal data and usage patterns; posting one's thoughts and daily activities online	Constant inspections by others of user's responsivity, membership; user's desire to be seen and observed; greater presence in public sphere with less engagement

Nysveen, Pedersen, & Thorbjornsen, 2005; Rice & Katz, 2008; Runnel, Pruulmann-Vengerfeldt, & Keller, 2006; Strocchi, 2003; Wei, 2008; Wirth et al., 2008). For example, in Japan, "PC email is exchanged with psychologically and geographically distant friends, whereas mobile email is exchanged with more intimate friends" (p. 53), and "mobile Internet use has more in common with time-enhancing home appliances such as the telephone, while PC Internet use has more in common with the time-displacing technology of TV" (p. 57) (Ishii, 2004; see also Ishii, 2006).

Extensions of this research focus would analyze what specific features and uses of these media, associated with pervasiveness, personalness and portability, in what social, national and cultural contexts, reinforce or change forms of social connectivity and social control. Such a concern would require both quantitative and qualitative approaches, a deeper understanding of the nature of each medium's characteristics (a media ecology approach), how media become domesticated (both within and outside households), and how users, their context, and the technologies influence each other (reinvention, technology duality) (Berker, Hartmann, Punie, & Ward, 2006; Johnson & Rice, 1987; Meyrowitz, 1985; Orlikowski, 1992; Postman, 1993). Related to this focus on contextuality would be a deeper investigation of how media convergence, social connectivity, and social control influence each other.

Acknowledgements

Thanks to Katy Pearce of UCSB for help in providing references and article summaries, and to Miriam Metzger of UCSB for thoughtful comments on a much earlier draft. Thanks to four anonymous reviewers for their insightful critiques, and to Editor Charles Salmon for his encouragement and suggestions.

Notes

1. Throughout, we make the simple distinction between mediated communication (human communication between two or more participants occurring through one of these technologies) and unmediated communication (direct face-to-face, or "co-present" interaction in the same place and same time).
2. The chapter does not attempt to analyze or summarize the wide research on influences on adoption of these media, such as from a diffusion of innovations perspective (Rice & Webster, 2002; Rogers, 2003) or a uses and gratifications perspective (even though several studies cited here do so: Campbell, 2007; Flanagin & Metzger, 2001; Leung & Wei, 2000; Livingstone & Bober, 2005; Lonkila & Gladarev, 2008; Vincent & Basil, 1997; and Wei, 2008).
3. Any review of a large amount of research is necessarily limited in terms of conceptual scope and simple page length. A different version, or another dimension, of this review would discuss and analyze the implications of the widely varying methodologies used to generate the various usage statistics and patterns noted throughout. The studies cited range from surveys to controlled experiments, from ethnographies to personal interviews, from the United States to Scandinavia and India, using a wide range of measures and evidence. While quantitative meta-analyses are very useful, they require studies that report effect sizes across somewhat similar measures. The main approach of this chapter was to assemble and integrate just such a range to illuminate the diversity of social connectivity and social control implications. This approach necessarily hides distinctions between as well as commonalities across results due to different methods.

References

Akiyoshi, M., & Ono, H. (2008). The diffusion of mobile Internet in Japan. *The Information Society, 24*(5), 292–303.

Anckar, B., & D'Incau, D. (2002). Value creation in mobile commerce: Findings from a consumer survey. *Journal of Information Technology Theory and Application, 4*, 43–64.

Aoki, K., & Downes, E. J. (2003). An analysis of young people's use of and attitudes toward cell phones. *Telematics and Informatics, 20*, 349–364.

Baron, N. (2008). Adjusting the volume: Technology and multitasking in discourse control. In J. E. Katz (Ed.), *Handbook of mobile communication studies* (pp. 177–193). Cambridge, MA: The MIT Press.

Bates, B., Albright, K., & Washington, K. (2002). Not your plain old telephone: New services & new impacts. In C. Lin & D. Atkin (Eds.), *Communication technology & society* (pp. 91–124). Cresskill, NJ: Hampton Press.

Baym, N., Zhang, Y., & Lin, M. (2004). Social interactions across media: Interpersonal communication on the Internet, telephone and face-to-face. *New Media & Society, 6*(3), 299–318.

Bell, G. (2005). The age of the thumb: A cultural reading of mobile technologies from Asia. In P. Glotz & S. Bertschi (Eds.), *Thumb culture: Social trends and mobile phone use* (pp. 67–87). Bielefeld, Germany: Transcript Verlag.

Berker, T., Hartmann, M., Punie, Y., & Ward, K. (Eds.). (2006). *Domestication of media and technology*. Berkshire, UK: Open University Press.

Bluedorn, A. C. (2002). *The human organization of time*. Stanford, CA: Stanford University Press.

Boneva, B. S., Quinn, A., Kraut, R. E., Kiesler, S., & Shklovski, I. (2006). Teenage communication in the instant messaging era. In R. E. Kraut, N. Brynin, & S. Kiesler (Eds.), *Computers, phones, and the Internet: Domesticating information technology* (pp. 201–218). Oxford: Oxford University Press.

Brown, B. (2001). Studying the use of mobile technology. In B. Brown, N. Green, & R. Harper (Eds.), *Wireless world* (pp. 3–15). London: Springer.

Brown, J. D., & Cantor, J. (2000). An agenda for research on youth and the media. *Journal of Adolescent Health, 27*(2), 2–7.

BurstMedia. (2006). *Online insights, 6*(4). Retrieved May 1, 2006, from www.burstmedia.com/assets/newsletter/items/2006_05_01.pdf

Campbell, S. W. (2007). A cross-cultural comparison of perceptions & uses of mobile telephony. *New Media & Society, 9*, 343–363.

Caronia, L., & Caron, A. H. (2004). Constructing a specific culture: Young people's use of the mobile phone as a social performance. *Convergence, 10*, 28–61.

Cascio, J. (2005, May 7). The rise of the participatory panopticon. http://www.worldchanging.com/archives/002651.html

Castells, M. (2001). *The Internet galaxy: Reflections on the Internet, business and society*. New York: Oxford University Press.

Castells, M., Fernandez-Ardevol, M., Qiu, J. L., & Sey, A. (2006). *Mobile communication and society: A global perspective*. Cambridge, MA: The MIT Press.

CBC News. (2009, June 15). Younger Canadians lead migration away from land lines: StatsCan. Retrieved from http://www.cbc.ca/technology/story/2009/06/15/cellphones-statistics-canada-survey.html?ref=rss

Chae, M., & Kim, J. (2003). What's so different about the mobile Internet? *Communications of the ACM, 46*(12), 240–247.

Christensen, T. H. (2009). 'Connected presence' in distributed family life. *New Media & Society, 11*(3), 433–451.

Cooley, H. R. (2004). It's all about the fit: The hand, the mobile screenic device and tactile vision. *Journal of Visual Culture, 3*(2), 133–155.

Cummings, J., Lee, J., & Kraut, R. E. (2006). Communication technology and friendship during the transition from high school to college. In R. E. Kraut, M. Brynin, & S. Kiesler (Eds.), *Computers, phones and the Internet: Domesticating information technology* (pp. 265–278). New York: Oxford University Press.

van Dijk, Jan A. G. M. (2005). *The deepening divide: Inequality in the information society.* Thousand Oaks, CA: Sage.

Donath, J. & boyd, d. (2004). Public displays of connection. *BT Technology Journal, 22*(4), 71–82.

Donner, J. (2007). The rules of beeping: Exchanging messages via intentional "missed calls" on mobile phones. *Journal of Computer-Mediated Communication, 13*(1), article 1. Retrieved from http://jcmc.indiana.edu/vol13/issue1/donner.html

Donner, J., Rangaswamy, N., Steenson, M. W., & Wei, C. (2008). 'Express yourself' and 'stay together': The middle-class Indian family. In J. E. Katz (Ed.), *Handbook of mobile communication studies* (pp. 325–337). Cambridge, MA: The MIT Press.

Dunkels, E. (2009). *Vad gör unga på nätet?* [What are adolescents doing on the net?] Malmö, Sweden: Gleerups.

Durkheim, E. (1995). *The elementary forms of religious life.* New York: Free Press. (Original work published 1912)

Dutton, W. H., Helsper, E. J., & Gerber, M. M. (2009). The Internet in Britain: 2009. Oxford: Oxford Internet Institute. Retrieved from http://digital-scholarship.org/digitalkoans/2009/06/24/the-internet-in-britain-2009/

Elmer, G. (2003). A diagram of panoptic surveillance. *New Media & Society, 5*(2), 231–247.

Fernback, J. (2007). Selling ourselves? Profitable surveillance and online communities. *Critical Discourse Studies, 4*(3), 311–330.

Flanagin, A., & Metzger, M. (2001). Internet use in the contemporary media environment. *Human Computer Research, 27*, 153–181.

Foucault, M. (1977). *Discipline and punish: Birth of the prison* (A. Sheridan, Trans.). New York: Pantheon.

Fox, S., & Lewis, O. (2001, April 2). *Fear of online crime: Americans support FBI interception of criminal suspects' email and new laws to protect online privacy.* Washington, DC: Pew Internet & American Life Project. Retrieved from http://www.pewinternet.org

Gaither, C. (2006, August 11). They do it all while studying: At homework time, many students also are playing games, e-mailing friends and watching TV. Scientists say that is bad for learning. *Los Angeles Times.* Retrieved from http://www.latimes.com/business/la-fi-pollhomework11aug11,0,7979479.story?coll=la-home-business

Gandy, O. (1993). *The panoptic sort.* Boulder, CO: Westview Press.

Gergen, K. (2008). Mobile communication and the transformation of the democratic process. In J. E. Katz (Ed.), *Handbook of mobile communication studies* (pp. 297–309). Cambridge, MA: The MIT Press.

Glotz, P., & Bertschi, S. (2005). People, mobiles and society. Concluding insights from an international expert survey. In P. Glotz, S. Bertschi, & C. Locke (Eds.), *Thumb culture: The meaning of mobile phones for society* (pp. 259–285). New Brunswick, NJ: Transaction Publishers.

Goffman, E. (1967). *Interaction rituals: Essays on face-to-face behavior.* New York: Pantheon.

Goggin, G. (2006). *Cell phone culture: Mobile technology in everyday life.* New York: Routledge.

de Gournay, C. (2002). Pretense of intimacy in France. In J. E. Katz & M. Aakhus (Eds.), *Perpetual contact* (pp. 193–206). Cambridge, UK: Cambridge University Press.

Green, N. (2002). On the move: Technology, mobility, and the mediation of social time and space. *The Information Society, 18,* 281–292.

Grinter, R. E., & Eldridge, M. A. (2001). y do tngers luv 2 txt msg? In *Proceedings of the 7th European Conference on Computer-Supported Cooperative Work (ECSCW'01)* (pp. 219–238). Dordrecht, The Netherlands: Kluwer Academic Publishers.

Grinter, R. E., & Palen, L. (2002). Instant messaging in teen life. In *Proceedings of CSCW'02* (pp. 21–30). New York: ACM Press.

Gross, E., Juvonen, J., & Gable, S. (2002). Internet use and well-being in adolescence. *Journal of Social Issues, 58,* 75–90.

Gyorgy, P. (2003). Virtual distance. In K. Nyiri (Ed.), *Mobile communication: Essays on cognition and community* (pp. 97–115). Vienna: Passagen Verlag.

Haddon, L. (2004). *Information and communication technology in everyday life: A concise introduction and research guide.* Oxford: Berg.

Haddon, L., & Vincent, J. (2009). Children's broadening use of mobile phones. In G. Goggin & L. Hjorth (Eds.), *Mobile technologies: From telecommunication to media* (pp. 37–49). London: Routledge.

Hafner, K. (2009, May 25). Texting may be taking a toll. *New York Times.* Retrieved from http://www.nytimes.com/2009/05/26/health/26teen.html?_r=1&emc=eta1

Hagen, I. (2007). 'We can't just sit the whole day watching TV': Negotiations concerning media use among youngsters and their parents. *Young: Nordic Journal of Youth Research, 15*(4), 369–393.

Hagen, I. & Wold. T. (2009). *Mediegenerasjonen. Barn og unge i det nye medieland-skapet* [The media generation: Children and young people in the new media landscape]. Oslo, Norway: Samlaget.

Hargittai, E. (2002). Second-level digital divide: Differences in people's online skills. *First Monday, 7*(4). Retrieved April 10, 2008, from http://firstmonday.org/htbin/cgiwrap/bin/ojs/index.php/fm/article/view/942

Harper, R. (2010). *Texture: Human expression in the age of communications overload.* Cambridge, MA: The MIT Press.

Harper, R., & Hamill, L. (2005). Kids will be kids: The role of mobiles in teenage life. In L. Hamill, & A. Lasen (Eds.), *Mobile world: Past, present and future* (CSCW series; pp. 61–72). London: Springer-Verlag.

Henke, L. L. (1985). Perceptions and use of news media by college students. *Journal of Broadcasting & Electronic Media, 29*(4), 431–436.

Hernwall, P. (2003). *Barn@com — att växa upp I det nya mediasamhället* [children@com—Growing up in the new media society]. Stockholm, Sweden: HLS Förlag.

Holm Sørensen, B. (2001). Børns hverdagsliv med de nye medier [Children's everyday lives with the new media]. In B. Holm Sørensen, L. Audon, & B. R. Olesen (Eds.),

Det hele kører parallelt. De nye medier i børns hverdagsliv [It's all runnung parallel: The new media in children's everyday lives] (pp. 9–47). Copenhagen, Denmark: Gads Förlag.

Holmes, M., Papper, R. A., Popovich, M. N., & Bloxham, M. (2005). *Middletown media studies II: Concurrent media exposure.* Muncie, IN: Ball State University Center for Media Design.

Howard, P. N., Anderson, K., Busch, L., & Nafus, D. (2009). Sizing up information societies: Toward a better metric for the cultures of ICT adoption. *The Information Society, 25,* 1–9.

Huberman, B. (2001). *The laws of the web: Patterns in the ecology of information.* Cambridge, MA: The MIT Press.

Humphreys, I. (2005). Cellphones in public: Social interactions in a wireless era. *New Media & Society, 7*(6), 810–833.

Igarashi, T., Takai, J., & Yoshida, T. (2005). Gender differences in social network development via mobile phone text messages: A longitudinal study. *Journal of Social and Personal Relationships, 22,* 691–713.

International Telecommunications Union. (2009a). Internet usage by region. Retrieved April 20, 2009, from http://www.itu.int/ITU-D/icteye/Reporting/ShowReport Frame.aspx?ReportName=/WTI/InformationTechnologyPublic&RP_ intYear=2008&RP_intLanguageID=1

International Telecommunications Union. (2009b). Mobile usage by region. Retrieved April 20, 2009, from http://www.itu.int/ITU-D/icteye/Reporting/ShowReport Frame.aspx?ReportName=/WTI/CellularSubscribersPublic&RP_ intYear=2008&RP_intLanguageID=1

Internet World Stats. (2007). Usage and population statistics. Retrieved October 24, 2007, from http://internetworldstats.com

Internet World Stats. (2009). Usage and population statistics. Retrieved April 20, 2009, from http://www.internetworldstats.com

Ishii, K. (2004). Internet use via mobile phone in Japan. *Telecommunications Policy, 28,* 43–58.

Ishii, K. (2006). Implications of mobility: The uses of personal communication media in everyday life. *Journal of Communication, 56*(2), 346–365.

Ito, M., Horst, H., Bittanti, M., boyd, d., Herr-Stephenson, B., Lange, P. G., et al. (2008, November). *Living and learning with new media: Summary of findings from the digital youth project.* The John D. and Catherine T. MacArthur Foundation Reports on Digital Media and Learning. Retrieved April 20, 2009, from www.macfound. org/atf/cf/%7BB0386CE3-8B29-4162-8098-E466FB856794%7D/DML_ETH-NOG_WHITEPAPER.PDF

Ito, M., & Okabe, D. (2005). Technosocial situations: Emergent structuring of mobile e-mail use. In M. Ito, D. Okabe, & M. Matsuda (Eds.), *Personal, portable, pedestrian* (pp. 257–273). Cambridge, MA: The MIT Press.

Ito, M., Okabe, D., & Matsuda, M. (Eds.). (2005). *Personal, portable, pedestrian.* Cambridge, MA: The MIT Press.

Jenson, S. (2005). Default thinking: Why consumer products fail. In R. Harper, L. Palen, & A. Taylor (Eds.), *The inside text: Social perspectives on SMS in the mobile age* (pp 1–19). New York: Springer.

Johnson, B., & Rice, R. E. (1987). *Managing organizational innovation: The evolution from word processing to office information systems.* New York: Columbia University Press.

Kalba, K. (2008). *The global adoption and diffusion of mobile phones*. Cambridge, MA: Harvard University Program on Information Resources Policy. Retrieved from http://www.pirp.harvard.edu/pubs_pdf/kalba/kalba-p08-1.pdf

Katz, J. E. (2006). *Magic in the air: Mobile communication and the transformation of social life* (pp. 87–101). New Brunswick, NJ: Transaction Publishers.

Katz, J. E., & Aakhus, M. (2002a). Framing the issues. In J. E. Katz & M. Aakhus (Eds.), *Perpetual contact: Mobile communication, private talk, public performance* (pp. 1–13). Cambridge: Cambridge University Press.

Katz, J. E., & Aakhus, M. (2002b). Conclusion: Making meaning of mobiles: A theory of Apparatgeist. In J. E. Katz & M. Aakhus (Eds.), *Perpetual contact: Mobile communication, private talk, public performance* (pp. 301–318). Cambridge: Cambridge University Press.

Katz, J. E., & Rice, R. E. (2002). *Social consequences of Internet use: Access, involvement and interaction*. Cambridge, MA: The MIT Press.

Katz, J. E., Rice, R. E., Acord, S., Dasgupta, K., & David, K. (2004). Personal mediated communication and the concept of community in theory and practice. In P. Kalbfleisch (Ed.), *Communication Yearbook 28* (pp. 315–370). Mahwah, NJ: Erlbaum.

Katz, J. E., & Sugiyama, S. (2006). Mobile phones as fashion statements: Evidence from student surveys in the U.S. and Japan. *New Media & Society, 8*, 321–337.

Kennedy, T. L. M., Smith, A., Wells, A. T., & Wellman, B. (2008, October). *Networked families*. Pew Internet & American Life Project. Retrieved from http://www.pewinternet.org/Reports/2008/Networked-Families.aspx

Kim, H., Kim, G. J., Park, H. W., & Rice, R. E. (2007). Configurations of relationships in different media: FtF, Email, Instant Messenger, Mobile Phone, and SMS. *Journal of Computer-Mediated Communication, 12*(4). doi: 10.1111/j.1083-6101.2007.00369.x

Kleinman, S. (2007). *Displacing place: Mobile communication in the twenty-first century*. New York: Peter Lang.

Klosek, J. (2000). *Data privacy in the information age*. Westport, CT: Quorum.

Koskinen, I. (2007). *Mobile media in action*. New Brunswick, NJ: Transaction Publishers.

Koskinen, I. (2008). Mobile multimedia: Uses and social consequences. In J. E. Katz (Ed.), *Handbook of mobile communication studies* (pp. 241–255). Cambridge, MA: The MIT Press.

Lee, S. J. (2009). Online communication and adolescent social ties: Who benefits more from Internet use? *Journal of Computer-Mediated Communication, 14*, 509–531.

Lenhart, A., Kahne, J., Middaugh, E., Macgill, A. R., Evans, C., & Vitak, J. (2008, September 16). *Teens, video games and civics*. Retrieved September 17, 2008, from http://www.pewinternet.org/Reports/2008/Teens-Video-Games-and-Civics.aspx

Lenhart, A., Madden, M., & Hitlin, P. (2005, July 27). *Teens and technology: Youth are leading the transition to a fully wired and mobile nation*. Retrieved September 17, 2008, from http://www.pewinternet.org/Reports/2005/Teens-and-Technology.aspx

Lessig, L. (1999). *Code and other laws of cyberspace*. New York: Basic Books.

Leung, L. (2007). Stressful life events, motives for Internet use, and social support among digital kids. *CyberPsychology & Behavior, 10*(2), 204–214.

Leung, L. (2008). Linking psychological attributes to addiction and improper use of the mobile phone among adolescents in Hong Kong. *Journal of Children & Media, 2*(2), 93–113.

Leung, L., & Wei, R. (2000). More than just talk on the move: A uses and gratification study of the cellular phone. *Journalism & Mass Communication Quarterly, 77*(2), 308–320.

Licoppe, C. (2004). 'Connected' presence: The emergence of a new repertoire for managing social relationships in a changing communication technoscape. *Environment and Planning D: Society and Space, 22*(1), 135–156.

Licoppe, C., & Smoreda, Z. (2005). Are social networks technologically embedded? How networks are changing today with changes in communication technology. *Social Networks, 27*(4), 317–335.

Liestøl, G., & Rasmussen, T. (2007). *Digitale medier. En innføring* [Digital media. An introduction]. Oslo: Universitetsforlaget.

Ling, R. (2004). *The mobile connection.* Frankfurt, Germany: Elsevier.

Ling, R. (2005a). Mobile communications vis-à-vis teen emancipation, peer group integration and deviance. In R. Harper, A. Taylor, & L. Palen (Eds.), *The inside text: Social perspectives on SMS in the mobile age* (pp. 175–189). New York: Springer.

Ling, R. (2005b). The socio-linguistics of SMS: An analysis of SMS use by a random sample of Norwegians. In R. Ling & P. Pedersen (Eds.), *Mobile communications: Renegotiation of the social sphere* (pp. 335–349). London: Springer.

Ling, R. (2008a). The mediation of ritual interaction via the mobile telephone. In J. E. Katz (Ed.), *Handbook of mobile communication studies* (pp. 165–176). Cambridge, MA: The MIT Press.

Ling, R. (2008b). *New tech, new ties: How mobile communication is reshaping social cohesion.* Cambridge, MA: The MIT Press.

Ling, R., & Haddon, L. (2003). Mobile telephony, mobility and the coordination of everyday life. In J. Katz (Ed.), *Machines that become us* (pp. 245–266). New Brunswick, NJ: Transaction Publishers.

Ling, R., & Haddon, L. (2008). Children, youth and the mobile phone. In K. Drotner & S. Livingstone (Eds.), *The international handbook of children, media and culture* (pp. 137–151). London: Sage.

Ling, R., & Julsrud, T. (2005). The development of grounded genres in multimedia messaging systems (MMS) among mobile professionals. In K. Nyíri (Ed.), *The global and the local in mobile communication* (pp. 329–338). Vienna: Passagen Verlag.

Ling, R., & Yttri, B. (2002). Hyper-coordination via mobile phones in Norway. In J. E. Katz & M. Aakhus (Eds.), *Perpetual contact: Mobile communication, private talk, public performance* (pp. 139–169). Cambridge: Cambridge University Press

Ling, R., & Yttri, B. (2005). Control, emancipation, and status: The mobile telephone in teens' parental and peer relationships. In R. E. Kraut, M. Brynin & S. Kiesler (Eds.), *Computers, phones and the Internet: Domesticating information technology* (pp. 219–234). New York: Oxford University Press.

Livingstone, S. (2002). *Young people and new media.* London: Sage.

Livingstone, S., & Bober, M. (2005). *UK children go online: Final report of key project findings.* London: The London School of Economics and Political Science, Department of Media and Communications. Retrieved November 14, 2009, from http://www.lse.ac.uk/collections/children-go-online/UKCGO_Final_report.pdf

Livingstone, S., & Bovill, M. (2001). *Children and their changing media environment. A European comparative study.* London: Erlbaum.

Lonkila, M., & Gladarev, B. (2008). Social networks and cellphone use in Russia: Local consequences of global communication technology. *New Media & Society, 10*, 273–293.

Lyon, D. (2001). *Surveillance society: Monitoring everyday life.* Buckingham, UK: Open University Press.

Macgill, A. R. (2007, October 24). *Parent and teenager Internet use.* Pew Internet & American Life Project. Retrieved October 25, 2007, from http://www.pewinternet. org/Reports/2007/Parent-and-Teen-Internet-Use.aspx

Mansell, R., & Collins, B. S. (Eds.). (2007). *Trust and crime in information societies.* Conventry, UK: Edward Elgar.

Mante-Meijer, E., & Haddon, L. (2001). *Checking it out with the people — ICT markets and users in Europe,* Eurescom Project Report EDOM 0161-903. Eurescom project P903. Heidelberg, Germany: Eurescom.

Mathiesen, T. (1997). The viewer society: Michel Foucault's "Panopticon Revisited". *Theoretical Criminology, 1*(2), 215–234.

Matsuda, M. (2005). Mobile communication and selective sociality. In M. Ito, D. Okabe, & M. Matsuda (Eds.), *Personal, portable, pedestrian* (pp. 123–142). Cambridge, MA: The MIT Press.

McMillan, S. J., & Morrison, M. (2006). Coming of age with the Internet: A qualitative exploration of how the Internet has become an integral part of young people's lives. *New Media and Society, 8*(1), 73–95.

Mesch, G., & Talmud, I. (2008). Cultural differences in communication technology use: Adolescent Jews and Arabs in Israel. In J. E. Katz (Ed.), *Handbook of mobile communication studies* (pp. 313–324). Cambridge, MA: The MIT Press.

Meyrowitz, J. (1985). *No sense of place: the impact of electronic media on social behavior.* New York: Oxford University Press.

Miller, M. (2001). A snapshot of the Class of 2001. *Public Relations Tactics, 8*(9), 21–22.

Nathanson, A. (2001). Parents versus peers: Exploring the significance of peer mediation of antisocial television. *Communication Research, 28,* 251–274.

Norris, P. (2001). *Digital divide: Civic engagement, information poverty, and the Internet worldwide.* Cambridge, UK: Cambridge University Press.

Nysveen, H., Pedersen, P. E., & Thorbjornsen, H. (2005). Intentions to use mobile services: Antecedents and cross-service comparisons. *Journal of the Academy of Marketing Science, 33,* 330–346.

Oksman, V., & Turtianen, J. (2004). Mobile communication as a social stage: Meanings of mobile communication in everyday life among teenagers in Finland. *New Media & Society, 6*(3), 391–339.

Orlikowski, W. (1992). The duality of technology: Rethinking the concept of technology in organizations. *Organization Science, 3*(3), 398–427.

Østergaard Madsen, C., & Stald, G. (Eds.). (2005). *Mobile medier — Mobile unge* [Mobile media — mobile youth]. Copenhagen, Denmark: Formidlingsrapport. Film & Medievitenskap, København Universitet.

Ozcan, Y. Z., & Kocak, A. (2003). A new or status symbol? Use of cellular telephones in Turkey. *European Journal of Communication, 18,* 241–254.

Pew Internet & American Life Project. (2002). *The Internet goes to college: How students are living in the future.* Retrieved November 15, 2009, from http://www. pewinternet.org/Reports/2002/The-Internet-Goes-to-College.aspx

Pew Internet & American Life Project. (2007, August 1). *U.S. lags behind: Why it will be harder to close the broadband divide.* Retrieved October 19, 2007, from http:// www.pewinternet.org/pdfs/Broadband_Commentary.pdf

Postman, N. (1993). *Technopoly: The surrender of culture to technology.* New York: Vintage.

Quan-Haase, A. (2007). University students' local and distant social ties: Using and integrating modes of communication on campus. *Information, Communication & Society, 10*(5), 671–693.

Reid, D., & Reid, F. (2005). Textmates and text circles: Insights into the social ecology of SMS text messaging. In L. Hamill & A. Lasen (Eds.), *Mobile world: Past, present and future* (pp. 105–118). London: Springer-Verlag.

Rice, R. E. (1987). Computer-mediated communication and organizational innovation. *Journal of Communication, 37*(4), 65–94.

Rice, R. E., & Katz, J. E. (2003a). Comparing Internet and mobile phone usage: Digital divides of usage, adoption, and dropouts. *Telecommunications Policy, 27*(8/9), 597–623.

Rice, R. E., & Katz, J. E. (2003b). Mobile discourtesy: National survey results on episodes of convergent public and private spheres. In K. Nyíri (Ed.), *Mobile democracy: Essays on society, self and politics* (pp. 53–64). Vienna: Passagen Verlag.

Rice, R. E., & Katz, J. E. (2008). Assessing new cell phone text and video services. *Telecommunications Policy, 32*(7), 455–467.

Rice, R. E., & Webster, J. (2002). Adoption, diffusion and use of new media in organizational settings. In C. Lin & D. Atkin (Eds.), *Communication technology and society* (pp. 191–227). Cresskill, NJ: Hampton Press.

Rideout, V., Roberts, D. F., & Foehr, U. (March, 2005). *Generation M: Media in the lives of 8–18 year olds.* A Kaiser Family Foundation Study. Retrieved April 10, 2005, from http://www.kaiserfamilyfoundation.org/entmedia/7250.cfm

Rogers, E. M. (2003). *Diffusion of innovations* (5th ed.). New York: Free Press.

Rule, J. B. (2002). From mass society to perpetual contact: Models of communication technologies in social context. In J. E. Katz & M. Aakhus (Eds.), *Perpetual contact: Mobile communication, private talk, public performance* (pp. 242–254). Cambridge: Cambridge University Press.

Runnel, P., Pruulmann-Vengerfeldt, P., & Keller, M. (2006). A mobile phone isn't a mobile phone any more: Case study of Estonian mobile phone use practices. In *Proceedings of the 5th conference on cultural attitudes toward technology and communication* (pp. 606–621). Retrieved November 22, 2006, from http://www.jrnl.ut.ee/~pille/PhD/5-VI-runnel-pruulmann-vengerfeldt-keller.pdf

Seepersad, S. (2004). Coping with loneliness: Adolescent online and offline behavior. *CyberPsychology & Behavior, 7,* 35–39.

Skog, B. (2002). Mobiles and the Norwegian teen: Identity, gender and class. In J. E. Katz & M. Aakhus (Eds.), *Perpetual contact: Mobile communication, private talk, public performance* (pp. 255–273). Cambridge: Cambridge University Press.

Smoreda, Z., & Thomas, F. (2001). Social networks and residential ICT adoption and use. In *Proceedings of EURESCOM Summit 2001.* Retrieved November 14, 2009, from http://www.eurescom.de/~public-web-deliverables/P900-series/P903/ICT_use_Smoreda.pdf

Spink, A., Cole, C., & Waller, M. (2008). Multitasking behavior. In B. Cronin (Ed.), *Annual Review of Information Science and Technology, 42,* 93–118. Medford, NJ: Information Today, Inc.

Sprint. (2004, July 7). *Sprint survey finds nearly two-thirds of Americans are uncomfortable overhearing wireless conversations in public.* Retrieved December 26, 2005, from http://www2.sprint.com/mr/news_dtl.do?id=2073

Stald, G. (2008). Mobile identity: Youth, identity, and mobile communication media. In D. Buckingham (Ed.), *Youth, identity and digital media* (pp. 143–163). Boston: The MIT Press.

Steadman, P. (2007). The contradictions of Jeremy Bentham's panopticon penitentiary. *Journal of Bentham Studies, 9.* Retrieved July 6, 2007, from http://www.ucl.ac.uk/Bentham-Project/journal/Steadman_panopt.htm

Strocchi, G. (2003). The next frontier of technology: Awaiting UMTS. In L. Fortunati, J. E. Katz, & R. Riccini (Eds.), *Mediating the human body: Technology, communication & fashion* (pp. 133–138). Mahwah, NJ: Erlbaum.

Taylor, A. S., & Harper, R. (2003). The gift of the gab?: A design oriented sociology of young people's use of mobiles. *Journal of Computer Supported Cooperative Work, 12*(3), 267–296.

Tichenor, P. J., Donohue, G. A., & Olien, C. N. (1970). Mass media flow and differential growth in knowledge. *Public Opinion Quarterly, 34,* 159–170.

Tønnessen, E. S. (2007). *Generasjon.com. Mediekultur blant barn og unge* [Generation.com. Media culture among children and adolescents]. Oslo, Norway: Universitetsforlaget.

Totten, J., Lipscomb, T., Cook, R., & Lesch, W. (2005). General patterns of cell phone usage among college students: A four-state study. *Services Marketing Quarterly, 26*(3), 13–39.

Turkle, S. (2008). Always-on/Always-on-you: The tethered self. In J. E. Katz (Ed.), *Handbook of mobile communication studies* (pp. 121–137). Cambridge, MA: The MIT Press.

Vincent, R. C., & Basil, M. D. (1997). College students' news gratifications, media use, and current events knowledge. *Journal of Broadcasting & Electronic Media, 41*(3), 380–392.

Walther, J. B. (1996). Computer-mediated communication: Impersonal, interpersonal, and hyperpersonal interaction. *Communication Research, 23,* 1–43.

Wei, C., & Kolko, B. E. (2005). Resistance to globalization: Language & Internet diffusion patterns in Uzbekistan. *The New Review of Multimedia & Hypermedia, 11,* 205–220.

Wei, R. (2008). Motivations for using the mobile phone for mass communications & entertainment. *Telematics & Informatics, 25,* 36–46.

Wei, R., & Lo, V-H. (2006). Staying connected while on the move: Cell phone use and social connectedness. *New Media & Society, 8*(1), 53–72.

Wellman, B. (2001). Physical place and cyberplace: The rise of personalized networking. *International Journal of Urban and Regional Research, 25*(2), 227–252.

Wirth, W., von Pape, T., & Karnowski, V. (2008). An integrative model of mobile phone appropriation. *Journal of Computer Mediated Communication, 13,* 593–617.

World Internet Project. (2009). *Summary report.* (13 countries across North America, South America, Europe, Asia, the Middle East, and Oceania). Los Angeles, CA: Center for the Digital Future, Annenberg School for Communication, University of Southern California. Retrieved November 14, 2009, from http://www.digitalcenter.org/pages/current_report.asp?intGlobalId=43

Yao, M. Z., Rice, R. E., & Wallis, K. (2007). Predicting user concerns about online privacy. *Journal of the American Society for Information Science & Technology, 58*(5), 710–722.

Yoon, K-W. (2003). Retraditionalizing the mobile: Young people's sociality and mobile phone use in Seoul, South Korea. *European Journal of Cultural Studies, 6*(3), 327–343.

Yoon, K-W. (2006). Local sociality in young people's mobile communications: A Korean case study. *Childhood, 13*(2), 155–174.

CHAPTER CONTENTS

2   A Few Transparent Liars

Explaining 54% Accuracy in Deception Detection Experiments

Timothy R. Levine

Michigan State University

Deception detection experiments consistently find that people are statistically significantly, but only slightly, better than chance. The stability of this finding and the lack of variance in judge ability are at odds with current and classic deception theory that explains accuracy in terms of message recipient's ability to spot leaked deception cues. An alternative explanation based on limited variance in message source transparency provides a more coherent account of deception detection findings and has important implications for past and future deception theory.

Introduction

Research consistently finds that people are only slightly better than chance at detecting deception. Meta-analysis of more than 200 experiments finds that people are, on average, 54% accurate when they have a 50–50 chance of being right (Bond & DePaulo, 2006). This level of accuracy is statistically better than could be obtained by chance alone, but it also suggests that people are not much better than a random coin flip at correctly distinguishing honest communication from outright lies.

There are a number of intriguing aspects of the deception detection accuracy literature. First, one of the more curious facets of the literature is the across-study stability of accuracy results. The slightly-better-than-chance accuracy finding appears to be among the most reliable, consistent, and robust finding in all of social science. Ninety-eight percent of all accuracy results fall between 39% and 67%, and more than 90% of studies produce results within 10% of the across-study mean. Figure 2.1, adapted from the results of Bond and DePaulo (2006), visually depicts the across-study consistency of this finding with a frequency distribution of study results. In Figure 2.1, the percent accuracy reported in each study is plotted on the horizontal axis and the number of studies obtaining a given result is presented on the vertical axis. A normal curve is superimposed on the distribution. As the reader can see, previous findings in the literatures are neatly and normally distributed around the across-study grand mean. As those familiar with meta-analysis know, the distributions of

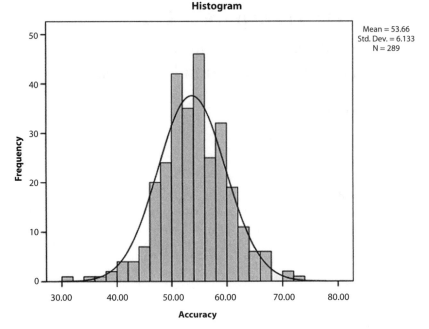

Figure 2.1 Percent accuracy observed in deception detection experiments (adapted from Bond & DePaulo, 2006).

study findings in social scientific literatures are rarely so orderly. Instead, "messy" literatures with multiple moderators and much unresolved heterogeneity are much more typical.

A second, related feature of the literature is that individual-study deviation from the across-study 54% average appears to be a simple function of the number of judgments made in the study (Bond & DePaulo, 2006). Studies involving larger numbers of judgments lawfully produce accuracy levels closer to the across-study mean. This means that study-to-study differences are more a function of mere reliability than substantive factors such as the population that was sampled, the theoretical orientation of the authors, the hypotheses being testing, or the specific independent variables under study. Usually, in social science, such things as hypotheses, theories, participants, and independent variables matter, so it is most curious that the deception detection literature is different from its parent fields of inquiry in these regards.

A third unusual feature of the literature is that small differences routinely produce statistically significant results even with small samples. The difference between the observed 54% accuracy and the 50% accuracy expected by mere chance is not only statistically significant in meta-analysis, but also at the level of the individual study. In social science, it usually takes large sample sizes to produce small, but statistically significant findings because the standard errors in social data tend to large. Standard errors, in turn, tend to be large when sample sizes are small because meaningful individual differences almost always exist in how humans respond in social situations. In contrast, the tight confidence intervals typical in the deception detection literature result from unusually small standard errors which, in turn, are a function of an unusual degree of homogeneity across judges.

Perhaps what makes the deception detection literature most intriguing, however, is the theoretical puzzle of adequately explaining these findings. If currently accepted theory is correct, there should be more variance in the findings from study to study, findings should not be just a mere function of reliability, there should be more variance in judge ability, and the accuracy ceiling should be higher. Decades of accumulated data systemically and persistently defy theoretical expectations, and this lack of theory-data correspondence begs explanation.

The difference between 54% observed accuracy and the 50% chance accuracy is highly statistically significant and thus clearly reflects some systematic causal mechanism. Veracity judgments are not solely attributable to chance, and consequently there must be a reason for the pattern of results. Simply finding that people do better than chance is not surprising. Most people, social scientists and otherwise, believe that some people are astute social observers and most of the rest of us have at least modest skill at reading others. What is perplexing is why people systematically do better than chance, but seldom much better than chance. Why not higher accuracy? And why is the just over chance accuracy finding so persistent and stable? In short, a viable explanation for this robust finding must not only account for why people systematically exceed chance, but also why people do not exceed chance by very much.[1]

Current theory interprets and explains accuracy results in terms of the individual message receiver's skill, competence, and ability to ferret out lies based on observing the behavior of the message source. The presumption is that these experiments provide a reasonable test of people's ability to distinguish truths from lies and that it is possible for the participants in these experiments to do well at their task. Given this, accuracy findings are usually interpreted as informative about people's ability (or lack there of) to detect deception. The message recipients are, after all, the subjects in these experiments, and consequently their performance is the focus.

Accuracy findings, however, may tell us as much or more about the message sources being judged and the conditions under which they are judged than about the people doing the judging. Along these lines, the current paper explains accuracy in deception detection findings in terms of variance in message source performance rather than variance in judge ability. It is argued that in the context presented by typical deception detection experiments, a "few transparent liars" model provides a better account of detection accuracy findings than a judge ability model or a source-receiver interaction model. Simply stated, stable and slightly better than chance accuracy is a function of a few transparent liars.

A Test-Taking Analogy

Many readers are likely familiar with giving and taking tests. Imagine that a class of 100 students is given four 100 question true-false exams over a semester. The standard interpretation of scores on tests like these is that scores of 50% reflect mere chance performance and no knowledge of class material, and that as scores approach 100%, systematic increases above chance levels reflect increasing mastery of course content. There is no reason to expect scores systematically below 50% because students do not intentionally seek a low grade by purposely missing questions that they know. Simply put, test scores are most often thought of as telling us about student performance: how much they studied, how effectively they studied, how smart they are, their testing taking ability, and the like.

Such true-false tests provide a reasonable analogy for deception detection experiments. In such experiments, participants are exposed to a series of truths and lies and are asked to distinguish which are which by making dichotomous truth-lie judgments. In these experiments there is an equal probability of a message being honest or deceptive and accuracy is scored as the percent of judgments correct across truths and lies, so the chance rate in these experiments is 50% just like a true-false test (Levine, Park, & McCornack, 1999). Honest sources have no reasons to fool judges in believing that they are really lying, and judges have nothing to gain by intentionally making incorrect judgments, so there is no reason to expect a systematic mechanism that would produce worse than chance performance. Thus, 50% minus chance variation should provide a basement for scores, and systematic variance above a 50% level would reflect the extent to which people accurately distinguish truths from lies in the context of these experiments.

Back to the true-false test analogy: imagine that students take a series of tests like the one described above and the average score on each of the tests is around 55%, with all four tests producing approximately the same outcome and a similar distribution of scores. The average student performs significantly better than chance, but in an absolute sense, fails miserably. Also, the standard deviations are consistently small. Over the four tests, all students tend to hover around the mean that varies little from test to test. What kind of explanation might best explain this pattern of test scores?

Again, this analogy is reasonably comparable to the deception detection literature. Across more than 200 separate experiments spanning several decades, average accuracy hovers around 54% (Bond & DePaulo, 2006). Findings from study to study are remarkably homogeneous and standard errors both between and across studies are small. A number of statistically significant moderators exist, but the impact of known moderators is small in an absolute sense and the results of most studies fall within plus or minus 10% regardless of the particular independent variables included in the study, the communication medium involved, who the research participants are, and the characteristics of the deceptive messages judged (Bond & DePaulo, 2006).

A test-taker explanation for this outcome might hold that the students studied only a little. They learned just enough to do better than mere chance but not nearly enough to do well. For example, the students may have learned and remembered about 10% of the class content. So, if students knew the answers to 10 questions and guessed on the other 90 questions, then they would get the 10 they knew for sure right and get 50% of the 90 they guessed on producing a 55% on the exam (10 + 45 = 55). So, a "little bit of knowledge" model can explain the outcome. But, it seems very odd that all the students would only know a little on all four tests. Usually, some students do better than other students. The lack of variance is odd indeed.

An alternative explanation is that the scores tell us more about the test than the test takers. Imagine a true-false test with 90 questions that are impossibly difficult necessitating guessing by everyone and ten questions that are so easy that everyone gets them correct whether or not they took the class, studied, etc. This test tells us nothing at all about what was learned, and it does not matter who takes the test. Regardless of knowledge, motivation, and ability, everyone does pretty much the same. People consistently do better than 50%, but no one does much better. Such a test always produces an average of 55% plus or minus chance variation. Now the lack of test taker variance is not at all odd. It is expected. The nature of the test makes test taker ability irrelevant so that little variance in ability is observed.

Explaining 54% Accuracy

Conventional Wisdom Regarding Reasons for Accuracy and Inaccuracy

The current thinking about deception detection has largely evolved from Ekman and Friesen's (1969) idea of "leakage." The original idea was that there are emotional correlates of deception, emotions are conveyed nonverbally, and emotional expression is not entirely under conscious control. Compared to the honest message source, deceivers are apt to experience guilt, fear of detection, and perhaps other emotions created by the act of lying. Deceivers try to control behavioral displays so as not to give themselves away, but cues associated with deception-linked emotion leak out anyway, often through nonverbal channels that are more difficult to control. Consequently, a message recipient who is actively looking for the right leaked cues should be fairly adept at distinguishing truth from lie.

The leakage idea was expanded upon by Zuckerman, DePaulo, and Rosenthal's (1981) four-factor theory. The four factor framework specifies four internal psychological states that differentiate truths and lies. These four include emotions, arousal, cognitive effort, and over control. Relative to truth-tellers, liars are more likely to experience greater levels of arousal, emotions like fear and guilt, greater cognitive effort, and more effort to control of non-verbal displays. Because each of these internal states is thought to be associated with specific nonverbal behaviors, clues to deception are leaked nonverbally. For example, the increased cognitive effort associated with lying is thought to lead to an increased number of speech errors and longer response latencies that signal deceit.

A contemporary iteration of this thinking is reflected in Interpersonal Deception Theory (IDT) (Burgoon & Buller, 1996). Liars strategically present themselves as honest, but non-strategically leak deception cues. Message receivers pick up on these cues and become suspicious. Liars, however, pick up on leaked suspicion, and strategically adapt. So do receivers. Net accuracy depends on the liar's encoding skill relative to the receiver's decoding skill and how the interaction progresses dynamically over time. IDT, therefore, is a source-receiver interaction model that rests on variance in both sender and receiver ability. Both senders and receivers are leaky, both senders and receivers are adept at spotting and correctly interpreting leakage, and both senders and receivers strategically use the information gained from leakage to adjust their own behavioral performance.

Thus, according to these dominant theoretical perspectives, the reason people are systematically better than chance accuracy is that verbal and nonverbal cues indicative of deceit are inevitably and inadvertently leaked, these leaked behaviors signaling deceit (and suspicion in the case of IDT) are perceived, and consequently truth is correctly distinguished from lie. Accuracy is a function of a message judge's ability to recognize valid leakage relative to the sender's ability to mask leakage.

The accepted reasons why people are far from perfect is that (a) there is an imperfect link between any given behavioral display and veracity, and (b) lay people rely on cues that lack diagnostic utility in addition to, or instead of, authentic cues. That is, there are no perfectly reliable deception cues and people often look for the wrong things. Consistent with this latter point, research finds that the most common belief about deception is that liars avoid eye contact (Bond & The Global Deception Research Team, 2006) whereas meta-analysis finds no link between gaze and honesty (DePaulo et al., 2003; Sporer & Schwandt, 2007). IDT further adds that liars engage in strategic countermoves, constantly adapting their performance to appear more honest and misleading less skilled judges (Burgoon & Buller, 1996). The net result is above chance accuracy that is far from perfect.

There are many findings consistent with this view. Meta-analysis of deception cues finds that there are behaviors that probabilistically distinguish truths from lies, but no behavior or set of behaviors that does so perfectly (DePaulo et al., 2003). Further, there is a less than perfect but non-zero correspondence between what people look for when detecting deception and the behaviors that have actual diagnostic utility (Zuckerman et al., 1981). Thus, above chance but less than ideal accuracy makes much sense from this perspective, and there is a wealth of supportive findings that can be cited as evidence in favor of this stance.

Not all findings in the literature, however, fall neatly in line with the ability-to-spot-leakage account. First, efforts to enhance accuracy through nonverbal training have failed to document much in the way of improvement. Meta-analysis finds only marginal improvements from non-verbal training (Frank & Feeley, 2003), and studies offering additional controls find even more meager results (Levine, Feeley, McCornack, Harms, & Hughes, 2005). If low accuracy findings stemmed simply from looking for the wrong cues, one would expect much better results from training studies. Further, the training approaches that appear most effective are not based on nonverbal leakage (Blair, Levine, & Shaw, in press; Hartwig, Granhag, Stromwall, & Kronkvist, 2006).

A judge ability account would also predict that professional expertise would be a strong determinant of accuracy. If accuracy is a skill, people should get better with practice and experience. People also tend to self-select into professions where they have aptitude. Thus, police, military interrogators, customs officials, etc. should be better at detecting deception than the average college sophomore. Yet, meta-analysis suggests that this is not the case. Neither age, nor expertise, nor specific occupation meaningfully impact accuracy (Aamodt & Custer, 2006; Bond & DePaulo, 2006).

Further, both judge ability accounts and source-receiver interaction explanations suggest substantial within and between study variance in accuracy. Ability and relative ability should vary from person to person and situation to situation. Such variance should not only stem from training and experience, but also from other individual differences such as self monitoring, perspective taking, emotional intelligence and the like. If some substantial proportion of message sources leak subtle cues to deception, more socially adroit people should be more accurate than their socially oblivious counterparts producing variance, increasing standard errors, and making findings generally more variable than they are. Yet, meta-analysis again shows that cognitive and social abilities have little impact on accuracy (Aamodt & Custer, 2006). The within- and across-study consistency of findings is difficult to reconcile with the leakage-based, perceptive judge perspective. In short, ability-based explanations can be stretched to explain the average effects but not the lack of variance apparent in the existing data.

Advocates of sender leakage and judge ability perspectives frequently blame methodological scapegoats for the failure to achieve theoretically predicted variance in accuracy. The three most frequently blamed culprits are the use of low stakes lies, sanctioned lies, and dichotomous (rather than continuous) deception judgments. Although it is axiomatic from within the logic of the leakage perspective that sanctioning and stakes make a substantial difference, the one published study directly testing cues from unsanctioned lies against the behaviors observed during truth and sanctioned lying found little evidence that sanctioning made a meaningful difference (Feeley & deTurck, 1998). In fact, the behavior for which the largest differences were observed produced differences that were in the direction opposite to that predicted by leakage and four-factor theories. Sanctioned lies were characterized by more speech errors and unsanctioned lies by fewer speech errors than the truthful control. Furthermore, detection accuracy studies using unsanctioned, higher stakes lies report results that are no different from the literature as a whole (e.g., Levine, Kim, Park, & Hughes, 2006). Studies that produce results falling farther for the 54% average are not those using better, presumably more valid stimulus materials, but are instead those studies involving few judgments, producing less stable results (Bond & DePaulo, 2006). As the number of judgments made in a study increases, estimates approach the across-study average. If substantial moderators existed, methodological or otherwise, this finding simply would not be the case. Finally, once converted to a common metric, meta-analysis shows that studies using continuous scaling find comparable results to dichotomously scored accuracy studies (Bond & DePaulo, 2006). Thus, not only do the usual methodological suspects appear innocent of any substantial sabotage, their failure to make the predicted differences offers further evidence inconsistent with the prevailing theoretical views.

The Psychometrics of Veracity Judgments

Finally, and most important, findings from the most recent meta-analysis are decisively incongruent with the judge ability perspective. Bond and DePaulo (2008) looked at the variance in accuracy judgments rather than just average accuracy levels. They decomposed veracity judgments into four components: demeanor, truth-bias, transparency, and ability.[2] *Demeanor* is the tendency of a person being judged to appear honest (or deceptive) independent of whether or not the person is lying. Variance in demeanor indicates that some people are more (or less) believable than others. *Truth-bias* is the tendency to believe others whether or not they are telling the truth. Variance in truth-bias means some people are more gullible than others; others are more skeptical. *Transparency* refers to how leaky people are when lying and how sincere they are when they are telling the truth. People who are transparent leak the fact that they are lying and it is relatively easier to distinguish when they are lying from when they are telling the truth than those who are less transparent. Finally, *ability* is an individual difference in skill at telling if someone is lying or not. Thus, demeanor and transparency reflect variance in the message source, whereas truth-bias and ability reflect variance in the message judge. Further, demeanor and truth-bias reflect variance in *bias*; that is, they are tendencies to believe (or not) that are independent of actual veracity, whereas transparency and ability reflect variance in *openness or skill* in presenting or discriminating between honest and deceptive messages. Because deception detection experiments average across an equal number of truths and lies, demeanor and truth-bias do not affect overall accuracy (Levine et al., 2006) whereas transparency and ability do impact overall accuracy. Thus, systematically above-chance accuracy stems from transparency, ability, or both.

Bond and DePaulo (2008) found that variance in demeanor is large, both in an absolute sense and relative to the other three sources of variation. Some people are just more believable than others, and this aura of believability has a large impact on judges. There are also individual differences in truth-bias and transparency, with these differences being much smaller than the variance in demeanor, but much larger than the variance in ability. Individual differences in ability contribute very little to overall accuracy. Comparatively, the variance in demeanor was 200 times as large as the variance in judge ability. Thus, variance in believability and accuracy stems more from the message source than the person judging the message, and the variance in bias swamps variance in ability. This explains why accuracy values within studies are so stable. The lack of individual differences in judge ability leads to small standard errors and even small differences can be statistically significant. This finding also renders theoretical accounts of deception detection based on either judge ability or source-receiver interactions impotent. Variables that do not vary cannot co-vary, and variables to that do not co-vary do not explain anything. The finding of only trivial variance in judge ability means that deception detection accuracy cannot be explained in terms of judge ability or source-receiver interactions.

A Few Transparent Liars

The thesis of the current essay is that deception detection accuracy findings are the result of a few transparent senders. Important to the argument is Bond and DePaulo's (2008) finding that the variance in sender transparency in detection accuracy studies is massively larger than the variance in judge ability, although variance in transparency is not large in an absolute sense. This suggests that above-chance accuracy is not a function of individual differences in judge's ability to recognize leakage, but instead a function of individual differences in how much is leaked independent of who is doing the judging. In terms of the previous test taking analogy, the variance in test results is attributable to test question difficulty rather than student knowledge or competence. Returning to deception, the current perspective holds that most people can lie seamlessly without diagnostically useful leakage, but a few people tend to give themselves away and consequently are systemically detected by most observers. There are enough transparent senders to produce accuracy rates that statistically exceed chance level, but too few (under the conditions in most deception detection experiments) to allow for accuracy rates that exceed chance by much. Those few transparent senders are seen as transparent by almost everyone so there is much more variance in transparency than ability. Hence, accuracy findings tell us more about the sender than the detector. The slightly-better-than-chance finding is a function of a relatively few transparent liars.

The Few Transparent Liars explanation fits the literature more neatly and cleanly than theories predicated on the ability to spot leakage. A Few Transparent Liars accounts both for the mean levels of accuracy observed in deception detection experiments and for the lack of variability observed around mean levels (see Bond & DePaulo, 2006, 2008). It explains the lack of large effects for professional experience (see Bond & DePaulo, 2006) and nonverbal training (see Frank & Feeley, 2003). It explains why cue studies fail to find evidence of substantial leakage (see DePaulo et al., 2003; Sporer & Schwandt, 2006, 2007). In short, the few transparent liars explanation makes previously puzzling anomalous findings cohere.

The current view does not deny the existence of leakage. Instead, leakage in some form or another is what makes some liars leaky. However, slightly above chance accuracy means that although leakage sometimes happens, it does not characterize the lies told by most of the people most of the time, at least in quantities that would be diagnostically useful even to a trained and experienced eye. Thus, one key difference between the current view and traditional leakage-based theory is the prevalence and centrality of leakage. Traditional leakage perspectives portray leakage as typical of lies, or at least unsanctioned, high-stakes lies. Leakage is presumed to characterize deceptive communication such that it can be used by a skilled and knowledgeable judge to distinguish truths from lies. This traditional view has been recently re-articulated by O'Sullivan (2009):

> In the previous chapter, Mark Frank reviewed how the disruptions in feeling and thinking caused by lying can result in observable clues that lie detectors could use to detect deceit. Quite surprisingly, few people seem to use these clues. (p. 74)

Leakage perspectives hold that deception cues exist, but low accuracy stems from a failure of judges to correctly use the information available to them. In contrast to leakage theory where leakage is seen as a given and judge ability as variable, the Few Transparent Liars Model views leakage as variable and judge ability as near constant.

Consistent with this perspective, recent meta-analyses of nonverbal deception cues find small and inconsistent effects for objective nonverbal deception cues (DePaulo et al., 2003; Sporer & Schwandt, 2006; 2007). Sporer and Schwandt (2007), for example, note that of the 154 tests of specific nonverbal behaviors predicted by four-factor theory that are reported in the literature, only 28 (18%) are statistically significant. Leakage findings thus occur at rates better than chance, but non-supportive results out-number supportive findings more than 5 to 1. Thus, leakage can very plausibly account for the statistically significant difference between 50% and 54% in accuracy, but not much more than that. Forty years of accumulated evidence shows that leakage-based accounts have little explanatory power, and consequently research findings do not support the prominent place nonverbal leakage has in deception theory.

The Few Transparent Liars Model is notably inconsistent with source-receiver interaction models such as IDT as accounts of deception detection accuracy. IDT views deception detection as a function of sender *and* receiver skill. Senders and receivers are theoretically specified to be sensitive to each other's leakage, and deception success or failure depends on the skills of each relative to the other. In the current perspective, judge ability does not meaningfully vary. Since it does not vary, it cannot co-vary, and it cannot *statistically interact* with receiver skill. This view does not deny that senders and receivers interact in a more general communication sense, but it does specify that deception detection accuracy is typically a function of limited sender variance and not variance in message judge ability or the statistical interaction sender-judge ability.

Several important qualifications and clarifications to the current argument need to be made explicit. First, in the test-taking analogy and so far in this essay, transparency was described as an all-or-nothing phenomenon for the sake of simplicity. Few, if any, people, however, are likely to be perfectly transparent. The point of the model is that within the typical deception detection experiment, some small proportion of people is at least somewhat transparent while the majority of people are not very transparent. The model need not, and does not, literally presume all or nothing transparency. Instead, it is based on more variance in sender transparency than judge ability.

A second qualification relates to the generality or boundary conditions of the model. The few transparent liars model applies to the context and ecology of typical deception detection experiment in the leakage tradition. Most previous deception detection experiments were designed with the ability to spot leakage perspective firmly ingrained, and hence these experimental designs test the ability to spot deception-produced leakage. Other types of information are typically precluded by design (Park, Levine, McCornack, Morrison, & Ferrara, 2002). For example, one way people are likely to assess the probability of deception is by considering if a person has reason to lie. That is, people project motive (Levine, Kim, & Blair, 2010). In deception detection experiments, however, no motive for lying is usually apparent. Or if there is a motive, it is constant across all sources. Thus, consideration of motive is of no use in determining truth from fabrication. Deception detection experiments also preclude useful prior factual knowledge, diagnostically useful information from informants, access to physical evidence, use of context information, use of communication content in context, the strategic use of evidence, and knowledge of confessions. Research indicates that outside the lab, lies are usually detected well after the fact on the basis of information other than leaked behavioral cues, such as those listed in the previous sentence (Park et al., 2002). Thus, the ecology of the deception detection experiment makes sense from an ability to spot leakage orientation, but makes less sense if the ability to spot leakage is largely irrelevant to how lies are actually detected. Consistent with this, recent experiments have reported higher levels of accuracy, but these elevated accuracy findings are not obtained from passive observations of deception generated nonverbal leakage. Instead, recent experiments reporting impressive accuracy findings are based on the strategic use of evidence (Granhag, Stromwal, & Hartwig, 2007; Hartwig et al., 2006), strategic questioning designed to increase transparency (Levine & Blair, 2010; Levine, Shaw, & Shulman, 2010), or content in context (Blair et al., in press) approaches.

It does not follow, however, that the leakage-based deception detection literature is therefore uninformative. To the contrary, these experiments provide a very consistent picture of the extent to which people can distinguish truths from lies in near real time based only on passive observation of sender performance. The contention here is that, except for a few inept liars, people cannot and do not detect deception under such conditions. These findings are theoretically important because accepted theory clearly predicts otherwise. Thus, alternative theory is needed to which the current perspective will contribute. These findings also have important practical implications. Knowing what does not work is highly valuable in preventing wasted effort, discouraging a false sense confidence, and in prompting new directions.

A third qualification is that while "a few transparent liars" provides a catchy phrase for the current model, the reader is reminded that transparency applies to truths and lies. Consequently, slightly-above-chance accuracy is specified to result from a few transparent *senders*. Traditional leakage is something liars do, but the idea of transparency applies to honest and deceptive senders alike. Both leaky lies and exculpatory statements enhance transparency.

The reader is cautioned that although accuracy in deception detection experiments is typically better than chance for honest sources and below chance for liars (the "veracity effect," Levine et al., 1999), it does not follow that above chance accuracy results only from transparent honest senders. The veracity effect stems from the tendency to believe a source independent of message veracity (Levine et al., 1999). The veracity effect and base-rate effects can be explained well by "mere chance" models (Levine et al., 2006). The current transparency model, in contrast, was created to explain systematic improvements over and above chance. Transparent sources are believed when they are honest and doubted when they are lying. Thus, judgments based on sender transparency, unlike sender demeanor and judge truth-bias, are contingent on message veracity. So, the more a given judge is truth-biased, the more that judge will get honest messages correct and lies wrong creating the well documented difference between truth and lie accuracy. As long as judges view an equal number of truths and lies, however, truth-bias does not affect average accuracy (Park & Levine, 2001; Levine et al., 2006). Gains in truth accuracy and degradations in lie accuracy average out. Transparency, on the other hand, leads to improvement over chance. In the Park-Levine model, truth-bias affects the slope of the regression of truth-lie base-rates onto total accuracy. Transparency is hypothesized to affect the y-intercept in Park-Levine model. A complete lack of transparency would produce 50% accuracy at the 50–50 truth-lie base-rate regardless of truth-bias. Because accuracy is 54% at the 50–50 base-rate, a little (but not zero) transparency is posited here. Applied to Park-Levine, the current thesis is that it is sender transparency, not judge ability, which accounts for the y-intercept in the Park-Levine model. Thus, the current model is consistent with Park and Levine (2001) but the focus is different. A few transparent liars can be thought of a modular add-on to the veracity effect and Park-Levine models, all of which will fit under the more general logic of the forthcoming Truth-Bias Theory.

Methodological Implications

Testing the few transparent liars logic in future research requires, at minimum, a research design that allows for sender and judge variance to be partitioned. This, in turn, requires that multiple judges assess multiple senders with senders as a repeated factor in the design. In such designs, accuracy can be scored both for individual judges and for individual senders, and judge variance can be compared to sender variance. In a first study based on the current logic, Levine, Shaw, & Shulman (2010) used this sort of design with 128 participants each judging 44 different senders who either were deceptive or honest. Consistent with predictions, variance in sender transparency was ten times larger than variance in judge ability, and a strategic questioning induction designed to alter detection accuracy increased variance in transparency but not variance in judge ability.

A stronger test of the few transparent liars idea, however, would not only partition sender and judge variance, but also fully distinguish between transparency, demeanor, ability, and truth-bias variance. Research accomplishing this would require a design like that described above except that additionally each sender would need to produce both honest and deceptive messages. Such a design would allow research to partition variance into sender effect, judge effect, and sender-judge interaction effects.

Some Explanatory Speculation

Presuming that the Few Transparent Liars Model is accurate, one interesting question is why so few people are transparent. Although admittedly speculative, perhaps the most plausible explanation is simply practice. Humans develop the cognitive abilities needed for deception in early childhood, between the ages of 3 and 5 (Peskin, 1992). The lies young children tell are likely to be highly transparent, and those transparent lies are likely to be punished or at least discouraged. Rather than abstaining from lies, however, children gradually learn to avoid detection through trial and error, and improve (i.e., lower transparency) with repeated practice over the years. By early adulthood, most people have had considerable practice in lying so it makes sense that they would be good at telling lies.

Why then are a few people transparent? One possibility is that since some people lie more than others (Serota, Levine, & Boster, 2010), some people are more practiced than others. A second explanation is that similar to most other skill sets, there are individual differences in natural ability and thus some people benefit more from practice than others. Further, these two explanations may interact so that people with less aptitude practice less and this exacerbates individual differences in transparency over time. Third, transparency is likely not limited to a stable, trait-like individual difference. Instead, transparency also probably varies within individuals as a result of situational and chance factors. Even the most seamless liars may slip up and reveal their lies on occasion. The net result of these three forces produces some small percentage of lies that are transparent and a large percentage that are not.

The Few Transparent Liars Model is not only predicated on some small variance in transparency, but also on a corresponding lack of variance in judge ability. Evolutionary perspectives on deception often presume that because human ability to deceive is highly evolved, the ability to detect must also have evolved. As Smith (1987) puts it, there must exist "a coevolutionary struggle between the deceiver and the deceived. There is an evolutionary arms race to develop better deception tactics and subsequently the pressure to develop better deception detection devices" (p. 59). Such a perspective makes the few transparent liar model seemingly at odds with evolutionary perspectives. Yet, this need not be the case. Whether the human ability to deceive evolved due to providing some unique evolutionary advantage, or as "a parasitism of the preexisting system for correct communication" (Smith, p. 59), it may well be the case that human susceptibility to being duped reflects a highly adaptive trade-off that has and does serve our species well.

As Gilbert (1991) argued, a cognitive system that evaluated all incoming information for veracity would be radically less efficient than a system that presumed truth as a default, then subsequently "unbelieved" information that was later discovered to be false. From an evolution of communication perspective, "it is well-known that group living, that has characterized the course of development of genus *Homo*, guarantees a series of noteworthy advantages" (Adenzato & Adrito, 1999, p. 10), and the development of language and communication greatly facilitates group functioning (Dunbar, 1988). It is the contention here that efficient communication requires a presumption of honesty. Although this presumption of honesty enables social exploitation and deception, it is most plausible that the net evolutionary advantage of efficient communication and social functioning greatly outweigh the occasional costs of being duped. Further it may be vastly more efficient to have social systems that discourage deceit than to either evolve real time deception detection ability or forsake efficient communication and cognitive function.

To the extent that this current evolutionary take on deception and deception detection has merit, it is predicted that parents everywhere will teach their children that lying is wrong and that all human cultures and religions will develop prohibitions against deception, at least within the salient in-group. Perhaps this is why the "a liar won't look you in the eye" belief transcends culture (Bond & The Global Deception Research Team, 2006). A lack of eye contact may not be associated with actual deception and consequently has no utility as a deception detection tool, but gaze aversion is associated with shame. All human cultures benefit if deception is discouraged, at least within the in-group, and propagating the belief that deception is a shameful practice serves this end. In any case, evolving a finely toned cognitive system adept at spotting leakage need not be an evolutionary mandate just because we get duped once in a while. Readers skeptical of the profound gullibility that characterizes the human species are directed to Farquhar (2005). Readers preferring experimental evidence may prefer Levine et al. (1999, 2006) for evidence of the strong impact of truth-bias in deception detection research findings.

Some Further Implications

To the extent to which better-than-chance accuracy rests on sender transparency, an interesting question is if sender transparency is a stable, trait-like individual difference, a fleeting behavioral response that is time and situation specific, or both. While either of these possibilities is consistent with the current thinking, it is perhaps most likely that transparency has both stable and situational properties. Some people may be chronically transparent while others may exhibit transparency in one instance but not another. Because there is limited variance transparency, it would likely to difficult to track longitudinally. But, the possibility that transparency might, in part, be situational suggests that transparency might be something that could be prompted or triggered. Consistent with this speculation, Levine, Shaw, & Shulman (2010) report success in increasing transparency with strategic questioning.

To the extent that transparency is also, in part, attributable to a few chronically leaky liars, then an implication of a few leaky liars is that chronically leaky liars probably realize that they are poor liars and consequently try not to lie. Whereas research indicates that people, on average, tell one to two lies per day (DePaulo, Kashy, Kirkendol, Wyer, & Epstein, 1996), the frequency of lie telling is not normally distributed across the population (Serota et al., 2010).

Because prevalence data are highly positively skewed, most lies are told by a few prolific liars and the modal number of lies per day is zero (Serota et al., 2010). It is likely that prolific liars are low on transparency and high on honest demeanor making them not only prolific but also highly successful. Thus, the type of people who create the better-than-chance accuracy findings in the lab (were random assignment of participations to truth-lie experimental condition predominates) may self-select out outside the lab and simply avoid putting themselves in situations where they need to lie. Alternatively, the people who keep accuracy scores near chance and inflate truth bias may be those most likely to lie outside the lab in everyday life.

This prediction was recently tested by Levine and Blair (2010) and Levine, Shaw, and Shulman (2010). Senders self-selected into deception or honest conditions, and under indirect questioning judges rated the demeanors of the dishonest sources as significantly more honest than the honest senders. This suggests that unlike most deception detection experiments, if liar and truth-tellers decide for themselves rather or not to lie, the ability to distinguish truth for lie may drop to below chance levels because the few transparent liars don't lie, and those with the most honest demeanors do lie.

Second, if the current thinking is correct, one way to obtain high accuracy using a traditional deception detection experimental design is for the researcher to purposely select leaky liars for inclusion in the experiment. If a few transparent liars typically exist, they could be selected though pre-screening and the researcher could stack the deck to obtain any specific accuracy result as a function of the ratio to transparent to non-transparent liars used. If a large number of sources were screened, and if only transparent liars were selected, very high accuracy will result.

Further, if mean accuracy could be experimentally altered by increasing transparency, the thinking presented in this paper predicts that individual differences in ability might emerge. In the task-taking analogy, reducing test item difficulty would allow variance in student ability to emerge. That is, if the test questions were not impossibly difficult, then students who studied well would do better than other students. Applied to deception, a substantial increase in transparency would allow expertise effects to immerge. Preliminary support for this reasoning was obtained by Levine and Blair (2010).

A third implication is that if poor accuracy is a result of a few transparent liars, then deception accuracy might be enhanced by prompting additional variance in transparency. Levine, Shaw, and Shulman (2010) attempted to increase sender transparency with strategic and direct interrogative questioning designed to challenge liars. Detection accuracy was 68% when sources were subjected to direct, strategic questioning compared to 44% accuracy under indirect background questioning. More importantly, the improvement in accuracy under direct questioning as associated with a 50% gain in variance in transparency but less than a 10% gain in judge ability variance. Further still, in the direct questioning condition were accuracy exceeded chance by a substantial margin, the variance in sender transparency was 15 times larger than the variance in judge ability. These findings suggest that it is transparency variance that explains accuracy and those strategies that increase transparency increase accuracy independent of judge ability.

Finally, although the few transparent liars model was created to explain the results of deception detection experiments, the model has implications for deception detection outside the research context. The model suggests that the passive observation of nonverbal behavior has little merit as a deception detection technique. If most people are not very leaky, watching for leakage makes little sense. This does not mean, however, that deception detection efforts are pointless. Instead, it suggests that deception detection practitioners need to rely on techniques other than the passive observation of nonverbal leakage. For example, approaches based on the strategic use of evidence (Granhag et al., 2007) and content in context (Blair et al., in press) have been producing accuracy rates above 70% in recent studies.

Summary and Conclusion

Past and current deception theory explains deception detection accuracy in terms of people's ability to recognize and interpret leaked behavioral cues indicative of deceit. Accepted theory specifies that people leak diagnostically useful behavioral clues that can used to distinguish truths from lies. From this traditional perspective, people attentive and sensitive to other's behavior can spot a liar. This view is predicated on some constancy in sender transparency but variance in judge ability.

Research on deception detection suggests people are poor lie detectors, at least when all they have to go on is the nonverbal and linguistic behavior of potential liars. Whereas people typically do better than chance, they seldom do much better than chance. Across studies, average accuracy hovers around 54%, and most results fall neatly within 10% of this average regardless of the features of the truths and lies judged, who the research participants are, and the specific independent variables under consideration. These findings present a perplexing puzzle for current theory because if current theories have verisimilitude, then research findings should be more variable and have a higher ceiling. Simply put, if clues to deception are leaked, people should, at least under favorable conditions, be able to spot leakage cues and make accurate judgments.

One often invoked explanation for the poorer than expected performance in accuracy experiments is that while authentic cues exist, people simply rely on the wrong cues. If this were the case, however, training would substantially improve accuracy. It does not. Another explanation (e.g., O'Sullivan, 2008) blames the use of student samples, arguing that adults in certain professions can spot a liar. Again, this is simply not the case. Age, education, and profession have little impact. At this point, the failure of the data to coincide with theoretical expectations is attributed to methodological limitation. Yet, once again, studies with these limitations removed are no more supportive of leakage theory than the literature as a whole. All this suggests that it is time to question the theory rather than the data.

This chapter explains slightly above chance accuracy in deception detection experiments by the existence of a few transparent senders. The existence of leakage is not denied, but leakage is presumed to be the exception rather than the rule. There are enough leaky liars so that people can do a little better than chance, but not enough to allow for much better than chance performance. If approximately 10% of liars were transparent, then 55% accuracy is both expected and understandable. Opposite from leakage-based theories, the current view is predicts more variance in sender transparency than judge ability.

Part of the theoretical beauty of this argument lies in its ability to reconcile findings in the literature that otherwise seem odd and anomalous. Specifically, the few transparent liars explanation makes sense out of findings that are inconsistent with current theory based on individual differences in the ability to spot pervasive leakage. Not only does the few transparent liars explanation account for slightly better than chance accuracy, it is also accounts for the across-study stability of accuracy findings, the sender and receiver variance findings, the lack of individual differences in accuracy, the lack of effects for nonverbal training, sanctioning, and stakes, and the findings from meta-analyses of deception cue studies. In short, the few transparent liars explanation provides a more coherent account of deception findings than can be obtained with currently accepted theory.

The current model also leads to the derivation of interesting new predictions. For example, if a lack of naturally occurring transparency explains poor accuracy, and if transparency has a situational component, then deception detection accuracy might be improved by strategies designed to enhance sender transparency. This could be done with strategic questioning designed to make liars more leaky, with questioning that allows honest sources the opportunity to provide exculpatory answers, or, ideally, both. As a second example, if transparency also has a trait-like component, then below chance accuracy might be expected in certain situations where people have the choice to lie or not because transparent liars will not lie, and those who do chose to lie will be those with honest demeanors. Thus, the Few Transparent Liars model provides a new conceptual framework that both reconciles existing findings and generates exciting new avenues for future research.

Author's Note

This chapter was completed with support from the *National Science Foundation* (SBE0725685). Correspondence can be addressed to Tim Levine, Department of Communication, Michigan State University, East Lansing, MI, 48824, levinet@msu.edu.

Notes

1. Since the publication of the Bond and DePaulo (2006) meta-analysis, there have emerged a handful of recent studies which report levels of accuracy that are well above chance (e.g., Blair et al., in press; Levine & Blair, 2010; Granhag et al., 2007). These studies involved techniques that rest on strategic question asking, reliance on message content, and reliance on prior knowledge instead of traditional nonverbal leakage. The implications of these recent findings will be discussed later in this chapter.
2. Three of these four labels were adopted by the current author and not Bond and DePaulo (2008). These labels were chosen both because they seem more intuitively descriptive, and because they are more consistent with conventional usage in the previous literature.

References

Aamodt, M. G., & Custer, H. (2006). Who can best catch a liar? *Forensic Examiner, 15*, 6–11.

Adenzato, M., & Ardito, R. B. (1999). The role of theory of mind and deontic reasoning in the evolution of deception. In M. Hahn & S. C. Stoness (Eds.), *Proceedings of the Twenty First Conference of the Cognitive Science Society* (pp. 7–12). Mahwah, NJ: Erlbaum.

Blair, J. P., Levine, T. R., & Shaw, A. J. (in press). Content in context improves deception detection accuracy. *Human Communication Research*.

Bond, C. F., Jr., & DePaulo, B. M. (2006). Accuracy of deception judgments. *Review of Personality and Social Psychology, 10*, 214–234.

Bond, C. F., Jr., & DePaulo, B. M. (2008). Individual differences in judging deception: Accuracy and bias. *Psychological Bulletin, 134*, 477–492.

Bond, C. F., & The Global Deception Research Team (2006). A world of lies. *Journal of Cross-Cultural Psychology, 37*, 60–74.

Burgoon, J. K., & Buller, D. B. (1996). Interpersonal deception theory. *Communication Theory, 6*, 203–242.

DePaulo, B. M., Kashy, D. A., Kirkendol, S. E., Wyer, M. M., & Epstein, J. A. (1996). Lying in everyday life. *Journal of Personality and Social Psychology, 70*, 979–995.

DePaulo, B. M., Lindsay, J. J., Malone, B. E., Muhlenbrick, L., Charlton, K., & Cooper, H. (2003). Cues to deception. *Psychological Bulletin, 129*, 74–118.

Dunbar, R. (1988). Theory of mind and the evolution of language. In J. R. Hurtford, M Studdert-Kennedy, & C. Knight (Eds.,) *Approaches to the evolution of language* (pp. 92–110). Cambridge: Cambridge University Press.

Ekman, P., & Friesen, W. V. (1969). Nonverbal leakage and clues to deception. *Psychiatry, 32*, 88–106.

Farquhar, M. (2005). *A treasury of deception: Liars, misleaders, hoodwinkers, and the extraordinary true stories of history's greatest hoaxes, fakes and frauds.* New York: Penguin.

Feeley, T. H., & deTurck, M. A. (1998). The behavioral correlates of sanctioned and unsanctioned deceptive communication. *Journal of Nonverbal Behavior, 22,* 189–204.

Frank, M. G., & Feeley, T. H. (2003). To catch a liar: Challenges for research in lie detection training. *Journal of Applied Communication Research, 31,* 58–75.

Gilbert, D. T. (1991). How mental systems believe. *American Psychologist, 46,* 107–119.

Granhag, P. A., Stromwal, L. A., & Hartwig, M. (2007). The Sue technique: The way to interview to detection deception. *Forensic Update, 88,* 25–29.

Hartwig, M., Granhag, P. A., Stromwall, L. A., & Kronkvist, O. (2006). Strategic use of evidence during police interviews: When training to detect deception works. *Law and Human Behavior, 30,* 603–619.

Levine, T. R., & Blair, J. P. (2010). *Questioning strategies, diagnostic utility, and expertise interactions in deception detection.* Manuscript submitted for publication.

Levine, T. R., Feeley, T., McCornack, S. A., Harms, C., & Hughes, M. (2005). Testing the effects of nonverbal training on deception detection accuracy with the inclusion of a bogus training control group. *Western Journal of Communication, 69,* 203–218.

Levine, T. R., Kim, R. K., & Blair, J. P. (2010). (In)accuracy at detecting true and false confessions and denials: An initial test of a projected motive model of veracity judgments. *Human Communication Research, 36,* 81–101.

Levine, T. R., Kim, R. K., Park, H. S., & Hughes, M. (2006). Deception detection accuracy is a predictable linear function of message veracity base-rate: A formal test of Park and Levine's probability model. *Communication Monographs, 73,* 243–260.

Levine, T. R., Park, H. S., & McCornack, S. A. (1999). Accuracy in detecting truths and lies: Documenting the "veracity effect." *Communication Monographs, 66,* 125–144.

Levine, T. R., Shaw, A., & Shulman, H. (2010). Increasing deception detection accuracy with strategic questioning. *Human Communication Research, 36,* 216–231.

O'Sullivan, M. (2008). Home runs and humbugs: Comments on Bond and DePaulo (2008). *Psychological Bulletin, 134,* 493–497.

O'Sullivan, M. (2009). Why most people parse palters, fibs, lies, whoppers, and other deception poorly. In B. Harrington (Ed.), *Deception: From ancient empires to Internet dating* (pp. 74–94). Stanford, CA: Stanford University Press.

Park, H. S., & Levine, T. R. (2001). A probability model of accuracy in deception detection experiments. *Communication Monographs, 68,* 201–210.

Park, H. S., Levine, T. R., McCornack, S. A., Morrison, K., & Ferrara, M. (2002). How people really detect lies. *Communication Monographs, 69,* 144–157.

Peskin, J. (1992). Ruse and representation: On children's ability to conceal information. *Developmental Psychology, 28,* 84–89.

Serota, K. B., Levine, T. R., & Boster, F. J. (2010). The prevalence of lying in America: Three studies of reported deception. *Human Communication Research, 36,* 1–25.

Sporer, S. L., & Schwandt, B. (2006). Paraverbal indicators of deception: A meta-analytic synthesis. *Applied Cognitive Psychology, 20,* 421–446.

Sporer, S. L., & Schwandt, B. (2007). Moderators of nonverbal indicators of deception: A meta-analytic synthesis. *Psychology, Public Policy, and Law, 13,* 1–34.

Smith, E. O. (1987). Deception and evolutionary biology. *Cultural Anthropology, 2,* 50–64.

Zuckerman, M., DePaulo, B. M., & Rosenthal, R. (1981). Verbal and nonverbal communication of deception. In L. Berkowitz (Ed.), *Advances in experimental social psychology* (Vol. 14, pp. 1–59). New York: Academic Press.

CHAPTER CONTENTS

3 From Dispositional Attributions to Behavior Motives

The Folk-Conceptual Theory and Implications for Communication

Natalya N. Bazarova and Jeffrey T. Hancock

Cornell University

This chapter introduces a new theoretical account of attribution—the *folk-conceptual theory of behavior explanations* (Malle, 1999)—to communication and discusses its implications for understanding communication phenomena. This new perspective has emerged from concerns about classic attribution theory, based on the person-situation distinction, and its ability to account for the cognitive complexity and social functions of attributions. The folk-conceptual theory distinguishes between explanations for intentional and unintentional behaviors, capturing different types of motives that can be inferred for intentional behaviors, and links explanations with their social and communicative functions. We lay out several directions for the theory to be usefully explored in communication to extend the field's thinking about how attributions are affected by, affect, and are communicated in social interaction. At the same time, we discuss how communication perspectives can enrich the folk-conceptual theory by integrating the socio-communicative context more fully into the analysis of explanations in social interaction.

Introduction

Attribution theory addresses questions of how people judge the causes of behaviors or events. Their perceptions of causes—attributions—can reflect on an individual action or a societal problem; be private or expressed in public; accurate or erroneous; concern one's own action or that of others; related to the event they witness directly or portrayed by someone else. According to Heider (1958), regarded as the "father" of attribution theory, people go through life as amateur scientists, piecing together information in an effort to make sense of the social and physical world they encounter by assigning causes to them.

This concern with interpreting events in the world, especially the meaning of social behaviors, is shared by communication scholars, who have recognized "myriad paths through which communication and attributions are intertwined" (Manusov, 2007, p. 157), including interpersonal relations (Manusov & Harvey, 2001), media studies (e.g., Gunther, 1991; Power, Murphy, & Coover, 1996; Sotirovic, 2003), persuasion (e.g., Andrews, 1987; Rucinski & Salmon, 1990), intercultural (e.g., Ehrenhaus, 1983), instructional (e.g., Luo, Bippus,

& Dunbar, 2005), and risk communication (e.g., Griffin et al., 2008; Kahlor, Dunwoody, & Griffin, 2002). These myriad paths can be organized along the lines of how attributions are affected by, affect, or are expressed in communication (Manusov, 2007; Manusov & Spitzberg, 2008).

First, the study of how attributions are affected by communication can shed light on how people interpret and construct the meaning of messages, including their perceptions of identities, relationships, and situations (Seibold & Spitzberg, 1982). In this sense, attributions provide the meaning ascribed to communication behaviors (Manusov, 2001; Metts, 2001). For instance, media studies have shown how the content and presentation style of news stories affect readers' attributions (e.g., Kanouse & Hanson, 1972; Knobloch-Westerwick & Taylor, 2008; Nerb & Spada, 2001). Interpersonal research has found links between communication behaviors and attributions in nonverbal dynamics (e.g., Manusov, Floyd, & Kerssen-Griep, 1997; Manusov & Rodriguez, 1989), affectionate communication (e.g., Floyd & Voloudakis, 1999; Vangelisti & Young, 2000), initial interactions (Town & Harvey, 1981), and interpersonal conflicts (e.g., Bippus, 2003; Sillars, Roberts, Dun, & Leonard, 2001).

Second, attributions can affect subsequent communication behaviors and social actions. Sillars (1982) characterized attributions as "the context in which we respond to social situations and [attributions] often determine the practical consequences of interaction" (p. 73). For instance, the types of attributions people make for societal problems affect their support for social programs (e.g., Sotirovic, 2003) or their siding with agents in the news (e.g., Knobloch-Westerwick & Taylor, 2008). At the interpersonal level, attributions about partners' actions can determine the attributor's subsequent communication behaviors during conflicts (e.g., Sillars, 1980).

Finally, attributions expressed in communication reflect how people are interpreting their social world in conversation. Communicated attributions are a major part of discourse; both in natural conversations (Burleson, 1986; Weber & Vangelisti, 1991) and in media stories that suggest causes or attribution frames for a news story (e.g., Gross, 2008; Gross & D'Ambrosio, 2004). Expressed attributions can be used in a strategic way (see for review, Manusov, 2007). For instance, communication research has studied how expressed attributions can serve impression management goals, often focusing on defensive explanations for a negative event (e.g., McLaughlin, Cody, & O'Hair, 1983; McLaughlin, Cody, & Read, 1992).

Taken together, attribution theory has had an important influence on communication research, offering insights into the interpretative processes fundamental to human communication. At the same time, communication scholars have recognized important limitations of attribution theory, including (a) scope and generalizability issues (Manusov & Spitzberg, 2008); (b) a focus on attributions as purely cognitive processes with limited attention to interaction and social-communicative functions (McLaughlin et al., 1992; Sillars, 1982; Weber & Vangelisti, 1991); (c) a theoretical ambiguity about "the nature, number, and exact function of the basic attributional dimensions" (Spitzberg, 2001, p. 360); and (d) verifiability and falsifiability issues in light of contradictory evidence (Manusov & Spitzberg, 2008; Spitzberg, 2001).

Perhaps more importantly, the traditional distinction of causes into dispositional or situational types does not appear to fully capture the complexity of attributions in social contexts. In social situations, perceivers are often interested in behavior intentionality and specific types of motives for an action. Seibold and Spitzberg (1982) saw the greatest potential of attribution theory in how it could shed light on aspects of communication "involving inference of intentionality, motive, and causality for another's behavior" (p. 87). Yet classic attribution theory stops short of addressing motives for behaviors and instead points to the person's disposition as a finite cause of an intentional behavior. That is, a dispositional attribution only suggests that something about the actor has prompted an intentional action without illuminating specific motives. For instance, when a listener interrupts a speaker, the speaker can attribute the interruption to a variety of motives; perhaps the listener needed a clarification, did not agree with the speaker, did not want to be late for class, or was simply fed up with the conversation. These reasons are likely to produce very different effects on communication, but classifying them as simply dispositional causes glosses over their differences.

The challenges to attribution theory brought up by communication scholars do not, however, undermine the importance of attributions for communication. As Manusov and Spitzberg (2008) wrote, "Despite our concerns with attribution theory as a *theory*, we contend that attribution processes have great potential for additional study and application by scholars interested in interpersonal communication and relationship" (p. 46). At the same time, scholars have pointed to the absence of superior options that could provide viable alternatives to attribution theory (Harvey & Omarzu, 2001).

Recently, however, an alternative to attribution theory has emerged in the work of Bertram Malle and his colleagues whose criticisms of classic attribution theory echo many of the concerns raised by communication scholars. Specifically, the traditional attribution approach is criticized for misinterpreting Heider's concepts of *personal causality* (intentional and purposive) and *impersonal causality* (without intervention of intention) as the more simplistic dispositional versus situational dichotomy, "confounding intentional and unintentional behavior … and ignoring many finer-grained types and forms of explanations" (Malle, 2007, p. 14). The proposed alternative framework—the folk-conceptual theory of behavior explanations—offers a revised picture of attributions where intentionality is a precursor to classes of explanations. The folk-conceptual theory divides up classes of explanations for intentional behaviors very differently than for unintentional behaviors. For intentional behaviors it goes beyond dispositional-situational categories to capture motives that lead up to the intention. A central assumption of the folk-conceptual theory is that people consider the specific desires, goals, and beliefs that presumably drive one's own or someone else's intentional behavior (Malle, 2007).

The folk-conceptual theory also addresses psychological and linguistic aspects of explanations. The psychological aspect refers to psychological factors that affect how people come to understand behavior causes and express them in conversation, such as an explainer's pragmatic goals or available information resources. The linguistic aspect is concerned with linguistic forms of explanations that, although they do not change the content of explanations, serve important socio-communicative functions in conversation (e.g., impression management). Thus, the folk-conceptual theory presents an integrative approach to explanations that recognizes them both as cognitive and communicative acts that fulfill social functions and communication goals.

As a more precise description of explanation processes, the folk-conceptual theory is expected to account more accurately for social functions and psychological phenomena related to attributions than the traditional attribution theory. Indeed, recent empirical tests contrasting predictions from the folk-conceptual theory and classic attribution theory support the new framework and give only limited or no support to traditional attribution dimensions (Malle, 2006; Malle, Knobe, & Nelson, 2007). For instance, recent empirical studies have supported predictions flowing from the folk-conceptual theory on a variety of phenomena, including the actor-observer bias (Malle et al., 2007), self-serving biases (Malle & Nelson, 2006), explanation asymmetries for group versus individuals (O'Laughlin & Malle, 2002), and rational self-presentation (Malle, Knobe, O'Laughlin, Pearce, & Nelson, 2000).

The distinctions laid out in the folk-conceptual theory may also inform a new look at the connections between communication and explanations. The goal for this chapter, therefore, is to present an alternative model of attributions, the folk-conceptual theory of explanations, and its potential contributions for understanding communication processes. Following the seminal pieces by Seibold and Spitzberg (1982) and Sillars (1982), which introduced classic attribution theory to communication, the present chapter provides an overview of the folk-conceptual theory and suggests implications for communication. To these ends, the chapter has the following organization. First, it briefly summarizes limitations of the traditional attribution approach from a communication perspective. The next section provides an overview of the folk-conceptual theory and how it addresses previous limitations. After the theory presentation, the chapter discusses its implications for communication, focusing on group communication, interpersonal deception, close relationships, interpersonal conflict, and account-giving research. The final section suggests ways how communication perspectives can inform the folk-conceptual theory by integrating the socio-communicative context more fully into the analysis of behavior explanations.

Limitations of the Traditional Attribution Approach

Communication settings stretch traditional attribution theory beyond its typical boundaries by bringing in a rich context of social interaction and active interaction rather than passive observation of a target. Sillars (1982) argued that causality in social interactions is "exceedingly complex" due to several factors (p. 93). First, in social interaction different causes can be confounded, including personality, relationship, reciprocal attributions, and reciprocal effects of behaviors. Second, the type and quality of a social relationship, the depth and breadth of self-disclosure, and partners' interdependence can affect attribution processes (e.g., Sillars, 1982; Town & Harvey, 1981; Vangelisti & Young, 2000). Therefore, the exclusively cognitive focus of traditional attribution theory and its primary concern with observers in non-social and non-interactive settings raise concerns about whether it can provide an adequate account of behavior explanations in communication contexts.

Treating attributions as purely intrapersonal cognitive phenomena also confines the scope of attribution theory by it failing to consider how people communicate and negotiate their spoken attributions in interaction (Hilton, 1990; Weber & Vangelisti, 1991). Spoken attributions reflect not only social, cognitive, and motivational factors (Cody & Braaten, 1992; Slugoski, Lalljee, Lamb, & Ginsburg, 1993), but they can also develop collaboratively in conversations as jointly constructed causal accounts (Burleson, 1986). Spitzberg (2001) argues that only through paying attention to interaction, and how attributions are negotiated in conversation, can attribution theory inform the development of relationships in ongoing interactions.

In addition to extending attribution theory to social and interactive settings, communication studies also expand the range of contexts and behaviors to which attributions are assigned. Manusov and Spitzberg (2008) noted that most attribution research focuses on "contexts involving actual or potential negative consequences and violations of expectations" (p. 45), and that traditional attribution's limitation to negative events makes it unclear how attributional processes operate in other contexts, such as explanations for positive behaviors. Behavior valence is often linked with judgments about behavior intentionality (see for review, Manusov, 2007), such as negative behaviors in achievement-oriented situations are commonly regarded as unintentional (e.g., an exam failure). Whereas the dispositional-situational attribution dimension may adequately describe causes of unintentional behaviors, attributions for intentional behaviors may not work the same way.

Furthermore, the traditional attributional dimensions of locus (dispositional-situational causes), controllability (controllable-uncontrollable causes), and stability (permanent or unstable causes) have received mixed empirical research, with many studies failing to find support for these dimensions (see for review, Bradbury & Fincham, 1990; Spitzberg, 2001). Despite contradictory evidence, however, attributions continue to be seen as having "three, and indeed only three, underlying causal properties that have cross-situational generality ... locus, stability, and controllability" (Weiner, 2004, p. 17). Manusov and Spitzberg (2008) expressed concerns about attribution theory's verifiability and falsifiability because accumulating contradictory evidence has not prompted scholarship to question attribution theory as a theory.

The Folk-Conceptual Theory of Behavior Explanations

In light of these rather serious issues for traditional attribution theory in communication contexts, we describe the folk-conceptual theory as a potentially useful alternative for communication scholars. As mentioned before, the folk-conceptual theory integrates conceptual, psychological, and linguistic aspects of behavior explanations. Conceptually, the folk-conceptual theory differentiates between explanations for intentional and unintentional behaviors. As shown in Table 3.1, unintentional behaviors are explained by causes, and intentional behaviors can be explained by one of the three modes: reasons, causal history factors, and enabling factors. There are further distinctions within reasons, which refer to the type of motive (desire, belief, or valuing) in light of which the agent formed an intention to act. Linguistically, reasons can be expressed in two different ways: with or without a mental marker that marks the type of reason cited in the behavior explanation. The psychological aspect of the folk-conceptual theory deals with psychological and communication factors that affect the choice of an explanation mode, reason type, and a linguistic form. The next section describes each of these aspects of the theory in more detail.

Differentiating between Intentional and Unintentional Behavior

The theoretical starting point for the folk-conceptual model is that people distinguish between intentional and unintentional behaviors and explain intentional behaviors differently than unintentional behaviors. While absent from classic attribution theory, the distinction between intentional and unintentional behaviors and its influence on causal explanations is recognized across a range of allied disciplines, such as philosophy and development psychology (see for review Malle, 1999). For instance, philosophy of human action distinguishes between intentional and unintentional actions, pointing to people's mental states, such as beliefs, desires, and intentions, as causes of intentional behaviors (Davidson, 1980; Mele, 2001).

According to the folk-conceptual theory, before perceivers start thinking about behavior causes, they first spontaneously decide whether it was an inten-

Table 3.1 Construction of Explanations According to the Folk-Conceptual Theory of Behavior Explanations

Behavior Type	Explanation Mode	Type of Reason	Linguistic Form
Unintentional behavior	Causes		
Intentional behavior	Reasons	Belief Desire Valuing	Expressed with or without a mental marker
	Causal history factors		
	Enabling factors		

tional or unintentional act. Judgments of behavior intentionality demonstrate a high degree of agreement across perceivers because people have a *shared concept of intentionality*, which is a cognitive ability to distinguish between intentional and unintentional behavior developed in early childhood (Malle & Knobe, 1997). Experimental studies in developmental psychology demonstrate that even young children (as early as five years old) are able to recognize the difference between intentional and unintentional actions (Astington, 2001; Moses, 2001).

A series of experimental studies examining the criteria that perceivers use to decide an agent's intentionality revealed that a perceiver must see the behavior to satisfy five requirements: (a) the agent must have a desire for an outcome, (b) the agent must have beliefs about the action leading to that outcome, (c) the agent must have an intention to perform the behavior, which is a decision to act based on appropriate beliefs and desires, (d) the agent must be aware of performing a particular behavior, and (e) the agent must have necessary skills for performing this behavior (Malle & Knobe, 1997).

Consider the following example to illustrate intentional and unintentional behaviors in this framework: A man yells to scare away a dog versus a man yells because a dog scared him. Yelling to scare away the dog in the first sentence is an intentional act because it satisfies all five criteria of the shared concept of intentionality. In contrast, the scared yelling in the second example is likely to have occurred without the person's desire, intention, or even awareness of the act, which suggests an unintentional action. This judgment about behavior intentionality is central to the type of explanations that people then use to infer what caused the behavior.

Explanation Modes

The folk-conceptual theory proposes different modes for explaining intentional and unintentional behaviors. The mode for explaining unintentional behavior is causes, and the modes for explaining intentional behavior are (a) reasons, (b) causal history factors, and (c) enabling factors (see Table 3.1).

Explanation Modes for Unintentional Behaviors.   Causes are factors that bring about behavior in a mechanical way or "impersonal" way, without the intervention of the agent's will, desire, or intention for the action (Malle, 2007). Because perceivers view behavior as unintentional—occurring independent of agent's reasoning process—they cannot attribute it to the agent's reasons (i.e., beliefs or desires). Instead, they refer to other causes, in the person or the environment, which in their view can account for the behavior, such as the dog causing the scared yelling in the example above. Causes of unintentional behaviors can be characterized along the traditional attribution dimensions (i.e., locus, stability, controllability) that describe whether the cause has an external or internal origin, temporary or permanent, controllable or uncontrollable. Thus, classic attribution theory and the folk-conceptual theory characterize causes of unintentional behaviors similarly. The real difference between these two frameworks lies in how they approach explanations for intentional behaviors.

Explanation Modes for Intentional Behaviors.   There are three explanation modes for intentional behaviors: reasons, causal history factors, and enabling factors (see Table 3.1). *Reasons* are the default way of explaining intentional behaviors because of their high frequency compared to the other two modes. Reasons are mental states (beliefs and desires), which the perceiver views as the agent's reasons and grounds for acting (Malle, 2007). To classify mental states as reasons, it is not enough for a perceiver to discern the agent's desire or belief for a certain action. The perceiver must assume that these mental states were the agent's *subjective* reasons for the action. That is, the perceiver thinks that (a) the agent has actively considered his/her reasons, beliefs, or desires during a reasoning process leading up to a decision to act, and (b) the agent him/herself regarded them as grounds for the action. When perceivers explain their own behavior, they are presumed to access their desires and beliefs directly. When perceivers explain someone else's behavior, they engage in the act of perspective taking by inferring beliefs and desires that presumably moved the agent to action.

Consider the interruption of a conversation, in which Art interrupts conversation partner Barbara and tells her that he has to go. First, according to the folk-conceptual theory, the perceiver—Barbara—initially identifies the interruption as an intentional act. What kind of explanation will be viewed as *reasons* within this framework? Barbara may infer a certain desire or belief that Art considered when deciding to interrupt her. For instance, from Barbara's perspective, Art had a certain desire (e.g., "He did not want to be late for class"), which he considered (e.g., "He had to interrupt me because he did not want to be late for class"), and for that reason interrupted her.

Perceivers can also explain an intentional action by *causal history factors* that have presumably shaped the agent's reasons, such as desires or beliefs. Causal history factors describe the origin of the agent's reasons without explicitly mentioning them. In the case of Art interrupting Barbara, causal history factors can include the immediate context (e.g., "Art interrupted Barbara because the background noise prevented him from hearing her"), childhood and cultural upbringing (e.g., "Interrupting is a conversational norm in his culture"), or personal traits (e.g., "He is ill-mannered"). Although the interruption is seen as an intentional act by the perceiver, the perceiver explains it by referring to causal background factors that have shaped the agent's reasons, rather than by Art's reasons directly. Importantly, the causal history factors are orthogonal to the dispositional-situational attribution distinction as they may refer to either disposition (e.g., personal traits) or situation (e.g., an immediate context) (Malle, 2006).

Certain psychological factors increase the likelihood of making causal history explanations. One of them is *behavior regularity*, which refers to a behavior trend versus a single act. According to the folk-conceptual theory, there is a tendency to explain a behavior trend by causal history factors because it can summarize a variety of reasons for different behaviors within this trend. For instance, "Professor Jones has monthly meetings with Rhonda because he is her advisor." The causal history explanation serves to summarize different reasons for the behaviors that Professor Jones and Rhonda accomplish through their monthly meetings: checking on the student's progress, addressing academic concerns, and helping with a research project.

Another factor that leads to causal history factors is *information availability*, which refers to a perceiver's information about the agent's reasons for behaviors. Perceivers typically attempt to attribute an intentional behavior to the agent's reasons, such as desires or beliefs that have presumably motivated the agent's behavior. When they have difficulty inferring the agent's specific reasons, a causal history explanation provides a cognitive shortcut by offering a general background factor that could account for the agent's behavior. For instance, a student explained why his classmate dropped out of school: "I did not know him that well, but he seemed like he had a lot of issues." Lacking knowledge of the dropout's reasons, the perceiver refers to a causal history factor to explain the behavior.

The third mode for explaining intentional behaviors is *enabling factors*, which applies specifically to difficult actions that get accomplished despite their difficulty. The focus of enabling factor explanations is on factors, such as abilities, effort, opportune circumstances, that facilitate turning the intention into a successful action (Malle, 2007). For example, when Brian is able to give a successful public speech performance, despite his public speech anxiety, an enabling factor explanation addresses how it was possible (e.g., "Because he practiced a lot").

Of particular interest to communication, the choice of an explanation mode (reasons, causal history factors, and enabling factors) can also be affected by conversational rules and social factors. In conversations speakers adjust their explanations to their audience's presumed interest and knowledge in order to fill in the audience's knowledge gap with the explanation (Grice, 1975; Turnbull, 1986). For instance, a question of "How was it possible" invites enabling factor explanations, whereas a question "How come?" tends to prompt causal history explanations because it signals the audience's interest in general background factors explaining the agent's reasons (Malle et al., 2000).

Strategically, people use communicated explanations for impression management and conveying a certain attitude towards the behavior agent (Antaki, 1994; Hilton, 1995; Todorov, Lalljee, & Hirst, 2000). Because the primary purpose of explanations is to create meaning for the audience, explanations provide a subtle way to manage impressions by concealing explicit impression management goals (Malle, 2004). For instance, by drawing attention to how difficult it was to perform a certain action (by explaining it in terms of enabling factors rather than the actor's reasons), the explainer can create a favorable impression of the agent who succeeded despite those difficulties.

Similarly, the use of causal history explanations can be used as mitigating factors in explanations of negative behaviors because they draw attention away from the agent's subjective reasons to more distant and objective causes that have presumably shaped those reasons, such as traits, emotions, cultural and family upbringing, intoxication, and immediate context (Malle, 2004). The use of reasons, on the other hand, highlights the agent's rationality because the explainer presents the agent's beliefs or desires that have motivated the agent's behavior (Malle et al., 2000).

Types of Reasons: Beliefs, Desires, and Valuings

The folk-conceptual theory outlines further distinctions within the reason explanation mode into three types (see Table 3.1): *beliefs* (knowledge and thinking), such as "He interrupted because he did not agree with the speaker"; *desires* (wants and needs), such as "He interrupted because he needed clarification," and *valuings* (likes and dislikes), such as "He interrupted because he did not like the joke."

Much as with the explanation modes, information availability and pragmatic goals affect the choice of reason sub-type. Belief reasons require detailed knowledge of the agent and his/her circumstances; desire reasons, in contrast, can be inferred from basic behavior perceptions, social rules, or cultural norms (Malle et al., 2000). Therefore, it is easier for perceivers to infer someone else's desires (e.g., "A stranger approached me because he needed directions to the bus stop") than beliefs (e.g., "A stranger approached me because he thought I was lost and needed help").

For explanations communicated in conversations, a choice of beliefs versus desires also reflects the speaker's pragmatic goals, such as impression-management goals. Reason explanations highlight the agent's reasoning processes, whereas desire explanations may imply self-centeredness because they refer to the agent's desires and needs (Malle et al., 2007). Indeed, the impression management goal to appear rational often leads people to increase the use of belief reasons in their explanations (Malle et al., 2000).

It is important to note that although the folk-conceptual theory argues that people reliably distinguish between different explanation modes and reason types, they are presumed to do so implicitly. In other words, people do not consciously think, "I will choose belief reasons over desire reasons." Instead, explanation types are presumed to be non-consciously selected and rely on automatic process (see Malle, 2005).

Linguistic Expression of Explanations

To recap, there are three explanation modes for intentional behaviors: reasons, causal history factors, and enabling factors. Reasons include three sub-types: beliefs, desires, and valuings. In addition to these conceptual distinctions between explanation modes and reason types, there is also a linguistic layer that deals specifically with how attributions are communicated in the discourse. According to the folk-conceptual theory, a perceiver can express reasons with or without *mental state markers*, which are verbs, such as "think," "believe," "want," "need," or "like." These verbs signal a reason type inferred by the perceiver, such as desire, belief, or valuing, which can be added to (marked form) or omitted (unmarked form) from a sentence. Compare the following two sentences: "He interrupted his partner because *he thought* it was time for him to go" versus "He interrupted his partner because it was time for him to go." Although the reason content is the same for these two sentences, the speaker expresses the reason explanation differently: with or without the mental marker "he thought."

The presence or omission of mental markers is important because of the psychological and communicative functions they serve in a conversation, such as expressing attitudes toward the agent and for self-impression management (Malle, 1999; Malle et al., 2000; Malle et al., 2007). In describing someone else's behavior, the use of a mental marker signals subjectivity about the agent's reasons. As signals of subjectivity, mental markers communicate different implications, such as distancing from the beliefs of the agent or expressing attitudes. Because we always infer other's belief states, explicitly mentioning them highlights the belief. The mental marker in the sentence "She asked us to speak softer because *she thought* the children were asleep" highlights the fact that the speaker may not share the agent's belief that the children were asleep. Mental markers can also have a distancing function. The following markers vary from very distant to not distant: mistakenly believes, jumped to the conclusion, assumes/presumes, concluded/deduced, saw/discovered, realizes/knows. Finally, mental marker can also communicate attitudes regarding the agent's action, such as whether it was justified or reasonable. For instance, in the sentence "He left because *he thought* we were treating him unfairly" the mental marker "he thought" casts doubt on the agent's reason as being justified.

From a self-presentation point, when speakers provide explanations about their own actions they are not only providing information, they are also attempting to control how others perceive them (Malle, 2006). Mental markers focus attention on the self, especially when they refer to one's desires as action explanations. When people want to appear rational, on the other hand, they use more belief reasons (e.g., thought, believe) and tend to omit mental state markers of desire (e.g., want, need) (Malle et al., 2000).

Importantly, linguistic differences are frequently mistaken for conceptual dispositional-situation distinctions in the coding of open-ended statements following the traditional attribution approach (Malle, 1999; Malle et al., 2000). Consider, for example, two sentences: "She interrupted the speaker because he was not right" (situation) and "She interrupted the speaker because she knew he was not right" (disposition). Although the traditional attribution approach would treat the first cause as situation ("he was not right") and the second cause as dispositional ("she knew he was not right"), they have the same belief reason presented in the unmarked and marked form.

The Folk-Conceptual Theory and Criticisms of the Traditional Attribution Approach

Before discussing the implication of the folk-conceptual theory for the study of human communication, let us briefly consider whether the new framework passes the main criticisms of the traditional attribution approach raised by communication scholars. Let us begin with the conceptual limitations pointed out by communication scholars, starting with the traditional model suffering from theoretical ambiguity regarding the disposition-situational distinction and its ability to describe attributions. Mounting evidence suggests that this distinction is problematic for a host of different types of social behavior (see for review Bradbury & Fincham, 1990; Manusov & Spitzberg, 2008; Spitzberg, 2001). The folk-conceptual model proposes an entirely new framework for describing explanations of social behavior that moves beyond the dispositional-situational distinction, and recent research suggests that accounting for people's motives is a more accurate reflection of people's explanations in social contexts (Ames et al., 2001; Malle et al., 2007; Rosati et al., 2001).

A second conceptual issue was that the traditional framework treats explanations as a purely cognitive process. The folk-conceptual theory, in contrast, recognizes that people do not construct explanations in a vacuum. It explicitly treats explanations as social actions specifying linguistic and social aspects of explanations, along with their conceptual structure. The built-in ties between cognitive, social, and communicative facets of explanations are probably the greatest strength of the new theory with respect to communication research that open potentially fruitful applications for communication. In fact, the integration of cognitive and communicative functions of explanations in a social context is recognized as the most important direction for future research concerned with behavior explanations (Malle, 2001).

Despite these advances by the folk conceptual theory, there remain important unanswered questions about how the theory can fully integrate cognitive and communicatve functions of explanations. The folk-conceptual theory has been tested primarily in non-interactive contexts (e.g., through vignette techniques). Questions raised by communication scholars about reciprocal effects of explanations and behaviors, the influence of emotions on how people explain behaviors in emotionally charged interactions (e.g., an interpersonal conflict), or a joint development of explanations in conversations require the examinations of attributions in interactive settings. Further in the chapter we expand on how the socio-communicative context can be more fully integrated into the folk-conceptual analysis of explanations, including social influences on judgments about behavior intentionality and explanation as a collaborative process in conversations.

Summary of the Folk-Conceptual Theory

To summarize, the folk-conceptual theory presents a complex picture of how people explain behavior, choosing from multiple modes of explanations (causes, reasons, causal history factors, or enabling factors), different types within the mode of reasons (beliefs, desires, and valuings), and, finally, choosing among alternative linguistic forms for expressed reasons (with or without mental state markers). What type of explanations people use is determined by three psychological factors: (a) behavior attributes (intentional/unintentional, difficulty of intentional behavior, and a singular behavior versus a trend); (b) pragmatic goals, such as audience design and impression-management goals; and (c) information resources.

Implications of the Folk-Conceptual Theory for Communication

One of the primary purposes of this chapter is to draw out the implications of the folk-conceptual theory for communication research. There are, however, some examples of the folk-conceptual theory already being adopted in areas related to communication. One study examined how medical students explain behaviors related to the issues of informed consent in clinical procedures (Knight & Rees, 2008), revealing strong impression management pressures on the framing of the explanations. Students tended to omit mental markers with belief reasons to convey rationality and present their reasons as objective and factual. In another study, the folk-conceptual theory informed how situational uncertainty and attitudes towards a negotiation partner (trust, distrust, suspicion) affected explanations about the partner's behavior. Individuals suspicious of a negotiation partner tended to use more reasons than causal history or enabling factors in their explanations in an effort to understand the partner's motives and goals (Sinaceur, 2007).

Other studies have employed the folk-conceptual theory to examine perceptions of nonhuman actions (Kiesler, Lee, & Kramer, 2006; Wang, Lignos, Vatsl, & Scassellati, 2006). Wang and colleagues (2006), for example, examined how people gauge the motives of animated robots, and how explanations for robot behaviors affect the social experience of a robot. Kiesler et al. (2006) examined the role of emotional attachment to animals and animated objects on judgments of their behavior intentionality. They found that emotional attachment leads people to perceive behaviors of animals and animated objects as more goal-directed as reflected by an increase of reason explanations (valuings, beliefs, desires) for their actions.

At this point let us consider how the folk-conceptual theory may contribute to thinking in several other areas of communication research, including group communication, interpersonal deception, hurtful communication in close relationships, interpersonal conflict, and account-giving research.

Implications for Group Communication

The folk-conceptual theory can contribute to our understanding of group communication by informing how members explain one another's motives and how they communicate explanations in a group interaction. The bulk of traditional attribution research in small groups has focused on attributions as cognitive processes, as represented by dispositional-situational distinctions, and how different factors (e.g., information availability, number of group members, group leadership) may be responsible for attribution biases distorting perceptions of causality (e.g., Allison & Messick, 1987; Forsyth, Zyzniewski, & Giammanco, 2002; Leary & Forsyth, 1987; Zaccaro, Peterson, & Walker, 1987). Although group communication has acknowledged the interpersonal use of attributions (Forsyth, 1980), social-communicative functions of explanations remain largely unexamined within the traditional attribution paradigm. Furthermore, the dispositional-situational distinction overlooks questions related to how group members infer partners' goals and motives from their behaviors, and the potential consequences of motive inferences on group communication. The folk-conceptual theory with its emphasis on inferred motives and social-communicative functions of explanations may enhance our understanding of group interaction, as illustrated in three areas of group research: virtual groups, information sharing in groups, and social identification processes.

Virtual Groups.   Virtual groups use communication technology, such as email, to interact and accomplish group work. Recent research on virtual groups has focused on the misperceptions of dispositional-situational causes that arise from being physically separated (Bazarova & Walther, 2009; Cramton, 2001, 2002; Walther & Bazarova, 2007). Biased attributions are frequently put forth as a key mechanism through which virtual communication affects interpersonal dynamics in groups, with dispositional blame of other group members conceptually linked to relational damage, interpersonal conflict, and inferior task performance in virtual groups (Cramton, 2001; Mortensen & Hinds, 2001; Walther, Boos, & Jonas, 2002).

   The study of dispositional-situational attributions has been an important step in understanding virtual group dynamics. Classifying a cause as dispositional (also referred to as person or internal attributions), however, overlooks distinctions between different types of dispositional factors important for perceptions of intentional behaviors (e.g., members' personalities, motives, attitudes, and abilities). Accordingly, virtual group research has not discriminated between biased attributions to members' motives and dispositions because dispositional attributions have referred to both members' intentions (e.g., Mortensen & Hinds, 2001; Hinds & Bailey, 2003) and their dispositions (e.g., Cramton, 2001; Walther et al., 2002). Because the folk-conceptual theory distinguishes reasons (i.e., desires, beliefs, and valuings) from other internal causes, our understanding of how virtual group members judge intentional behaviors, and the effects of those judgments, can be advanced. For instance, there may be differences in how members assign intentionality to behaviors, such as a partner's sudden disengagement from an online conversation. Judgments about behavior intentionality depend on information about the situational context (Malle, Moses, & Baldwin, 2001), but distributed partners in virtual groups have limited information about one another's situational environments (Cramton, 2001). The limited knowledge of distributed partners and their situations may increase intentionality biases, which refer to "differences in the readiness to judge behaviors as intentional" (Malle, 2004, p. 176).

The existing approach to attributions in virtual groups is also premised on the basic assumption that virtual group members do not know each other well, and in the absence of direct information about others' behavior they make guesses about what is the most likely and plausible explanation for their behaviors (Bazarova & Walther, 2009). This view has so far failed to take into account the role of communicated attributions. Although virtual members may not directly observe of one another's behaviors, they can communicate the causes of their actions. Future research needs to examine how group members explain their own and others' behaviors in virtual groups. For example, given that speakers tailor the content of explanations to the audience's presupposed knowledge (Hilton, 1995; Slugoski et al., 1993), do members of distributed or culturally diverse virtual groups explain behavior causes differently than members of collocated or culturally homogeneous groups? Drawing on the folk-conceptual theory, members of physically separated or culturally diverse virtual teams should use more causal history factors to fill background gaps for their partners rather than referring to their desires and goals directly. Attention to how virtual members construct explanations in their communication can facilitate our understanding of the "socially develop[ed] interpretations of events, and socially constituted negotiated processes" that have been largely ignored by virtual group research (Gibbs, Nekrassova, Grushina, & Wahab, 2008, p. 199).

Information Sharing. How group members assign motives and goals to one another is important for information sharing in groups. Recent research on information sharing has moved away from the cooperative sharing assumption to recognizing that group members may have a variety of goals and motives that impact how they share information, such as cooperative, competitive, and mixed motives (Wittenbaum, Hollingshead, & Botero, 2004). In addition to a member's own motives, however, one's willingness to share information may also be affected by how a group member perceives other members' motives, such as whether they pursue cooperative or competitive goals. The folk-conceptual theory can be applied to study how group members explain others' motives and potential effects of those explanations on information sharing in groups. For instance, using mental markers to explain another group member's behavior can reveal whether the explainer is suspicious of that partner's beliefs or motives. Suspicion about hidden motives is likely to decrease information sharing (Kramer, 1998) and reduce susceptibility to biases in seeking information (Schul, Burnstein, & Bardi, 1996).

Social Identification. The folk-conceptual theory can contribute to our understanding of how people explain behaviors of social groups and use their explanations to influence the audience' attitudes and behaviors towards a particular social group. Specifically, a distinction between causal history factors and reason explanation when explaining behaviors of outgroup members may be more useful the dispositional-situational distinction derived from classic attribution theory. For example, research suggests that explainers make more dispositional attributions for behaviors of outgroups than ingroups (Hewstone, 1990). This phenomenon has been explained by the limited contextual information one has about outgroup members, which leads perceivers to generalize to personalities and traits as their behavior causes. However, the distinction into dispositional versus situational attributions overlooks differences between personal characteristics and reasons (i.e., motives), both of which refer to factors internal to the agent. The underspecification of the dispositional-situation distinction leaves it unclear whether perceivers tend to explain behaviors of outgroup members by shared reasons or by similar personalities. In contrast, the folk-conceptual distinction between reasons and causal history factors can disentangle motives from dispositions.

For instance, a recent study examined how people explain behaviors of an aggregate of individuals differently from behaviors of a jointly acting group (O'Laughlin & Malle, 2002). The findings suggest that the more coordinated and unified a group is perceived to be, the more likely explanations of the group's action will be in terms of shared reasons, such as desires or beliefs that generalize to all members (e.g., "Members of this group work very hard because they want to win a competition"). In contrast, explanations for aggregates of unconnected individuals, such as high school seniors nationwide, tend to refer to causal history factors (e.g., their age or stereotypical characteristics). The differential use of reasons versus causal history factors flows from the fact that reasons are unlikely to generalize to unconnected individuals while a causal history factor can provide a single explanation for a variety of different reasons that those individuals might have. Reason explanations for a jointly acting group, on the other hand, highlight the joint nature of the group action and perception of the group as a unified agent that acts on shared reasons.

Because reasons and causal history factors imply a different level of a group unity and coordination, explainers can use them strategically to manage the audience's impression of a particular group (O'Laughlin & Malle, 2002). Abelson, Dasgupta, Park, and Banaji (1998) argued that seeing a group as unified and coordinated increases perceptions of out-group threat, negative judgments about it, and defensive behaviors towards it. Assuming that people can influence others' attitudes and behaviors towards social groups through explanations of their behaviors (Gross & D'Ambrosio, 2004), undesirable shared reasons for a group action (e.g., a hate group's propaganda) can intensify ingroup/outgroup conflict, create antagonistic perceptions of the outgroup, and instill feelings of fear in the audience and rejection of the outgroup. The strategic use of explanations can potentially open up useful ways for examining how media affect perceptions of social groups through the differential use of reasons and causal history factors, including propagandistic and persuasive use of explanations for their actions.

Implications for Interpersonal Deception

Interpersonal deception involves one person intentionally misleading another, and such an act is central to several communication theories (e.g., Buller &

Burgoon, 1996). Communication research has examined both the production of deception, namely when, where, and why people lie, as well as the much more frequently studied detection of deception. The folk-conceptual theory has potential implications for both of these approaches to interpersonal deception.

Causal explanations of deception are most obviously related to the task of detecting deception. Typically in a deception detection task, people are asked to judge whether another person has lied or told the truth. A large body of research suggests that people are quite poor at detecting deception in most situations, performing effectively at chance (see Bond & DePaulo, 2008; DePaulo, Lindsay, Malone, Muhlenbruck, Charlton, & Cooper, 2003; Vrij, 2008). Our poor deception detection ability is often attributed to the *truth bias,* an attributional bias in which we tend to believe our conversational partners (Levine, Park, & McCornack, 1999). Although the truth bias is well-documented, it is perhaps surprising that the explanations that perceivers hold when attempting to detect deception are not well understood. Most studies examining deception detection stop short of understanding the kinds of causal explanations that may go into truthful versus deceptive judgments.

The folk-conceptual theory can provide some guidance on how to approach this problem. Given that deception, by definition, cannot be an unintentional behavior, judgments about deception fall firmly into the intentional part of the folk-conceptual theory. An important question flowing from the folk-conceptual theory, therefore, is how people explain their partner's potentially deceptive behavior. When people make judgments regarding deception, do they rely on reasons (e.g., "He lied to me because he needed the money") or causal history factors (e.g., "He lied to me because he's a liar")? An example question that could be asked here is whether different types of causal explanations differentially affect detection success. That is, do people that rely on causal history factors when making judgments about deception perform better than those considering reasons?

Regardless of what exact theoretically important questions are raised, the folk-conceptual theory also raises an important methodological limitation in deception research: Deception detection protocols must go beyond asking simply whether or not the participant believes the other person was lying or not and begin delving into the kinds of explanations that participants provide when judging potentially deceptive behavior. This kind of research could lead to deeper insights into the truth bias that go beyond simply assuming that people are inherently cooperative communicators (Grice, 1975). For instance, is the truth bias affected by the kind of causal explanation that one makes when judging the veracity of a statement?

The folk-conceptual theory also has implications for understanding the production of deception, or how people go about lying, especially the linguistic components of the folk-conceptual theory. Over the last decade, there has been renewed interest in the language of deception (see Galasinski, 2000; Vrij, 2008). Several communication theories (e.g., Interpersonal Deception Theory, Buller & Burgoon, 1996) assume that the cognitive effects of lying may be reflected in language. For instance, one empirical finding that has emerged in several studies suggest that when people lie they often use fewer first person references, presumably due to an attempt to psychological distancing from the lie (Bond & Lee, 2005; Hancock, Curry, Goorha, & Woodworth, 2008; Newman, Pennebaker, Berry, & Richards, 2003).

These kinds of findings are particularly relevant to the mental markers described by the folk-conceptual theory. In particular, mental markers can serve to distance the agent from stated beliefs. For example, in the statement "My girlfriend is dieting because *she thinks* she's gaining weight" the belief mental marker *she thinks* distances the speaker from the beliefs of his girlfriend to a greater degree than if he said "My girlfriend is dieting because she's gaining weight" (Malle et al., 2000). Using a mental marker in this fashion implies that the speaker does not agree with the agent's belief. Given that belief markers distance the speaker from the agent's beliefs, speakers may rely on mental markers in deceptive explanations to distance themselves from their own deceptive statements. That is, when people are lying about why someone else did something (e.g., providing a false alibi for a friend), we should see more belief mental markers in their explanation. The folk-conceptual theory's linguistic aspects may be helpful in theoretically grounding how language may reflect deception.

Implications for Hurtful Communication in Close Relationships

Attribution research on hurtful communication has been in many ways consistent with the folk-conceptual theory because of its emphasis on the role of motives and goals in explanations for hurtful messages (e.g., McLaren & Solomon, 2008; Vangelisti, 1994, 2001; Vangelisti & Young, 2000). Vangelisti and Young's (2000) work, for instance, illustrates the importance of perceived motives on the emotional and relational effects incurred by a hurtful message. According to their findings, explanations of hurtful messages falling on the same dispositional dimension produce very different effects on emotional distance, relationship quality, and satisfaction, when different motives are inferred for the speaker, such as the speaker's desire to hurt, support, achieve an interpersonal goal, or express concern with a hurtful message.

The folk-conceptual theory can contribute to research on close relationships by providing an organizing frame for different types of causes inferred for an intentional speech act, such as a hurtful message. For instance, Vangelisti and Young (2000) conceptualized the intentionality of hurtful communication based on whether the consequences of a hurtful message (i.e., to hurt) were intentionally or unintentionally elicited. According to their approach, a hurtful message was considered intentional only when the speaker's inferred intent was to hurt; hurtful messages with other types of intent inferred on the part of the speaker (e.g., intent to help/support, achieve an interpersonal goal, or fulfill one's need) were considered unintentional. The folk-conceptual theory would suggest, however, that different types of intents for a hurtful message reflect the contents of reasons, such as the speaker's goals and desires, rather than judgments about the message intentionality. In other words, a speech act with any type of inferred intent (e.g., to hurt or express concern) is an intentional behavior, which causes can be classified by using explanation modes and reason types offered within the folk-conceptual theory. For instance, explaining a hurtful message by a partner's emotional state is an example of a causal history factor; explaining a hurtful message by a partner's desire to achieve a selfish goal is an example of a desire reason; and explaining a hurtful message by a partner's perception of a situation is an example of a belief reason (e.g., "He said it because he thought I needed to lose weight").

The folk-conceptual categories can extend close relationships research to predict the interpersonal effects of hurtful communication. For instance, explaining a hurtful message by causal history factors can portray a hurtful action as part of a larger pattern (e.g., "The partner said hurtful words because he is arrogant"), which has stronger implications about the quality of the relationships than specific reasons given for a one-time act (e.g., "The partner said hurtful words because he wanted to show his superiority"). Similarly, framing a negative message as reflecting a belief reason (e.g., "He yelled at me because he thought I deserved it") should reduce blame for a hurtful message compared to a message framed as a desire reason (e.g., "He yelled at me because he wanted to punish me").

Implications for Interpersonal Conflict

Communication scholars have drawn on attribution theory to examine the dynamics of interpersonal conflict (e.g., Bippus, 2003; Canary & Spitzberg, 1990; Sillars, 1980). Although classic attribution theory has provided a framework for studies of interpersonal conflict, communication research has often gone beyond dispositional and situational attributions to examine the role of perceived motives in interpersonal conflict. For instance, extending sociological approaches to conflict, Sillars (1980) examined inferred motives about a partner's desire to cooperate versus to exploit the relationship. According to Sillars' findings, inferences about a partner's cooperative-competitive intent were related to choices of communicative strategies in conflict, satisfaction with the relationship, and conflict outcomes.

At the same time, attributional analyses of interpersonal conflict have relied on attributional biases, especially the actor-observer bias (see for review, Seibold & Spitzberg, 1982; Sillars, 1982). The robustness of the traditional actor-observer bias, however, has been disputed in a comprehensive meta-analysis that revealed that actors and observers did not differ on their likelihood of making dispositional or situational attributions across studies (Malle, 2006). Furthermore, a recent set of empirical studies examining the actor-observer bias across different contexts and methods gave limited or no support to the traditional actor-observer hypothesis (Malle et al., 2007).

The disconfirmation of the actor-observer bias along dispositional and situational attributions does not imply, however, that there are no differences in how actors and observers explain behaviors. Indeed, there is strong evidence that there are three actor-observer asymmetries predicted by the folk conceptual theory that flow from differences in information access and motivation across actors and observers: (a) actors use more reasons and fewer causal history factors than observers do (*reason asymmetry*); (b) actors use more belief reasons and fewer desire reasons than observers (*belief asymmetry*); and, (c) finally, actors express belief reasons without a mental marker more often than observers do (*marker asymmetry*).

There are several ways to reconcile the disconfirmation of the traditional actor-observer bias with communication research on interpersonal conflict that draws on this bias. Consider, for instance, why biases towards a partner's personality, as suggested by the traditional actor-observer bias, may have negative consequences for conflict resolution. According to Sillars (1980),

> Personality constructs assume cross-situational consistency. Therefore, conflicts that are attributed to basic differences in personality are seen as irreconcilable. More proximal causes of difficulty which may be less stable, such as perceptions, goals, and interaction patterns, are overlooked. (p. 184)

Sillar (1980) distinguishes between personality characteristics that have "cross-situational consistency" and "more proximal" causes, such as goals and motives, both of which reflect on a person rather than a situation, and these distinctions map more clearly onto the folk-conceptual model than the traditional dispositional-situational distinction. Specifically, proximal causes reflect reason explanations, and actors use more reasons and fewer causal history factors than observers (i.e., the *reason asymmetry*). Personality factors that contribute to the perception of conflict being "irreconcilable" reflect factors captured by causal history factors, such as personality, the culture someone grew up in, or his/her family upbringing. Explaining one's own behavior in terms of reasons and partners' behaviors in terms of causal history factors should increase perceptions of irreconcilable differences between self and partner, and, therefore, interfere with conflict resolution.

Implications for Account-Giving

While much of this chapter has focused on how perceivers explain the causes of *other's* social behaviors, people also use explanations to account for their *own* behaviors. The explanation of one's own behavior, especially in the context of a failure event (e.g., being late for work) and the potential for reproach (e.g., the boss getting angry), has been referred to collectively as *account-giving* by communication scholars (see Cody & Braaten, 1992). Account episodes typically include excuses that explain how a failure event was not the explainer's fault or responsibility. Because responsibility is determined by whether a behavior was intentional and controllable, the folk-conceptual model is ideally suited to advancing our understanding of account-giving, especially given the traditional dispositional-situational framework's focus on unintentional behavior.

The folk-conceptual model, for example, emphasizes the importance of impression management in the strategic use of communicated explanations. Impression management is a non-trivial motivation for account-giving, with several studies indicating that managing one's impression to minimize social punishment and maximize social reward is the most important rationale for account-giving (see Weiner, 1992). As noted earlier, speakers can use different modes of explanations to subtly accomplish impression management goals, such as deflecting blame and responsibility (Malle, 2004; Todorov et al., 2000). In an account-giving episode, for example, a speaker may explain that he/she was late for work because of situational factors, such as bad traffic, rather than dispositional factors, such as not being a conscientious person.

While this traditional distinction between situational and dispositional explanations gets at the core of deflecting blame, it fails to differentiate amongst the wide range of explanation strategies available to an account giver when some intentionality for the failure event is admitted. For example, using reason explanations can highlight the rationality of the account giver's actions (e.g., "I was late because I needed to assist an injured cyclist") while causal history factors can draw attention away from the account giver to other causes. Further, when providing reason explanations, accounts can be divided between beliefs (e.g., "I was late because I thought the meeting had been cancelled"), desires (e.g., "I was late because I wanted to see the end of the show"), and valuings (e.g., "I was late because I hate coming here").

Finally, the folk-conceptual model's linguistic elements may also have a role to play in account giving. As noted earlier, mental markers such as "I think" serve to distance the speaker from the explanation. Although to date no studies have examined the use of mental markers in account giving, it seems likely that mental markers may be another strategy that account givers may use to provide excuses or rationales for undesired behaviors. As these brief examples make clear, the folk-conceptual model can contribute to a much richer understanding of accounts that goes beyond the dispositional-situational distinction.

Extensions of the Folk-Conceptual Theory from Communication Research

While the previous discussion highlights the implications of the folk-conceptual theory for communication research, it is also the case that communication perspectives may, in turn, inform the folk-conceptual theory by integrating the socio-communicative context more fully into the analysis of behavior explanations. Specifically, communication research can contribute to our understanding of how people make judgments of intentionality in social interactions and to the joint development of communicated explanations in ongoing conversation.

Social Influences on Judgments about Behavior Intentionality

Recall that the starting point in the explanation process outlined by the folk-conceptual theory is a judgment about behavior intentionality, which sets off perceivers on different explanation modes. Although the folk-conceptual theory considers the effect of social factors on how people choose distinct modes for explaining *intentional* behaviors, it does not specify how social influences may determine judgments about behavior intentionality in the first place (i.e., judgments of whether a behavior is intentional or not).

Consider, for instance, the utterance "Ann pushed somebody." Although it is possible that Ann pushed somebody intentionally, it is equally plausible to assume a lack of intention for the above action (e.g., Ann's push was the result of her slipping). The folk-conceptual theory considers the role of contextual influences on judgments about behavior intentionality, such as cues in the immediate context, prior knowledge about the person, and general information about the situational environment in which the action is embedded (Malle et al., 2001). In addition to this contextual information, communication research provides evidence that social factors also affect judgments about behavior intentionality. Based on the studies of how people explain hurtful communication in close relationships, Vangelisti and Young (2000) concluded that "the quality of people's interpersonal associations creates a context for the interpretation of their messages" (p. 407). For instance, judgments of nonverbal behaviors suggest that people who are satisfied with their relationship are less likely to see partners' negative actions as intentional than those who are not satisfied with their relationship (Manusov, 1990, 1996). The valence of behavior may also influence how people perceive behavior intentionality. Summarizing empirical results from several studies on judgments of intentionality in nonverbal communication, Manusov (2007) concluded that "whether a behavior was judged as positive or negative is often linked with intentionality attributions, with positive cues more commonly seen as intentional, especially if directed toward the attributor" (p. 147).

The effects of social influences on intentionality judgments suggest that some behaviors in social interaction can be characterized as *potentially* purposeful or intentional, as suggested by Manusov (2007), rather than intentional. Future research should examine how different socio-communicative factors, such as relational interdependence, trust, group membership, and conversational audience, affect judgments about behavior intentionality in social interaction.

Explanations as a Collaborative Process

Although the folk-conceptual theory describes explanations as both social and cognitive phenomena, more attention should be paid to a dynamic and joint construction of explanations through interaction. According to Burleson (1986), people frequently talk to one another about why someone behaved a certain way, which he refers to as "motive-seeking" conversations (p. 64). Burleson's analysis of attribution in conversation reveals a dynamic and collaborative nature of explanations in motive-seeking conversations:

> Although the attributions made about others are frequently the product of an individual consciousness, when two or more people collectively interpret the action of another through talk, the resulting attribution assumes the character of a collaboratively constructed social product. (p. 64)

The outcome of the collaborative, publicly conducted attribution process is a *consensually established* product, which is "socially constructed, tested, and verified" (Burleson, 1986, p. 79). Whereas Burleson (1986) applies traditional attribution dimensions to analyze conversational attribution processes, the folk-conceptual theory offers categories that capture inferred motives in motive-seeking conversations, which should enhance our understanding of how people arrive at joint explanations of behaviors. At the same time, future research needs to examine the extent to which publicly conducted attribution processes are different from individual attribution processes. Although the folk-conceptual theory treats explanations as both cognitive and social events, it captures a static and individual, rather than dynamic and collaborative, account of explanations. Future research needs to examine the impact of conversational roles, expectancies, perspective taking, interaction goals, and information exchange on how people arrive at joint explanations of events and behaviors in conversations.

Conclusion

This chapter lays out a new perspective on attributions based on the folk-conceptual theory of behavior explanations (Malle, 1999). This new perspective has emerged because of the concerns about classic attribution theory to properly address a cognitive complexity and social functions of attributions, which are also shared by communication scholars. The revised framework distinguishes between explanations for intentional and unintentional behaviors and disentangles between reasons (goals and motives) and causal factors, such as personality, that shape those reasons. It also links distinctions within explanations with psychological and communication factors that determine which type of explanation is used. Finally, it specifies language forms of explanations and their social functions. The new framework has already garnered empirical support and has shown to have predictive power for various psychological phenomena, including the actor-observer bias and individual versus group explanations (Malle et al., 2007; O'Laughlin & Malle, 2000).

   This chapter presents the folk-conceptual theory as a promising alternative to classic attribution theory for understanding communication phenomena. It points out several directions in which the folk-conceptual theory could be usefully explored in communication, showing how the new theory can extend our thinking about how attributions are affected by, affect, and are communicated in communication. At the same time, communication perspectives suggest ways to integrate the socio-communicative context more fully into the analysis of explanations in social interaction.

We conclude with a quote, "If the folk-conceptual theory of explanation is an improvement over traditional attribution theory (at least in the domain of intentional behavior), then we should see a variety of fruitful applications of the folk-conceptual theory in the near future" (Malle, 2004, p. 232). It is our hope that this chapter will stimulate fruitful applications of the folk-conceptual theory to communication phenomena and advance our knowledge of the intricate relationship between behavior explanations and human communication.

References

Abelson, R. P., Dasgupta, N., Park, J., & Banaji, M. R. (1998). Perceptions of the collective other. *Personality and Social Psychology Review, 2,* 243–250.

Allison, S. T., & Messick, D. M. (1987). From individual inputs to group outputs, and back again: Group processes and inferences about members. In C. Hendrick (Ed.), *Group processes* (pp. 111–143). Newbury Park, CA: Sage.

Ames, D. R., Knowles, E. D., Morris, M. W., Kalish, C. W., Rosati, A. D., & Gopnik, A. (2001). The social folk theorist: Insights from social and cultural psychology on the contents and contexts of folk theorizing. In B. F. Malle, L. J. Moses, & D. A. Baldwin (Eds.), *Intentions and intentionality: Foundations of social cognition* (pp. 308–329). Cambridge, MA: MIT Press.

Andrews, P. H. (1987). Gender differences in persuasive communication and attribution of success and failure. *Human Communication Research, 13,* 372–385.

Antaki, C. (1994). *Explaining and arguing: The social organization of accounts.* London: Sage.

Astington, J. W. (2001). The paradox of intention: Assessing children's metarepresentational understanding. In B. F. Malle, L. J. Moses, & D. A. Baldwin (Eds.), *Intentions and intentionality: Foundations of social cognition* (pp. 85–103). Cambridge, MA: MIT Press.

Bazarova, N. N., & Walther, J. B. (2009). Attributions in virtual groups: Distances and behavioral variations in computer-mediated discussions. *Small Group Research, 40,* 138–162.

Bippus, A. M. (2003). Humor motives, qualities, and reactions in recalled conflict episodes. *Western Journal of Communication, 67,* 13–27.

Bond, C. F. Jr., & DePaulo, B. M. (2008). Individual differences in detecting deception. *Psychological Bulletin, 134,* 501–503.

Bond, G. D., & Lee, A. Y. (2005). Language of lies in prison: Linguistic classification of prisoners' truthful and deceptive natural language. *Applied Cognitive Psychology, 19,* 313–329.

Bradbury, T. N., & Fincham, F. D. (1990). Attributions in marriage: Review and critique. *Psychological Bulletin, 107,* 3–33.

Buller, D. B., & Burgoon, J. K. (1996). Interpersonal deception theory. *Communication Theory, 6,* 203–242.

Burleson, B. R. (1986). Attribution schemes and causal inference in natural conversations. In D. G. Ellis & W. A. Donohue (Eds.), *Contemporary issues in language and discourse processes* (pp. 63–85). Mahwah, NJ: Erlbaum.

Canary, D. J., & Spitzberg, B. H. (1990). Attribution biases and associations between conflict strategies and competence outcomes. *Communication Monographs, 57,* 139–151.

Cody, M. J., & Braaten, D. O. (1992). The social-interactive aspects of account-giving. In M. L. McLaughlin, M. J. Cody, & S. Read (Eds.), *Explaining the self to others* (pp. 225–244). Hillsdale, NJ: Erlbaum.

Cramton, C. D. (2001). The mutual knowledge problem and its consequences for dispersed collaboration. *Organization Science, 12,* 346–371.

Cramton, C. D. (2002). Attribution in distributed work groups. In P. J. Hinds & S. Kiesler (Eds.), *Distributed work* (pp. 191–212). Cambridge, MA: MIT Press.

Davidson, D. (1980). *Essays on actions and events.* New York: Oxford University Press.

DePaulo, B. M., Lindsay, J. J., Malone, B. E., Muhlenbruck, L., Charlton, K., & Cooper, H. (2003). Cues to deception. *Psychological Bulletin, 129,* 74–118.

Ehrenhaus, P. (1983). Culture and the attribution process: Barriers to effective communication. In W. B. Gudykunst (Ed.), *Intercultural communication theory* (pp. 259–270). Beverly Hills, CA: Sage.

Floyd, K., & Voloudakis, M. (1999). Affectionate behavior in adult platonic friendships. *Human Communication Research, 25,* 341–369.

Forsyth, D. R. (1980). The function of attributions. *Social Psychology Quarterly, 43,* 184–189.

Forsyth, D. R., Zyzniewski, L. E., & Giammanco, C. A. (2002). Responsibility diffusion in cooperative collectives. *Personality and Social Psychology Bulletin, 28,* 54–65.

Galasinski, D. (2000). *The Language of deception: A discourse analytical study.* Thousand Oaks, CA: Sage.

Gibbs, J. L., Nekrassova, D., Grushina, Y., & Wahab, A. (2008). Reconceptualizing virtual teaming from a constitutive perspective: Review, redirection, and research agenda. In C. S. Beck (Ed.), *Communication yearbook 32* (pp. 187–229). New York: Routledge.

Griffin, R. J., Yang, Z., ter Huurne, E., Boerner, F., Ortiz, S., & Dunwoody, S. (2008). After the Flood: Anger, attribution, and the seeking of information. *Science Communication, 29*(3), 285–315.

Grice, H. P. (1975). Logic and conversation. In P. Cole & J. Morgan (Eds.), *Syntax and semantics* (Vol. 3, pp. 41–53). New York: Academic Press.

Gross, K. (2008). Framing persuasive appeals: Episodic and thematic framing, emotional response, and policy opinion. *Political Psychology, 29,* 169–192.

Gross, K., & D'Ambrosio, L. (2004). Framing emotional response. *Political Psychology, 25,* 1–29.

Gunther, A. C. (1991). What we think others think: Cause and consequence in the third-person effect. *Communication Research, 18,* 355–372.

Hancock, J. T., Curry, L., Goorha, S., & Woodworth, M. T. (2008). On lying and being lied to: A linguistic analysis of deception. *Discourse Processes, 45,* 1–23.

Harvey, J. H., & Omarzu, J. (2001). Are there superior options? In V. Manusov & J. H. Harvey (Eds.), *Attribution, communication behavior, and close relationships* (pp. 372–380). Cambridge, UK: Cambridge University Press.

Heider, F. (1958). The psychology of interpersonal relations. New York: Wiley.

Hewstone, M. (1990). The 'ultimate attribution error'? A review of the literature on intergroup causal attribution. *European Journal of Social Psychology, 20*, 311–335.

Hilton, D. J. (1990). Conversational processes and causal explanation. *Psychological Bulletin, 107*, 65–81.

Hilton, D. J. (1995). The social context of reasoning: Conversational inference and rational judgment. *Psychological Bulletin, 118*, 248–271.

Hinds, P. J., & Bailey, D. E. (2003). Out of sight, out of sync: Understanding conflict in distributed teams. *Organization Science, 14*, 615–632.

Kahlor, L., Dunwoody, S., & Griffin, R. J. (2002). Attributions in explanations of risk estimates. *Public Understanding of Science, 11*, 243–257.

Kanouse, D., & Hanson, L. (1972). Negativity in evaluation. In E. Jones, D. Kanouse, H. Kelly, R. Nisbett, S. Valins, & B. Weiner (Eds.), *Attribution: Perceiving the causes of behavior* (pp. 121–135). Morristown, NJ: General Learning Press.

Kiesler, S., Lee, S. L., & Kramer, A. (2006). Relationship effects in psychological explanations of nonhuman behaviors. *Anthronzoös, 19*, 335–352.

Knight, L. V., & Rees, C. E. (2008). "Enough is enough, I don't want any audience": Exploring medical students' explanations of consent-related behaviors. *Advances in Health Sciences Education, 13*, 407–426.

Knobloch-Westerwick, S., & Taylor, L. D. (2008). The blame game: Elements of causal attribution and its impact on siding with agents in the news. *Communication Research, 35*, 723–744.

Kramer, R. M. (1998). Paranoid cognition in social systems: thinking and acting in the shadow of doubt. *Personality Social Psychology Review, 2*, 251–275.

Leary, M. R., & Forsyth, D. R. (1987). Attributions of responsibility for collective endeavors. *Review of Personality and Social Psychology, 8*, 167–188.

Levine, T. R., Park, H. S., & McCornack, S. A. (1999). Accuracy in detecting truths and lies: Documenting the "veracity effect." *Communication Monographs, 66*, 25–144.

Luo, L., Bippus, A., & Dunbar, N. (2005). Causal attributions for collaborative public speaking presentations in college classes. *Communication Reports, 18*, 65–73.

Malle, B. F. (1999). How people explain behavior: A new theoretical framework. *Personality and Social Psychology Review, 3*, 23–48.

Malle, B. F. (2001). Attribution processes. In N. J. Smelser & P. B. Baltes (Eds.), *International encyclopedia of the social and behavioral sciences* (Vol. 14, pp. 913–917). Amsterdam: Pergamon/Elsevier.

Malle, B. F. (2004). *How the mind explains behavior: Folk explanations, meaning, and social interaction.* Cambridge, MA: MIT Press.

Malle, B. F. (2005). Folk theory of mind: Conceptual foundations of human social cognition. In R. Hassin, J. S. Uleman, & J. A. Bargh (Eds.), *The new unconscious* (pp. 225–255). New York: Oxford University Press.

Malle, B. F. (2006). The actor-observer asymmetry in causal attribution: A (surprising) meta-analysis. *Psychological Bulletin, 132*, 895–919.

Malle, B. F. (2007). Attributions as behavior explanations: Toward a new theory. In D. Chadee & J. Hunter (Eds.), *Current themes and perspectives in social psychology* (pp. 3–26). St. Augustine, Trinidad: SOCS, The University of the West Indies.

Malle, B. F., & Knobe, J. (1997). The folk concept of intentionality. *Journal of Experimental Social Psychology, 33*, 101–121.

Malle, B. F., Knobe, J., & Nelson, S. E. (2007). Actor-observer asymmetries in explanations of behavior: New answers to an old question. *Journal of Personality and Social Psychology, 93*, 491–514.

Malle, B. F., Knobe, J., O'Laughlin, M., Pearce, G. E., & Nelson, S. E. (2000). Conceptual structure and social functions of behavior explanations: Beyond person–situation attributions. *Journal of Personality and Social Psychology, 79*, 309–326.

Malle, B. F., Moses, L. J., & Baldwin, D. A. (2001). Introduction: The significance of intentionality. In B. F. Malle, L. J. Moses, & D. A. Baldwin (Eds.), *Intentions and intentionality* (pp. 1–24). Cambridge, MA: MIT Press.

Malle, B. F., & Nelson, S. E. (2006). *How bad is it? The role of explanations and intentionality in evaluations of objectionable behavior.* Invited symposium paper presented at the Society of Personality and Social Psychology Annual Convention, Palm Springs, California.

Manusov, V. (1990). An application of attribution principles to nonverbal messages in romantic dyads. *Communication Monographs, 57*, 104–118.

Manusov, V. (1996). Changing explanations: Investigating the process of account-making over time. *Research on Language and Social Interaction, 29*, 155–179.

Manusov, V. (2001). Introduction. In V. Manusov & J. H. Harvey (Eds.), *Attribution, communication behavior, and close relationships* (pp. xvii–xxi). Cambridge, UK: Cambridge University Press.

Manusov, V. (2007). Attributions and interpersonal communication: Out of our heads and into behavior. In D. R. Rosko-Ewoldson & J. Monahan (Eds.), *Communication and social cognition: Theories and methods* (pp. 141–169). Mahwah, NJ: Erlbaum.

Manusov, V., Floyd, K., & Kerssen-Griep, J. (1997). Yours, mine, and ours: Mutual attributions for nonverbal behaviors in couples' interactions. *Communication Research, 24*, 234–260.

Manusov, V., & Harvey, J. H. (Eds.). (2001). *Attribution, communication behavior, and close relationships.* Cambridge, UK: Cambridge University Press.

Manusov, V., & Koenig, J. (2001). The content of attributions in couples' communication. In V. Manusov & J. H. Harvey (Eds.), *Attribution, communication behavior, and close relationships* (pp. 134–152). Cambridge, UK: Cambridge University Press.

Manusov, V., & Rodriguez, J. S. (1989). Intentionality behind nonverbal cues: A perceiver's perspective. *Journal of Nonverbal Behavior, 13*, 15–24.

Manusov, V., & Spitzberg, B. H. (2008). Attributes of attribution theory: Finding good cause in the search for theory. In D. O. Braithwaite & L. A. Baxter (Eds.), *Engaging theories in interpersonal communication* (pp. 37–49). Thousand Oaks, CA: Sage.

McCornack, S.A. (1999). Information manipulation theory. *Communication Monographs, 59*, 1–16.

McLaughlin, M. L., Cody, M. J., & O'Hair, H. D. (1983). The management of failure events: Some contextual determinants of accounting behavior. *Human Communication Research, 9*, 208–224.

McLaughlin, M. L., Cody, M. J., & Read, S. J. (Eds.). (1992). *Explaining the self to others.* Hillsdale, NJ: Erlbaum.

McLaren, R. M., & Solomon, D. H. (2008). Appraisals and distancing responses to hurtful messages. *Communication Research, 35*, 339–357.

Mele, A. R. (2001). Acting intentionally: Probing folk notions. In B. F. Malle, L. J. Moses, & D. A. Baldwin (Eds.), *Intentions and intentionality: Foundations of social cognition* (pp. 27–43). Cambridge, MA: MIT Press.

Metts, S. (2001). Extending attribution theory: contributions and cautions. In V. Manusov & J. H. Harvey (Eds.), *Attribution, communication behavior, and close relationships* (pp. 338–350). Cambridge, UK: Cambridge University Press.

Mortensen, M., & Hinds, P. (2001). Conflict and shared identity in geographically distributed teams. *International Journal of Conflict Management, 12,* 212–238.

Moses, L. J. (2001). Some thoughts on ascribing complex intentional concepts to young children. In B. F. Malle, L. J. Moses, & D. A. Baldwin (Eds.), *Intentions and intentionality: Foundations of social cognition* (pp. 69–83). Cambridge, MA: MIT Press.

Nerb, J., & Spada, H. (2001). Evaluation of environmental problems: A coherence model of cognition and emotion. *Cognition and Emotion, 15,* 521–551.

Newman, M. L., Pennebaker, J. W., Berry, D. S., & Richards, J. M. (2003). Lying words: Predicting deception from linguistic style. *Personality and Social Psychology Bulletin, 29,* 665–675.

O'Laughlin, M. J., & Malle, B. F. (2002). How people explain actions performed by groups and individuals. *Journal of Personality and Social Psychology, 82,* 33–48.

Power, J. G., Murphy, S. T., & Coover, G. (1996). Priming prejudice: How stereotypes and counter-stereotypes influence attribution of responsibility and credibility among ingroups and outgroups. *Human Communication Research, 23,* 36–58.

Rosati, A. D., Knowles, E. D., Kalish, C. W., Gopnik, A., Ames, D. R., & Morris, M. W. (2001). The rocky road from acts to dispositions: Insights for attribution theory from developmental research on theories of mind. In B. F. Malle, L. J. Moses, & D. A. Baldwin (Eds.), *Intentions and intentionality: Foundations of social cognition* (pp. 287–303). Cambridge, MA: MIT Press.

Rucinski, D., & Salmon, C. (1990). The "other" as the vulnerable voter: A study of the third-person effect in the 1988 U.S. presidential campaign. *International Journal of Public Opinion Research, 2,* 345–368.

Schul, Y., Burnstein, E., & Bardi, A. (1996). Dealing with deceptions that are difficult to detect: Encoding and judgment as a function of preparing to receive invalid information. *Journal of Experimental Social Psychology, 32,* 228–253.

Seibold, D. R., & Spitzberg, B. (1982). Attribution theory and research: Review and implications for communication. In B. J. Dervin & M. J. Voight (Eds.), *Progress in Communication Sciences III* (pp. 85–125). Norwood, NJ: Ablex.

Sillars, A. L. (1980). Attributions and communication in roommate conflicts. *Communication Monographs, 47,* 180–200.

Sillars, A. L. (1982). Attribution and communication: Are people "naïve scientists" or just naïve? In M. E. Roloff & C. R. Berger (Eds.), *Social cognition and communication* (pp. 73–106). Beverly Hills, CA: Sage.

Sillars, A. L., Roberts, L. J., Dun, T., & Leonard, K. (2001). Stepping into the stream of thought: Cognition during marital conflict. In V. Manusov & J. H. Harvey (Eds.), *Attribution, communication behavior, and close relationships* (pp. 193–210). Cambridge, UK: Cambridge University Press.

Sinaceur, M. (2007). *Suspending judgment to create value: Suspicion and trust in negotiations.* Unpublished manuscript, INSEAD, Fontainebleau, France.

Slugoski, B. R., Lalljee, M., Lamb, R., & Ginsburg, G. (1993). Attribution in conversational context: Effects of mutual knowledge on explanation-giving. *European Journal of Social Psychology, 23,* 219–238.

Sotirovic, M. (2003). How individuals explain social problems: The influences of media use. *Journal of Communication, 53,* 122–137.

Spitzberg, B. H. (2001). The status of attribution theory qua theory in personal relationships. In V. Manusov & J. H. Harvey (Eds.), *Attribution, communication behavior, and close relationships* (pp. 353–371). Cambridge, UK: Cambridge University Press.

Todorov, A., Lalljee, M., & Hirst, W. (2000). Communication context, explanation and social judgment. *European Journal of Social Psychology, 30,* 199–209.

Town, J. P., & Harvey, J. H. (1981). Self-disclosure, attribution, and social interaction. *Social Psychology Quarterly, 44,* 291–300.

Turnbull, W. (1986). Everyday explanation: The pragmatics of puzzle resolution. *Journal of the Theory of Social Behavior, 16,* 141–160.

Vangelisti, A. L. (1994). Messages that hurt. In W. R. Cupach & B. H. Spitzberg (Eds.), *The dark side of interpersonal communication* (pp. 53–82). Hillsdale, NJ: Erlbaum.

Vangelisti, A. L. (2001). Making sense of hurtful interactions in close relationships. In V. Manusov & J. H. Harvey (Eds.), *Attribution, communication behavior, and close relationships* (pp. 38–58). Cambridge, UK: Cambridge University Press.

Vangelisti, A. L., & Young, S. L. (2000). When words hurt: The effects of perceived intentionality on interpersonal relationships. *Journal of Social and Personal Relationships, 17,* 393–424.

Vrij, A. (2008). *Detecting lies and deceit: The psychology of lying and the implications for professional practice.* Chichester, UK: Wiley.

Walther, J. B., & Bazarova, N. N. (2007). Misattribution in virtual groups: The effects of member distribution on self-serving bias and partner blame. *Human Communication Research, 33,* 1–26.

Walther, J. B., Boos, M., & Jonas, K. J. (2002). Misattribution and attributional redirection in distributed virtual groups. *Proceedings of the 35th Hawaii International Conference on System Sciences.* Washington, DC: ICEE Computer Society.

Wang, E., Lignos, C., Vatsal, A., & Scassellati, B. (2006). Effects of head movement on perceptions of humanoid robot behavior. *Proceedings of the 1st ACM SIGCHI/ SIGART Conference on Human-Robot Interaction, USA,* 81–85.

Weber, D. J., & Vangelisti, A. L. (1991). Because I love you…: The tactical use of attributional expressions in conversation. *Human Communication Research, 17,* 606–624.

Weiner, B. (1992). Excuses in everyday interaction. In M. L. McLaughlin, M. J. Cody, & S. J. Read (Eds.), *Explaining one's self to others* (pp. 131–146). Hillsdale, NJ: Erlbaum.

Weiner, B. (2004). Attribution theory revisited: Transforming cultural plurality into theoretical unity. In D. M. McInerney & S. V. Etten (Eds.), *Big theories revisited* (Vol. 4, pp. 13–29). Greenwich, CT: Information Age Publishing.

Wittenbaum, G. M., Hollingshead, A. B., & Botero, I. (2004). From cooperative to motivated sharing in groups: Going beyond the hidden profile paradigm. *Communication Monographs, 71,* 286–310.

Zaccaro, S. J., Peterson, C., & Walker, S. (1987). Self-serving attributions for individual and group performance. *Social Psychology Quarterly, 50,* 257–263.

CHAPTER CONTENTS

4 Raising the Specter of Death

What Terror Management Theory Brings to the Study of Fear Appeals

Susanna Dilliplane

University of Pennsylvania

How do people respond to persuasive appeals that invoke the threat of death? This chapter calls attention to Terror Management Theory (TMT), a theoretical framework that considers the unique effects of raising the salience of one's mortality and yet has remained largely outside the focus of inquiry into the effects of fear appeals. The distinct conceptual and predictive features of TMT, as well as their relevance to health and political communication research, are discussed and then juxtaposed with those found in the dominant strains of the fear appeal literature. The analysis articulates the theoretical and empirical implications of these conceptual differences and offers a set of testable predictive contrasts, with the goal of stimulating and facilitating new lines of fear appeal scholarship.

Imagine you are watching television and an ad comes on the screen.[1] A video of the twin towers on September 11th zooms in on the gaping, burning holes from the hijacked planes, bringing to mind the horrific fates of those on the planes and trapped in the World Trade Center buildings. Warning that the threat of terrorist attacks still looms large, the narrator urges you to support a particular political candidate. Or your TV screen is filled by the pained face of a man who has been hospitalized with throat and lung cancer, and yet doggedly expresses his intent to be alive for his daughter's upcoming visit. This scene is followed by the stark message that the man died before his daughter arrived, as well as an appeal for viewers to quit smoking.[2]

How do people react to such appeals that invoke the threat of death? One class of answers to this question may be found in the literature on fear appeals. A number of existing theoretical frameworks from the health and political arenas, well known to communication researchers, could readily classify the above examples as high-fear appeals and derive predictions about likely message responses. However, different answers are emerging from research that specifically focuses on fear of death, rather than fear generally. The purpose of this chapter is to call attention to Terror Management Theory (TMT), a theoretical framework that has remained largely outside the focus of communication research, and to juxtapose its distinct conceptual and predictive features with those found in the dominant strains of the literature on fear and persuasion.

I begin with an explication of Terror Management Theory and its relevance to research on fear appeals. I then discuss major constructs within the existing fear appeal research, with a particular emphasis on two prominent theoretical frameworks that exemplify how these constructs and their interrelationships are conceptualized in the health and political arenas. These highlighted models are then used to consider conceptual comparisons and contrasts with TMT, along with the implications of these differences for understanding responses to persuasive appeals invoking the threat of death. Based on the key conceptual distinctions among the frameworks, the analysis concludes with a series of testable predictive contrasts, which is offered as a first step toward productively incorporating TMT into future scholarship in health and political communication.

This chapter is not about presenting an original theoretical model. TMT is a well-established theory in psychology, and various TMT studies have either hinted at or articulated some of the same points that I make here, particularly in the health context, where the theory's authors have offered a model of health behavior decisions that integrates TMT with more traditional approaches to health psychology (see Goldenberg & Arndt, 2008). Nonetheless, prior TMT scholarship has very rarely been explicitly situated in a persuasive communications context. Thus, my central aim here is to discuss TMT's potential contributions from a communication perspective, with a particular emphasis on comparing and contrasting TMT's core constructs, their interrelationships, and corresponding predictions with those of existing theoretical frameworks in the fear communication literature.

By focusing on theoretical comparison, this chapter is oriented toward understanding how to leverage the unique features of TMT in relation to prior research on fear appeals—a body of work that is concerned not only with predicting attitudes and behaviors, but also with communication and persuasion processes involved in the use of emotional appeals and with questions of message design. In addition, this comparison brings to light a number of intriguing questions about how to understand responses to fear appeals invoking the threat of death, such as the possibility of a two-part sequential response that is not mediated by fear arousal. In positioning TMT relative to important themes in the health and political literature on persuasion and fear appeals, this chapter seeks to bring terror management more squarely into the focus of communication scholars.

Terror Management Theory: An Overview

Terror Management Theory seeks to explain the motivational underpinnings of human behavior, positing that concerns about the inevitability of death affect a broad array of attitudes and behaviors that have no logical or semantic relationship with mortality (Greenberg, Pyszczynski, & Solomon, 1986; Solomon, Greenberg, & Pyszczynski, 1991; see also Pyszczynski, Solomon, & Greenberg, 2003). Although TMT has generated a vast number of studies, it appears to have been almost entirely neglected in communication research, including the fear appeal literature.[3] Given the theory's focus on terror—generally defined as intense or overwhelming fear—its potential contributions to the study of fear appeals deserve consideration. In this section, I provide an overview of the theory and its relevance to health and political communication.

Based on insights derived from Ernest Becker's work (1962, 1973, 1975), TMT begins with an existential dilemma facing humans: as animals, we possess a general orientation toward continued life or self-preservation, but our unique mental ability of consciousness and self-consciousness, which enables reflection on the past and anticipation of the future, unfortunately renders us conscious of the disturbing inevitability of our own deaths (Goldenberg, Pyszczynski, Greenberg, & Solomon, 2000; Pyszczynski, Greenberg, Solomon, & Maxfield, 2006). It is human awareness of the inevitability of death and the possibility of total annihilation of one's being upon death that creates the potential for existential terror. TMT's conception of fear of death, which has roots in evolutionary theorizing, thus generally encompasses all humans; put simply, humans fear death (Pyszczynski, Greenberg, et al., 2006).

According to TMT, cultural beliefs systems save us by mitigating the horror and dread caused by awareness of our own mortality.[4] Terror is managed via a "dual-component cultural anxiety-buffer" consisting of a cultural worldview and self-esteem (Arndt, Greenberg, Pyszczynski, & Solomon, 1997, p. 379). A cultural worldview provides an explanation for one's existence, standards through which individuals can attain a sense of personal value, and the potential for literal or symbolic immortality if one lives up to those standards. An individual acquires and maintains self-esteem by believing in the cultural worldview and living up to the standards it sets.

Although cultural worldviews—which provide order, permanence, and meaning to reality and one's existence in it—obviously differ from culture to culture (and from individual to individual), their *purpose* is the same: "cultural worldviews set up the path to immortality, to transcendence of one's own death. By being valued contributors to such a meaningful world, we become permanent constituents of an eternal symbolic reality, instead of just corporeal beings in a wholly material reality" (Pyszczynski et al., 2003, p. 19). Thus, existential terror is managed through belief systems that deny that death is the end of one's existence, either by promising literal immortality (e.g., heaven, reincarnation) or by enabling a person to feel that he or she is an important part of a significant and enduring reality (Pyszczynski, Greenberg, et al., 2006).

In the context of this chapter, it is important to note that the death-denying function of worldviews is not simply about controlling fear of an immediate physical threat; the problem of mortality represents an existential threat that also operates on a more abstract level. When one thinks about what happens to oneself when one dies, it is not necessarily the imminent threat of death that drives existential terror, but rather knowledge of the inevitability of one's own death, which may be non-imminent but nonetheless terrifying due to its potential finality (for consideration of the physical versus abstract components of existential threat, see Pyszczynski, Greenberg, et al., 2006; Hirschberger, Pyszczynski, & Ein-Dor, 2009).

Given the vast diversity in cultural worldviews and standards by which self-esteem is obtained, TMT views the two components of the cultural anxiety buffer as relatively fragile social constructions requiring continual consensual validation; hence, many behaviors focus on attaining this validation (Pyszczynski, Greenberg, & Solomon, 1999). To the extent that cultural worldviews protect against deep-rooted fears of death, reminders of mortality are hypothesized to lead to an increased need for these beliefs and, by extension, more positive responses to things that validate it and more negative responses to things that threaten it (Pyszczynski et al., 1999). More specifically, TMT posits that a two-stage defense process kicks in when one's mortality becomes salient (Greenberg, Arndt, Simon, Pyszczynski, & Solomon, 2000). First, a person puts conscious thoughts of death out of his or her mind by engaging in threat-focused cognitive maneuvers such as distraction strategies, alteration of beliefs to deny vulnerability, or reassuring thoughts about one's health and the remoteness of the threat (Pyszczynski et al., 2003). These proximal defenses are the direct, rational (though not necessarily unbiased) psychological defenses that are activated to cope with conscious awareness of death—i.e., active suppression.

Once thoughts of death are out of focal attention, but are still accessible, distal defenses are activated. At this stage, people bolster faith in their cultural worldviews and their self-esteem to defend against unconscious thoughts of death. For example, individuals may derogate those who violate or challenge their beliefs, increase regard for those who validate or praise their beliefs, subscribe more strongly to group stereotypes, or exhibit greater in-group favoritism and out-group hostility or prejudice (e.g., Das, Bushman, Bezemer, Kerkhof, & Vermeulen, 2009; Greenberg et al., 1990; Hoyt, Simon, & Reid, 2009; Schimel et al., 1999; Halloran & Kashima, 2004). Such worldview bolstering reduces the accessibility of thoughts of mortality (Arndt, Greenberg, Solomon, et al., 1997). Given that the physical reality of the inevitability of death cannot, in the end, be rationally denied, it is posited that these distal defenses enable the individual to attack the problem at a more abstract level. The confirmation of culturally constructed conceptions of reality and a corresponding sense of self-esteem functions to symbolically control the problem of inevitable death and protect against the potential terror it engenders (Pyszczynski et al., 2003).

The latent accessibility of thoughts of mortality is critical to the theory's predictions. Defensive distortions caused by suppression should occur immediately after mortality is made salient, while worldview and self-esteem bolstering should be greatest once thoughts of mortality are no longer in focal consciousness. Experimental manipulations have provided support for the temporal sequence of this dual process (Greenberg, Arndt, Simon, Pyszczynski, & Solomon, 2000). Active suppression occurs directly after mortality salience is induced, pushing thoughts of death from conscious awareness. Following a delay and distraction, the death concerns that are accessible—but beneath one's conscious radar—provoke distal terror management defenses (see Arndt, Cook, & Routledge, 2004, for a model of the cognitive architecture of terror management). Unlike the individual's conscious suppression of mortality-related thoughts (proximal defenses), distal defenses occur without the individual's awareness of the connection between the threat of death and worldview defense (or the motivation that underlies this response) (Pyszczynski et al., 1999).

A typical TMT experiment manipulates mortality salience (MS) by asking people to respond to two open-ended questions: "Please briefly describe the emotions that the thought of your own death arouses in you" and "Jot down, as specifically as you can, what you think will happen to *you* as you physically die" (Solomon, Greenberg, & Pyszczynski, 2004). Other operationalizations of MS induction, also relevant to a communication context, include subliminal death primes (e.g., flashing the word "death," as in Arndt, Greenberg, Pyszczynski, et al., 1997, or flashing the words "9/11" and "WTC," as in Landau et al., 2004), gory footage of a fatal automobile accident (Nelson, Moore, Olivetti, & Scott, 1997), news reports about terrorist attacks (Das et al., 2009), and even insurance brand logos (Fransen, Fennis, Pruyn, & Das, 2008).[5] Control groups either receive an innocuous version of this treatment (e.g., asking open-ended questions about television use, or subliminally flashing a neutral word like "field") or a non-death-related treatment with a negative valence (e.g., asking people to think about intense physical pain, social exclusion, general anxieties, or dental pain), neither of which appears to produce the same distal defense effects as an MS induction (Pyszczynski et al., 2003).

Following the MS treatment, a delay is introduced, typically in the form of a distracter task or an opportunity to engage in proximal defenses, in order to allow for death thoughts to recede from focal attention. No delay is required if subliminal priming is used because death-related thoughts are not brought to conscious awareness. Next, latent accessibility of death-thoughts is assessed through a word fragment completion task, asking respondents to fill in a series of words, some of which may be completed into death-related words. For example, "coff _ _" could be *coffin* or *coffee*, and "gra _ _" could be *grave* or *grape*. Alternative measures of death thought accessibility, such as reaction times, have been used to provide validation of this word fragment completion task (Arndt, Cook, Greenberg, & Cox, 2007). According to TMT, accessibility should be *higher* among those whose mortality is primed prior to the delay. (Note, however, that accessibility measured directly after mortality salience is raised, as opposed to after a delay, is expected to be *lower* due to active suppression involved in proximal defenses.)

Defense of cultural worldviews (distal defenses) is then assessed through attitudinal and behavioral measures, with the expectation that defense will be greater among people whose mortality was made accessible. For example, thinking about death led respondents to evaluate a source of pro-American views more positively and a source of anti-American views more negatively compared to a control group, demonstrating how MS influences responses to those who support or oppose important aspects of cultural worldviews (Greenberg et al., 1990, Study 3). A similar pro-American bias was found when people's personal mortality was made salient by a video of a fatal car accident, as opposed to a neutral driving video (Nelson et al., 1997).

This overview of TMT has aimed to provide a broad understanding of the theory's core concepts and propositions. More in-depth treatments of the theory's nuances and the kinds of research questions they have inspired may be found elsewhere. In addition, while theoretical critiques of TMT are certainly important to recognize and consider (e.g., Baron, 1997; Buss, 1997; Mikulincer & Florian, 1997; Wicklund, 1997; McGregor, 2006; Proulx & Heine, 2006; Kirkpatrick & Navarrete, 2006; see Pyszczynski, Greenberg, et al., 2006, for a response), as are ethical and philosophical questions regarding the use of fear appeals (e.g., Pfau, 2007), these issues lie somewhat beyond the immediate objective of this chapter. The focus here is on laying out TMT's basic tenets in order to facilitate a discussion of its relevance to the study of fear appeals and its conceptual comparison to other frameworks.

Intuitively, TMT's conceptualization of how people respond when their mortality is made salient seems directly relevant to fear appeal research. Based on the theory's propositions, a fear appeal that raises the salience of personal mortality will elicit an initial suppression response to remove thoughts of death from focal awareness. In addition, if the appeal advocates views that challenge a person's worldview as a relevant source of self-esteem, it will encourage message rejection once thoughts of death are accessible but latent, while an appeal that validates the person's beliefs should receive an especially positive evaluation, enhancing the likelihood of message acceptance. TMT thus has the potential to provide new insights for understanding and predicting responses to fear appeals.

Further, this framework is applicable to both health and political contexts—indeed, to any context in which death and fear appeals are employed. For example, reminders of death in conjunction with health-related behaviors are quite commonplace in health persuasion campaigns, as well as experimental manipulations in which death-related appeals serve as a "high" fear condition (Henley & Donovan, 2003). In recognition of this fact, Goldenberg and Arndt (2008) have recently integrated terror management into a model for predicting health decisions, which revolves around the impact of conscious versus unconscious death thoughts on health behaviors. Their model posits that either defensive avoidance or health-promoting behavior may serve the same function of removing conscious thoughts of death by reducing a perceived health-related threat (i.e., proximal defenses), and that distal defenses activated by nonconscious thoughts of death can motivate behavior that is either beneficial or antithetical to physical health, depending not on the implications for health but on the implications of the behavior for worldview and self-esteem.[6] This work represents an important contribution toward making TMT a useful tool in health promotion campaigns and illustrates the need for further consideration of terror management's relevance to research on fear communications in the health domain.

Death-related themes also arise in the context of political persuasion. Although political studies have largely focused on non-death-related appeals (or do not differentiate among specific types of fear appeals), reminders of death are not unfamiliar features of political persuasive appeals. Among the examples that readily come to mind are post-9/11 speeches made by President Bush that sounded themes of death (see Merskin, 2004) and campaign appeals containing reminders of 9/11, which have appeared in a number of political contests. However, references to death have certainly been used in war-related contexts prior to 9/11, both in presidential rhetoric (see, e.g., Ivie, 1999) and in campaign appeals (e.g., the famous "Daisy Girl" TV ad). They also appear in non-war policy contexts; for example, in the recent U.S. debate over health care reform, an ad by the conservative Independent Women's Forum warned that 300,000 American women could have died if the United States had a "government-run" health insurance plan similar to that of England.[7]

Given that mortality salience has been found to produce greater nationalistic bias, enhanced endorsement of values associated with a salient social identity, greater out-group hostility or prejudice, increased ingroup bias, and greater support for extreme military force or violence (Das et al., 2009; Greenberg et al., 1990, 2000; Halloran & Kashima, 2004; Hoyt et al., 2009; Pyszczynski, Abdollahi, et al., 2006; see also Pyszczynski, Rothschild, & Abdollahi, 2008), the potential ramifications of political appeals containing reminders of death could be significant for outcomes such as policy support, candidate support, and other political attitudes or actions. Indeed, in the context of politics—an arena often associated with the use of tactics intended to subtly manipulate the public—it is worth noting that persuasive messages need not hammer people over the head with an MS treatment in order to produce worldview defense. More subtle treatments, including some outside of conscious awareness, show stronger effects than when people are made to ponder death extensively (Pyszczynski et al., 2003, p. 56). In addition, reminders of the 9/11 terrorist attacks have been found to raise mortality salience and provoke worldview defense among American students in a manner akin to standard MS inductions (Landau et al., 2004; Pyszczynski, Abdollahi, et al., 2006; see also Das et al., 2009, for a non-American example). Real-world messages whose text, imagery, or audio provide reminders of death thus seem well equipped to produce terror management responses.

Major Constructs in Fear Appeal Research

A number of theoretical frameworks have been developed to account for the impact of fear—and persuasive appeals that seek to elicit fear—on attitudes and behaviors in both health and political contexts. Although there is variation among these models, they have in common an interest in delineating the role of key constructs such as environmental (message) threat, threat appraisal, fear arousal, and cognition in shaping outcomes such as information seeking and processing, attitudes, and behaviors. The following discussion provides an overview of the major constructs within prior fear communication research, drawing particular attention to two dominant frameworks in the health and political science literatures—the Extended Parallel Process Model (Witte, 1992, 1994, 1998) and the Theory of Affective Intelligence (Marcus, Neuman, & MacKuen, 2000)—in order to more fully illustrate the concepts and their theoretical relationships.

Theorizing in a Health Context

In the health communication context, fear appeals have inspired a wealth of studies, along with a number of theoretical frameworks for explaining the effects of these appeals. Examples include the drive models proposed by Janis (1967; Hovland, Janis, & Kelly, 1953) and McGuire (1968, 1969), which were followed by Leventhal's (1970, 1971) parallel response model and subjective expected utility approaches such as Rogers' (1975, 1983) protection motivation theory (PMT) and Sutton's (1982) subjective expected utility (SEU) model. Each of these theoretical perspectives placed varying degrees of emphasis on the cognitive versus emotional processes involved in people's reactions to fear appeals. The drive models focused on fear, positing a curvilinear (inverted U-shaped) relationship between fear and attitude change. Leventhal's parallel response model (later called the parallel process model) took theorizing in a new direction by separating the emotional and cognitive processes involved in responses to fear appeals. Subjective expected utility approaches largely ignored fear in favor of the cognitive side of fear appeals, focusing on the perceived utility of the threat and subjective probabilities of its occurrence (Sutton's SEU model) and perceptions of threat and efficacy (Rogers' PMT).

Witte (1992, 1994) advanced these earlier approaches with her proposal for the Extended Parallel Process Model (EPPM). Drawing on Leventhal's parallel process model, Witte's EPPM differentiates between danger control processes, which lead to message acceptance, and fear control processes, which lead to message rejection. The EPPM also builds on PMT in its use of the key concepts of perceived threat (the additive effects of perceived susceptibility to the threat and perceived severity of the threat) and perceived efficacy (self-efficacy and response efficacy). According to the model, a rapid sequential appraisal process takes place: threat appraisal comes first, followed by an appraisal of efficacy, provided that the threat meets a certain threshold (Witte, 1998). Thus, a fear appeal may produce one of three responses: (a) no response if perceived threat is low; (b) message acceptance, produced by a high threat/high efficacy interaction; or (c) message rejection, produced by a high threat/low efficacy interaction. The combination of high perceived threat and efficacy is hypothesized to lead to cognitions about the threat and ways to avoid it, which leads to behavior change (i.e., message acceptance). This response represents a deliberate effort to control the danger. By contrast, high perceived threat coupled with low perceived efficacy is hypothesized to produce message rejection and even boomerang responses, as people deal with the overwhelming fear of a danger they think they cannot control by engaging in defensive avoidance, message minimization, or reactance. This is a potentially unconscious response to control the emotion of fear.

The EPPM posits that the role of fear is contingent on perceived efficacy. Fear directly causes message rejection when efficacy is low; message threat leads to greater perceived threat, which leads to fear that then causes message rejection. Put simply, as perceived threat increases when perceived efficacy is low, people will do the opposite of what the message advocates (Witte, 1998, p. 439). As a result, persuasion or message acceptance should be *lowest* among those in high threat/low efficacy conditions relative to all other conditions (suggesting a boomerang effect), or at the very least message acceptance should not be significantly different from low threat conditions (which is more akin to a null effect). Fear also can indirectly influence message acceptance when efficacy is high; the fear produced by perceived threat is cognitively appraised, causing a further increase in perceived threat that then increases message acceptance. Thus, a person may experience a great deal of fear in a high threat/high efficacy situation, but the "critical point" at which fear outweighs cognitions has not been reached. Overall, affect drives the fear control responses characterizing message rejection, while cognitions (beliefs about severity, susceptibility, self-efficacy, and response efficacy, as well as cognitive appraisals of fear) characterize the danger control processes associated with message acceptance. Moreover, danger control and fear control responses are treated as competing: "if one is defensively responding to a fear appeal and rejecting it, one is not making attitude, intention, or behavior changes" (Witte & Allen, 2000, p. 601).

More recently, further modifications to these theoretical approaches were proposed in the stage model of the processing of fear-arousing communications (Das, de Wit, & Stroebe, 2003; de Hoog, Stroebe, & de Wit, 2005, 2007). The stage model bears some similarities to the EPPM, but distinguishes itself by incorporating aspects of dual process theories of persuasion (e.g., Chaiken, 1980; Chaiken, Liberman, & Eagly, 1989; Petty & Cacioppo, 1986), building on the proposition that fear arousal can both act as a motivator to encourage systematic (in-depth) processing and induce defense motivation (information processing that is positively or negatively biased in order to support one's own beliefs or preferences). Further, the stage model hypothesizes different effects of defense motivation on primary appraisal of the threat (Stage 1) and secondary appraisal of the action recommendation (Stage 2).[8] While this and other frameworks represent important streams of theorizing about fear appeals, I focus on the EPPM because it is an elegant model that incorporates major constructs in the health-related fear appeal literature and concisely maps out their relationships. As a result, it not only provides a useful model with which to set up a theoretical comparison with TMT, but it has fostered a great deal of research and continues to be influential in the fear appeal domain.

For example, in a meta-analysis of studies in the health context, Witte and Allen (2000) found a positive linear function for all independent variables; messages with stronger fear appeals, stronger severity and susceptibility, and stronger response efficacy and self-efficacy produced a greater persuasive impact on attitude, intention, and behavior (danger control responses). High threat/high efficacy appeals produced the greatest persuasive impact, as predicted by the EPPM (as well as the SEU model). Further, this meta-analysis was the first to examine fear control responses, or the defensive tactics used to resist a message. The authors found that (a) the stronger the fear appeal (i.e., the greater the threat), the greater the defensive response; (b) the weaker the efficacy message, the greater the defensive response; and (c) fear control responses were negatively correlated with danger control responses.

However, not all of the EPPM's predictions have garnered empirical support. For example, the EPPM predicts that high threat/low efficacy appeals should produce the strongest fear control responses (i.e., the least persuasion, the most message rejection), but Witte and Allen's meta-analysis (2000) revealed no difference between high threat/low efficacy and low threat/high efficacy messages—both types were less persuasive than high threat/high efficacy messages but more persuasive than low threat/low efficacy messages. Other empirical research based on the EPPM has found a similar pattern of consistent support for the persuasiveness of high threat/high efficacy messages (although see Muthusamy, Levine, & Weber's 2009 study in Namibia for an interesting exception), but greater ambiguity regarding other propositions of the model. For example, people who perceived high threat and efficacy showed greater cognition about cardiovascular disease (indicative of danger control response) compared to people who perceived high threat and low efficacy, but the latter group exhibited greater cognition as well as greater health media use and discussion than those with low perceived threat (Rimal, 2001).[9]

Similarly, a recent study of anti-smoking appeals found partial support for the superior persuasiveness of high threat/high efficacy messages, but no boomerang effect (message rejection) in response in the high threat/low efficacy conditions relative to the low threat conditions (which would be hypothesized to have a null effect) (Wong & Cappella, 2009). Interestingly, respondents with low readiness to quit, who would be expected to be the least open to an appeal advocating smoking cessation, showed the greatest intention to quit in the high threat/high efficacy condition and the lowest intention to quit in the low threat conditions, with the high threat/low efficacy condition squarely in the *middle*—a pattern that does not reflect the fear control response to high threat/low efficacy appeals predicted by the EPPM. In addition, Witte's initial test of the EPPM (1994) produced some unexpected results, including a *negative* relationship between fear and message minimization and defensive avoidance (rather than a positive relationship between fear and message rejection) and a non-significant relationship between perceived threat and attitude and behavior (only behavioral intent showed the predicted significant positive relationship).

These patterns in the empirical research suggest room for speculation about whether terror management processes may enhance explanations of fear appeal responses in cases where mortality salience is raised. For example, *lower* fear may be related to *higher* fear control responses such as message minimization or defensive avoidance (as found by Witte, 1994) if people are engaging in proximal defenses aimed at immediately reducing mortality salience. Further, message acceptance in the form of information searching or behavioral modification may be observed after exposure to a high threat/low efficacy message that raises the salience of death if such responses serve to validate cultural beliefs and symbolically reduce the threat of death. On the flip side, perceived threat may sometimes fail to be related to message acceptance if worldview defense manifests in message rejection.

Theorizing in a Political Context

Theorizing about the impact of fear appeals on political attitudes and behaviors has been somewhat limited compared to the health context. In part, the relative dearth of models that specifically focus on fear communications is reflective of the fact that a significant stream of political science research has employed a bipolar valence approach to modeling affect, which lumps together positively valenced emotions (e.g., enthusiasm, hope, pride) and negatively valenced emotions (e.g., anger, guilt, fear, sadness). For example, research on campaign advertising effects has tended to use this positive/negative model of affect (e.g., Ansolabehere & Iyengar, 1995; Lau, Sigelman, Heldman, & Babbit, 1999; Brooks, 2006). The "hot cognition hypothesis" of Lodge and Taber's dual-process model of motivated political reasoning similarly seems to map onto a bipolar valence approach (Lodge & Taber, 2000, 2005). This hypothesis suggests that all sociopolitical concepts (e.g., political leaders, issues, groups) have an affective charge (positive or negative), an evaluative tally that automatically comes to mind upon exposure to the associated object and thus influences the judgment process (Lodge & Taber, 2005). Other theories of emotion and politics include Affect Transfer, which posits that a stimulus that provokes negative emotion causes more negative evaluations of that stimulus and vice versa for a stimulus that elicits positive emotion, and Endogenous Affect, which predicts the reverse causal direction so that preexisting candidate evaluations induce corresponding emotional reactions (Ladd & Lenz, 2008).

A significant departure from this approach to modeling the role of affect in political judgments is found in the Theory of Affective Intelligence (Marcus et al., 2000). Drawing on the circumplex model of affect, which represents affective states as a circle in a two-dimensional bipolar space (Russell, 1980; Neuman, Marcus, MacKuen, & Crigler, 2007), Affective Intelligence (AI) models emotional variation along two axes (a dual unipolar model). The theory also departs from a dominant view of affect in politics that equates emotion with irrationality. AI envisions a marriage of emotion and reason in which affective and cognitive processes are intertwined, not mutually exclusive.

The theory predicts political behavior as a function of two physiological subsystems in the brain—the preconscious emotional systems of disposition and surveillance.[10] The disposition system provides feedback on whether an ongoing sequence of habitual actions is successfully advancing one's plans or failing to do so. Emotional assessments (enthusiasm or frustration/despair) control the execution of habits, which can be relied upon in a safe, familiar, and rewarding environment. The surveillance system scans the environment for novel or threatening stimuli. If no threat is detected, a person's affective reaction is a sense of calm or tranquility. If a threat is detected, the person experiences anxiety, which has a notable impact on attention: current activity is suspended and attention is oriented to the threat in order to facilitate learning. Key to AI's conceptualization of threat is its novelty, or the uncertainty involved in the nature or consequences of the threat. Anxiety thus revolves around uncertainty about an unknown, rather than aversion to a known negative entity.

Emotions—which are generated by affective appraisal processes that precede conscious awareness—serve as key mediators of political judgment and behavior. The disposition system's signal of enthusiasm leads to reliance on enduring political habits, while the surveillance system's signal of fear leads to less reliance on habits as well as greater motivation to gather contemporary information about issues and candidates' positions on those issues.[11] According to AI, anxiety creates the conditions for rational reconsideration of one's "normal" vote choice, thus leaving the door open for "candidates of all political stripes to have a plausible shot at persuasion"—i.e., possible defection (Marcus et al., 2000, p. 61). In sum, contrary to the notion that a calm mind is best equipped for reasoned, thoughtful judgment, the central tenet of AI is that anxiety produces a more "rational" voter—one who sets aside habit and carefully considers the options to decide on the best course of action (Marcus et al., 2000, p. 58).

Support for the theory has been provided by survey data on vote choice in U.S. elections: anxiety (about the candidate of one's party) appeared to reduce reliance on partisanship and ideology and increase the impact of specific and contemporary information about candidate qualities and issue positions on vote choice (Marcus et al., 2000; MacKuen, Marcus, Neuman, & Keele, 2007). Moreover, while anxiety alone was not found to motivate greater defection, it interacted with voters' assessments of candidates' issue distances and qualities, thereby influencing the probability of defection (MacKuen et al., 2007). Other research found that anxiety was positively associated with greater willingness to learn more about specific issue debates and to learn more about the perspectives of opponents, even regarding a contentious issue like affirmative action (Wolak, Marcus, & Neuman, 2003). The experimental findings of Redlawsk, Civettini, and Lau (2007) also provided some support for the idea that anxiety affects information processing and learning in a campaign context. Exposure to a significant amount of negative information about one's preferred candidate (i.e., a high-threat environment) was found to increase anxiety, resulting in more careful information processing, greater efforts to learn about that candidate, and greater accuracy in issue placement of that candidate. Though this study did not examine subsequent changes in vote preference, AI points to the possibility that such behaviors—driven by anxiety—could lead to defection from one's original candidate choice.

Studies with a stronger communications bent have provided more specific links between Affective Intelligence and the fear appeal literature. For example, messages that included a high-anxiety prime, as opposed to a low-anxiety prime, were found to increase the influence of contemporary information (the message's argument), and decrease the influence of predispositions, on attitudes regarding tolerance toward racist groups (Marcus et al., 2005). Though not presented as a specific test of AI, another study found that anxiety produced by a threatening news article increased attention to a campaign, online information seeking, and learning (Valentino, Hutchings, Banks, & Davis, 2008). Supportive of AI's conceptualization of the role of anxiety, the authors found that anxiety functioned as a mediator between the high-threat message and behavioral outcomes.

Expanding Affective Intelligence to a campaign advertising context, Brader (2006) manipulated television ads involving candidates in a real election in order to examine the effects of emotionally evocative (i.e., high) fear appeals and enthusiasm appeals. In expressing subsequent candidate assessments and preferences, people exposed to a high fear appeal tended to rely less on their predispositions or prior candidate preferences and more on recent information or contemporary evaluations, as shaped by the ad. The high fear appeal produced a greater shift toward the ad's sponsor, particularly among those initially opposed or indifferent toward that candidate. It also led to greater interest in relevant information such as political news, suggesting support for the predicted impact of fear on information seeking and learning processes.

More recently, Brader, Valentino, and Suhay (2008) tested the theory's propositions in a policy-oriented communications context. They found that a negative news story on immigration that incorporated a cue for a stigmatized immigrant group (Latinos) increased anxiety compared to the same story with a cue for a European immigrant group, particularly when Latinos were depicted in a stereotypic manner (low-skill). Elevated anxiety in turn affected policy opinions, information seeking, and political action. Mediation analyses suggested that anxiety mediated the relationship between message threat and outcomes, while perceived threat to the self or the nation did not. Though this study focused on a news article rather than a persuasive appeal, its finding that anxiety facilitated attitudinal and behavioral change in the direction of the currently available information points to the potential impact of persuasive fear appeals in a policy debate.

It should be noted that Affective Intelligence is not specifically a communication theory, though it has been adapted to this area of research. Additionally, AI is not the only theory that speaks to the role of anxiety in a political persuasion context. For example, Nabi's Cognitive-Functional Model

(Nabi, 1999, 2002), which integrates a discrete emotions approach and dual process cognitive response models of persuasion, considers the impact of fear on persuasion. Straddling the health and political contexts, Nabi specifically highlights differences between the CFM and the EPPM, yet also tests the model by studying responses to manipulations of a news article on domestic terrorism and related proposed legislation (Nabi, 2002).

That being said, this chapter focuses on Affective Intelligence because it is a dominant framework for understanding the role of anxiety in the political science literature. Unlike the health context, the literature on politics and affect contains few if any direct inquiries into the effects of fear appeals that incorporate the threat of death. Prior research in this area therefore provides less guidance for isolating a significant block of studies or empirical patterns that may gain explanatory clarity through the application of a TMT perspective. The relative influence of Affective Intelligence in the field thus served as a dominant criterion in its selection as an appropriate model to compare with TMT in a political context. Moreover, similar to the EPPM, Affective Intelligence presents a clear conceptualization of major constructs that are central to fear appeal research—such as environmental (message) threat, threat perception, anxiety, and cognition—as well as their interrelationships and effects on attitudinal and behavioral outcomes, which makes the theory a useful representative framework against which to compare TMT.

Comparing and Contrasting Theoretical Frameworks

How does the conceptual framework provided by TMT compare to how major constructs in the fear appeal research are defined and interconnected in the EPPM and Affective Intelligence? Four important areas of conceptual contrast distinguish terror management from the other theoretical frameworks: (a) the conceptualization of threat and fear, (b) the temporal sequence of fear appeal response, (c) the role of rationality and consciousness, and (d) the impact of individual differences.

The Conceptualization of Threat and Fear

Threat and fear are core constructs in the fear appeal literature, providing for the communication processes that link the environment (which produces a threat) and an individual (who perceives threat, feels fear, and responds accordingly). Stripped down to the simplest of terms, a persuasive message communicates a threat to an individual, who, upon perception of the threat, experiences fear as a result, and that arousal of fear then shapes attitudes and behaviors in a manner that is either congruent or incongruent with the message advocacy. TMT's conceptualization of the roles of threat and fear in producing responses serves to distinguish it from the EPPM and AI, but also points to how this theory may be integrated into prior fear appeal scholarship.

As discussed earlier, the EPPM conceptualizes perceived threat as an additive construct consisting of perceived susceptibility and perceived severity—perceptions that respond to the threat embedded in the message. In addition to this communication of threat, the EPPM also views efficacy as an important message component, which affects individuals' perceptions of self-efficacy and response efficacy. Greater perceived threat leads to greater fear arousal, which is followed by either fear or danger control responses depending on the level of perceived efficacy. In Affective Intelligence, perception of threat occurs initially as a preconscious affective response to a novel or unsettling stimulus in the environment, such as messages communicating alarming information about one's preferred candidate or frightening imagery and sounds. Greater anxiety triggered by the perception of threat functions as a mediator that strengthens responsiveness to contemporary information, including the immediate message, and potential persuasion in a direction congruent with that information. Generally speaking, in both AI and the EPPM, message threat, perceived threat, and fear arousal work in tandem, such that as the information in the message becomes progressively more threatening, threat perception and fear arousal should increase correspondingly (allowing for moderation by individual differences).

Also important is the manner in which emotional variation is modeled by AI and the EPPM. As noted earlier, AI models emotional variation along two axes, each of which ranges from absence of emotion to greater emotionality (i.e., from calm to increasing levels of anxiety, and from depression to increasing levels of enthusiasm). The EPPM similarly models fear arousal along a low-to-high continuum, from absence of fear to high fear.[12] This approach to modeling emotional variation has important implications for the classification of fear appeals. For example, in the EPPM, a message that invokes the threat of severe pain and a message that invokes the threat of death would be similarly classified as high threat messages, or "high fear" appeals because of their intended effect on emotional arousal, and to the extent that fear arousal was comparable for these two messages, predicted outcomes would be expected to be similar. Although Affective Intelligence does not directly address the threat of death, it seems reasonable to extrapolate that predictions about the effects of death-related fear appeals would be similar as those for other frightening appeals. To the extent that a death-related appeal generates uncertainty due to the novelty of the threatening information—for example, information that a repeat of 9/11 will happen if the Democratic candidate is elected makes a Democratic voter uncertain about his usual vote choice (see also the example described in Marcus et al., 2000, p. 43)—the message should be expected, within an AI framework, to influence anxiety arousal and subsequent behavioral outcomes in a manner similar to other highly threatening appeals.

Interpreted within a TMT framework, the constructs of threat and fear are imbued with new meaning and give rise to a different set of implications. To begin with, given that awareness of the inevitability of death is a human ability, perceived susceptibility to the threat is universal (though perhaps moderated by individual differences, as discussed in a later section). Humans perceive more than risk or degree of vulnerability to that outcome; they perceive the inevitability of their own deaths. Thus, a message that contains the threat of death may be internalized not only in terms of level of risk that this negative consequence will be experienced (as in the EPPM) or as uncertainty about the negative consequences of the threat (as in AI), but as an eventual outcome that is inescapably inevitable and a physical certainty.[13] In addition, threat severity may be understood differently. Given that death signals the end to physical existence, threat severity encompasses both the (maximal) physical threat as well as a more abstract threat to symbolic constructs. That is, existential threat represents more than the prospect of a negative (albeit more extreme) physical outcome; it represents concerns about what happens to a person when he or she inevitably dies.

Thus, TMT suggests that the threat of death is not the same as the threat of any other negative outcome, just in the extreme; there is something qualitatively different about death that makes it more than just a question of degree. By extension, fear of death, as conceptualized in TMT, uniquely pertains to existential anxieties about the inevitability and potential finality of physical death: "Whereas fears of clear and present dangers or possible future threats are adaptive because they motivate action to avert the threat, or at least reduce the chances of it happening, fear of the inevitability of death is uniquely problematic, and qualitatively different from fears of not finding a mate or virtually any other aversive event, because there is nothing one can do to reduce the probability of death to less than 100% certain" (Pyszczynski, Greenberg et al., 2006, p. 342). Of course, just because a message contains reference to death does not mean that it will raise the salience of mortality (see Nelson et al., 1997; Ullrich & Cohrs, 2007). However, to the extent that a message communicating the threat of death is internalized as implicating personal mortality (i.e., raises thoughts of one's own death), a terror management perspective suggests that it may belong in a separate class of appeals rather than at the extreme end of a low-to-high continuum.

TMT also speaks to the concept of efficacy and its relationship with threat, a central fulcrum for the EPPM's predictions. While some theorizing has proposed that response efficacy could function as a moderator of proximal defenses (Goldenberg & Arndt, 2008), the concept of efficacy may also be conceived as playing a symbolic role in distal defenses. If TMT's perspective is articulated within the language of the EPPM, individuals are faced with a situation in which perceived threat is maximized, but perceived efficacy cannot fully make up for the fact that death is ultimately inevitable. That is, to the extent that thoughts of one's eventual demise are made salient, efficacy revolving around behavioral modification may address the delay of death but cannot prevent its inevitable arrival. In that sense, TMT would suggest the need for something akin to *symbolic* efficacy through validation of cultural worldviews, which allows people to control the threat posed by awareness of mortality. If an appeal focuses on values that are relevant to the target audience, this message component could be understood as providing symbolic efficacy, encouraging people to bolster those values in order to reduce the accessibility of death-related thoughts. However, although it may function as a mechanism for threat control, such worldview defense will not necessarily lead to message acceptance (e.g., if the message attacks one's beliefs).

In terms of the theoretical linkages between perceived threat, fear, and outcomes, TMT contrasts with the EPPM and Affective Intelligence in that it does *not* assume fear arousal to be at the heart of the relationship between mortality salience and subsequent behaviors. Recall that in the EPPM, fear aroused by a threatening appeal is a direct cause of message rejection, as well as an indirect cause of message acceptance, while in AI, predicted effects on political decision-making (i.e., greater reliance on contemporary information) are driven by the arousal of anxiety, which mediates the relationship between message threat and outcomes. This prescribed role for fear arousal is consistent with an interest in issues of message reception in the persuasion and communication literature; fear-arousing content is a tool used to grab a receiver's attention and motivate him or her to process the message. Within the EPPM and AI, the arousal of fear is understood to be an important influence on the receiver's attention to and processing of the message, stages in the persuasion process that help determine the ultimate message response (null effect, message-congruent response, or message-incongruent response).

By contrast, TMT specifically rejects the proposition that fear arousal mediates the relationship between MS induced by the threat of death and worldview defense. The theory's proponents argue that the theory is about "how we cope with our knowledge of mortality *without* perpetual anxiety," drawing on Erdelyi's argument (1974) that the brain is a multistage processing system involving conscious and unconscious monitoring of stimuli, which allows defensive reactions to be triggered by the "informational value of stimuli" prior to affect arousal (Solomon et al., 2004, p. 25, emphasis added). It is not suggested that thoughts of death never produce affect, but rather that subjective affect is not necessary for terror management effects to occur. TMT posits that mortality salience can intensify worldview defense without arousing higher levels of anxiety because the defensive reactions control the threat posed by the stimulus, thereby averting the experience of affect. It is the *potential* for experiencing fear (or terror inspired by awareness of death's inevitability) that mediates MS effects rather than the actual subjective experience of affect.

TMT research has provided support for the contention that fear arousal does not mediate the relationship between MS and worldview defense, primarily by showing that raising MS does not arouse significantly greater levels of negative affect (using scales such as the PANAS as well as physiological measures) (see Pyszczynski et al., 2003, p. 55). The effects of an MS treatment are compared to those of treatments that raise the salience of other severe threats or sources of fear, such as intense physical pain, paralysis, failure, worries about life after college, and intense uncertain future bouts of pain. While terror management defenses are found to occur only in response to the MS treatments, not in response to other serious threats, fear arousal is not found to differ significantly across conditions (see, e.g., Shehryar & Hunt, 2005). Such studies that compare an MS treatment and a non-death treatment that is associated with strong negative affect (such as intense pain) have also helped to demonstrate that MS specifically, rather than negative affect more generally, explains the observed effects (Arndt et al., 2007).

TMT thus suggests a new way of thinking about the role of fear in persuasive appeals. If greater fear arousal is not what motivates the distinct terror management responses, as proposed by TMT, then death-related fear appeals and responses to such messages may not fit into a classification system that conceptualizes threat and fear in terms of levels. Rather, persuasive appeals that raise the salience of mortality may involve a modified set of communication and psychological variables, such as priming of cultural values relevant for maintaining a symbolic buffer against existential anxiety. The theory therefore provides reason for caution in assuming that fear appeals that raise the salience of death have the same persuasive outcomes as other fear appeals, including "high fear" messages that invoke other serious negative outcomes such as physical harm, arrest, or economic hardship.

The Temporal Sequence of Responses to Fear Appeals

The three theoretical frameworks may also be compared in terms of how they conceptualize the temporal nature of fear appeal responses. As noted earlier, the EPPM treats the two responses to fear appeals—fear control processes and danger control processes—as competing. The more one is engaged in defensive avoidance or message minimization (message rejection), the less one is thinking about attitude or behavior changes to address the threat (message acceptance). This posited inverse relationship assumes simultaneity of responses; the impact on attitude or behavior outcomes—whatever the degree of message acceptance or rejection—is understood to be measurable at one time. AI's predictions are similarly oriented toward a single measurable response, by which I mean that people are assumed to have one reaction to a given fear appeal, rather than two entirely different responses depending on a temporal sequence (the latter of which is not the same as allowing for deterioration of effects over time). The EPPM also hypothesizes an appraisal process involving a rapid two-step sequence: threat appraisal, followed by efficacy appraisal (Witte, 1998). For Affective Intelligence, the preconscious processes of threat appraisal and anxiety arousal—and their impact on attention—may be understood to be similarly immediate.

By contrast, TMT proposes a sequential response consisting of proximal defenses (active suppression) followed by distal defenses (worldview and self-esteem bolstering). Proximal defenses involve people's conscious and rational efforts to defend against the threat of mortality by removing death-thoughts from focal attention. Distal defenses involve an unconscious response that bears no logical relationship to the threat of mortality and only occurs once thoughts of death have drifted from conscious focus. When mortality salience is raised by a fear appeal, responses measured immediately after exposure to the appeal would be expected to be different from responses measured after a delay and distraction.

A number of studies provide support for this sequential response. For example, to test the temporal sequence of proximal and distal defenses, Greenberg and colleagues (2000) assessed proximal defenses by giving respondents a chance to bias their responses in order to indicate that they were not the type of person with a short life expectancy (rational minimization); distal defenses were assessed by respondents' evaluations of pro- and anti-American essays. Greater vulnerability-denying bias was found among those assessed immediately after mortality salience was induced, compared to those assessed after a distraction or delay. Further, those respondents who were distracted or engaged in proximal defenses between MS induction and essay evaluation showed greater pro-American bias (worldview defense) than those who evaluated the essays directly after MS. In fact, the latter participants, who evaluated the essays directly after thinking about death, showed no more worldview defense than those who were in a control condition. These findings suggest that proximal defenses are the immediate response to mortality salience, while symbolic terror management does not occur until conscious thoughts of death have been removed from focal awareness by proximal defenses or distraction. Other research has similarly found worldview defense to occur only after a delay, but not before (e.g., Shehryar & Hunt, 2005).

In a study examining the effects of priming thoughts of cancer, Arndt and colleagues (2007) provided further insight into the proximal-distal sequential response. They found that respondents who were under low cognitive load exhibited lower accessibility of death-related thoughts directly after cancer was primed (indicative of active suppression), compared to respondents under high cognitive load (simultaneously mentally rehearsing a 10-digit number). From a TMT perspective, this makes sense because proximal defenses are conscious cognitive efforts to push thoughts of death from focal attention; people with a low cognitive load were better able to focus on suppressing thoughts of death than those with a high cognitive load. Providing an intriguing linkage to the EPPM, the authors also manipulated perceived vulnerability and measured perceived threat. They found that increased vulnerability led respondents to perceive an article on cancer as more threatening, which then led to greater immediate suppression. Interestingly, the fear control responses that the EPPM would predict in a situation where perceived threat exceeds perceived efficacy, particularly defensive avoidance and message minimization, are similar to the psychological suppression maneuvers posited to serve as proximal defenses. A terror management perspective thus suggests that death-related appeals may produce EPPM-predicted effects in the initial stage of proximal defense, while leaving open the possibility of other message effects as part of distal defenses.

The sequential nature of the responses predicted by TMT has important repercussions for the measurement of responses to fear appeals and expectations about when message acceptance or rejection will be most likely. Notably, neither proximal defense nor distal defense is synonymous with message acceptance or rejection. For example, suppression of death-related thoughts was related to greater intention to engage in cancer-preventive behavior, which suggests that initial proximal defense can have *positive* effects if it enables people to engage in healthy behaviors more than when they are not able to suppress these thoughts (Arndt et al., 2007; see also Goldenberg & Arndt, 2008). With regard to distal defenses, a source who validated important cultural views was evaluated more positively after a delay, suggesting the potential for message acceptance as a consequence of distal defenses (Greenberg et al., 2000). On the other hand, message acceptance of a drunk-driving fear appeal that invoked the threat of death was found to be *lower* among a target population (those who value drinking alcohol) after a delay, which suggests that distal defenses produced greater message rejection (Shehryar & Hunt, 2005).

The Role of Rationality and Consciousness

Comparisons and contrasts may also be drawn between TMT and the other frameworks in their conceptualization of the role of "rationality" and consciousness in the emotional and cognitive processes underlying responses to fear appeals. The EPPM portrays danger control processes as a largely cognitive effort geared toward appraisal of the threat and how best to avoid it through behavioral modification. In contrast to this more conscious, rational process, efforts to control one's fear may be more unconscious. Further, while fear control processes are dependent on fear arousal, danger control processes are more cognition-oriented and do not depend on fear, though fear can indirectly affect danger control responses. As Witte has argued (1994), "fear must be present for fear control processes to occur, while danger control processes can occur with or without the production of fear" (p. 118). Affective Intelligence envisions a somewhat different role for consciousness and rationality. Anxiety arousal affects attention as part of a preconscious response to environmental stimuli. It also directly increases the rationality of predicted attitude and behavior outcomes insofar as the person becomes more responsive to relevant current information in the environment that will help to alleviate the threat.

TMT distinguishes between a rational mode of thinking and a more "experiential" mode of thinking, the latter being characterized as neither conscious nor logical. The theory argues that fear of death is an "unconscious, primal concern," so distal defenses occur when a person is in an experiential mode of processing rather than a rational mode (Pyszczynski et al., 2003, p. 65). The individual therefore does not make a conscious connection between worldview defense and the thoughts of death raised by the stimulus. It is the proximal defenses that deal directly and logically with the problem of mortality through active suppression of conscious thoughts of death.

In some ways, this cognitive and rational approach to dealing with the threat of death is reminiscent of the EPPM's danger control responses. Indeed, Goldenberg and Arndt (2008) specifically allow for the possibility that health-promoting behavior could serve as a form of proximal defense (e.g., eating healthier to reduce conscious vulnerability to death), which would represent a conscious message-congruent response akin to danger control. However, as noted earlier, psychological defensive maneuvers such as distraction and denial are also posited to serve as proximal defenses, and this type of response bears greater similarity to the EPPM's conceptualization of fear control processes. Moreover, it is possible that expressing an intent to engage in healthy behavior after exposure to a fear appeal is sufficient to remove thoughts of death from consciousness, allowing for subsequent actual behavior to be unconsciously shaped by distal defenses. Thus, there is somewhat of a mismatch between the two theories in terms of how cognitive reasoning is thought to interact with threat to produce responses. For TMT, conscious cognitive efforts may be directed toward a message response that the EPPM would classify as potentially unconscious fear control caused by fear arousal (a direct role for affect that TMT denies), and a response that TMT views as *un*consciously occurring as part of distal defenses could be categorized by the EPPM as deliberate cognitive danger control.

Meanwhile, Affective Intelligence and TMT share a common focus on unconscious responses. However, AI sees the actual experience of anxiety as integrated in unconscious responses, rather than the potential for anxiety. Moreover, while Affective Intelligence portrays anxiety's effects on behavior as a rational adjustment of attention and information seeking in response to threat, the worldview defense responses predicted by TMT are produced by an essentially irrational process with no conscious connection to the source of fear (death). Indeed, subliminal priming of mortality has been found to lead to worldview defense, despite the fact that respondents are not consciously aware of the increased accessibility of death-related thoughts (Arndt, Greenberg, Pyszczynski, et al., 1997).

The Impact of Individual Differences

The final area of conceptual comparison among the theoretical frameworks concerns the impact of individual differences. All three theories provide accommodation for factors that distinguish individuals, including direction and strength of predispositions (e.g., political views, personal relevance of message components) and characteristics like gender, age, and cultural or ethnic group identity. Comparing the frameworks is a challenge, given the range of individual differences that may be integrated into any given model's predictions. In the interests of clarity and relative brevity, the present discussion is limited to a selection of differences that suggest linkages among the theories.

A few broad contrasts may be noted upfront in how the models conceptualize the role of individual differences. The EPPM sees individual differences as having an indirect effect on outcomes such that they affect perceived threat and efficacy, which in turn affect message response (Witte, 1998). For example, differences in readiness to quit smoking were found to moderate some of a fear appeal's effects on message acceptance in a three-way interaction with threat and efficacy (Wong & Cappella, 2009), though trait anxiety (Witte & Morrison, 2000) and cultural orientation (Murray-Johnson, Witte, Wen-Ying, & Hubbell, 2001) did not moderate the relationships as predicted. Affective Intelligence incorporates individual differences such as political predispositions as moderators of the effects of a fear appeal. For example, increased information searching was contingent on hearing threatening information about one's favored candidate (a predisposition) (Redlawsk et al., 2007), while message acceptance was increased among people exposed to a fear appeal sponsored by a candidate whom they were predisposed to oppose (Brader, 2006).

TMT strives for universality and breadth of explanation, but also acknowledges the importance of individual differences in culturally shaped beliefs and their relevance to maintaining self-esteem. As stated earlier, self-esteem derived from living up to the standards of one's cultural worldviews buffers against death-related anxiety. It follows, then, that individuals with higher self-esteem will be less defensive after mortality salience is raised—a proposition that initially seems straightforward. The role of individual differences is more complicated than this, however, in part because cultural values made salient by a message interact with individual differences in value relevance and self-esteem (see, e.g., Das et al., 2009; Arndt et al., 2009). For example, Arndt and Greenberg (1999) showed that a self-esteem boost can reduce worldview defense in response to MS, but suggested that the protective capacity of self-esteem to reduce worldview defense depends on the type of threat and the individual's source of self-esteem: "When the source of value on which self-esteem is predicated is undermined, self-esteem is diluted of its anxiety-buffering capacity and is unable to provide protection"—hence, the need for worldview defense (p. 1339; see also Schmeichel et al., 2009, on explicit versus implicit self-esteem, and Landau et al., 2009, on situations where self-esteem enhancement and worldview bolstering are in conflict).

The role of individual differences within a TMT framework is also complicated by the two-part sequential response. For example, worldview defense in the form of message rejection is expected if the source attacks a belief that is relevant to the individual. Shehryar and Hunt (2005) found this pattern in their study of reactions to drunk-driving fear appeals. Only those with a strong prior commitment to drinking alcohol (compared to those who did not view alcohol as relevant to self-esteem) exhibited worldview defense in the form of significantly lower message acceptance. On the surface, the obvious response to that finding is, so what? It is unsurprising that a person who is highly committed to a behavior will be more likely to reject a message attacking that behavior. However, what is distinct about this finding is that it *only* occurred after exposure to a fear appeal that invoked the threat of death, not after exposure to fear appeals invoking other severe threats such as arrest or serious injury. Moreover, worldview defense among those committed to drinking alcohol was observed only after a delay between message exposure and assessment of message acceptance (for a comparable finding for smoking behavior, see

Hansen, Winzeler, & Topolinski, in press, especially note 2). This is a potentially important insight from the standpoint of message effects and persuasion, suggesting a three-way interaction between mortality salience, time of measurement, and individual differences in the personal relevance to self-esteem of values primed by an appeal.

The role that TMT prescribes for individual differences in value relevance may have implications for two important individual-level moderators in health communication research: gender and age. For example, one area of inquiry has focused on testing a common belief that young people, particularly young men, are especially prone to engage in risky behaviors because they believe in their own invulnerability. Henley and Donovan (2003), for instance, compared responses of two age groups (ages 16–25 and 40–50) to fear appeals about emphysema that either included death as a consequence or did not. The authors interpreted the null difference between young people's responses to death and non-death appeals, even among men, as evidence that feelings of invulnerability do not drive risky behavior in youth. Another study of alcohol use among adolescents suggested that young people are not simply irrationally engaging in risky behavior (i.e., illegal alcohol consumption) because they believe they are invulnerable; rather, they *rationally* perceive the benefits of performing risky behaviors as outweighing the risks (Goldberg, Halpern-Felsher, & Millstein, 2002).

TMT may offer new insights for this area of research by suggesting how defense against thoughts of death may paradoxically lead to greater risky behavior. In a twist on the explanation offered in the above-mentioned study by Goldberg and colleagues (2002), some TMT research has suggested that symbolic benefits to self-esteem, as a buffer against mortality-related anxiety, may *irrationally* drive risky behaviors due to *sensitivity* to vulnerability to death, rather than a sense of invulnerability (Hirschberger, Florian, Mikulincer, Goldenberg, & Pyszczynski, 2002). For example, Hirschberger and colleagues (2002) found that U.S. male students exhibited significantly greater intention to engage in a range of risky behaviors after mortality salience compared to a control condition, even controlling for sensation-seeking. Their follow-up study revealed that Israeli male students were more willing to try illicit drugs in three hypothetical scenarios after MS compared to a control condition, controlling for baseline attitudes toward drug use. The authors suggested that the cultural values relevant to men's self-esteem (e.g., courage, valor, thumbing one's nose at danger) are more oriented toward risk-taking compared to women, who did not exhibit these effects after MS. This interpretation is consistent with other work suggesting that cultural emphasis on different values for men versus women (e.g., the ideal of thinness for women) may contribute to gender differences in responses when mortality is salient (Goldenberg, Arndt, Hart, & Brown, 2005), as well as research linking MS to increased engagement in risky behaviors (Arndt et al., 2009).

TMT's conceptualization of the role of individual differences is also relevant to a number of key political variables. For example, consider the potential implications of an interaction between mortality salience and age, which is an important predictor of political participation. If more youthful feelings of invulnerability do tend to attenuate with age, then older people may respond differently to a political appeal invoking the threat of death. This may be particularly true if the message content relates most directly to the personal mortality of older people—an illustration of which is aptly provided by the rhetoric of "death panels" in the recent debate over end of life issues and health care insurance reform in the United States. Moreover, given that older people tend to participate in politics more, their responses to appeals raising the salience of mortality may have a disproportionately strong impact on policy and electoral outcomes.

TMT also speaks strongly to the relationship between mortality salience and individual differences in national, ethnic, cultural, and ideological orientation—all of which play central roles in domestic as well as international politics. A number of studies have shown how values attached to membership or identification with various groups may interact with MS to produce responses with important political implications. For example, as noted earlier, mortality salience increased pro-American bias in evaluations of a person who voiced negative views of the United States and a person who voiced positive views of the United States, producing significantly more negative and positive evaluations, respectively (Greenberg et al., 1990). That study also found that MS increased in-group favoritism and out-group hostility based on religious affiliation. Similarly, news reports on terrorist attacks were found to raise MS and to increase out-group prejudice – not only prejudice against Arabs among non-Muslims, but prejudice against Europeans among Muslims (Das et al., 2009). Priming mortality along with different in-group identities (e.g., Australian, Aboriginal) led to corresponding out-group value rejection and in-group value endorsement (Halloran & Kashima, 2004). Worldview defense can also come in the form of bolstering faith in one's political ideology. A study of American conservatives and liberals found that both groups showed greater aggression against and derogation of critics of their political orientation after reminders of mortality (McGregor et al., 1998). Further, recent research has shown that that MS can enhance evaluations of charismatic political candidates, but only if their rhetoric bolsters one's pre-existing ideological values, while evaluations of candidates espousing the opposing ideology can be diminished by MS (Kosloff, Greenberg, Weise, & Solomon, in press).[14]

Given that a great deal of politics revolves around conflicts between groups, it is important to emphasize the ramifications of TMT's propositions about the role of belief systems in shaping people's responses to reminders of mortality. As noted earlier, cultural worldviews differ widely across individuals and cultures, and yet they may serve the same purpose insofar as confirmation of one's belief system can serve as a buffer against existential terror engendered by awareness of mortality. Thus, TMT's predictions for worldview bolstering after mortality salience has been raised apply as much to a Western nation such as the United States as they do to an Islamic country such as Iran (see Pyszczynski, Abdollahi et al., 2006; Pyszczynski et al., 2008). Indeed, Pyszczynski,

Abdollahi, and colleagues (2006) found that, when MS was raised, Iranian students preferred a student expressing pro-martyrdom (attacking the U.S.) views over an anti-martyrdom student and showed greater interest in joining the pro-martyrdom cause than the anti-martyrdom cause; these patterns were reversed in the control condition (dental pain). These authors also examined American students' support for extreme military force as an appropriate tactic in the war on terrorism, and found that support was significantly higher after reminders of mortality and 9/11 compared to the dental pain condition, though this pattern only occurred among conservatives. These findings not only suggest the cross-cultural explanatory potential of TMT, but also highlight how terror management responses can revolve around intergroup value differences; in the face of reminders of mortality, hostility toward out-groups who threaten one's cultural worldviews and enhanced regard for in-group members who validate one's views provide symbolic protection against fear of death. (Note, though, that priming values such as tolerance or compassion may mitigate out-group hostility in response to MS; see Pyszczynski et al., 2008.)

Together, these patterns found in TMT research suggest that mortality salience will *increase* the influence of people's preexisting political values and beliefs on their attitudes and behaviors. This proposition stands in contrast to the predictions of Affective Intelligence that a fear appeal arousing anxiety will decrease reliance on predispositions and increase the influence of contemporary information, opening the door for message acceptance by those with oppositional preexisting views (Brader, 2006; Wolak et al., 2003). In this way, AI allows for fear appeals to encourage greater crossover among groups with conflicting standing decisions (e.g., policy positions), while TMT suggests that appeals invoking fear of death may lead to reinforced subscription to preexisting beliefs and polarization along group lines.

Toward New Directions in Fear Communication Research

This chapter's discussion of TMT and its conceptual contrasts with dominant frameworks in existing fear communication scholarship is intended to stimulate new directions in fear appeal research. To that end, I have constructed a summary table that depicts the major constructs and their relationships as conceptualized by TMT, the EPPM, and Affective Intelligence (Table 4.1). A summary cannot capture all of the theoretical nuances unique to each model, but the virtue of a simplified and easily comprehendible comparative overview is its utility in suggesting new empirical research questions.

Taking some initial steps toward generating such questions, I suggest two sets of predictive contrasts derived from the theoretical comparison (Table 4.2). TMT is juxtaposed against the EPPM and Affective Intelligence in a health context and a political context, respectively. Given that TMT is more of a new kid on the block from a communications perspective, testing its predictive contrasts with existing models is an appropriate first step in a research agenda integrating TMT into the study of fear appeals. Indeed, because there

Table 4.1 Conceptual Summary of the EPPM, Affective Intelligence, and TMT

EPPM	Affective Intelligence	TMT
Message: Threat and efficacy.	*Message:* Threat (novel).	*Message:* Threat.
Appraisal: Individual appraises threat and, if perceived threat is high enough, appraises efficacy.	*Appraisal:* Individual experiences preconscious affective response (fear).	*Appraisal:* Individual perceives threat of own death, raising the salience of mortality.
Affect: Greater perceived threat leads to greater fear, which has direct and indirect effects on subsequent response.	*Affect:* Greater perceived threat leads to greater fear, which mediates subsequent response.	*Affect:* Death-related threat does not arouse greater fear than non-death-related threat.
Response: If perceived threat and perceived efficacy are high, cognitions about the threat and recommendations for behavioral modification dominate, leading to message acceptance. If perceived threat is high and efficacy is low, fear dominates, leading to message rejection. Low threat leads to a null response.	*Response:* Attention is oriented toward contemporary information, lessening reliance on predispositions and increasing the likelihood of attitude and behavioral change in the direction of the message.	*Response (proximal defense):* Individual suppresses thoughts of death, which may initially affect message acceptance. *Response (distal defense):* Individual bolsters self-esteem by engaging in worldview defense, which may increase message acceptance or rejection depending on which cultural values are made salient by the message.
Individual differences: Perceived threat and perceived efficacy are affected by individual differences.	*Individual differences:* What is considered threatening information is affected by individual differences (e.g., threatening information diverges from expectations based on preexisting beliefs).	*Individual differences:* Mortality salience and worldview defense are affected by individual differences (e.g., relevance of cultural values and valence of arguments made in message).

has been so little research specifically attempting to study the potential for fear appeals to produce terror management responses, it makes sense to test the predictions of TMT against the predictions of other theories, where contrasts arise, rather than moving directly to the development of hybrid models.

A number of competing predictions are embedded in Table 4.2, which could be tested in an experimental context. For example, TMT predicts effects for a death-related appeal that are distinct from the effects of a non-death-related fear appeal, yet are not driven by greater fear arousal. Both the EPPM and Affective Intelligence do not specifically predict distinct effects for a death-related

Table 4.2 Contrasting Predictions by the EPPM, Affective Intelligence, and TMT

Health Context	
EPPM	**TMT**
Death versus neutral (non-fear) appeals: Exposure to a death appeal will increase perceived threat, leading to message acceptance if perceived efficacy is high and message rejection if perceived efficacy is low. Personal relevance of the message qualifies these responses such that greater personal relevance leads to stronger effects.	*Death versus neutral appeals:* Exposure to a death appeal will significantly increase worldview defense, regardless of efficacy level, leading to message acceptance if the advocacy is congruous with validation of cued cultural values and message rejection if the advocacy is incongruous with validation. Personal relevance of the message qualifies the responses such that greater personal relevance leads to stronger worldview defense.
Fear (non-death) versus death appeals: Exposure to a fear appeal will produce the same effects as a death appeal.	*Fear versus death appeals:* Exposure to a fear appeal will *not* produce the same effects as exposure to a death appeal.
The role of fear arousal: Greater fear will be directly related to message rejection and indirectly related to message acceptance. Only to the extent that a death appeal arouses greater fear will that appeal produce different effects from a fear appeal.	*The role of fear arousal*: The distinct effects of a death appeal will *not* be mediated by a significantly greater arousal of fear compared to the fear appeal.
Time of response measurement: The hypothesized effects will not change if assessed before or after a delay.	*Time of response measurement:* The worldview defense effects of a death appeal will only obtain if measured after a delay.* Suppression effects akin to fear control may emerge if response is measured immediately after exposure to a death appeal.
Political Context	
Affective Intelligence	**TMT**
Death versus neutral appeals: Exposure to a death appeal will significantly increase favorable attitudes toward the advocated candidate or policy position, particularly among people who were predisposed against that preference or who had no strong predisposition.	*Death versus neutral appeals:* Exposure to a death appeal will significantly increase favorable attitudes toward the advocated candidate or policy position among those who were predisposed toward that preference (message validates values), while exposure to a death appeal will significantly decrease favorable attitudes toward the advocated candidate or policy position among those who were predisposed against that preference (message challenges values).
Fear versus death appeals: Exposure to a fear appeal will produce the same effects as a death appeal.	*Fear versus death appeals:* Exposure to a fear appeal will *not* produce the same effects as exposure to a death appeal.

(*continued*)

Table 4.2 Continued

Political Context	
Affective Intelligence	*TMT*
The role of fear arousal: The effects of exposure to death and fear appeals will be mediated by elevated levels of fear. Only to the extent that a death appeal arouses greater anxiety will that appeal create stronger effects than a fear appeal.	*The role of fear arousal*: The distinct effects of a death appeal will *not* be mediated by a significantly greater arousal of fear compared to the fear appeal.
Time of response measurement: The hypothesized effects will not change if assessed before or after a delay.	*Time of response measurement:* The distinct effects of a death appeal will only obtain if measured after a delay.*

*Provided that death-related thoughts are brought to focal attention; a delay is not needed if thoughts of death are primed but not brought to conscious awareness.

Note: In this table, a "death" appeal is one that raises the salience of personal mortality, a "fear" appeal is one that primes non-death-related fears, and a "neutral" appeal is one that does not arouse fear. Note that while Affective Intelligence does not directly address death as a threat, its predictions for a death-related fear appeal may be reasonably extrapolated as similar to those for other highly threatening fear appeals. Also, in a political context, a "predisposition" is not necessarily limited to party identification or ideological orientation; in either AI or TMT, it could theoretically refer to other group-based identification or values (e.g., associated with one's race/ethnicity, nationality, religion).

fear appeal unless it produces greater threat perception and thus fear arousal. Timing of measurement also points to predictive contrasts, with TMT proposing different responses to a death-related appeal depending on whether outcomes are assessed immediately after message exposure or following a delay, and the EPPM and AI proposing no difference. More specifically, in response to an appeal invoking the threat of death, TMT allows for delayed message rejection when personally relevant values are attacked, even if efficacy is high, and delayed message acceptance when relevant values are validated, even if efficacy is low; by contrast, the EPPM predicts message acceptance in the former case and rejection in the latter case. TMT's predictions of delayed message acceptance among those whose beliefs are validated and delayed rejection among those whose beliefs are attacked also contrast with expectations based on Affective Intelligence—i.e., greater message acceptance among those who were predisposed *against* the views articulated in a message and relatively little effect on those who already agreed with the message.[15]

Differentiation of fear appeals by quality of consequence (i.e., death versus some other fear-inducing consequence) and differentiation of response by temporal sequence have not been part of prior fear appeal theorizing. TMT thus offers strong hypotheses about this class of appeals and a new set of considerations for evaluating the persuasive value of the threat of death. At the same time, great care must be taken in integrating this theory into the fear appeal literature and testing it against other frameworks. Attentiveness to detail is essential in the design of studies that test contrasting predictions derived from separate theories, including a systematic approach to measurement timing and careful pretesting and manipulation checks (e.g., mortality salience, fear arousal, and salience of relevant values cued by the messages). Sensitivity to cued values is important because worldview defense will reflect validation of whichever values provide the greatest protection against death-related anxiety in a given context (Weise et al., 2008; Halloran & Kashima, 2004). For example, a persuasive appeal priming mortality and national identity may be expected to increase support for a counterterrorism policy if the source validates important national values, while an appeal priming mortality and political orientation may decrease support for the same policy among those who feel their ideological values have been attacked and increase support among those whose ideological beliefs have been validated.

From a message design perspective, drawing on TMT may help researchers determine what types of appeals work best in different circumstances. Identifying message design principles that do not rely on audience evaluation as a proxy (e.g., what makes a "strong" versus "weak" argument, what makes a message emotionally evocative) is notoriously difficult (Cappella, 2006). Conceptualizing death as a qualitatively different threatening consequence, distinct from the more nebulous continuum of low to high fear-arousing content, may contribute to efforts to define message factors that produce reliable responses. That said, further investigation is needed regarding whether, when, and how messages that communicate the threat of death raise the salience of mortality. For example, do some reminders of mortality, such as images embedded in an appeal, make death-related thoughts accessible at an unconscious level, rather than bringing them to focal attention? Recall that, as conceptualized by TMT, fear of death may not revolve solely around the threat of its imminence, but also around the more abstract threat that its inevitability poses. The persuasive influence of reminders of death communicated in messages therefore may not be limited to increasing perceptions of risk, but may also be exerted by triggering more abstract-level thinking about what happens when one dies. That is, reminders of death, even relatively subtle message features, could produce worldview defense and thus affect message acceptance without necessarily convincing people that death is lurking around the corner.

At the same time, it is not a given that any reminder of death will lead people to think about their own mortality. Indeed, priming mortality more generally, as opposed to personal mortality, does not appear to bring about terror management responses (Nelson et al., 1997; Ullrich & Cohrs, 2007). Further, reminders of death may be more likely to raise the salience of personal mortality among some populations compared to others, depending on individual-level and contextual factors. This limitation is not particularly troublesome from a persuasive communications perspective. Appeals are almost never expected to be universally persuasive; in fact, the trend is toward greater microtargeting based on audience characteristics likely to maximize message reception.[16] The fact that worldview defense is predicated on raising mortality salience does not limit TMT's contribution to fear appeal research; it simply defines the parameters of terror management's potential influence on message response.

In sum, terror management theory represents a promising yet underused source of theoretical predictions in fear appeals research. Its integration into the communication research agenda would provide a complement to, not a replacement of, existing theoretical frameworks for analyzing people's responses to fear appeals. Obviously, in terms of appeals that employ threats other than death, TMT does not necessarily pose a challenge to frameworks such as the EPPM or Affective Intelligence. It is when the salience of mortality is raised that TMT provides a distinct perspective that parts ways with other theoretical frameworks. Its potential contribution lies with its recognition of human fears of death and the way that these fears might uniquely affect reactions to messages.

The communications context encompasses a wealth of message features through which mortality may be primed, from text to imagery to audio, and situations in which mortality salience may be raised in the service of persuasive appeals are abundant, both within and outside the United States. Indeed, given the theory's emphasis on cultural values and their relevance to self-esteem and symbolic immortality, using a TMT framework to explore cross-cultural and cross-national differences in responses to fear appeals priming mortality may prove particularly fruitful. Though its application to fear appeal research requires sensitivity to the specific factors involved in the prediction of different types of attitudes and behaviors among different populations, TMT offers a rich and versatile framework whose integration into communication research may make unique empirical and conceptual contributions to the study of fear communications and persuasion.

Notes

1. The author is indebted to Joseph N. Cappella for his many insightful comments and continual encouragement throughout the writing of this paper. Special thanks also to Russell Neuman, the editor, and the anonymous reviewers for their very thoughtful and constructive feedback.
2. These ad descriptions are only partly hypothetical. In the 2008 U.S. presidential election, the National Republican Trust PAC aired an attack ad against Barack Obama that incorporated images invoking 9/11; the ad may be viewed at http://www.npr.org/blogs/secretmoney/2008/10/pac_ties_obamas_policies_to_se.html (accessed Aug. 28, 2009). The anti-smoking example is taken directly from an ad developed by the Department of Health United Kingdom in 2004. The ad may be downloaded from the Cancer Institute NWS website, at http://www.cancerinstitute.org.au/cancer_inst/campaigns/anthony.html   (accessed Aug. 28, 2009).
3. Exceptions include studies by Shehryar and Hunt (2005) and Ben-Ari, Florian, and Mikulincer (2000) in the health context, Miller and Hansen (2007) in the political context, and Solomon et al. (1995) in a college campus context. These studies specifically tested TMT propositions using fear appeals. Other theoreti-

cal (e.g., Miller & Landau, 2005, 2008; Pfau, 2007) and empirical (Goldenberg et al., 1999, 2007; Magee & Kalyanaraman, 2009; Das et al., 2009) work has drawn on TMT in a communication context, but not with a specific focus on either fear appeals or conceptual comparisons between TMT and existing fear appeal models.

4. The theory's authors recognize that cultural worldviews can serve purposes other than terror management (see Pyszczynski, Greenberg, et al., 2006).

5. As Fransen et al. (2008) emphasize, MS effects induced by messages may be unintentional, such as with brands whose associations with death (in their study, insurance) induce MS and then affect consumer behaviors (e.g., preference for domestic products over foreign products).

6. Note that this model brings a more specific focus to health-promoting behaviors as a form of proximal defenses, in addition to the psychological defensive maneuvers (e.g., denial of vulnerability, distraction) emphasized in other TMT research (e.g., Pyszczynski et al., 2003; Greenberg et al., 2000).

7. This ad may be viewed at the FactCheck.org website: http://www.factcheck. org/2009/09/a-false-appeal-to-womens-fears/ (accessed Sept. 4, 2009).

8. The authors of the stage model emphasize a number of differences from earlier models. For example, severity and vulnerability are seen as having separate effects (as well as interaction effects) on persuasion outcomes, as well as main and interaction effects on information processing. The model also predicts that any recommendation, so long as the action is somewhat plausible and not impossible to carry out, will be seen as effective when vulnerability and severity are high due to biased processing. Thus, defensive reactions such as minimization of threat do not necessarily impede message acceptance (as found by Witte & Allen, 2000), but can actually enhance message acceptance.

9. Because this study used the terminology of perceived risk (internalization of a threat) and self-efficacy and did not include threat severity or response efficacy, it does not map perfectly onto the EPPM. However, perceived risk is conceptually closely related to perceived susceptibility, and the author drew on the EPPM as a theoretical framework for the study (see also Rimal & Real, 2003, for a discussion of the risk perception attitude (RPA) framework, which is derived from the predictions of the EPPM).

10. The authors do not suggest that all behaviors are driven by affective systems; some may be influenced more by conscious considerations (Marcus et al., 2000, pp. 51-52).

11. Although AI focuses on anxiety and enthusiasm, it should not be confused with discrete emotion models, which represent another established approach to modeling affect in the political science literature (Neuman et al., 2007). Discrete emotion models view various affects as associated with distinct signal values and functions (Dillard & Meijnders, 2002; Dillard & Peck, 2000; Dillard, Plotnick, Godbold, Freimuth, & Edgar, 1996).

12. With some minor variations, fear arousal has been operationalized in similar ways by studies based on Affective Intelligence and the EPPM. Marcus and colleagues (2000, Appendix B) recommended drawing on affect items in the PANAS (Positive and Negative Affect Schedule; Watson, Clark, & Tellegen, 1988) to measure anxiety, including how much respondents feel afraid, scared, anxious, upset, distressed, nervous, frightened, and uneasy. Witte and colleagues (Witte,

      1994; Witte & Morrison, 2000) have incorporated similar items in assessments of fear arousal.

13. In TMT research, the theoretical role of perceived vulnerability is open to debate (see, e.g., Goldenberg & Arndt, 2008, who viewed it as a moderator of proximal defenses, and Hirschberger, Pyszczynski, & Ein-Dor, 2009, who examined its role as a moderator of distal defenses).

14. By "charismatic," the authors refer to leadership characteristics such as self-confidence, a visionary outlook, readiness for risk-taking, and an emphasis on a collective identity (Kosloff et al., in press). In addition, some studies have examined the effects of MS and reminders of 9/11 on attitudes toward President George W. Bush and other political figures (e.g., Landau et al., 2004; Cohen, Ogilvie, Solomon, Greenberg, & Pyszczynski, 2005; Miller & Hansen, 2007; Weise et al., 2008). While the results seem to replicate other findings of pro-American bias after MS—increasing regard for Bush as a symbolic protector of the American value system, particularly among liberals—a TMT interpretation is vulnerable to alternative explanations due to the specific circumstances involved in this case. Further research in this vein that moves beyond a focus on Bush is needed (see, e.g., Kosloff et al., in press).

15. From AI's perspective, it would make sense if those who were initially supportive of the advocacy showed no movement, given that the information provided by the anxiety-producing ad was congruent with predispositions and thus posed no novel threat.

16. At the same time, the Internet has created new opportunities for reaching a greater portion of the target audience, easing some of the traditional constraints of time, money, and space. Consider, for example, a recent PSA produced by a local police department in South Wales. The 4-minute video, which depicts in detail the fatal consequences of texting and driving, went viral on the Internet, attracting millions of viewers as well as news coverage in the United States. (See S. Morris, "Made in Gwent with £10,000: the road safety video taking YouTube by storm," *The Guardian*, Sept. 3, 2009, http://www.guardian.co.uk/uk/2009/sep/03/gwent-road-safety-film.)

References

Ansolabehere, S., & Iyengar, S. (1995). *Going negative: How political advertisements shrink and polarize the electorate*. New York: Free Press.

Arndt, J., Cook, A., & Routledge, C. (2004). The blueprint of terror management: Understanding the cognitive architecture of psychological defense against the awareness of death. In J. Greenberg, S. L. Koole, & T. Pyszczynski (Eds.), *Handbook of experimental existential psychology* (pp. 35–53). New York: Guilford Press.

Arndt, J., Cook, A., Greenberg, J. L., & Cox, C. R. (2007). Cancer and the threat of death: The cognitive dynamics of death-thought suppression and it impact on behavioral health intentions. *Journal of Personality and Social Psychology, 92*(1), 12–29.

Arndt, J., Cox, C. R., Goldenberg, J. L., Vess, M., Routledge, C., Cooper, D. P., & Cohen, F. (2009). Blowing in the (social) wind: Implications of extrinsic esteem contingencies for terror management and health. *Journal of Personality and Social Psychology, 96*(6), 1191–1205.

Arndt, J., & Greenberg, J. (1999). The effects of a self-esteem boost and mortality salience on responses to boost relevant and irrelevant worldview threats. *Personality and Social Psychology Bulletin, 25*, 1331–1341.

Arndt, J., Greenberg, J., Pyszczynski, T., & Solomon, S. (1997). Subliminal exposure to death-related stimuli increase defense of the cultural worldview. *Psychological Science, 8*(5), 379–385.

Arndt, J., Greenberg, J., Solomon, S., Pyszczynski, T., & Simon, L. (1997). Suppression, accessibility of death-related thoughts, and cultural worldview defense: Exploring the psychodynamics of terror management. *Journal of Personality and Social Psychology, 73*, 5–18.

Baron, R.M. (1997). On making terror management theory less motivational and more social. *Psychological Inquiry, 8*(1), 21–58.

Becker, E. (1962). *The birth and death of meaning.* New York: Free Press.

Becker, E. (1973). *The denial of death.* New York: Free Press.

Becker, E. (1975). *Escape from evil.* New York: Free Press.

Ben-Ari, O. T., Florian, V., & Mikulincer, M. (2000). Does a threat appeal moderate reckless driving? A terror management theory perspective. *Accident Analysis and Prevention, 32*, 1–10.

Brader, T. (2006). *Campaigning for hearts and minds: How emotional appeals in political ads work.* Chicago: University of Chicago Press.

Brader, T., Valentino, N. A., & Suhay, E. (2008). What triggers public opposition to immigration? Anxiety, group cuts, and immigration threat. *American Journal of Political Science, 52*(4), 959–978.

Brooks, D. J. (2006). The resilient voter: Moving toward closure in the debate over negative campaigning and turnout. *Journal of Politics, 68*(3), 684–696.

Buss, D. M. (1997). Human social motivation in evolutionary perspective: Grounding terror management theory. *Psychological Inquiry, 8*(1), 22–26.

Cappella, J. N. (2006). Integrating message effects and behavior change theories: Organizing comments and unanswered questions. *Journal of Communication, 56,* S265–S279.

Chaiken, S. (1980). Heuristic versus systematic information processing and the use of source versus message cues in persuasion. *Journal of Personality and Social Psychology, 39*, 752–766.

Chaiken, S., Liberman, A., & Eagly, A. H. (1989). Heuristic and systematic information processing within and beyond the persuasion context. In J. S. Uleman & J. A. Bargh (Eds.), *Unintended thought* (pp. 212–252). New York: Guildford Press.

Cohen, F., Ogilvie, D.M., Solomon, S., Greenberg, J., & Pyszczynski, T. (2005). American roulette: The effect of reminders of death on support for George W. Bush in the 2004 presidential election. *Analyses of Social Issues and Public Policy, 5*(1), 177–187.

Das, E. H. H. J., Bushman, B. J., Bezemer, M.D., Kerkhof, P., & Vermeulen, I. E. (2009). How terrorism news reports increase prejudice against outgroups: A terror management account. *Journal of Experimental Social Psychology, 45*, 452–459.

Das, E. H. H. J., de Wit, J. B. F., & Stroebe, W. (2003). Fear appeals motivate acceptance of action recommendations: Evidence for a positive bias in the processing of persuasive messages. *Personality and Social Psychology Bulletin, 29*, 650–663.

De Hoog, N., Stroebe, W., & de Wit, J. B. F. (2005). The impact of fear appeals on processing and acceptance of action recommendations. *Personality and Social Psychology Bulletin, 31,* 24–33.

De Hoog, N., Stroebe, W., & de Wit, J. B. F. (2007). The impact of vulnerability to and severity of a health risk on processing and acceptance of fear-arousing communications: A meta-analysis. *Review of General Psychology, 11*(3), 258–285.

Dillard, J. P., & Meijnders, A. (2002). Persuasion and the structure of affect. In J. P. Dillard & M. Pfau (Eds.), *The persuasion handbook* (pp. 309–327). Thousand Oaks, CA: Sage.

Dillard, J. P., & Peck, E. (2000). Affect and persuasion: Emotional responses to public service announcements. *Communication Research, 27*(4), 461–495.

Dillard, J. P., Plotnick, C. A., Godbold, L. C., Freimuth, V. S., & Edgar, T. (1996). The multiple affective outcomes of AIDS PSAs: Fear appeals do more than scare people. *Communication Research, 23*(1), 44–72.

Erdelyi, M. H (1974). A new look at the new look: Perceptual defense and vigilance. *Psychological Review, 81,* 1–25.

Fransen, M. L., Fennis, B. M., Pruyn, A. T. H., & Das, E. (2008). Rest in peace? Brand-induced mortality salience and consumer behavior. *Journal of Business Research, 61,* 1053–1061.

Goldberg, J. H., Halpern-Felsher, B. L., & Millstein, S. G. (2002). Beyond invulnerability: The importance of benefits in adolescents' decision to drink alcohol. *Health Psychology, 21*(5), 477–484.

Goldenberg, J. L., & Arndt, J. (2008). The implications of death for health: A terror management health model for behavioral health promotion. *Psychological Review, 115*(4), 1032–1053.

Goldenberg, J. L., Arndt, J., Hart, J., & Brown, M. (2005). Dying to be thin: The effects of mortality salience and body mass index on restricted eating among women. *Personality and Social Psychology Bulletin, 31*(10), 1400–1412.

Goldenberg, J. L., Pyszczynski, T., Johnson, K. D., Greenberg, J., & Solomon, S. (1999). The appeal of tragedy: A terror management perspective. *Media Psychology, 1,* 313–329.

Goldenberg, J. L., Pyszczynski, T., Greenberg, J., Solomon, S. (2000). Fleeing the body: A terror management perspective on the problem of human corporeality. *Personality and Social Psychology Review, 4*(3), 200–218.

Goldenberg, J. L., Goplen, J., Cox, C. R., & Arndt, J. (2007). "Viewing" pregnancy as an existential threat: The effects of creatureliness on reactions to media depictions of the pregnant body. *Media Psychology, 10,* 211–230.

Greenberg, J., Arndt, J., Simon, L., Pyszczynski, T., & Solomon, S. (2000). Proximal and distal defenses in response to reminders of one's mortality: Evidence of a temporal sequence. *Personality and Social Psychology Bulletin, 26,* 91–99.

Greenberg, J., Pyszczynski, T., & Solomon, S. (1986). The causes and consequences of a need for self-esteem: A terror management theory. In R. F. Baumeister (Ed.), *Public self and private self* (pp. 189–212). New York: Springer-Verlag.

Greenberg, J., Pyszczynski, T., Solomon, S., Rosenblatt, A., Veeder, M., Kirkland, S., et al. (1990). Evidence for terror management theory II: The effects of morality salience on reactions to those who threaten or bolster the cultural worldview. *Journal of Personality and Social Psychology, 58*(2), 308–318.

Halloran, M. J., & Kashima, E. S. (2004). Social identity and worldview validation: The effects of ingroup identity primes and mortality salience on value endorsement. *Personality and Social Psychology Bulletin, 20,* 915–925.

Hansen, J., Winzeler, S., & Topolinski, S. (In press). When the death makes you smoke: A terror management perspective on the effectiveness of cigarette on-pack warnings. *Journal of Experimental Social Psychology.*

Henley, N., & Donovan, R. J. (2003). Young people's response to death threat appeals: Do they really feel immortal? *Health Education Research, 18*(1), 1–14.

Hirschberger, G., Florian, V., Mikulincer, M., Goldenberg, J. L., & Pyszczynski, T. (2002). Gender differences in the willingness to engage in risky behavior: A terror management perspective. *Death Studies, 26*, 117–141.

Hirschberger, G., Pyszczynski, T., & Ein-Dor, T. (2009). Vulnerability and vigilance: Threat awareness and perceived adversary intent moderate the impact of mortality salience on intergroup violence. *Personality and Social Psychology Bulletin, 35*(5), 595–607.

Hovland, C., Janis, I., & Kelly, H. (1953). *Communication and persuasion.* New Haven, CT: Yale University Press.

Hoyt, C. L., Simon, S., & Reid, L. (2009). Choosing the best (wo)man for the job: The effects of mortality salience, sex, and gender stereotypes on leader evaluations. *Leadership Quarterly, 20*, 233–246.

Ivie, R. L. (1999). Fire, flood, and red fever: Motivating metaphors of global emergency in the Truman doctrine speech. *Presidential Studies Quarterly, 29*(3), 570–591.

Janis, I. L. (1967). Effects of fear arousal on attitude change: Recent developments in theory and experimental research. In L. Berkowitz (Ed.), *Advances in experimental social psychology* (Vol. 3, pp. 166–225). New York: Academic Press.

Kirkpatrick, L. A., & Navarrete, C. D. (2006). Reports of my death anxiety have been greatly exaggerated: A critique of terror management theory from an evolutionary perspective. *Psychological Inquiry, 17*(4), 288–298.

Kosloff, S., Greenberg, J., Weise, D., & Solomon, S. (In press). The effects of mortality salience on political preferences: The roles of charisma and political orientation. *Journal of Experimental Social Psychology.*

Ladd, J. M., & Lenz, G. S. (2008). Reassessing the role of anxiety in vote choice. *Political Psychology, 29*(2), 275–296.

Landau, M. J., Greenberg, J., & Sullivan, D. (2009). Managing terror when self-worth and worldviews collide: Evidence that mortality salience increases reluctance to self-enhance beyond authorities. *Journal of Experimental Social Psychology, 45*, 68–79.

Landau, M. J., Solomon, S., Greenberg, J., Cohen, F., Pyszczynski, T., Arndt, J., et al. (2004). Deliver us from evil: The effects of mortality salience and reminds of 9/11 on support for President George W. Bush. *Personality and Social Psychology Bulletin, 30*, 1136–1150.

Lau, R. R., Sigelman, L., Heldman, C., & Babbit, P. (1999). The effects of negative political advertisements: A meta-analytic assessments. *American Political Science Review, 93*(4), 851–875.

Leventhal, H. (1970). Findings and theory in the study of fear communications. In L. Berkowitz (Ed.), *Advances in experimental social psychology* (Vol. 5, pp. 119–186). New York: Academic Press.

Leventhal, H. (1971). Fear appeals and persuasion: The differentiation of a motivational construct. *American Journal of Public Health, 61*, 1208–1224.

Lodge, M., & Taber, C. (2000). Three steps toward a theory of motivated political reasoning. In A. Lupia, M. McCubbins, & S. Popkin (Eds.), *Elements of reason:*

Cognition, choice, and the bounds of rationality (pp. 183–213). Cambridge, UK: Cambridge University Press.

Lodge, M., & Taber, C. (2005). The automaticity of affect for political leaders, groups, and issues: An experimental test of the hot cognition hypothesis. *Political Psychology, 26*(3), 455–481.

MacKuen, M., Marcus, G. E., Neuman, W. R., & Keele, L. (2007). The third way: The theory of affective intelligence and American democracy. In W. R. Neuman, G. E., Marcus, A. N. Crigler, & M. MacKuen (Eds.), *The affect effect: Dynamics of emotion in political thinking and behavior* (pp. 124–151). Chicago: University of Chicago Press.

Magee, R. G., & Kalyanaraman, S. (2009). Effects of worldview and mortality salience in persuasion processes. *Media Psychology, 12*(2), 171–194.

Marcus, G. E., Neuman, W. R., & MacKuen, M. (2000). *Affective intelligence and political judgment.* Chicago: University of Chicago Press.

Marcus, G. E., Sullivan, J. L., Theiss-Morse, E., & Stevens, D. (2005). The emotional foundation of political cognition: The impact of extrinsic anxiety on the formation of political tolerance judgments. *Political Psychology, 26*(6), 949–963.

McGregor, I. (2006). Offensive defensiveness: Toward an integrative neuroscience of compensatory zeal after mortality salience, personal uncertainty, and other poignant self-threats. *Psychological Inquiry, 17*(4), 299–308.

McGregor, H., Lieberman, J., Greenberg, J., Solomon, S., Arndt, J., Simon, L., et al. (1998). Terror management and aggression: Evidence that mortality salience promotes aggression toward worldview-threatening individuals. *Journal of Personality and Social Psychology, 74*, 590–605.

McGuire, W.J. (1968). Personality and susceptibility to social influence. In E. Borgatta & W. Lambert (Eds.), *Handbook of personality theory and research* (pp. 1130–1187). Chicago: Rand McNally.

McGuire, W.J. (1969). The nature of attitudes and attitude change. In G. Lindzey & E. Aronson (Eds.), *The handbook of social psychology* (Vol. 3, pp. 136–314). Reading, MA: Addison-Wesley.

Merskin, D. (2004). The construction of Arabs as enemies: Post-September 11 discourse of George W. Bush. *Mass Communication & Society, 7*(2), 157–175.

Mikulincer, M., & Florian, V. (1997). Do we really know what we need? A commentary on Pyszczynski, Greenberg, and Solomon. *Psychological Inquiry, 8*(1), 33–36.

Miller, C., & Hansen, G. (2007). *The effects of mortality salience on response to presidential campaign ads: An application of terror management theory.* Paper presented at the annual meeting of the NCA 93rd Annual Convention, November 15. Chicago, IL.

Miller, C., & Landau, M. J. (2005). Communication and terrorism: A terror management theory perspective. *Communication Research Reports, 22*, 79–88.

Miller, C., & Landau, M. J. (2008). Communication and the causes and costs of terrorism: A terror management theory perspective. In H. D. O'Hair, R. L. Heath, K. J. Ayotte, & G. R. Ledlow (Eds.), *Terrorism: Communication and rhetorical perspectives* (pp. 93–128). Cresskill, NJ: Hampton Press.

Murray-Johnson, L., Witte, K., Wen-Ying, L., & Hubbell, A. P. (2001). Addressing cultural orientations in fear appeals: Promoting AIDS-protective behaviors among Mexican immigrant and African American adolescents and American and Taiwanese college students. *Journal of Health Communication, 6*, 335–358.

Muthusamy, N., Levine, T. R., & Weber, R. (2009). Scaring the already scared: Some problems with HIV/AIDS fear appeals in Namibia. *Journal of Communication, 59,* 317–344.

Nabi, R. L. (1999). A cognitive-functional model for the effects of discrete negative emotions on information processing, attitude change, and recall. *Communication Theory, 9*(3), 292–320.

Nabi, R. L. (2002). Anger, fear, uncertainty, and attitudes: A test of the cognitive-functional model. *Communication Monographs, 69*(3), 204–216.

Nelson, L. J., Moore, D. L., Olivetti, J., & Scott, T. (1997). General and personal mortality salience and nationalistic bias. *Personality and Social Psychology Bulletin, 23,* 884–892.

Neuman, W. R., Marcus, G. E., MacKuen, M., & Crigler, A. N. (2007). Theorizing affect's effects. In W. R. Neuman, G. E., Marcus, A. N. Crigler, & M. MacKuen (Eds.), *The affect effect: Dynamics of emotion in political thinking and behavior* (pp. 1–20). Chicago: University of Chicago Press.

Petty, R. E., & Cacioppo, J. T. (1986). The elaboration likelihood of persuasion. *Advances in Experimental Social Psychology, 19,* 193–205.

Pfau, M. W. (2007). Who's afraid of fear appeals? Contingency, courage, and deliberation in rhetorical theory and practice. *Philosophy and Rhetoric, 40*(2), 216–237.

Proulx, T., & Heine, S. J. (2006). Death and black diamonds: Meaning, mortality, and the meaning maintenance model. *Psychological Inquiry, 17*(4), 309–318.

Pyszczynski, T., Abdollahi, A., Solomon, S., Greenberg, J., Cohen, F., & Weise, D. (2006). Mortality salience, martyrdom, and military might: The great Satan versus the axis of evil. *Personality and Social Psychology Bulletin, 32,* 525–537.

Pyszczynski, T., Greenberg, J., & Solomon, S. (1999). A dual-process model of defense against conscious and unconscious death-related thoughts: An extension of terror management theory. *Psychological Review, 106*(4), 835–845.

Pyszczynski, T., Greenberg, J., Solomon, S., & Maxfield, M. A. (2006). On the unique psychological import of death: Theme and variations. *Psychological Inquiry, 17*(4), 328–356.

Pyszczynski, T., Rothschild, Z., & Abdollahi, A. (2008). Terrorism, violence, and hope for peace. *Current Directions in Psychological Science, 17*(5), 318–322.

Pyszczynski, T., Solomon, S., & Greenberg, J. (2003). *In the wake of 9/11: The psychology of terror.* Washington, DC: American Psychological Association.

Redlawsk, D. P., Civettini, A. J. W., & Lau, R. R. (2007). Affective intelligence and voting: Information processing and learning in a campaign. In W. R. Neuman, G. E. Marcus, A. N. Crigler, & M. MacKuen (Eds.), *The affect effect: Dynamics of emotion in political thinking and behavior* (pp. 152–179). Chicago: University of Chicago Press.

Rimal, R. N. (2001). Perceived risk and self-efficacy as motivators: Understanding individuals' long-term use of health information. *Journal of Communication, 51*(4), 633–654.

Rimal, R. N., & Real, K. (2003). Perceived risk and efficacy beliefs as motivators of change: Use of the risk perception attitude (RPA) framework to understand health behaviors. *Human Communication Research, 29*(3), 370–399.

Rogers, R.W. (1975). A protection motivation theory of fear appeals and attitude change. *Journal of Psychology, 91,* 93–114.

Rogers, R.W. (1983). Cognitive and physiological processes in fear appeals and attitude change: A revised theory of protection motivation. In J. Cacioppo & R. Petty (Eds.), *Social psychophysiology* (pp. 153–176). New York: Guildford Press.

Russell, J. A. (1980). A circumplex model of affect. *Journal of Personality and Social Psychology, 39*(6), 1161–1178.

Schimel, J., Simon, L., Greenberg, J., Pyszczynski, T., Solomon S., Waxmonski, J., et al. (1999). Support for a functional perspective on stereotypes: Evidence that mortality salience enhances stereotypic thinking and preferences. *Journal of Personality and Social Psychology, 77*(5), 905–926.

Schmeichel, B. J., Gailliot, M. T., Filardo, E., McGregor, I., Gitter, S., & Baumeister, R. F. (2009). Terror management theory and self-esteem revisited: The roles of implicit and explicit self-esteem in mortality salience effects. *Journal of Personality and Social Psychology, 96*(5), 1077–1087.

Shehryar, O., & Hunt, D. M. (2005). A terror management perspective on the persuasiveness of fear appeals. *Journal of consumer psychology, 15*(4), 275–287.

Solomon, S., Greenberg, J., & Pyszczynski, T. (1991). A terror management theory of social behavior: The psychological functions of self-esteem and cultural worldviews. In M. Zanna (Ed.), *Advances in experimental social psychology* (Vol. 24, pp. 91–159). Orlando, FL: Academic Press.

Solomon, S., Greenberg, J., & Pyszczynski, T. (2004). The cultural animal: Twenty years of terror management theory and research. In J. Greenberg, S. L. Koole, & T. Pyszczynski (Eds.), *Handbook of experimental existential psychology* (pp. 13–34). New York: Guilford Press.

Solomon, S., Greenberg, J., Pyszczynski, T., & Pryzbylinski, J. (1995). The effects of mortality salience on personally-relevant persuasive appeals. *Social Behavior and Personality, 23*(2), 177–190.

Sutton, S. R. (1982). Fear-arousing communications: A critical examination of theory and research. In J. R. Eiser (Ed.), *Social psychology and behavioral medicine* (pp. 303–337). London: Wiley.

Ullrich, J., & Cohrs, J. C. (2007). Terrorism salience increases system justification: Experimental evidence. *Social Justice Research, 20*(2), 117–139.

Valentino, N. A., Hutchings, V. L., Banks, A. J., & Davis, A. K. (2008). Is a worried citizen a good citizen? Emotions, political information seeking, and learning via the Internet. *Political Psychology, 29*(2), 247–273.

Watson, D., Clark, L. A., & Tellegen, A. (1988). Development and validation of brief measures of positive and negative affect: The PANAS scales. *Journal of Personality and Social Psychology, 54*(6), 1063–1070.

Weise, D. R., Pyszczynski, T., Cox, C. R., Arndt, J., Greenberg, J., Solomon, S., & Kosloff, S. (2008). Interpersonal politics: The role of terror management and attachment processes in shaping political preferences. *Psychological Science, 19*(5), 448–455.

Wicklund, R. A. (1997). Terror management accounts of other theories: Questions for the cultural worldview concept. *Psychological Inquiry, 8*(1), 54–58.

Witte, K. (1992). Putting the fear back into fear appeals: The extended parallel process model. *Communication Monographs, 59*, 329–349.

Witte, K. (1994). Fear control and danger control: A test of the extended parallel process model (EPPM). *Communication Monographs, 61*, 113–133.

Witte, K. (1998). Fear as motivator, fear as inhibitor: Using the extended parallel process model to explain fear appeal successes and failures. In P. A. Andersen & L. K. Guerrero (Eds.), *Handbook of communication and emotion* (pp. 423–451). San Diego, CA: Academic Press.

Witte, K., & Allen, M. (2000). A meta-analysis of fear appeals: Implications for effective public health campaigns. *Health Education & Behavior, 27*(5), 591–615.

Witte, K., & Morrison, K. (2000). Examining the influence of trait anxiety/repression-sensitization on individuals' reactions to fear appeals. *Western Journal of Communication, 64*(1), 1–27.

Wolak, J., Marcus, G. E., & Neuman, W. R. (2003). *How the emotions of public policy affect citizen engagement, public deliberation, and the quality of electoral choice.* Paper presented at the Annual Meeting of the American Political Science Association, Philadelphia, PA.

Wong, N. C. H., & Cappella, J. N. (2009). Antismoking threat and efficacy appeals: Effects on smoking cessation intentions for smokers with low and high readiness to quit. *Journal of Applied Communication Research, 37*(1), 1–20.

5 *Commentary*
Toward the Development
of Interdisciplinary Theory

Matthew J. Hornsey and Cindy Gallois

The University of Queensland

The four chapters we reviewed for this section all start with fascinating questions—we deal with them in reverse order: What can public health and political communicators learn from understanding responses to reminders of death? Why the puzzling lack of variability in success rates among studies examining deception detection? Has our attention to traditional attribution dimensions blinded us to the complex ways in which people assume motives in social interaction? How have new media changed the way we connect with (and control) each other? In each chapter the reader is guided through a twisting plot to a plausible conclusion. Each one also speaks to a broader narrative about researchers operating on inter-disciplinary margins. In two cases—Dilliplane's synthesis of terror management theory with work on fear appeals, and Bazarova and Hancock's critical review of attribution theory—the authors incorporate work from social psychology and thus bring new theory into communication. In Rice and Hagen's work on new media and Levine's essay on deception, the authors mine territory that has long lain in the "third spaces" between (and across) disciplines. Many would argue that scholars like these are the best equipped to take science forward: In a world of excessive specialization, those who operate on inter-disciplinary boundaries may well take theory and research to the next level.

Recently we contributed to a *Journal of Communication* special issue devoted to exploring connections between communication and other disciplines; our brief was communication and social psychology (Hornsey, Gallois, & Duck, 2008). In that paper, we discussed the paradox that although the fields of communication and social psychology cover very similar territory, the two fields seem to insiders as if they occupy distinct spaces, with different heritages, journals, icons, theories, and languages. For example, whereas social psychologists see text primarily as a stimulus from which data flow, communication scholars are more likely to see text *as* data. Likewise social psychologists tend to view communication in static "snapshots"; communication scholars treat it as an evolving, dynamic and reciprocal process. Theoretical development is the raison díetre of most research in social psychology, whereas communication scholars see descriptive research as equally valid. Finally, communication scholars take a diverse and eclectic approach to methods, emphasizing both consistency and variability, but in social psychology there is a heavy reliance on correlational and experimental methods to search out consistencies. All four chapters here reflect these tensions, and show the advantages of changing the lens from one field to the other.

For a clear example of the parallel research universes in social psychology and communication, one need look no further than the curious case of terror management theory (TMT). TMT begins with the premise that humans are probably alone on the planet in being cognizant of our own demise—unlike sheep, cats, or fish, we suffer the crushing certainty that we will one day die, as will everyone we know and love. This rather unfortunate talent causes an existential "terror" which we ward off with psychological defense mechanisms. Our first line of defense (as Dilliplane notes) is suppression of and distraction from death-related thoughts. The next line of defense is to conform to the prevailing cultural worldview, because this deepens our connections with others and makes us contributors to an "eternal symbolic reality". Self-esteem rests in part on the ability to make peace with and converge to the cultural worldview articulated in our culture. Reinforcing the cultural worldview and bolstering self-esteem lends substance, meaning, and permanence to our experience of reality, creating a sense of symbolic immortality (in the case of religious beliefs about the afterlife, potentially *literal* immortality).

The relevance of this for communication lies in the well-documented tendency for reminders of mortality to have significant effects on people's responses to arguments and messages from others. For example, Americans are more negative toward a critic of their country when they have been reminded of their mortality compared to a control. Similarly, in these conditions people are more supportive of a conservative leader and of anti-terrorism messages.

The question that Dilliplane raises is this: How can these ideas inform what we know about political and public health messages? Reflection tells us that most public health messages trade implicitly or explicitly on the fear of death. It is not advisable to take drugs, to drink and drive, or to smoke because these activities can kill you—and in case you're not paying attention, the message is hammered home with images of victims being zipped up in body bags, bleeding on the street, wasting away in hospitals, or being lowered into graves. Many political messages also play on fears of death (e.g., campaigns relating to terrorism or health care). The success or otherwise of these strategies has traditionally been explained through theories of how fear and/or anxiety shape persuasion. TMT raises the tantalizing prospect that at least some of these effects may be driven by a qualitatively different psychological ingredient: the raising of mortality salience and the resultant defenses. Because fear campaigns and mortality issues are usually conflated, it is difficult to disentangle their unique contributions. Dilliplane, however, presents a clear map of the points at which the two traditions of literature make different predictions, as well as constructing an agenda to enrich future research through a TMT perspective.

The case that Dilliplane makes is so compelling and potentially generative of future research questions that one wonders why it took so long for the synthesis to be made. TMT is not a niche or obscure area in social psychology; it has been around for 20 years, and for the last decade has been a ubiquitous presence in social psychology's best journals. It is true that TMT's success was somewhat slow to arrive, partly because its basic concepts lay outside social psychology's traditional preoccupations. Adapted from the work of Ernest Becker (a cultural anthropologist and inter-disciplinarian who only received significant recognition after his death), TMT is unusual for a social psychological theory in that its underlying mechanisms are abstract and difficult to measure. It also has a temporal quality, unusual for a discipline that is typically more comfortable assuming simultaneous or rapid two-step processes. Finally, TMT combines a big-picture existential approach with an evolutionary twist and experimental methodologies that people normally associate with more micro-level theories of human behavior. Once social psychology embraced this rather unusual mix, however, it did so with enthusiasm.

Given this transformational success, there has apparently been a long and circuitous route for TMT to enter the communication literature. For approximately 20 years, TMT and research in communication on fear appeals have co-existed with little acknowledgement of each other (Dilliplane points to some rare and isolated exceptions). This gulf was partly bridged in 2008 with Goldenberg and Arndt's paper in *Psychological Review,* drawing out the implications of TMT for health promotion. Dilliplane's chapter is a welcome companion piece, bringing TMT to an examination of key papers in health communication in an outlet that communication scholars will certainly read.

It is not yet clear how useful TMT will be for investigations of fear appeals. Dilliplane's spells out when and why the two traditions might make different predictions. A cogent criticism of TMT, however, is that it is more powerful in explaining data post hoc than in predicting behavior. TMT can also be slippery because what people understand to be the cultural worldview can change from culture to culture, individual to individual, and context to context. Thus, there may be a misleading sense of precision about how the major research traditions intersect and differ in their predictions. Nevertheless, the chapter offers tremendous opportunities for those with the interest (and courage) to explore these complexities.

Like Dilliplane, Bazarova and Hancock present a social psychological theory and explore its implications for communication scholars. The theoretical heritage here is somewhat different. Whereas TMT's focus on existential defense mechanisms was not familiar to most communication scholars, the folk-conceptual theory treads very familiar ground: attributions for behavior. Attribution theory is threaded throughout communication research, addressing the fact that people are not passive information processors but rather actively reflect on and discuss what causes behavior and media messages. From the earliest days, communication scholars have been alive to theorizing on attribution, particularly Heider's famous distinction between situational and dispositional causes.

They have not always felt comfortable with the theoretical framework that social psychology has offered, however. Bazarova and Hancock outline some key concerns for communication scholars, which reflect the tensions raised earlier. For example, social psychology is criticized for treating attribution as a one-way cognitive process, without adequately considering the interactive, reciprocal, and social-communicative functions of attribution. Some work, beginning with Hilton and Slugoski (1986), questioned this approach, invoking (in their analysis) Gricean notions of conversational implicature. It would be fair to say, however, that such extensions gained relatively little currency within psychology. Perhaps more importantly, attribution theory is criticized as being overly broad and lacking granulation. People's understandings of specific motives for behavior are extraordinarily complex, and there is value in mapping out this complexity. Communication scholars have long argued that people are more sophisticated than classic attribution theory can account for.

Interestingly social psychologists seem to have listened to these concerns, and Malle's (e.g., 1999) theory is a promising response: Folk-conceptual theory acknowledges and accounts for the complexity of the attributional process. In this view, people choose from multiple modes of explanation, using many linguistic forms to express them. According to Malle and colleagues, one of the key attributions shaping responses to messages and events is intentionality. Indeed, when interpreted through this framework, attributions of intentionality appear to engulf the attributional field. Strikingly, they argue that the actor-observer bias along dispositional and situational attributions evaporates when intentionality is taken into account.

This work, and Bazarova and Hancock's chapter, remind us of the dangers of reifying early seminal work. When a theory has been in introductory textbooks for decades it can begin to feel part of the ether rather than a contestable intellectual construct. Many of us may have been guilty of using Heider as a compass rather than as a theory. This has the potential to limit researchers' imaginations, and in that context Malle's folk-conceptual theory is a breath of fresh air. Bazarova and Hancock lay out compellingly the opportunities that this development provides in terms of our understanding of a range of communication phenomena.

Folk-conceptual theory also integrates cognitive and communicative dimensions in a social context. Bazarova and Hancock argue that the theory could develop further along these lines, integrating the socio-communicative context more fully. For example, research could examine how understanding of messages and behaviors can be negotiated and developed jointly through interaction and conversation. This message gives evidence of communication and social psychology researchers collaborating on ways to take our understanding of communication to the next level.

This collaboration is something that researchers in deception may take for granted. Work in this and related domains in interpersonal interaction have crossed disciplinary boundaries quite naturally, with key figures and developments acknowledged in multiple literatures. The field has been built on the boundaries across disciplines. This cross-fertilization is arguably one of the reasons why the area continues to thrive four decades after Ekman's pioneering work on emotional leakage. If any area provides a counter-example to our generalizations about differences between communication and social psychology it is this one.

In his review of the deception detection literature, Levine highlights the fact that people typically are successful at detecting deception about 54% of the time—statistically significantly above chance, but a relatively modest improvement on chance all the same. Furthermore, the slightly-above-chance accuracy effect is remarkably consistent across studies, with small standard errors in each study. From a classic social-psychological point of view, these are good things: Cross-study consistency and small amounts of error speak to a reliable and robust effect.

For Levine, however, this lack of variability is a red flag. Like Bond and DePaulo (2006), he sees the small amount of variance as sending a message in its own right. Specifically, he argues that the consistencies in accuracy should be unlikely to occur from the perspective of classic deception theory. If detection accuracy is a function of the recipient's ability to spot leaked cues, then we should see greater variability in detection performance, and we should also see increases in accuracy after training. Rather, Levine argues that the data are consistent with a "few transparent liars" theory. Most liars in the laboratory are impossible to read, whereas a small percentage leak significantly. Thus, people consistently perform above chance, but not much. The variance lies in the message senders, not receivers, which is why accuracy does not improve substantially after training in detecting leakage. Levine argues that future research should be oriented toward examining why people are so good at concealing leakage.

Levine's thesis is simple and compelling. It also makes a good case for why a blend of social psychology and communication sensibilities can lead to good science. As we noted earlier, there is a tendency for experimentalists in the social psychological tradition to focus on consistencies and patterns, leaving them relatively blind to variability. In addition, there is a tendency to focus on message recipients. Messages (and senders) are considered as stimuli, to which recipients (the participants) are asked to react. This approach to communication can sometimes mean that senders are forgotten as a key part of communication. Communication scholars may be less prone to this bias because they are more alive to mapping out variability, and careful to avoid static approaches to communication.

Levine points out that classic experimental paradigms, which rely on passive observations of leakage in nonverbal behavior, are designed implicitly to assess the ability-to-spot-leakage perspective. Having cast doubt on whether the ability to spot leakage plays an important role in deception detection, he goes on to argue that these paradigms need to be complemented by studies that take a more ecologically valid approach. Like Bazarova and Hancock, Levine argues that attributions about motive provide a powerful tool to guide research on deception. Message receivers also have available prior factual knowledge, access to physical evidence, use of strategic questioning, and contextual information. Recent research by Levine and others suggests that, when given the chance, people are quite sophisticated at using "content in context" approaches to detect deception, with impressively high accuracy rates.

The parallels with Malle's folk-conceptual theory are interesting. In both chapters the authors make the case that researchers have worked from a classic perspective, assuming certain received wisdoms and then using paradigms and intellectual frames that are implicitly designed to reinforce these frames. Dissenting voices are needed to flush the field out of a rut and to usher it into a new era of growth and creativity. The more diversity within a field, the more likely it is to auto-correct in the face of flawed or incomplete assumptions. In the case of research on attributions and deception detection, the mix of sensibilities appears to have helped provide the necessary diversity of approach to catalyze growth.

Research in new media, like the areas of the other three chapters in this section, is also a field that overlaps with both communication and psychology. In their review, Rice and Hagen address one of the biggest social science questions of our age: How do new media (mobile phones and the internet in particular) change the way that we connect with (and control) our family, friends, and acquaintances? This frontier question by definition would appear to warrant a cross-disciplinary approach, and it has attracted the interest of senior scholars in both psychology and communication, including these authors. Nonetheless, Rice and Hagen's comprehensive reference list indicates that little of this research has been published in either psychology or communication outlets. Instead, with a few exceptions (including one review paper by Katz, Rice, Acord, Dasgupta, and David in the 2004 *Communication Yearbook*), research on new media has appeared in specialist, often e-technology, journals—the closest to mainstream communication research are probably *New Media and Society* and ICA's *Journal of Computer-Mediated Communication*.

Is this highly specialized publication pattern a good or bad thing? New areas may need a fresh new space in which to innovate and grow. Certainly, interesting and informative work is being done in this new space: Rice and Hagen lay out a cornucopia of studies from many parts of the world using an impressive range of methodologies. Even so, much of the research is heavily descriptive, with a relative lack of new theory or extensions of existing theory to tie it together. This is not to say there is no theoretical engagement. Rice and Hagen discuss (at least briefly) a number of existing communication theories. Indeed, one of the memorable sections involves an inversion of Foucaldian notions of surveillance and the argument that, rather than being a Panopticon, new media operate as a *Peropticon*, promoting the observation of self though the system. Compared to the other chapters in this section, however, the prioritization of data over theory in this research is notable. This could be an optimal strategy. It is as though scholars have taken a *tabula rasa* approach to theory, preferring instead to build from the bottom up with data. One can't help but wonder, though, whether the field could benefit from drawing more explicitly from mainstream communication, social psychology, or related disciplines, to obtain insights on identity construction, community, multi-tasking, the divide between public and private spaces, and so forth. At the very least, this might help provide a common language and an entry point that would help social scientists to engage with this work. Furthermore, as the authors note, the lack of convergence in research approaches undercuts the ability to conduct meta-analyses, meaning that at times the forest is hard to see for the trees. In the meantime, however, Rice and Hagen have done the field a favor by condensing this broad and complex work, drawing links where possible, and offering it to communication scholars.

All the chapters in this section present coherent reviews that make sense of the past while at the same time offering a solid platform and great opportunities for the future. All of them show the advantages of combining approaches, and the dangers of looking too much through the lens of one theory or one methodology, however powerful it may be. We hope that the new opportunities are pursued vigorously, and that they form part of a conversation in which researchers across all disciplines of the social sciences can listen in, contribute to, and be heard.

References

Bond, C. F., Jr., & DePaulo, B. M. (2006). Accuracy of deception judgments. *Review of Personality and Social Psychology, 10*, 214–234.

Goldenberg, J. L., & Arndt, J. (2008). The implications of death for health: A terror management health model for behavioral health promotion. *Psychological Review, 115,* 1032–1053.

Hilton, D. J., & Slugoski, B. R. (1986). Knowledge-based causal attribution: The abnormal conditions focus model. *Psychological Review, 93*, 75–88.

Hornsey, M. A., Gallois, C., & Duck, J. M. (2008). The intersection of communication and social psychology: Points of contact and points of difference. *Journal of Communication, 58,* 749–766.

Katz, J. E., Rice, R. E., Acord, S., Dasgupta, K., & David, K. (2004). Personal mediated communication and the concept of community in theory and practice. In P. Kalbfleisch (Ed.), *Communication Yearbook 28* (pp. 315–370). Mahwah, NJ: Erlbaum.

Malle, B. F. (1999). How people explain behavior: A new theoretical framework. *Personality and Social Psychology Review, 3*, 23–48.

Part II:

Communication Processes, Normative Ideals, and Political Realities

CHAPTER CONTENTS

6 Emerging Agendas at the Intersection of Political and Science Communication

The Case of Nanotechnology

Dietram A. Scheufele and Anthony Dudo

University of Wisconsin-Madison

The continued disconnects between science and the mainstream public have received renewed attention from policymakers and academics in recent years as scientific and technological innovations increasingly commingle science and politics. Nanotechnology is the most recent example in a long line of emerging technologies that have produced applications with tremendous ethical, legal, and social implications. It is therefore particularly surprising that our discipline has not played as much of a leadership role in closing potential communication gaps between science and the public as it should have. So where have we fallen short? And where are the most obvious contributions that communication theory and research can make to the unresolved questions surrounding communication about emerging technologies, in general, and nanotechnology, in particular? This chapter provides an overview of the state-of-the-art literature on communication about nanotechnology and highlights areas of convergence from conceptual models in political and science communication that help us build a better theoretical understanding of how science and technology get communicated in modern societies.

[T]here are two ways, I think, science can learn from the arts—at least two ways: one, very concretely, in terms of ideas, and the other in terms of communication.

> Adam Bly, Founder & Editor-in-Chief, Seed Magazine
> (http://www.bigthink.com/science-technology/7283)

It has taken more than a hundred scientists two years to find out how to make the product in question; I have been given thirty days to create its personality and plan its launching. If I do my job well, I shall contribute as much as the hundred scientists to the success of this product.

> David Ogilvy (1963, p. 69)

... [C]ommunication is not just one element in the struggle to make science relevant. It is the central element.

> Randy Olson, biologist-turned-filmmaker (2009, p. 9)

Modern democracies have long been faced with difficulties in communicating science, engineering, and medicine to the general public (Cicerone, 2007; Skapinker, 2007). This challenge has received renewed attention from policymakers and academics in recent years, given the fact that numerous scientific and technological innovations are increasingly commingling the realms of science and politics. More competitive funding environments and political opposition to specific areas of research have further highlighted the need for improving the connections between science and the mainstream public via better communication about emerging technologies (Scheufele, 2007). These realities press social scientists to explore certain research questions. For example, how do citizens make sense of complex scientific and technological issues and the ethical, legal, and social challenges inherent with the rapid developments they pose? And how can we, as communication researchers, help establish sustainable channels of communication between science and the public, especially for increasingly controversial, politically charged issues such as global warming, regenerative medicine, synthetic biology, agricultural biotechnology, and nanotechnology?

While some of the issues that bring these communication questions to the foreground are only now emerging, the underlying theoretical and conceptual questions about science communication are not new. Scholars in arts and humanities, the social sciences, and the natural sciences are all trying to find answers. Many of these efforts, however, have focused narrowly on providing more or better public education and have paid limited attention to the vast body of research and theorizing in communication that has gone beyond simple educational efforts, and offers insights into the mechanisms through which lay publics connect with and make sense of science. As a result, we are faced with a scenario in which more than a fifth of all respondents in a recent survey of AAAS scientists (Mervis, 2009) pointed to problems related to communicating with young people and members of the public as one the greatest U.S. scientific failures of the past 20 years (Kohut, Keeter, Doherty, & Dimock, 2009).

These failing or at least frail connections between scientists and the public—or what we hereafter refer to as "communication gaps"—have become particularly salient for recent emerging technologies, such as nanotechnology. The formation of public opinion about these issues is, in fact, anything but straightforward. Instead, research suggests that a tapestry of factors and considerations influence individuals' awareness, knowledge, and perceptions related to such issues. For example, when forming opinions about these technological breakthroughs public concerns often focus on the moral or ethical dimensions that arise from applications that these new technologies make possible. As a result, normative considerations about science (i.e., ideas about how science *ought* to function within society) often clash with the scientific potential of emerging technologies to fundamentally change everyday life. And the greater the technical possibilities and the speed with which applications of new technologies hit the end market, the greater the challenges are that new technologies pose for people's value systems and their views of what science should and should not do (e.g., Khushf, 2006).

In short, closing the communication gap between science and the mainstream public—that is, fostering a more fluid and mutually beneficial connection between these two entities at a time when scientific and technological issues are increasingly political—requires, first, a more thorough understanding of how the public think and feel about science and, second, necessarily more complex attempts to bring science to the public, and vice versa. This is both good news and bad news. The good news is that communication scholars are uniquely equipped to help address these problems. The bad news is that our discipline has done an inadequate job, so far, in providing the intellectual leadership for bridging potential gaps between science and lay publics.

With these considerations in mind, we aim to accomplish a few goals in this chapter. After providing a brief primer on the science and proliferation of nanotechnology, we discuss the state of current public awareness, interest, and knowledge related to nanotechnology. Second, we discuss examples of previous controversial technologies, highlighting the disconnect (or "communication gap") that so often exists between science and the mainstream public regarding scientific and technological issues. We then make a case for how communication researchers can help reduce this communication gap.

It is important to note that this chapter is not meant to be an exhaustive review of the social dimensions of nanotechnology (for one such attempt, see, Anderson, Peterson, Wilkinson, & Allan, 2009). Instead, using what empirical research has revealed thus far about communication and nanotechnology, we will outline key models from communication theory that can guide communication researchers to help build more promising bridges between science and the public.

Nanotechnology and the Public

Nanotechnology is the most recent example in a long line of emerging technologies that will produce and has already produced applications with tremendous ethical, legal, and social implications (ELSIs). The term "nanotechnology" has been used for more than 30 years and serves as an umbrella for a broad range of technological activity that focuses on the engineering and use of objects at the nanoscale, up to 100 nanometers (each nanometer is one billionth of a meter) in size. To put this into perspective, an ant is about five millimeters or 50 million nanometers long. "Doing" nanotechnology involves combining components from various scientific disciplines (e.g., chemistry, biology, engineering, etc.) (Wood, Jones, & Geldart, 2007), making it, in practice, an interdisciplinary endeavor with much definitional obscurity (Anderson, Petersen, Wilkinson, & Allan., 2009).

Despite nanotechnology's definitional ambiguity and potential ELSIs, it has commonly been referred to as the next Industrial Revolution. Indeed, federal funding for nanotechnology has roughly quadrupled during the past eight years (National Nanotechnology Initiative, 2008), and corporate consultancies predict nanotechnology to develop into a $3.1 trillion global industry by 2015. Although today the technology is used in more than 1,000 consumer end products in the United States, from golf clubs to toothpaste to cleaning fluids, large and sustained levels of federal funding for nanotechnology got under way only in 2000 with President Clinton's National Nanotechnology Initiative.

Research on the educational and societal dimensions of nanotechnology as defined by the National Nanotechnology Coordination Office (National Nanotechnology Initiative, 2008) currently comprises about 2% of all federal funding of nanotechnology ($33.5 million across all agencies, estimated for FY 2009). This research has included work in public policy dealing with real-time technology assessment (Guston & Sarewitz, 2002) and regulatory frameworks for nanotechnology (Corley, Scheufele, & Hu, 2009), analyses of the themes that have dominated media coverage (Corley et al., 2009) and public debates (Berube, 2008) of nanotechnology, research on risk perceptions among lay publics (Bainbridge, 2002; Burri & Bellucci, 2008; Peter D. Hart Research Associates, 2006, 2007; Pidgeon, Harthorn, Bryant, & Rogers-Hayden, 2009; Scheufele, Corley, Shih, Dalrymple, & Ho, 2009; Scheufele & Lewenstein, 2005) and experts (Corley et al., 2009), and comparisons between the two (Scheufele et al., 2007; Siegrist, Keller, Kastenholz, Frey, & Wiek, 2007; Siegrist, Wiek, Helland, & Kastenholz, 2007).

Surveys of the public have demonstrated that most Americans are largely unaware of the technology (see, for example, Cobb & Macoubrie, 2004; Peter D. Hart Research Associates, 2007) and that levels of actual knowledge about nanotechnology among the U.S. public, measured with a series of true/false questions, have remained low and overall stagnant since 2004 (see online supplementary materials to Scheufele, Corley, et al., 2009).

These findings, of course, are not too surprising given how disengaged many Americans are from science in general. During the 2004 election, for example, almost 7 out of 10 Americans (69%) reported that scientific findings are often "hard for people like me to understand," and almost two thirds (60%) of the public thought that they did not know a lot about the issue of stem cell research, which was brought up by both presidential candidates during the debates (data set described in Ho, Brossard, & Scheufele, 2008). For issues such as nanotechnology, levels of self-reported knowledge are even lower, and 4 out of 5 Americans (81%) think that they are not well informed about nanotechnology, with about a fifth of all respondents (21%) thinking of themselves as "not informed at all" (data set described in Scheufele et al., 2007).

Part of the explanation for low levels of real and perceived knowledge lies in the lack of attention that the U.S. public pays to science as an issue. Half of all respondents (50%) in the same national survey (Scheufele et al., 2007) report that they watched "stories related to science, technology, and medicine" on TV only once or not at all during the past week. The numbers are similar for science stories read in newspapers (49%), and even higher for web content, where 4 out of 5 Americans (82%) report that they read "stories related to science, technology, and medicine" only once or not at all during the past week.

Despite the limited levels of public literacy, a number of nano-based applications have received news coverage and policy discussions about the unforeseeable consequences of nanotechnology-related research. These concerns are driven in part by more general concerns about insufficient regulatory structures for nanotechnology (e.g., Maynard et al., 2006) and its applications (e.g., Berube, 2008), and in part by worries about the specific risks to human health and the environment (e.g., Scheufele et al., 2007). In order to understand the emerging communication environment surrounding nanotechnology, it is important to first examine some lessons communication researchers learned from previous technologies.

The Politicization of Science: Lessons for Communication Research from Previous Controversies

One helpful illustration of the communication disconnects between science and large cross-sections of society is the issue of agricultural biotechnology, and particularly the debate surrounding genetically modified Bt corn. In 1999, Cornell Entomologist John Losey and colleagues (Losey, Rayor, & Carter, 1999) published a *Scientific Correspondence* in the journal *Nature* outlining results from lab studies that suggested that Bt-transgenic corn might have harmful effects on Monarch butterfly larvae. The report triggered an intense academic debate, including criticism from some of Losey's own colleagues at Cornell, who raised methodological concerns about the generalizability of lab-based findings (Shelton & Roush, 1999). Other allegations focused on the fact that the article had been rejected by the journal *Science* (Delborne, 2005), but—contrary to some reports—the *Correspondence* piece in *Nature* had in fact undergone peer review before publication (Beringer, 1999).

This technical debate among a small group of specialized scientists, of course, went largely unnoticed by the general public. Instead, the public's attention was drawn to the issue when *USA Today*'s front page made the sweeping announcement that "Engineered corn kills butterflies" (Fackelmann, 1999, p. 1A), and the *Washington Post* pitted "biotech" against the monarch butterfly—the "'Bambi' of insects" (Weiss, 1999, p. A3).

This disconnect between scientific discourse and mediated public debates highlights two important points. First, many scientists and public information officers at universities are unaware of the important role that cultural references and imagery play for how lay audiences interpret new technologies or make decisions about public funding for science. A recent column by Earle Holland, Director of Communications at the Ohio State University, highlights this problem by referring to effective communication as an ancillary task for science (Holland, 2009). Second, the success of *Greenpeace*'s "Frankenfood" campaign is a good example of how important media effects models—such as framing (Tewksbury & Scheufele, 2009)—are for explaining and predicting effects of science communication efforts. Framing refers to the idea that the presentation of an issue, rather than the information itself, can shape interpretations among audiences by creating resonance between the message frame and underlying cognitive schemas held by audiences. We will discuss framing in greater detail below, but, for now, the importance of framing is best illustrated by recent research comparing the relative impacts of survey questions framed around the labels "climate change" and "global warming" on public attitudes (Whitmarsh, 2009). Consistent with framing theory, hearing the term "Frankenfood" likely triggers a series of socially and culturally shared interpretive schemas in that person's head, ranging from "playing God" to "runaway science" and the notion of "unnatural, artificial" food, regardless of how factually accurate one may think Greenpeace's campaign on the topic really was (Nisbet & Scheufele, 2007). The idea that culturally shared imagery or terminology is often at the center of how we debate science as a society (Kirby, 2003) and how we make sense of emerging technologies as individuals (Scheufele, 2006) is not new. Many scientists, however, continue to see their work as largely divorced from these debates and from the cultural values underlying them. When pressed by a journalist about the impacts of Bt-transgenic corn on larvae of monarch butterflies, Cornell Entomologist Tony Shelton, for instance, dismissed the concerns by asking "[h]ow many monarchs get killed on the windshield of a car?" (as cited in Fedoroff & Brown, 2004, p. 209). This highly-publicized statement unintentionally distilled two competing frames: the beloved monarch as the "Bambi" of butterflies (Weiss, 1999, p. A3), and the image of a heartless scientist who is not concerned about the impacts that his or her work has on society.

The second point highlighted by the Bt corn controversy is the immense impact that a potential disconnect between science and the public can have on markets and policy debates. In fact, a number of scholars warned almost immediately about the consequences of a news wave that provided little opportunity for a dialogue between science, policy makers, and the public:

> [I]mmediately after publication of the *Nature* correspondence, there was a nearly 10% drop in the value of Monsanto stock, possible trade restrictions by Japan, freezes on the approval process for Bt-transgenic corn by the European Commission (Brussels), and calls for a moratorium on further planting of Bt-corn in the United States. (Shelton & Roush, 1999, p. 832)

This overview, of course, is meant mostly as an illustration of the importance of communication among all stakeholders for deliberative societal decision-making about science. We therefore caution against a number of potential misperceptions. One is the notion that citizens' personal values and beliefs are inherently problematic, especially if they seem to be at odds with traditional pro-science viewpoints. As we will discuss later, this assumption makes little sense for many emerging technologies, especially those that raise new ethical and moral concerns about their potential applications. A second misperception relates to the assumption that nanotechnology and previous technologies, such as agricultural biotechnology, are directly comparable. There are (and will be) differences between nanotechnology and biotechnology in terms of public opinion. Although we have drawn comparisons in this chapter to help articulate some suggestions for closing communication gaps between science and the mainstream public broadly and within the context of nanotechnology, communication researchers should also recognize that nanotechnology and biotechnology are not the same animal. For example, Priest (2008) discusses how these technologies might raise different ethical issues for people and advocates that researchers "continue to expect, and look for, differences as well as similarities" when using biotechnology as a model for studying the public opinion dynamics of nanotechnology (p. 223). We echo these sentiments and urge researchers to be mindful of the unique properties nanotechnology poses for communication.

Science and the Public: A Leadership Role for Communication Research?

Given the increasing prominence of scientific issues, such as climate change, on the public agenda, it is surprising that the communication discipline has not provided more intellectual leadership to the debates about how to effectively address science-public gaps. And data from a recent survey commissioned by the American Association for the Advancement of Science (AAAS; Mervis, 2009) and conducted by the Pew Center for the People and the Press (Kohut, Keeter, Doherty, & Dimock, 2009) raised concerns that things are worse than ever. In fact, the polling data suggested that few scientists are even making an effort to close communication gaps with the general public. Only about 2 in 5 AAAS scientists, for instance, report that they "often" talk with non-scientists about research findings, and only 3% "often" talk to reporters (Kohut et al., 2009).

The good news is that these data are somewhat inconsistent with more systematic surveys of scientific experts in different fields (Corley et al., 2009; Dunwoody, Brossard, & Dudo, 2009; Dunwoody & Scott, 1982; Peters et al., 2008; Scheufele et al., 2007; Wilkes & Kravitz, 1992) and countries (Peters et al., 2008). For example, a survey of productive epidemiologists and stem cell researchers shows that approximately two out of three scientists surveyed had at least one interaction with media in the previous three years, and that more than one quarter (29%) had more than five interactions (Dunwoody et al., 2009). Additionally, data from a survey of the leading nanotechnologists in the United States (Scheufele et al., 2007) suggest that these scientists often recognize the importance of science-public connections. More than half of the surveyed nanotechnologists "strongly" or "somewhat" agree that "[s]cientists should pay attention to the wishes of the public, even if they think citizens are mistaken or do not understand their work." And these scientists believe that communication can make a difference, with more than 80% disagreeing that "[c]ommunicating with the public does not affect public attitudes toward science" (for an overview of these results, see Scheufele, Brossard, et al., 2009).

These survey results should be inspiring to communication researchers for at least two reasons. On the one hand, they highlight the immense potential for (science) communication to provide the leadership and expertise that has been missing from many previous efforts to improve communication among various stakeholders during public debates about science and emerging technologies. And many of these debates are more salient on the public agenda now than they were 40 or 50 years ago when issues related to science and technology were at the bottom of many public rankings of the most important problem facing the country (e.g., Funkhouser, 1973). The most powerful illustration of this shift is a series of recent initiatives and reform efforts by U.S. President Barack Obama in the areas of stem cell funding, health care, and climate change.

The data from the scientist surveys also serves as a reminder that our discipline can do a better job performing this leadership role. So where have we fallen short? And where are the most obvious contributions that communication theory and research can make to the unresolved questions surrounding communication about emerging technologies, in general, and nanotechnology, in particular. At least three areas are worth highlighting.

Worldviews and Attitudes

Communication scholars have known for a long time that "cultivation effects" matter, i.e., the idea that public perceptions of how science functions are shaped heavily by media portrayals in popular culture (Gerbner, 1987; Gerbner, Gross, Morgan, & Signorielli, 1981). Cultivation effects are particularly pronounced for issues where lay citizens have limited personal experience, and where public perceptions are therefore shaped heavily by media portrayals (for an overview, see Shanahan & Morgan, 1999). Given the limited experience that most citizens have with bench scientists and their daily work, it is not too surprising that their perceptions of science (Dudo, Brossard, et al., 2009; Nisbet et al., 2002) and science-related risks (Dahlstrom & Scheufele, in press) are shaped, in part, by television portrayals, that one in four (25%) members of the general public understands the concept of a scientific study, and only about two in five can correctly describe a scientific experiment (42%) or the scientific process more broadly (41%) (National Science Board, 2008).

It could be argued that these cultivation effects are the root of misconstrued public opposition to emerging technologies and should be countered with educational campaigns to correct potentially biased views of how science works. Consistent with this view, many science communication initiatives start with the (implicit) premise that deficits in public knowledge are the central culprit driving societal conflict over science, when, in fact, science literacy has only a limited role in shaping public perceptions and decisions (Allum, Sturgis, Tabourazi, & Brunton-Smith, 2008; Brossard, Lewenstein, & Bonney, 2005;

Rodgers, 2007, 2009). And research on cultivation effects in the realm of science suggests that the cultural influences of television on perceptions of science cannot simply be explained by levels of scientific training, formal education, or scientific literacy (e.g., Dudo, Brossard, et al., 2009; Nisbet et al., 2002).

Emerging technologies, such as nanotechnology, have exacerbated this problem by challenging moral belief systems (Scheufele, Corley, et al., 2009) and raising questions about the responsible development and use of breakthrough science (Kahan et al., 2008). These questions and concerns have been most salient for the intersection of nanotechnology and biotechnology, and in particular with respect to Nano-Bio-Info-Cogno (NBIC) technologies (i.e., research at the intersection between nanotechnology, biotechnology, and information technology) (Roco & Bainbridge, 2003). NBIC technologies may, in the future, enable scientists to create life and intelligence at the nanoscale without divine intervention (Khushf, 2006; Roco & Bainbridge, 2003) thereby threatening people's religious beliefs and making some groups more likely to oppose further research in nanotechnology on moral or religious concerns (Pearson, 2006; Scheufele, Corley, et al., 2009). Again, this does not mean that one group of stakeholders is "right" or "justified" in their beliefs, but rather highlights the increasing complexity of influences on judgments about nanotechnology.

At the same time, recent U.S. surveys have shown that the public's knowledge about nanotechnology, for instance, has few direct effects on attitudes or support for funding. Part of the explanation for this phenomenon, of course, is the low and static level of knowledge described earlier. But, more importantly, recent research has shown that the way audiences make sense of nanotechnology and the risks associated with it are often a complex interaction of worldviews (Kahan, Braman, Slovic, Gastil, & Cohen, 2009; Kahan et al., 2008), religious beliefs (Scheufele, Corley, et al., 2009), emotional variables (Lee, Scheufele, & Lewenstein, 2005; Siegrist, Cousin, Kastenholz, & Wiek, 2007), message frames (Cobb, 2005; Schütz & Wiedmann, 2008), and deference toward scientific authority (Brossard & Nisbet, 2007; Brossard, Scheufele, Kim, & Lewenstein, 2009; Lee & Scheufele, 2006).

Figure 6.1, for example, shows the influence of factual scientific knowledge (measured through a series of true false questions) on support for federal funding for nanotechnology (for details on data collection and statistical tests, see Brossard et al., 2009). Higher levels of knowledge, in this figure, were significantly related to increased support for research among less religious respondents. For more religious respondents, however, there was no significant link, and highly knowledgeable religious respondents did not differ from less knowledgeable ones with respect to their attitudes on funding for nanotechnology research. These findings held across different attitudinal indicators, suggesting that ideology serves as a "perceptual filter" that audiences use when they need to balance existing values and worldviews against what they *know* to be scientific facts.

When it comes to data on real-world examples of cultivation effects in the emerging field of nanotechnology, evidence is limited. There have been

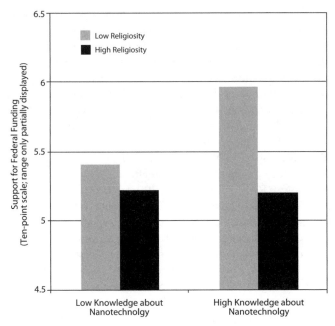

Figure 6.1 Religiosity as a "filter" of knowledge (data based on Brossard et al., 2009).

speculative accounts of potential influences of popular novels, such as Michael Crichton's *Prey*, or motion pictures, such as the *Terminator* series (Gregory, 2009). At this point, however, there are no studies that have shown empirically that public views on nanotechnology are cultivated by exposure to popular media (i.e., that heavy exposure to popular media messages is significantly related to more negative perceptions). This may be due in part to the portrayal of nanotechnology in mass media so far, which appears to be mostly positive (Dudo, Dunwoody, & Scheufele, 2009; Gaskell, Ten Eyck, Jackson, & Veltri, 2005; Gorss & Lewenstein, 2005; Laing, 2005; Stephens, 2005; Wilkinson, Allan, Anderson, & Petersen, 2007) or neutral (Friedman & Egolf, 2005; Friedman & Egolf, 2007), and also the fact we have yet to see nanotechnology emerge as a salient issue in mainstream media.

Widening Knowledge Gaps

Regardless of the limited empirical support for a link between scientific knowledge and more positive attitudes toward science, there are strong normative arguments to be made in favor of an informed citizenry that is capable of making well-reasoned policy decisions and ethical choices about scientific issues, such as nanotechnology (Krieghbaum, 1967). And K–12 education, teacher training, and informal science education are absolutely critical tools for raising science literacy (Shamos, 1995), recruiting the scientists of tomorrow (Committee on Public Understanding of Engineering Messages, 2008), and providing interested voters with policy-relevant information (Miller, 1992).

And all of these tools are also being used in the informal science education efforts that many museums are spearheading in the area of nanotechnology and other emerging technologies (Bell, 2009). Unfortunately, the effects of these efforts on public understanding of nanotechnology have been limited. Many of the previous attempts to connect wide cross sections of the public with science have in fact resulted in *widening* gaps between the already information rich and the information poor. This is partly due to likelihood of exposure. Almost 40% of college-educated respondents, for instance, visited a science or technology museum in 2006, compared to less than 10% for respondents with a high school education or less (National Science Board, 2008).

As a result, exhibits and similar outreach efforts may inherently favor elite audiences. Widening gaps between the information rich and information poor are also a function of the way issues like nanotechnology play out in public discourse. In their research on "knowledge gaps" Tichenor and his colleagues (Tichenor, Donohue, & Olien, 1970) found that audiences with high socioeconomic status (SES) showed much stronger learning effects from health related information than low-SES audiences. This effect is in part due to the fact that TV shows like *NOVA* or the Science section of the *New York Times* tailor their content to highly educated elite audiences. As a result, learning effects for mass audiences are minimal, even if these audiences happen to tune in to *NOVA* or read an article in the *Times*.

Regardless of what the mechanisms may be, however, the current infrastructure for informal science education puts too much of a burden on museums and similar organizations, and—as a result—may inadvertently widen the very gaps it is attempting to close. Figure 6.2, for instance, plots comparisons

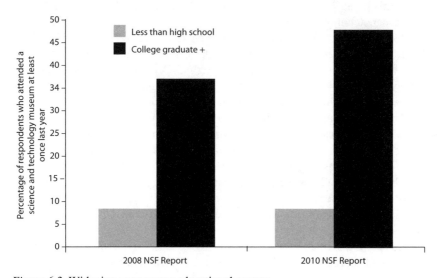

Figure 6.2 Widening gaps across educational groups.

of attendance in science and technology museums as reported in the 2008 (National Science Board, 2008) and 2010 (National Science Board, 2010) Science and Engineering Indicators reports.

As Figure 6.2 shows, efforts to increase exposure to informal science education efforts among the most educated segments of the population have been successful, with almost half of the most highly educated respondents reporting that they had been to a museum at least once during the previous year, an increase of more than 10% compared to the report 2 years earlier. Among respondents with less than a high school degree, however, only 1 in 10 had visited a science or technology museum last year, and that number did not change since the release of the 2008 report. This suggests that we are not only witnessing differentials in exposure to informal science communication efforts, but also widening gaps over time.

These widening gaps in terms of message exposure likely exacerbate the phenomenon that Tichenor et al. (1970) described as "the knowledge gap." As outlined earlier, Tichenor and his colleagues argued that exposure to the same message would produce weaker learning effects among respondents of lower SES than among respondents with higher SES; and their predictions hold, even in modern election campaigns (Eveland & Scheufele, 2000). It is reasonable to assume, of course, that museums and other sites for informal science education play a key role in producing the more integrated understanding of issues (Neuman, 1981; Neuman, Just, & Crigler, 1992) that allows audiences to efficiently process new information from mass media. In other words, without the contextualized understanding that museums can provide through exhibits and other popularizations of science, audiences may also not be able to understand the complexities of emerging technologies, such as nanotechnology, and their ethical, legal, and societal implications.

At this point in the issue cycle (Downs, 1972), levels of public understanding of nanotechnology are low overall (National Science Board, 2008) with what seems like no changes overall between 2004 and 2007 (National Science Board, 2008; Scheufele, Corley, et al., 2009). What is particularly interesting, however, is the pattern illustrated in Figure 6.3. A comparison of two national surveys from 2004 (for more details on questions and sampling, see Scheufele & Lewenstein, 2005) and 2007 (for more details on questions and sampling, see Scheufele et al., 2007) shows that there is a widening gap between the two SES distinguished in the NSF Science and Engineering Indicators reports. These gaps were statistically significant, even after controlling for demographic differences among respondents. Highly educated respondents showed a slight increase in knowledge about nanotechnology, measured as the number of correct responses on a series of six true/false quiz-type questions. The least educated respondents, however, showed a slight decrease in the number of questions they were able to answer correctly.

This pattern is important for at least two reasons. First, it highlights the fact that current approaches to science communication and public education are not working as well as they could. The gap between the two groups is widening

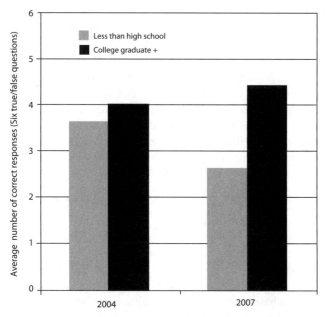

Figure 6.3 Widening knowledge gaps for nanotechnology (Graph based on work reported in Corley & Scheufele, 2010).

in part because highly educated respondents were more informed in the first place and are beginning to understand nanotechnology better now that more information about it is becoming available in mass media (Dudo, Dunwoody, et al., 2009). But the gap may also be widening because less educated groups are increasingly less informed, especially as nanotechnology enters a stage in the issue cycle where the initial excitement about its economic and scientific potential is replaced by increasingly complex debates about regulatory frameworks, toxicological studies, and blurring lines between nanotechnology and other emerging technologies that may be particularly confusing to those segments of the audience that were less informed to begin with (Dudo, Dunwoody, et al., 2009; Nisbet, Brossard, & Kroepsch, 2003; Nisbet & Huge, 2006).

Research on public attitudes on nanotechnology and related emerging technologies has demonstrated that how people think about emerging technologies is much more complex and multifaceted than many traditional outreach models assume (Rodgers, 2007, 2009). But many of these data also show that there are some very stable factors when it comes to public opinion. One of them is who the public trusts when it comes to providing the best information about these new technologies. One of the more recent studies in this area (Corley et al., 2009) shows that the general public ranks university researchers among the most trusted sources for information about nanotechnology. In other words, scientists may be in a unique position to close knowledge gaps.

This raises a second important point. Communication scholars have not done a particularly good job in developing research programs and theoretical models that would help scholars in other disciplines and practitioners in their efforts to close these gaps. As a result, many efforts to communicate about science with lay publics are characterized by a noticeable absence of communication-related theorizing and data. Shamos (1995) puts it more succinctly: "[T]he reasoned approach that supposedly characterizes the practice of science has not carried over very well into science education" (p. xi). In fact, initial research from the national surveys about nanotechnology cited earlier suggests that exposure to online news sources has the potential to close knowledge gaps among the least educated audiences, after controlling for demographic variables and exposure to traditional news media.

Framing Nanotechnology—Negotiation Models of Media Effects

The lack of attention that our discipline has paid to the subfield of science communication—relative to political communication, history, or other subdisciplines—is surprising for a number of reasons.

First, the communication disconnects we are dealing with in the area of nanotechnology are not new. Nonetheless, many scientists continue to seek solutions that are based on outdated stimulus-response models of the 1920s and 30s and assume that the scientific accuracy of messages will ultimately overcome perceptual or informational gaps. Some nano scientists, for instance, have argued that the communication disconnects between the public and scientists are to a large degree due to the public not understanding the relative size of nanoparticles (Batt, 2008). It is surprising how unsuccessful the communication discipline has been in introducing decades of relevant communication research to the debates that has the potential to help guide and inform science outreach and communication efforts across disciplines.

This also leads us to a second surprising fact. Science journalists have long bemoaned the chronic communication problems about scientific issues, such as nanotechnology. In the 1960s, Hillier Krieghbaum (1967) argued that "[w]hat science news 'consumers' want from the mass media is a bit of the essence of the experiment, not its detailed nuts and bolts. This relatively simple idea is not understood by many non-journalists" (p. 39). And journalists, such as Lippmann (1922/1997) or Krieghbaum (1967), introduced the field of communication early on to their intuitive but accurate understanding of what it means to write for different audiences with different worldviews, values, and prior knowledge of an issue. They argued that in order to make a complex issue, such as nanotechnology, accessible to a casual news audience, they needed metaphors or narratives that allow citizens to tie new information about a complex scientific topic (conveyed in a 500-word newspaper story or a 30-second local TV news segment) with what they already know or understand about the world. And their intuitive understanding was confirmed by a series of studies in the 1970s and 1980s (Gans, 1983; Gitlin, 1980; Shoemaker & Reese, 1996; Tuchman, 1978) that examined many of these narratives and metaphors as part of the news production process.

This work quickly became part of a growing tradition of media effects research that McQuail (2005) later described as negotiation models of media effects. McQuail saw these negotiation models as a departure from or at least modification of some of the powerful effects theories that had dominated the 1970s, including Elizabeth Noelle-Neumann's Spiral of Silence model (Noelle-Neumann, 1973, 1984), and George Gerbner's concept of Cultivation (Gerbner & Gross, 1974). Rather than powerful effects of what both Gerbner and Noelle-Neumann assumed to be slanted news coverage, these negotiation models assume that characteristics of audiences (e.g., predispositions, schema, etc.) strongly influence how they process the content of mass media.

Communicating with lay publics about complex scientific issues directly falls under the umbrella of these negotiation models. How can journalists and science communicators present issues in ways that resonate with audiences' existing knowledge structures or value systems? And how does that help audiences to make sense of complex scientific issues, even though they are not experts? Some answers to these questions have been provided by communication researchers as part of the prominent communication subfield of "framing" (Bryant & Miron, 2004; Entman, 1993; Scheufele, 1999; Scheufele & Tewksbury, 2007). But, unfortunately, the concepts and theorizing developed by scholars in our discipline are finding their way only slowly into the area of science communication and outreach (Nisbet & Scheufele, 2007; Scheufele, 2006).

As mentioned earlier, framing refers to how the presentation characteristics of information influence how individuals' interpret that information. More specifically, frames are interpretative storylines that help communicate why an issue might be a problem, who or what might be responsible, and what should be done. The earliest formal work on framing traces back four decades to the sociologist Erving Goffman (1974), who described words and non-verbal interactions as helping individuals negotiate meaning through the lens of existing cultural beliefs and worldviews. In the 1970s and 1980s, cognitive psychologists Daniel Kahneman and Amos Tversky discovered that the different ways in which a message is presented can result in very different responses, depending on the terminology used to describe the problem or the visual context provided in the message (Kahneman, 2003). This work—which won Kahneman the Nobel Prize—demonstrated that all human perception is reference dependent and that this is particularly true for ambiguous stimuli (i.e., issues or objects that can be interpreted in different ways, Kahneman, 2003).

Frames are therefore about applicability; the idea that the effects of a message are particularly strong if various frame devices within the message (imagery, metaphors, etc.) resonate with an underlying schema (value system, beliefs, etc.) held by an audience member (Price & Tewksbury, 1997; Tewksbury & Scheufele, 2009). The notion of applicability is therefore an extremely useful explanatory mechanism for how specific media frames can influence audience reactions and interpretations. Moreover, for lay audiences, many emerging technologies are the equivalent of an ambiguous stimulus, especially when they seem tinged with uncertainty or controversy (Nisbet & Scheufele, 2007). As a result, the frame that is being used to describe a scientific or technological issue can serve as a powerful heuristic when audiences are being asked to make judgments about associated risks or regulatory policies to attenuate the risks (Scheufele, 2006).

Greenpeace's "Frankenfood" frame during the debates surrounding genetically modified organisms (GMOs) is a particularly good example. It resonates with culturally-shared descriptions from Mary Shelley's *Frankenstein* and visual images from various movie adaptations. It also activates an intuitive understanding of the dangers of "runaway science," and the risks of science going too far. And it does all of that simply by introducing a new label for GMOs, and not by making a persuasive argument or offering new information.

Frames therefore have very little to do with actual information. Rather, their effects are very subtle and work by activating cognitive schema that increase or decrease the likelihood that audiences interpret the issue in certain ways (e.g., as an issue of "morality" or "economics"). Nanotechnology, in a similar fashion, was described early on in its issue cycle mostly in terms of its economic and scientific promise, and attitudes toward the new technology were shaped mostly by these positive frames offered by mass media (Scheufele & Lewenstein, 2005). However, with the recent discovery suggesting a link between carbon nanotubes and asbestos-like pathogenicity (Poland et al., 2008), it seems that nanotechnology is now beginning to be framed as the "next asbestos" in public debate (see, for example, Dean, 2008), indirectly triggering a *public accountability* link to a past well-known health controversy, specifically the absence of regulatory oversight of asbestos. The phrase also activates the notion that emerging nanotechnologies may open a Pandora's box of long-term effects that will be unknown for years to come.

Given their experiences with Greenpeace's "Frankenfood" campaign and the health scare surrounding "Magic Nano" in Germany, Austria, and Switzerland (Weiss, 2006), European corporations have been extremely sensitive to these framing efforts and have engaged in very successful pre-emptive image campaigns. Magic Nano is a cleaning product that was sold by Kleinmann GmbH in Germany and was linked to respiratory problems of dozens of consumers in Germany, Austria, and Switzerland (Weiss, 2006). The health problems allegedly caused by Magic Nano were later found to be caused by an interaction of the coating of the metal spray cans and the cleaning liquid, and were unrelated to the use of nanoparticles.

Communication efforts by corporations in Europe have therefore often been characterized by a consistent framing of new product releases and other marketing materials around a "nano is nature" theme. This frame device activates a *social progress* interpretation of nanotechnology as a process that is in harmony with nature, existing for thousands of years. European firms have also expanded these efforts beyond current market applications, launching pre-emptive campaigns to brand entire industries. The Chemie-Wirtschaftsförderungs-Gesellschaft, a German Industry Group, for instance, has rolled out a broad online and print campaign featuring an alternative application of the *social progress* frame: "Chemie macht Zukunft [chemistry makes future]." While these frames are focused very narrowly on persuasive corporate goals, they—once again—highlight the effectiveness of the framing mechanism for how lay audiences make sense of emerging technologies.

Where Our Discipline Has Underdelivered: Agendas for Future Research

Back in 2007, Google cofounder Larry Page gave a keynote speech at the annual meeting of the American Association for the Advancement of Science. His message was simple: science is at a critical junction because of the promise that it increasingly holds for changing the world as we know it, in ways that can trigger deep fears among the general public, but also great enthusiasm (Ham, 2007). As a result, public reactions to breakthrough technologies boil down to a communication issue. And, although there are signs that scientific organizations are increasingly trying to help scientists become better communicators (Dunwoody et al., 2009; Olson, 2009), scientists have so far been unable to establish effective channels of communication with the general public. This chapter outlined at least three areas in which our discipline faces both challenges and opportunities related to this goal. The challenges stem from our inability so far to make intellectual contributions to larger societal efforts to close the science-public divide. But they also stem from at least two developments.

First, nanotechnology (and all new emerging technologies) are moving targets. This is partly a function of new scientific developments that increasingly merge these different research areas with one another. Their intersections include NBIC technologies, but also fields like medicine and material science. The changing nature of emerging technologies, such as nanotechnology, is also a function of how widely disseminated they are and will be in society. In fact, some experts have predicted that the notion of nanotechnology will soon disappear as it infiltrates most areas of science and society. And the fact that corporations like BASF already invest more than 80% of their R&D budget on nanotech-related applications supports this prediction. Research on public reactions to these technologies will therefore have to deal with a rapid proliferation of applications and also with increasing overlaps between technologies, such as biotechnology, nanotechnology, and stem cell research (Cacciatore, Scheufele, & Corley, in press).

Second, many traditional approaches to communicating with the public about science may have outlived their purpose. What we need are innovative and creative approaches to meaningfully connect with increasingly hard-to-reach and therefore underserved publics. And these efforts to connect science and the public need to adapt to the realities of a new information environment. Many traditional approaches to science communication and science outreach have relied on traditional channels, such as television or newspapers. Recent data by the Pew Research Center for the People and the Press (2008), however, suggest that we are seeing significant shifts from television (which is still the primary source of information for three quarters of respondents 65 years or older) to online sources (which are the preferred medium for more than half of the under 24 year olds). The same data from earlier this year also show that interest in science-related issues is highest among respondents who rely mainly on new information technologies for news, as opposed to traditional mass media channels.

Many corporations are already investing significant amounts of time and effort into researching new ways of reaching these younger, online audiences. In doing so, they apply insights from traditional communication theory to the opportunities that emerge from new social media. Using concepts like opinion leadership and two-step-flow of information (Lazarsfeld, Berelson, & Gaudet, 1948), Victoria's Secret and other corporate players, for example, recruit influential students who are central nodes in their social networks as "campus ambassadors" (Schweitzer, 2005). Drawing from basic (Weimann, 1994) and applied (Keller & Berry, 2003) research in communication and related disciplines they conclude that centrally and densely connected nodes can serve as particularly effective spokespeople for brands and products, especially for younger demographics that are chronically difficult to reach through traditional media channels. And while there is little publicly available research that attests to the effectiveness of this approach for commercial products, data from the most recent U.S. presidential race suggests that almost one third (28%) of all users of social networking sites between ages 18 and 29 report having received "any candidate or campaign information" through these networked information channels (Smith & Rainie, 2008). We do not provide this example to imply that scientists and science communicators should behave like corporations pushing their products, but rather to highlight that scientists and science communicators who desire to bolster the frequency and quality of interactions with the public about emerging technologies need to be increasingly creative, strategic, and theory-driven.

In sum, effective public communication is not a guessing game; it is a science—a science in which communication as a discipline should play a much more prominent role than it has so far. Public opinion and communication research allows us to get a very accurate picture over time of exactly what different groups in society want to know about nanotechnology and other emerging technologies, about potential implications for their daily lives, about what their concerns are, and who they are looking to for answers. Relying on empirical research to understand and communicate strategically with different publics will therefore be a key mission of the theme. This will address at least three of the problems raised earlier. (a) It will provide us with a systematic understanding of how the public thinks about new technologies, what they know, and what the channels are to connect with them. (b) It will provide us with insights into the social-psychological processes that determine how the public forms attitudes, based on information, visual cues, popular representations of science, etc. (c) These insights from basic research will also help us develop, test, and assess innovative ways of reaching and engaging various publics through different art forms, communication campaigns, or informal outreach.

References

Allum, N., Sturgis, P., Tabourazi, D., & Brunton-Smith, I. (2008). Science knowledge and attitudes across cultures: A meta-analysis. *Public Understanding of Science, 17*(1), 35–54.

Anderson, A., Petersen, A., Wilkinson, C., & Allan, S. (2009). *Nanotechnology, risk and communication.* London: Macmillan.

Bainbridge, W. S. (2002). Public attitudes toward nanotechnology. *Journal of Nanoparticle Research, 4*(6), 561–570.

Batt, C. A. (2008). Thinking small is not easy. *Nature Nanotechnology, 3*(3), 121–122.

Bell, L. (2009). Engaging the public in public policy: How far should museums go? *Museums & Social Issues, 4*(1), 21–36.

Beringer, J. E. (1999). Cautionary tale on safety of GM crops. *Nature, 399*(6735), 405–405.

Berube, D. M. (2008). Rhetorical gamesmanship in the nano debates over sunscreens and nanoparticles. *Journal of Nanoparticle Research, 10*, 23–37.

Brossard, D., Lewenstein, B. V., & Bonney, R. (2005). Scientific knowledge and attitude change: The impact of a citizen science project. *International Journal of Science Education, 27*(9), 1099–1121.

Brossard, D., & Nisbet, M. C. (2007). Deference to scientific authority among a low information public: Understanding U.S. opinion on agricultural biotechnology. *International Journal of Public Opinion Research, 19*(1), 24–52.

Brossard, D., Scheufele, D. A., Kim, E., & Lewenstein, B. V. (2009). Religiosity as a perceptual filter: Examining processes of opinion formation about nanotechnology. *Public Understanding of Science, 18*(5), 546–558.

Bryant, J., & Miron, D. (2004). Theory and research in mass communication. *Journal of Communication, 54*(4), 662–704.

Burri, R. V., & Bellucci, S. (2008). Public perception of nanotechnology. [Editorial Material]. *Journal of Nanoparticle Research, 10*(3), 387–391.

Cacciatore, M. A., Scheufele, D. A., & Corley, E. A. (in press). From enabling technology to applications: The evolution of risk perceptions about nanotechnology. *Public Understanding of Science.*

Cicerone, R. J. (2007). Celebrating and rethinking science communication. *In Focus, 6*(3), 3.

Cobb, M. D. (2005). Framing effects on public opinion about nanotechnology. *Science Communication, 27*(2), 221–239.

Cobb, M. D., & Macoubrie, J. (2004). Public perceptions about nanotechnology: Risks, benefits and trust. *Journal of Nanoparticle Research, 6*(4), 395–405.

Committee on Public Understanding of Engineering Messages. (2008). *Changing the conversation: Messages for improving public understanding of engineering.* Washington, DC: The National Academies Press.

Corley, E. A., & Scheufele, D. A. (2010). Outreach gone wrong? When we talk nano to the public, we are leaving behind key audiences. *The Scientist, 24*(1), 22.

Corley, E. A., Scheufele, D. A., & Hu, Q. (2009). Of risks and regulations: How leading U.S. nanoscientists form policy stances about nanotechnology. *Journal of Nanoparticle Research, 11*(7), 1573–1585. doi:10.1007/s11051-009-9671-5

Dahlstrom, M. F., & Scheufele, D. A. (in press). Prime time risks: A cultivation look at effects of channel diversity and exposure purpose on environmental risk perceptions. *Environmental Communication.*

Dean, C. (2008, December 10). Panel criticizes U.S. effort on nanomaterial risks. *New York Times.* Retrieved December 10, 2008, from http://www.nytimes.com/2008/12/11/science/11nano.html

Delborne, J. A. (2005). *Pathways of scientific dissent in agricultural biotechnology.* (Unpublished doctoral dissertation). University of California, Berkeley.

Downs, A. (1972). Up and down with ecology—the "issue-attention cycle." *Public Interest* (28), 38–50.

Dudo, A., Brossard, D., Shanahan, J., Scheufele, D. A., Morgan, M., & Signorielli, N. (2009, August). *Science on television in the 21st century: Recent trends in portrayals and their contributions to public attitudes toward science.* Paper presented at the annual convention of the Association for Education in Journalism & Mass Communication, Boston, MA.

Dudo, A., Dunwoody, S., & Scheufele, D. A. (2009, August). *The emergence of nano news: Tracking thematic trends and changes in media coverage of nanotechnology.* Paper presented at the annual convention of the Association for Education in Journalism & Mass Communication, Boston, MA.

Dunwoody, S., Brossard, D., & Dudo, A. (2009). Socialization or rewards? Predicting U.S. scientist-media interactions. *Journalism & Mass Communication Quarterly, 86*(2), 299–314.

Dunwoody, S., & Scott, B. T. (1982). Scientists as mass media sources. *Journalism Quarterly, 59*(1), 52–59.

Entman, R. M. (1993). Framing: Toward clarification of a fractured paradigm. *Journal of Communication, 43,* 51–58.

Eveland, W. P., & Scheufele, D. A. (2000). Connecting news media use with gaps in knowledge and participation. *Political Communication, 17*(3), 215–237.

Fackelmann, K. (1999, May 20). Engineered corn kills butterflies, study says. *USA Today,* p. 1A.

Fedoroff, N. V., & Brown, N. M. (2004). *Mendel in the kitchen: A scientist's view of genetically modified food.* Washington, DC: National Academies Press/Joseph Henry Press.

Friedman, S. M., & Egolf, B. P. (2005). Nanotechnology: Risks and the media. *IEEE Technology & Society Magazine, 24,* 5–11.

Friedman, S. M., & Egolf, B. P. (2007). *Changing patterns of mass media coverage of nanotechnology risks.* Paper presented at the Project on Emerging Nanotechnologies, Woodrow Wilson Center for International Scholars, Washington, DC.

Funkhouser, G. R. (1973). The issues of the sixties: An exploratory study in the dynamics of public opinion. *Public Opinion Quarterly, 37*(1), 62–75.

Gans, H. J. (1983). News Media, News Policy, and Democracy—Research for the Future. *Journal of Communication, 33*(3), 174–184.

Gaskell, G., Ten Eyck, T., Jackson, J., & Veltri, G. (2005). Imagining nanotechnology: Cultural support for technological innovation in Europe and the United States. *Public Understanding of Science, 14*(1), 81–90.

Gerbner, G. (1987). Science on television - How it affects public conceptions. *Issues in Science and Technology, 3*(3), 109–115.

Gerbner, G., & Gross, L. (1974). System of cultural indicators. *Public Opinion Quarterly, 38*, 460–461.

Gerbner, G., Gross, L. P., Morgan, M., & Signorielli, N. (1981). Scientists on the TV screen. *Culture and Society, 42*, 51–54.

Gitlin, T. (1980). *The whole world is watching: Mass media in the making & unmaking of the new left*. Berkeley, CA: University of California Press.

Goffman, E. (1974). *Frame analysis: An essay on the organization of experience*. New York: Harper & Row.

Gorss, J., & Lewenstein, B. (2005). *The salience of small: Nanotechnology coverage in the American press, 1986–2004*. Paper presented at the annual International Communication Association conference, New York, NY.

Gregory, O. (2009). Artificial life: Top five examples from film and fiction. *The Telegraph*. Retrieved March 28, 2009, from http://www.telegraph.co.uk/science-andtechnology/science/4986533/Artificial-life-top-five-examples-from-film-and-fiction.html

Guston, D. H., & Sarewitz, D. (2002). Real-time technology assessment. *Technology in Society, 24*(1-2), 93–109.

Ham, B. (2007). Science has a "serious marketing problem," says Google founder Larry Page. AAAs 2007 Annual Meeting News Blog. Retrieved February 17, 2007, from http://www.aaas.org/news/releases/2007_ann_mtg/127.shtml

Ho, S. S., Brossard, D., & Scheufele, D. A. (2008). Effects of value predispositions, mass media use, and knowledge on public attitudes toward embryonic stem cell research. *International Journal of Public Opinion Research, 20*(2), 171–192.

Holland, E. (2009). Research, not relations: Why scientists should leave communications to the pros. *Columbia Journalism Review*. Retrieved September 21, 2009, from http://www.cjr.org/the_observatory/research_not_relations.php.

Kahan, D. M., Braman, D., Slovic, P., Gastil, J., & Cohen, G. (2009). Cultural cognition of the risks and benefits of nanotechnology. *Nature Nanotechnology, 4*(2), 87–90.

Kahan, D. M., Slovic, P., Braman, D., Gastil, J., Cohen, G., & Kysar, D. (2008). *Biased assimilation, polarization, and cultural credibility: An experimental study of nanotechnology risk perceptions*. Project on Emerging Nanotechnologies Research [Brief No. 3]. Washinton, DC: Woodrow Wilson Center for Scholars and The Pew Charitable Trusts.

Kahneman, D. (2003). Maps of bounded rationality: A perspective on intuitive judgment and choice. In T. Frängsmyr (Ed.), *Les Prix Nobel: The Nobel Prizes 2002* (pp. 449–489). Stockholm, Sweden: Nobel Foundation.

Keller, E., & Berry, J. (2003). *The influentials*. New York: The Free Press.

Khushf, G. (2006). An ethic for enhancing human performance through integrative technologies. In W. S. Bainbridge & M. C. Roco (Eds.), *Managing nano-bio-info-cogno innovations: Converging technologies in society* (pp. 255–278). Dordrecht, The Netherlands: Springer.

Kirby, D. A. (2003). Science consultants, fictional films, and scientific practice. *Social Studies of Science, 33*(2), 231–268.

Kohut, A., Keeter, S., Doherty, C., & Dimock, M. (2009). Scientific achievements less prominent than a decade ago: Public praises science; scientists fault public, media.

The Pew Research Center For The People & The Press. Retrieved July 14, 2009, from http://pewresearch.org/pubs/1276/science-survey

Krieghbaum, H. (1967). *Science and the mass media.* New York: New York University Press.

Laing, A. (2005). A report on Canadian and American news media coverage of nanotechnology issues. Retrieved March, 30, from http://www.nanotechproject. org/events/archive/new_page/

Lazarsfeld, P. M., Berelson, B. R., & Gaudet, H. (1948). *The people's choice: How the voter makes up his mind in a presidential campaign* (2nd ed.). New York: Duell, Sloan & Pearce.

Lee, C. J., & Scheufele, D. A. (2006). The influence of knowledge and deference toward scientific authority: A media effects model for public attitudes toward nanotechnology. *Journalism & Mass Communication Quarterly, 83*(4), 819–834.

Lee, C. J., Scheufele, D. A., & Lewenstein, B. V. (2005). Public attitudes toward emerging technologies—Examining the interactive effects of cognitions and affect on public attitudes toward nanotechnology. *Science Communication, 27*(2), 240–267.

Lippmann, W. (1922/1997). *Public opinion.* New York: Simon & Schuster.

Losey, J. E., Rayor, L. S., & Carter, M. E. (1999). Transgenic pollen harms monarch larvae. *Nature, 399*(6733), 214–214.

Maynard, A. D., Aitken, R. J., Butz, T., Colvin, V., Donaldson, K., Oberdörster, G., et al. (2006). Safe handling of nanotechnology. *Nature, 444*(7117), 267–269.

McQuail, D. (2005). *Mass communication theory* (5th ed.). London: Sage.

Mervis, J. (2009). An inside/outside view of U.S. science. *Science, 325*(5937), 132–133.

Miller, J. D. (1992). Toward a scientific understanding of the public understanding of science and technology. *Public Understanding of Science, 1*(1), 23–26.

National Nanotechnology Initiative. (2008). FY 2009 budget & highlights. Retrieved March 28, 2009, from http://www.nano.gov/NNI_FY09_budget_summary.pdf

National Science Board. (2008). Science and Engineering Indicators 2008 (Chapter 7). *National Science Foundation.* Retrieved January 21, 2008, from http://www.nsf. gov/statistics/seind08/

National Science Board. (2010). Science and Engineering Indicators 2010 (Chapter 7). *National Science Foundation.* Retrieved February 16, 2010, from http://www.nsf. gov/statistics/seind10/

Neuman, W. R. (1981). Differentiation and integration: Two dimensions of political thinking. *The American Journal of Sociology, 86*(6), 1236–1268.

Neuman, W. R., Just, M. R., & Crigler, A. N. (1992). *Common knowledge: News and the construction of political meaning.* Chicago: University of Chicago Press.

Nisbet, M. C., Brossard, D., & Kroepsch, A. (2003). Framing science — The stem cell controversy in an age of press/politics. *Harvard International Journal of Press-Politics, 8*(2), 36–70.

Nisbet, M. C., & Huge, M. (2006). Attention cycles and frames in the plant biotechnology debate: Managing power and participation through the press/policy connection. *The Harvard International Journal of Press/Politics, 11*(2), 3–40.

Nisbet, M. C., & Scheufele, D. A. (2007). The future of public engagement. *The Scientist, 21*(10), 38–44.

Nisbet, M. C., Scheufele, D. A., Shanahan, J., Moy, P., Brossard, D., & Lewenstein, B. V. (2002). Knowledge, reservations, or promise? A media effects model for public perceptions of science and technology. *Communication Research, 29*(5), 584–608.

Noelle-Neumann, E. (1973). Return to the concept of powerful mass media. *Studies in Broadcasting, 9*, 67–112.

Noelle-Neumann, E. (1984). *The spiral of silence: Public opinion, our social skin.* Chicago: University of Chicago Press.

Ogilvy, D. (1963). *Confessions of an advertising man.* New York: Ballantine Books.

Olson, R. (2009). *Don't be such a scientist: Talking substance in an age of style.* Washington, DC: Island Press.

Pearson, T. D. (2006). The ethics of nanotechnology: A Lutheran reflection. *Journal of Lutheran Ethics, 6*(2). Retrieved from http://archive.elca.org/ScriptLib/dcs/jle/article.asp?aid=629

Peter D. Hart Research Associates. (2006). Public awareness of nano grows — majority remain unaware. *The Woodrow Wilson International Center for Scholars Project on Emerging Nanotechnologies.* Retrieved October 3, 2006, from http://www.nanotechproject.org/78/public-awareness-of-nano-grows-but-majority-unaware

Peter D. Hart Research Associates. (2007). Awareness of and attitudes toward nanotechnology and federal regulatory agencies. Retrieved October 10, 2007, from http://www.nanotechproject.org/138/9252007-poll-reveals-public-awareness-of-nanotech-stuck-at-low-level

Peters, H. P., Brossard, D., de Cheveigné, S., Dunwoody, S., Kallfass, M., Miller, S., et al. (2008). Science communication: Interactions with the mass media. *Science, 321*(5886), 204–205.

Pidgeon, N., Harthorn, B. H., Bryant, K., & Rogers-Hayden, T. (2009). Deliberating the risks of nanotechnologies for energy and health applications in the United States and United Kingdom. *Nature Nanotechnology, 4*(2), 95–98.

Poland, C. A., Duffin, R., Kinloch, I., Maynard, A., Wallace, W. A. H., Seaton, A., et al. (2008). Carbon nanotubes introduced into the abdominal cavity of mice show asbestos-like pathogenicity in a pilot study. *Nature Nanotechnology, 3*(7), 423–428.

Price, V., & Tewksbury, D. (1997). News values and public opinion: A theoretical account of media priming and framing. In G. A. Barett & F. J. Boster (Eds.), *Progress in communication sciences: Advances in persuasion* (Vol. 13, pp. 173–212). Greenwich, CT: Ablex.

Priest, S. H. (2008). Biotechnology, nanotechnology, media, and public opinion. In K. David & P. B. Thompson (Eds.), *What can nanotechnology learn from biotechnology? Social and ethical lessons for nanoscience from the debate over agrifood biotechnology and GMOs* (pp. 221–234). Burlington, MA: Elsevier.

Roco, M. C., & Bainbridge, W. S. (2003). *Converging technologies for improving human performance.* Dordrecht, The Netherlands: Kluwer.

Rodgers, P. (2007). A little knowledge. *Nature Nanotechnology, 2*(12), 731.

Rodgers, P. (2009). Getting to know the public. *Nature Nanotechnology, 4*(2), 71.

Scheufele, D. A. (1999). Framing as a theory of media effects. *Journal of Communication, 49*(1), 103–122.

Scheufele, D. A. (2006). Messages and heuristics: How audiences form attitudes about emerging technologies. In J. Turney (Ed.), *Engaging science: Thoughts, deeds, analysis and action* (pp. 20–25). London: The Wellcome Trust.

Scheufele, D. A. (2007). Nano does not have a marketing problem — yet. *Nano Today, 2*(5), 48.

Scheufele, D. A., Brossard, D., Dunwoody, S., Corley, E. A., Guston, D. H., & Peters, H. P. (2009). Are scientists really out of touch? *The Scientist.* Retrieved from http://www.the-scientist.com/news/display/55875/

Scheufele, D. A., Corley, E. A., Dunwoody, S., Shih, T.-J., Hillback, E., & Guston, D. H. (2007). Scientists worry about some risks more than the public. *Nature Nanotechnology, 2*(12), 732–734.

Scheufele, D. A., Corley, E. A., Shih, T.-J., Dalrymple, K. E., & Ho, S. S. (2009). Religious beliefs and public attitudes to nanotechnology in Europe and the US. *Nature Nanotechnology, 4*(2), 91–94.

Scheufele, D. A., & Lewenstein, B. V. (2005). The public and nanotechnology: How citizens make sense of emerging technologies. *Journal of Nanoparticle Research, 7*(6), 659–667.

Scheufele, D. A., & Tewksbury, D. (2007). Framing, agenda setting, and priming: The evolution of three media effects models. *Journal of Communication, 57*(1), 9–20.

Schütz, H., & Wiedemann, P. M. (2008). Framing effects on risk perception of nanotechnology. *Public Understanding of Science, 17*(3), 369–379.

Schweitzer, S. (2005, October 24). Building a buzz on campus. *The Boston Globe,* p. A1.

Shamos, M. H. (1995). *The myth of scientific literacy.* New Brunswick, NJ: Rutgers University Press.

Shanahan, J. E., & Morgan, M. (1999). *Television and its viewers: Cultivation theory and research.* New York: Cambridge University Press.

Shelton, A. M., & Roush, R. T. (1999). False reports and the ears of men. *Nature Biotechnology, 17*(9), 832–832.

Shoemaker, P. J., & Reese, S. D. (1996). *Mediating the message: Theories of influences on mass media content* (2nd ed.). White Plains, NY: Longman.

Siegrist, M., Cousin, M.-E., Kastenholz, H., & Wiek, A. (2007). Public acceptance of nanotechnology foods and food packaging: The influence of affect and trust. *Appetite, 49*(2), 459–466.

Siegrist, M., Keller, C., Kastenholz, H., Frey, S., & Wiek, A. (2007). Laypeople's and experts' perception of nanotechnology hazards. *Risk Analysis, 27*(1), 59–69.

Siegrist, M., Wiek, A., Helland, A., & Kastenholz, H. (2007). Risks and nanotechnology: The public is more concerned than experts and industry. *Nature Nanotechnology, 2*(2).

Skapinker, M. (2007, October 29). Scientists must learn to talk to the media. *Financial Times,* p. 11.

Smith, A., & Rainie, L. (2008). The Internet and the 2008 election. *Pew Internet & American Life Project.* Retrieved June 16, 2008, from http://www.pewinternet.org/PPF/r/252/report_display.asp

Stephens, L. F. (2005). News narratives about nano S&T in major US and non-US newspapers. *Science Communication, 27*(2), 175–199.

Tewksbury, D., & Scheufele, D. A. (2009). News framing theory and research. In J. Bryant & M. B. Oliver (Eds.), *Media effects: Advances in theory and research* (3rd ed., pp. 17–33). Hillsdale, NJ: Erlbaum.

The Pew Research Center For The People & The Press. (2008). Audience segments in a changing news environment: Key news audiences new blend online and traditional sources. Retrieved August 17, 2008, from http://people-press.org/reports/pdf/444.pdf

Tichenor, P. J., Donohue, G. A., & Olien, C. N. (1970). Mass media flow and differential growth in knowledge. *Public Opinion Quarterly, 34*(2), 159–170.

Tuchman, G. (1978). *Making news: A study in the construction of reality.* New York: The Free Press.

Weimann, G. (1994). *The influentials: People who influence people.* New York: State University of New York Press.

Weiss, R. (1999, May 20). Biotech vs. 'Bambi' of insects? Gene-altered corn may kill Monarchs. *Washinton Post,* p. A3.

Weiss, R. (2006, April 6). Nanotech product recalled in Germany. *Washington Post,* p. A2.

Whitmarsh, L. (2009). What's in a name? Commonalities and differences in public understanding of "climate change" and "global warming." *Public Understanding of Science, 18*(4), 401–420.

Wilkes, M. S., & Kravitz, R. L. (1992). Medical researchers and the media. Attitudes toward public dissemination of research. *Journal of the American Medical Association, 268*(8), 999–1003.

Wilkinson, C., Allan, S., Anderson, A., & Petersen, A. (2007). From uncertainty to risk?: Scientific and news media portrayals of nanoparticle safety. *Health Risk & Society, 9*(2), 145–157.

Wood, S., Jones, R., & Geldart, A. (2007). Nanotechnology, from the science to the social: The social, ethical, and economic aspects of the debate. Swindon: Economic and Social Research Council. Retrieved August 14, 2009, from http://www.esrcsocietytoday.ac.uk/ESRCInfoCentre/Images/ESRC_Nano07_tcm6-18918.pdf

CHAPTER CONTENTS

7 Public Deliberation on Policy Issues
Normative Stipulations and Practical Resolutions

Nurit Guttman

Tel Aviv University

Public deliberation forums on policy issues are increasingly employed as a means to engage citizens in discussions on a wide range of public policy issues that traditionally were entrusted to experts. Philosophically these forums draw on deliberative democracy theory, but their application can be found in diverse social and organizational contexts. This chapter summarizes concerns regarding limitations and pitfalls that can characterize public deliberation and discusses how the broad normative conditions for a democratic public deliberation have been translated to actual procedures in various public deliberation initiatives. Several types of deliberation methods and examples on topics such as planning, nanotechnology, and budgets are presented to illustrate how different public deliberation initiatives aimed to realize these stipulations. The chapter concludes with theoretical and pragmatic challenges.

Introduction

Across the globe, government agencies and not-for-profit organizations convene civic forums in which citizens deliberate public policy issues. These forums, referred to by some as "mini-publics" (e.g., Fung, 2003; Skorupinski, Baranzke, Ingensiep, & Meinhardt, 2007), commonly take place outside the formal political process but are meant to influence it, if indirectly, by introducing the public's views into the policy arena and broadening public discourse on the topic (Delli Carpini, Lomax, Cook, & Jacobs, 2004). Participants in these forums are asked to deliberate on issues that traditionally have been entrusted to experts, such as municipal budgets, new biomedical technologies, environmental regulations, transportation, energy policy, genetically modified foods, and healthcare reform. Often these issues are controversial or can be characterized as wicked social problems (Rittel & Webber, 1973). The methods employed in the different forums are varied; some are implemented on a grand scale, involving sophisticated communication technologies and hundreds or even thousands of people assembled for a long weekend, while other forums may consist of small groups of about 15 to 20 people that meet over a period of several months, or of groups that convene over a period of several days simultaneously in different locations. The various types of public deliberation forums are predicated on the shared belief that citizens have the right and capacity to engage in a democratic process that results in policy recommendations, and that this process benefits society and policy decision making (Gutmann & Thompson, 1996; Abelson et al., 2003).

At the heart of these public deliberation forums are conversations among the participants. Whereas conversation among citizens with different views has been hailed as an essential component of democracy (Wyatt, Katz, & Kim, 2000), proponents of public deliberation share the assumption that regular conversations among citizens are not sufficient for reaching understandings or assessing policy proposals (Fishkin, 1991; Gastil & Levine, 2005; Webler, 1995). Further, scholars caution that the goal of realizing democratic ideals through public deliberation forums can be undermined by the actual practice of these forums and by certain dominant conversation modes that may emerge (Abelson et al., 2003; Sanders, 1997; Young, 1996). In particular, critics are concerned about participants' capacities to discuss issues for which they possess no technical knowledge, to listen to others' views, or to refrain from promoting their own interests (Abeslon et al., 2003). In addition, critics maintain that their practices may not meet egalitarian ideals (Sanders, 1997). The development of methods to meet democratic ideals in public deliberation forums and addressing unintended consequences, therefore, is inundated with theoretical and pragmatic challenges. Further, advances in the uses of communication technologies present new challenges and opportunities for public deliberations that employ modes other than face-to-face interactions (Gastil, 2000; Hass, 2004).

Existing theories of public deliberation incorporate a broad normative framework for the implementation of public deliberation (Bohman, 1996; Cohen, 1997), but how to actually implement these normative stipulations has been left to the ingenuity of practice-oriented scholars and practitioners (Abelson et al., 2003; Buttom & Mattson, 1999; Delli Carpini et al., 2004; Fung, 2003). Consequently, various deliberative models have been developed and multiple types of deliberative forums have emerged. The design of these forums includes a combination of features typically chosen to help create a venue that is egalitarian, reflective, and that enables learning and careful examination of policy issues (Burkhalter, Gastil, & Kelshaw, 2002; Gastil, 2000; Yankelovich, 1991).

This chapter has three main purposes: (a) to examine how the broad normative goals of public deliberation delineated by scholars have been articulated as more specific normative conditions, (b) to explore how these have been translated to actual procedures employed by various public deliberation initiatives, and (c) to identify challenges to theory and practice that emerge from these types of applications. This chapter is organized in four sections. First, it presents a brief overview of the philosophical rationale for deliberative public discussions and of definitions of deliberation. Second, it summarizes concerns regarding the limitations and pitfalls that can characterize public deliberation initiatives on policy issues and normative conditions proposed by theorists and practical applications to address them. Third, it offers examples of how different types of public deliberation initiatives have aimed to address these conditions. Fourth, it concludes with several propositions regarding new theoretical and pragmatic challenges.

Philosophical and Theoretical Rationales for Public Deliberation

Normative and philosophical arguments for engaging citizens in a discussion for the purpose of influencing public policy draw on broad democratic ideals of liberty, equality, and the right of citizens to influence decisions that affect their lives (Buttom & Mattson, 1999). The normative justification for public deliberation draws on these broad ideals but is also typically associated with conceptions of deliberative democracy. Chambers (2003) characterizes deliberative democratic theory as a normative theory that proposes ways in which we can enhance democracy and criticize institutions that do not live up to democratic normative standards. She characterizes it as a talk-centric (rather than voting-centric) democratic theory that turns away from liberal individualist or economic understandings of democracy and toward a view anchored in conceptions of accountability and discussion. Although visions of deliberative democracy differ, they typically share an emphasis on discussions among citizens that aim to produce reasonable, well-informed opinions, which participants are willing to revise—in light of these discussions—as a means to advance public policy and increase accountability (Chambers, 2003). Chambers also proposes that currently there is a general endorsement of deliberation outside discussions of deliberative democracy per se, and that also constitutional democracy is increasingly conceived as entailing deliberation in some fundamental way. Similarly, Buttom and Mattson (1999) explain that in a representative democracy some level of citizen deliberation is viewed as important because citizens need to make representatives aware of their interests and concerns. Dryzek (2000) adds that public deliberations actually take place mostly in forums linked to liberal political institutions because deliberative democracy is typically limited to a small number of occasions in which wideranging popular deliberation can occur. In practice, public deliberation forums on policy issues take place in a multitude of settings (Fung, 2003). Therefore, the challenge of developing theory and practice regarding conditions for public deliberation is not confined to the debate on deliberative democracy. It can have relevance to the formation of forums in a variety of contexts created for the purpose of engaging people in discussion pertaining to a wide spectrum of policy-related issues.

Drawing on the normative assumptions of democratic processes (Bohman, 1996; Bracci, 2001; Burkhalter et al., 2002; Price, Cappella, & Nir, 2002), public deliberation can be defined as a process with the following features:

- it typically begins with a problematic situation that elicits different value considerations and dilemmas;
- participants devote time to learn about the issues at hand;

- participants must engage in careful problem analysis and prioritization of values;
- participants engage in attentive listening and consider available data and alternative points of views; and
- participants are accorded adequate and equitable speaking opportunities in a safe dialogical space, in which they can champion and challenge a range of alternative viewpoints.

These features distinguish public deliberation initiatives from other types of discussions on social issues that may take place among citizens, such as debates, arguments, informal meetings, or even typical "town hall" meetings that usually do not include a learning and dialogical process. Thus, even when deliberative public initiatives are limited by various institutional or geographical constraints, public deliberation remains a unique type of public discussion, rooted in deliberative democratic theory.

For both normative and pragmatic reasons, public deliberation advocates believe it is essential to engage citizens in the deliberation of public policy issues. Discussions on public policy, they maintain, should not be left only to specialized, technically informed elites or to elected representatives (Barber, 1984; Fiorino, 1990; Yankelovich, 1991). Public deliberative consultation forums are viewed as a new wave in policy-making theory that departs from what critical theorists refer to as "instrumental rationality" of policy making, and makes progress toward a "communicative turn" in the relationship between citizens and decision makers (Forester, 1989). As Chambers (2003) notes, there is a wide endorsement of deliberation in some form or other; however, its rising appeal has also attracted criticisms and concerns. The next sections present major arguments in favor of public deliberation followed by criticisms and concerns.

Arguments in Favor of Public Deliberation Forums on Policy Issues

In one of the earlier writings on the rationale and practice of consulting the public on policy issue from the perspective of practitioners, Daniel Fiorino (1990), a director at the U.S. Environmental Protection Agency, outlined three main types of arguments in support of public deliberation on policy issues: (a) a substantive argument, i.e., that non-experts' views may be as sound than those of experts because they can see problems, issues and solutions that experts may miss, they have a sensitivity to social and political values that experts' models often do not acknowledge, and they may have a better capacity than experts for accommodating uncertainty; (b) a normative argument, i.e., drawing on democratic ideals that to be a citizen is to be able to participate in decisions that affect oneself and one's community; and (c) an instrumental argument, i.e., that citizens' participation on policy decisions regarding controversial and difficult decisions makes policy decisions more legitimate to the public.

Beyond the benefits specified by Fiorino (1990), scholars have noted additional benefits to the practice of public deliberation forums. Participation in public deliberation can serve to develop participants' capacities as citizens, which in turn, can contribute to the normative and substantive benefits of public deliberation on policy issues (Barber, 1984; Bohman, 1996; Fishkin, 1991; Forester, 1999; Gastil & Dillard, 1999; Mansbridge, 1999; Milner, 2002). Engaging citizens in deliberations is believed to benefit individuals by providing them with an opportunity to develop and express their views, learn about the positions of others, identify shared concerns and preferences, and come to understand and reach judgments about matters of public concern. These individual benefits, in turn, benefit society. Citing C. Wright Mills, scholars maintain that one of the requirements of democracy is to have articulate and knowledgeable publics; participation in deliberative forums can serve this purpose (Buttom, & Mattso, 1999).

Another benefit attributed to public deliberation forums is providing venues in which citizens acquire knowledge regarding policy options and express their preferences in a civic process beyond the act of voting (Milner, 2002). Some theorists view participation in public deliberation initiatives as a necessary condition for individuals to develop morally as citizens, arguing that the public deliberation experience enables citizens to become an articulate and knowledgeable public, helps create a greater sense of political efficacy, and enhances participants' civic literacy by enabling them to gain more in-depth knowledge of policy issues. Participation in deliberation is believed to increase people's motivation to participate in the political process, help predispose them to perceive a potential for common ground in future encounters, encourage a collective mode of thinking, and enhance participants' sense of altruism (Barber, 1984; Bohman, 1996; Fishkin, 1991; Forester, 1999; Gastil & Dillard, 1999; Mansbridge, 1999; Milner, 2002). Further, scholars note that an important benefit of public deliberation is that participants are exposed to a range of perspectives. This can enable them not only to change their mind, but also to broaden their range of reasons or to deepen their own articulation of their support for particular views as they relate to core values (Cappella et al., 2002; Gastil & Dillard, 1999; Price et al., 2002).

An additional potential benefit concerns the topics raised in the discussion. Scholars propose that public deliberations can elicit discussions pertaining to divisions in society that typically do not occur because many citizens are not part of regular political discussions and do not have the opportunity to meet people who are outside their social milieu (Benhabib, 1992; Gutmann & Thompson, 1996). Gutmann and Thompson (1996) add that although public deliberation cannot make incompatible values compatible, it can help participants recognize the moral merit in opponents' claims and help them distinguish between disagreements that arise from genuinely incompatible values and those that are more resolvable than they first appear.

Participation in public deliberation is also viewed as having an educative benefit, by helping people learn about issues that policy makers grapple with.

This benefit can be viewed as a normative benefit that is related to the development of participants as citizens. From the perspective of policy makers it could also be viewed as an instrumental benefit because it refers to citizens gaining a better understanding of the policy issues and of policy making, According to this view, public deliberations' main contribution would be to create a process through which citizens learn about the complexity of policy issues and the need to make trade-offs and compromises (Buttom & Mattson, 1999). This kind of learning is likely to lead to participants' enhanced trust in political institutions, which some scholars view as an important benefit, in an era in which people have relatively little faith in government (Cooke, 2000; Fung, 2003).

To briefly summarize, advocates of public deliberative forums argue that deliberation produces informed policy decisions that are more legitimate, fairer, potentially wiser, and more publicly oriented. The process is also believed to contribute to improving participants' civic skills and to their sense of political self-efficacy. Notwithstanding general support for public deliberation, even its proponents raise both theoretical and pragmatic concerns, which present challenges to the realization of public deliberation. The next section summarizes four types of major concerns regarding potential limitations and pitfalls of public deliberation initiatives on policy issues and normative conditions proposed by theorists, and practical applications to address them.

Normative Concerns, Conceptual Conditions, and Pragmatic Procedures to Realize Democratic Ideals of Public Deliberation

Criticisms regarding public deliberation mainly concern whether the deliberation process can be free of explicit and implicit forms of coercion or of power relations in society, and whether the citizen-participants can discuss complex policy issues. Further, critics are concerned whether the deliberation process can indeed be egalitarian and whether it is likely to exclude members of interest groups, who are the very actors in democratic societies, and whose passion, interests, and knowledge are central to democratic life (Barnes, 2005; Hendriks, 2006; Sanders, 1997; Young; 1996, 2001). These broad concerns have been categorized as related to issues of (a) power, (b) fairness, (c) competence, and (d) the discursive process (Abelson et al., 2003; Webler, 1995; Webler & Tuler, 2002; Webler, Tuler, & Kreuger, 2001).

Concerns and Conditions Regarding Power

Perhaps the most prominent concern in public deliberation is that participation and communication should be free from coercion. Thus, public deliberation forums need to create a space for discussion in which participants will feel that they are free from coercion, and can express views that may not be popular or ask questions about assertions made by others. Yet, as noted in the critiques of public deliberation, this outcome may not be fully achievable, because, as underscored by critical theorists, no situation can be completely "free of power" (Forester, 1989).

Drawing on philosophical and democratic ideals, scholars have outlined several major stipulations for egalitarian and non-coercive deliberative processes. Most notably Habermas (1989, 1992) articulated a vision of discursive norms that he proposed would ensure that none of the participants in a democratic discourse would be privileged due to power relations. These norms can be found in what he referred to as the "the ideal speech situation" and can be summarized briefly as: the right of anyone affected by results of the discourse to have an equal opportunity to attend and participate in it; the right of every participant to have an equal opportunity to make different types of claims regarding the issue that pertain to facts, norms, etc.; the right of each person to have an equal opportunity to challenge claims made by others; and the opportunity to influence the decision-making process (Bohman, 1996; Webler, 1995). For the purpose of articulating conditions for deliberation that address issues of power, six more specific concerns are noted. These concerns relate to the choice, framing and mode of discussion of the issues, the tendency of lay participants to defer to the experts, the potential of forums to merely serve as a "fig leaf" for those in power, the co-optation of participants' views, and not challenging the status quo.

Influencing the Agenda and Modes of Discussion.   The topic of most pubic deliberations is chosen by sponsoring agencies or organizations. This raises concerns associated with power because participants are confined to the chosen issues and will not be able to discuss any related issues. By implication, stipulations related to power would include the conditions that participants should have a say in the topics chosen as well as in the choice of moderators and method of facilitation (e.g., Webler & Tuler, 2000). However, these conditions are not likely to be realized in most public deliberation forums because participants typically arrive after the topics and the moderators were selected and they are unlikely to have influence on the pre-determined agenda and facilitation method. Acknowledging the significance of these stipulations can have important implications because it raises the issue of the extent to which participants can control the issues, which kind of facilitation strategies may be less coercive, and should participants have say in the facilitation method. An example of participants' lack of control can be found in the case of the Health Parliament initiative in Israel, in which participants in one group were unhappy with their facilitator but the community center organizers who hired him refused to replace him, and this left them discontent with the process (Guttman, 2007).

Framing of the Issues.   Policy-related issues may be framed various ways, and the way they are framed can influence the types of solutions proposed. For example, in the case of new technologies alternative frames can refer to the issue in terms of scientific progress, economic prospect, ethical issues, a

Pandora's box, or public accountability. Each framing can influence the type of discourse and perspective taken (Besley, Kramer, Yao, & Toumey, 2008). Thus, the way the issue is framed can enable or inhibit the discussion. Further, the way the policy questions are phrased can serve to inhibit the discussion on relevant issues and to exclude alternative interpretations (Bracci, 2001; Walmsley, 2009). The critique on the way the issues are framed in public deliberation corresponds to critiques on the way questions may be phrased in public opinion polls which are used to gauge public opinion, but do not provide all possible policy alternatives (Herbst, 1991; Salmon & Glasser, 1995). Thus, a condition associated with framing is that participants need to be provided with alternative framings of the issue.

Deferring to the Experts.   A common practice in public deliberations is to invite people considered to be experts on relevant topics to explain the issues or express their views. This raises the concern that participants are likely to defer to experts' assertions (Abelson et al., 2003). Inviting people because of their presumed expertise may present them as authoritative figures, which consequently, may influence the process. This was noted by participants in a Swiss forum on genetically modified foods. They observed that referring to the professionals as "experts" could be manipulative, and they suggested it would be better to refer to them as "informants" (Skorupinski et al., 2007). Thus, the procedures of public deliberation need to include a method to show the limitations of experts' knowledge. One suggestion, made by participants, is to invite experts with different views, and have them discuss the issues among themselves, which could enable participants to see how people with knowledge on the topics challenge alternative perspectives (Skorupinski et al., 2007). Other suggestions that are implemented in some initiatives are to provide participants with training sessions that demystify the authority of experts (Davies & Burgess, 2004; Kashefi & Mort, 2004).

Serve as a 'Fig Leaf'.   A common critique is that public deliberation initiatives forums serve the agenda of decision makers by bolstering their credibility or justifying and legitimizing unpopular policies (Abelson et al., 2003; Dryzek, Goodin, Tucker, & Reber, 2009; Kashefi & Mort, 2004). Scholars list several reasons why deliberations initiated by government agencies may not necessarily serve democratic ideals: the motives of government agencies that initiate public deliberations are typically instrumental; forums could be used to gauge potential public opposition to policy proposals; forums may help government to buy time and postpone decisions on a thorny issue; forums could be used as a way to bypass troublesome "usual suspects" who show up for more standard forms of public consultation, thus excluding views of people who have a more partisan position, the forum that is set up can generate a more favorable picture of public opinion; the timing of the forum is such that it is too late in order to make a significant difference, and the discussion concerns minor aspects of the issues (Dryzek et al., 2009; Parkinson, 2004a; Pidgeon & Rogers-Hayden, 2007).

Regarding the critique that public deliberation is likely to take place when the main decisions regarding the issues have already been made, one example is the issue of new technologies. Critics maintain that the public is usually involved too late in the decision-making process in order to make a real difference, and invited to a consultation initiative only after the technology under consideration is already in development or even in the application stages. They maintain that public consultation is often used only for token purposes, or worse, as a means to manipulate public attitudes and force acceptance of certain risks (Pidgeon & Rogers-Hayden, 2007). Drawing on these critiques, conditions for deliberation should include the stipulation that the deliberation should not take place in relatively late stages of the decision-making process and should not serve as an alternative to forums that include members of interest groups.

Co-Optation. Researchers have noticed that in public deliberation on healthcare policies, once participants were exposed to the complexities of the system, they became more sympathetic to the challenges faced by decision makers who deal with these types of issues on a daily basis. They also saw that participants found that the challenges decision-makers had to face were inspiring, and they became more appreciative of the dilemmas decision makers encounter (Abelson et al, 2003; Fishkin, Luskin, & Jowell, 2000; Guttman, 2007). Whereas this may serve to enhance participants' faith in government, it raises concerns regarding the impact this may have on their views, in particular, that they may lose their lay perspective and this may result in a closer alignment of their views with those of the professionals or policy makers. Thus, participants in public deliberation forums may become co-opted to the views of decision-makers by a deliberative process that was intended to make them more informed (Guttman, 2007; Mullen, 2000). To avoid a co-optation process, public deliberation procedures need to include methods for participants to become aware of and critically appraise potential processes of co-optation that may take place as they become more informed about the challenges associated with the policy issue.

Not Challenging the Status Quo. Related to issues of power, another concern is that participants in deliberative public forums are unlikely to challenge the status quo (e.g., of the distribution of power and resources in society). This may result from the way issues are framed to begin with and also because the standards of the discourse are not likely to encourage participants from challenging the status quo, or may even prohibit them from doing so (Mansbridge, 1999; Sanders, 1997). As suggested regarding the concern about co-optation, participants would need to be provided with means to critically discuss issues concerning power and the status quo.

Concerns and Conditions Regarding Fairness and Inequity

Deliberative democracy theorists state a broad and general concern regarding the ability of public deliberation to be egalitarian because contemporary society is highly complex, diverse, and marred by social and economic inequities. This, they believe, limits the ability of deliberative forums to engage people from diverse backgrounds in an equitable way (Bohman, 1996). Webler and Tuler (2000) explain that the stipulation for fairness requires an equal distribution of opportunities to act meaningfully in all aspects of the deliberation process. This includes having an equal chance to be present in the discourse and to be able to critique the claims made by other participants.[1] These broad concerns are further elaborated regarding four specific issues: inequitable representation, privileging a rational and dispassionate mode of talk, and inequity in persuasive ability.

Achieving Equitable Representation.   Equity in representation is difficult to achieve because public forums—even those that recruit a relatively large number of people—cannot accommodate all those who would like to participate. Further, they cannot claim to be representative of members of diverse groups, in particular those from marginalized populations who may find it difficult to attend because of physical or economic reasons, or who would feel socially isolated (Levine, Fung, & Gastil, 2005). A repeated finding is that many public deliberation forums tend to have an under-representation of people from lower income populations or minorities (e.g., Einsiedel, 2002). Organizers of public deliberation forums have tried to meet the challenge of representation in numerous ways. One common approach is the use of statistical sampling methods. Another is to recruit participants through community outreach activities by local organizations, in order to reach people who typically do not attend public meetings and are outside the political process. Various procedures such as compensation for work days or child care, and providing transportation, are also used to encourage the participation of low-income participants. In one forum, a participant from a minority group who was selected through a random sample said he would agree to participate if his nephew could participate as well, and his request was accepted. This was part of the approach to encourage the participation of minorities and individuals from economically disadvantaged populations (Guttman et al., 2008).

Avoiding Privileging a Rational and Dispassionate Mode of Talk.   Another stipulation related to fairness and equity is that people should have equitable opportunities to contribute to the discussion, to introduce any assertion they believe is relevant from their point of view, and to express their views (Webler & Tuler, 2000). A critique related to this stipulation and to power differentials among participants concerns the mode of talk expected to take place in public deliberations. People's views are likely to be respected only if they adhere to talk that is considered rational, contained, and oriented to a shared problem. Thus, a major criticism and concern regarding public deliberations is the value placed on a rational and dispassionate mode of discourse, which is perceived as legitimate and preferable. Though personal stories and impassioned accounts inevitably emerge in deliberative forums' discussions, the views expressed in these modes may be discredited. Since these are often modes preferred by people from minority, new immigrant, or elderly populations, their views and credibility may be diminished, and equity in the deliberative process may be undermined, because of the devaluation of modes of expression of people from minority and other marginalized populations (Barnes, 2005; Black, 2009; Gastil, Reedy, Braman, & Kahan, 2008; Ryfe, 2006; Young, 1996). Another criticism associated with the focus on rational arguments is that emotional arguments can be devalued as well, and their importance in reasoning will be obscured (Nussbaum, 1995). A related critique is that a deliberative discourse that emphasizes rationality and "the better argument" can serve to delegitimize or "tame" the expression of passion, which is related to a sense of moral urgency (Sanders, 1997).

In order to enable different styles of making claims or to present testimony as part of the deliberative process, the design may need to include particular procedures that actually encourage various modes of talk and testimony (Sanders, 1997; Young, 1996). Further, because members from economically and socially disadvantaged or minority populations may not feel they can express their true views when they are alone in the forum, including at least two participants from such groups can help them feel they can freely express themselves, even if this entails a statistical over-representation of a particular group. This condition draws on social psychology research and community development (Guttman, 2007). Further, to enable narrative styles of expression the design of the forum would need to ensure that there is sufficient time for all participants to express themselves.

Address Inequity in Persuasive Ability.   Some critics emphasize the fact that people differ in their argumentation and persuasive rhetoric capacities and this will create a situation of inequity in the deliberative process. This concern is based on the assumption that participants may change their attitudes as a result of listening to those who are more persuasive in their argumentation style, rather than by "the better argument" (Sanders, 1997). The procedures or mode of facilitation therefore would need to help participants who are less articulate to present their perspectives.

Concerns Regarding Competence

A major concern often voiced by critics of public deliberation on policy issues is that lay participants or regular citizens lack competence to discuss or understand the policy issue, to critically assess its implications, or to look beyond their personal interests (e.g., Arnstein, 1969; Bohman, 1996; Mansbridge,

1999; Webler & Tuler, 2000; Yankelovich, 1991). Three particular concerns regarding competence are typically specified: (a) cognitive limitations, (b) not knowing about the issues, and (c) not considering the policy issues from a public good perspective and looking beyond personal interests. These are briefly outlined, followed by a framework developed by Webler and his colleagues (Webler & Tuler, 2000) and a list of stipulations and examples of procedures that have been employed to address the challenge of competence in public deliberations on policy issues.

Cognitive Limitations.   One argument against public deliberation forums is that lay people have limited cognitive capacities to understand discuss and assess complex and difficult issues that involve technical knowledge and value dilemmas, and therefore these issues should be discussed only by people with expertise on the topics (Abelson et al., 2003; Bates, Lynch, Bevan, & Condit, 2005; Bohman, 1996; Cohen, 1997). Proponents of public deliberation counter this argument by saying that elected officials themselves do not always possess technical knowledge, and that this is one of the challenges that need to be addressed in the design and procedures of the deliberation initiative.

Limited Knowledge about the Issue.   Because participants are not familiar with the policy issues and their complexity, critics are concerned that their knowledge will be too limited to discuss complex policy issues. To address this concern various means of providing background information have been implemented (Abelson et al., 2003). These are elaborated in the stipulations and examples described in the following sections.

Not Looking beyond Personal Interests.   Some opponents of involving the public in policy issues believe that participants are likely to form their opinions mainly on what they perceive would be best for them rather than on considerations that encompass the public good. This type of criticism is often voiced by opponents of public deliberation and decision makers who say that residents are likely to reject socially-minded proposals because of the NIMBY ("not in my back yard") approach (Arnstein, 1969). However, outcomes of public deliberation often show that when public deliberative forums adopt procedures that enable participants to consider alternative sides of the issue, participants tend to adopt a broader and public good perspective (Buttom & Mattso, 1999). The philosophical work of Rawls (1971, 1997) underscores the importance of getting participants to adopt a more public goods perspective. In his discussion of public deliberation of justice, Rawls presents an approach to steer citizens away from considering issues mainly from a perspective of self-interest. Whereas this approach and an emphasis on commonalities have been criticized by some scholars, others maintain that moving participants to a more pubic good perspective should be a condition for public deliberation (Buttom & Mattso, 1999; Mansbridge, 1999; Sanders, 1997).

Stipulations and Procedures to Address Competence

The concerns regarding the competence of participants to consider policy issues present both normative and pragmatic challenges: How to devise a competent deliberation process that stems from the democratic ideal to expose citizens to a wide array of competing arguments, and thereby provide them with an opportunity to consider these when working towards a solution (Gutmann & Thompson, 1996). To address these challenges, various forums have employed procedures such as those described in the sections that follow. Before presenting a series of specific stipulations regarding competence, this section begins with a brief overview of a theoretical framework that provides a conceptual approach to the notion of competence in public deliberation.

Drawing on the work of Habermas (1984, 1987, 1989, 1992), Webler (1995) and his colleagues (Ren & Webler, 1995; Webler & Tuler, 2000) adapted Habermas's normative framework on "communicative competence" to the context of public deliberative forums. This framework specifies communication qualities needed to discuss issues in a manner that reflects the competence of the speaker and creates understanding and agreement with others. Its focus is on people making "validity claims" that can be distinguished accroding to four types: (a) comprehension and language (communicative), (b) factuality and correctness (cognitive), (c) issues of morality (regulative), and (d) people's own subjective feelings (expressiveness). The framework underscores the need to attend to each facet of competence, and Webler and his colleagues adapt these as normative stipulations for public deliberation forums. Thus, to meet conditions for competence, the process should enable participants to critically assess the different types of arguments made about the policy issue and the way people express them. Rather than focus on the comptence of the individual, Webler and his colleagues focus on the competence of the process and the procedures coordinating the interactions, and they propose that a competent process will lead to a competent discussion of the issues.[2]

Another stipulation, which is not mentioned by Webler and his colleagues, is articualted by Mansbridge (1999), who assigns public deliberation an emancipatory critical role. According to this perspective, public deliberation needs to enable citizens to identify conflicts and help participants better understand their interests. By implication, an additional condition for public deliberation would be to include methods to enhance participants' critical capacities. Overall, five main stipulations for public deliberation can be noted as important to the creation of a competent pubic deliberation process: (a) participants need the opportunity to learn about the policy issue and its complexity; (b) the process needs to enhance their abilities to scrutinize relevant information and claims about the issues; (c) participants need to be presented with alternative perspectives of interest groups; (d) values and ethical dilemmas need to be identified; and (e) participants need to have enough time to reflect. These stipulations and examples of procedures employed to realize them are specified in the following sections.

Participants Need the Opportunity to Learn about the Policy Issue and Its Complexity.   Scholars of deliberative democracy emphasize that deliberative processes require procedures that enable each individual participant and the group as a whole to learn about the issue and understand its different aspects (Cohen, 1997; Priest, 1995). Public deliberation procedures thus aim to employ methods that will provide participants with information that meets the following conditions: background information about the issue, different types of arguments and perspectives, presentation of the information in a way that participants from diverse backgrounds can comprehend, and presentation of information in ways that will not be considered biased. For this purpose two common procedures are employed in many public deliberation initiatives: the preparation of print and audiovisual background materials provided to participants, and bringing people with professional or technical expertise or specialized knowledge about the issues, or "witnesses," as they are referred to in forums that follow a model called "citizens' juries" (described in the examples section). Each type of procedure can be employed to provide participants with knowledge about the issue poses additional challenges. For example: How should technical aspects of the issues be presented? Whose views should be included? How should experts/professionals be selected?

Participants Need the Opportunity to Enhance Their Abilities to Scrutinize Relevant Information and Claims about the Issues.   A central challenge in public deliberations is how to enhance participants' capacities to critically assess claims and arguments about the issues (Barber, 1984; Roberts, 2004; Yankelovich, 1991) and the framing of the issues (Dryzek et al., 2009). One approach used in deliberative forums is to present participants with several alternative scenarios, each describing the implications of adopting a particular course of action or policy, and arguments for and against it (Maxwell, Rosell, & Forest, 2003; Pimbert & Wakeford, 2002). Several scholars emphasize that deliberative forums should enhance participants' critical capacities to identify implicit assumptions embedded in the way the issues are framed (Walmsley, 2009). Similarly, others maintain that participants should be able to identify their own interests, particularly when they are members of disadvantaged social groups (Sanders, 1997). Thus, from a critical theory perspective, an important normative requirement is to enhance participants' capacities to scrutinize claims that support dominant suppositions. In this respect, the deliberative process should move participants beyond what can be considered an unreflective acceptance of conventional ways of thinking about the issues (Benhabib, 1992). This stipulation serves as a particular challenge when participants are asked to deliberate topics that involve new technologies or issues with which they are unfamiliar, and they may not know how to connect them to their own lives (Einsiedel, Jelsøe, & Breck, 2001; Pidgeon & Rogers-Hayden, 2007).

Participants Need to be Presented with Alternative Perspectives of Interest Groups.   A condition related to the stipulation to enhance participants' knowledge on the issue is the representation of views from diverse interest.[3] Typical procedures to meet this condition are that the background materials or the people invited to present their views and their expertise should represent different positions and interests, including the positions of various partisan groups. Presenting issues as they are framed by partisan or advocacy groups should not be avoided and is believed to be beneficial to the deliberative process, because it can help clarify and illustrate the range of perspectives surrounding an issue (Walmsley, 2009). To address fairness in the preparation of the information resources, some forums create advisory committees to oversee the task of creating background information; these committees can include representatives from different stakeholder groups, and are described in some of the examples presented in the sections that follow. Challenges associated with the condition of representation of different perspectives include choosing whose perspective should be included or excluded and which experts should be invited to present their view (Hendriks, 2006).

Participants Need the Opportunity to Identify Values and Ethical Dilemmas.   Several scholars emphasize the central role of values and ethical dilemmas in public deliberation. This implies that the deliberative process should engage participants in a discussion that elicits awareness of values and ethical dilemmas associated with the issues. Various forums employ specific procedures such as dilemma activities and alternative scenarios for this purpose (e.g., Campbell, 1995; Hadron & Holmes, 1997; Maxwell et al., 2003). Yet, even the use of ethical dilemma activities may frame the issue in a certain way (Guttman, 2007). Similarly, as Skorupinski and his colleagues (2007) point out, even bringing an ethicist to present an ethical approach can be biased. Skorupinski and his colleagues maintain that the role of ethical experts should not be to introduce a moral point of view, but to reflect upon potential conflicts between several moral perspectives or ethical approaches. Therefore, they suggest that it is not sufficient to invite only one ethical expert. They propose that at least two ethicists are necessary in order to expose participants to the ethical controversies related to the issue, and to help them realize that there are different ethical approaches. They add that ethical experts should be encouraged to defend their own moral conviction in terms of their preference of a certain ethical approach instead of playing a neutral role. They compare this to inviting different scientific experts in order show that even in science there are different perspectives.

Participants Need to Have Enough Time to Reflect.   Allowing time for people to obtain information, learn the materials, and listen to others is part of the design of public deliberative forums. This differentiates them from other participative events that have a relatively short duration, and do not provide participants with sufficient time to reflect. The design may include relatively long sessions (e.g., full day meetings, meetings over consecutive days) and intervals between meetings (weeks or even months) to enable participants to develop their listening skills and to discuss the issues with others (Lenagham et al., 1996). For example, in the Israeli Health Parliament initiative, one participant created a survey to learn her community's views, which she administered between the meetings (Guttman et al., 2008). Webler and Tuler (2000) add that time is needed to ensure that people have opportunity to reflect and get in touch with their own feelings and concerns.[4]

Concerns and Conditions Regarding the Discursive Process

Public deliberation is essentially a group process, and, as such, concerns can be raised regarding the methods of deliberation and processes that occur as a result of group dynamics. That can include the tendency of participants to try to make their point rather than to listen, opinion polarization, the influence of the group facilitation, and pressure on participants to pursue commonalities and the common good. These are further elaborated below.

Argumentation versus Fostering Listening and Deliberation.   Listening to others' views, as emphasized by Barber (1984) and Yankelovich (1991), is an essential component in public deliberation, but it may not be easily accomplished. A common concern is that participants in public deliberation may adopt a mode of argumentation rather than listening. Researchers propose that non-judgmental listening often is an acquired skill, and therefore presents an additional methodological challenge to the design of the public deliberation process. An attempt to address this challenge is illustrated in the ground rules of a Canadian public deliberation on the Ontario budget (Nolté, Maxwell, & MacKinnon, 2004). These rules state that participants need to be open and to listen to others even when they disagree, and to suspend judgment. Similarly, the handbook they received shows contrasts between a dialogue and a debate and explains that in a debate the purpose of listening is to find flaws in the arguments of others, whereas in a dialogue listening is for understanding others' views. Creating a good deliberation process, in which people are presented with information, listen to each other, ask questions, and assess options is not self-generating, and therefore needs planning and facilitation. Young (1996) proposes that deliberations include a form of greeting that corresponds to Ryfe's (2002) notion of a (feminist) relational form of deliberation. In this approach, participants recognize that there is discursive equality and mutual respect among them. By acknowledging the presence and points of view of others they are obligated to listen carefully to others' views and take them seriously into consideration (Haas, 2004). A common procedure is to engage professional facilitators to help promote a fair process of turn-taking, to ensure that discussions focus on the issues, to encourage participants to engage in mutual learning and to be attentive to each other (Levine et al., 2005). Webler and Tuler (2000) also stipulate that the discursive method should be designed to resolve disputes among participants.

Opinion Polarization.   Research findings on small-group processes indicate that in certain instances people's views may shift and become more extreme, because of factors relating to conformity and personal identity (Myers & Lamm, 1976). Thus, participating in a group process may move people's negative views to a more extreme position polarize their initial inclination, instead of opening them to other perspectives. This may explain shifts in opinions found in deliberative initiatives (Price et al., 2006). By implication, facilitation methods would need to attend to the potential tendency of polarization, which relates to other concerns associated with facilitation noted in the following section.

Influence of Facilitation.   Discussions in public deliberation are typically moderated by professional facilitators to enhance the participation of all members, to help focus on the issues, and to challenge assertions (Levine et al., 2005). Concerns about the process of facilitation parallel the concerns about inhibiting or devaluating stories and narratives. Gastil (2008) observes that in public deliberation processes that are strongly solution-oriented and heavily facilitated, facilitators may cut stories short or even discourage them. They may also summarize participants' stories in a way that reduces their potential power. Aakhus (2001) reports that facilitators in public forums did not tend to acknowledge the influence they exercised on the group decision process. They were unaware that their adoption of practices they believed represented professional norms of expert group facilitation influenced the process. When asked, public deliberation forum participants tend to praise the facilitation process and to view the role of facilitators as unbiased (Einsiedel, 2002). However, clearly, facilitators have a strong impact on the deliberative process.

Avoid Pressure to Pursue Commonalities and the Common Good.   One of the goals of public deliberation is to identify and seek commonalities. This is typically the case in deliberations that use a consensus approach. In general, group decision-making processes lead to seeking a commonly agreed upon solution (Levine et al., 2005). This process has both advantages and limitations according to the literature. Theorists maintain that deliberation should ideally shape the identity and interests of citizens in ways that contribute to the formation of a public conception of the common good (Barber, 1984; Cohen, 1997). However, aiming to reach a consensus can exert pressure on participants to belittle not only differences, but also the articulation of possible conflicts of interest. Thus, striving to channel participants' views toward those that prioritize the public good is contested by critics on grounds that it may be detrimental to the interests of members of marginalized social groups (Sanders, 1997; Mansbridge, 1999). One suggestion to address this dilemma is to find ways to help participants in deliberative forums to articulate potential differences, by giving them an opportunity to retreat from the more general discussion and deliberate among themselves. Scholars suggest that this would enable them to discover their true interests, which may conflict with those considered to be the common good. This type of solution, however, is unlikely to be feasible in public deliberation forums based on a relatively small numbers of participants. Therefore, an important but potentially a contested role of public deliberation forums, would be to help citizens identify and understand their own interests better, before deliberation leads them into discussions that emphasize the public good (Mansbridge, 1999).

To briefly summarize the main conditions presented in the literature,[5] deliberative forms that aim to realize deliberative ideals (within limitations) would need to employ procedures to ensure fair access in terms of (a) attendance (e.g., to overcome barriers related to economic factors, location, time, and cultural prohibitions); (b) materials and information on the topic that are accessible to all and that enable all to have a working knowledge of the issues; (c) enable expressiveness, or the confidence to express one's self; and (d) participation in the discussion in terms of turn-taking and the decision-making process. These conditions generally concern fairness in physical, psychological, cognitive as well as cultural access in the discursive processes. Next, in order for the deliberation process to ensure *competence* of the process it would need to employ procedures that (a) provide participants with methods and materials that can enable them to understand, analyze, and discuss the issues; (b) elicit deliberation rather than mere argumentation; (c) create discursive processes to help enhance critical thinking and identification of values and ethical dilemmas; (d) provide participants with sufficient time for contemplation and discussions; and (e) ensure the process does not advance an uncritical adoption of dominant assumptions.

Developers of the methods of various deliberative forums have taken these stipulations into consideration, and have aimed to address the challenges associated with them. These stipulations thus serve as the basis for the development of recruitment and group facilitation procedures, as well as the provision of information resources. Clearly, it is not feasible to design and implement a public deliberation forum that addresses all the concerns raised by theorists and practitioners. Further, certain concerns and the ways employed to address them conflict with others. For example, design features that aim to realize a normative condition of offering a fair chance to participate in the forum by using a random sample are likely to conflict with the stipulation to include people who have vested interest in the issue (Fung, 2003). The section that follows presents examples of various designs and procedures of actual public deliberation initiatives and the types of challenges that have emerged from their implementation, both for theory and practice.

From Theory to Practice

Despite the cost and organizational effort required to implement deliberate public forums and awareness of their limitations, hundreds of such initiatives have taken place in the past three decades. Preparation often includes disputes regarding whether to invite particular stakeholder groups, how to present different perspectives of the issues, what technical facts should be included in background materials, and how to present background information to people with limited literacy skills. Participants need to be recruited in a way that would be viewed as fair; experts or representatives of interest groups need to be invited and willing to participate, and facilitators need to be trained. In some cases, as in the deliberative poll method (described below), participants may need to be flown in from distant locations. The following section presents a brief overview of several prominent types of deliberative methods employed in the past several decades; each employs particular procedures aimed to fulfill the conditions for public deliberation. These are the citizens' jury method, planning cells, scenario workshops, consensus conferences, deliberative polls, citizens' dialogues, the town meeting, and an Internet forum. In addition, several examples of specific initiatives are described to illustrate the types of issues that the public has been asked to deliberate, how certain procedures were employed, or dilemmas that had arisen in the attempts to realize conditions for public deliberations on policy issues. It should be noted that numerous adaptations of deliberative designs have been employed, drawing on these and other methods (Carson & Hartz-Karp, 2005).

The Citizens' Jury and Planning Cells

A relatively prevalent model in public deliberation forums is called the citizens' jury, which draws on the analogy of the jury system used in the legal system. It puts a particularly strong emphasis on enabling participants to hear and question people who are considered to be experts or represent interest/stakeholder groups, and often they are referred to as "witnesses." This procedure was developed to meet conditions of competence by providing participants opportunities to both hear testimonyor professional expertise, and to question the witnesses. The goals of the forum differ from those of a jury in the legal system and participants are not expected to come up with a yes or no answer. Instead, they are asked to produce detailed opinions and recommendations or to outline a value framework that can be used as a basis for policy making. The model was originally developed in the in the United States in the 1970s, and hundreds of citizens' juries have been implemented in numerous variations around the world. In this method, between 12 and 25 participants are recruited through a random sample, using a quota determined by age, gender, ethnicity, and other demographic variables that might be important on a given issue to help ensure fairness. Participants meet for several days, sometimes over a period of months, to discuss policy questions. Though they are usually presented with background materials to meet stipulations of competence, the focus is on what are called "expert witnesses" that participants can question. Participants may even ask to invite witnesses on their own initiative. The meetings are facilitated by professional facilitators and overseen by steering groups that usually are composed of the commissioning body and key stakeholders, including sometimes media representatives (Smith & Wales, 2000).

A model similar to the citizens' jury, also developed in the 1970s, is termed the "planning cells" method that was developed and implemented in Germany. It had institutional support from government and agency sponsors, who commissioned the German Research Institute for Citizen Participation to organize citizens' deliberations to provide input to policy makers on topics related to local planning, national energy, technology and communication. In the planning cells, deliberation takes place among approximately 25 randomly selected citizens who meet several times over a period of weeks or months. Their recommendations are presented to the sponsor, the media, and other interested groups. In contrast to many other pubic deliberation initiatives, planning cells initiatives include an accountability requirement, according to which the sponsors agree to consider the decisions produced by the planning cell (Dienel & Renn, 1995).

Numerous citizens' juries took place in Britain, many of them on healthcare topics (over 200 in Britain). One example is a 1998 citizens' jury in Belfast, whose mission was to develop a response to a White Paper regarding the government's modernization agenda for the National Health Services. The jury was asked to consider questions about values surrounding health and social services, and opinions on public involvement in health decision making. This is an example of a government agency seeking to consider values that can serve as a basis for policy decisions. In contrast, in 1999 a citizen jury was convened by the British Leicestershire Health Authority to discuss a bitter public controversy: the health authority's proposal to reconfigure services at Leicester's three main hospitals. After four days of hearing witnesses and deliberating, the jury accepted the case for a planned care site, but made various recommendations. These two applications of citizens' jury method are examples of how it has been used for different purposes, each presenting different kinds of challenges. The Belfast forum was asked to consider a broad policy agenda, and to focus on values, whereas the Leicester forum was asked to make recommendations regarding a specific and disputed policy, which raised concerns regarding the forum serving the agenda of the authorities (Parkinson, 2004b).

Scenario Workshops Involving Members of Marginalized Groups

A common critique of public deliberation forums is that they tend to fail to involve members of marginalized groups. This presents challenges related to recruitment, representation, provision of information, as well as a discursive method that enables participants to express themselves in culturally familiar ways. A scenario workshop initiative carried out in India in 2001 in the state of Karnataka illustrates some procedures adapted to address these challenges. It was organized by the ActionAid organization on the controversial topic of genetically modified organisms (GMOs) as they relate to agriculture. Participants were asked to deliberate the possible future role of GMOs and to consider the topic in the context of reducing rural poverty and promoting sustainable agriculture. The design of the forum included several procedures to help realize deliberative goals. The location of the forum was chosen to be in a place familiar to the participants, and it took place on a farm in a small village. To address conditions of representation, the participants were 14 farmers: six men and eight women representing *Dalit* (untouchable caste) and indigenous (known as *adivasi*) people. The selection of participants aimed to include farmers who would represent various farming traditions. To allow time for deliberation, the meetings took place over four days. In order to enable participants to gain knowledge about the issues from the perspective of different stakeholders, the procedures included testimony by various stakeholders and experts who presented evidence for and against GMOs from scientific institutes, commercial biotechnology corporations, non-government organizations working on development issues, farmers' unions, and government agencies. In addition to hearing the views of witnesses, participants were presented with three different scenarios, each developed by different stakeholders to help elicit thinking from different types of perspectives. These were mainly presented through the use of videos (not all participants had a formal education) in a current affairs format, and each framed the issues differently. The scenarios were intended to provide a wider understanding of linkages between biotechnology, corporate control, and local power structures and to encourage participants to create different visions of farming. To help ensure a fair process in terms of the views participants were exposed to, the process was overseen by a panel of several interest groups (donors, government, civil society organizations), and presided over by a retired Chief Justice from India's Supreme Court. Media professionals were involved in relaying information on the event to a larger audience; to ensure transparency the deliberations were recorded on video and made publicly available. The forum concluded with most participants rejecting the use of GMO seeds in the near future, while providing a list of actions they recommended government and transnational corporations should adopt in order to gain better acceptance by the farmers. This initiative illustrates procedures employed to elicit the voice of members of marginalized groups, and the diversity among them and to facilitate critical analysis of the way the issues are framed by dominant stakeholders. It raises questions regarding the types of scenarios that were not offered, and the extent to which participants' recommendations may nonetheless mainly serve to support the interests of economically powerful stakeholders.

Eliciting Citizens' Views on New Technologies Using the Consensus Conference Model

Another prevalent public deliberation model similar in its design to the citizens' jury is called the consensus conference. The consensus conference model was originally developed in the mid-1980s by the Danish Board of Technology and financed by the Danish government with an independent board of governors working closely with Parliament (Andersen, & Jæger, 1999; Einsiedel, Jelsøe, & Breck, 2001; Jensen, 2005). Its approach is similar to the citizens' jury model in that it convenes a small number of people, usually selected through a random sample, in order to represent varied socio-demographic characteristics, and, like the citizens' jury model, it is also based on discussions and the presentations of invited experts who serve as an information resource for participants. However, as its name indicates, a consensus conference focuses on working towards consensus. It also typically includes in its design the involvement of the media and the public in an open session when experts are questioned and when its main conclusions are presented to policymakers. It also differs in its meeting schedules from the citizens' juries. Consensus conference participants are typically convened for several consecutive days, though it is also common for them to have several meetings beforehand in order to study the issues together. Thus, the consensus conference model, similarly to the citizens' jury model, aims to address challenges related to competence by emphasizing study of the issues and questioning experts. Consensus conference initiatives often deal with topics related to the use of new technologies that may have profound social implications and characterized as controversial. Therefore, their procedures typically aim to help ensure that the views and interests of various stakeholders are presented. In Denmark, these forums mainly have been used to discuss scientific or technical issues. Topics addressed in these forums include electronic surveillance, noise and technology, gene therapy, electronic identity cards, food irradiation, transportation, and educational technology. Numerous consensus conferences that have adopted the Danish model with variations have been implemented around the world (e.g., Sclove, 2000), including the United States (e.g., the Citizens' Panel on Telecommunications; Guston, 1998), Argentina, Australia, Austria, Belgium, Brazil, Canada, Israel, Japan, The Netherlands, New Zealand, Norway, and South Korea.[6]

A Statistically Representative Sample: Deliberative Polling

A method that operates on a larger scale in terms of the number of the participants convened to discuss policy issues and which uses a statistically representative sample is deliberative polling. This method was conceptualized by Fishkin (1991, 1999) in the early 1990s and designed to incorporate a deliberative process into traditional public opinion polls. One of the main features that distinguishes the deliberative poll from the consensus conference and the citizens' jury methods is that it convenes a relatively large representative random sample of participants. Similarly to the other public deliberation methods, it provides participants with background materials as an information resource as well as opportunities for discussions in small groups. It typically takes place in a 2- to 3-day period over a weekend. Topics addressed by deliberative polls include crime, the future of the monarchy, the future of Europe, Britain's National Health Service, and U.S. presidential campaigns. It also enables participants' to question stakeholders, experts, or political candidates, sometimes in a larger setting that can be characterized as a town hall meeting with the flair of a media event. Organizers of these initiatives pride themselves that this type of event enables ordinary citizens to face and even confront politicians. Politicians who participated in such meetings were the Danish Prime Minister and the opposition leader; the Prime Minister of Australia; Britain's prime ministers Tony Blair and John Major, then-U.S. Vice-President Al Gore, U.S. senators, and media publishers, some of whom appeared by satellite.

The deliberative polling initiatives also typically have a mass media component, including television broadcasts intended to generate public attention, and they may even strive to become a variation of a media event. Some initiatives were shown live by national broadcasting outlets. In the 1996 U.S. presidential election, the national public broadcasting stations broadcast eleven hours of town hall meetings, including live footage of the discussions with candidates followed by a 90-minute national broadcast. The events are usually also covered by print media. A major component of the design is that participants are asked to fill out survey questionnaires regarding their views and knowledge regarding the issues before and after the process. The post-deliberation views are usually presented as survey findings but with an emphasis that these data differ substantially from those obtained in regular surveys because they represent considered public opinion (Fishkin et al., 2000). Empirical studies of this method suggest that in many cases participants' views may shift as a result of the deliberative process or that their views become what researchers describe as more sophisticated or consistent (Gastil & Dillard, 1999; Luskin, Fishkin, & Jowell, 2002).

The deliberative polling model aims to address challenges of representation by using a relatively large sample of people, and fairness, by employing a random method of choosing people. But this method may need to be modified in order to enable people from marginalized groups to participate in a way that equalizes their chances to have an impact in the group. Other challenges, which need to be addressed by other types of methods as well, are what to include in the background materials and who should be invited as an informant or as an expert. Some initiatives have a steering committee that oversees the process of including the views of different stakeholders in the background materials. An additional challenge relates to the kinds of views that are elicited. Because the views of the public in the deliberative poll method essentially are reported through aggregated responses to closed-ended questionnaire item, rather than the development of open-ended recommendations, the method may not put an emphasis on providing alternative scenarios or framing of the issues, or on novel approaches that can emerge in the deliberation process. It also differs from approaches (e.g., the citizens' dialogues) that focus on the articulation and prioritization of values.

An example of a forum that used the deliberative poll model is a European initiative called "Tomorrow's Europe,"[7] which convened 362 citizens from 27 European Union nations [EU] in October 2007 using random sampling procedures. This was the first time a deliberative poll was conducted with a transnational sample. Participants arrived at Brussels for a weekend of deliberation, for the purpose, as implied in the name of the initiative, to discuss the future of the European Union. The initiative took place in parallel to institutional EU discussions and ahead of the European parliamentary election. Participants were provided with background materials and met in group sessions. The logistics of this particular initiative necessitated having translators in many languages to enable participants to hear the experts, politicians and stakeholders, and to discuss the issues among themselves. As in other Deliberative Polling initiatives, participants filled out questionnaires before and after the meetings. Some of the changes that took place in participants' opinions reflect an increased willingness to make sacrifices to secure economic security. This illustrates scholars' contention that the public deliberation process can move people's views toward conceptions of the public good. Additionally, the deliberation decreased differences between views of participants from old and new EU member states. Knowledge gains were found to be dramatic for the whole sample. It should be noted that other public engagements took place in Europe on similar issues in addition and over 3,000 people were polled separately.[8]

Large Scale Town Meeting: Listening to the City

A method that convenes an even larger number of people than the Deliberative Polling method is the 21st Century Town Meeting. It was developed in the United States during the mid-1990s and implemented by a not-for-profit organization America*Speaks*. This method utilizes computer technology to synchronize and connect a large number of people—up to several thousands—gathered in a large space in order to engage in a deliberative process. A relatively unique design feature in the 21st Century Town Meeting is using technology to enable participants to know about the views of members in other groups. This procedure aims to enable moving back and forth between intimate small group dialogues and the collective work of thousands of people. For this purpose, it employed networked computers that recorded discussions and ideas generated by each group; the views and themes that emerged in the discussion were condensed and then disseminated to all other group members. The network enables participants to learn about the views generated in all of the groups and get a sense of what occurs in the larger group of which they are a part. Participants can also use electronic key pads to vote on issues and learn about the aggregated votes of others. Large screens projected data, themes, and information in real-time to the entire gathering. At the end of the day, a summary report is produced and distributed to the participants, sponsors, and officials.

A prominent deliberate consultation initiative was on the topic of plans to reconstruct the New York City World Trade Center site that was destroyed in a terrorist attack in September 11, 2001. The forum took place in 2002 in New York City with more than 4,000 participants. Participants were divided into small groups, each moderated by a facilitator. An important focus in the design was the elicitation of values. Thus, the discussions centered initially on values, and only later on specific recommendations. After the recommendations were presented, officials stated that current development plans would be revised along the lines suggested by the participants. It was reported that New York's governor adopted the participants' conclusions to seek new design options according to particular directives. Media interest in to the Listening to the City project, as in other large-scale events, was reported as relatively high and included coverage in international media outlets. This coverage was probably also due to its interest to international audiences (Lukensmeyer & Brigha, 2002).

Online Deliberation: A Follow-Up of the Face-to-Face Listening to the City

The face-to-face Listening to the City deliberation was followed by an online discussion. Polletta, Ching, Chen, and Anderson (2009) report on the Internet-based deliberation—Listening to the City Online. The deliberation took place in a time period of 2 weeks in an asynchronous format, and the topics included preliminary plans for the site, as well as housing, transportation, economic development issues, and plans for a memorial to the victims of the attack. Participants were recruited through emails sent by civic organizations to their members and were assigned to groups consisting of about 30 members, with the intention that members would have a similar socio-demographic background but would not know each other. It was found that in each group some people did not actively participate, and those who did tended to have more formal education and a higher income, when compared to the average income of residents of the New York metropolitan region.

As in face-to-face deliberative forums, participants were provided with background materials. Sixteen of the groups were actively facilitated by one or two facilitators, who provided information, encouraged participants to provide an input; responded to and summarized participants' responses, and helped solve technical problems. The researchers believe facilitators in an on-line deliberation can play an important role, both in encouraging and helping people to post and respond to links (relating to conditions of equity), and to help participants jointly evaluate the credibility of information sources (relating to conditions of competence). In this case it was found that people posted more links when a facilitator was present, but did not participate more in terms of comments. In all groups the organizers introduced questions at regular intervals. Similarly to the face-to-face forum, participants had the opportunity to learn about the views expressed by others, in other groups. Participants could read the posts in other groups but were restricted to posting within their group. Periodically, they were asked as a group to summarize areas of agreement and difference and were also asked to respond to a poll. As noted by the researchers, this procedure could help those with minority opinions understand that others also shared their views, and thus it can help meet the condition of equity. It was found that participants availed themselves to information resources on the Internet, including those posted by other groups, and used them not only to support their own arguments but to share information, present other perspectives, brainstorm, generate ideas or to expand the array of options that were being discussed. Thus, being exposed to the posts of the other groups allowed participants, according to the researchers, a sense that they could access a wide range of ideas and opinions while operating mainly within a more intimate group. In addition, the Internet was used to encourage participants to take action outside the forum by joining advocacy groups or signing petitions order to influence decision makers. This may be a particular feature of the Internet deliberation, or it may result from recruiting participants through community organizations. It should be noted that across the globe numerous Internet forms of deliberations are developed and implemented and present new opportunities and challenges (e.g., Price et al., 2006; Wright & Street, 2007).

Citizens' Dialogues: Values and Trade-Offs

Another model that focuses on values is called the citizens' dialogue, which has been implemented in Canada on various topics, including budget and healthcare services. Some of the initiatives have been led by prominent politicians, such as the initiative on the future of Canadian healthcare (Maxwell et al., 2003). The typical design features of the citizens' dialogue include multiple regional meetings that take place nearly simultaneously in different geographical locations, each including about 30 to 50 participants. Conducting separate forums in different locations is done to meet the normative condition of access because of the wide geographical spread of citizens in Canada. The citizens' dialogues method draws on two inter-related assumptions regarding competence. One is that an important condition in public deliberation is identification and articulation of values. The second is that participants need to identify and consider various trade-offs of potential policy solutions. For this purpose, a workbook is developed that includes background materials and several policy-related scenarios with implications and arguments for and against each. The goal of these procedures is to have participants work through the issues, identify and articulate basic values that can guide decision making, and discuss trade-offs associated with each alternative. Another goal is to get participants to shift from an individual to a community-based point of view (Maxwell et al., 2003).

One example is the Citizens' Dialogue on the Ontario Budget that took place in 2004. This initiative was part of a broader program of engaging the public through town hall meetings between residents who self-selected to participate and elected officials, including the Premier and members of parliament. The deliberative initiative was commissioned by the government and conducted by the Canadian Policy Research Networks. This was the first time citizens in Canada were given a chance to discuss large government budget strategy. Between January and March 2004, over 250 randomly selected residents were convened for a full day in six cities around the province. The consultation documents state that the purpose was to engage unaffiliated citizens who would participate as individuals and not as representatives of stakeholder or advocacy groups. Thus, the emphasis is, as in the deliberative polls and other forums, to recruit un-affiliated and unconnected participants. The sessions were guided by professional facilitators and participants worked for nine hours in large and small groups to formulate advice to Ontario's government on its budget strategy. This advice drew on their articulation of six core values (Nolté, et al., 2004). The method in these citizens' dialogues is to get participants to articulate relevant core values and to compel them to examine alternative scenarios in order to get them to identify and take into consideration inevitable trade-offs. As in the other types of methods, the degree to which the value-elicitation methods (e.g., the types of scenarios) meet conditions for a democratic public deliberation depends on the types of information provided and the procedures of articulating values and alternative policy-related visions.

Bottom-Up Approach in a Public Deliberation on Nanotechnology

Similarly to developments in genetically modified food or biomedical technology, advances in the development of nanotechnologies present the prospect of exciting opportunities in the domains of new materials, the environment, medicine, and information technology, alongside concerns about the uncertainly of long-term risks (Pidgeon & Rogers-Hayden, 2007). A British initiative called the NanoJury UK was implemented in the summer of 2005. The project was initiated and jointly funded by the Interdisciplinary Research Collaboration in Nanotechnology based at Cambridge University and non-government environmental organizations. The initiative differed from other citizens' juries by not asking participants to address a specific problem or question, but instead presenting four related topics on which participants generated their own concerns and issues. This was done in an attempt to stimulate a bottom-up approach, and to allow participants more control over the process. The recruitment goal was to involve people from marginalized groups and to hear from people whose voices are usually part of discussions on these topics. Because this initiative sought to recruit members from low-income populations who may not be predisposed to participate, it enlisted community outreach activities and a word-of-mouth method. Participants were selected from people who had volunteered in response to publicity as well as through personal recommendations (Pidgeon & Rogers-Hayden, 2007).

For the purpose of providing diverse perspectives a panel was created to oversee the consultation process. It consisted of members from various stakeholder groups, including representatives from government, civil society, nanotechnologies experts, funding bodies, and academia, and was responsible for planning, publicity, and decision making. In addition, a science panel was created to provide technical guidance. The initiative consisted of 16 participants who met for two and a half hours, twice a week for 5 weeks between June and July 2005. The format of the 10 sessions involved an introduction to nanotechnology followed by several sessions with witnesses in which participants heard the witnesses and were given time to meet as a group to decide on additional questions. Researchers who observed these sessions suggested that the serial format may have limited the ability of the participants to critically analyze the claims they heard, in particular because the topic was new to them. Some of the participants suggested that if they had been able to meet with more than one of the witnesses at a time and see how witnesses would have critiqued each other, they could have assessed the opposing claims better. The final sessions were devoted to developing their recommendations (Pidgeon & Rogers-Hayden, 2007).

One of the main criticisms of public deliberation on issues related to new technologies is how participants may assess the risk. The assumption is that group discussions on new technologies are likely to lead to what risk perception researchers call an "amplification" of risk concerns. Yet it was found that the group discussions on technologies did not necessarily lead to amplification of risk perceptions, and may in fact create the opposite effect (attenuation rather than amplification). The researchers conclude that the participants were capable of debating the risks currently identifiable with nanotechnologies and that their recommendations can be characterized as balanced by showing both support and caution for the development of nanotechnologies (Pidgeon & Rogers-Hayden, 2007).

As illustrated in these examples, there are numerous variations of methods that aim to realize normative stipulations for public deliberation and dozens of initiatives. The scenario workshop in Karnataka, India, and the NanoJury UK illustrate initiatives that aimed to recruit mainly members of marginalized or low-income groups; the Deliberative Polling method used a relatively large number of people to serve as a statistically representative sample; the large group assembled in the 21st Century Town Meeting method and its online version enabled participants to see others' minority views, which could strengthen the expression of people who hold them; and the Citizen's Dialogue method used multiple regional meetings as a means to enhance access and a focus on values and trade-offs as a method to enhance analytic competence. A brief summary of the conditions or stipulations and the procedures used to address them is presented in Table 7.1. This summary is not intended to provide a comprehensive list, but rather to illustrate the types of conditions that have been underscored in the literature and the way several public deliberation initiatives have tried to meet them in practice.

Practices, Procedures, and Challenges to Normative Theory

To summarize, public deliberation forums on policy issues carry with them a promise of advancing democratic processes in local and national settings.

Table 7.1 Normative Stipulations and Practical Resolutions in Public Deliberations on Policy Issues*

Broad Normative Stipulations	Specific Normative Stipulations	Features/Practices/Procedures Used in Forums	Examples**
Power: Elimination of coercion and authority, creating a 'space' for discussion in which participants feel they can freely express their views, and not using the public deliberation as a tool to bolster decision-makers' credibility	Participants should be able to influence the agenda and the modes of discussion	• Participants formulate the issues • Participants determine the role of the moderator • Influence of facilitation	In the NanoJury UK on nanotechnology organizers left open the questions and issues were defined by the participants (Pidgeon & Rogers-Hayden, 2007). However, in most cases the agenda of the discussion was determined before the recruitment of participants and the roles of the moderator were pre-determined.
	Participants need to be provided with alternative framings of the issue	• Provide participants with different ways the issue is framed by different stakeholders	Participants are provided with the views of different stakeholders on the issues, including alternative ways of framing. This is one of the goals of the background materials produced, for example, for the Deliberative Polls (Fishkin, Luskin, & Jowell, 2000).
	Participants should not be made to feel they need to defer to experts	• Enable participants to see different experts discuss the issues among themselves • Training sessions demystify expertise • Refer to 'experts' as 'informants'	Referring to experts as 'informants' was a suggestion made by participants in a Swiss forum on genetically modified foods (Skorupinski, et al., 2007). Training sessions for participants to demystify the authority of experts are reported by Davies and Burgess (2004) and Harrison and Mort (2004).

(continued)

Table 7.1 Continued

Broad Normative Stipulations	Specific Normative Stipulations	Features/Practices/Procedures Used in Forums	Examples**
	The forum should not be used as a "fig leaf" by the organizers	• Ensure public deliberation takes place early enough in the process of decision making • Ensure the forum is not used to eliminate the voice of stakeholders and advocates	The 21st Century Town Meeting "Listening to the City" was not an alternative to other forums, and it took place in a time that enabled decision makers to change the plans (Lukensmeyer & Brigha, 2002).
Fairness and equity: Provision of egalitarian access and means of expression	Provide equitable access for participants from diverse social groups	• Invitation to participate in the forum is based on random sampling to ensure equal chance • Recruitment of a relatively larger percent of minorities • Outreach activities through local and civic organizations • Offer compensation for work days • Help with child care • Provide transportation Regional meetings	The Karnataka forum in India recruited farmers from marginalized groups (Pimbert, Wakeford, & Satheesh, 2001). The British NanoJury UK participants from low income populations were recruited through local organizations and by word of mouth (Pidgeon & Rogers-Hayden, 2007). The "Listening to the city" internet forum recruited participants through civic organizations (Polletta, et al., 2009). The Canadian Citiznes' Dialogue on the future of healthcare held regional meetings (Maxwell, Rosell, & Forest, 2003).

There should be fairness in the opportunity to participate in the forum	• Use of statistical sampling methods to ensure a fair chance to participate • Create forums that enable participation of a large number of people • Create additional modes of participation for those who cannot attend the face-to-face forum (e.g., internet outlet; other types of forums)	Random sampling methods are typically used in Deliberative Polling, Citizens' Juries, Consensus Conferences and Citizens' Dialogues. In the British "GM Nation?" open community meetings took place in addition to the forum (Pidgeon, et al., 2005). Large scale events such as The 21st Century Town Meeting "Listening to the City" enabled a large number of people to participate (over 4,000; Lukensmeyer & Brigha, 2002).
There should be egalitarian speaking opportunities	Professional moderators facilitate the group discussion to help ensure fair turn-taking	Professional moderators were employed in the various forums.
Participants from minority groups should have the confidence to express their views	Have more than one (at several participants) from a minority population to encourage participants to express their views	The British NanoJury UK recruited mainly participants from low income populations (Pidgeon & Rogers-Hayden, 2007). The Indian Karnataka forum, recruited mainly farmers from low-income populations (Pimbert, Wakeford, and Satheesh, 2001).
There should be equity in expression: Certain types of rationality or mode of expression should not be privileged	Encourage participants to express themselves through stories, narratives and testimonials	In a British forum on health care services' policy elderly participants were encouraged by facilitators to tell stories (Barnes, (2005).
Information should be provided in modes that address literacy needs and are culturally appropriate	• Using media that do not require reading skills, such as videos, photographs, songs • Using formats such as personal stories, proverbs, myths	The Karnataka forum in India used videos in 'current event' formats (Pimbert, Wakeford, and Satheesh, 2001).

(continued)

Table 7.1 Continued

Broad Normative Stipulations	Specific Normative Stipulations	Features/Practices/Procedures Used in Forums	Examples**
	There should be opportunities to pursue the true interests of members, in particularly those from marginalized populations	Give participants an opportunity to deliberate in a way that enables them to discover their true interests, which may conflict with those considered to be 'the common good' (Sanders, 1997; Mansbridge, 1999)	This stipulation is noted by some scholars but was not raised in the cases reviewed. It may have occurred in the Karnataka forum in India, which recruited only farmers (Pimbert, Wakeford, & Satheesh, 2001).
Competence: Participants should be able to carefully and critically assess the information, views and arguments about the policy issue in order to provide 'considered' views and recommendations	Participants need the opportunity to learn about the policy issue and its complexity: Provision of relevant information and different perspectives on the topic should be provided	• Provision of background materials in print or video; including survey findings, newspaper articles, videos. • Time allocated to learning the issues • Informants or experts on the topic present the issues and are available for questions and clarifications • Convene people from diverse backgrounds	Background materials and informants that presented information and different perspectives are featured in all cases. The Karnataka forum in India used different scenarios composed by different stakeholders (Pimbert, Wakeford, & Satheesh, 2001). An expert panel was created to oversee the process in xenotransplantation dialogue in Canada and there was diversity in the types of 'informants' solicited, including patients (Einsiedel, 2002). In the "Tomorrow's Europe" Deliberative Poll of the European Union translators were used so that participants from different countries could communicate with each other. In the NanoJury UK several sessions were allocated to learning the issues (Pidgeon & Rogers-Hayden, 2007).

The process should help enhance participants' capacities to analyze the information and assess the claims made by other participants and the informants or experts	• Informants available for questions • Have experts on the topic or different stakeholders debate the issues among themselves	In most cases, across the different models, informants/experts were available for questions. At the British GM Nation forum the participants selected the presenters they wanted to hear (Pidgeon, et al., 2005).
The process should help enhance the consideration of the public good beyond personal interest	• Presenting alternative scenarios • Providing policy makers' point of view	Alternative scenarios were used in the Canadian Citizens' Dialogues (Maxwell, Rosell, & Forest, 2003) and the Karnataka forum in India on GM agriculture (Pimbert, Wakeford, & Satheesh, 2001).
The process should help enhance participants' capacities to articulate, conceptualize, and identify value issues and dilemmas	• Dilemma activities • Alternative scenarios and discussion of trade-offs	Dilemma activities were used in the Health Parliament in Israel (Guttman et al., 2008). Values were identified as a basis for policy recommendations in the Belfast Citizens' Jury on 'modernizing' the health services agenda (Barnes 1999); the 2002 'Listening to the City' in New York City (Lukensmeyer & Brigha, 2002). Values and trade-offs were discussed in the "Citizens'" Dialogue on the Ontario Budget" (Nolté, Maxwell, & MacKinnon, 2004).

(continued)

Table 7.1 Continued

Broad Normative Stipulations	Specific Normative Stipulations	Features/Practices/Procedures Used in Forums	Examples**
	The process should help enhance participants' critical capacities	• Presenting alternative frames, for example from the point of view of advocates • Having stakeholders with different perspectives debate among each other • Develop as a group questions to be addressed to experts, candidates or decision makers	In the Citizens' Dialogues, participants are given work books with 'pro' and 'con' arguments, and lists of trade-offs to consider for various claim or propositions (Maxwell, Rosell, & Forest, 2003).
	Participants need to have enough time to reflect	• Sessions are allocated at least a day. In most models meetings take place over days, sometimes weeks of months.	
Discursive Process: The process should encourage attentive listening and consideration of others' views and perspectives	The process should encourage attentive listening to and consideration of others' views and perspectives	• Professional facilitators that encourage listening • Materials on listening	In the Citizens' Dialogue forums the 'work books' given to participants as background materials make a distinction between dialogue and debate and the importance of listening (Maxwell, Rosell, & Forest, 2003).
	The process should encourage the elicitation of minority views	Enable exposure to views of the minority in other groups	The "Listening to the city" face-to-face and internet forums enabled participants to view the views of members of other groups (Lukensmeyer & Brigha, 2002; Polletta, et al., 2009).

| The facilitation should not influence people's views | Facilitators need to be made aware and trained to avoid the influence of their own facilitation on participants' views | This was likely to occur in the Karnataka forum in India that consisted of farmers from marginalized groups (Pimbert, Wakeford, & Satheesh, 2001). It may have been facilitated in the 'Listening to the City' deliberations—both the face-to-face and online—because they enabled exposure to minority views in other groups (Lukensmeyer & Brigha, 2002; Polletta, Ching, Chen, &Anderson, 2009) |
| Avoid pressure to pursue commonalities and the 'common good' and enable participants to identify their own interests, while considering the common good. This is particularly important for participants from disadvantaged populations. | • Enable participants to work in groups of people with the same interests
• Be exposed to advocates | |

* Adapted from Webler and Tuler (2002) and Guttman (2007).
** Not all procedures are illustrated with specific examples because not all were found in the cases described in this paper. The examples draw on the examples described or referred to in the paper.

Numerous public deliberation initiatives on policy issues have proliferated across nations and focused on diverse topics. Proponents view public deliberations as a welcome exercise in democracy and a necessary component of important public policy decision making. Yet the enthusiasm public deliberation initiatives generate among their proponents is also marked with numerous challenges and several types of criticisms. Clearly, theoretical ideals cannot be realized in practice in a way that meets all normative stipulations. Numerous and serious concerns have been noted. Briefly, one concern is that lay participants will not be able to comprehend and discuss complex policy issues and may focus on their own interests (competence issues). Another concern is that instead of promoting equitable opportunities for members of diverse groups to express their views it will serve to reinforce social inequities (equity issues). An additional concern is that public deliberations may be subjected to manipulations or mainly serve institutional goals (power issues). And yet other concerns refer to how the discussion will take place in order to elicit substantive recommendations (discursive issues). These types of concerns are the backdrop for the articulation of conditions and stipulations by public deliberation theorists.

Attempts to realize the normative stipulations formulated to address the concerns regarding power, competence, equity and discursive issues can be found in the various procedures employed by a multitude of public deliberation initiatives.[9] The specific procedures employed in public deliberation initiatives are the means practitioners have used to resolve theoretical stipulations (Aakhus, 2001). The various types of deliberative models illustrate different interpretations of theoretical stipulations. This is reflected in differences in the details of procedures employed by each type of forum, for example, in different modes of facilitation or in variations in the interactions scheduled to take place between participants and the informants. A theoretical challenge with practical implications to public deliberation therefore, concerns the strategic design of public deliberation forums, and how this design can provide practical answers to the normative stipulations, drawing on philosophical theories of democracy. From a theoretical perspective, an important question is whether the differences that have emerged between the different types of public deliberation models should be explained theoretically as well. It is also important to study the deliberative processes that take place when different types of procedures are adopted to meet the various normative stipulations articulated by theorists. One question is whether different types of procedures represent the same or different types of normative stipulations. A related question is: what are the theoretical conceptualizations of the practices employed in different types of public deliberation forums regarding the way they aim to address normative conditions?

Because the application of each procedure involves a certain compromise of the normative condition (Levine et al., 2005), it invariably raises additional normative concerns and perhaps new types of theoretical questions. For example, one question is, which types of compromises can be acceptable and under which conditions? As Ashcraft (2001) proposes, a distinction can be made

among three levels. The first is the problem: in the context of public deliberation, how to achieve the normative goals of an egalitarian and competent deliberative process that is free of power influences? The second is the technical: in
the context of public deliberation, what procedures are necessary and feasible?
The third is the philosophical and ethical: in the context of public deliberation,
what is an acceptable compromise in normative conditions, and which kinds of
dilemmas may emerge from contradictions in the application of public deliberation procedures (e.g., when attempts to achieve competence may lead to a bias
in favor of decision makers; Guttman, 2007; Levine et al., 2005)?

Two additional important and possibly contentious normative and pragmatic challenges concern the quality of the opinions generated (e.g., Price et
al., 2002) and the impact of the recommendations on actual policies (Fung,
2003). Some advocates of public deliberation suggest that the success of public
deliberation forums should be inferred by how participants discuss and present recommendations on topics about which they had no previous knowledge.
Similarly, others maintain that successful deliberative processes are those in
which participants challenge the framing of the issue as it is conceived by the
government agencies or technical experts (Besley et al., 2008; Dryzek et al.,
2009; Pimbert et al., 2001). Such diverse conceptions of success indicate that
there is a need for further theorizing on the meaning of a successful public
deliberation and the types of tools needed to assess it. Further, it raises questions such as from whose perspective should success be assessed: the organizers' or the client organization for whom the policy issue is of particular
relevance.

In conclusion, the increasing interest in the implementation of public
deliberation forums points to the need to advance the theory, to study current applications, and to further develop mechanisms for public deliberation
that take into account the numerous challenges specified by scholars, critics
and the participants themselves (Gastil & Levine, 2005). This is amplified by
on-going developments in communication technologies that have resulted in
the creation of new formats of public deliberation that can enable the use of
more varied information resources, including on-line resources and interactive
media. In the past decade a vast numbers of online forums have already been
created, yielding new formats of numerous kinds, on which there is a growing literature (e.g., Howard & Gaborit, 2007; Gantwerk, 2005; Levine, 2001;
Morrison & Newman, 2001; Price et al., 2006; Wright & Street, 2007). Public
deliberation conducted through online forums also raises new challenges both
from theoretical and pragmatic perspectives: deliberation that is not face-to-
face and may cross geographical boundaries may require new types of normative stipulations and procedures to realize them.

Notes

1. Webler and Tuler (2000) outline three main discursive standard criteria for fairness. The first concerns agenda and process rules. It includes the conditions

that everyone should get an equal chance to put their concerns on the agenda, approve or propose rules for discussion, debate and critique proposals, and influence decision making. However, some of these conditions are not likely to be implemented in many public deliberative forums because such forums tend to have a predetermined agenda. Nonetheless, they can serve as a guideline for the faciliation method so that it can provide a greater degree of participant control over the discussion and decision-making procedures.

2. Webler (1995) proposes, that drawing on Habermas's conception of competence, there are pragmatic and ethical difficulties in focusing on the competence of the individual, because it necessitates finding ways to assess people's competence and this may serve to exclude those deemed not to be competent, thus depriving them of an opportunity to learn to be competent through a communicative process.

3. As noted by Webler and Tuler (2000) this can correspond to normative claims according to Habermas's conceptualization.

4. This is related to Habermas's conception of expressive claims (Webler & Tuler, 2000).

5. This discussion of conditions focuses on the deliberative aspects, and therefore does not include condtions for impact of the deliberation (see, for example Fung, 2003).

6. Source: The Loka Institute http://www.loka.org/TrackingConsensus.html

7 Http://www.tomorrowseurope.eu/

8. Europe. http://europa.eu/debateeurope/

9. Often these are the result of the work of national and transnational organizations that have been developing public deliberation methods as a means to translate public deliberation ideals into practice. These organizations tend to be affiliated with academic institutions or research centers. For example, in Canada, The Canadian Community for Dialogue and Deliberation, working with The W. Maurice Young Centre for Applied Ethics at the University of British Columbia or the Simon Fraser University's Dialogue Programs. In the United States America*Speaks* a nonpartisan organization based in Washington, DC, or The Jefferson Center, the Deliberative Democracy Consortium, The Loka Institute, The National Coalition for Dialogue and Deliberation, The National Issues Forums Institute, The Center for Deliberative Democracy, at the Department of Communication at Standford University in California.

References

Aakhus, M. (2001). Technocratic and design stances toward communication expertise: How GDSS facilitators understand their work. *Journal of Applied Communication Research, 29*(4), 341–371.

Abelson, J., Eyles, J., Forest, P., Smith, P., Martin, E., & Gauvin, F. (2003). Deliberations about deliberative methods: Issues in the design and evaluation of public participation processes. *Social Science and Medicine, 57*(2), 239–251.

Andersen , I. E., & Jæger, B. (1999). Danish participatory models, scenario workshops and consensus conferences: Towards more democratic decision-making. *Science and Public Policy, 26*(5), 331–340.

Arnstein, S. R. (1969). A ladder of citizen participation. *Journal of the American Institute of Planning, 35,* 216–224.

Ashcraft, K. L. (2001). Feminist organizing and the construction of "alternative" community. In G. J. Shepherd & E. W. Rothenbuhler (Eds.), *Communication and community* (pp. 79-110). Mahwah, NJ: Erlbaum.

Barber, B. (1984). *Strong democracy: Participatory politics for a new age.* Berkeley: University of California Press.

Barnes, M. (2005). The same old process? Older people, participation and deliberation. *Ageing and Society, 25(2),* 245–259.

Bates, B. R., Lynch, J. A., Bevan, J. L., & Condit, C. M. (2005). Warranted concerns, warranted outlooks: A focus group study of public understandings of genetic research. *Social Science and Medicine, 60*(2), 331–344.

Benhabib, S. (1992). *Situating the self: Gender, community, and postmodernism in contemporary ethics.* New York: Routledge.

Besley, J. C., Kramer, V. L., Yao, Q., & Toumey, C. (2008). Interpersonal discussion following citizen engagement about nanotechnology: What, if anything, do they say? *Science Communication, 30*(2), 209–235.

Black, L. W. (2009). Listening to the city: Difference, identity, and storytelling in online deliberative groups. *Journal of Public Deliberation, 5*(1), Article 4. Retrieved September 5, 2009, from http://services.bepress.com/jpd/vol5/iss1/art4

Bohman, J. (1996). *Public deliberation: Pluralism, complexity, and democracy.* Cambridge, MA: MIT Press.

Bracci, S. L. (2001). Managing health care in Oregon: The search for a civic bioethics. *Journal of Applied Communication Research, 29*(2), 171–194.

Burkhalter, S., Gastil, J., & Kelshaw T. (2002). A conceptual definition and theoretical model of public deliberation in small face-to-face groups. *Communication Theory, 12*(4), 398–422.

Buttom, M., & Mattson, K. (1999). Deliberative democracy in practice: Challenges and prospects for civic deliberation. *Polity, 31,* 609–637.

Campbell, A. V. (1995). Defining core health services: The New Zealand experience. *Bioethics, 9*(3-4), 252–258.

Cappella, J. N., Price, V., & Nir, L. (2002). Argument quality as a reliable and valid measure of opinion quality: Electronic dialogue during campaign 2000. *Political Communication, 19,* 73–93.

Carson, L., & Hartz-Karp, J. (2005). Adapting and combining deliberative designs: Juries, polls, and forums. In J. Gastil (Ed.), *The deliberative democracy handbook: Strategies for effective civic engagement in the twenty-first century* (pp. 120–138). San Francisco: Jossey-Bass.

Chambers, S. (2003). Deliberative democratic theory. *Annual Review of Political Science, 6,* 307–326.

Cohen, J. (1997). Deliberation and democratic legitimacy. In J. F. Bohman & W. Rehg (Eds.), *Deliberative democracy: Essays on reason and politics* (pp. 67–91). Cambridge, MA: MIT Press.

Cooke, M. (2000). Five arguments for deliberative democracy. *Political Studies, 48*(5), 947–969.

Davies, G., & Burgess, J. (2004). Challenging the 'view from nowhere': Citizen reflections on specialist expertise in a deliberative process. *Health and Place, 10*(4), 349–361.

Delli Carpini, M. X., Lomax Cook, F., & Jacobs, L. R. (2004). Public deliberation, discursive participation, and citizen engagement: A review of the empirical literature. *Annual Review of Political Science, 7,* 315–344.

Dienel, P. C., & Renn, O. (1995). Planning cells: A gate to 'fractal' mediation. In O. Renn, T. Webler, & P. Wiedemann (Eds.), *Fairness and competence in citizen participation* (pp. 117–140). Dordrecht, The Netherlands: Kluwer.

Dryzek, J. S. (2000). *Deliberative democracy and beyond: Liberals, critics, contestations.* Oxford, UK: Oxford University.

Dryzek, J. S., Goodin, R. E., Tucker, A., & Reber, B. (2009). Promethean elites encounter precautionary publics: The case of GM foods. *Science, Technology & Human Values, 34*(3), 263–288.

Einsiedel, E. F. (2002). Assessing a controversial medical technology: Canadian public consultations on xenotransplantation. *Public Understanding of Science, 11*(4), 315–331.

Einsiedel, E. F., Jelsøe, E., & Breck, T. (2001). Publics at the technology table: The Australian, Canadian and Danish consensus conferences on food biotechnology. *Public Understanding of Science, 10*(1), 83–98.

Fiorino, D. J. (1990). Citizen participation and environmental risk: A survey of institutional mechanisms. *Science, Technology & Human Values, 15*, 226–243.

Fishkin, J. (1991). *Democracy and deliberation: New directions for democratic reform.* New Haven, CT: Yale University Press.

Fishkin, J. S. (1999). Toward a deliberative democracy: Experimenting with an ideal. In S. Elkin & K. E. Soltan (Eds.), *Citizen competence and democratic institutions* (pp. 279–290). State College, PA: Pennsylvania State University Press.

Fishkin, J. S., Luskin, R. C., & Jowell, R. (2000). Deliberative polling and public consultation. *Parliamentary Affairs, 53*(4), 657–666.

Forester, J. (1989). *Planning in the face of power.* Berkeley: University of California Press.

Forester, J. (1999). *The deliberative practitioner.* Cambridge, MA: MIT Press.

Fung, A. (2003). Recipes for public spheres: Eight institutional design choices and their consequences. *Journal of Political Philosophy, 11*(3), 338–367.

Gantwerk, H. (2005). Fly into the future: An on-line dialogue about the future of San Diego's airport. A report to the San Diego County Regional Airport Authority. Retrieved November 15, 2009, from Viewpoint Learning http://www.viewpoint learning.com/publications/reports/fly_future_0805.pdf

Gastil, J. (2000). Is face-to-face citizen deliberation a luxury or a necessity? *Political Communication, 17*(4), 357–361.

Gastil, J. (2008). *Political communication and deliberation.* Thousand Oaks, CA: Sage.

Gastil, J., & Levine, P. (Eds.). (2005). *The deliberative democracy handbook: Strategies for effective civic engagement in the 21st century.* San Francisco: Jossey-Bass.

Gastil, J., & Dillard, J. P. (1999). Increasing political sophistication through public deliberation. *Political Communication, 16*(1), 3–23.

Gastil, J., Reedy, J., Braman, D., & Kahan, D. M. (2008). Deliberation across the cultural divide: Assessing the potential for reconciling conflicting cultural orientations to reproductive technology. *The George Washington Law Review, 76*, 1772–1794.

Guston, D. H. (1998). Evaluating the first U.S. consensus conference: The impact of the citizens' panel on telecommunications and the future of democracy. *Science, Technology, & Human Values, 24*(4), 451–482.

Gutmann, A., & Thompson, D. (1996). *Democracy and disagreement.* Cambridge, MA: Harvard, Belknap Press.

Guttman, N. (2007). Dilemmas and contradictions in the practices and procedures of public deliberation initiatives that aim to get "ordinary citizens" to deliberate policy issues. *Communication Theory, 17*(4), 411–438.

Guttman, N., Shalev, C., Kaplan, G., Abulafia, A., Bin-Nun, G., Goffer, R., et al. (2008). What should be given a priority — costly medications for relatively few people or inexpensive ones for many? The health parliament public consultation initiative in Israel. *Health Expectations, 11*(2), 177–188.

Haas, T. (2004). The public sphere as a sphere of publics: Rethinking Habermas's theory of the public sphere. *Journal of Communication, 54*(1), 178–184.

Habermas, J. (1984). *The theory of communicative action, Vol.1: Reason and the rationalization of society* (T. McGarthy, Trans.). Boston: Beacon Press.

Habermas, J. (1987). *The theory of communicative action, Vol. 2: Lifeworld and system: A critique of functionalist reasoning* (T. McGarthy, Trans.). Boston: Beacon Press.

Habermas, J. (1989). *The structural transformation of the public sphere* (T. Burger, Trans.). Cambridge, MA: MIT Press.

Habermas, J. (1992). Further reflections on the public sphere (T. Burger, Trans.). In C. Calhoun (Ed.), *Habermas and the public sphere* (pp. 421–460). Cambridge, MA: MIT Press.

Hadron, D., & Holmes, A. C. (1997). The New Zealand priority criteria project. Part 1: Overview. *British Medical Journal, 314*, 131–134.

Hendriks, C. M. (2006). When the forum meets interest politics: Strategic uses of public deliberation. *Politics & Society, 34*(4), 571–602.

Herbst, S. (1991). Classical democracy, polls, and public opinion: Theoretical frameworks for studying the development of public sentiment. *Communication Theory, 1*(3), 225–238.

Howard, T., & Gaborit, N. (2007). Using virtual environment technology to improve public participation in urban planning process. *Journal of Urban Planning and Development, 133*(4), 233–241.

Jensen, C. B. (2005). Citizen projects and consensus-building at the Danish Board of Technology. *Acta Sociologica, 48*(3), 221–235.

Kashefi, E., & Mort, M. (2004). Grounded citizens' juries: A tool for health activism? *Health Expectations, 7*(4), 290–302.

Lenagham J., New, B., & Mitchell, E. (1996). Setting priorities: Is there a role for citizens' juries? *British Medical Journal, 312*, 1591–1593.

Levine, P. (2001). Civic renewal and the commons of cyberspace. *National Civic Review, 90*(3), 205–212.

Levine, P., Fung, A., & Gastil, J. (2005). Future directions for public deliberations. *Journal of Public Deliberation, 1*(1), Article 3.

Lukensmeyer, C. J., & Brigha, S. (2002). Taking democracy to scale: Creating a town hall meeting for the twenty-first century. *National Civic Review, 91*(4), 351–366.

Luskin, R., Fishkin, J. S., & Jowell, R. (2002). Considered opinions: Deliberative polling in Britain. *British Journal of Political Science, 32*, 455–487.

Mansbridge, J. (1999). Everyday talk in the deliberative system. In S. Macedo (Ed.), *Deliberative politics: Essays in democracy and disagreement* (pp. 211–239). New York: Oxford University Press.

Maxwell, J., Rosell, S., & Forest, P. (2003). Giving citizens a voice in healthcare policy in Canada. *British Medical Journal, 326*, 1031–1033.

Milner, H. (2002). *Civic literacy: How informed citizens make democracy work.* Hanover, NH: University Press of New England.

Morrison, J., & Newman, D. (2001). On-line citizenship: Consultation and participation in new labour's Britain and beyond. *International Review of Law, 15*(2), 171–194.

Mullen, P. (2000). Public involvement in health care priority setting: Are the methods appropriate and valid? In C. Ham & A. Coulter (Eds.), *The global challenge of health care rationing* (pp. 163–174). Buckingham, UK: Open University Press.

Myers, D. G., & Lamm, H. (1976). The group polarization phenomenon. *Psychological Bulletin, 83*, 602–662.

Nolté, J., Maxwell, J., & MacKinnon, M. P. (2004). "Trust and Balance": Citizens' dialogue on the Ontario budget strategy 2004–2008. Ottawa, ON: Canadian Policy Research Networks.

Nussbaum, M. C. (1995). Emotions and women's capabilities. In M. C. Nussbaum & J. Glover (Eds.), *Women, culture, and development* (pp. 360–395). Oxford, UK: Oxford University Press.

Parkinson, J. (2004a). Hearing voices: Negotiating representation claims in public deliberation. *The British Journal of Politics and International Relations, 6*, 370–388.

Parkinson, J. (2004b). Why deliberate? The encounter between deliberation and new public managers. *Public Administration, 82*(2), 377–395.

Pidgeon, N., & Rogers-Hayden, T. (2007). Opening up nanotechnology dialogue with the publics: Risk communication or 'upstream engagement'? *Health, Risk & Society, 9*(2), 191–210.

Pimbert, M., Wakeford, T., & Satheesh, P. V. (2001, December). Citizens' juries on GMOs and farming futures in India. *LEISA Magazine*, 27–29. Retrieved September 5, 2009, from http://www.leisa.info/index.php?url=getblob.php&o_id=12549&a_id=211&a_seq=0

Pimbert, M. P., & Wakeford, T. (2002). *Prajateerpu: A citizens jury/scenario workshop on food and farming futures for Andhra Pradesh, India*. London: IIED.

Polletta, F., Ching, P., Chen, B., & Anderson, C. (2009). Is information good for deliberation? Link-posting in an online forum. *Journal of Public Deliberation, 5*(1), Article 2. Retrieved Septemeber 5, 2009, from http://services.bepress.com/jpd/vol5/iss1/art2

Price, V., Cappella, J. N., & Nir, L. (2002). Does disagreement contribute to more deliberative opinion? *Political Communication, 19*(1), 95–112.

Price, V., Nir, L., & Cappella, J. N. (2006). Normative and informational influences in online political discussions. *Communication Theory, 16*(1), 47–74.

Priest, S. H. (1995). Information equity, public understanding of science and the biotechnology debate. *Journal of Communication, 45*(1), 39–54.

Rawls, J. (1971). *A theory of justice*. Cambridge, MA: Belknap Press.

Rawls, J. (1997). The idea of public reason. In J. Bohman & W. Rehg (Eds.), *Deliberative democracy: Essays on reasons and politics* (pp. 93–141). Cambridge, MA: MIT Press.

Rittel, H., & Webber, M. (1973). Dilemmas in a general theory of planning. *Policy Sciences, 4*, 155–169.

Roberts, N. (2004). Public deliberation in an age of direct citizen participation. *The American Review of Public Administration, 34*(4), 315–353.

Ryfe, D. M. (2002). The practice of deliberative democracy: A study of 16 deliberative organizations. *Political Communication, 19*(3), 359–377.

Ryfe, D. M. (2006). Narratives and deliberation in small group forums. *Journal of Applied Communication Research, 34*(1), 72–93.

Salmon, C. T., & Glasser, T. L. (1995). The politics of polling and the limits of consent. In T. L. Glasser & C. T. Salmon (Eds.), *Public opinion and the communication of consent* (pp. 437–458). New York: Guilford Press.

Sanders, L. M. (1997). Against deliberation. *Political Theory, 25*(3), 347–376.

Sclove, R. E. (2000). Town meetings on technology: Consensus conferences as democratic participation. In D. L. Kleinman (Ed.), *Science, technology & democracy* (pp. 33–48). Albany: State University of New York Press.

Skorupinski, B., Baranzke, H., Ingensiep, H. W., & Meinhardt, M. (2007). Consensus conferences — A case study: Publiforum in Switzerland with special respect to the role of lay persons and ethics. *Journal of Agricultural and Environmental Ethics, 20*(1), 37–52.

Smith, G., & Wales, C. (2000). Citizen juries and deliberative democracy, *Political Studies, 48*(1), 51–65.

Walmsley, H. L. (2009). Mad scientists bend the frame of biobank governance in British Columbia. *Journal of Public Deliberation, 5*(1), Article 6. Retrieved September 5, 2009, from http://services.bepress.com/jpd/vol5/iss1/art6

Webler, T. (1995). "Right" discourse in citizen participation. In O. Renn, T. Webler, & P. Wiedmann (Eds.), *Fairness and competence in citizen participation: Evaluating models for environmental discourse* (pp. 35–86). Dordrecht, The Netherlands: Kluwer.

Webler, T., & Tuler, S. (2000). Fairness and competence in citizen participation: Theoretical reflections from a case study. *Administration and Society, 32*(5), 566–595.

Webler, T., & Tuler, S. (2002). Unlocking the puzzle of public participation. *Bulletin of Science, Technology and Society, 22*(2), 179–189.

Webler, T., Tuler, S., & Kreuger, R. (2001). What is a good public participation process? Five perspectives from the public. *Environmental Management, 27*(3), 435–450.

Wright, S., & Street, J. (2007). Democracy, deliberation and design: The case of online discussion forums. *New Media & Society, 9*(5), 849–869.

Wyatt, R. O., Katz, E., & Kim, J. (2000). Bridging the spheres: Political and personal conversation in public and private spaces. *Journal of Communication, 50*(1), 71–92.

Yankelovich, D. (1991). *Coming to public judgment: Making democracy work in a complex world.* Syracuse, NY: Syracuse University Press.

Young, M. (1996). Communication and the other: Beyond deliberative democracy. In S. Benhabib (Ed.), *Democracy and difference: Contesting the boundaries of the political* (pp. 120–135). Princeton, NJ: Princeton University Press.

Young, I. M. (2001). Activist challenges to deliberative democracy. *Political Theory, 29*, 670–690.

CHAPTER CONTENTS

8 Personalization of Politics

A Critical Review and Agenda for Research

Silke Adam

University of Bern

Michaela Maier

University of Koblenz-Landau

In this chapter we develop an agenda for future research on the personalization of politics. To do so, we clarify the propositions of the personalization hypothesis, critically discuss the normative standard on which most studies base their evaluation of personalization, and systematically summarize empirical research findings. We show that the condemnation of personalization is based on a trivial logic and on a maximalist definition of democracy. The review of empirical studies leads us to question the assumption that personalization has steadily increased in all areas of politics. Finally, our normative considerations help us develop new research questions on how personalized politics affects democracy. Moreover, this review also makes clear that another weakness of today's empirical research on the personalization of politics lies in methodological problems and a lack of analysis of the impacts of systemic and contextual variables. Consequently, we suggest methodological pathways and possible explanatory factors for the study of personalization.

Introduction

The term "personalization" in politics evokes media pictures of French presidents who, freshly divorced, whisper sweet nothings to former top-models, or of German Ministers of Defence who pose for photographs with their girlfriends in a swimming pool while the military troops are preparing for an assignment abroad. However, these examples represent only one aspect of the phenomenon that is discussed under the label "personalization of politics" in the scientific literature. Personalization in this broader perspective refers to a development in which politicians become the main anchor of interpretations and evaluations in the political process (Holtz-Bacha, Lessinger, & Hettesheimer, 1998)—be it as individuals with political or non-political traits. The claim is that personalization is changing the focus of politics from topics to people and from parties to politicians.

Debates about and studies dealing with processes of political person-alization show a strong, but mostly implicit normative focus (Hoffmann & Raupp, 2006). These normative considerations—if indeed articulated—claim that political personalization creates human pseudo events (Boorstin, 1964), downplay the big social/political picture in favor of human triumphs and trag-edies (Bennett, 2002, p. 45) and consequently have negative consequences for democracy (e.g., Holtz-Bacha et al., 1998; Kaase, 1994; Keeter, 1987). A con-cern uttered in such discussions is that the complexity of political processes is reduced to achievements and standpoints of individual politicians instead of a reinforcement of rational opinion-building and decision making. Personaliza-tion seems to hamper these rational processes as it is claimed to weaken the influence of current issues and party programs on voting decisions. This con-cern becomes even more prominent if not only individual people, but their non-political or even private lives, become the focus of attention. In this situation, "aspects of credibility and the humanization of politicians seem more impor-tant than e.g. the professional capability of a politician" (Lass, 1995, p. 10; also see Sarcinelli, 1987). This focus on candidates as "attractively packaged com-modities" (Dalton & Wattenberg, 1993, p. 208) seems to seduce people into making superficial judgments based on candidates' styles and looks—casting votes "on feeling" (Keeter, 1987, p. 356). Finally, elections based on such judg-ments are claimed to be irrational and undemanding, thereby hindering pub-lic control of the political process (Keeter, 1987). In addition, such decisions are assumed to be conducted by voters with little political interest and under-standing (Dalton & Wattenberg, 1993; Kindelmann, 1994; Page, 1978). Linden (2003) summarizes the concerns underlying most research on personalization in politics: "One is apt to believe that due to the personalization the political parties, along with the parties the political culture, and along with the political culture the democracy would go to the dogs" (p. 1206, own translation).

Many books and articles have been written about the phenomenon of the personalization of politics (e.g., Kepplinger, 1998; Wattenberg, 1995; also see the literature review in this chapter), indicating that this topic has become cen-tral to political scientists as well as scholars of political communication (Rahat & Sheafer, 2007). So what can we add? We think that it is time to critically review the state of the literature regarding personalization in politics. From this review we seek to develop an agenda that points to future paths research needs to take to understand the process, the reasons for, and the consequences of personalization. To develop such a research agenda, we proceed in four steps. First, we intend to clarify the propositions of the personalization hypothesis and thus define our object of investigation. Second, we critically discuss the normative standard on which most studies on personalization of politics are based. It is against this normative standard that concerns about personaliza-tion are uttered. Third, we systematically summarize the empirical state of the art of personalization. In doing so, we concentrate our efforts on quantitative results referring to Western democracies as it would definitely go beyond the scope of this chapter to also review all qualitative work. In addition, we focus on comparisons across time because personalization is regarded as an increasing phenomenon in politics, and its analysis thus requires a longitudinal perspective. We are aware of the fact that such an endeavor always runs the risk of missing some studies and not taking account of the most current research projects as the publication process takes its time.[1] However, we are confident that the identified normative and empirical shortcomings lead us towards a research agenda for the future (a fourth step). The shortcomings of today's empirical research show us how we need to proceed if we seek to describe and explain the degree and development of personalization. The discussion of the normative standard against which personalization is evaluated allows us to make progress in understanding the consequences of personalization for democracy. We can show that the assumed negative consequences of personalization are not confirmed empirically and are based on a standard that must be challenged on theoretical grounds. Consequently, we believe that if future research intends to say something about the positive or negative effects of personalization for democratic politics, we need to develop our research questions from more than one normative theory and link them to citizens' empirical beliefs in legitimacy. Such a broadened perspective will help us to obtain a more balanced evaluation of personalization in politics.

The Personalization Hypothesis

Personalization of politics is a popular concept. Some even claim that "personalization of politics will remain a—perhaps *the*—central feature of democratic politics in the twenty-first century" (McAllister, 2007, p. 585).[2] However, neither the concept itself nor research related to it are new phenomena: Researchers agree that "personalization of politics is as old as politics itself" (Radunski, 1980, p. 15; see also Briggs & Burke, 2002) as there have always been political actors representing political ideas, goals, and parties, and even empirical evidence for full-fledged image campaigns on the occasion of U.S. presidential elections going back as far as 1840 (Jamieson, 1996). As Halldén (1998, pp. 131–133) puts it, "the course of history is directed by Great Men and Women," and their "emotional and motivational states" are given as explaining factors for political and social change. Political science has always taken into account this relevance of "political personae" (van Zoonen & Holtz-Bacha, 2000, p. 47). Weber, for example, has compared the charismatic leadership of political actors with wizards (Weber, 2005). And the question regarding the standards on which voters judge political candidates has been crucial to electoral research for many years (for prominent examples see Campbell, Converse, Miller, & Stokes, 1980; Converse & Dupeux, 1966).

However, interest in the phenomenon of personalization was certainly boosted by changes in the political process as well as its framework, e.g., the media system and especially the introduction of television, as well as by some especially meaningful academic contributions in this field (see, for example, Iyengar and Kinder (1987) on priming theory, Hallin (1992a, 1992b) on sound bite news, and Patterson (1993a) and Jamieson (1996) on horse race journalism and strategic game coverage; below). These developments and insights made personalization a central topic of political communication attention and research in recent years.

Despite the popularity of the concept, there is no consensus on the exact definition of personalization. Holtz-Bacha et al. (1998, p. 241) describe the idea of personalization in a relatively broad manner when they stress that (a) it involves a development over time and that (b) "a person turns into an interpretative framework for complex political facts" constructing political reality. That implies two perspectives (e.g., Brettschneider, 2002; Gabriel & Keil, 2007; Gabriel & Vetter, 1998; Langer, 2007; Lass, 1995; Marcinkowski & Greger, 2000; Reinemann & Wilke, 2007; Stern & Graner, 2002). On the one hand, personalization refers to a stronger focus on candidates/politicians instead of parties, institutions, or issues. On the other hand, the personalization hypothesis claims that it is not only individuals per se, but it is their personal, non-political characteristics that become more relevant. The first form of personalization thus identifies the main development from institutions and issues to people; the second form refers to a change in the criteria for the evaluation of politicians from features regarding their professional competence and performance to features concerning non-political personality traits (also see Holtz-Bacha, 2000, 2001a, 2004; van Zoonen, 2006).

This latter proposition of political personalization is problematic. Gabriel and Vetter (1998) have stressed that it is rather complicated to distinguish between political and non-political traits. They suggest that the criteria could be operationalized on a continuum with two opposite endpoints. One end can be described by performance-related features such as leadership qualities and professional or problem-solving competences, which Lass (1995, p. 60) refers to as "role-near, instrumental" criteria (also see Iyengar & Kinder, 1987). The other end summarizes appearance and family circumstances, which Lass (1995, p. 60) refers to as "role-distant" or "value-expressive." In between these two extremes a number of characteristics could be located that can be subsumed under the broader heading of political trust, e.g., credibility and fairplay.

Distinguishing these two perspectives on personalization allows us to point out that the personalization hypothesis is based on at least two propositions. These propositions do not only necessitate different empirical research settings, but also different normative evaluations. To further clarify the personalization hypothesis, we need to address the areas of politics for which these propositions are relevant. Holtz-Bacha et al. (1998) have summarized the corresponding set of research findings and identified three areas that are the subject of studies on personalization in politics[3]: personalization of election campaigns, personalization of media reporting and commentating,[4] and personalization of voting behavior (also see Brettschneider, 2002; Gabriel & Vetter, 1998; Holtz-Bacha, 2003). In all of these areas, research on both propositions can be conducted.

In studying the change from institutions/issues to people (Proposition 1) with regard to election campaigns, this form of personalization means that the top-candidates become more important for the campaign compared to the political parties and to the issue positions. This becomes apparent in communication strategies focusing on the candidates (Brettschneider, 2001, 2002)—also to attract the attention of the media (Schulz & Zeh, 2003)—as well as in candidates' freedom to increasingly present themselves as relatively independent from their parties. The stronger autonomy of the candidates vis-à-vis the party also becomes visible in the organization of the election campaign (Brettschneider, 2002; Mancini & Swanson, 1996). Professional consultants and campaign managers often replace political parties and their permanent staff in the planning and implementation of election campaigns (also see Holtz-Bacha, 2003). In the context of media's reporting and commentating, research investigates, for example, whether the attention given to candidates increases compared to the attention to political parties or the attention given to issue coverage. Last but not least, Proposition 1 of the personalization hypothesis is also applied to voting behavior. It is stated that the importance of candidate voting has increased compared to issue voting and voting along party lines. Candidate voting in this perspective is based on candidates' evaluation, whereas issue voting results from a comparison between the perceived issue positions of political parties and voters' own viewpoints (Fuchs & Kühnel, 1994).

Proposition 2 can also be applied to all the above-mentioned research areas. Researchers interested in election campaigns study the question of whether politicians are presented in light of non-political traits rather than their competence and performance (Brettschneider, 2008). Similar questions are relevant if one looks for changes in media's reporting and commentating. Also here one can ask whether political candidates are increasingly portrayed in light of their non-political personality traits (Lass, 1995; also see Brettschneider, 2002; Holtz-Bacha et al., 1998). Finally, Proposition 2 is relevant in research on voting behavior. Here, we study whether non-political personality traits have become more important for citizens' decision making at the expense of political character traits (Brettschneider, 2002).

The personalization hypothesis with its two propositions applied to three areas was first developed in the United States. Here, the conditions for processes of personalization are ideal. The candidates running for presidency stand in the center of political campaigns, media coverage, and voting, as they are directly elected by citizens. However, most researchers assume that processes of personalization are not limited to presidential systems like the United States, but also take place in semi-presidential or parliamentary systems, which by their nature are more strongly focused on parties.

Changes in the political process itself are often claimed to foster personalization across political systems (Swanson & Mancini, 1996). The first line of reasoning in this tradition refers to changes in culture, the second line to changes in institutions. Researchers underlining the importance of cultural changes claim that processes of personalization take place as traditional ties between the political system and citizens weaken (Hallin & Mancini, 2003;

Sarcinelli, 1990). Long-term identification with parties declines (Pennings & Lane, 1998; Wiorkowski & Holtz-Bacha, 2005), the number of floating voters increases (Ersson & Lane, 1998), and traditional partisan cleavages or strong ideologies vanish (Mazzoleni, 2000). As a consequence thereof, parties use personalization strategies to win their votes. This chosen strategy, however, is assumed to change parties themselves: from mass or catch-all parties to media parties, minimal parties, or professional parties (e.g., Beyme, 1997; for a summary of the party change literature see Wiesendahl, 2001).

The second line of reasoning refers to institutional changes. These changes refer to "the adoption of rules, mechanisms, and institutions that put more emphasis on the individual politician and less on political groups and parties" (Rahat & Sheafer, 2007, p. 66). Examples are the introduction of primaries for the selection of political candidates, the launch of televised debates, or the replacement of closed lists by open lists that allow for intra-party competition in elections. For example, when explaining the emergence of two phenomena closely connected with the concept of personalization, i.e., horse race and game schema coverage, Patterson (1993a, 1993b) and Jamieson (1992, 1993; Jamieson & Birdsell, 1988) show that the institutional change of introducing primaries in the United States not only increased the individual campaign activities of the candidates but also boosted personalized media coverage during the nomination process. In several studies the media interest in this phase was shown to be even stronger than during the convention and the general election (see Patterson, 1993a; Robinson & Sheehan, 1983; Lichter, Amundson, & Noyes, 1988; Center for Media and Public Affairs, 1992). In the case of Israel, Rahat and Sheafer (2007) showed that changes in candidate selection led to personalization in media coverage, which fostered personalization in the behavior of politicians in parliament. In Germany, Reinemann and Wilke (2007) showed that with the introduction of televised debates, the physical appearance of a candidate gained in importance.

Taking these changes into account, the personalization hypothesis is assumed to be valid in all types of political systems. It assumes an increase in personalization over time. For a hard test of the hypothesis we need to look for processes of personalization within parliamentary systems as these systems are inherently driven by a party logic (Karvonen, 2007). However, the hypothesis does not claim that the total amount of personalized campaigning, media coverage, or voting is the same across different political systems. Moreover, we expect differences in the total amount depending on political context factors, a topic on which we elaborate further in the final section of this chapter.

Changes in the political process are not regarded as the sole reason for the prominence of the personalization hypothesis. Researchers claim that the increase in personalization is connected to at least two developments (Iyengar & Kinder, 1987; Karvonen, 2007; Schulz, Zeh, & Quiring, 2005; Swanson & Mancini, 1996): (a) changes in politics and (b) changes in the journalistic and media systems. Which of these developments proves to be more important is an unsolved question (Schulz, Zeh, & Quiring, 2005). Regarding the media system, the rise of television has often been connected to processes of personalization (e.g., Hallin, 1992a; Jamieson, 1996, p. 25; Iyengar & Kinder, 1987; Schoenbach, 1994; van Zoonen & Holtz-Bacha, 2000). With its picture-oriented style of presentation and its problems in conveying complex information, television is regarded as a main instrument of personalization (Wiorkowski & Holtz-Bacha, 2005). However, Patterson (1993a, p. 81) has pointed out that the television model of journalism "gradually affected the print media, to the point where the difference in the styles of television and newspaper reporting is now relatively small" as newspapers today also "heavily rely on the interpretative style of reporting," at least in the United States.

Turning to more recent developments, Patterson (1993a, pp. 78–81; also see Hallin, 1992a) points to a significant change in U.S. journalism since the 1960s, which is a part of Americanization or modernization also affecting other Western societies. First, he argues that journalists' role perception changed from "silent sceptics" to "vocal cynics" (p. 79) in the relationship to politicians as a result of, for example, the Watergate scandal. Second, this higher self-esteem was additionally boosted by the growing public esteem of the profession, which increased with a growing number of TV programs and the number of well-known journalists and reporters. Third, commercial TV further boosted the aggressive style of reporting. As a consequence of these changes in journalism, political campaigns have become "increasingly packaged for television, with a heavy reliance on pacing and visual imagery" (p. 13). The journalists' reaction was no longer to give political actors the opportunity to make extensive verbal statements but rather to ask questions and to answer and commentate themselves while providing only a symbolic visual of the politician, a phenomenon being examined by sound-bite research (Hallin, 1992a). Further on, journalists increasingly focus on campaigns as a strategic game or horse race between the leading candidates (e.g., Foley, 2000; Genz, Schoenbach, & Semetko, 2001; Jamieson, 1993; Keeter, 1987; Patterson, 1991, 1993a; Scammell & Langer, 2006).

The media logic is said to have become more prominent with the introduction of private, commercial television, which occurred more or less simultaneously in all of Europe during the 1980s and 1990s (also see Curran, Iyengar, Lund, Salovaara-Moring, 2009). Since these profit-oriented channels aim to meet the needs and expectations of the average audience, "a short, simple and people-oriented" presentation of politics (Brettschneider, 2002, p. 22) with a focus on infotainment, human-interest stories, and emotions (van Zoonen & Holtz-Bacha, 2000) is assumed to be the result (also see Gabriel & Vetter, 1998; Schoen, 2005, Holtz-Bacha, 2004). In addition, certain media trends such as specific forms of professional up-to-date campaigning are said to boost personalization (e.g., interactive Internet-communication on the one side, but also forms of personal direct-marketing; both seem to become more important due to the individualization of society) (Gronbeck & Wiese, 2005; Holtz-Bacha, 2006b; Langer, 2007; Schmitt-Beck, 2007). However, parallel to differences in political systems, the absolute amount of personalized politics might well differ according to differences in the media systems (e.g., differences in the importance of private versus public television), as we will also elaborate further in the final section of this chapter.

A Critical Assessment of the Normative Standard Used for Evaluating Personalization

Many studies dealing with the phenomenon of personalization of politics are implicitly or explicitly based on the standards of classic democratic theory, which require that voters' decision making is rational and informed (Berelson, 1966; Dalton, 2000; Sears & Chaffee, 1979). Such decision making postulates that a voter must have ample information about current political issues and the standpoints of the competing political parties in order to be able to compare his own issue positions with those of the parties to come to a rational voting decision. A prerequisite for citizens' informed and rational decision making is a functioning information flow from the elite to the public (Beierwaltes, 2000); only if citizens acquire information on the positions and decisions of those responsible can they effectively control the political elite. The critical evaluation of the personalization of politics is directly related to these ideas. If election campaigns and/or media reporting and commentating focus on people instead of issues, on non-political traits instead of political qualities, citizens will lack information for qualified decision making in elections. This curtailing of the information flow to means of symbolic politics calls the basic tenet of democratic decision making into question (Beierwaltes, 2000; Langer, 2007). The focus on the political candidates or even their personality traits is seen as lacking substance, whereas issue voting is seen as superior and better suited for informed decision making (Brettschneider, 2002; Dalton & Wattenberg, 1993).

Yet the normative evaluation of personalization of politics is based on a *trivial logic:* more personalization automatically is assumed to mean less information about issue positions (for a critical discussion, see Hoffmann & Raupp, 2006). However, Iyengar and Kinder (1987) have found convincing empirical evidence that issue salience is linked to citizens' evaluation of the political competencies as well as to perceived character traits of political actors, and vice versa. And election research until today points to very complex interactions between orientations towards parties, candidates, and issues (e.g., Brettschneider, 2002; Oegema & Kleinnijenhuis, 2000; Pan & Kosicki, 1997). Consequently, the process of electoral decision making is not a zero-sum game in which stronger candidate orientation necessarily means a loss of the normatively more significant issue and party orientation (see also Lass, 1995). Iyengar and others (Iyengar, 1989; Iyengar & Kinder, 1987; also see Holtz-Bacha, 1999, 2003; Schulz & Zeh, 2003) argue that issues are actually used for the image construction of candidates, and that campaign managers try to determine the issue contexts in which candidates are presented. Kim, Scheufele, and Shanahan (2005) support this idea when they show that information about candidates fosters knowledge on the candidates' positions regarding issue positions and therefore contributes to issue voting. In addition, Johnston and Kaid (2002) show that political ads do not just focus on issues or images, but in reality always contain information on both.

In addition, theories of democracy have always acknowledged that the idea of politically well-educated voters who make their voting decision with full information and certainty is unrealistic. As a consequence thereof, researchers have *challenged this maximalist definition of democracy*:

> [We] now understand that this maximalist definition of the prerequisites for informed decision making is unnecessary. Instead, our models should look at whether citizens can manage the complexities of politics and make reasonable decisions given their political interests and positions. (Dalton, 2000, p. 922)[5]

One of the front-runners in this tradition is Downs (1968), who highlights the problem of information costs for the average citizen. Consequently, decisions can be rational even though citizens may not be fully informed. In addition, mechanisms are sought to minimize the costs of information gathering. "A rational voter therefore seeks to minimize his information costs by applying mechanisms of information simplification or 'informational shortcuts'" (Fuchs & Kühnel, 1994, p. 315; also see Lau & Redlawsk, 2001; Page, 1978; Popkin, 1991; Wirth & Voigt, 1999).

Voters' reliance on informational shortcuts instead of a rational weighing of standpoints on different issues is not a new phenomenon. Before discussions on political personalization started dominating the field, another shortcut was—and still is—studied intensively: party identification. In contrast, however, to the short-term shortcut personalization, party identification is regarded as a long-term shortcut—a kind of psychological party membership (Campbell et al., 1980). Party identification can impact voting decisions directly or have an indirect influence on short-term attitudes about candidates and issues. Party identification therefore is a classical informational shortcut. As Campbell and colleagues (1980, p. 128) state: "the complexities of politics and government increase the importance of having relatively simple cues to evaluate what cannot be matters of personal knowledge." Some authors even conclude that, from the standpoint of classical democratic theory, short-term shortcuts may come closer to the ideal of an informed, independent voter (Dalton, 2000) than voting according to party identification. Voting along party lines is problematic in the sense that new information on issues, people, or parties is not likely to change voting decisions. Consequently, the likelihood of an effective control of political elites by the electorate is small if long-term party identification is dominant, as governments are not necessarily deselected when they do not represent the will of the electorate (Linden, 2003).

In contrast, different criteria for a person's evaluation have been identified as not only cost-saving, but also rational, relevant, and valuable for decision making for at least three reasons: (a) in complex decision-processes it seems reasonable to apply evaluation concepts which have proven their worth in everyday life,[6] (b) it also seems reasonable to draw conclusions on the basis of retrospective experience when making assumptions about the future (also see Mughan, 2000), and (c) even seemingly non-political information can convey politically relevant information. Voting decisions are complex because diverse information about issues, candidates, parties, and political programs has to be evaluated and weighed against long-term political attitudes. In such complex decision processes it seems reasonable that voters rely on criteria that they also apply in more day-to-day evaluations, e.g., when making up their minds about other individuals (Gabriel & Vetter, 1998; Lane, 1978; Lass, 1995; Jamieson & Waldman, 2003). Moral traits such as integrity, honesty, reliability, accountability, credibility, and trustworthiness have been repeatedly named as possible relevant criteria in this context (Dalton & Wattenberg, 1993; Downs, 1968; Gabriel & Vetter, 1998; Just et al., 1996; Kinder, 1986; Langer, 2006; Miller, Wattenberg, & Malanchuk, 1986; Page, 1978; Rahn, Aldrich, Borgida, & Sullivan, 1990; Street, 2004; van Zoonen, 2005). As a second group, Popkin (1991; see also Corner, 2000) introduces candidates' demographic characteristics such as race, ethnicity, age, and localism as important cues "because the voter observes the relationship between these traits and behavior as part of his daily experience" (p. 794). Several researchers (Fuchs & Kühnel, 1994; Gabriel & Vetter, 1998; Mughan, 2000; Popkin, 1991) have specifically pointed out the relevance of retrospective experiences when trying to assess the behavior of a politician after election day. Gabriel and Vetter (1998), for example, stress the importance of trustworthiness: a voter needs to trust that the candidates will represent the interest of the voters on a variety of issues, even those not yet known. For this reason, information about qualities and traits of politicians are recognized as retrospective experiences which voters may use as informational shortcuts. This is not to say that all information about candidates is actually valuable for every voting decision (also Patterson, 1993a). But even a purely visual presentation may contain valuable cues (Bucy & Grabe, 2007, p. 670). And non-political information may become politically relevant depending on the context of the election—e.g., if it is related to political issues or programs—and the priorities of the individual voter (Fuchs & Kühnel, 1994; Lass, 1995; Wirth & Voigt, 1999). For example, the family situation of a politician may not be totally disconnected from his or her vision on child care and gender questions.[7] Popkin (1991, p. 789) has recognized that "by employing such a cost-saving strategy, the voter does not sacrifice his basic issue orientations; he simply deals with them in a more economic way." Therefore, in summary, we support Kaltefleiter's (1981) view that personalization may be seen as a mechanism that bundles a variety of available information in a political person and helps make democracy work—as we would like to add—by providing a short-term shortcut for voters.

Last but not least, we argue that it is not well-justified that most normative evaluations of political personalization *solely refer to classic democratic theory.* This one-sidedness overemphasizes the possible problems of personalization discussed here but omits other risks and chances that might be just as relevant. If one evaluates personalization in politics from the standpoint of other strands of democratic theory, we can find not only new benchmark for evaluation, but also new questions that empirical research needs to answer. This broadened perspective will be addressed in the concluding section of this chapter.

A Critical Assessment of the Empirical Evidence for Personalization

Not only is the normative basis for the evaluation of political personalization shaky and one-sided, but also the empirical question of whether personalization actually develops and what consequences it suggests, is not yet answered. However, those who talk about or evaluate it often regard the degree and form of personalization as a new, increasing problem that has developed over time. Langer (2006) criticizes these ready-made preconceptions:

> Moreover, because there are stunning instances of the exposure of leaders' personal lives 'everywhere', it has become natural to believe that these suffice as evidence of the strength of the phenomenon, obscuring the need for systematic empirical evidence. (p. 98)

In the following we shed light on the empirical—mostly quantitative—state of research regarding personalization in politics—personalization in election campaigning, in media reporting, and in voting behavior. As the hypothesis is based on a development over time, we are less interested in the absolute amount of personalization than in longitudinal comparisons. The first part of this review deals with Proposition 1, which assumes that the relevance of candidates/politicians has increased over time when compared to political organizations and issues. The second part of this review focuses on Proposition 2, which assumes that non-political traits have become more important over time for the evaluation of political actors than political and management competences and achievements. We will inspect these propositions on the basis of existing empirical research.

From Institutions/Issues to People?

Election Campaigns.   It is difficult to assess whether the emphasis in election campaigns has changed from institutions and issues to people and personalities. In this field, few studies have been conducted so far, not many of which cover a long time frame and have an internationally comparative perspective. Often, the research reports contain only qualitative descriptions of the campaigns and the underlying strategies.

One of the few longitudinal studies that cover at least one aspect of election campaigns (i.e., televised ads) has been conducted by Holtz-Bacha and colleagues (Holtz-Bacha, 2000; Holtz-Bacha et al., 1998; Holtz-Bacha & Lessinger, 2006) for German national elections between 1957 and 2005. The results of this study point out that personalization is not a new phenomenon in political advertising and that there is no continuous trend towards more strategic personalization in the context of elections. Instead, strategies of personalization applied in political advertising depend on the context of the election, e.g., the type of candidates and issues, the party in power in government or the opposition (Holtz-Bacha, 2000; Holtz-Bacha, 2001b; Holtz-Bacha, 2006a). Thus, at least for Germany, it seems that one might agree with Kaltefleiter (1981), who claims that personalized election campaigns have taken place ever since the first national elections. In 1953, for example, the Christian Democratic party canvassed the electorate with the slogan "Germany votes for Adenauer."

Johnston and Kaid (2002) come to a similar conclusion in their study of U.S. presidential campaign ads between 1952 and 2000. They show that political ads have not increasingly focused on candidates' images. In contrast, the campaigns in the 1990s and the first years of 2000 contain the highest percentage of issue ads ever. Instead of a linear time trend, the campaigns differ from election to election. They show, for example, that Eisenhower's campaign in 1952 was strongly focused on issues, whereas in 1956 he ran a campaign based on image constructions. Also Gilens, Vavreck, and Cohen (2007) support this view showing that political ads in the United States have become less character-oriented. From his study of TV ads in the U.S. presidential races between 1952 and 1996, West (1997, p. 47) concludes that emphases on candidates' qualities in specific elections "were more a matter of defusing or highlighting personal qualities important in a particular race than a manifestation of any general trend toward personalistic politics." The trend he describes is one of diminishing party appeals in the ads, which are not necessarily replaced by a stronger emphasis on candidates.

From his comparison of the United States, Germany, and the U.K., Brettschneider (2002) draws similar conclusions: he cannot observe systematic changes in election campaigns that point toward personalization. It is the specific institutional design of the United States (i.e., a presidential system combined with primaries) that gives candidates a very prominent role. Above that, from time to time campaigns are personalized in all countries—e.g., the campaigns of Gladstone and Disraeli in the U.K., Adenauer in Germany, or Eisenhower in the United States. Hodess, Tedesco, and Kaid (2000) come to somewhat different conclusions from their analysis of British party election broadcasts in 1992 and 1997. They characterize the latter election as more candidate driven (Hodess et al., 2000) and thus claim that personalization is increasing, a position that is supported by Scammell and Langer (2006) after analyzing British party election broadcasts between 1992 and 1997. However, it is questionable if such a short time span warrants such a strong conclusion.[8] In addition, both research teams clearly show that the focus of the ads is still on issues and not on people (Hodess et al., 2000; Scammell & Langer, 2006). Finally, qualitative studies based on expert opinions of 14 countries claim to find an increase in leader-centered election campaigns (Webb & Poguntke, 2005).

Media Reporting and Commentating. Strong evidence exists that election news coverage in the United States has become increasingly dominated by an emphasis on candidate and party strategy, focusing more on the "horserace" and candidate personalities and very little on campaign issues (Farnsworth & Lichter, 2007; Graber, 2006; Patterson, 1993a). In their analysis of articles appearing in the *New York Times* from 1952 to 2000, Gilens et al. (2007) show that character content has steadily increased, whereas policy content has decreased. Similar patterns have emerged in analyses of election coverage around the world, suggesting that most news coverage tends to focus on campaign strategy and personalization at the cost of issues or party policies (Kaid & Strömbäck, 2008). This finding is supported by a comparative study of Dalton, McAllister, and Wattenberg (2000). They show that the ratio of candidate to party mentions in the media coverage during elections has increased in four out of five countries, namely the United States, the U.K., Austria, and France, between 1952 and 1997. The strongest increase was in the United States: From 1.7 candidate mentions for every 1 party mention in 1952, this ratio has increased to 5.6 in 1996. However, in Canada, for example, no increase was observed. However, it needs to be mentioned that the levels of personalization between countries still differ drastically. In presidential systems (U.S. and France) the level of personalization is about four times as high as in parliamentary systems.

Studies focusing only on the U.K. also support the first proposition of the personalization hypothesis. Using Harrison's studies on broadcasting coverage, a time series going back to 1964, Foley (2000) and Mughan (2000) reach the conclusion that there was an increase in the visibility of political leaders in television reporting in the 1980s and 1990s (also see Scammell & Semetko, 2008). On the basis of an analysis of *The Times* between 1945 and 1999, Langer (2006) also agrees with this argument, as do Rahat and Sheafer (2007) when analyzing media coverage of 16 election campaigns in Israel from 1949 to 2003. In the early years of these election campaigns in Israel, media coverage focused on the parties, followed by a combined focus on parties and candidates. Since the 1981 election, however, the candidates themselves became the focus of attention. This personalized media coverage is accompanied by a focus on conflicts internal to the parties instead of inter-party struggles (Shenhav & Sheafer, 2008). Following the overview of Karvonen (2007) on the state of empirical research, it seems that studies on the Finnish case also support Proposition 1 regarding media reporting. On the basis of a content analysis of TV newscasts in the context of German elections between 1990 and 2005, Schulz and Zeh (2005, 2006) also come to the conclusion that candidates have become more important for the media coverage since 1990. These findings are supported by expert opinions in 14 countries (Webb & Poguntke, 2005). Bucy and Grabe (2007) show that personalization in U.S. TV coverage takes on a specific form. It is a visual form of personalization as candidates' sound bites are overshadowed by journalists' voices, whereas candidates' image bites (their presentation without necessarily being heard) gain in importance (see also Hallin, 1992a; Patterson, 1993a).

However, there are studies which point to contrary results regarding personalization in media reporting. In their analysis of the campaign coverage of four quality newspapers in Germany from 1949 to 1998 Wilke and Reinemann (2001, p. 302) could not observe a trend towards personalization: "Neither the amount of references to the candidates, nor the number of candidates' photos or the amount and content of evaluative statements displayed a linear increase in course of time." Although the average degree of personalization has increased in the years after 1980, compared to this slight trend towards personalization, the differences found among the individual elections seem to be far more important (Wilke & Reinemann, 2001). Genz et al. (2001) reach a similar conclusion: For the time period between 1990 and 1998 they did not find a general increase of personalization in the TV news coverage of German national elections at all, but a much stronger focus on the two top-candidates compared to other political actors in 1998 than in 1990 or 1994. In a continuation of their long-term study of German election coverage in quality newspapers, Reinemann and Wilke (2007) show that the relative number of references to candidates in election coverage did not increase drastically with the introduction of televised debates. What it did, however, was to boost the absolute amount of media coverage devoted to the overall campaign. Thus, these data do not support a clear-cut change from institutions/issues to people. In contrast, they indicate that people have been important in election coverage since the beginning: 79% of all campaign coverage made reference to candidates in 1961; 71% in 2005. Jucknat's findings (2007) point in a similar direction. Analyzing media coverage in five German elections (1953, 1961, 1972, 1987, 2002), she underlines the importance of individual candidates in all elections but cannot identify a linear trend. Also Binderkrantz and Green-Pedersen (2009) raise a critical voice regarding personalization of media reporting. In their analysis of public radio news in Denmark between 1984 and 2005, they found no discernible trend outside of election times.

With the exception of the German case, empirical results seem to support Proposition 1 regarding media reporting, at least during election campaigns. However, an agreed upon methodology of how to study personalization is lacking. It therefore becomes extremely difficult to judge whether differences found between countries are real or a methodological artifact. These methodological problems become apparent if one compares studies within one country on the same election. Reinemann and Wilke (2007), for example, identify the election coverage of 1990 as one of the most personalized ones in the history of post-war Germany. In contrast, Kaase (1994, p. 220), who analyzed a broad spectrum of German media, concluded that personalization in 1990 "was not a widespread phenomenon in media information."

Voting Behavior. From a normative point of view, this last area of personalization is the most interesting as it touches upon the question of whether voters' decision making is rational and informed. The role of personalization for the voting decision, the so-called "candidate voting," as well as the orientation of voters to current political issues ("issue voting") are short-term determinants of voting behavior.[9] A hypothesis formulated in many studies is that in times of decreasing attachments to specific parties, such short-term variables might have gained significant impact (also see Gabriel & Keil, 2007). Whether this hypothesis holds true or not is somewhat hard to judge, since few studies have examined the relevance of candidate voting in parliamentary democracies (also see Brettschneider, 2002).

Existing research, however, points in the direction that candidate orientations have not gained in importance over time, and that they are far less important than is widely believed. In summarizing the results of elections in the United States, the U.K., France, Germany, and Canada from 1960 to 2001, King (2002) does not find a linear trend towards more personalized election outcomes and concludes that "the almost universal belief that leaders' and candidates' personalities are almost invariably hugely important factors in determining the outcomes of elections is simply wrong" (p. 216). Interested in the question of whether candidates actually impact the outcome of elections— not individual votes—he identifies only very few elections where the winning party would not have won any way irrespective of their candidate (King, 2002). In this finding he is supported by various authors conducting empirical studies. In their analysis of open-ended candidate likes/dislikes items in national election studies, Gilens et al. (2007) show that for the United States character-based considerations have even decreased in importance between 1952 and 2000 compared to issue considerations. For all German national elections between 1961 and 2005, Brettschneider, Neller, and Anderson (2006, p. 495) conclude: "the evaluations of the candidates for chancellor play only a small role on the behavior of voters" (also see Falter & Rattinger, 1983; Gabriel & Vetter, 1998; Kaase, 1994; Lass, 1995; Schulz & Zeh, 2005). In her overview of the respective research, Karvonen (2007) also comes to the conclusion that "personalities of party leaders are not among the prime determinants of electoral outcomes in parliamentary democracies" (pp. 8–9, Table 3), and in the same vein Linden (2003) concludes that voting is not becoming more personalized over the course of time.[10] Schoen (2007, 2009) reaches the same result analyzing German national elections between 1980 and 2005 showing that candidate effects varied considerably across elections. This result is also supported by experts' judgments in 14 countries. It is not clear whether voters in parliamentary systems actually cast their ballot in a personalized manner (Webb & Poguntke, 2005).

If candidate voting neither clearly increases over time nor has a strong impact in general, the questions arise (a) whether there is an indirect impact, and (b) whether specific situations exist, in which it may play a crucial role. Turning to the indirect impact first, Lass (1995) points out that although political parties are more important than candidates in voting, it is the attitudes towards candidates that influence voters' attitudes towards parties. Consequently, "candidates do not occasionally influence the voting behavior independent from party evaluations but they are an integral and permanent part of the perception and evaluation of political parties" (Lass, 1995, p. 191). As well, Brettschneider (2002) points in a similar direction by showing that party identification, issue preference, and candidate voting usually go hand in hand and do not contradict one another. Therefore, he concludes that the direct impact of candidates on the voting decision is very small. Turning to the specific situations in which candidate voting may be important and therefore to understand the variation from election to election and from country to country (and even from region to region; Pappi & Shikano, 2001), Brettschneider (2002) differentiates institutional, situational, and individual factors for explanation. Personalized voting is stronger in institutional settings resembling presidential systems compared to parliamentary systems (see also Pappi & Shikano, 2001). In the presidential voting system of the United States, voting is more strongly determined by the candidates than in the U.K. and Germany (Brettschneider, 2002). The situational factor (see also Kaase, 1994; King, 2002) refers to the current political issues and the people running for office. If parties are hard to differentiate, but the candidates show clear-cut differences, candidate voting becomes more likely. In a study of U.S. presidential elections between 1964 and 1984, Romero (1989) showed that where the electorate's issue responsiveness rises, its responsiveness to party and candidates is lessened. He concludes: "There is an inverse relationship in single elections between the impact of issue evaluations and party and candidate evaluations. Depending upon the specific campaign, issues, party, or the candidates become salient" (Romero, 1989, p. 417). Kellermann's study (2007) must also be interpreted in light of situational factors. Between 1990 and 2005 the relevance of candidate-voting decreased in Germany for the Christian Union parties, while it increased for the Social Democrats. These opposite trends could be explained with the fading importance of former Chancellor Kohl for the CDU/CSU, whereas Gerhard Schröder's star as new "media chancellor" was still rising. Personal factors refer to the party identification of each voter (see also Lass, 1995; Schulz & Zeh, 2005). Those strongly identifying with a party evaluate the candidate of the own party more positively irrespective of the actual person. For these citizens, candidate voting becomes relatively unlikely.

From Political to Non-Political Personality Traits?

The second proposition we want to examine on the basis of empirical studies at hand is whether personalization is a problem because candidates are increasingly portrayed and evaluated on the basis of non-political, symbolic criteria that do not refer to any substantial issue positions. Research has shown that candidates can be evaluated on different dimensions, e.g., issue competence, integrity, leadership qualities, and non-political traits like appearance and taste (for overviews see Brettschneider, 2002; Kindelmann, 1994; Rahn, Aldrich, Borgida, & Sullivan, 1990; Sigel, 1969; Wirth & Voigt, 1999). The thesis is that non-political characteristics of a person have become more important for the evaluation of a candidate than aspects regarding his or her issue positions, political and management qualities, and achievements. In the following the way in which candidates are presented and evaluated will be analyzed again for the three areas campaign strategies, media reporting, and voting behavior.

Election Campaigns. The question whether election campaigns increasingly build on non-political features of candidates is difficult to answer because there is even less empirical research available for Proposition 2 compared to Proposition 1. Again, the only empirical study that compares election campaigns over a longer time span is to our knowledge the one of Holtz-Bacha and colleagues (Holtz-Bacha, 2000; Holtz-Bacha et al., 1998; Holtz-Bacha & Lessinger, 2006). From this study she concludes that parties hardly use personal attributes of candidates in their campaign strategies. Only 8% of their presentations of party candidates consist of candidates' personal traits (Holtz-Bacha, 2000). However, one can observe differences between the Social Democrats and the Conservatives: Whereas the latter try to connect their candidates with attributes of "competence," the campaigns of the Social Democrats use attributions to a lesser degree although there has been an increase in the attributions made to personal traits since 1990 (Holtz-Bacha, 2000). However, it is doubtful if this is sufficient to speak of a trend towards non-political personalization in election campaigns.

Media Reporting and Commentating. In the field of media content analysis, the data base regarding the longitudinal development of the relevance of non-political traits is better but definitely in need of further development (also see Langer, 2006). The long-term analysis of the press coverage on national elections in Germany between 1961 and 1998 by Wilke and Reinemann (2001) brought the insight that "evaluative statements concerning the personality of a candidate had not received more attention over the years by the media when compared to statements about their competences" (p. 302). The authors found that issue competence and leadership-/manager-skills were reported on more often (43% of all statements) than the personality of the candidates (trustworthiness, decisiveness, honesty, intelligence, sympathy, serenity; 33%), while 11% dealt with the appearance (talent for public speaking, physical appearance), and 4% with their values (e.g., religiousness and conservatism).[11] In 2002 and 2005, however, the number of evaluative statements about the candidates in the quality media exploded, which was partly a result of the introduction of televised debates in those years (Reinemann & Wilke, 2007). Compared to previous elections, it is not only the total number of evaluative statements that increased, but the dimensions for candidate evaluation also changed (Reinemann & Wilke, 2007): 23% (2002) and 22% (2005) of all evaluative statements about the candidates dealt with their appearance (e.g., rhetorical skills, media performance, and looks). This is the highest number in Germany since 1949.

In the case of Israel, Rahal and Sheafer (2007) could not find a trend towards a stronger focus on personal characteristics and private lives in their analysis of the election coverage between 1949 and 2003. Coverage of personal traits never exceeded 15% of the news items analyzed. After her analysis of *The Times* for the period between 1945 and 1999, Langer (2006, p. 253) states that "references to leaders' personal lives and associated private qualities are not as prominent as generally assumed." As the portion of statements referring to the persona of a politician did not exceed 12%, she argues that this figure is not large enough "to claim that the personal has taken over the political" (Langer, 2006, p. 254). And even in U.S. presidential elections, Sigelman and Bullock (1991), who analyzed election coverage over 100 years, were not able to find such a trend. All of these studies refer to verbal statements when analyzing candidates' traits, although research shows that, at least for TV, it is the visual image and less the verbal that characterizes personalization (Bucy & Grabe, 2007, p. 669; also see Kepplinger, 1982; Kepplinger & Donsbach, 1987; Kepplinger & Maurer, 2005; Kepplinger, Brosius, & Dahlem, 1994). Which candidate traits, however, are best supported by which visual presentations is so far a question that has not been tackled empirically. Certainly, image bites do not contain arguments or policy positions. Yet, whether they contain information about leadership qualities or only about hair color has not been studied as yet.

Voting Behavior.   Most of the empirical studies dealing with the question of which dimensions of candidate evaluation are decisive for voting behavior have concluded that political and management skills, rather than non-political traits, influence voters' decision making.

One of the earlier comprehensive studies in this field was presented by Lass (1995), who found that the perceived integrity of candidates had the strongest impact on the evaluation of the politicians in three German elections (1969, 1976, and 1987). Non-political evaluations, in contrast, turned out to play an inferior role: "Candidate-oriented thinking cannot be disqualified as superficial" (Lass, 1995, p. 192). According to Lass (1995), over time, citizens' images have become significantly more complex and have a stronger cognitive foundation compared to the 1960s. The studies by Brettschneider (2002), Gabriel and Vetter (1998), and Pappi and Shikano (2001) support the findings of Lass. In Brettschneider's (2001, 2002) study, a rare comparative study, non-political character traits had the lowest impact of all candidate characteristics on the candidate-evaluation in Germany, Great Britain, the United States, and their importance did not increase over time. Instead, the competence to solve political problems, integrity, and leadership qualities were the most important determinants. Brettschneider (2002) therefore recapitulated that non-political traits of a candidate might be taken into account by voters, but that they would not be decisive for voting-decisions if the candidate could not convince by his or her issue competence and leadership-qualities.[12] Also for the United States, Miller et al. (1986) could not detect a trend towards an increasing importance of candidates' personal characteristics compared to performance characteristics. The findings of Mughan (2000), in a study of British elections between 1987 and 1997, show that the "character traits" effectiveness and caring had become more important in the voting decision but are not strong supports for the second proposition of the personalization hypothesis. First, from our point of view, effectiveness in particular can hardly be seen as a non-political trait, and second, the author himself limits his findings by acknowledging that the influence of these traits varies with the political circumstances of individual elections.

One widespread assumption regarding the relevance of non-political traits for the voting decisions in different groups of the electorate is that citizens with fewer cognitive resources are more oriented toward non-political traits of candidates than voters with a very pronounced political knowledge. For the German elections between 1998 and 2005, however, Gabriel and Keil (2007) have shown that this does not hold true. They state that, again, it seems to depend more on the context of a specific election than on the cognitive engagement of a voter whether personality traits or political competences are more important for the voting decision. In contrast, Keeter (1987) was able to detect differentiated effects by analyzing open-ended questions in eight national election studies in the United States. Whereas candidates' personal qualities and traits gained in importance for television-dependent voters since 1964, no such effect could be detected for those who relied on newspapers.

Personalization Revisited

A critical review of the state of empirical research leads us to question McAllister's (2007, p. 584) statement that there is "little doubt that politics has become more personalized over the past half-century." There is only one area of politics where the empirical state of research supports this statement: media coverage. For this we find relatively clear evidence of a movement from parties and issues to people (see also Karvonen, 2007). This finding may be explained by the fact that personalization is one of the most important news factors determining journalistic selection processes (e.g., Galtung & Ruge, 1965; Schulz, 1997). Beyond, media organizations themselves can create new personalized media formats to which they amply refer to within their other programs (Reinemann, 2007; Siegert, 2001).

For the other areas of politics as well as for the second proposition, which claims a development toward non-political evaluation standards, it is questionable whether politics has actually shifted dramatically towards stronger personalization. Hardly any evidence for Proposition 1 is found in respect to voting—even in those countries in which personalization has shaped other areas (for a similar evaluations, see Gabriel & Keil, 2005; Schoen & Weins, 2005). Campaigns, as much as we can tell from the scarce number of studies at hand, lie between (for a similar evaluation, see Brettschneider & Vollbracht, 2009). It thus seems that the area of politics on which most critical evaluations of political personalization are based—voting behavior—has not changed from parties and issues to people. It is, therefore, a myth on which today's condemnation of personalization in politics is based. This myth refers to the logic that personalization is something exceptionally new. However, it seems to us that candidates for political office and elected politicians have always been very visibly personalized. Wilke and Sprott (2009), for example, even show that already in 1925 and 1932 more than 80% of media articles in the election campaigns for the president of the German Reich were personalized and that journalists were highly interested in politicians' private lives. This visibility is changing depending on different contexts but is not necessarily showing a steady increase over time.

Regarding the second proposition of the personalization hypothesis, we hardly find any evidence of a change from political to non-political personality traits for a candidate's or politician's evaluation, In regard to campaigning, we cannot confirm Proposition 2, although the basis for this evaluation is thin as there are hardly any quantitative analyses available concerning aspects of the form of personalization in political campaigns over the course of time. Therefore, major research efforts are necessary to investigate whether election campaigns are shifting the focus towards non-political traits of politicians. Also, regarding media coverage, we do not observe a stronger focus on non-political evaluation criteria. Thus, the conclusion of Wirth and Voigt (1999) seems to be justified. According to these researchers, the rational choice model of political simplification seems to be confirmed in most studies on media coverage, perhaps with the exception of Germany after the introduction of the televised debates in 2002. Last but not least, the major strand of research also rejects Proposition 2 regarding the influence of personalization on voting behavior. There is hardly any evidence that non-political attributes have become more important for candidate evaluation, preference, or even voting behavior (also see Bartels, 2002; Fiorina, Abrams, & Pope, 2003; Schoen & Weins, 2005). Table 8.1 provides an overview of the empirical status quo.

This empirical review of the state of the art challenges the popular conviction that personalization of politics is an overarching phenomenon that increases sharply in all Western societies. Personalization—at least as far as we can tell from the sparse data available—has not strongly affected voting decisions, and personalization has not yet transformed the political process

Table 8.1 Empirical Evidence for Personalization

Areas Dimensions	Campaigns	Media	Voting
Proposition 1: Institutions / issues → persons	–/+*	+	–
Proposition 2: Political → non-political traits	–*	–	–

* few studies available

into a depoliticized contest in which non-political traits, such as physical appearance, have become increasingly important:

> Modern elections, despite what is often said and written about them, are only very seldom beauty contests ... Modern elections remain overwhelmingly *political* contests, and political parties would do well to choose their leaders and candidates in light of that fact. (King, 2002, p. 221)[13]

Political Personalization: Toward a Theoretically Grounded Research Agenda

Our review has shown that personalization research is characterized by research lacunas in many areas, by methodological problems when measuring personalization, and by an underlying normative (negative) evaluation that can be challenged on theoretical grounds. Consequently, a future research agenda needs to address three core tasks. The first is to improve our ability to *describe* and measure the degree and development of personalization; the second is to *explain* the conditions under which it occurs; and the third is to *evaluate* how personalization might affect democracy.

In order to *describe* the degree and development of personalization and thus overcome today's "inconsistencies" (Rahat & Sheafer, 2007, p. 66) in research going beyond the conclusion that the topic is "genuinely unsettled" (Karvonen, 2007, p. 9), it is necessary to standardize the instruments that are employed. As yet, an agreement upon methodology of how one might operationalize personalization is lacking (Kaid & Strömbäck, 2008). The resulting methodological problems lead to research artifacts claiming different levels and degrees of personalization even if one looks at the same elections (e.g., Reinemann & Wilke, 2007; Kaase, 1994). This standardization is especially challenging in reference to Proposition 2 of the personalization hypothesis. The review has made clear that there is neither consensus on the dimensions on which candidates are evaluated nor on how to differentiate these dimensions on political versus non-political traits (Gabriel & Vetter, 1998). Graber (1972), for example, qualifies only 23% of all mentions of presidential qualities in the media coverage of the U.S. campaign of 1968 as referring to professional capacities, whereas the rest describes candidates' personal attributes, style, and professional image. However, other authors apply a much stricter definition of non-political characteristics. To truly measure whether there is a trend towards the non-political, a good starting point to classify candidates' characteristics on a continuum has been proposed by Gabriel and Vetter (1998; for ideas of how to develop such scales, see Sears & Chaffee, 1979; Miller & MacKuen, 1979; Lang, & Lang, 1979; Dennis, Chaffee, & Choe, 1979; Simons & Leibowitz, 1979; Jamieson & Waldman, 2003). In addition, research on personalization needs to go beyond its focus on verbal statements and also take into account visuals (see e.g., Bucy & Grabe, 2007) and ask which candidate traits are best carried through which form of presentation (see e.g., Kepplinger, 1982; Kepplinger & Donsbach, 1987; Mutz, 2007).

As the personalization hypothesis implies a development over time, a longitudinal research design is necessary (Kaase, 1994; Krewel, 2008; Langer, 2006, 2007). Only such a research design would allow us to test whether personalization actually increases. If we were to reject this claim, the consequence would not be that people or even their personal traits are irrelevant. Instead, it could just mean that it is an old phenomenon which occurs in variable degrees at certain times, and we should more strongly head towards an understanding of the conditions which explain the degrees and forms of personalized campaigns, news coverage, or voting behavior[14] and of the effects on today's democracies.[15]

In this context the *explanation* of personalization or of the different levels of personalized politics requires not only conducting comparative research across time but also across countries. Within such comparative research, countries or time-points need to be replaced by variables that have explanatory power. Future research needs to specify the cultural and institutional factors in regard to the political and media systems that explain under which conditions personalized politics evolves (see also Schoen, 2007).

Earlier in the chapter we described the cultural and institutional changes attributed to the boost in personalization as a longitudinal trend. We described the weakening of political identification and the increase of voters' volatility as such a cultural development and changes in the process of candidate selection as such an institutional development. In regard to media, we referred to the changes in role-perceptions of journalists (cultural) and the introduction of commercial television (institutional). As we concluded, these factors are often claimed to be responsible for the increase of personalization of politics over time. Yet, these trends do not affect all countries equally because system-level variables still differ (see for the limits of homogenization, Hallin & Mancini, 2004; Benson & Hallin, 2007). A closer look at these system-level variables may therefore help us to (a) understand the differences in the absolute amount of personalization in different countries and (b) predict how system-level changes impact upon personalization.

Important macro-level variables can be identified with regard to the political system. Those political systems rooted in *parties* with loose ideological and organizational ties to the electorate more easily allow for personalization compared to those with clear ideological orientations (Hallin & Mancini, 1984; Schoen & Weins, 2005). Most Western democracies have experienced a decline of party loyalty. However, large differences prevail. For the United States, for example, Hallin (1992a, b) sees dramatic shifts with the breakdown of the political consensus leading to a fragmented and adversarial political system that is accompanied by a journalist-centered form of critical reporting, which shows the visuals of politicians while leaving the interpretations to journalists.

Further, differences between countries prevail also regarding the *selec-*

tion of candidates running for presidency or prime minister. Personalization is boosted in those systems in which members or supporters of a party can directly decide on a party's candidate in primaries or caucuses compared to those systems in which leading party committees internally decide who is going to run. Primaries or caucuses—as introduced in the United States as a result of the McGovern-Fraser Commission Report in the early 1970s—force candidates to convince party members, supporters, campaign sponsors, and the media of their competence, experience, leadership qualities, and integrity. These are all person-centered heuristics (Brady & Johnston, 1987). In such a system, traditional party functions are handed over to the mass media, which serve as an intermediary to inform rank-and-file voters about potential candidates (Patterson, 1993a, pp. 34–37).

In addition, *presidential systems* (e.g., U.S., France) with their directly elected, single executive who is independent of parliamentary majorities (see Lijphardt, 1999) are more strongly focused on the person compared to *parliamentary systems* (see also Hallin & Mancini, 1984). In the latter, personalization is hampered because prime ministers share power with their cabinet, and they are dependent on the parliament for election and potential dismissal. Consequently, any institutional change towards a stronger presidential type of democracy (e.g., the introduction of direct elections of the prime minister in Israel in 1996) is likely to trigger the process of personalization.

Furthermore, political systems can be differentiated into *majoritarian* (e.g., the U.K.) and *consensus democracies* (e.g., Switzerland; Lijphardt, 1999).[16] Majoritarian democracies are responsive to the majority of citizens, whereas consensus democracies are responsive to as many people as possible and therefore based on inclusiveness, bargaining and compromise. One may expect that majoritarian democracies show stronger tendencies for personalization compared to consensus democracies. Why? Classical majoritarian democracies are characterized by (a) a stronger leader focus on the prime minister as (s)he can govern without being bound into coalitions in the executive and is superior in power compared to the parliament, (b) a two-party system which allows focusing on two leaders only (see Hallin & Mancini, 1984), and (c) an electoral system in which the winning candidate takes it all. In contrast, consensus democracies are linked to proportional representation based on party lists (see also Strömbäck & Dimitrova, 2006).

In addition, one might also expect variation in the degree of personalization in consensus democracies because these differ regarding the *mode of election*: Some combine proportional representation based on party lists with personalized modes of elections (e.g., mixed member proportional formula in Germany and New Zealand or single transferable vote in Ireland; see Lijphardt, 1999, p. 148f.). In those systems where there are personalized modes of elections, we expect stronger personalization than in party-list proportional systems. With a focus on Germany, Klingemann and Wessels (1999, p. 18) show that the mixed electoral system contributes to a "personal vote at the grass roots." According to Holtz-Bacha (2006b, p.18), it is specific parties that personalize their campaigns: In mixed member proportional systems, where the first vote is for the candidate and the second for the party, smaller parties normally go for the second vote and therefore have less personalized campaigns.

Finally, political systems differ regarding their habitual *style of campaign communication*. In countries with televised debates between the leading candidates, personalization is promoted. Latest evidence here comes from Germany. With the introduction of televised debates in 2002, personalization of national campaigns has increased (Maurer & Reinemann, 2007; Wilke & Reinemann, 2006, pp. 321–323; Holtz-Bacha, 2006b, p. 21). However, as the number of these debates has declined in 2005 and 2009, it becomes clear that this is an institutional factor likely to affect short-term changes in the degree of personalization.

With regard to the national media systems as possible explanatory factors, Hallin and Mancini (1984, p. 830, 2004; see also Wiorkowski & Holtz-Bacha, 2005, p. 175) argue that the degree of commercialization of the media system affects not only the media content but also the form of representation and in both ways determines the degree of personalization. A "commercial imperative" in general leads to an "essentially cinematic [style of reporting], combining visual imagery with narrative structure" (Hallin & Mancini, 1984, p. 839). As commercialization is most prominent in what Hallin and Mancini (2004) call "liberal media systems" (U.S., Canada, Ireland—and to a lesser degree the U.K.), one can expect a more dramatized, personalized, and popularized style of reporting there. The pioneering case in this respect is the United States. Yet, with the rise of private broadcasters, commercialization has also invaded European media systems. Research shows that a higher degree of commercialization seems to boost personalization even in public broadcasting (Curran et al., 2009; Schulz & Zeh, 2006, p. 300). However, countries still differ regarding the importance of public broadcasters. In countries with solid public funding, market pressures are less severe for public broadcasters, which might let us expect less personalization.

These macro-level factors are important to consider in future research seeking to understand differences and changes in the degree of personalization between countries. What needs to be done is to analyze the relative importance of these factors and their interactions. However, these system-level variables are not suitable to account for variation between different elections within the same country and between different organizations/parties. To understand such variation in personalized politics, future research must also focus on meso-level and situational factors.

On an organizational level, we might expect that catch-all parties, or parties with a loose ideological profile, conduct more personalized campaigns compared to single-issue parties, as a clear focus on issue positions might be risky taking into account the diverging interests and expectations of catch-all parties' heterogeneous voter-groups (Wiorkowski & Holtz-Bacha, 2005). On this organizational level, we may also expect differences between media organizations. Those news organizations that need to cater to a mass taste (e.g., the boulevard press) are more likely to rely on people and their non-political traits in transporting information compared to those news organizations that cater more strongly to the elites. Personalization in this perspective is not an exclusive feature of television, but of popular commercial media in general (Hallin & Mancini, 2004, p. 278).

And third, the degree of personalization of election campaigns and media coverage may also vary due to the specific context of an election (e.g., the constellation of parties, candidates, and topics; see Holtz-Bacha, 2000; Wilke & Reinemann, 2000; Schulz & Zeh, 2006). One interesting example for how the party constellation may influence the degree of personalized politics is the emergence of new political parties, a phenomenon which is not so infrequent at all (e.g., when looking at the spectrum of parties competing in the European parliamentary elections 2009 in many south and eastern European countries). Holtz-Bacha (2006b, p. 10) has described that the interest of the media is especially high in the top candidates of such new parties due to the novelty factor.

But independent from the novelty factor, the candidate constellation itself also seems to have a significant influence on the decision to choose a personalized campaign strategy or not. The question of whether a candidate is willing to participate in a strongly personalized campaign or prefers to focus on issues instead is a momentous decision (Holtz-Bacha, 2006b). Besides personality traits and strategic convictions, candidates' experiences in former elections might boost or hinder personalization. Further, the popularity of the candidates has implications for the interests of the parties. If a candidate is significantly more popular than the opposite candidate, the party will, of course, try to build on this advantage. Also, if the candidate is more popular than his/her own party, the attempt to transfer this positive image to the party by focusing on the candidate makes sense. This seems to be especially promising if the image of the candidate is linked with positive memories of his actions and achievements during his term in office. Such memories very often also provide good opportunities for visual representation (see also Holtz-Bacha, 2006b).

A rather new field of research looks at whether the involvement of women in election campaigns fosters personalization. Holtz-Bacha (2006b, p. 24) argues that female candidates receive more attention in campaigns, which leads to a higher degree of personalization (e.g., of the media coverage) simply because the uncommonness of their involvement makes them more interesting than male candidates. But there are also those who suggest that the physical attraction of female candidates and the possibilities this offers for visualization boost personalization (e.g., Dillenburger, Holtz-Bacha, & Lessinger, 2005). Schulz and Zeh (2006, pp. 280–281) argue that women are judged more often on the basis of "emotions, appearance and gender... They are represented rather on the basis of female characteristics and put in context with 'female' topics. Their family lives and personality get more attention than their political program."

As a last situational factor, the constellation of issues and topics has been identified as a good predictor for personalized election campaigns. In general, Holtz-Bacha (2006b) has identified the economic and political situation of a country as relevant context factors. More specifically, Wiorkowski and Holtz-Bacha (2005; see also Holtz-Bacha, 2006b) have found personalization to be a strategy with the goal to distract from unpleasant issues either at present or those may arise after the election (e.g., possible coalition partners).

Finally, research needs to tackle the question of how personalization or personalized politics *impact* upon democracy—and thus how one might evaluate personalization/personalized politics. It is not sufficient to study the impact of the verbal dimension of personalized politics while totally neglecting the impact of visuals (see for this claim Lowry & Shidler, 1995). The visuals might be the trigger that actually makes the difference. Although widely assumed to change politics, to date researchers have hardly been able to document how TV differs from other media in its content and implications (Mutz, 2007, p. 632). This search for consequences of personalization/personalized politics has methodological as well as normative implications. From a methodological point of view, one has to go beyond solely relying on surveys or content analysis, which for themselves are not sufficient to detect effects. For determining such effects, one needs to combine content analysis and surveys, or one needs to conduct experimental research (Holtz-Bacha, 2003; Kaase, 2000; Klein & Ohr, 2001; Mutz, 2007).

To evaluate how personalization/personalized politics affect democracy, there are in general two ways to proceed. First, one may study the impact of personalized politics on citizens' attitudes towards the political system and regime. In this perspective democracies would be affected by personalized politics as citizens' empirical beliefs in legitimacy change (Nohlen, 2002). Second, one may derive normative standards from theories of democracy and ask how personalization/personalized politics affect the quality of democracy as described by these normative standards. In this perspective the normative core of a democracy would be affected by personalized politics (Nohlen, 2002). These two paths for research pose different research questions. Yet, to answer them we need to draw on empirical research.

Turning to possible effects on citizens' empirical beliefs in the legitimacy of a political system, one may rely on Easton (1965). He distinguishes three relevant types of attitudes towards a democracy: attitudes towards the authorities who are responsible for day-to-day politics, the regime, which equals the constitutional order, and the political community. Personalized politics is likely to be connected to the attitudes towards the authorities. Research on second-level agenda-setting, for example, states that media's emphasis on substantive and affective attributes of candidates is linked to opinions about these candidates (e.g., Kim & McCombs, 2007). Other researchers have shown that the visual presentation of political elites in the media influences their evaluations (e.g., Kepplinger & Donsbach, 1987; see also Bucy, 2000; Bailenson, Iyengar, Yee, & Collins, 2008). In addition, research has shown that the type of framing influences responsibility attributions (Iyengar, 1989). Episodic framing, which is often used by personalized reports (for this connection, see Boykoff & Boykoff, 2007), leads citizens to emphasize individual responsibility, whereas thematic framing points to the responsibility of the state, the authorities. Further, we might hypothesize that such attitudes towards the authorities have the potential to also affect the empirical beliefs in the legitimacy of the regime and the political community. Yet until today, there are no empirical studies that have validated this claim.[17] Positive evaluations of political candidates might foster citizens' beliefs in the legitimacy of the regime or the community, whereas negative evaluations might have the opposite effect. We would assume that a negative impact of personalized politics on empirical beliefs in democracy is most likely in parliamentary systems because here the focus on a person does not go along with the power of this person in the political process. Personalized politics without political power and responsibility (Campus, 2002) might easily lead to frustration (Bartolini, 2006) on the side of the electorate.

Whether personalized politics affects the quality of a democracy as defined by normative theories has often been assumed but hardly ever been empirically tested. So far most researchers have connected personalization/personalized politics with the basic standard for a liberal democracy: an informed and rational control of the elites by citizens. If election campaigns and/or media reporting and commenting focus on people instead of issues, on non-political personality traits instead of political qualities, citizens are assumed to lack the information necessary for qualified decision making in elections. Following up on our critique of the normative standards for evaluation that such reasoning is trivial and neglects the importance of informational shortcuts for citizens, we want to propose a counter-hypothesis, which will hopefully help place the effect of personalized politics on the quality of information flows on the top of future research agendas.

This counter hypothesis builds on the experiences with the European Union. Research on recent European Parliament elections has clearly validated that national parties avoid placing emphasis on the leaders and personalities who would represent the party in Strasbourg to avoid shedding light on parties' internal disputes on EU integration (e.g., for the German party TV ads in 2004 see: Esser, Holtz-Bacha, & Lessinger, 2008; Maier & Maier, 2008; Wiorkowski & Holtz-Bacha, 2005). In addition, this lack of personalized politics does not only shape parties' communication but also media coverage. The lack of familiar faces in Europe accompanied by the lack of clear-cut accountability has been identified as one crucial factor in explaining why it is so difficult for the EU to gain the attention of national mass media (e.g., Gerhards, 1993; Peter & de Vreese, 2004). In this vein Meyer (1999) concludes that "[w]ithout the personalization of political debate and decision processes, political accountability remains invisible" (p. 633). Adam (2007a, 2007b) also points in a similar direction when she shows that it is national politicians who give European politics a face and therefore influence whether European issues are debated in a country or not. Politics without personalization thus runs the risk of being ignored in public debate as its logic does not fit with the news value of the main transmitters, the mass media. Further research, therefore, needs to address the question whether personalization and/or personalized politics is fostering the existence of the normatively desirable informed citizen. So far empirical research has focused on the general ability of mass media to foster citizens' political knowledge (for an overview see Maier, 2009). Yet, even here the results are inconsistent. The same holds for research on the effects of paid advertisement on voters' knowledge (e.g., Freedman, Franz, & Goldstein, 2004; Huber & Arceneaux, 2007; see also Jamieson et al., 2000 for ads and TV debates). Even more limited is our knowledge on how personalized information affects citizens' knowledge: Does it increase knowledge acquisition (e.g., Fiske & Taylor, 1984; Graber, 2001; Beniger & Jones, 1990) or not (e.g., Prior, 2003)?

However, as argued previously, to focus only on the informed and rational control of the elites proposed by classic democratic theory is narrow and does not adequately take into account the breadth of today's theories of democracy. To deal with this plurality and thus to truly examine the question of the impact of personalized politics/personalization on the core standards of our democracies, we also consider basic ideas of pluralist, participatory, and discursive theories. Since these strands of theory are sometimes hard to clearly differentiate and the views of some authors even shift over time in the course of their writings, we confine ourselves to several principle ideas to widen the research agenda on the consequences of personalization.

Pluralist theories of democracy are founded on the idea that the state allows all interests to equally access the political system, thereby avoiding power concentration (e.g., Fraenkel, 1991; for a summary, see Beierwaltes, 2000; Schmidt, 1995). In reference to the criterion access, personalization/personalized politics could be evaluated critically. One might argue that personalized politics has the potential to increase the inequality of interest representation in politics. Personalized politics gives those with high status and prominence an advantage. It is easier for them to access the media (Wolfsfeld, 1997), because they better fit the news values. This is also what Kernell (1988) refers to when he shows that only few politicians are prominent enough to directly address the public instead of negotiating in parliament. This strategy as part of personalized politics is called "going public." As a consequence, democracies are assumed to become more populist when focused on leader personalities (Kriesi, 2001). Personalized politics might also give specific people an advantage in campaigning, with possible effects, for example, on the candidate recruitment process (Freedman et al., 2004) money-wise or appearance-wise. Thus, personalization/personalized politics might increase the inequality in access to the political system. In this perspective it is not only the fact that interests have different potentials to be organized (Olson, 1965), but also that those interests promoted by the prominent and the prestigious or the more active have better chances to be articulated. Yet, empirical research needs to show whether and how personalized politics contributes to inequalities in access.

From the standpoint of participatory democracy (e.g., Barber, 1984; for a summary see Ferree, Gamson, Gerhards, & Rucht, 2002; Schmidt, 1995), participation is a value per se. Personalization in this perspective might be valuable as it has the potential to foster participation of those normally less involved in the political process (e.g., Langer, 2007; Schulz, Zeh, & Quiring, 2005). Mazzoleni (2000), for example, claims that personalized leadership is one of the main factors that accounts for political motivation and participation. Personalization, he claims, "appeals to symbolic politics, to political emotions and the deeper needs of personal and subcultural identification" (Mazzoleni, 2000, p. 328) and thus might "drive substantial sectors of lukewarm electors to cast a ballot in favor of political leaders" (p. 328). Empirical research, so far, still struggles with the question whether and how mass media usage in general affects participation (e.g., Scheufele, 2002) or the question of the impact of paid political ads on participation (e.g., Freedman et al., 2004; Huber & Arceneaux, 2007; Jamieson, 2000). Research is needed to understand the specific effects of personalized information on voter participation.

Finally, turning to discursive theories of democracy (for this term, see Ferree et al., 2002), which are closely linked to participatory theories (see Schmidt, 1995), participation alone is not sufficient but needs to be accompanied by a well-functioning process of opinion formation. "The notion of a deliberative democracy is rooted in the intuitive ideal of a democratic association in which justification of the terms and conditions of association proceeds through public argument and reasoning among equal citizens" (Cohen, 1989, p. 17). A prerequisite for this process is the acceptance of others as legitimate speakers. To date only few studies (e.g., Moy & Gastil, 2006) have tackled the question of how mass media affect deliberative conversions. Even less empirical studies (e.g., Mutz, 2007) search for the role of personalized information for deliberations. Whether personalized politics supports such discursive reasoning is questionable. Personalized politics is likely to give those arguments that are supported by prestigious and prominent speakers an advantage and thus might contradict the idea that the quality of an argument is more important than the person giving voice to it (Ferree et al., 2002). In addition, one may ask how specific forms of personalized presentations affect our acceptance of others as legitimate speakers. In this vein, Mutz (2007) has shown in her experimental research that television discourses that portray public actors in an intimate way and in which the actors interact disrespectfully with each other, do indeed increase citizens' knowledge about the arguments of the opposition. At the same time this personalized presentation of politics lowers the regard for the other side, and therefore citizens "come to perceive that the opposition is unworthy and illegitimate" (Mutz, 2007, p. 633). If this finding holds, today's presentation of candidates on TV would hinder political deliberation as it degrades those with opposing views. An overview how the discussed normative standards link to an empirical research program is presented in Table 8.2.

By critically reviewing the empirical and normative state of the art regarding personalization of politics we have developed an agenda for future research. Such research needs to overcome methodological weaknesses (describe), to systematically use comparative research in order to understand personalization as a dependent variable (explain), and to study the consequences of personal-

Table 8.2 Linking Normative Standards to Empirical Research Questions

Normative standard	Empirical questions: Personalization / personalized politics
Informed / rational control of elites (classic theory of democracy)	… hinders or fosters information flows?
Equal access to the political process (pluralist theory of democracy)	… increases the inequality because those with high status have an advantage?
Participation in the political process (participatory theory of democracy)	…fosters participation?
Discursive reasoning (discursive theory of democracy)	… hampers discursive reasoning because the status of a person is more important than the strength of the argument … weakens the acceptance of others as legitimate speakers?

ization/personalized politics for our democracies (evaluate). This last step is decisive if we want to go beyond a simple condemnation of personalization/ personalized politics. Only after having clarified how personalization or personalized politics affects citizens' empirical beliefs in the legitimacy of the political system, the informed and rational control of the elites, the access to the political system, citizens' participation, and the quality of discursive reasoning, can we arrive at a sound judgment of the issue under discussion. These old and new questions can only be answered if empirical research broadens its focus and overcomes its existing deficits.

Notes

1. For a summary of the state of the art, in addition to a standard literature research including a search in the ISI Web of Knowledge and in Communication Abstracts, the following scientific journals were systematically searched for publications dealing with personalization for all volumes between 2000 and 2008: *Communication Research; Communication Theory; Communications; Communication, Culture and Critique; Communication Yearbook; European Journal of Communication; Global Media and Communication; Human Communication Research; Information, Communications and Society; International Communication Gazette; Journal of Applied Communication Research; Journal of Broadcasting and Electronic Media; Journal of Communication; Journalism and Mass Communication Quarterly; Journalism and Communication Monographs; Journal of Public Relations Research; Mass Communication and Society; Media, Culture and Society; Medien & Kommunikationswissenschaft; Media Perspektiven; Media Psychology; New Media and Society; Nordicom Review; Political Communication; Publizistik; Television and New Media; Visual Communication; Visual Communication Quarterly; Zeitschrift für Medienpsychologie.*
2. Most authors look for personalization during election campaigns. However,

the question of personalization in politics could as well be studied—and would probably be as relevant—in between elections.

3. Rahat and Sheafer (2007) propose a slightly different classification: They distinguish between institutional, media, and behavioral personalization. The latter can be observed in the behavior of politicians or of the public. The most distinct feature of this typology compared to the one used here is institutional personalization, which means the "adoption of rules, mechanisms, and institutions that put more emphasis on the individual politicians" (Rahat & Sheafer, 2007, p. 66), e.g., an open list in elections, primaries. This stronger focus on developments within politics per se is also reflected in research on the "presidentialization" (e.g., Webb & Poguntke, 2005). Here, the growth of leadership power is not only studied in the electoral face (campaigns, media coverage, voting) but also regarding the power distribution within parties and political executives.

4. The authors acknowledge that personalization might also be taking place in media genres not usually covered in the studies analyzing media reporting and commentating (e.g., TV-infotainment formats and magazines, etc.). However, the normative concerns regarding personalization usually address the development of classical news formats of TV and newspapers.

5. Berelson (1966) comes to a similar conclusion when he writes: "Actually the major decisions the ordinary citizens is called upon to make in a modern representative democracy involve basic simplifications which need not rest upon a wide range of information so long as they are based upon a certain amount of crucial information, reasonably interpreted" (p. 494).

6. That personalization can help reduce the complexity of the political process and thus also the costs of information seeking is underlined not only by political scientists, but also by various other disciplines (Hoffmann & Raupp, 2006). Psychologists, for example, describe this complexity reduction of personalization in schema theories and sociologists refer to this mechanism of complexity reduction when systems need to communicate.

7. A similar argument is proposed by Holtz-Bacha (2000) who points out that only through personalization can difficult political concepts be communicated to the citizens.

8. Johnston and Kaid's (2002) results covering a period of 50 years show us how cautious one needs to be about trends. Whereas one finds an increase in personalization in the 1970s and 80s, this trend seems to have reversed in later years.

9. For a variant of the social-psychological model of voting behavior, see Brettschneider (2002).

10. Only few studies come to the conclusion that personalized voting has become more important respectively has increases over time. Kaltefleiter (1981), for example, claims that about 50% of the changes in voting behavior between two elections can be explained by the evaluation of the top candidates. Analyzing time series from the years 1961 to 1998 (Ohr, 2000), respectively 1972 to 1998, Ohr (2002) comes to the conclusion that the overall evaluation of the top candidates of the two major German parties has a significant impact on the voting decision and has significantly increased since 1994.

11. Regarding the ratio of personalized versus non-personalized news items, these findings are in line with the results from a content analysis of German TV-news reports during the 1998 German elections by Wirth and Voigt (1999; also see Kindelmann, 1994).

244 COMMUNICATION YEARBOOK 34

12. This conclusion is also supported by a number of cross-sectional analyses by Klein and Ohr (2000, 2001; Ohr, 2000, 2002) in the context of the German national elections 1998 and 2002. Although in the specific constellation of the 1998 election they found that in the case of Gerhard Schröder non-political traits, such as the evaluation of his private life and physical attraction, in addition to his trustworthiness and integrity, were more important for the voting decision than were the political competences of the candidate. In their analysis of the 2002 German national elections their results were more in line with the mainstream. In the latter analysis they concluded that for the voting decision party identification and the competence of the parties to solve problems ranked ahead of the personality traits of the candidates.

13. The widespread discussion on personalization might lead to a paradoxical effect that has been formulated by Webb and Poguntke (2005): "Indeed one may say that this perception of the importance of leaders is what really matters: even if leaders actually only have a modest direct effect on voting behavior, the fact that the strategists tend to be convinced of their importance nevertheless results in campaigns which are increasingly centered on party leaders" (p. 346; also see Blumler, 1990; Patterson, 1989).

14. We speak of personalized politics if voters substitute issues/parties (Proposition 1) or non-political traits substitute political traits of candidates (Proposition 2). Yet, here we do not assume a linear trend in the course of time.

15. In this context Dalton and Wattenberg (1993) have called for a stronger focus on the new democracies of Eastern Europe, because here strong ties and images of parties are lacking and therefore images of individual candidates might be more important.

16. In principal, presidential as well as parliamentary systems fit into these categories (Lijphardt, 1999).

17. Cappella and Jamieson (1996) have made a first step in this direction when they show that the exposure to strategy frames (part of such frames is an emphasis on the candidates' performance, style, and perceptions) increases citizens' cynicism.

References

Adam, S. (2007a). Domestic adaptations of Europe. A comparative study of the debates on EU enlargement and a common constitution in the German and French quality press. *International Journal of Public Opinion Research, 19*(4), 409–433.

Adam, S. (2007b). *Symbolische Netzwerke in Europa. Der Einfluss der nationalen Ebene auf europäische Öffentlichkeit. Deutschland und Frankreich im Vergleich* [Symbolical networks in Europe. The influence of the national level on the European public sphere. A comparison of Germany and France]. Köln, Germany: Halem.

Bailenson, J. N., Iyengar, S., Yee, N., & Collins, N. A. (2008). Facial similarity between voters and candidates causes influence. *Public Opinion Quarterly, 72*(5), 935–961.

Barber, B. R. (1984). *Strong democracy: Participatory politics for a new age.* Berkeley: University of California Press.

Bartels, L. M. (2002). The impact of candidate traits in American presidential elections. In A. King (Ed.), *Leaders' personalities and the outcomes of democratic elections* (pp. 44–69). Oxford, UK: Oxford University Press.

Bartolini, S. (2006). Mass politics in Brussels: How benign could it be? *ZSE, 1*, 28–56. doi:10.1515/ZSE.2006.002

Beierwaltes, A. (2000). *Demokratie und Medien. Der Begriff der Öffentlichkeit und seine Bedeutung für die Demokratie in Europa* [Democracy and the media. The concept of the public and its relevance for democracy in Europe]. Baden-Baden, Germany: Nomos Verlag.

Beniger, J. R., & Jones, G. (1990). Changing technologies, mass media, and control of the pictures in people's heads: A preliminary look at U.S. presidential campaign slogans, 1800–1984. In S. Kraus (Ed.), *Mass communication and political information processing* (pp. 149–170). Hillsdale, NJ: Erlbaum.

Bennett, W. L. (2002). *News: the politics of illusion* (5th ed.). New York: Longman.

Benson, R., & Hallin, D. C. (2007). How states, markets and globalization shape the news: The French and US national press, 1965–97. *European Journal of Communication, 22*(1), 27–48.

Berelson, B. (1966). Democratic theory and public opinion. In B. Berelson & M. Janowitz (Eds.), *Reader in public opinion and communication* (pp. 489–504). New York: Free Press.

Beyme, K. von (1997). Funktionenwandel der Parteien in der Entwicklung von der Massenmitgliederpartei zur Partei der Berufspolitiker [Changing functions of political parties in the evolution from member parties to parties of professional politicians]. In O. W. Gabriel, O. Niedermayer & R. Stöss (Eds.), *Parteiendemokratie in Deutschland* (pp. 359–383). Opladen, Germany: Westdeutscher Verlag.

Binderkrantz, A. S., & Green-Pedersen, C. (2009). Policy or process in focus? *The International Journal of Press/Politics, 14*(2), 166–185.

Blumler, J. G. (1990). Elections, the media and the modern publicity process. In M. Ferguson (Ed.), *Public communication: The new imperatives: Future directions for media research* (pp. 101–114). London: Sage.

Boorstin, D. J. (1964). *Das Image oder Was wurde aus dem Amerikanischen Traum?* [The image or what happened to the American dream?] Hamburg: Rowohlt.

Boykoff, M., & Boykoff, J. (2007). Climate change and journalist norms: A case-study of US mass-media coverage. *Geoforum, 38*, 1170–1204.

Brady, H. E., & Johnston, R. (1987). What's the primary message: Horse race or issue journalism. In G. R. Orren & N. W. Polsby (Eds.), *Media and momentum: The New Hampshire primary and nomination politics* (pp. 127–186). Chatham, NJ: Chatham House.

Brettschneider, F. (2001). Candidate-Voting. Die Bedeutung von Spitzenkandidaten für das Wahlverhalten in Deutschland, Großbritannien und den USA von 1960 bis 1998 [Candidate-Voting. The significance of top candidates for the electoral behaviour in Germany, Great Britain and the USA from 1960 till 1998]. In H.-D. Klingemann & M. Kaase (Eds.), *Wahlen und Wähler. Analysen aus Anlass der Bundestagswahl 1998* (pp. 351–100). Wiesbaden, Germany: Westdeutscher Verlag.

Brettschneider, F. (2002). *Spitzenkandidaten und Wahlerfolg: Personalisierung — Kompetenz — Parteien; ein internationaler Vergleich* [Top candidates and electoral success: Personalization — competence — parties; an international comparison]. Wiesbaden, Germany: VS.

Brettschneider, F. (2008). Personalization of campaigning. In W. Donsbach (Ed.), *The international encyclopedia of communication* (Vol. 8, pp. 3583–3585). Oxford, UK: Blackwell.

Brettschneider, F., & Vollbracht, M. (2009). Personalisierung der Unternehmensberichterstattung [Personalization of news coverage of business companies]. In M. Eisenegger & S. Wehmeier (Eds.), *Personalisierung der Organisationskommunikation. Geschäft mit der Eitelkeit oder sozialer Zwang?* (pp. 133–158). Wiesbaden, Germany: VS Verlag.

Brettschneider, F., Neller, K., & Anderson, C. J. (2006). Candidate images in the 2005 German national election. *German Politics, 15*(4), 481–499.

Briggs, A., & Burke, P. (2002). *A social history of the media. From Gutenberg to the Internet.* Cambridge, UK: Blackwell.

Bucy, E. P. (2000). Emotional and evaluative consequences of inappropriate leader displays. *Communication Research, 27*(2), 194–226.

Bucy, E. P., & Grabe, M. E. (2007). Taking television seriously: A sound and image bite analysis of presidential campaign coverage, 1992–2004. *Journal of Communication, 57*(4), 652–675.

Campbell, A., Converse, P. E., Miller, W. E., & Stokes, D. E. (1980). *The American voter.* Chicago: University of Chicago Press.

Campus, D. (2002). Leaders, dreams and journeys: Italy's new political communication. *Journal of Modern Italian studies, 7*(2), 171–191.

Center for Media and Public Affairs (1992). Battle of the sound bites. *Media Monitor August/September 1992, 6*(7).

Cohen, J. (1989). Deliberation and democratic legitimacy. In A. Hamlin & P. Pettit (Eds.), *The good polity* (pp. 17–34). Cambridge, MA: Blackwell.

Converse, P. E., & Dupeux, G. (1966). De Gaulle and Eisenhower: The public image of the victorious general. In A. Campbell, P. E. Converse, W. E. Miller & D. E. Stokes (Eds.), *Elections and the political order* (pp. 292–345). New York: Wiley.

Corner, J. (2000). Mediated persona and political culture. Dimensions of structure and process. *European Journal of Cultural Studies, 3*(3), 386–402.

Curran, J., Iyengar, S., Lund, A. B., & Salovaara-Moring, I. (2009). Media systems, public knowledge and democracy: A comparative study. *European Journal of Communication, 24*(1), 5–26.

Dalton, R. J. (2000). Citizen attitudes and political behaviour. *Comparative Political Studies, 33*(6/7), 912–940.

Dalton, R. J., & Wattenberg, M. P. (1993). The not so simple act of voting. In A. W. Finifter (Ed.), *Political science: The state of the discipline II* (pp. 193–218). Washington, DC: American Political Science Association.

Dalton, R. J., McAllister, I., & Wattenberg, M. P. (2000). The consequences of partisan dealignment. In R. J. Dalton & M. P. Wattenberg (Eds.), *Parties without partisans: Political change in advanced industrial democracies* (pp. 37–63). Oxford, UK: Oxford University Press.

Dennis, J., Chaffee, S. H., & Choe, S. Y. (1979). Impact on partisan, image, and issue voting. In S. Kraus (Ed.), *The Great Debates. Carter vs. Ford 1976* (pp. 314–330). Bloomington: Indiana University Press.

Dillenburger, M., Holtz-Bacha, C., & Lessinger, E.-M. (2005). It's Yourope! Die Plaktakampagnen der Parteien im Europawahlkampf 2004 [It's Yourope! The parties' campaign posters in the EP elections 2004]. In C. Holtz-Bacha (Ed.), *Europawahl 2004. Die Massenmedien im Europawahlkampf* (pp. 35–64). Wiesbaden, Germany: VS.

Downs, A. (1968). *Ökonomische Theorie der Demokratie* [Economic theories of democracy]. Tübingen, Germany: Mohr.

Easton, D. (1965). *A systems analysis of political life*. New York: Wiley.

Ersson, S., & Lane, J.-E. (1998). Electoral instability and party system change in Western Europe. In P. Pennings & J.-E. Lane (Eds.), *Comparing party system change* (pp. 23–39). London: Routledge.

Esser, F., Holtz-Bacha, C., & Lessinger, E.-M.. (2008). A low-key affair: German parties' political advertising. In L. L. Kaid (Ed.), *The EU expansion: Communicating shared sovereignty in the parliamentary elections* (pp. 65–84). New York: Peter Lang.

Falter, J. W., & Rattinger, H. (1983). Parteien, Kandidaten und politische Streitfragen bei der Bundestagswahl 1980: Möglichkeiten und Grenzen der Normal-Vote-Analyse [Parties, candidates and political issues in the Bundestag elections 1980: Opportunities and limitations of the normal-vote-analysis]. In M. Kaase & H.-D. Klingemann (Eds.), *Wahlen und politisches System. Analysen aus Anlaß der Bundestagswahl 1980* (pp. 320–421). Opladen, Germany: Westdeutscher Verlag.

Farnsworth, S. J., & Lichter, S. R. (2007). *The nightly news nightmare: Television's coverage of U.S. presidential elections, 1988–2004* (2nd ed.). Lanham, MD: Rowman & Littlefield.

Ferree, M. M., Gamson, W. A., Gerhards, J., & Rucht, D. (2002). *Shaping abortion discourse. Democracy and the public sphere in Germany and the United States.* Cambridge, UK: Cambridge University Press.

Fiorina, M. P., Abrams, S., & Pope, J. (2003). The 2000 U.S. presidential election: Can retrospective voting be saved. *British Journal of Political Science, 33,* 163–187.

Fiske, S. T., & Taylor, S. E. (1984). *Social cognition*. New York: Random House.

Foley, M. (2000). *The British presidency. Tony Blair and the politics of public leadership.* Manchester, UK: Manchester University Press.

Fraenkel, E. (1991). Strukturanalyse der modernen Demokratie [Structural analysis of modern democracy]. In E. Fraenkel (Ed.), *Deutschland und die westlichen Demokratien* (pp. 326–359). Frankfurt a. M., Germany: Suhrkamp.

Freedman, P., Franz, M., & Goldstein, K. (2004). Campaign advertising and democratic citizenship. *American Journal of Political Science, 48*(4), 723–741.

Fuchs, D., & Kühnel, S. (1994). Wählen als rationales Handeln: Anmerkungen zum Nutzen des Rational-Choice-Ansatzes in der empirischen Wahlforschung [Voting as rational action: Notes on the use of the rational choice approach in empirical election research]. In H.-D. Klingemann & M. Kaase (Eds.), *Wahlen und Wähler. Analysen aus Anlass der Bundestagswahl 1990* (pp. 305–334). Opladen, Germany: Westdeutscher Verlag.

Gabriel, O. W., & Keil, S. I. (2005). Empirische Wahlforschung in Deutschland: Kritik und Entwicklungsperspektiven [Empirical election research in Germany: Critical summary and perspectives for the future]. In J. W. Falter & H. Schoen (Eds.), *Handbuch Wahlforschung* (pp. 611–641). Wiesbaden, Germany: VS.

Gabriel, O. W., & Keil, S. I. (2007). Kandidatenorientierungen in Teilelektoraten und Wahlverhalten [Orientations towards candidates in parts of the electorate and electoral behaviour]. In H. Rattinger, O. W. Gabriel & J. W. Falter (Eds.), *Der gesamtdeutsche Wähler. Stabilität und Wandel des Wählerverhaltens im wiedervereinigten Deutschland* (pp. 357–384). Baden–Baden, Germany Nomos.

Gabriel, O. W., & Vetter, A. (1998). Bundestagswahlen als Kanzlerwahlen? Kandidatenorientierungen und Wahlentscheidungen im parteienstaatlichen Parlamentarismus [German national elections as chancellor elections? Orientations towards candidates and voting decisions in parliamentarism]. In M. Kaase & H.-D. Klingemann (Eds.), *Wahlen und Wähler. Analysen aus Anlass der Bundestagswahl 1994* (pp. 505–536). Opladen, Germany: Westdeutscher Verlag.

Galtung, J., & Ruge, M. H. (1965). The structure of foreign news. The presentation of the Congo, Cuba and Cyprus crises in four Norwegian newspapers. *Journal of Peace Research, 2,* 64–91.

Genz, A., Schoenbach, K., & Semetko, H. A. (2001). "Amerikanisierung"? Politik in den Fernsehnachrichten während der Bundestagswahlkämpfe 1990–1998 ["Americanization"? Politics in the TV news during the German national election campaigns 1990–1998]. In H.–D. Klingemann & M. Kaase (Eds.), *Wahlen und Wähler. Analysen aus Anlass der Bundestagswahl 1998* (pp. 401–414). Wiesbaden, Germany: Westdeutscher Verlag.

Gerhards, J. (1993). Westeuropäische Integration und die Schwierigkeiten der Entstehung einer europäischen Öffentlichkeit [Western European integration and the difficulties of the emergence of a European public sphere]. *Zeitschrift für Soziologie, 22*(2), 96–110.

Gilens, M., Vavreck, L., & Cohen, M. (2007). The mass media and the public's assessments of presidential candidates, 1952–2000. *The Journal of Politics, 69*(4), 1160–1175.

Graber, D. A. (1972). Personal qualities in presidential images. The contribution of the press. *Midwest Journal of Political Science, 16,* 46–76.

Graber, D. A. (2001). *Processing politics. Learning from television in the Internet age.* Chicago: University of Chicago Press.

Graber, D. A. (2006). *Mass media and American politics* (7th ed.). Washington, DC: CQ Press.

Gronbeck, B. E., & Wiese, D. R. (2005). The repersonalization of presidential campaigning in 2004. *American Behavioural Scientist, 49*(4), 520–534.

Halldén, O. (1998). Personalization in historical descriptions and explanations. *Learning and Instruction, 8*(2), 131–139.

Hallin, D. C. (1992a). Sound bite news: Television coverage of elections, 1968–1988. *Journal of Communication, 42*(2), 5–24.

Hallin, D. C. (1992b). The passing of the "High Modernism" of American journalism. *Journal of Communication, 42*(3), 14–25.

Hallin, D. C., & Mancini, P. (1984). Speaking of the president. *Theory and Society, 13,* 829–850.

Hallin, D. C., & Mancini, P. (2003). Amerikanisierung, Globalisierung und Säkularisierung: Zur Konvergenz von Mediensystemen und politischer Kommunikation in westlichen Demokratien [Americanization, globalization and secularization: On the convergence of media systems and political communication in Western democracies]. In F. Esser & B. Pfetsch (Eds.), *Politische Kommunikation im internationalen Vergleich. Grundlagen. Anwendungen. Perspektiven* (pp. 35–55). Opladen, Germany: Westdeutscher Verlag.

Hallin, D. C., & Mancini, P. (2004). *Comparing media systems. Three models of media and politics.* Cambridge, UK: Cambridge University Press.

Hodess, R., Tedesco, J. C., & Kaid, L. L. (2000). British party election broadcasts. A comparison of 1992 and 1997. *The Harvard International Journal of Press/Politics, 5*(4), 55–70.

Hoffmann, J., & Raupp, J. (2006). Politische Personalisierung [Political personalization]. *Publizistik, 51*(4), 456–478.

Holtz-Bacha, C. (1999). Mass media and elections. An impressive body of research.

In H.-B. Brosius & C. Holtz-Bacha (Eds.), *The German Communication Yearbook* (pp. 39–68). Cresskill, NY: Hampton Press.

Holtz-Bacha, C. (2000). *Wahlwerbung als Politische Kultur. Parteienspots im Fernsehen 1957–1998* [Canvassing as political culture. Party ads on TV 1957–1998]. Wiesbaden, Germany: Westdeutscher Verlag.

Holtz-Bacha, C. (2001a). Das Private in der Politik: Ein neuer Medientrend? [The private in politics: A new media trend?] *Aus Politik und Zeitgeschichte, B41–42*, 20–26.

Holtz-Bacha, C. (2001b). Selbstdarstellung der Politik: Die Präsentation von Themen und Kandidaten in den Fernsehspots der Parteien [Selfpresentation of politics: The presentation of topics and candidates in the parties' TV ads]. In H. Oberreuter (Ed.), *Umbruch '98: Wähler, Parteien, Kommunikation* (pp. 123–137). München, Germany: Olzog.

Holtz-Bacha, C. (2003). Bundestagswahlkampf 2002: Ich oder der [German national election campaign 2002: Me or him?]. In C. Holtz-Bacha (Ed.), *Die Massenmedien im Wahlkampf. Die Bundestagswahl 2002* (pp. 9–28). Wiesbaden, Germany: Westdeutscher Verlag.

Holtz-Bacha, C. (2004). Germany: How the private life of politicians go into the media. *Parliamentary Affairs, 57*(1), 41–52.

Holtz-Bacha, C. (2006a). Personalisiert und emotional: Strategien des modernen Wahlkampfes [Personalized and emotional: Strategies of modern election campaigns]. *Aus Politik und Zeitgeschichte, 7*, 11–19.

Holtz-Bacha, C. (2006b). Bundestagswahl 2005 — Die Überraschungswahl [German national election 2005 — The surprising election]. In C. Holtz-Bacha (Ed.), *Die Massenmedien im Wahlkampf. Die Bundestagswahl 2005* (pp. 5–31). Wiesbaden, Germany: VS.

Holtz-Bacha, C., & Lessinger, E.-M. (2006). Wie die Lustlosigkeit konterkariert wurde: Fernsehwahlwerbung 2005 [How the Inactivity was foiled: Political advertising on TV 2005]. In C. Holtz-Bacha (Ed.), *Die Massenmedien im Wahlkampf. Die Bundestagswahl 2005* (pp. 164–182). Wiesbaden, Germany: VS.

Holtz-Bacha, C., Lessinger, E.-M., & Hettesheimer, M. (1998). Personalisierung als Strategie der Wahlwerbung [Personalization as strategy of political advertisement]. In K. Imhof & P. Schulz (Eds.), *Die Veröffentlichung des Privaten — Die Privatisierung des Öffentlichen* (pp. 240–250). Wiesbaden, Germany: Westdeutscher Verlag.

Huber, G. A., & Arceneaux, K. (2007). Identifying the persuasive effects of presidential advertising. *American Journal of Political Science, 51*(4), 957–977.

Iyengar, S. (1989). How citizens think about national issues: A matter of responsibility. *American Journal of Political Science, 33*(4), 878–900.

Iyengar, S. (2008). Priming theory. In W. Donsbach (Ed.), *The International Encyclopedia of Communication*. Blackwell Reference Online.

Iyengar, S., & Kinder, D. R. (1987). *News that matters*. Chicago: University of Chicago Press.

Jamieson, K. H. (1992). *Dirty politics: Deception, distraction and democracy*. New York: Oxford University Press.

Jamieson, K. H. (1993). The subversive effects of a focus on strategy in news of presidential campaigns. In *1-800-President. The Report of the Twentieth century fund task force on television and the campaign of 1992* (pp. 35–61). New York: The Twentieth Century Fund Press.

Jamieson, K. H. (1996). *Packaging the presidency. A history and criticism of presidential campaign advertising* (3rd ed.). Oxford, UK: Oxford University Press.

Jamieson, K. H. (2000). *Everything you think you know about politics... And why you're wrong.* New York: Basic Books.

Jamieson, K. H., & Birdsell, D. (1988). *Presidential debates: The challenge of creating an informed electorate.* New York: Oxford University Press.

Jamieson, K. H., & Waldman, P. (2003). *The press effect: Politicians, journalists and the stories that shape the political world.* New York: Oxford University Press.

Jamieson, K. H., Hagen, M. G., Orr, D., Sillaman, L., Morse, S., & Kirn, K. (2000). What did the leading candidate say and did it matter? *Annals AAPSS, 572,* 12–16.

Johnston, A., & Kaid, L. L. (2002). Image ads and issue ads in U.S. presidential advertising: Using videostyle to explore stylistic differences in televised political ads from 1952 to 2000. *Journal of Communication, 52*(2), 281–300.

Jucknat, K. (2007). Köpfe statt Themen? Köpfe und Themen!: Die Personalisierung der Wahlkampfberichterstattung in Deutschland und in den USA [Heads instead of topics? Heads and topics!: The Personalization of the election campaign coverage in Germany and the USA]. *Zeitschrift für Parlamentsfragen (ZParl), 38*(1), 147–159.

Just, M., Crigler, A., Alger, D., Cook, T., Kern, M., & West, D. (1996). *Crosstalk. citizens, candidates, and the media in a presidential campaign.* Chicago: University of Chicago Press.

Kaase, M. (1994). Is there personalization in politics? Candidates and voting behavior in Germany. *International Political Science Review, 15*(3), 211–230.

Kaase, M. (2000). Entwicklung und Stand der Empirischen Wahlforschung in Deutschland [Development and status quo of empirical election research in Germany]. In M. Klein, W. Jagodzinski, E. Mochmann & D. Ohr (Eds.), *50 Jahre Empirische Wahlforschung in Deutschland. Entwicklung, Befunde, Perspektiven, Daten* (pp. 17–40). Wiesbaden, Germany: Westdeutscher Verlag.

Kaid, L. L., & Strömbäck, J. (2008). Election news coverage around the world: A comparative perspective. In L. L. Kaid & J. Strömbäck (Eds.), *The Handbook of election news coverage around the world* (pp. 421–431). New York: Routledge.

Kaltefleiter, W. (1981). Personalisierung [Personalization]. In M. Greiffenhagen, S. Greiffenhagen & R. Prätorius (Eds.), *Handwörterbuch zur politischen Kultur in Deutschland. Ein Lehr- und Nachschlagewerk* (pp. 296–299). Opladen, Germany: Westdeutscher Verlag.

Karvonen, L. (2007, September). *The personalization of politics. What does research tell us so far, and what further research is in order?* Paper presented at the ECPR Conference, Pisa, Italy.

Keeter, S. (1987). The illusion of intimacy: Television and the role of candidate personal qualities in voter choice. *Public Opinion Quarterly, 51,* 344–358.

Kellermann, C. (2007). Trends and Constellations: Klassische Bestimmungsfaktoren des Wahlverhaltens bei den Bundestagswahlen 1990–2005 [Trends and constellations: Classical determinants of the electoral behaviour in the German national elections 1990–2005]. In H. Rattinger, O. W. Gabriel & J. W. Falter (Eds.), *Der gesamtdeutsche Wähler. Stabilität und Wandel des Wählerverhaltens im wiedervereinigten Deutschland* (pp. 297–328). Baden–Baden, Germany: Nomos.

Kepplinger, H. M. (1982). Visual biases in television campaign coverage. *Communication Research, 9*(3), 432–446.

Kepplinger, H. M. (1998). *Die Demontage der Politik in der Informationsgesellschaft* [The disassembly of politics in the information society]. Freiburg, Germany: Alber.

Kepplinger, H. M., & Donsbach, W. (1987). The influence of camera perspectives on the perception of a politician by supporters, opponents, and neutral viewers. In D. L. Paletz (Ed.), *Political communication research: Approaches, studies, assessments* (pp. 62–72). Norwood, NJ: Ablex.

Kepplinger, H. M., & Maurer, M. (2005). *Abschied vom rationalen Wähler* [Goodbye to the rational voter]. Freiburg, Germany: Alber.

Kepplinger, H. M., Brosius, H. B., & Dahlem, S. (1994). Charakter oder Sachkompetenz von Politiker. Woran orientieren sich die Wähler? [Character or issue competence of politicians. What do voters use for orientation?]. In H.-D. Klingemann & M. Kaase (Eds.), *Wahlen und Wähler. Analysen aus Anlaß der Bundestagswahl 1990* (pp. 472–505). Opladen, Germany: Westdeutscher Verlag.

Kernell, S. (1988). *Going public. New strategies of presidential leadership.* Washington, DC: CQ Press.

Kim, K., & McCombs, M. (2007). News story descriptions and the public's opinions of political candidates. *Journalism and Mass Communication Quarterly, 84*(2), 299–314.

Kim, S., Scheufele, D. A., & Shanahan, J. (2005). Who cares about the issues? Issue voting and the role of news media during the 2000 U.S. presidential election. *Journal of Communication, 55*(1), 103–121.

Kindelmann, K. (1994). *Kanzlerkandidaten in den Medien. Eine Analyse des Wahljahres 1990* [Candidates for chancellor in the media. An analysis of the election year 1990]. Opladen, Germany: Westdeutscher Verlag.

Kinder, D. (1986). Presidential character revisited. In R. R. Lau & D. O. Sears (Eds.), *Political cognition: the 19th annual Carnegie Symposium on cognition* (pp. 233–255). Hillsdale, NJ: Erlbaum.

King, A. (2002). Conclusions and implications. In A. King (Ed.), *Leaders' personalities and the outcomes of democratic elections* (pp. 210–221). Oxford, UK: Oxford University Press.

Klein, M., & Ohr, D. (2000). Gerhard oder Helmut? 'Unpolitische' Kandidateneigenschaften und ihr Einfluss auf die Wahlentscheidung bei der Bundestagswahl 1998 [Gerhard or Helmut? 'Unpolitical' traits of the candidates and their impact on the voting decisions in the German national elections 1998]. *Politische Vierteljahresschrift, 41*(2), 199–224.

Klein, M., & Ohr, D. (2001). Die Wahrnehmung der politischen und persönlichen Eigenschaften von Helmut Kohl und Gerhard Schröder und ihr Einfluss auf die Wahlentscheidung bei der Bundestagswahl 1998 [The perception of Helmut Kohl's and Gerhard Schröder's political and personal traits and their impact on the voting decisions in the German national elections 1998]. In H.-D. Klingemann & M. Kaase (Eds.), *Wahlen und Wähler. Analysen aus Anlass der Bundestagswahl 1998* (pp. 91–132). Wiesbaden, Germany: Westdeutscher Verlag.

Klingemann, H. D., & Wessels, B. (1999). Political consequences of Germany's mixed-member system: Personalization at the grass-root? *Wissenschaftszentrum Berlin für Sozialforschung (WZB): Discussion Paper FS III, 99–205.*

Krewel, M. (2008). Wahlkampfkommunikation im intertemporalen Vergleich [Campaign communication in a longitudinal comparison]. In E. Aydin, M. Begenat, C. Michalek, J. Schemann & I. Stefes (Eds.), *Düsseldorfer Forum Politische Kommunikation. Schriftenreihe DFPK* (Vol. 3, pp. 169–197). Berlin, Germany: LIT.

Kriesi, H. (2001). Die Rolle der Öffentlichkeit im politischen Entscheidungsprozess. Ein konzeptueller Rahmen für ein international vergleichendes Forschungsprojekt

[The public's role in the process of political decision-making. A conceptual frame for an international comparative research project]. *Wissenschaftszentrum Berlin für Sozialforschung (WZB): Discussion Paper*, 1–701.

Lane, R. E. (1978). Interpersonal relations and leadership in a "cold society." *Comparative Politics, 10*, 443–459.

Lang, G. E., & Lang, K. (1979). Immediate and mediated responses: First debate. In S. Kraus (Ed.), *The Great Debates. Carter vs. Ford 1976* (pp. 298–313). Bloomington: Indiana University Press.

Langer, A. I. (2006). *The politicisation of private persona: The case of Tony Blair in historical perspective.* Submitted for the PhD in Media and Communication, London School of Economics.

Langer, A. I. (2007). A historical exploration of the personalisation of politics in the print media: The British Prime Ministers (1945–1999). *Parliamentary Affairs, 60*(3), 371–387.

Lass, J. (1995). *Vorstellungsbilder über Kanzlerkandidaten. Zur Diskussion um die Personalisierung der Politik* [Images of candidates for chancellor. On the discussion about the personalization of politics]. Wiesbaden, Germany: Deutscher Universitätsverlag.

Lau, R. R., & Redlawsk, D. P. (2001). Advantages and disadvantages of cognitive heuristics in political decision making. *American Journal of Political Science, 45*, 951–971.

Lichter, R., Amundson, D., & Noyes, R. (1988). *The video game: Network coverage of the 1988 primaries.* Washington, DC: American Enterprise Institute.

Lijphardt, A. (1999). *Patterns of democracy. Government forms and performance in thirty-six countries.* New Haven, CT: Yale University Press.

Linden, M. (2003). Abschied von der Volkspartei?: Zur These von der "Personalisierung der Politik" [Goodby to the catch-all party?: On the thesis about the "personalization of politics"]. *Zeitschrift für Politikwissenschaft, 13*(3), 1205–1234.

Lowry, D. T., & Shidler, J. A. (1995). The biters and the bitten: An analysis of network TV news bias in campaign '92. *Journalism & Mass Communication Quarterly, 69*, 341–361.

Maier, J. (2009). Was die Bürger über Politik (nicht) wissen — und was die Massenmedien damit zu tun haben — ein Forschungsüberblick [What citizens (do not) know about politics — and what mass media have to do with it — a state of research]. In B. Pfetsch & F. Marcinkowski (Eds.), *Politik in der Mediendemokratie* (pp. 393–414). Wiesbaden, Germany: Verlag für Sozialwissenschaften.

Maier, J., & Maier, M. (2008). The reception of European election campaigns and political involvement. In L.L. Kaid (Ed.), *The EU expansion: Communicating shared sovereignty in the parliamentary elections* (pp. 85–100). New York: Peter Lang.

Mancini, P., & Swanson, D. L. (1996). Politics, media, and modern democracy: Introduction. In D. L. Swanson & P. Mancini (Eds.), *Politics, media, and modern democracy. An international study of innovations in electoral campaiging and their consequences* (pp. 1–26). Westport, CT: Praeger.

Marcinkowski, F., & Greger, V. (2000). Die Personalisierung politischer Kommunikation im Fernsehen. Ein Ergebnis der—"Amerikanisierung" [The personalization of political communication on TV. A result of the "Americanization"]. In K. Kamps (Ed.), *Trans-Atlantik — Trans-Portabel? Die Amerikanisierungsthese in der politischen Kommunikation* (pp. 179–197). Wiesbaden, Germany: Westdeutscher Verlag.

Maurer, M., & Reinemann, C. (2007). Personalisierung durch Priming. Die Wirkungen des TV-Duells auf die Urteilskriterien der Wähler [Personalization through priming. The effects of televised debates on citizens' evaluation standards]. In M. Maurer, C. Reinemann, J. Maier, & M. Maier (Eds.), *Schröder gegen Merkel. Wahrnehmung und Wirkung des TV-Duells 2005 im Ost-West-Vergleich* (pp. 111–128). Wiesbaden, Germany: VS.

Mazzoleni, G. (2000). A return to civic and political engagement prompted by personalized political leadership? *Political Communication, 17*, 325–328.

McAllister, I. (2007). The personalization of politics. In R. J. Dalton & H.-D. Klingemann (Eds.), *The Oxford handbooks of political science: The Oxford handbook of political behaviour* (pp. 571–588). Oxford, UK: Oxford University Press.

Meyer, C. O. (1999). Political legitimacy and the invisibility of politics: Exploring the European Union's communication deficit. *Journal of Common Market Studies, 9*(1), 617–639.

Miller, A. H., & MacKuen, M. (1979). Informing the electorate: A national study. In S. Kraus (Ed.), *The Great Debates. Carter vs. Ford 1976* (pp. 269–297). Bloomington: Indiana University Press.

Miller, A. H., Wattenberg, M. P., & Malanchuk, O. (1986). Schematic assessments of presidential candidates. *American Political Science Review, 80*(2), 521–540.

Moy, P., & Gastil, J. (2006). Predicting deliberative conversation: The impact of discussion networks, media use, and political cognitions. *Political Communication, 23*(4), 443–460.

Mughan, A. (2000). *Media and the presidentialization of parliamentary elections.* New York: Palgrave.

Mutz, D. C. (2007). Effects of "in-your-face" television discourse on perceptions of a legitimate opposition. *American Political Science Review, 101*(4), 621–635.

Nohlen, D. (2002). Legitimität [Legitimacy]. In D. Nohlen (Ed.), *Kleines Lexikon der Politik* (pp. 275–277). Bonn, Germany: C.H. Beck.

Oegema, D., & Kleinnijenhuis, J. (2000). Personalization in political television news: A 13-wave survey study to assess effects of text and footage. *Communications, 25*(1), 43–60.

Ohr, D. (2000). Wird das Wählerverhalten zunehmend personalisierter, oder Ist jede Wahl anders? Kandidatenorientierungen und Wahlentscheidung in Deutschland 1961 bis 1998 [Is the voters' behaviour increasingly personalized, or is each election different? Orientation towards candidates and voting decision in Germany 1961 till 1998]. In M. Klein, W. Jagodzinski, E. Mochmann & D. Ohr (Eds.), *50 Jahre empirische Wahlforschung in Deutschland. Entwicklung, Befunde, Perspektiven, Daten* (pp. 272–307). Wiesbaden, Germany: Westdeutscher Verlag.

Ohr, D. (2002). Der personalisierte Wähler. Welche Rolle die Bewertung politischer Kandidaten für das Wählerurteil spielt [The personalized voter. The role of the evaluation of political candidates for the voters' decision]. *Planung & Analyse, 1*, 16–20.

Olson, M. (1965). *The logic of collective action.* Cambridge, MA: Harvard University Press.

Page, B. I. (1978). *Choices and echoes in presidential elections: Rational man and electoral democracy.* Chicago: University of Chicago Press.

Pan, Z., & Kosicki, G. M. (1997). Priming and media impact on the evaluation of the president's performance. *Communication Research, 24*(1), 3–30.

Pappi, F. U., & Shikano, S. (2001). Personalisierung der Politik in Mehrparteiensystemen am Beispiel deutscher Bundestagswahlen seit 1980 [Personalization of politics in multi-party systems using the example of German national elections since 1980]. *Politische Vierteljahresschrift, 42*(3), 355–387.

Patterson, T. E. (1989). The press and candidate images. *International Journal of Public Opinion Research, 1*(2), 123–135.

Patterson, T. E. (1991). More style than substance: Television news in U.S. national elections. *Political Communication and Persuasion, 8*, 145–161.

Patterson, T. E. (1993a). *Out of order.* New York: Vintage.

Patterson, T. E. (1993b). Let the press be the press: Principles of campaign reform. In *1-800-President. The report of the twentieth century fund task force on television and the campaign of 1992* (pp. 91–109). New York: The Twentieth Century Fund Press.

Pennings, P., & Lane, J.-E. (1998). Introduction. In P. Pennings & J.-E. Lane (Eds.), *Comparing party system change* (pp. 1–19). London: Routledge.

Peter, J., & de Vreese, C. H. (2004). In search of Europe. A cross-national comparative study of the European Union in national television news. *The Harvard International Journal of Press/Politics, 9*(3), 3–24.

Popkin, S. L. (1991). *The reasoning voter: communication and persuasion in presidential campaigns.* Chicago: University of Chicago Press.

Prior, M. (2003). Any good news in soft news? The impact of soft news preferences on political knowledge. *Political Communication, 20*, 149–171.

Radunski, P. (1980). *Wahlkämpfe. Moderne Wahlkampfführung als politische Kommunikation.* München, Germany: Olzog.

Rahat, G., & Sheafer, T. (2007). The personalization(s) of politics: Israel, 1949–2003. *Political Communication, 41*(1), 65–80.

Rahn, W. M., Aldrich, J. H., Borgida, E., & Sullivan, J. L. (1990). A social-cognitive model of candidate appraisal. In J. A. Ferejohn & J. H. Kuklinski (Eds.), *Information and democratic processes* (pp. 136–159). Urbana: University of Illinois Press.

Reinemann, C. (2007). Völlig anderer Ansicht. Die Medienberichterstattung über das TV-Duell [Completely different views. The media news coverage about the televised debate]. In M. Maurer, C. Reinemann, J. Maier, & M. Maier (Eds.), *Schröder gegen Merkel. Wahrnehmung und Wirkung des TV-Duells 2005 im Ost-West-Vergleich* (pp. 167–194). Wiesbaden, Germany: VS.

Reinemann, C., & Wilke, J. (2007). It's the debates, stupid! How the introduction of televised debates changed the portrayal of chancellor candidates in the German press, 1949–2005. *The Harvard International Journal of Press/Politics, 12*(4), 92–111.

Robinson, M. J., & Sheehan, M. A. (1983). *Over the wire and on TV: CBS and UPI in campaign '80.* New York: Sage.

Romero, D. W. (1989). The changing American voter revisited: Candidate evaluations in presidential elections, 1952 to 1984. *American Politics Research, 17*, 409–421.

Sarcinelli, U. (1987). *Symbolische Politik* [Symbolic politics]. Opladen, Germany: Westdeutscher Verlag.

Sarcinelli, U. (1990). Auf dem Weg in eine kommunikative Demokratie? Demokratische Streitkultur als Element politischer Kultur [On the track to a communicative democracy? Democratic debating culture as an element of political culture]. In U. Sarcinelli (Ed.), *Demokratische Streitkultur. Theoretische Grundpositionen und*

Handlungsalternativen in Politikfeldern (pp. 29–51). Bonn, Germany: Bundeszentrale für politische Bildung.

Scammell, M., & Langer, A. I. (2006). Political advertisement in the United Kingdom. In L. L. Kaid (Ed.), *The SAGE Handbook of political advertising* (pp. 65–82). Thousand Oaks, CA: Sage.

Scammell, M., & Semetko, H. A. (2008). Election news coverage in the U.K. In J. Strömbäck & L. L. Kaid (Eds.), *The handbook of election news coverage round the world* (pp. 73–89). New York: Routledge.

Scheufele, D. A. (2002). Examining differential gains from mass media and their implications for participatory behaviour. *Communication Research, 29*(1), 46–65.

Schmidt, M. (1995). *Demokratietheorien. Eine Einführung* [Theories of democracy. An introduction]. Opladen, Germany: Westdeutscher Verlag.

Schmitt-Beck, R. (2007). New modes of campaigning. In R. J. Dalton & H.–D. Klingemann (Eds.), *The Oxford handbooks of political science: The Oxford handbook of political behaviour* (pp. 744–764). Oxford, UK: Oxford University Press.

Schoen, H. (2005). Wahlkampfforschung [Research on election campaigns].In J. W. Falter & H. Schoen (Eds.), *Handbuch Wahlforschung* (pp. 503–542). Wiesbaden, Germany: VS.

Schoen, H. (2007). Campaigns, candidate evaluations, and vote choice: Evidence from German federal election campaigns, 1980–2002. *Electoral Studies, 26*(2), 324–337.

Schoen, H. (2009). Wahlsoziologie [Political sociology]. In V. Kaina & A. Römmele (Eds.), *Political Sociology* (pp. 181–208). Wiesbaden, Germany: VS.

Schoen, H., & Weins, C. (2005). Der sozialpsychologische Ansatz zur Erklärung von Wahlverhalten [The socialpsychological approach to voting behavior]. In J. W. Falter & H. Schoen (Eds.), *Handbuch Wahlforschung* (pp. 187–242). Wiesbaden, Germany: VS.

Schoenbach, K. (1994). The "Americanization" of German election campaigns: Any impact on the voters? In D. L. Swanson & P. Mancini (Eds.), *Politics, media and modern democracy. An international study of innovations in electoral campaigning* (pp. 91–104). Westport, CT: Praeger.

Schulz, W. (1997). *Politische Kommunikation: theoretische Ansätze und Ergebnisse empirischer Forschung* [Political communication: Theoretical approaches and results of empirical research]. Opladen, Germany: Westdeutscher Verlag.

Schulz, W., & Zeh, R. (2003). Kanzler und Kanzlerkandidaten in den Fernsehnachrichten [Chancellors and candidates for chancellor in TV news]. In C. Holtz–Bacha (Ed.), *Die Massenmedien im Wahlkampf. Die Bundestagswahl 2002* (pp. 57–79). Wiesbaden, Germany: Westdeutscher Verlag.

Schulz, W., & Zeh, R. (2005). The changing election coverage of German television. A content analysis: 1990–2002. *Communications, 30*, 385–407.

Schulz, W., & Zeh, R. (2006). Die Kampagne im Fernsehen — Agens und Indikator des Wandels. Ein Vergleich der Kandidatendarstellung [The campaign on TV — medium and indicator of change. A comparison of the candidates' presentation]. In C. Holtz-Bacha (Ed.), *Die Massenmedien im Wahlkampf. Die Bundestagswahl 2005* (pp. 277–305). Wiesbaden, Germany: VS.

Schulz, W., Zeh, R., & Quiring, O. (2005). Voters in a changing media environment. *European Journal of Communication, 20*(1), 55–88.

Sears, D. O., & Chaffee, S. H. (1979). Uses and effects of the 1976 Debates: An overview of empirical studies. In S. Kraus (Ed.), *The Great Debates. Carter vs. Ford 1976* (pp. 223–261). Bloomington: Indiana University Press.

Shenhav, S. R., & Sheafer, T. (2008). From inter-party debate to inter-personal polemic: Media coverage of internal and external party disputes in Israel, 1949–2003. *Party Politics, 14*(6), 706–725.

Siegert, G. (2001). *Medien, Marken, Management: Relevanz, Spezifika und Implikationen einer medienökonomischen Profilierungsstrategie* [Media, brands, management: Relevance, specifics and implications of a media ecomomic profil strategy]. München, Germany: Fischer.

Sigel, R. S. (1969). Image of the American presidency: Part II of an exploration into popular views of presidential power. In A. Wildavsky (Ed.), *The Presidency* (pp. 296–309). Boston: Little, Brown & Company.

Sigelman, L., & Bullock, D. (1991). Candidates, issues, horse races, and hoopla: Presidential campaign coverage, 1888–1988. *American Politics Quarterly, 19*, 5–32.

Simons, H. W., & Leibowitz, K. (1979). Shifts in Canadian images. In S. Kraus (Ed.), *The Great Debates. Carter vs. Ford 1976* (pp. 398–404). Bloomington: Indiana University Press.

Stern, E., & Graner, J. (2002). It's the candidate stupid? Personalisierung der bundesdeutschen Wahlkämpfe [It's the candidate stupid? Personalization of the German national election campaigns]. In T. Berg (Ed.), *Moderner Wahlkampf. Blick hinter die Kulissen* (pp. 145–170). Opladen, Germany: Leske + Budrich.

Street, J. (2004). Celebrity politicians: Popular culture and political representation. *The British Journal of Politics & International Relations, 6*, 435–452.

Strömbäck, J., & Dimitrova, D. V. (2006). Political and media systems matter: A comparison of election news coverage in Sweden and the United States. *The Harvard International Journal of Press/Politics 11*(4), 131–147.

Swanson, D. L., & Mancini, P. (1996). Patterns of modern electoral campaigning and their consequences. In D. L. Swanson & P. Mancini (Eds.), *Politics, media, and modern democracy. An international study of innovations in electoral campaigning and their consequences* (pp. 247–267). Westport, CT: Praeger.

Van Zoonen, L. (2005). *Entertaining the citizen. When politics and popular culture converge.* Lanham, Boulder, MD: Rowman & Littlefield.

Van Zoonen, L. (2006). The person, the political and the popular. A woman's guide to celebrity politics. *European Journal of Cultural Studies, 9*(3), 287–301.

Van Zoonen, L., & Holtz-Bacha, C. (2000). Personalisation in Dutch and German politics: The case of talk show. *The Public, 7*(2), 45–56.

Wattenberg, M. P. (1995). *The rise of candidate-centered politics.* Cambridge, MA: Harvard University Press.

Webb, P., & Poguntke, T. (2005). The presidentialization of contemporary democratic politics: Evidence, causes, and consequences. In T. Poguntke & P. Webb (Eds), *The presidentialization of politics in democratic societies* (pp. 336–356). Oxford, UK: Oxford University Press.

Weber, M. (2005). *Die Wirtschaftsethik der Weltreligionen* [Economic ethics of the world religions]. Tübingen, Germany: Mohr.

West, D. (1997). *Air wars. Television advertising in election campaigns 1952–1996* (2nd ed.). Washington, DC: Congressional Quarterly.

Wiesendahl, E. (2001). Sammelrezension: Parteien im Epochenwechsel? Neue Literatur zum organisatorischen Strukturwandel politischer Parteien [Parties in the change of epochs? New literature about the organizational change of political parties]. *Politische Vierteljahresschrift, 42*, 734–743.

Wilke, J., & Reinemann, C. (2000). *Kanzlerkandidaten in der Wahlberichterstattung. Eine vergleichende Studie zu den Bundestagswahlen 1949–1998* [Candidates for chancellor in the campaign coverage. A comparative study of German national elections from 1949 to 1998]. Köln, Germany: Böhlau.

Wilke, J., & Reinemann, C. (2001). Do the candidates matter? Long-term trends of campaign coverage: A study of the German press since 1949. *European Journal of Communication, 16*(3), 291–314.

Wilke, J., & Reinemann, C. (2006). Die Normalisierung des Sonderfalls? Die Wahl-kampfberichterstattung der Presse 2005 im Langzeitvergleich [The normalization of the exception? Campaign coverage in the press 2005 — a long-term comparison]. In C. Holtz-Bacha (Ed.), *Die Massenmedien im Wahlkampf. Die Bundestagswahl 2005* (pp. 306–337). Wiesbaden, Germany: VS.

Wilke, J., & Sprott, C. (2009). "Hindenburg wählen, Hitler schlagen!" Wahlkampf-kommunikation bei den Reichspräsidentenwahlen in der Weimarer Republik. [Elect Hindenburg, win against Hitler. Campaign communication in the German Reich election in the Weimar Republic]. In H. Kaspar, H. Schoen, S. Schumann, & J.R. Winkler (Eds.), *Politik — Wissenschaft — Medien. Festschrift für Jürgen W. Falter zum 65. Geburtstag* (pp. 277–306). Wiesbaden, Germany: VS.

Wiorkowski, A., & Holtz-Bacha, C. (2005). Und es lohnt sich doch. Personal-isierungsstrategien im Europawahlkampf [However it's profitable. Personaliza-tion strategies in the European election campaign]. In C. Holtz-Bacha (Ed.), *Europawahlkampf 2004 Die Massenmedien im Europawahlkampf* (pp. 174–196). Wiesbaden, Germany: VS.

Wirth, W., & Voigt, R. (1999). Der Aufschwung ist meiner! Personalisierung von Spitzenkandidaten im Fernsehen zur Bundestagswahl 1998 [The boom is mine! Personalization of top candidates on TV during the German national election 1998]. In C. Holtz-Bacha (Ed.), *Wahlkampf in den Medien — Wahlkampf mit den Medien. Ein Reader zum Wahljahr 1998* (pp. 136–161). Opladen, Germany: West-deutscher Verlag.

Wolfsfeld, G. (1997). *Media and political conflict. News from the Middle East.* Cam-bridge, UK: Cambridge University Press.

Commentary
Mediating the Public Sphere
Democratic Deliberation, Communication
Gaps and the Personalization of Politics

Robin Mansell

London School of Economics and Political Science

The three chapters in this section are concerned, each in their own way, with the relationship between the media, political communication, and the public sphere. In this chapter, I offer a short synopsis of the main arguments presented by the authors based on their extensive assessments of the state of the art in each of the fields of scholarship they address. I follow this with a reflection on the directions for future research that are suggested in the light of ongoing debates surrounding the theorization of the public sphere in modern politics. My comments begin with a discussion of chapter 7 on public deliberation, followed by that on nanotechnology (chapter 6), and finally the review of research on personalization in politics as presented in chapter 8.

Theory and Practice of Public Deliberation

In her contribution, Nurit Guttman provides a comprehensive assessment of the gaps between the ideal theory of the public sphere as conceived by Habermas and his critics and the practice of public deliberation as it has been instantiated in a variety of deliberative forums. She draws very effectively on case studies to suggest that the standards of practice deemed most likely to foster rational-critical debate often are contradictory. The result is that the ideals of communicative action cannot be achieved. Nevertheless, she finds that research is needed to discern how those who provide such forums can foster improved contexts for inclusive debates that are the essential foundation of deliberative democracy. Guttman's (2000) research on public health communication has been centrally concerned with whether media campaigns should seek to alter people's values, raising issues around contested power relations. In the present chapter, she assesses the extent to which the institutionalized practices of deliberative forums across a range of issues succeed in mitigating asymmetrical power relations.

The empirical question Guttman addresses is how well do forums for public deliberation fulfill the conditions for deliberation and compensate for deficiencies? She examines this question especially in relation to deliberations on public policy issues aimed at influencing decisions about "wicked" social problems.

Acknowledging that the outcomes of civic forums may simply conform to normative assessments of public welfare enhancing interventions, she suggests that there is a gap between the theoretical criteria for public engagement and the practice-based design of such forums. Her chapter offers an overview of the normative conditions which are said to adhere to the ideal, the procedures for public debate that have been espoused, and, based on an assessment of examples of deliberative forums, an analysis of the ways in which experience suggests insights and challenges to both theory and practice.

Guttman draws attention to the way potentially conflicting conditions aimed at achieving fair access and competence of process are operationalized in the practice of deliberative forums including citizens' juries, scenario workshops, consensus conferences, deliberative polls, citizens' dialogues, 21st century town hall meetings, and an Internet forum. Some of these approaches use computer technology and large scale survey techniques. They also may be informed or influenced by media coverage. Given the differences in approaches and insofar as compromise is acceptable, under what conditions is it acceptable and what should be established as the criterion for success? Although she does not examine online forums in depth, Guttman does ask whether these new electronic opportunities will give rise to improved possibilities for public deliberation, more consistent with those espoused theoretically for the public sphere.

Deliberative theories of democracy are founded upon the ideals of liberty, equality, and the right of citizens to influence decisions. In representative democracies, there is also a need for public dialogue to enable decision makers to become aware of the interests and concerns of citizens. Where deliberative forums are organized to address problems involving controversies over values, there must be a commitment on the part of participants to learn, listen and form opinions about issues in a safe dialogical space. Deliberative forums are expected to foster a knowledgeable public, to provide a space for deliberation that goes beyond the expression of opinions through voting, to enable exposure to a broader range of perspectives, and to encourage learning about the complexity of policy making and the trade-offs. The assumption is that this may lead to greater political efficacy, civic literacy, self-efficacy, and trust in political institutions. Guttman highlights the fact that departures from the ideal speech situation (Habermas, 1962/1989) may arise for many reasons including instances where the topics are not chosen by participants, they are framed by others who may appear to have greater expertise, they occur towards the end of a cycle of decision making, or if they fail to challenge the status quo.

In deliberative forums efforts to enhance the potential for rational discourse, include those to introduce informational strategies, measures to present alternative perspectives and to expose differences in value judgments and moral stance. The aim is to reach a view of the common good through consensus formation. On the basis of her review of a selection of cases, Guttman finds that no forum can be expected to meet all the criteria for an ideal speech situation but, in practice, much can be done to enhance the inclusion of normally excluded voices.

Deliberating on Science and Technology

In their review of the literature focusing on public debate around the introduction of nanotechnology applications, Dietram Scheufele and Anthony Dudo highlight a communication gap between scientific evidence and the public perception of the issues. What counts as legitimate evidence and what role do the media play in such debates? Scheufele and Dudo ask "how can we establish sustainable channels of communication between science and the public, especially for increasingly controversial, politically charged issues...?" (this volume, p. 144). In contrast to the preceding chapter in this section, these authors draw on research on how the public and scientists (and the media) frame potentially emotionally charged issues by drawing on culturally shared imagery.

The starting point in this chapter is not the idealized Habermasian public sphere but, instead, an assessment of whether citizen's worldviews and understandings of science and technology can be understood through the lens of cultivation theory, the processing of emotional insights, message framing and the authoritative status accorded to science in a given societal context. The authors review empirical evidence on widening communication or knowledge gaps with respect to nanotechnology, raising the possibility that interpretive models of the way audiences negotiate the meaning of information are likely to shed important light on the social-psychological processes that give rise to public attitudes. Like Guttman, Scheufele and Dudo suggest that the shift to online sources of information and debate may hold potential for new strategies and theoretically informed means of reducing the gaps and offering a more inclusive basis for the public understanding of science.

These authors are concerned about the relative absence of contributions by media and communication scholars to the "wicked" social controversies over nanotechnology. This issue has given rise to a host of moral and ethical issues that have been discussed extensively by those concerned with ethical, legal, and social implications (ELSIs). From media depictions of nanotechnology killing butterflies to the Greenpeace Frankenfood campaign, Scheufele and Dudo suggest that deliberative forums, together with a greater awareness on the part of scientists, could make a considerable difference to the way the public understands the potential and the risks of this new technology. They point to studies suggesting that individuals' moral belief systems may be challenged and that ideology serves as a perceptual filter when audiences need to balance values and worldviews against scientific facts. They argue that public opinion and communication research should be able to provide us with a more accurate picture of what groups in society want to know, their concerns, and the opinions they value.

Scheufele and Dudo argue that the goal of public deliberation and media coverage of the nanotechnology issues should be an informed citizenry that is capable of making well-reasoned policy decisions and ethical choices about scientific issues. If communication strategies are failing because scientists are working with the sender-receiver model of media effects, then it is important to make them aware of research by media and communication scholars into media framing. Drawing in part on the work of Tversky and Kahneman (1981), they suggest that people systematically violate requirements of consistency and coherence, normally assumed to be necessary for rational choice.

Thus, they suggest that empirical research in this area needs to focus on how the public forms attitudes based on information, visual cues, and popular representations of science. More creative public engagement might be achieved with the public through the use of art forms, communication campaigns and informal outreach aimed at introducing less threatening imagineries of nano-technology and other science-based technological innovations.

Personalizing Politics

Silke Adams and Michaela Maier evaluate the strengths and weaknesses of empirical research on what has been labeled the "personalization of politics." The focus in this chapter is on the normative standard that is invoked in assessments of the implications of the personalization of politics for democratic processes. Silke and Maier argue that, notwithstanding the (historial) presence of personal attributes concerning political leaders in the media, the evidence is at best ambiguous on the issue of whether personalization has been increasing.

The claims and counterclaims emerging from empirical studies are attributable to the absence of consistent definitions, methods, and assessments of systemic and contextual variables. Personalization in this chapter is broadly understood to encompass processes whereby politicians become the main sources of interpretations and evaluations of the political process, the concern being that this may have negative implications for democracy if it detracts from rational decision making. In the literature, personalization is said to result in a focus on candidates and politicians (and their non–political personal characteristics) to the detriment of issue-based deliberation in contexts such as election campaigns, media reporting, and voting behavior.

Adam and Maier's review of the literature suggests that there are complex interactions between parties, candidates, and issues. This complexity includes the possibility that decisions may be rational even if citizens do not achieve the highest standard of information. Citizens may economize on information based on criteria such as the perceived integrity and honesty of the source, enabling them to make short-cuts. Personalization may help citizens to bundle information in a political person in a way that enhances the democratic process. Their assessment is that: (a) there is relatively little research, (b) what there is generally is not based on longitudinal studies, and (c) there are contradictory claims in the literature.

Arguing that personalization has been a feature of media coverage for decades, they conclude that it "has not strongly affected voting decisions, and personalization has not yet transformed the political process into a depoliticized contest in which non-political traits....have become increasingly important" (this volume, pp. 232–233). A future research agenda needs to develop standardized research instruments and definitions and undertake longitudinal cross country comparisons to establish a stronger evidence base to explain the complexity of personalization in modern politics. Rather than an emphasis mainly on content analysis of the media and on surveys, they suggest that cultural and institutional changes in politics and the changing character of professional journalism, especially with respect to media framing, need to be better understood before conclusions about the strengthening or undermining of democracy are drawn. As in the two preceding chapters, research on economizing on information or "information shortcuts" needs to be located in a theoretical framework that acknowledges the interpretive capacities of citizens (audiences) and the implications for the informed citizen within the wider context of pluralist, participatory, and discursive theories of democracy. When deliberative theories of democracy are drawn upon, they argue it is important to consider questions about the role of intimacy and its implications for citizen's perceptions of candidates and political issues.

Interdisciplinary Research Agendas

In summary, all three chapters in this section raise questions about the normative standards for deliberative democracy, whether they are achievable, and whether it is necessary to include an understanding of the personal, the emotional, values, and the interpretative capacities of audiences/citizens to understand the implications of public deliberation. Each highlights issues of the legitimacy of political systems, the role of informed elites, access to decision making forums, participation, and the quality of discursive reasoning.

Guttman locates her work within the field of political communication focusing on the theory and practice of deliberative democracy; Scheufele and Dubo locate their work in the tradition of studies of public understanding of scientific communication; while Adam and Maier work within the field of political communication and studies of political candidates and leaders. These authors invoke the standard of rational-critical discourse as the foundation of the democratic ideal, but each suggests the need to draw upon theoretical insights into factors contributing to inconsistencies and departures from the normative ideal speech situation without concluding that such departures are necessarily detrimental to democracy. In so doing, they are implicitly suggesting an interdisciplinary research agenda for future research on the relations between public deliberation, the role of the media, and politics and democracy.

This strengthening of the research agendas is supported in each chapter by drawing upon insights from media and communication theories, but also from political theory, psychology, cultural studies, sociology, and the economics of information. In the remainder of this chapter, I contextualize the forward-looking research agendas proposed in each of these chapters, by pointing to lines of argument that serve to situate the arguments in the broader context of the relationship between the media and democratization.

Contextualizing the Media, Deliberation, and Democratization

In his analysis of strengths and weaknesses of Habermas's depiction of the public sphere, Calhoun (1992) highlights Habermas's main concern: "What are the social conditions ... for a rational-critical debate about public issues conducted by private persons willing to let arguments and not statuses determine decisions?" Calhoun suggests that for Habermas, "a public sphere adequate to a democratic polity depends upon both the quality of discourse and quantity of participation" (p. 2).

The three chapters in this section speak to the extent to which formal and informal procedures for public deliberation are influenced by the media and by the practices and sense-making or interpretative strategies of citizens.

Habermas (1962/1989, 1996) was concerned that as private organizations became historically powerful, especially in the production of the mass media, and as the state became more influential in the private realm of citizens' lives, the public sphere underwent a "refeudalization" such that relatively passive consumption of culture and the media became the norm in contrast to rational-critical debate. Modern media (information and entertainment) consumption entails a process whereby the personal becomes more visible making it difficult to achieve the ideal of this form of argument. As Calhoun explains, "the media are used to create occasions for consumers to identify with the public positions or personas of others" (1992, p. 26). The public may agree, disagree, or ignore, but engages less and less in the critical discourse required for the normative ideal of democracy. The struggle today for political decision making is to enable consensus formation through communication in ways that are not dominated by powerful actors. The research question then is whether there are mediated contexts and deliberative strategies that facilitate the emergence of rational-critical discourse.

A conception of science and politics as objective and disinterested is central to this normative notion of the public sphere. As Calhoun (1992) suggests,

> The very idea of the public was based on the notion of a general interest sufficiently basic that discourse about it need not be distorted by particular interests (at least in principle) and could be a matter of rational approach to an objective order, that is to say, truth. (p. 9)

Or, put another way, of harmony and consensus. Readers will be aware that Habermas has been criticized, not the least for his neglect of diverse identities and their politics, whether associated with feminism, religion, nationalism, or social movements (Dean, 2003; Thompson, 1993). One radical departure, while similarly concerned with the functioning of democracy, suggests a different standard for the assessment of the quality and quantity of public deliberation. Mouffe (1999) offers this alternative through her conception of agonistic pluralism (Laclau & Mouffe, 1985).

In contrast to the public sphere envisaged by Habermas, Mouffe (1999) argues that when the public sphere is principally concerned with the moral grounds for decision making, this downplays the contested interests of citizens. She suggests that this conception "... consists in replacing the market-inspired view of the public sphere by another conception that conceives political questions as being of a moral nature and therefore susceptible of being decided rationally" (1999, p. 746). But, in politics conditions of power and antagonism remain ever-present suggesting that any consensus must be provisional and partial. "Political practice in a democratic society does not consist in defending the rights of preconstituted identities, but rather in constituting those identities themselves in a precarious and always vulnerable terrain" (Mouffe, 1999, p. 753). It is in this context then that the research question becomes one of how to constitute or institutionalize power relationships in ways that are consistent with democracy.

Instead of seeking to attain the highest standard of an objective commensurability of views and opinions (consistent with an objective science), it is crucial to seek means of acknowledging diversity and difference, of allowing passionate debate, and of providing the means for enabling conflict among adversaries to be expressed. This, Mouffe, argues can lead to insight and mobilization toward democratic practice in a way that is consistent with a multiplicity of voices. This offers a theoretical model that contrasts with the goal of deliberative democracy that tends to repress passion and to elevate standards of rationality and morality.

The chapters in this section are principally located in the tradition of research informed by the deliberative conception of the public sphere, but they all acknowledge the extent to which the media and political processes fall short of the normative ideal. It is therefore helpful to juxtapose this view with the alternative offered by Mouffe. This invites us to consider how power relations between citizen and state are organized in different contexts and to assess whether we should extend the range of criteria used to assess how political practices either facilitate consensus formation or vigorous debate among adversaries.

The Habermasian view of the public sphere is more in line with a conception of power in which power is visible through observed behavior, decision making (as well as non-decision making), and observable conflict on issues or potential issues where citizen's subjective interests are regarded as policy preferences to be revealed through their political participation, e.g., voting, participation in deliberative forums (Lukes, 1974/2005). Another view of power focuses on issues and potential issues and on observable and covert issues, but also on *latent conflict* so as to distinguish between subjective and real interests.

> The three dimensional view of power involves a thoroughgoing critique of the behavioural focus of the first two views as individualistic and allows for considerations of the many ways in which potential issues are kept out of politics, whether through the action of social forces and institutional practices, or through individual's decisions. (Lukes, 1974/2005, p. 24)

In this view, the interpenetration of the media with political processes suggests that mediation processes have the power to frame issues, to prime people through cultivation, and to engage in agenda setting. They are also implicated in the extent to which latent and observable conflicts are resolved through, following Mouffe, emotionally charged adversarial debate in multiple contexts (place based deliberative forums, voting and elections, and online discussions) in which such debate may occur. When we consider issues such as the standards to be achieved by deliberative forums (Guttman), the communicative relations between scientists and lay publics on nanotechnology futures (Scheufele & Dudo), or the implications of personalization for democracy (Adam & Maier), a forward looking research agenda arguably would be enhanced by considering the merits and disadvantages of both these conceptions—that is consensus and agonism—of the articulation of the political with the media in modern democracies.

Acknowledging the potential explanatory power of both these theoretical models, suggests that we should understand the mediated environment as one in which both reason and emotion are in play. In Castells' work on *Communication Power* (2009), for example, he argues that "the most fundamental form of power lies in the ability to shape the human mind. The way we feel and think determines the way we act, both individually and collectively. Yes, coercion, and the capacity to exercise it, legitimate or not, is an essential source of power. But coercion alone cannot stabilize domination" (p. 3). Although individuals interpret media materials in diverse ways, their mental processing is conditioned by the communications environment. In other words, it is this broad context that matters in examining the factors influencing public opinion and decision making. And as Silverstone (1999, p. 143) observed, "It is all about power, of course. In the end." There are other conceptions of the public and the nature of public discourse and publicity, following, for example, Arendt and developing the notion of theatricality (Villa, 1999). There are debates about the legitimacy of place based and non-place based forums for dialogue within the democratic sphere (Barnett, 2003) and about the role of rationality, objectivity as well as subjectivity, and the personal or private boundaries (Ferree, Gamson, Gerhrard, & Rucht, 2002; Warner, 2002) of decision making. These cannot be pursued here.

In the light of this broader (and contested) theoretical framework, however, we can revisit the chapters in this section. In the case of Guttman's discussion of public deliberative forums, we might ask whether standards aimed at achieving fairness and equity and which privilege rational discourse might be complemented by those designed to encourage other forms of narration and storytelling, even if they are passionate and emotional. This is important in the light of Janssen and Kies's (2005) observation that the evaluation of the quality of online political forums requires that we operationalize what quality means and clarify the range of conditions for a public sphere. And given the increasing reliance of the public on Internet-based sites for the exchange of information and communication, we might also extend consideration of these criteria to research on these online sites. Albrecht (2006), for example, calls for more empirical studies of online deliberation, since it is not clear who participates or who is represented. Just as in offline forums, the Habermasian deliberative ideal of a more informed public is clearly not being achieved very extensively. While some barriers to deliberation may be reduced, others come to the fore including play with identity and conflictual behavior.

While some studies in this area continue to work with the framework of rational-critical deliberation there is contradictory evidence as to whether online and offline deliberation yields increases in participants' knowledge, political efficacy, and willingness to participate in politics (Min, 2007). There is a growing body of research on e-democracy but this rarely focuses on who participates or what the consequences of such deliberation online may be. Haque and Loader's work on *Digital Democarcy* (1999) indicates that it is no less difficult to create the conditions for the ideal speech situation in e-democracy initiatives than it is in the offline world. Similarly, Wilhelm's (2000) *Democracy in the Digital Age* suggests that political participation online in the United States at least is neither inclusive nor deliberative. Coleman and Gotze's (2001) review of representation, engagement, and democracy online similarly suggests that government representatives find it very hard to build relationships with the proliferation of online communities. To understand whether a deliberative or agonistic model best explains developments in this area it also may be useful to draw upon the large literature on the way the contexts of online communication interact with beliefs and actions (Delli-Carpini, Cook, & Jacobs, 2004; Rice, 1993; Tidwell & Walther, 2006; Walther, 1992) in the field of computer mediated communication.

Studies of online social movements are suggesting that, despite the unbounded nature of the Internet, when transnational civil society groups seek to construct a transnational public sphere they encounter constraints:

> … the power-shift from the nation states towards regional/global political or indeed economic institutions and the lack or rather weak democratic controls on these 'higher' levels of governance, have promoted civil society organisations—and more specifically social movement organisations—to organise themselves beyond the nation states in order to critically question the legitimacy of international economic and political actors. (Cammaerts & Van Audenhove, 2005, p. 149)

Whether in national or transnational contexts, the conflictual or agonistic model seems an essential complement to the rational–deliberative model. Cammaerts' (2008) work offers insight into the larger scale online interactive processes in connection with debates in the context of World Summit on the Information Society and on the European Convention, suggesting a mixed picture where participants appear to learn and become more informed about issues, but rarely are able to influence the outcomes of debates, indicating the importance of analyzing exclusions from democratic processes (Cammaerts & Carpentier, 2007).

In general, research on forums for deliberative online dialogue suggests that if the criteria are: "exchange and critique of reasoned moral–practical validity claims ... reflexivity ... ideal role taking ... sincerity... discursive inclusion and equality ... autonomy from state and economic power" (Dahlberg, 2001, p. 623), then these are not met as a result of the shift from offline to online forums. Dahlgren (2000) distinguishes between the structures (how online spaces are configured), representation (media output in terms of fairness, accuracy, agenda setting), and interaction (citizens engaged in talk with each other) offered by the online public sphere. He observes that criticism of the Habermasian public sphere generally runs as follows:

> The rationalist bias tends to discount a wide array of communicative modes that can be of importance for democracy, including the affective, the poetic, the humorous, the ironic, and so forth ... [and] that adherence to the perspective of deliberative democracy risks downplaying relations of power that are built into communicative situations. (Dahlgren, 2005, pp. 156–157)

He turns to a consideration of civic culture, constituted by values, affinity, knowledge, identities, and practices, thereby opening up the range of criteria for assessment to admit both the rational–critical and the potentially agonistic.

The foregoing suggests a more inclusive theoretical agenda for considering the relationships between scientists, the media, and citizens than that proposed by Scheufele and Dudo in their assessment of public understanding of nanotechnology. In line with the tensions between the two theoretical approaches to public debate outlined here, individuals can be expected to interpret science and media stories on the basis of both information and emotion as they suggest in their chapter. When these authors point to the theoretical insights that can be drawn from the field of media and communication studies, they may, however, in addition to recourse to cultivation and related theories, consider drawing upon insights into the complexity of mediation processes and the ways these inform decision making about highly controversial, ethically charged social and political issues (Silverstone, 2007).

Castells' (2009) work suggests that there are lessons to be drawn from experimental cognitive neuropsychology, and we also know that the media can be understood to offer a particular mode of representation through its texts and images, serving as a form of government which is engaged in the "elaboration of a language for depicting the domain in question that claims both to grasp the nature of that reality represented, and literally to *re*present it in a form amenable to political deliberation, argument and scheming" (Miller & Rose, 2008, p. 31).

Sociological studies of the relations between science, technology, and public understanding reveal the extent to which scientists' self–understanding is resistant to the idea of reflexivity and often modeled on a theoretical conception of truth and progressive innovation for the common good (MacKenzie, 1996). It may be that the problematic nature of the knowledge or communication gap highlighted by Scheufele and Dudo would benefit from studies drawing upon research in the field of science and technology studies, once again, emphasizing the need for media and communication scholars to reach out to draw upon the insights in cognate fields of study. For instance, Rogers-Hayden and Pidgeon (2007) emphasize the importance of engaging in new forms of risk communication in the context of nanotechnology debates, arguing that there is a need for more than attention to the standards of deliberative forums or to holding them earlier in the innovation process. They suggest that such dialogue may open up differences or conflictual visions as much as it may move towards public consensus (Rogers-Hayden & Pidgeon, 2007). And Macnaghten, Keames, and Wynne (2005, p. 270) argue that in addition to focusing on issues of media framing, there is a need to ask questions about covert and latent power relations. "Why these technologies? Why not others? Who needs them, and what human purposes are driving them? Under what conditions will they be enacted; and who sets those conditions? Who is controlling them? Who benefits from them? Can they be trusted?" Like Scheufele and Dudo in their chapter in this section, they call for research that would seek to understand how nanotechnologies are imagined noting that imaginaries are "mobilized through ongoing public discourses and enacted in everyday practices" (Macnaghten et al., 2005, p. 279). Importantly, they ask "how do they mobilize public and private interest and opposition?" recalling a concern about latent and potentially conflictual relationships.

In recent work, analysis of visionary images has been undertaken by Losch (2008) who focuses on media representations of alternative futures for nanotechnology, by Bennett-Woods (2008) in *Nanotechnology: Ethics and Society,* and by Schummer and Baird (2006) in *Nanotechnology Challenges,* taking up some of these issues. Perhaps the most comprehensive work to date is by Anderson, Petersen, Wilkinson, and Allan (2009) who examine *Nanotechnology, Risk and Communication* in the United Kingdom, focusing on media framing as well as on the way policy makers and scientists represent developments in this area. The strongly interdisciplinary flavor of research in this area is emphasized again here as these authors work within the fields of Sociology, Science Communication and Journalism/Media Studies.

In their research on personalization Adam and Maier suggest a research agenda that calls for definitional clarity, longitudinal comparative studies, and consideration of the informational short-cuts that voters may employ that may be rational, relevant, and valuable for decision making, adhering closely to the wider precepts of the deliberative norm offered by Habermas's concept of the public sphere. This suggests a rich and important forward–looking research agenda. The comparative research agenda is one for which there has been strong demand especially by Gurevitch and Blumler (2004), but this is an area of political communication that has remained underdeveloped. In many instances, scholars based in the United States have led the way in tackling issues in the field of political communication and the questions around personalization are no exception. Others have contributed country studies examining similarities or differences with U.S. trends. In this area there are few comparative frameworks such as is the case more generally in political science, for example, where there are comparisons of democratic institutions and electoral or party systems (Johansen, 2009). Comparisons offered by scholars in the media and communication field tend to be organized around themes such as trends in the professionalization of politics, in media logics, and in personalization. Arguably, work in this field would benefit from being located within the broader disputed territory of the theories about power and discourse outlined at the beginning of this section.

There is a "driving democracy" agenda (Norris, 2008) in the field of political communication that seeks to compare different types of political institutions including the electoral system, parliamentary or presidential executives, unitary or federal states, and the structure and independence of the media. This work often relates to new democracies and the process of entrenching or consolidating democracy but also has implications for issues of civic engagement and participation in older democracies. There is a comparative agenda in this area, but although studies of personalization are underway, this work is still marginal. For example, the youngish democracies in Latin America, nearly all post-military dictatorships—have without exception opted for presidential systems which are personalized to one degree or another—for various reasons including the absence of well–developed civil society organizations. In these contexts, personalization emerges in tension: it may be a necessary step towards democratization but it may also be a source of vulnerability as charismatic leaders take on more power and weaken sources of opposition. These developments juxtapose two images of personalization—the classic Weberian "big" charisma associated with a strong, heroic populist leader; a form that is arguably distinct from the Western/Northern anxieties about the intrusion of the private, that is, the "small" charisma of the intimate, personal charm, sincerity, and personal affinity.

In addition, Adam and Maier's call for a renewed focus on the description, explanation, and evaluation of personalization needs to be pursued. In addition to the definitional clarify that they call for, there is scope to go further to build on the work of Langer (2006, 2007). She analytically separates the dimensions of personalization to consider: (a) "presidentialization" (concentration of power in the person of a leader at the expense of cabinet/parliament) through constitutional change without effective deliberation and (b) personality politics (increased attention from media, citizens, and parties to the personal qualities of leaders). These might include attention to qualities deemed "legitimate" for voters to exercise rational choices or they might entail a focus on private characteristics such as whether a leader is a good parent (Smith, 2008). In the latter case, Langer refers to this as the politicization of private persona (Langer, in press). In the first case, the changes may result in a redistribution of executive power as in the case of Chavez in Venezuela and Putin in Russia. Although these dimensions of personalization may be linked, it is analytical useful to separate them as each may imply different normative consequences for the public sphere.

Lastly, it may be productive to consider personalization from the "demand" side. Most research approaches this concept as a characteristic that emerges from the top down as a result either of a media logic and understanding of media power and the needs of television and journalism professionals, or of campaigning strategy where the goal is to create a competitive advantage under conditions of considerable ideological/policy similarity between rivals (Scammell & Semetko, 2001). This downplays the bottom–up contributions to personalization. Personalization may enable citizens to connect with leaders and therefore may facilitate their engagement with politics and the democratic process. There is relatively little work on how leader images are constructed and created in part from the bottom up (Scammell, 2003) through branding. Leader images may be regarded as a form of brand equity, something in the gift of consumers that, while influenced by the media, is distinct. There is increasing interest in the bottom-up creation of leader image as in the 2008 Obama campaign using social media such as YouTube and other social networking sites such designforobama.org, also suggesting the importance of charisma and heroic leadership.

Conclusion

Overall, the synthesis of the state of the art of research in the field of public deliberation, media, politics and political outcomes presented in this section demonstrates that there is a need for future research that is designed to encompass longitudinal, comparative research based on a wider range of empirical methodologies. In each of the areas of concern in this section, the researchers are exploring outwards to acknowledge findings in related disciplines and fields of inquiry. They are also challenging scholars in the media and communication field to widen their investigation to embrace issues of substantial public concern that raise new issues of risk both for individuals and society.

While the contributors to this section work predominantly within a theoretical framework informed by Habermas's conception of the public sphere, they all find it essential to reach beyond this framework if we are to understand how better to create inclusive opportunities for citizens to engage in political decision making. In this chapter, I have suggested the need to acknowledge the tension between those concerned with power and consensus formation around those issues and interests that rise to the surface of public life and those which frequently lie concealed or latent, but which belie ongoing contestations over power in society. In all of these cases, the media play a significant role in representing political leaders, scientists and lay publics. Research that reveals greater insight into how publicity and opinion formation interact in today's mediated environment is clearly essential to democratic functioning and its results offer the foundations for political practice in many diverse areas.

References

Albrecht, S. (2006). Whose voice is heard in the virtual public sphere? A study of participation and representation in political debates on the Internet. *Information, Communication & Society, 9*(1), 62–82.

Anderson, A. G., Petersen, A., Wilkinson, C., & Allan, S. (2009). *Nanotechnology, risk and communication*. Basingstoke, UK: Palgrave Macmillan.

Barnett, C. (2003). *Culture and democracy: Media, space and representation*. Edinburgh, Scotland: Edinburgh University Press.

Bennett-Woods, D. (2008). *Nanotechnology: Ethics and society*. Boca Raton, FL: CRC Press.

Calhoun, C. (1992). *Habermas and the public sphere*. Cambridge, MA: MIT Press.

Cammaerts, B. (2008). *Internet-mediated participation beyond the nation state*. Manchester, UK: Manchester University Press.

Cammaerts, B., & Carpentier, N. (Eds.). (2007). *Reclaiming the media: Communication rights and democratic media roles*. Bristol, UK: Intellect Books.

Cammaerts, B., & Van Audenhove, L. (2005). Online political debate: Unbounded citizenship and the problematic nature of a transnational public sphere. *Political Communication, 22*(2), 147–162.

Castells, M. (2009). *Communication power*. Oxford, UK: Oxford University Press.

Coleman, S., & Gotze, J. (2001). *Bowling together: Online public engagement in policy deliberation*. London: Hansard Society.

Dahlberg, L. (2001). The Internet and democractic discourse: Exploring the prospects for online deliberative forums extending the public sphere. *Information, Communication & Society, 4*(4), 613–633.

Dahlgren, P. (2000). The Internet and the democratization of civic culture. *Political Communication, 17*(4), 335–340.

Dahlgren, P. (2005). The Internet, public spheres, and political communication: Dispersion and deliberation. *Political Communication, 22*(2), 147–162.

Dean, J. (2003). Why the Internet is not a public sphere. *Constellations, 10*(1), 95–112.

Delli-Carpini, M. X., Cook, F. L., & Jacobs, L. R. (2004). Public deliberation, discursive participation, and citizen engagement: A review of the literature. *Annual Review of Political Science, 7*(1), 315–344.

Ferree, M., Gamson, W., Gerhrard, J., & Rucht, D. (2002). Four models of the public sphere in modern democracies. *Theory and Society, 31*(3), 289–324.

Gurevitch, M., & Blumler, J. G. (2004). State of the art of comparative political communication reseach. In F. Esser & B. Pfetsch (Eds.), *Comparing political communications: Theories, cases, and challenges* (pp. 325–343). Cambridge, UK: Cambridge University Press.

Guttman, N. (2000). *Public health communication interventions*. London: Sage.

Habermas, J. (1962/1989). *The structural transformation of the public sphere*. Cambridge, UK: Polity Press.

Habermas, J. (1996). *Between facts and norms: Contributions to a discourse theory of law and democracy* (W. Rehq, Trans.). Cambridge, MA: MIT Press.

Haque, B. N., & Loader, B. D. (Eds.). (1999). *Digital democracy: Discourse and decision making in the information age*. London: Routledge.

Janssen, D., & Kies, R. (2005). Online forums and deliberative democracy. *Acta Politica, 40*(2), 317–335.

Johansen, H. (2009). *Re–conceptualising party-centred politics in terms of market: A relationship marketing approach*. Unpublished PhD thesis, London, London School of Economics and Political Science.

Laclau, E., & Mouffe, C. (1985). *Hegemony and socialist strategy: Towards a radical democratic politics*. London: Verso.

Langer, A. I. (2006). *The politicisation of private persona: The case of Tony Blair in historical perspective*. Unpublished PhD thesis, London, London School of Economics and Political Science.

Langer, A. I. (2007). A historical exploration of the personalisation of politics in the print media: The British prime ministers 1945–1999. *Parliamentary Affairs, 60*(3), 371–387.

Langer, A. I. (In press). *Personality politics in the United Kingdom*. Manchester, UK: Manchester University Press.

Losch, A. (2008). Anticipating the futures of nanotechnology: Visionary images as a means of communication. *Technology Analysis and Strategic Management, 18*(3-4), 393–409.

Lukes, S. (1974/2005). *Power: A radical view* (2nd ed.). London: Macmillan.

MacKenzie, D. (1996). Economic and sociological explanations of technological change. In D. MacKenzie (Ed.), *Knowing machines: Essays on technical change* (pp. 49–66). Cambridge MA: The MIT Press.

Macnaghten, P., Keames, M. B., & Wynne, B. (2005). Nanotechnology, governance and public deliberation: What role for the social sciences? *Science Communication, 27*(2), 268–291.

Miller, P., & Rose, N. (2008). *Governing the present: Administering economic, social and personal life*. Cambridge, MA: Polity Press.

Min, S.-J. (2007). Online vs. face-to-face deliberation: Effects on civic engagement. *Journal of Computer Mediated Communication, 12*(4), 1369–1387.

Mouffe, C. (1999). Deliberative democracy or agonistic pluralism? *Social Research, 66*(3), 746–758.

Norris, P. (2008). *Driving democracy: Do power-sharing institutions work?* Cambridge, UK: Cambridge University Press.

Pidgeon, N., & Rogers-Hayden, T. (2007). Opening up nanotechnology dialogue with the publics: Risk communication or 'upstream engagement'? *Health, Risk & Society, 9*(2), 191–210.

Rice, R. E. (1993). Media appropriateness: Using social presence theory to compare traditional and new organisational media. *Human Communication Research, 19*, 451–484.

Rogers-Hayden, T., & Pidgeon, N. (2007). Developments in nanotechnology public engagement in the UK: 'Upstream' toward sustainability. *Journal of Cleaner Production, 16*(8-9), 1010–1013.

Scammell, M. (2003). Citizen consumers: Towards a new marketing of politics? Unpublished manuscript, University of Washington, retrieved November 15, 2009, from http://depts.washington.edu/gcp/pdf/citizenconsumers.pdf

Scammell, M., & Semetko, H. (Eds.). (2001). *Media, journalism and democracy*. Dartmouth, NH: Dartmouth Publishing.

Schummer, J., & Baird, D. (Eds.). (2006). *Nanotechnology challenges: Implications for philosophy, ethics and society.* Singapore: World Scientific Publishing.

Silverstone, R. (1999). *Why study the media?* London: Sage.

Silverstone, R. (2007). *Media and morality: On the rise of the mediapolis.* Cambridge, UK: Polity Press.

Smith, A. (2008). 'New Man' or 'Son of Manse'? Gordon Brown as a reluctant celebrity father. *British Politics, 3*(4), 556–575.

Thompson, J. (1993). The theory of the public sphere. *Theory Culture & Society, 10*(3), 173–189.

Tidwell, L. C., & Walther, J. B. (2006). Computer-mediated communication effects on disclosure, impressions, and interpersonal evaluations: Getting to know one another a bit at a time. *Human Communication Research, 28*(3), 317–348.

Tversky, A., & Kahneman, D. (1981). The framing of decisions and the psychology of choice. *Science Communication, 211*(4481), 453–458.

Villa, D. (1999). Theatricality and the public realm. In D. Villa (Ed.), *Politics, philosophy, terror: Essays on the thought of Hannah Arendt* (pp. 128–155). Princeton, NJ: Princeton University Press.

Walther, J. B. (1992). Interpersonal effects in computer-mediated interaction: A relational perspective. *Communication Research, 19*, 52–90.

Warner, M. (2002). Publics and counterpublics. *Public Culture, 14*(1), 49–90.

Wilhelm, A. (2000). *Democracy in the digital age: Challenges to political life in cyberspace.* London: Routledge.

Part III

Communication and Societies in Transition

CHAPTER CONTENTS

10 The New Arab Cyberscape

Redefining Boundaries and Reconstructing Public Spheres

Sahar Khamis

University of Maryland, College Park

Vít Šisler

Charles University in Prague

This chapter analyzes the new Arab media landscape, with a special focus on the growing influence of the Internet in redefining boundaries and reconstructing public spheres in contemporary Arab societies. This includes: preserving authentic cultural norms and religious values while opening the door for more modern and liberal influences; appealing to a pan-Arab audience with its own regional interests and cultural specificities while addressing a broader, transnational audience; asserting conformity and compliance with existing political order and traditional authorities while fueling resistance and public discontent; and engaging in confrontations with external forces and international powers while advocating dialogue and engaging in media diplomacy. Special attention is paid to how and why this complex and hybrid Arab cyberscape may overlap with, or diverge from, the Habermasian notion of the public sphere. These similarities and differences are explored and examined in light of three contemporary challenges confronting the Arab cyberscape: democratization, dialogue, and diaspora.

Introduction

This chapter analyzes the new Arab media landscape, with a special focus on the growing influence of the Internet on redefining boundaries and reconstructing public spheres in contemporary Arab societies. In exploring this process, we explain how this new Arab cyberscape is oscillating between, and often times even synthesizing, the bipolar opposites of regionalization and globalization, traditionalism and modernity, as well as conformity and resistance.

Before discussing the general structure and organization of this chapter, we must first shed light on two important conceptual notions. The first is the overlap between the notions of Arab and Muslim public spheres (Zayani, 2008). The research on the role of new media and the Internet in the Arab world oftentimes entangles with broader research concerning the Middle East and/or the Muslim world in general. In many cases research conducted within the framework of Islamic and/or Middle Eastern studies deals directly with issues related to the Arab cyberscape. Conversely, many new Arab media play an important role in the production of global Islamic knowledge, transcending national, regional, and language boundaries. This is particularly relevant to the situation of Muslim minorities living in non-Muslim countries, where the Internet and new media have become an important adjunct to traditional means of communicating about Islam and facilitate "a new form of Islamic discourse" (Bunt, 2006, p. 13). Many prominent Islamic websites are maintained and/or operate from Arab countries, so besides being part of the "emerging Muslim public sphere" (Eickelman & Anderson, 2003, p. 1), they also form an inseparable part of the Arab media landscape. Therefore, although this chapter focuses primarily on the Arab cyberscape, it also incorporates research originated in the framework of Islamic and/or Middle Eastern studies, as long as it is directly related to the topic of new media and the public sphere in the Arab world.

The second issue deserving clarification is our operational definition of cyberscape. The term *cyberscape* stems from the combination of the words cyberspace and landscape and describes the emerging convergence of the Internet with new media outlets. These new media outlets encompass, but are not limited to, video blogs, audio lectures, and sermons, video games, and social networking sites. At the same time, the term *cyberscape* refers to a broader media landscape, in which the Internet and the new media outlets proliferate, with its social, cultural, and linguistic context. Therefore, we have to explore how and why the emerging Arab cyberscape, with all its complexities and dynamics, is invoking dramatic changes in both media form and communication content simultaneously. In terms of form, cyberscape intersects the blurry boundaries between mainstream media and new media and media producers and media consumers; it also converts and combines different types of new media. In terms of content, cyberscape intersects boundaries between the public and private spheres, local and global spheres, and traditional and modern spheres. As such, it reformulates and reconstructs ongoing debates, discourses, and public spheres in the Arab world.

In investigating the relationship between the proliferation of new media outlets in the Arab world and the construction of new types of media and multiple public spheres, we assess whether the notion of the public sphere, as envisioned by Habermas, is a valid interpretative framework for analyzing these processes in the Arab mediascape.

Therefore, the chapter starts with a brief explication of the Habermasian notion of the public sphere and discusses the applicability of this theoretical framework to the contemporary Arab media context. We then provide an overview of the emerging Arab mediascape, with a focus on the implications of Internet boundaries, as well as changing public spheres. Special attention will be paid to how and why the Arab cyberscape may overlap with, or diverge from, the Habermasian notion of the public sphere. These similarities and differences will be discussed in light of three contemporary challenges confronting the Arab cyberscape, namely: the democratization challenge, the dialogue challenge, and the diaspora challenge.

The Habermasian Public Sphere: Theoretical Insights, Critiques, and Limitations

The term *public sphere* was defined by Habermas as "a sphere between civil society and the state, in which critical public discussion of matters of general interest" take place (1989, p. xi). For the purpose of this chapter, we will focus on the communication-related aspects of Habermas's theory. For political communication, Habermas idealizes the concept of rational-critical deliberations. He developed his notion around "how the classical bourgeois public sphere of the seventeenth and eighteenth centuries was constituted around rational critical argument, in which the merits of the arguments and not the identities of arguers were crucial" (Calhoun, 1992, p. 2). Therefore, the fact that his theory developed among the European bourgeois elites, in particular, triggers a main criticism of Habermas's public sphere, which is its Eurocentric bias (Gunaratne, 2006; Salvatore, 2007). This criticism revolves around several aspects of Habermas's notion of the public sphere that are perceived to be culture-bound and, therefore, would not necessarily fit non-Western societies. This includes the fact that his theory mainly referred to the political, economic, cultural, and technological developments in seventeenth and eighteenth century Europe, with a special focus on Britain, France, and Germany (Goode, 2005, p. 4).

In this respect, Salvatore (2007) has expressed concern that the Western Habermasian notion of public sphere could not easily "apply" to the Arab Muslim world, mainly because Habermas "significantly underplayed the role of religious traditions in its formation" (p. 2). Similarly, other authors argue that some of the underlying assumptions which place political discussions at the heart of public deliberations, while restricting religion are not applicable in most of the Arab world, where religion forms a very central part of all ongoing discourses and debates, both online and offline (El-Nawawy & Khamis, 2009; Etling, Kelly, Faris, & Palfrey, 2009; Hofheinz, 2005; Hamzah, 2005).

Additionally, while the emphasis on political speech confines personal, domestic, and family matters to the private domain, many of the websites in the Arab/Muslim world today, especially websites issuing *fatwa* (religious and legal advice), are full of questions which touch upon private, domestic, and family affairs, thus, placing them at the center of ongoing public discussions in this new mediascape (El-Nawawy & Khamis, 2009; Šisler, 2007, 2009a). Therefore, the private versus public dichotomy in the Habermasian public sphere, which institutionalizes "not just a set of interests and an opposition between state and society but a practice of rational-critical discourse on political matters" (Calhoun, 1992, p. 9) is very different from the reality of civil society in most of the Arab world. (Fandy, 2007; El-Nawawy & Khamis, 2009). That's mainly because many of the prerequisites for creating these notions of civil society and the public sphere are largely absent in this part of the world, due to low levels of political participation, the domination of authoritarian ruling regimes, low literacy levels that are associated with low newspapers circulation rates, and the reliance on oral and interpersonal forms of communication.

Another important point is what Calhoun (1992) describes as "Habermas's two-sided constitution of the category of public sphere as simultaneously about the quality or form of rational-critical discourse and the quantity of, or openness to, popular participation" (p. 4). The latter aspect of openness and wider participation based on equal access and equal chances of inclusion is certainly materializing in the Arab world at a fast pace, thanks to new communication technologies, especially the Internet and its interrelated media outlets. However, the former aspect of rational-critical deliberations seems largely absent in the new Arab media scene, as clearly demonstrated by the proliferation of ideological sites (Selnow, 1998), proselytizing audio sermons (Allievi, 2003; Hirschkind, 2006), and propagandistic video games (Šisler, 2008).

Most of these computer-mediated dialogues do not fit Habermas's theory of communicative action, which assumes that "modern individuals are oriented in the world not simply as strategic, but, above all, as communicative actors. Their actions are coordinated not only through egocentric calculations of success but through acts of reaching understanding" (Johnson, 2006, p. 48). Habermas defines communicative action as a process where "participants are not primarily oriented to their own individual successes; they pursue their individual goals under the condition that they can harmonize their plans of action on the basis of common situation definitions" (Johnson, 2006, p. 48). This idealistic vision of the communication process was also found to be largely absent in many of the online discourses in the contemporary Arab mediascape, where the opposite notion of strategic action that is based on persuasion and communicating with the purpose of shaping or changing the other party's views and/ or asserting the superiority and righteousness of one's own position, seemed to be the dominant pattern (Lynch, 2006; El-Nawawy & Khamis, 2009).

Despite the various criticisms of the Habermasian notion of the public sphere, mainly on the grounds that it is "idealistic, Eurocentric and unwittingly patriarchal" (Goode, 2005, p. 1), it continues to be a useful framework for "thinking about how wider social and cultural issues are addressed; and for trying to make sense of how agreement about what is acceptable in a culture is reached" (McKee, 2005, p. 6). This paradox is highly relevant to this essay, which tries to examine the various aspects of overlap with, as well as divergence from, the Habermasian public sphere within the realm of the equally paradoxical and transformative Arab media landscape. On one hand, we argue, in line with the findings of a number of authors (Eickelman & Anderson, 2003; Lynch, 2005, 2006; Hafez, 2008; Mellor, 2007; Al-Saggaf, 2006; Zayani, 2008; El-Nawawy & Khamis, 2009) that the new Arab cyberscape meets some of the basic requirements for the existence of a Habermasian public, such as equal access, openness to popular participation, and the diversity that allows individuals with heterogeneous, and sometimes even clashing, backgrounds and opinions to define the nature and course of interaction. On the other hand, we argue that the contemporary Arab cyberscape with its increasing tide of Islamization, gender inclusiveness, and growing transnationalism, differs significantly from the Eurocentric, bourgeois, male-dominated, and secular Habermasian public sphere. However, in order to better understand the nature and extent of these similarities and differences, we have to first shed light on the rapidly changing Arab mediascape, in general, and the transformative Arab cyberscape, in particular.

The Changing Arab Mediascape and the Transformative Arab Cyberscape

The high level of media hybridization and interdependency, together with determining social, political, and economic factors, implies that any analysis of the impact of the Internet and new media on the Arab public sphere has to transcend the "media-centric logic" (Allievi, 2003, p. 12) and should be contextualized within the broader context of Arab media developments.

Prior to 1990, most media ownership in the Arab world rested largely with governments, and most media functioned under strict governmental supervision and control. A number of authors (Rugh, 2004; Boyd, 1999; Mellor, 2007; Abdel Rahman, 1985, 2002) argued this was to keep lay people largely uninformed and, thus, incapable of effectively participating in political controversies and rational debates. This prevailing pattern was especially true in the case of broadcast media, which were strictly controlled through direct ownership, censorship, and various forms of economic incentives and disincentives (Rugh, 2004; Boyd, 1999; Sakr, 2007). The importance of controlling broadcast media, in particular, across the Arab world stems from the "obvious political importance in communicating with most of the population across the literacy barriers that prevail in the area" (Rugh, 2004, p. 255; see also Abdulla, 2007, p. 3). This meant that there was generally some evidence of tolerance of press freedom and diversity in print media, especially in some countries, such as Lebanon and Kuwait, which was not witnessed in broadcast media (Rugh, 2004; Boyd, 1999; Khamis, 2007; Sakr, 2007). The restrictions imposed by local governments led to a high level of media localization and audience isolation, because the only way Arab audiences heard news, other than what was locally approved, was by cross border radio or cross border television (Rugh, 2004, p. 255).

A "new media revolution" erupted in the Arab world after 1990 inspired by a number of factors and their accompanying shifts in the media landscape. First, significant political changes took place in a number of Arab countries, which led to increasing the margin of pluralism, diversity, and liberalism. This had a direct effect on modifying the media systems in these countries (Rugh, 2007). The second factor was the 1990 Iraqi invasion of Kuwait and the Gulf war that followed it in 1991, which was accompanied by the availability of

CNN network's news coverage of the war throughout the Arab region free of charge for the first time. This phenomenon had multiple implications on the media scene in the region, since it inspired many Arab countries to revolutionize their own television coverage by allowing privatized satellite television channels as well as professionalizing their own patterns of television coverage along the lines of Western television journalism (El-Nawawy & Iskander, 2002, 2003).

At the same time, the Internet penetration started to spread throughout the Arab world. Although the region generally suffered from "being on the low end of the digital divide" (Abdulla, 2007, p. 35), facing many challenges, including the lack of human and economic IT resources, illiteracy and computer illiteracy, the lack of funds for IT research and development, and the lack of solid telecommunication infrastructures, this situation is rapidly changing, since many Arab countries are currently striving hard to increase Internet coverage. Overall, governments in the Arab world have adopted strikingly different approaches to the Internet (Alterman, 2000, p. 22). Whereas some countries, like Egypt, Jordan, and the United Arab Emirates avidly invest in global Internet connections and promote the establishment of local service providers (Abdulla, 2007, p. 41), others, such as Saudi Arabia, have been slow to adopt such measures, and the Internet there is subject to many restrictions to prevent access to what the government considers undesirable information (Alterman, 2000, p. 22). Therefore, Internet penetration rates vary greatly in different Arab states. According to recent estimations in March 2009 (Internet World Stats, 2009), the world average Internet penetration is 23.8%. Several Arab countries substantially exceed this figure, for example: the United Arab Emirates (48.9%), Qatar (42.6%), Lebanon (39.5%), and Kuwait (34.7%), whereas most of the Arab world falls slightly below it, like Saudi Arabia (22.7%), Morocco (19.2%), Jordan (18.2%), Syria (17.6%), and Egypt (12.9%). Only in Yemen (1.4%) and Iraq (1.0%) does Internet penetration remain far below the international average. Generally, the region as a whole witnessed an unprecedented rise in Internet penetration levels over the last few years (Abdulla, 2007, p. 45; Warf & Vincent, 2007). Ironically, although many Internet websites and blogs are used to defy and resist autocratic governments and dictatorial regimes in the Arab world, a number of these governments took steps to encourage Internet proliferation and accessibility, mainly in order to boost economic development, as in the case of the Egyptian (Abdulla, 2006, p. 94), Jordanian (Zelaky, Eid, Sami, & Ziada, 2006, pp. 18–23), and Syrian (Anderson, 2008b) governments. This provides additional evidence of the highly ambivalent and complex relationship between the Arab cyberscape and governments in the Arab world.

The introduction of satellite television channels and the Internet represented an important shift from the monolithic, state-controlled and government-owned, media pattern to a much more pluralistic and diverse media scene, where many diverse and competing voices representing different political positions and orientations could be heard at the very same time, adding to the richness of ongoing political debates and the formation of a wide array of public opinion trends (Khamis, 2007; Atia, 2006). This pluralistic media scene manifested itself in the fact that many Arab newspapers, both governmental and oppositional, created their own websites on the Internet. This clearly exemplified a coexistence between "state ownership" and "private ownership," "governmental control" and "individual or party control," as well as "old" and "new" forms of communication simultaneously. Many of these newly emerging online newspapers represented a wide array of diverse voices and conflicting political views, which were sometimes very critical of governments and top officials (Atia, 2006).

The introduction of these new media outlets signified not only a shift from a highly monolithic to a more pluralistic media scene, but they also represented a shift away from the previous patterns of media localization and audience isolation, due to the availability of a greater number of choices that were present in the pre-1990 era.

In fact, it is safe to say that one of the most important avenues through which public opinion trends and public spheres are both shaped, as well as reflected, in modern Arab societies, beside satellite television channels, is the Internet (Zelaky et al., 2006, p. 5). The significance of the introduction of the Internet stems from the fact that it defies boundaries, challenges governmental media censorship, and provides an alternative voice to traditional media outlets, which echo official, governmental policies and views.

Just like the case of satellite television channels, Internet use is rapidly among younger people, especially the 20- to 30-year-old age group, and those younger than 20 years old (Abdulla, 2007, p. 50). There is a shortage in reliable data on the income levels and educational backgrounds of Internet users in the Arab world, but it is safe to say that Internet use is the highest among urban, middle- and upper-class groups, as suggested in studies covering Morocco (Baune, 2005), Kuwait (Wheeler, 2006), Egypt (Abdulla, 2007), and Saudi Arabia (Sait, Al-Tawil, Sanaullah, & Faheemuddin, 2007). Similar to Western societies, the use of the Internet is a way of life for young, educated Arabs (Khalid, 2007). The Internet is used for many purposes beyond access to news and other information. Instrumental sites such as search engines, social contacts through the email, blogs, and Facebook, as well as the discussion of taboo topics are just some of the utilizations; along with entertainment, sports, and seeking moral guidance and religious advice through religious websites (Bunt, 2006; Hofheinz, 2005; Abdulla, 2007).

Journalists and non-governmental organizations (NGOs) were among the first in the Arab world to use the Internet professionally. NGOs use the Internet to communicate with their mother organizations and to create web pages to attract donors. Journalists use the Internet to "hunt for information, access wire stories and images, and issue online editions of newspapers that are primarily read by national diasporas in the Gulf States, Europe, or America" (Hofheinz, 2005, p. 84). These examples illustrate the fact that many competing voices and forces are struggling for survival and attention in the changeable Arab cyberscape, which opens the door, in turn, for the proliferation of multiple, contesting public spheres.

The widespread access to the Internet and the emerging Arabic blogosphere (Etling et al., 2009; Atia, 2006; Iskander, 2006) also means that a whole new arena is now available to the public that didn't exist before in which to express their own views, ideas, criticisms, and ambitions, through discussing various cultural, social, and religious topics, which opens the door for heated online debates (Hofheinz, 2005).

One of the strongest advantages of the Internet vis-à-vis other types of media lies in its liberalizing potential due to the fact that it is, to some extent, free from the system of clientelism, which continues to characterize even the nominally private Arab satellite channels. According to Fandy (2007), "Arab media outlets may at times give the impression that they are independent, but they are in-fact still government-controlled, whether directly or indirectly. This casts doubt on the analytical usefulness of the private vs. public dichotomy, often used to assess media in Western societies when examining Arab media" (p. 8). He justifies this claim in light of the fact that the owners of the media in most of the Arab world not only "have close political ties to the state based on ideological positions or self-interest, but also close family ties and religious affiliations that ultimately link them to their respective governments. Thus questions of ownership encompass economic, political, and family interests. These cannot be simply reduced to 'cultural context'. Strategic political and economic motives structure this context" (p. 9).

Therefore, even the new, private media outlets in the Arab world, such as satellite television channels, became in many cases captives of the prevailing patterns of clientelism and instrumentalism, whereby the media simply echo the interests and the agendas of their owners, whether they are government officials, members of the ruling families, or any other powerful public figures.

Analyzed within this context, the Internet emerges as an increasingly powerful and independent medium in the Arab world, mainly because of its ability to escape governmental ownership and hegemony, which makes it less likely to fall victim to the prevailing patterns of clientelism and instrumentalism that characterize most Arab media. Therefore, it can be argued that the Internet is changing the nature of the communication process and is consequently contributing to the proliferation of multiple public spheres, as well as the creation of numerous publics and counterpublics (Fraser, 1992; Warner, 2002). These counterpublics are, according to Warner (2002), publics too, but "because they differ markedly in one way or another from the premises that allow the dominant culture to understand itself as a public, they have come to be called counterpublics" (pp. 112–113). Some examples of counterpublics in the Arab world are religious minorities, such as Shi'ites and Druze, political minorities, such as opposition groups, and social minorities, such as homosexuals.

This transformative nature of the Internet is exhibited in a number of important ways. First, it allows media consumers to become producers, who can create their own "knowledge communities" (Jenkins, 2006) that "form around mutual intellectual interests; their members work together to forge new knowledge often in realms where no traditional expertise exists; the pursuit of and assessment of knowledge is at once communal and adversarial" (p. 20).

Second, the Internet's expanding audiovisual potentials help greatly in widening its appeal and accessibility among larger segments of the population in the Arab world, thus, challenging the illiteracy barrier and narrowing the digital divide (Norris, 2006) between the information haves and have-nots in various strata of Arab societies. This, in turn, contributes to an informational trickle-down process, whereby the Internet and new media can be made available to vast segments of the wider public, rather than being restricted only to elites, intellectuals, and those in power. This phenomenon can expand the pluralistic and multiple public spheres that can proliferate as a result of this growing, transformative Arab cyberscape.

This last point is linked closely to some scholars' (Thompson, 1990; Goode, 2005) criticism of Habermas's print-media bias that is expressed in his argument that the new broadcast media's immediacy might discourage distanced reflection and critical discussion among their audience. According to Goode (2005, p. 20), Habermas fails to account for the fact that new broadcast media have been more accessible to the general masses compared to print media.

Goode's (2005) claim is particularly relevant to the Arab world given the low literacy rates and the strong oral cultural heritage (Boyd, 2003, p. 241; Abdulla, 2007, p. 7; Salvatore, 2007, p. 164). Amin and Gher (2000) argue that the Arabic cultural heritage must be considered when evaluating the impact of digital communication in the Arab world. As they put it: "Primary among many cultural issues is the fact that the oral tradition is the preferred mode of communication among Arabic peoples" (p. 136). This, in turn, explains the large divide and the widening gap in the Arab world between official spheres, such as governmental institutions and political parties and their controlled media, on one hand, and popular spheres, where most of the everyday communication activities take place, on the other hand, through "informal institutions, such as interpersonal communication, the mosque, and the souq [marketplace]...where the validity of the message and the person delivering the message and their trustworthiness are verifiable" (Fandy, 2007, p. 132).

Many other authors expressed concern that focusing on written content in the research conducted on the Internet and information technologies is not necessarily representative of the communication realities in the Arab/Muslim context (Allievi, 2003; Boyd, 2003; Eickelman, 2003; Mernissi, 2006; Šisler 2007). Specifically regarding the production of Islamic knowledge, Allievi (2003) claims that non-written media are more pervasive and more consumed than others by Muslim audiences. Similar to Gunaratne's (2006) criticism of Habermas's Eurocentric bias, Allievi argues that the focus on written media is a consequence of "a Western cultural heritage" and the result of "a certain way of understanding cultural transmission and its methods" (p. 15).

As has been discussed above, the oral and audiovisual capacities of the

Internet and information and communication technology bridge the gap between different types of media, thus, creating media "convergence," as well as bridging different types of audiences. Media formats encompassed by the notion of cyberscape transcend the virtual borders of the Internet, such as audio sermons and lectures, which can be downloaded, burned, and disseminated in both online and offline contexts (Bunt, 2004); audio and video clips mixing popular culture with promoting Islamic piety and circulating on websites and CDs (Alim, 2005; Pond, 2006); or recently emerged Arab video games, available on DVDs or downloadable through P2P networks, which immerse players into recreation of real political events, thus reshaping the latter comprehension and evaluation (Šisler, 2008; Tawil-Souri, 2007). These examples problematize the focus on the written content of the Internet, and they also highlight the heterogeneous character of the new Arab cyberscape.

By the same token, Kraidy (2007), in his research on Lebanon and Saudi Arabia, explores how satellite TV, mobile phones, and the Internet merge into what he calls "hypermedia space" and argues that the latter contributes to shifts in the nature and boundaries of social and political agency, utilizing the combination of audiovisual and written content. This media hybridization and its social aspects redefine also traditional Internet formats, such as bulletin boards and social networking sites, functioning as online forums for young activists in Egypt and beyond (Eltahawy, 2008). Increasingly, posts on these sites are uploaded from mobile phones and include audiovisual material as well as short comments, pertaining in fact more into the oral mode of communication than to a written one. In his prescient work, Ong (1982) coined the term *secondary orality* to describe the tendency of electronic media to echo the communication patterns of oral culture, with its participatory, interactive, and communal aspects. Not only does the proliferation of these hybridized media platforms in the Arab world exemplify the multifaceted possible results of Ong's secondary orality and Allievi's (2003) non-written media, when translated into the cultural context of Arab oral tradition (Amin & Gher, 2000), it also echoes the previously discussed notions of convergence and interdependency. As Anderson (2008a) argues, convergence is the next phase of the information revolution in the Arab world. According to him, this process includes "media that morph into each other, messages that migrate across boundaries and technologies, and unanticipated assemblages" (p. 7). It is precisely this assemblage of remix culture, media interdependency, networked and oral communication, as well as individual agency that (re)shapes the transformative Arab cyberscape today.

Therefore, it is necessary here to revisit Habermas's (1989) argument that the new broadcast media's immediacy could discourage distanced reflection and critical discussion, since this argument pertains to most of the hybridized media platforms mentioned above, given their audiovisual (video clips, audio sermons) or performative (video games) nature. Essentially, we argue that Habermas's claim has to be nuanced, and the ability of digital audiovisual media to encourage critical reflection should be reconsidered. Indeed, many of the sermons, video clips, and games disseminated on the Internet or circulating off-line have a clear ideological and persuasive bent and are utilizing the media's potential to achieve various political or religious aims. Examples include pros-elytizing lectures of new charismatic preachers (Bunt, 2004, 2009), propagandistic videos from *jihadi* military operations (Bunt, 2009), or political video games released by the Lebanese Hezbollah movement (Šisler, 2008).

Yet, a substantial number of these new media outlets open space for social critique, participation, and discussion. So-called "video blogs," i.e., blogs containing user created videos, provide individuals with the opportunity to comment on what they consider as crucial political, social, or religious issues. Oftentimes, the posted videos trigger vibrant debates resulting in uploading video responses (Šisler, 2009b). In his research on video blogs in Cairo, Fahmi (2009) demonstrates how Egyptian bloggers have created spaces of protest within hybrid physical and virtual worlds, utilizing the combination of audio-visual technology and urban street activism for "the new civil society mobilization" (p. 104). Similarly, video games can be designed to immerse players into simulation of complicated and multifaceted issues, providing him/her with deeper understanding of social and political topics and/or encouraging critical reflection of the latter (Bogost, 2007). Kraidy's (2007) research on the above mentioned hypermedia space suggests that it promotes participatory practices like voting, campaigning, and alliance building, which can, under certain circumstances, translate into social or political actions. Therefore, one should consider the aims of the producers of these media's content and distinguish between whether they are engaging in communicative or strategic actions in Habermasian terms.

Finally, these new digital media platforms are particularly appealing to Arab youth (Gulvady, 2009; Hashem, 2009; Pond, 2006; Kraidy, 2007; Sait et al., 2007; Fahmi, 2009). Given the fact that some 50% of the total population of the Arab world is 18 years of age or under (Simonsen, 2005, p. 9), youth culture is of growing importance. The increasing participation of Arab youth in debates and opinion exchange, enabled by the Internet and the above mentioned digital media outlets, challenges not only the official Arab media broadcasting, but also the Habermasian notion of public sphere as adult and male dominated (Goode, 2005) as well as the clear distinction between the private and public spheres (Calhoun, 1992; Holub, 1991).

After providing this overview of the rapidly changing contemporary Arab mediasacpe, with a special focus on the highly transformative Arab cyberscape and its implications, we now shift our attention to three of the most pressing contemporary challenges confronting it.

The New Arab Cyberscape: Three Contemporary Challenges

In this section we focus on how the rapid developments in the Arab mediascape are directly linked to three contemporary challenges: the democratization challenge, the dialogue challenge, and the diaspora challenge. In analyzing the democratization challenge, we focus on the actors, i.e., the participants in this newly emerging Arab cyberscape, and the extent to which they can widen the scope of deliberative democratization, as envisioned by Habermas. The focus here is on the empowerment and introduction of these new actors and new voices via the emerging Arab cyberscape, and whether and/or how this can translate into broader political and social changes in the Arab world.

In discussing the dialogue challenge, we focus on the content, i.e., the nature of the ongoing online discussions in the contemporary Arab cyberscape and how far they fit Habermas's notion of communicative versus strategic action, and, how far they can contribute to the notions of dialogue of civilizations versus clash of civilizations. In other words, the focus is on the Arab cyberscape and its parallel, yet contradictory, functions of bridging tradition and modernity, while conserving social and religious order, and promoting dialogue with the West, while reinforcing bipolar and divisive discourses, such as Jihad vs. McWorld (Barber, 1995).

Finally, in our exploration of the diaspora challenge, we focus on the context, i.e., the international, globalized setting through which transnational communication is taking place via deterritorialized new media (Bunt, 2000, 2003; Cesari, 2004), such as the Internet. We investigate the implications of the emergence of heterogeneous globalized public spheres alongside more homogeneous localized public spheres. The diaspora section, explores the emerging transnational public sphere (Eickelman & Anderson, 2003) enabled by the Internet and its interrelated new media, and discusses its role in the recreation of an imagined global Arab *umma* (community), as well as shaping the identities of Arab and Muslim minorities living abroad.

First: The Democratization Challenge

As previously mentioned, the significant changes in the media environment in the Arab world since the early 1990s brought about a new era of diversity and relative freedom, away from direct state ownership and control (Napoli, Amin, & Napoli, 1995). Perceived primarily as alternatives, new media and information technologies raised many expectations over their revolutionary potentials. As Anderson (2008a) describes it, these technologies indicated alternative channels and discourses breaking into the public, therefore suggesting transformation of a public sphere. Many scholars have credited the Internet as a "forum for alternative voices" (Eickelman & Anderson, 2003, p. ii) empowering previously marginalized actors.

Therefore, in exploring the democratizing potential of the Arab cyberscape we must examine the role it plays in creating, reconstructing, or empowering public spheres on the local and international levels, as well as in the political, social and religious domains, in various Arab societies, by providing a voice to the voiceless (Lynch, 2006).

Regarding the social domain, Bunt (2000) and Poole (2002, p. 54) suggested that the openness of the Internet allows disenfranchised and marginalized groups to circumvent mainstream media and to subvert hegemonic discourses along the lines of gender, sexuality, and age. Similarly, Mernissi (2006, p. 121) argues that the introduction of the Internet in the Arab world has "destroyed the frontier that divided the universe into a sheltered private arena, where women and children were supposed to be protected, and a public one where adult males exercised their presumed problem-solving authority" (see also Hashem, 2009). More specifically, Wheeler (2008), in her study of the role of cybercafés in the lives of Egyptian women, shows that the Internet is said by participants to increase information access/professional development, expand or maintain social networks and social capital, and transform social and political awareness.

In his study of Internet bulletin boards in Saudi Arabia, Samin (2008) found that they can act as a "voice box for empowering the marginalized Saudi Shi'ite minority" (p. 213), as well as allow the expression and vocalization of long-silenced female voices. Thus, his study revealed that these Internet bulletin boards can largely act as vehicles for resisting "tribal exclusion and gender segregation" (p. 213), although, as he confirms, they can serve as a mechanism for reinforcing pre-existing norms within "newly networked traditional communities" simultaneously (Samin, 2008, p. 199).

This is closely related to the findings of El-Nawawy and Khamis's (2009) study on Islamic websites, which revealed that women are increasingly becoming active participants in the virtual public sphere, through posting in both general, as well as gender-restricted (women's only) Islamic websites. This creates an emerging form of Islamic feminism, which, they argue, differs from, and even challenges, the male-dominated Habermasian public sphere.

Regarding the religious domain, Anderson (2003, pp. 45–60) analyzed the emergence of "new Islam's interpreters" on the Internet and suggested that they can eventually contest the authority of traditional *ulama*, i.e. Islamic religious scholars (see also Norton, 2003, pp. 19–32). Similarly, Bunt (2003) argued that "greater number of people can take Islam into their hands, opening new spaces for debate and critical dialogue" (p. 14). Especially the already mentioned phenomenon of fatwa-issuing websites has been analyzed by number of studies (Bunt 2000, 2003; Caeiro, 2003, 2004; Mariani, 2006; Šisler 2007, 2009a; Kutscher, 2009). Some of these authors indicate that the Internet tends to displace the interpretive authority from religious scholars towards the individualized interpretation of the sacred texts (Caeiro, 2003). Others have argued that an opinion leadership exemplified in new religious authorities can be established using the mass support accumulated through the Internet and new communication technologies (Bunt, 2003; Šisler, 2009a).

A prominent example of the latter is the case of Amr Khaled, the young, charismatic, and modernized Egyptian Islamic televangelist, who was able to use his popular television show, *Sunaa' al Haya* (Life Makers), to act as the foundation for debates on his equally popular website amrkhaled.net (El-Nawawy & Khamis, 2009; Seib, 2007; Mariani, 2006). Both of these avenues target young Muslims and they both complement each other illustrating the impact of the media convergence and media merging processes. This process also provides evidence of how modernity, as represented in the utilization of new media technologies, such as the Internet and satellite television channels, can be utilized to serve the preservation of tradition, as represented in this case in the teachings of the Islamic religion, which form the essence of Amr Khaled's satellite program and Internet website (El-Nawawy & Khamis, 2009).

Another example is the Egyptian scholar Sheikh Youssef Al-Qaradawi, one of the most prominent and influential religious authorities in the Muslim world today, whose popularity among Muslims has skyrocketed over the past 10 years thanks to his regular appearance in a weekly show titled *Al-Shari'a wal Hayat* (Islamic Law and Life), which is broadcast on *Al-Jazeera* satellite channel. Interestingly, Al-Qaradawi's fame and credibility spilled over to the website islamonline.net. The fact that this website has been associated with his name and established under his guidance secured its huge popularity among Muslims everywhere (El-Nawawy & Khamis, 2009; Gräf, 2007; Mariani, 2006). Here again, this offers example of the overlap between different types of new media, on one hand, as well as building a bridge between the binary opposites of tradition and modernity, on the other.

Finally, regarding the political domain, Eid (2007) argued that the Internet in the Arab world allowed diversity of opinions and empowered journalists, political dissidents, and human rights activists, thus, promoting freedom of speech and democracy. In his essay on Egyptian opposition websites, Abdel-Latif (2004) likewise argued that the Internet has emerged as a platform for voices denied a place in the mainstream, state-owned media, enabling the opposition to "break the monopoly of the state over the articulation of the political and social agenda" (p. 1). Similarly, Zayani (2005) explained how new forms of media in the Arab world brought about a new era of diversity of opinions, vigorous public debates, as well as pluralism, which shifted away from the highly uniform and harshly controlled media in the pre-1990 era.

More recently, new expectations of the democratization potential of the Internet have been associated with the phenomenon of blogging (Anderson, 2009), which allows individuals holding different political, cultural, and religious opinions to debate and exchange views. Indeed, blog users in the Arab world started to develop an increasing self confidence and a growing belief in their own potential and their own individuality, because they became capable, for the first time, of developing and expressing their authentic views, which are separate from the traditional worldviews (Hofheinz, 2005, pp. 92–95). Examples of the increasing influence of the Arab blogosphere and its expanding role as a news source allowing marginalized political voices to be heard, not just locally but also internationally, include Arab bloggers' coverage of the War in Iraq in 2003 and its aftermath (Wall, 2006; Trammell, 2006; Johnson & Kaye, 2006) and the Israel-Hezbollah conflict in 2006 (Ward, 2007). In the last few years, blogs have made their way into mainstream press in the Arab world, enabling them to influence the agenda of traditional media coverage (Ward,

2007, pp. 2–11). Such examples provide clear proof of the symbiotic relationship between new and mainstream media outlets, on both an international and a regional scale (Ward, 2007; Hofheinz, 2005; Gulvady, 2009).

The fact that the content of popular blogs has begun to influence mainstream media content deserves further attention as there is a positive indication that the new Arab blogosphere could potentially challenge the content of mainstream media through purposefully covering those controversial events and topics that may not be tackled in mainstream media, or at least covering them with more frankness and aggressiveness. Bloggers also utilize mainstream media to establish more credibility with their audiences "by selectively linking to or quoting these mainstream media sites while adding their interpretations of a news story or an issue" (Berenger, 2006, p. 182; see also Etling et al., 2009, pp. 38–46).

Through influencing the agenda of mainstream media, "blogs threaten to unravel the carefully managed, state-controlled narrative which frames government policy" (Al Malky, 2008). Furthermore, blogs are relatively low-cost and easy to maintain, and the changes in readership structure and composition can have very little influence over content. With greater privatization and increasing competition in the post-1990 era, mainstream media in the Arab world sensed an increasing pressure to appeal to the tastes and interests of growing and diversified audiences in order to sustain themselves. Covering the war in Lebanon in 2006, the Iraq war in 2003, and even the sexual harassment of women on the streets of Cairo can set bloggers apart from mainstream media, attract more audiences, and increase public awareness. Thus, mainstream media's credibility can be seriously questioned and their popularity can be undermined if they fail to keep up with the controversial and sensitive topics covered in blogs (Al Malky, 2008).

These significant shifts in all the political, religious, social, and media arenas inspired the birth of new debates and discourses, the creation of new media effects, as well as a growing wave of expectation of liberalization and democratization in the Arab region, in addition to providing platforms for many forces to resist these waves simultaneously. This last point necessitates shedding some light on the democratization debate around the role of new cyberscape in the Arab world. This debate stems to a large extend from the above mentioned expectations associated with the emergence of new voices and the empowerment of marginalized actors in all the political, religious, and social domains. In other words, the essence of the "democratization debate," according to Rugh (2007), is that many observers predicted that new media developments, such as the increased level of Internet penetration and the spread of Arab satellite television, would intrinsically lead to a significant growth in Arab democracy.

The optimists regarding the democratizing potential of new Arab media, such as Telhami (2002), Alterman (2005), and Lynch (2005), herald the new media landscape in the Arab world as a potential agent of change and reform. For example, Alterman (2005) indicates that the new pluralistic media environment in the Arab world is a key stimulator behind shaping public opinion trends throughout the Arab region, while Telhami (2002) mentions that this newly erupting information revolution has empowered the Arab public on an unprecedented scale. Furthermore, Lynch (2005) expresses enthusiasm regarding the perceived role of new media in the Arab world in acting as motors of change, which have the capacity not just to shape and influence public opinion trends and attitudes, but also inspires them to take collective action, in order to vent their anger and frustration, as in the case of the potential impact of Arab satellite television channels on encouraging public protests and opposition against autocratic Arab regimes.

Similarly, Ebeid (2008) predicts that the true winds of change in the entire Arab world are most likely to result from the information revolution especially the proliferation of new information technologies, which she believes has the capacity to break the barriers to effective communication, challenge authoritarian governments' hegemony, and destroy traditional taboos. She also highlights the power of the Internet and new mobile communication devices in helping actual political participation and organization, as in the case of a number of young political activists in Egypt who used websites and cell phones to organize strikes and mobilize effective political participation in demonstrations and other forms of political expression on the streets of Cairo.

What can be observed here is a phenomenon whereby the Internet, alongside other new(er) types of media, is actually boosting not just the sharing and exchanging of political information, but also expanding the possibilities of formulating an active civil society (Diamond, 1999) and vibrant public spheres that translate effective political discussions into organized political action, thus, expanding the horizons of democratic participation.

Yet, on the other end of the spectrum, there are many scholars who voiced their concerns about the potential of the Internet and new media outlets to bring about democracy. Apart from the increasing possibilities of state control over the Internet, through such means as blocking websites, filtering content, or even the direct prosecution of posters (Kalathil & Boas, 2003; Eid, 2004; Zelaky et al., 2006; Abdulla, 2007, pp. 77–90), in the last few years established authorities, political as well as religious, have started to reclaim the public sphere created by the Internet and new media by setting up their own media projects, blogs, and websites (Mariani, 2006; Anderson, 2008a, 2009). Anderson (2008a) argues that many supposedly new actors turned out to have roots in old establishments. As he says: "Often it was the cadet generations of elites who brought the new technologies. Governments proved adept at deploying the underlying technologies to their own ends. [And] by the end of millennium established religious figures had their sermons, lessons, and outreach on the Internet for the populations it drew and aggregated" (p. 1). The increasing penetration of the Internet in the Arab world can also bolster the economic development, as well as increase general public satisfaction and thus favor institutions and authorities in an indirect manner (Kalathil & Boas, 2003, p. 8).

Therefore, many other scholars, such as Zayani (2005, 2008) and Seib (2007), are equally skeptical of the perceived trend of ascribing too much power to new media avenues in the Arab world in the process of mobilizing the public, or enforcing the required shift to democracy. Zayani (2008) warns of the tendency to perceive the influence of new media on shaping Arab public opinion in light of a simple cause and effect equation, by acknowledging the complexity and subtlety of the process of public opinion formation. He argues that in the Arab world channeling the energies of a public opinion that the media is making more pronounced poses noteworthy challenges, mainly because in Western democracies the news media are part of a political process that both enriches it and keeps it in check. Therefore, the media in these societies have the potential to enhance the interconnectedness between citizens and their governments. However, this is not the case in most Arab countries (Zayani, 2008).

Seib (2007) reminds us that new media in the Arab world are only part of a complex and interrelated set of variables, and while, indeed, they may act as catalysts or stimulators of change and reform, one should be careful not to assign too much power to them in the transition toward democratization. He contends that new media can facilitate transnational trends in politics and other facets of globalization, due to their own transnational nature, which can, in turn, affect the dynamics of democratization. Yet, he asserts that "The complexity of democratization should be respected, however, and no single factor's impact should be overrated" (Seib, 2007, p. 2). In other words, the media can only play the role of facilitators or accelerators of the transition to democracy.

Particularly the role of blogging in the Arab world, given the prominent expectations it created, has to be critically evaluated in light of the Habermasian concept of public sphere. In this respect, Anderson (2009) argues that blogs tend to cluster into what he calls "network neighborhoods" with long-standing solidarities but with relatively low information (or high redundancy), as all members share pretty much the same social location. Therefore, he contends that "network communication fosters not Habermas's ideal public sphere of rational communication ('speaking truth to power') but a politics, including cultural politics, that trades on knowing how and showing up."

Similarly, an extensive study exploring the structure and content of the Arabic blogosphere using link analysis and human coding of individual blogs (Etling et al., 2009) found that the Arabic blogosphere is organized primarily around specific countries (p. 3) with coherent clusters of blogs based on similarities in linking choices (p. 9), thereby confirming Anderson's claim of network neighborhoods. Yet, as Etling et al. (2009) argue, blogs form part of an emerging "networked public sphere" in which the power of elites to control the public agenda and bracket the range of allowable opinions is seriously challenged (p.7) and which can further support efficient interaction among important communities of interest, allowing them to negotiate agendas, process opinion, and broker knowledge (p. 49). Etling et al. (2009) demonstrate that blogging already shows signs of having an impact in the Arab world, such as "facilitating cooperation between secular and Islamist reformers in Egypt, and promoting discussion and reform within the Muslim Brotherhood" (p. 49).

We argue that the diversity and plurality in this transitional Arab cyberscape is matched by a high degree of coexistence of a number of parallel, albeit contradictory, phenomena. The first one of these bipolar opposites is authoritarianism versus resistance. While governmental hegemony and control are still widely exercised in the Arab region, without genuine political diversity or participation, yet many alternative, resistant voices are emerging and having their own media as platforms to express their political thoughts and oppositional views (Zayani, 2005, 2008). One example is the *kefaya* opposition movement in Egypt, which, like many other political and religious groups in Egypt, managed to have its views heard through Internet websites and blogging (Abdulla, 2006, 2007). Other prominent examples of the successful utilization of the Internet to disseminate information censored by the ruling regimes are the cases of the Saudi Arabian Shaykh Muhammad al-Mohaisany (Bunt, 2005) or the Egyptian online opposition newspaper *al-Sha'b* associated with the *Hizb al-amal* opposition party (Abdel-Latif, 2004).

Yet, as Rahimi (2008) points out, "However salient [...] the force of the Internet might have appeared to some in its initial developments, authoritarian states soon came to adopt creative ways to hold back potential challenges posed by the new technology." The report of the Arabic Network for Human Rights Information (Zelaky et al., 2006) about the Internet and freedom of expression in 18 Arab countries provides vast evidence on how Arab governments can (a) censor, block, or filter information on the Internet; (b) restrict free access to it; (c) prosecute and intimidate both Internet users and publishers; and (d) utilize the Internet to gather information about citizens. Although the situation varies significantly in different Arab countries in accordance with the respective political and judiciary systems, in many cases "communication and the Internet are restricted, opposition websites are blocked, and web-editors and writers are arrested and imprisoned" (p. 36). Moreover, the underlying development of the case studies mentioned in the report suggests that freedom of expression on the Internet witnessed a general relapse after September 2001, when most Arab governments took measures to restrict this freedom in the name of combating terrorism (p. 20).

Similarly, Kalathil and Boas's (2003) research on the United Arab Emirates, Egypt, and Saudi Arabia reveals that although "the use of the Internet may indeed pose challenges to information control in much of the Middle East, most of the region's governments are actively seeking to ensure that the Internet use does not threaten the political status quo" (p. 103). Kalathil and Boas summarize their findings as follows: "Several countries (including Saudi Arabia and the United Arab Emirates) feature elaborate censorship schemes for the Internet, employing advanced technology to block public access to pornographic or political web sites. Others, like Egypt [...], promote self-censorship in the population, making well-publicized crackdowns against uses of the Internet that are considered politically or socially inappropriate" (p. 103). Although they strongly argue for a nuanced conclusion about the impact of Internet use on particular authoritarian and semi-authoritarian regimes (p. 104), Kalathil and Boas suggest that on a general level "state propaganda grows sophisticated" (p. 139), "authorities learn to constrain politically threatening use" (p. 140), and "the Internet is important but not sufficient for successful activism" (p. 148).

Finally, the research by Abdulla (2007, pp. 71–90) mostly affirms the above mentioned findings, providing additional evidence on how Internet cafes can easily be monitored by security officers, as in Syria (p. 81), and how filtering circumvention tools can be blocked, as in Saudi Arabia (p. 79), thus, restricting the number of users who can possibly evade the control of the state.

Nevertheless, despite the censorship, prosecutions, and crackdowns, the Internet remains a prominent outlet for publishing dissenting political opinions (Zelaky et al., 2006, p. 5; Amin, 2007, p. x; Anderson, 2009). As Zelaky et al. (2006, p. 5) document, in several cases a number of sites were instantly established in order to compensate for the blocked ones (e.g., the website of Muslim Brotherhood). Yet, the fundamental problem of the democratization debate lies in the assumption of the direct link between information and political and social changes. As Kalathil and Boas (2003, p. 2) put it, information and communication technology can not have any social or political impact apart from its use by human beings. The mere presence of dissent discourse on the Internet doesn't necessarily have to lead to the undermining of established political and religious structures.

Indeed, in many recent cases we again witness the coexistence of an official sphere versus a popular sphere, due to the existence of official, mainstream views, representing the governmental policies and positions, alongside the popular, diverse views, which usually come from private, independent, and more outspoken channels of communication, such as blogs (Seymour, 2008; Weyman, 2007).

However, this pluralistic and, often times, paradoxical, Arab media environment, where many vibrant and alternative views and opinions are being shared and exchanged, has not been paralleled yet by an equal shift toward political democratization. Therefore, we can conclude that the pace of change in the media arena has been much faster than the pace of change in the political arena, and that there is a process of uneven development between press freedom and political freedom, whereby the accelerated rate of press freedom, despite its many handicaps, restrictions, and imperfections, is not equally matched by actual political reform or real democracy.

This paradox could be referred to as a case of "media schizophrenia" (Iskander, 2006), due to the widening gap between the very loud, critical, or even angry voices, which are heard through alternative media avenues, such as the opposition newspapers and their online websites and blogs, and the absence of true democratic practice and actual political participation, as a result of this increasing tide of media freedom.

Therefore, these new media in the Arab world are largely acting as safety valves through which to release the public's anger and frustration at many political, economic, and social ills and injustices, especially since the public is not granted the chance to exercise real political rights or to play an effective role in the most crucial decision-making processes. This poses an interesting phenomenon, whereby new media in the Arab world, could be said to "substitute" rather than "promote" actual democratic practice and the exercise of real political rights (Seib, 2007). This trend seems to be widely encouraged by many Arab governments for the purpose of either absorbing the public's anger and frustration at major political, economic, or social grievances, or diverting the public's attention away from them (Seib, 2007; Khamis, 2007). Yet, the mere existence of these oppositional and resistant voices in an unprecedented fashion offers a clear indication that "The potential is there for systematic change, but that will not happen unless and until the underlying political system becomes a more liberal and democratic one" (Rugh, 2004, p. 161).

The previous discussion necessitates shedding some light on the concepts of transition, transformation, and democratization and their applicability, or lack thereof, in the contemporary Arab media scene. According to Kleinsteuber (2010), the term *transition* refers to a passing from one state to another; while democratization only refers to the change of the political system from authoritarianism to democracy, which brings about the end of dictatorship; and transformation is a much broader concept, based on the assumption that change also includes other sectors like the economy, society, culture, or even the perception of a nation. Taking this analytical framework into consideration, we can argue that the new Arab media scene today is certainly transitional, partly transformative, but not yet democratized. Arab media systems could be described as transitional, due to the many waves of change that swept the Arab media scene, and which brought about some aspects of change into contemporary Arab societies, such as expanding the realms of public debates and discussions, thus, introducing a process of partial transformation, but without a spillover to the domain of actual democratic practice yet. Thus, we can describe this process as a phenomenon of transformation without democratization.

A number of authors (Rugh, 2007; Zayani, 2008; Sakr, 2007) argued that through challenging existing governments, confronting American hegemony in the Arab region, and allowing the expression of public anger and discontent, new media environments in the Arab world are offering a considerable promise for the improvement in human conditions, because issues of government accountability, individual rights, and press freedom become topics of public discussions and debates. However, if, and when, these anticipated improvements will actually translate into real democratic practice in the Arab world still remains to be seen.

So far, however, the persistence of patterns of governmental ownership and control over many media outlets in the Arab world do have negative implications and consequences, both on the internal degree of freedom and independence enjoyed by Arab journalists and media professionals, as well as on the external degree of trust and credibility enjoyed by these media internationally (Khamis, 2007; Al-Kallab, 2003; Rugh, 2004, 2007). Although the Internet enjoys the advantage of escaping the general patterns of clientelism and instrumentalism that restrict other media outlets in the Arab world, it would be naïve to assume that it provides a totally safe haven of free expression, which escapes any type of governmental interference or control. As demonstrated above, factors such as maltreatment, lack of transparency, protracted procedure, and, most importantly, threat of a legal precedent, or, even worse, actual legal punishment are do have their negative implications on new media in the Arab world, including the Arab blogosphere (Gharbeia, 2007; Zelaky et al., 2006). Such cases of arrests and trials of journalists and bloggers in the Arab world point to the crucial need for securing greater legal protection for journalists and media professionals to safeguard their freedom, independence, and human rights (El-Kalliny, 1998; Al-Kallab, 2003). These restrictions and impediments to freedom of expression, affecting both old and new media outlets alike, raise doubt on the potential of even the transformative Arab cyberscape to give birth to vibrant, dynamic, controversial, and truly democratized public spheres, as envisioned by Habermas.

Despite these legal and political restrictions, however, new media have significant transformative impacts on the Arab media scene today, through constructing new public sphere(s) and discourses and promoting new values. The Internet in the Arab world transcends boundaries and produces unstable aggregations of information, technologies, and actors. Although, as Anderson (2008b) argues, this does not necessarily translate into democratization of an electoral sort, but we should be careful not to undermine the Internet's potential for promoting change. This is particularly relevant to the emergence of blogs in the Arab world, where the networked communication and alliance-forming, as we have seen under certain conditions, can be translated into collective political action, such as the new civil society mobilization connecting urban activism with video blogging in Cairo (Fahmi, 2009).

To conclude this discussion, the answer to the question: "Will the Net help deliver a better democracy?" (Dahlgren 2001, p. 52), within the framework of the current Arab cyberscape and its interrelated contemporary Arab political context, with all its complexities and ambivalences, seems to fit Dahlgren's (2001) argument that "The Net does have a capacity to enhance the public sphere, though it seems not to dramatically transform political life. It allows new communicative spaces to develop—alternative public spheres—even if the paths to the centers of political decision making are often far removed" (p. 52).

Finally, regarding the potential of networked information technology in challenging authoritarian regimes and promoting democratization, Dean, Anderson, and Lovink (2006) emphasize that "What are often identified as the destabilizing effects of networked information technologies also destabilize the very presumptions of democratic action" (p. xxii). The essential characteristic of networked society, based on technical expertise and knowledge, and reputation management, promotes "unstable assemblages and contingent effects that can disrupt democratic processes of representation, which require a stable object, and accountability, which requires a stable subject, that are elements of democratic (constituency) politics" (p. xxiv). This claim is even more pertinent to the Arab cyberscape, given its previously discussed transitional character, where the underlying political system (Rugh, 2004) is in most cases not liberal and democratic, and where the reputation management of networked communication (Dean et al., 2006; Anderson, 2009) empowers liberal and democratic, as well as authoritarian and ideological, voices simultaneously, as will be discussed in the following section.

Second: The Dialogue Challenge

The challenge of dialogue stems from the fact that the Arab/Muslim world has been the center of the world's attention, especially after the 9/11 attacks. The increased media attention has created new media-generated images, new discourses in contextualizing the relationship between the West and the Arab/Muslim world, as well as media battles and media diplomacy efforts in the global public sphere. All these significant and overlapping factors have, on the one hand, reinforced negative stereotypes and misconceptions about Arabs and Muslims, through the indiscriminate association of their identities with the negative labels of fanaticism and terrorism. On the other hand, they generated interest in studying their identities, culture, religion, and communication patterns. In every case, the fact remains that the 9/11 attacks had profound implications on the prevailing images of Arabs and Muslims, as well as on their relationship with the rest of the world, especially the West. The stigmatizing labels of terrorists and fanatics in the post-9/11 era have been closely associated with both Arabs and Muslims, often times indiscriminately, which provoked a series of reactions and implications inside the Arab world and internationally (Hafez, 2008; Sardar & Davies, 2002; Poole & Richardson, 2006). A combination of international developments and tensions, such as the ongoing discourse of clash of civilizations, the war on terror, the war in Iraq, and the war in Lebanon, have all had profound impacts on the international images and perceptions of Arabs and Muslims (Khamis, 2007). After the 9/11 attacks, Arab and Muslim identities became "politicized through the ascribed interrelationship between Islam, Arab identity, and terrorism" (Witteborn, 2007, p. 572). As a result, many Arabs and Muslims found themselves increasingly misunderstood, either as an isolated and excluded minority of extremists and fanatics who resist interaction with other cultures and faiths, or, even worse, as a group of terrorists who are ready to violently attack others (El-Nawawy & Khamis, 2009). Therefore, many Arabs and Muslims had to make their identities more salient; they felt the need not just to educate people about their own culture and religion but also to defend being an Arab and/or a Muslim (Witteborn, 2007).

Most importantly, the 9/11 attacks and their aftermath invoked two predominant international discourses in contextualizing the relationship between the West and the Arab/Muslim world, namely: the discourse of clash of civilizations and the discourse of dialogue among civilizations. The first discourse was initially proposed by Huntington (1996), and it spoke of antagonistic civilizations in the West and Islam. This discourse, according to Hafez (2008), fuels conflicting ideologies of the West versus the Rest, which can be ignited through "nationalist and religiously fundamentalist hegemonies in the world's media systems" (p. 31). This can lead to the danger of feeding "cultural warfare" (Hafez, 2008, p. 31). Similarly, other authors proposed the scenario of Jihad vs. McWorld (Barber, 1995), whereby Jihad refers to the exacerbation of identities on the grounds of difference and exclusion, while McWorld alludes to market forces that erase national identities. Here again, the danger of this highly "polarized scenario" (Karim, 2003, p. 9) is that it widens the gap and magnifies the distance between the self and the other and, thus, diminishes the possibilities of cross-cultural empathy and dialogue.

To the contrary, the other discourse of dialogue among civilizations emphasizes the middle-ground of shared commonalities and the need for greater communication to promote better understanding. One of the advocates of this position, Hafez (2008) asserts that Huntington's notion of the clash of ancient civilizations is short sighted because it fails to understand that it is not "the 'clash of civilizations' but a 'lack of communication' that is at work" (Hafez, 2008, p. 31). Likewise, Lynch (2006) is optimistic about the possibility of sustaining dialogue in an age of terror through many voices in the global public sphere promoting mutual understanding. These two bipolar extremes of clash versus dialogue were reflected in both Arab and Western media, through media battles, on the one hand, and media diplomacy, on the other.

This reminds us that one of the true impediments to the construction of a Habermasian-style dialogue in the contemporary Arab cyberscape is the proliferation of "ideological site" (Selnow, 1998), which usually focus on one side of the debate, with little regard for evenhandedness, since this is not their mission. Rather, their main mission is "to state a position—often as strongly as possible—in order to reinforce the believers. They frequently overstate the urgency of conditions and the strength of the adversaries, and at the same time project a solidarity among supporters" (Selnow, 1998, p. 194).

As previously discussed, many of the contemporary websites in the Arab world, especially political and Islamic ones, fit under this category of ideological sites, taking into account the high degree of ideological uniformity, shared loyalty, and apparent coherence exemplified by the participants in these websites, as well as the absence of genuine, Habermasian-style critical-rational deliberations and the missing middle terrain of negotiation and debate in many of them (El-Nawawy & Khamis, 2009). Interestingly, this observation applies only to a small, albeit significant, cluster of the Arabic blogosphere, bloggers from the Islam-focus area who "write about Islam from a conservative perspective and frequently criticize other faiths" (Etling et al., 2009, p. 5).

The crowded Arab/Islamic Internet marketplace today displays a wide array of ongoing discourses and debates, which reflect the two opposing poles of divergence and consensus on different levels and in diverse forms. However, we should avoid the danger of overgeneralization regarding the prevalence of ideological sites in the contemporary Arab cyberscape. Noticeably, the Arabic blogosphere seems to be "a space populated with a broad diversity of views, many of which promote common international values such as free speech and human rights" (Etling et al., 2009, p. 50) and "overt support for violent global confrontation with the West appears to be exceedingly rare" (p. 4).

The dialogue challenge in contemporary Arab cyberscape is by no means limited to Internet websites only. In fact, other, oftentimes hybridized, new media outlets are utilized in the Arab world for both ideological persuasion and critical-rational deliberations simultaneously, be it in the form of social networking, video blogging, or video games.

Particularly video blogging, posting video clips created by users on the Internet through public venues like YouTube or on individual blogs, is becoming popular among Arab youth (Fahmi, 2009; Šisler, 2009b). Indeed, many of these videos share an agenda similar to Selnow's (1998) ideological sites in terms of political propaganda, proselytization, and loyalty enhancement. As Bunt (2009, p. 223) argues, the utilization of video clips has been an effective tool for the jihadi movements since the 1990s. Examples of ideological video blogging include postings by the Iraqi insurgency, al-Qaeda, the Lebanese Hezbollah movement, and, more recently, the widely circulated rap video clip "Dirty Kuffar" by Sheikh Terra, which eulogized Osama bin Laden and the events of 9/11 (Bunt, 2009, p. 224).

To the contrary, many video blogs successfully trigger genuine debate, interaction, and opinion exchange among Arabs and non-Arabs and Muslims and non-Muslims, encouraging viewers to post their comments and video responses (Šisler, 2009b). This form of video blogging affirms the Habermasian notion of rational deliberations and negotiation, thus, challenging his critique of broadcast media's immediacy. Additionally, the non-hierarchical and do-it-yourself character of the video blogging culture, combined with the affordability of mobile phone technology in the Arab world (Abdulla, 2007, p. 13), appeals to the Arab youth and provides them with a viable space for the construction and representation of their identities, which are challenged by Western mainstream media images (Poole & Richardson, 2006; Šisler, 2008).

Another prominent example of the dialogue challenge in the Arab cyberscape is the emerging phenomenon of engaged video games. Video games constitute a popular leisure time activity for a substantial segment of Arab youth, as suggested in the research conducted by Šisler (2008, 2009b) in Syria, Egypt, and Lebanon, and by Tawil-Souri (2007) in Palestine. Although the penetration of gaming consoles and personal computers remains relatively low in the Arab world compared to the United States and Europe, the growing emergence of cybercafés and game nets facilitates wide access to the latest products of the game industry to young generations (Baune, 2005; Abdulla, 2007). Several researchers (Bogost, 2007; Frasca, 2004) indicated that video games could act as a powerful, persuasive medium. As Bogost (2007, p. ix) argues: "Videogames open a new domain for persuasion, [...] the art of persuasion through rule-based representations and interactions rather than the spoken word, writing, images, or moving pictures."

In relation to the dialogue challenge, it is worth mentioning that a number of video games recently developed in the Arab world recreate real world events and immerse players in their virtual representations. Many of these games have a clear ideological or persuasive twist. For example, the "Special Force 2," produced by the Lebanese Hezbollah movement to comment on the July 2006 war with Israel, as well as "Jenin: Road of Heroes," which retells the story of the Battle of Jenin that took place in 2002 in the Jenin Palestinian refugee camp (Šisler, 2008, 2009b). These games constitute a direct response to war games produced in the United States and Europe, which feature Arabs and Muslims as enemies and exploit the schematizing concepts of religious fundamentalism and/or terrorism (Šisler, 2008). Essentially, the concept of these Arab games is not different from Western first-person shooters, it has merely reversed the polarities of the narrative and iconographical stereotypes mentioned above by substituting the Arab Muslim hero for the American soldier (Šisler, 2008, p. 211). At the same time, as is the case with Western war games, the reality is depicted in a very selective way, thus, reshaping the perception of the conflict, its cause, and its outcome in favor of one side.

Nevertheless, there exist other, significantly different, concepts of utilization of video games in the Arab world. For example, a Syrian company, Afkar Media, developed a strategy game which aims to educate both Arab and Western players about pre-Islamic Arab culture and early Islamic history (Šisler, 2009b). This game "Quraish," can be played from various perspectives, including Arab and Byzantine, and tries, according to its producers, to "contribute to the balance of cultures [and] mutual understanding" (Šisler, 2006, p. 81). In this respect, and taking into account Habermas's notion of communicative action, Frasca's (2004) suggestion that game simulations possess the potential for developing a tolerant attitude should be revisited. In fact, many video games have successfully appropriated the media potential in order to promote debate and rational-critical deliberation, particular in issues pertaining to the Arab world, such as the game "Global Conflicts: Palestine" (Egenfeldt-Nielsen & Buch, 2006).

Therefore, the previous discussion affirms that the dialogue challenge in the contemporary Arab cyberscape could not be limited to Internet sites only, but has to encompass more versatile, hybridized platforms and media outlets as well, which could combine the two bipolar extremes of undermining and enhancing tolerance and dialogue simultaneously.

In summing up this discussion on the challenges related to dialogue in the Arab cyberscape, we have to bear in mind that the 9/11 attacks and their aftermath did not bring about only the significance of the events themselves, rather, they also brought about "the rapidly evolving new media environment—for Europe and North America and for the Muslim world—and the increasing interconnectivity among producers, consumers, and subjects of all forms of media" (Eickelman & Anderson, 2003, p. i). Therefore, we can contend that this new era of media explosion, both on the regional and the international domains, is the product of, as well as the accelerator behind, the birth of new international images, discourses, reactions, as well as interesting paradoxes and challenges, including the democratization and dialogue challenge, as already explained, and the diaspora challenge, that will be tackled in the following section.

Third: The Diaspora Challenge

Our discussion of the diaspora challenge necessitates a deeper understanding of the nature of the Internet as a transnational medium and its potential for linking de-territorialized communities. This allows the Internet to play parallel, albeit contradictory, roles. On one hand, it contributes to audience fragmentation and plurality, through millions of websites, which reach large, heterogeneous audiences. On the other hand, it consolidates similarities among homogenous, special interest groups as "a medium that subdivides and stratifies its audiences" (Selnow, 1998, p. 186) into various layers, according to their shared loyalties.

The Internet simultaneously promotes dual, but contrasting, processes of pluralism and segmentation, on one hand, and unity and cohesion, on the other hand. In fact, in many cases the audiences of new media, especially the Internet, are significantly heterogeneous in terms of both demographic and psychographic traits, which makes the media exposure and usage experience their main unifying factor. For example the Internet as a unifying tool does not require uniformity. Members of dispersed groups can tie themselves tightly or loosely, as they choose, to a central cultural identity. The "Internet connects on its users' terms" (Seib, 2007, p. 13).

Additionally, by significantly reducing national and international boundaries, the Internet creates a global, transnational community that no media source has been able to establish before. Therefore, even with the relatively limited Internet access in the Arab world compared to Western societies, the Internet created a new virtual community unmatched by other sources (Bunt, 2000, 2003; Eickelman & Anderson, 2003; Mandaville, 2001, 2003, 2007).

These new forms of communication play an important role in formulating diasporic identities through "the simultaneous consumption of the same content by members of a transnational group" (Karim, 2003, p. 1). The Internet certainly has profound implications on the phenomenon of spreading new ideas, values, and beliefs among new generations of Arabs and Muslims, bridging geographical barriers, as well as social, political, and cultural differences. In other words, Internet technology is a key player in transforming the actual Arab and Muslim communities into imagined communities in cyberspace (Bunt, 2000, 2003; Mandaville, 2001, 2003, 2007). Such imagined worlds replace a "passive audience recipient with a potentially active-surfing public" (Dartnell, 2005).

It can be argued that the Internet plays a vital role in satisfying the inquisitive desire of young diasporic Arabs and Muslims to learn more about their own culture and faith. They surf the net to connect with each other and to get information on how to cope with various cultural encounters without deviating from their faith and how to set a good example for Islam in the Western world (Mandaville, 2001, 2003). Those young diasporic Arabs and Muslims who are utilizing the Internet technology to serve their religion are "inserting the normative discourse of Islam into the Western discourse of information technology. In this sense the use of the Internet by Muslim diaspora groups provides one of the best examples of … 'globalizing the local'" (Mandaville, 2001, p. 76). This provides evidence of the transformative power of the Internet in terms of cross-cutting the boundaries of the local and the global as well as the traditional and the modern.

The process of redefining and renegotiating local cultural and religious identities in a global context that often takes place among the younger-generation diasporic Arabs and Muslims in the cyber world can lead to three possible outcomes: (a) it can unify and integrate them under the banner of globality; (b) it can separate them by making them more aware of their own internal differences and magnifying their sense of otherness; (c) or it can create an in-between status, where a hybridized political identity embraces elements of both the diaspora and the homeland (Mandaville, 2001).

Favoring the first of these three options, Seib (2004) argues that the Internet succeeded to provide "a space for greater integration of the Arab community into the global community" (Seib, 2004, p. 81). That's mainly because many young Arabs, especially those in diasporic communities all over the world, can find out international news very quickly and effectively, and, at the same time, they can also retrieve news about the Arab world more easily and efficiently. Therefore, for these transnational Arab communities scattered over the globe, the Internet can actually provide an Arab global village (Khazen, 1999). It can be argued that the Internet serves the dual function of making them good global citizens, who are more effectively integrated into the global community, while remaining good Arab citizens, who are well connected with their own homelands, through enabling them to preserve their distinct religious, social, and cultural identities. The Internet also enables members of this Arab global village to engage in online discussions and deliberations, which can help in expressing, challenging, and negotiating their authentic, cultural identities and/ or constructing more modernized, contemporary versions of these identities (El-Nawawy & Khamis, 2009). This is closely linked to the notion of "mediazation of tradition" (Thompson, 1995, p. 180), whereby new media, especially the Internet, can act as a possible bridge between tradition and modernity, through aiding the creation of alternative voices in cyberspace and facilitating the spread of democratization and freedom of expression.

The Internet provides excellent avenues for diasporic Arab communities to remain connected and informed. This is especially true for younger generations of Arabs who are technically savvy and who are keen to re-establish connections with their own homeland, culture, and religion through the various media available for them. These new media have made available to migrant Arabs, those living in transnational communities, the relevant political, cultural, and religious information that can provide them with a sense of communalism and collectivism that would allow them to preserve their distinct identities as members of the same national, ethnic, and cultural group (Cesari, 2004). Consequently, these new media avenues act as a bridge between the local, regional sphere and the international, global sphere.

For example, Khalili (2005), who examined the Palestinian cyberculture in the refugee camps of Lebanon, argues that "Palestinian youth 'excorporate' the resources provided by high-tech capitalism and use the ideological concepts developed in their diaspora to form a cyberculture in which transnational nationalisms play the dominant role" (p. 127). Furthermore, she suggests that the Internet has facilitated cross-border connections, and that "quotidian virtual practices—visits to the Web cafés, online news gathering, virtual courtship, and game playing—have led to a revivification of political national identities already present in a nonvirtual social context" (p. 129). Khalili also shows that web cafés and Internet centers have become important public gathering places for young Palestinians, including women (p. 130), thus effectively connecting and online and offline public spheres. This interplay between virtual and real spaces manifests what Lim (2006) calls "cybercivic space" and provides one possible mechanism for translating electronic messages into social engagement and direct political action, as is often the case with Palestinian boycotts or demonstrations (Khalili, 2005, p. 130).

At the same time, as Khatib (2006) says that advocacy of a national identity has been in conflict with the views of many Islamic fundamentalists in the Arab world. She argues that the Internet, as a tool communicating global citizenship for Islamic fundamentalist movements worldwide, "becomes a means of constituting, representing, and influencing the existence and growth of various Islamic fundamentalist in a global context" (p. 70).

The previous discussion draws our attention to the fact that the globalization that is inspired and accelerated by new communication technologies does not necessarily result in a cultural convergence along the lines of Westernization and secularization. In fact, as in the case of young diasporic Arabs and Muslims who use the Internet to connect with their local culture and indigenous religion, we can conclude that it can paradoxically give birth to a process of cultural divergence, which challenges the connection between globalization, Westernization, and secularization. What is clear is the strong role played by the Internet in redefining local cultural and religious identities in a global context,, thus creating hybrid public spheres in both local and global contexts.

As Fraser (2009) reminds us, "It is commonplace nowadays to speak of 'transnational public spheres,' 'diasporic public spheres,' 'Islamic public spheres,' and even an emerging 'global public sphere... A growing body of media studies literature is documenting the existence of discursive arenas that overflow the bounds of both nations and states" (p. 76). However, she argues that these emerging concepts have theoretical challenges, mainly because the concept of the public sphere as originally envisioned by Habermas, that correlates mainly with a sovereign power, because it is based on the assumption that features such as "the normative legitimacy and political efficacy of public opinion—are essential to the concept of the public sphere in critical theory" (Fraser, 2009, pp. 76–77). These features, according to Fraser (2009), however, "are not easily associated with the discursive arenas that we today call 'transnational public spheres.' It is difficult to associate the notion of legitimate public opinion with communicative arenas in which the interlocutors are not fellow members of a political community... And it is hard to associate the notion of efficacious communicative power with discursive spaces that do not correlate with sovereign states" (p. 77).

Yet, Fraser (2009) argues that these realizations should not lead us to abandon the notion of a "transnational public sphere," rather to rethink public-sphere theory in a transnational frame (p. 78). This could be best achieved through adopting a critical-theoretical approach that seeks to locate normative standards and emancipatory political possibilities precisely within the historically unfolding constellation and reformulate accordingly (Fraser, 2009). In a similar fashion, Bohman (2004) proposes extending the issue of publics beyond the national arena towards global society, through envisioning the notion of a public of publics, which he defines as a global public sphere formed through the intersection of various more localized publics. The role of the Internet in enabling "the mediation of dialogue across borders and publics...in a complexly interconnected world" (Bohman, 2004, p.154) is certainly detected in today's hybrid Arab cyberscape and its expanding features of globalization, deterritorialization, and transnationalism (Cesari, 2004).

Concluding Remarks: A Post-Habermasian Arab Cyberscape?

In this chapter, we contextualized the ongoing waves of transformation in the Arab media landscape, in general, and the Arab cyberscape, in particular. In doing so, we acknowledge the need for generating more indigenous knowledge in the study of the paradoxical Arab cyberscape and contextualizing, change within a larger political, social, and cultural framework that takes the local context and its specificities into consideration in studying transnational media systems and their implications. Adopting such an approach is particularly important because oftentimes "the Internet is abstracted out of its social and cultural contexts: in particular, some of the relevant literature suffers from a lack of a 'media perspective,' not treating the Internet as part of a larger, integrated media environment" (Dahlgren, 2009, p. 160; see also Sreberny, 2008).

Furthermore, the different views mapped in this chapter oscillate between the two bipolar extremes of optimism, as a result of overestimating the role of the Internet and its capacity to induce change and to stimulate deliberative democracy, while underestimating its role in acting as an accelerator of political reform and as a catalyst for democratization. Indeed, as the studies reviewed in this chapter suggest, particularly in the context of a transitional society, the destabilizing effects of the Internet and networked communication (Dean et al., 2006) can translate into collective mobilization for political reform (see Lim, 2006; Fahmi, 2009; Khalili, 2005; Kraidy, 2007). Yet, such reform can promote both civil society and democratization in the Habermasian sense as well as forces which oppose civil society and the nation state, as is the case of Islamist jihadi movements (Khatib, 2006; Lim, 2006). As Lim (2006) argues, the interplay between the technology of the Internet and society neither derives from nor results in linear pathways of socio-political change. Instead, "the inherently democratic nature of the Internet can assist the civil society to burst into being; yet setting the foundations for democracy on the terrain of civil society is yet only one of many possibilities" (p. 103; see also Ess, 1996, p. 201).

Therefore, it is safe to say that networked communication technologies in the Arab world contribute to the unsettling of existing arrangements (Dean et al., 2006) and promote new organizational formats—coalitions, networks, campaigns, and mobilizations—which in turn have already manifested their impact on the Arab public, as was the case in Cairo urban protests (Fahmi, 2009), Palestinian boycotts in Lebanon (Khalili, 2005), or the Egyptian Kefaya movement (Abdulla, 2006, 2007).

We found abundant evidence in this chapter of the existence of overlapping local-global, traditional-modern, and religious-political discourses and public spheres, as a result of the introduction of the Internet as a new communication medium in the Arab mediascape and its multiple applications and implications. This new Arab cyberscape could be said to meet some of the basic requirements for the existence of a Habermasian public sphere; it provides a virtual space where participants "relate to reach others in a particular way that preserves perhaps the most essential feature of dialogue for democratic citizenship, in which each is equally entitled to participate in defining the nature and course of...interaction: all participants may mutually make claims upon each other (and) they address each other in the normative attitude in which all may propose and incur mutual obligations" (Bohman, 2004, p. 152). However, despite the overlap with the notion of the public sphere as envisioned by Habermas, the contemporary Arab cyberscape with its gender inclusiveness, increasing tide of Islamization, and growing transnationalism, provides a complex public space that differs significantly from the Eurocentric, bourgeois, male-dominated, and secular Habermasian public sphere. In this respect, we agree with Salvatore's (2007) claim that the Western notions of the public sphere could not simply apply to the Arab Muslim world and that we need to reconstruct a different genealogy of the public sphere, based on historical experiences other than those originating from the models of north-western, European modernity. In particular, Salvatore presents a genealogy of the public sphere departing from axial traditions, thus incorporating an Arab Islamic legacy to the construction of the symbolic-communicative link into the genealogy of the European, Christian and post-Christian self-under-standing that has shaped the bulk of the theoretical literature on the public sphere (p. 11).

The hybridization of the contemporary Arab cyberscape is evident in the proliferation of not just publics, but also counterpublics (Fraser, 1992; Warner, 2002) on a local level, as well as the creation of a "public of publics rather than a unified public sphere based in a common culture or identity" (Bohman, 2004, p. 152) on a global level. This intersectionality cross-cuts and (re)defines the blurry boundaries of race, class, gender, ethnicity, national identity, and geographic borders, as well as political, religious, and social orientations, con-tributes to the (re)construction of post-Habermasian public spheres.

As a result of this new Arab cyberscape, we can argue that a new form of Arab mediated public sphere (Zayani, 2008), or multiple public spheres, are being formed, which, combine different forms of new media where vari-ous Arab newspapers and satellite television channels are utilizing Internet websites to serve multiple functions and to reach different audiences, and where different blogs form symbiotic relationships with mainstream media to serve mutual interests. This, in turn, broadens the base of popular participa-tion, interactivity, and inclusion, which formulates growing mediated public spheres in the Arab world cross-cutting different forms of media, discourses and segments of the audience. Nevertheless, as the analysis of the Arab blogo-sphere (Etling et al., 2009) suggests, what is emerging in the Arab cyberscape is not necesarily the "Arab global village" as envisioned by Khazen (1999), but rather a network of parallel, yet interconnected, public spheres organized pri-marily along the lines of nationality and citizenship (Etling et al., 2009, p. 3).

The findings in this chapter provide evidence that academics need to enhance their ability to localize, globalize, synthesize, and contextualize their approaches in studying the transformative Arab media landscape, through adopting deep, comprehensive, flexible, porous, and comparative academic orientations and research methods. This holds true in analyzing the ongoing processes of media dynamics, public opinion formation, and public sphere reconstruction. In fact, the transformative and transitional Arab media scene today is restructuring and reconstituting itself, through being influenced by multiple forces, including globalization, regionalization, the information revo-lution, resurgence of religion, and cultural convergence, to mention only a few. In doing so, however, it is also giving birth to new phenomena, such as media convergences, media merges, public opinion formation, and public sphere construction, through an ongoing, interdependent, and interconnected cycle of reconstruction and transformation.

References

Abdel-Latif, O. (2004). Cyber-struggle: Islamist websites versus the Egyptian state. *Arab Reform Bulletin.* Retrieved on May 20, 2009, from http://www.mafhoum. com/press7/220T44.htm

Abdel Rahman, A. (1985). *Studies in contemporary Egyptian press.* (in Arabic). Cairo: Dar Al Fikr Al Arabi.

Abdel Rahman, A. (2002). *Issues of the Arab press in the 21*st *century* (in Arabic). Cairo: Al Arabi lil-Nashr wal Tawzi'.

Abdulla, R. A. (2006). An overview of media developments in Egypt: Does the internet make a difference? *Global Media Journal* (Mediterranean edition), *1*, 88–100.

Abdulla, R. A. (2007). *The Internet in the Arab world: Egypt and beyond.* New York: Peter Lang.

Alim, H. S. (2005). A new research agenda: Exploring the transglobal hip hop umma. In M. Cooke & B. B. Lawrence (Eds.), *Muslim networks from Hajj to hip hop* (pp. 264–274). Chapel Hill: University of North Carolina Press.

Al-Kallab, S. (2003). The Arab satellites: The pros and cons. *Transnational Broadcasting Studies Journal, 10.* Retrieved November 16, 2009, from http://www. tbsjournal.com

Allievi, S. (2003). Islam in the public space: Social networks, media and neocommunities. In S. Allievi & J. Nielsen (Eds.), *Muslim networks and transnational communities in and across Europe* (pp. 1–28). Leiden, The Netherlands: Brill.

Al Malky, R. (2008). Blogging for reform: The case of Egypt. *Arab Media and Society.* Retrieved November 25, 2008, from http://www.arabmediasociety.com

Al-Saggaf, Y. (2006). The online public sphere in the Arab world: The war in Iraq on the Al Arabiya website. *Journal of Computer-Mediated Communication, 12,* 311–334.

Alterman, J. (2000). The Middle East's information revolution. *Current History, 99*(633), 21–26.

Alterman, J. (2005). IT comes of age in the Middle East. *Foreign Service Journal, 36,* 42.

Amin, H. Y. (2007). Foreword to the Arabic edition. In R. A. Abdulla (Ed.), *The Internet in the Arab world: Egypt and beyond* (pp. ix–xi). New York: Peter Lang.

Amin, H. Y., & Gher, L. A. (2000). Digital communication in the Arab world entering the 21st century. In L. A. Gher & A. Y. Hussein (Eds.), *Civic discourse and digital age communications in the Middle East* (pp. 109–140), Stanford, CT.: Alex.

Anderson, J. W. (2003). The Internet and Islam's new interpreters. In D. F. Eickelman & J. W. Anderson (Eds.), *New media in the Muslim world* (2nd ed., pp. 1–19). Bloomington: Indiana University Press.

Anderson, J. W. (2008a, September 6). Convergence: Next phase of the information revolution. *NMIT Working Papers.* Retrieved April 25, 2009, from http://nmit. wordpress.com/2008/09/06/convergence-next-phase-of-the-information-revolution

Anderson, J. W. (2008b, September 15). Globalization, democracy, the Internet and Arabia. *NMIT Working Papers.* Retrieved April 25, 2009, from http://nmit.wordpress.com/2008/09/15/globalization-democracy-the-internet-and-arabia

Anderson, J. W. (2009, January 31). Blogging, networked publics and the politics of communication: Another free-speech panacea for the Middle East? *NMIT Working Papers*. Retrieved April 25, 2009, from http://nmit.wordpress.com/2009/01/31/197/

Atia, T. (2006, July 26). *Paradox of the free press in Egypt*. USEF Expert Panel Discussion Notes. Washington, DC: United States-Egypt Friendship Society.

Barber, B. R. (1995). *Jihad vs. McWorld*. New York: Times Books.

Baune, I. (2005). Youth in Morocco. In J. Simonsen (Ed.), *Youth and youth culture in the contemporary Middle East* (pp. 128–139). Aarhus, Denmark: Aarhus University Press.

Berenger, R. D. (2006). Introduction: War in cyberspace. *Journal of Computer-Mediated Communication, 12*, 176–188.

Bogost, I. (2007). *Persuasive games: The expressive power of videogames*. Cambridge, MA: The MIT Press.

Bohman, J. (2004). Expanding dialogue: The Internet, the public sphere and prospects for transnational democracy. In N. Crossley & J. M. Roberts (Eds.), *After Habermas: New perspectives on the public sphere* (pp. 131–155). Oxford, UK: Blackwell.

Boyd, D. (1999). *Broadcasting in the Arab world: A survey of the electronic media in the Middle East* (3rd ed.). Ames: Iowa State University Press.

Boyd, D. (2003). Impact of the electronic media on the Arab world. In K. Anokwa, C. Lin, & M. Salwen (Eds.), *International communication: Concepts and cases* (pp. 239–252). Belmont, CA: Wadsworth/Thompson.

Bunt, G. R. (2000). *Virtually Islamic: Computer-mediated communication and cyber Islamic environments*. Cardiff: University of Wales Press.

Bunt, G. R. (2003). *Islam in the digital age: E-jihad, online Fatwas and cyber Islamic environments*. London: Pluto Press.

Bunt, G. (2004). Rip, burn, pray: Islamic expressions online. In L. L. Dawson & D. E. Cowan (Eds.), *Religion online: finding faith on the Internet* (pp. 123–134). London: Routledge.

Bunt G. R. (2005). Defining Islamic interconnectivity. In M. Cooke & B. B. Lawrence (Eds.), *Muslim networks from Hajj to hip hop* (pp. 235–251). Chapel Hill: University of North Carolina Press.

Bunt, G. R. (2006). Towards an Islamic information revolution? In E. Poole & J. E. Richardson (Eds.), *Muslims and the news media* (pp. 153–164). London: I. B. Tauris.

Bunt, G. R. (2009). *iMuslims: Rewiring the house of Islam*. Chapel Hill: University of North Carolina Press.

Caeiro, A. (2003, August 7). Debating fatwas in the cyberspace: The construction of Islamic authority in four francophone Muslim Internet forums. *Sacred media — Transforming traditions in the interplay of religion and the media*. Retrieved April 25, 2009, from http://www.sacredmedia.jyu.fi/mainpage.php#caeiro

Caeiro, A. (2004). The social construction of Shari'a: Bank interest, home purchase, and Islamic norms in the West. *Die Welt des Islams, 44*(3), 351–375.

Calhoun, C. (1992). Introduction: Habermas and the public sphere. In C. Calhoun (Ed.), *Habermas and the public sphere* (pp. 1–50). Cambridge, MA: MIT Press.

Cesari, J. (2004). *When Islam and democracy meet: Muslims in Europe and in the United States*. New York: Palgrave Macmillan.

Dahlgren, P. (2001). The public sphere and the net: Structure, space, and communication. In W. L. Bennett & R. M. Entman (Eds.), *Mediated politics: Communication in the future of democracy* (pp. 33–55). Cambridge, UK: Cambridge University Press.

Dahlgren, P. (2009). *Media and political engagement: Citizens, communication, and democracy.* New York: Cambridge University Press.

Dartnell, M. (2009, July). Communicative practice and transgressive global politics. *First Monday, 10.* Retrieved from http://www.firstmonday.org/issues/issue10_7/dartnell/index.html

Dean, J., Anderson, J. W., & Lovink, G. (2006). *Reformatting politics: Information technology and global civil society.* New York: Routledge.

Diamond, L. (1999). *Developing democracy: Toward consolidation.* Baltimore, MD: Johns Hopkins University Press.

Ebeid, M. M. (2008, September). Reform in Egypt [Lecture]. College Park, MD: University of Maryland.

Egenfeldt-Nielsen, S., & Buch, T. (2006). The learning effect of 'global conflicts: Middle East'. In M. Santorineos & N. Dimitriadi (Eds.), *Gaming realities: A challenge for digital culture* (pp. 93–97). Athens: Fournos.

Eickelman, D. F. (2003). Communication and control in the Middle East: Publication and its discontent. In D. F. Eickelman & J. W. Anderson (Eds.), *New media in the Muslim world: The emerging public sphere* (2nd ed., pp. 33–44). Bloomington: Indiana University Press.

Eickelman, D. F., & Anderson, J. W. (2003). Redefining Muslim publics. In D. F. Eickelman & J. W. Anderson (Eds.), *New media in the Muslim world: The emerging public sphere* (2nd ed., pp. 1–18). Bloomington: Indiana University Press.

Eid, G. (2004). *The Internet in the Arab world: A new space of oppression?* Cairo: The Arabic Network for Human Rights Information.

Eid, G. (2007). Arab Activists and Information Technology. The Internet: Glimmer of light in a dark tunnel. *The Initiative for an Open Arab Internet.* Retrieved April 25, 2009, from http://www.openarab.net/en/node/268

Eley, G. (1992). Nations, publics, and political cultures: Placing Habermas in the nineteenth century. In C. Calhoun (Ed.), *Habermas and the public sphere* (pp. 289–339). Cambridge, MA: MIT Press.

El-Kalliny, S. (1998). The staff of Arab satellite channels: Training methods and election criteria (in Arabic). *Journal of Arts and Humanities, 15,* 30–50.

El-Nawawy, M., & Iskander, A. (2002). *Al-Jazeera: How the free Arab news network scooped the world and changed the Middle East.* Boulder, CO: Westview Press.

EL-Nawawy, M., & Iskandar, A. (2003). *Al Jazeera: The story of the network that is rattling governments and redefining modern journalism.* Boulder, CO: Westview Press.

El-Nawawy, M., & Khamis, S. (2009). *Islam dot com: Contemporary Islamic discourses in cyberspace.* New York: Palgrave Macmillan.

Eltahawy, M. (2008). The Middle East's generation facebook. *World Policy Journal, 25*(3), 69–77.

Etling, B., Kelly, J., Faris, R., & Palfrey, J. (2009). *Mapping the Arabic Blogosphere: Politics, Culture, and Dissent.* Retrieved November 16, 2009, from http://cyber.law.harvard.edu/publications/2009/Mapping_the_Arabic_Blogosphere

Ess, C. (1996). The political computer: Democracy, CMC, and Habermas. In C. Ess (Ed.), *Philosophical perspectives on computer-mediated communication* (pp. 197–230). Albany: State University of New York Press.

Fahmi, W. S. (2009). Bloggers' street movement and the right to the city: (Re)claiming Cairo's real and virtual "spaces of freedom". *Environment and Urbanization,* *21*(1), 89–107.

Fandy, M. (2007). *(Un)Civil war of words: Media and politics in the Arab world.* Westport, CT: Praeger Security International.

Frasca, G. (2004). Videogames of the oppressed: Critical thinking, education, tolerance, and other trivial issues. In P. Harrigan & N. Wardrip-Fruin (Eds.), *First person: New media as story, performance, and game* (pp. 85–94). Cambridge, MA: MIT Press.

Fraser, N. (1992). Rethinking the public sphere. In C. Calhoun (Ed.), *Habermas and the public sphere* (pp. 109–142). Cambridge, MA: MIT Press.

Fraser, N. (2009). *Scales of justice: Reimagining political space in a globalizing world.* New York: Columbia University Press.

Gharbeia, A. (2007). Lost in process. *Index on Censorship, 36,* 51–55.

Goode, L. (2005). *Jurgen Habermas: Democracy and the public sphere.* London: Pluto Press.

Gräf, B. (2007). Sheikh Yūsuf al-Qaradāwī in cyberspace. *Die Welt des Islams, 47*(3–4), 403–421.

Gulvady, S. (2009). Blogging — Redefining global modern journalism: An Omani perspective. *Global Media Journal, 8*(14). Retrieved from http://lass.calumet.purdue.edu/cca/gmj/sp09/gmj-sp09-gulvady.htm

Gunaratne, S. (2006). Public sphere and communicative rationality: Interrogating Habermas's eurocentrism. *Journalism & Communication Monographs, 8*(2), 93–156.

Habermas, J. (1989). *The structural transformation of the public sphere: An inquiry into a category of bourgeois society.* Cambridge, MA: MIT Press.

Hafez, K. (2008). European-Middle Eastern relations in the media age. *Middle East Journal of Culture and Communication, 1,* 30–48.

Hamzah, D. (2005). Is there an Arab public sphere? The Palestinian Intifada, a Saudi Fatwa, and the Egyptian press. In A. Salvatore & M. LeVine (Eds.), *Religion, social practice, and contested hegemonies: Reconstructing the public sphere in Muslim majority societies* (pp. 181–206). New York: Palgrave Macmillan.

Hashem, M. E. (2009). Impact and implications of new information technology on Middle Eastern youth. *Global Media Journal, 8*(14). Retrieved from http://lass.calumet.purdue.edu/cca/gmj/sp09/gmj-sp09-hashem.htm

Hirschkind, C. (2006). Cassette ethics: Public piety and popular media in Egypt. In B. Meyer & A. Moors (Eds.), *Religion, media, and the public sphere* (pp. 29–51). Bloomington: Indiana University Press.

Hofheinz, A. (2005). The Internet in the Arab world: Playground for political liberalization. *International Politics and Society, 3,* 78–96.

Holub, R. (1991). *Jürgen Habermas: Critic in the public sphere.* London: Routledge.

Huntington, S. P. (1996). *The clash of civilizations and the remaking of world order.* New York: Simon & Schuster.

Internet World Stats. (2009, March 31). Retrieved May 20, 2009, from http://www.internetworldstats.com

Iskander, A. (2006, July 26). *Paradox of the free press in Egypt.* USEF Expert Panel Discussion Notes. Washington, DC: United States-Egypt Friendship Society.

Jenkins, H. (2006). *Convergence culture: Where old and new media collide.* New York: New York University Press.

Johnson, P. (2006). *Habermas: Rescuing the public sphere.* London: Routledge.

Johnson, T. J., & Kaye, B. K. (2006). Blog day afternoon: Are blogs stealing audience away from traditional media sources? In R. D. Berenger (Ed.), *Cybermedia go to war* (pp. 316–335). Spokane, WA: Marquette Books.

Kalathil, S., & Boas, T. C. (2003). *Open networks, closed regimes: The impact of the Internet on authoritarian rule.* Washington, DC: Carnegie Endowment for International Peace.

Karim, K. H. (2003). Mapping diasporic meidasacpes. In K. H. Karim (Ed.), *The media of diaspora* (pp. 1–17). London: Routledge.

Khalid, M. (2007). Politics, power and the new Arab media. *Information Warfare Monitor.* Retrieved December 3, 2008, from http://www.infowar-monitor.net/modules

Khalili, L. (2005). Virtual Nation: Palestinian Cyberculture in Lebanese Camps. In R. L. Stein & T. Swedenburg (Eds.), *Palestine, Israel, and the politics of popular culture* (pp. 126–149). London: Duke University Press.

Khamis, S. (2007). The role of new Arab satellite channels in fostering intercultural dialogue: Can Al Jazeera English bridge the gap? In P. Seib (Ed.), *New media and the new Middle East* (pp. 39–52). New York: Palgrave Macmillan.

Khatib, L. (2006). Communicating Islamic fundamentalism as global citizenship. In J. Dean, J. W. Anderson, & G. Lovink (Eds.), *Reformatting politics: Information technology and global civil society* (pp. 69–83). New York: Routledge.

Khazen, J. (1999). Censorship and state control of the press in the Arab world. *The Harvard International Journal of Press/Politics, 4,* 87.

Kleinsteuber, H. J. (2010). Comparing West and East—A comparative approach to transformation. In B. Dobek-Ostrowska, M. Glowacki, K. Jakubowicz, & M. Sukosd (Eds.), *Comparartive media systems: European and global perspectives* (pp. 23–40). Budapest, Hungary: Central European University.

Kraidy, M. (2007). Saudi Arabia, Lebanon and the changing Arab information order. *International Journal of Communication, 1,* 139–156.

Kutscher, J. (2009). The politics of virtual fatwa counseling in the 21st century. *Masaryk University Journal of Law and Technology, 3*(1), 33–50.

Lim, M. (2006). Lost in transition: The Internet and reformasi in Indonesia. In J. Dean, J. W. Anderson, & G. Lovink (Eds.), *Reformatting politics: Information technology and global civil society* (pp. 85–106). New York: Routledge.

Lynch, M. (2005). Assessing the democratizing power of Arab satellite TV. *Transnational Broadcasting Studies Journal, 1,* 150–155.

Lynch, M. (2006). Dialogue in an age of terror. In M. A. Muqtader Khan (Ed.), *Islamic democratic discourse* (pp. 227–256). Lanham, MD: Lexington Books.

Mandaville, P. (2001). *Transnational Muslim politics: Reimagining the umma.* London: Routledge.

Mandaville, P. (2003). Communication and diasporic Islam: A virtual ummah? In K. Karim (Ed.), *The media of diaspora* (pp. 135–147). London: Routledge.

Mandaville, P. (2007). *Global political Islam.* London: Routledge.

Mariani, E. (2006). The role of states and markets in the production of Islamic knowledge on-line: The examples of Yusuf al-Qaradawi and Amru Khaled. In G. Larsson (Ed.), *Religious communities on the Internet* (pp. 131–149). Uppsala: Swedish Science Press.

McKee, A. (2005). *The public sphere: An introduction.* London: Cambridge University Press.

Mellor, N. (2007). *Modern Arab journalism: Problems and prospects.* Edinburgh: Edinburgh University Press.

Mernissi, F. (2006). Digital Scheherazades in the Arab world. *Current History,* *105*(689), 121–126.

Napoli, J., Amin, H., & Napoli, L. (1995). Privatization of the Egyptian media. *Journal of South Asian and Middle Eastern Studies, 18,* 30–57.

Norris, P. (2006). *Digital divide: Civic engagement, information poverty, and the Internet worldwide.* London: Cambridge University Press.

Norton, A. R. (2003). The new media, civic pluralism, and the struggle for political reform. In D. F. Eickelman & J. W. Anderson (Eds.), *New media in the Muslim world: The emerging public sphere* (2nd ed., pp. 19–32). Bloomington: Indiana University Press.

Ong, W. J. (1982). *Orality and literacy: The technologizing of the word.* London: Metheun.

Poole, E. (2002). Networking Islam: The democratizing potential of new technologies in relation to Muslim communities. *Diasporic Communication, 9*(1), 51–64.

Poole, E., & Richardson, J. E. (2006). Introduction. In E. Poole & J. E. Richardson (Eds.), *Muslims and the news media* (pp. 1–9). London: I.B. Tauris.

Pond, C. (2006). The appeal of Sami Yusuf and the search for Islamic authenticity. *TBS Journal.* Retrieved April 25, 2009, from http://www.arabmediasociety.com/topics/index.php?t_article=88

Rahimi, B. (2008, September 6). Internet and the state: The rise of cyberdemocracy in revolutionary Iran. *NMIT Working Papers.* Retrieved April 25, 2009, from http://nmit.wordpress.com/2008/09/06/internet-and-the-state-the-rise-of-cyberdemocracy-in-revolutionary-iran/

Rugh, W. A. (2004). *Arab mass media: Newspapers, radio, and television in Arab politics.* Westport, CT: Praeger.

Rugh, W. A. (2007). Do national political systems still influence Arab media? *Arab Media and Society.* Retrieved November 25, 2008, from http://www.arabmediasociety.com

Sait, S. M., Al-Tawil, K. M., Sanaullah, S., & Faheemuddin, M. (2007). Impact of Internet usage in Saudi Arabia: A social perspective. *International Journal of Information Technology and Web Engineering, 2*(2), 81–115.

Sakr, N. (2007). *Arab television today.* London: I. B. Tauris.

Salvatore, A. (2007). *The public sphere: Liberal modernity, Catholicism, Islam.* New York: Palgrave Macmillan.

Samin, N. (2008). Dynamics of Internet use: Saudi youth, religious minorities and tribal communities. *Middle East Journal of Culture and Communication, 1*(2), 197–215.

Sardar, Z., & Davies, M. W. (2002). *Why do people hate America?* Cambridge, UK: Icon Books.

Seib, P. (2004). The news media and the clash of civilizations. *Parameters: US Army War College, 34,* 71–85. Retrieved December 2, 2008, from Academic Search Premier Database.

Seib, P. (2007). New media and prospects for democratization. In P. Seib (Ed.), *New media and the new Middle East* (pp. 1–17). New York: Palgrave Macmillan.

Selnow, G. W. (1998). *Electronic whistle-stops: The impact of the Internet on America politics.* Westport, CT: Praeger.

Seymour, R. (2008). Middle East bloggers set cat among the pigeons. *Middle East,* 62–63.

Simonsen, J. (Ed.). (2005). *Youth and youth culture in the contemporary Middle East.* Denmark: Aarhus University Press.

Šisler, V. (2006). In videogames you shoot Arabs or aliens — Interview with Radwan Kasmiya. *Umelec/International, 10*(1), 77–81.

Šisler, V. (2007). The Internet and the construction of Islamic knowledge in Europe. *Masaryk University Journal of Law and Technology, 1*(2), 205–217.

Šisler, V. (2008). Digital Arabs: Representation in video games. *European Journal of Cultural Studies, 11*(2), 203–220.

Šisler, V. (2009a). European courts' authority contested? The case of marriage and divorce fatwas on-line. *Masaryk University Journal of Law and Technology, 3*(1), 51–78.

Šisler, V. (2009b). Video games, video clips and Islam: New media and the communication of values. In J. Pink (Ed.), *Muslim societies in the age of mass consumption* (pp. 231–258). Newcastle, UK: Cambridge Scholars Publishing.

Sreberny, A. (2008). The analytic challenges of studying the Middle East and its evolving media environment. *Middle East Journal of Culture and Communication, 1,* 8–23.

Tawil-Souri, H. (2007). The political battlefield of pro-Arab video games on Palestinian screens. *Comparative Studies of South Asia, Africa and the Middle East, 27*(3), 536–551.

Telhami, S. (2002). Public opinion could flare out of control in Arab nations. *San Jose Mercury News.* Retrieved on November 25, 2008, from http://www.brookings.edu/views/op-ed/telhami/2002

Thompson, J. (1990). *Ideology and modern culture: Critical social theory in the era of mass communication.* Palo Alto, CA: Stanford University Press.

Thompson, J. (1995). *The media and modernity: A social theory of the media.* Palo Alto, CA: Stanford University Press.

Trammell, K. D. (2006). Is this mic on? Celebrity use of blogs to talk politics during the war in Iraq. In R. D. Berenger (Ed.), *Cybermedia go to war* (pp. 304–315). Spokane, WA: Marquette Books.

Wall, M. A. (2006). Blogs over Baghdad: A new genre of war reporting. In R. D. Berenger (Ed.), *Cybermedia go to war* (pp. 294–303). Spokane, WA: Marquette Books.

Ward, W. (2007). Uneasy bedfellows: Bloggers and mainstream media report the Lebanon conflict. *Arab media & society.* Retrieved December 2, 2008, from http://www.arabmediasociety.com/ topics/index.php?t_article=54

Warf, B., & Vincent, P. (2007). Multiple geographies of the Arab Internet. *Area, 39*(1), 83–96.

Warner, M. (2002). *Publics and counterpublics.* New York: Zone Books.

Weyman, G. (2007). Western journalists report on Egyptian bloggers. *Nieman Reports, 61*(2). Retrieved from http://www.nieman.harvard.edu/reportsitem.aspx?id=100216

Wheeler, D. L. (2006). *The Internet in the Middle East: Global expectations and local imaginations in Kuwait.* Albany: State University of New York Press.

Wheeler, D. L. (2008). Empowerment zones? Women, Internet cafés, and life transformations in Egypt. *Information Technologies and International Development, 4*(2), 89–104.

Witteborn, S. (2007). The situated expression of Arab collective identities in the United States. *Journal of Communication, 57,* 556–575.

Zayani, M. (2005). *The Al-Jazeera phenomenon: Critical perspectives on new Arab media*. Boulder, CO: Paradigm.

Zayani, M. (2008). The challenges and limits of universalist concepts: Problematizing public opinion and a mediated Arab public sphere. *Middle East Journal of Culture and Communication, 1,* 60–79.

Zelaky, E., Eid, G., & Sami, S., & Ziada, D. (2006). *Implacable adversaries: Arab governments and the Internet*. Cairo: The Arabic Network for Human Rights Information.

CHAPTER CONTENTS

11 Between the Rejected Past and an Uncertain Future

Russian Media Studies at a Crossroads

Natalya Krasnoboka

University of Antwerp, Belgium

This chapter presents the state-of-the-art in the rapidly growing field of Russian media studies. It begins by discussing the major works in Soviet media studies, arguing that their potential contribution to the understanding of post-Soviet media developments is often overlooked. It proceeds by discussing the works by Russian and international researchers on the issues related to media change and post-Soviet media developments in the country. In order to produce an all-inclusive review of the works in the field, the chapter turns to the monitoring reports of international organizations. It also reflects upon research attempts to understand the role of the Internet in political and social processes in Russia. After a thorough mapping of the field, the chapter assesses current shortcomings and concludes by suggesting that comparative analysis and further conceptualization of post-totalitarian media evolution should become the next steps for scholarly endeavor.

Introduction

Almost two decades after the collapse of the Soviet Union, there is still a struggle to understand the processes in post-Soviet media[1] and their trajectory. Fluidity, changeability, vagueness, and inconclusiveness of many developments in those countries challenge research attempts to analyze them in a clear and orderly way. Theoretical and empirical contributions are scattered across journals and research fields.

This chapter attempts to present the state-of-the-art in the post-Soviet Russian media studies. Currently, research interest in Russian media is more advanced and better documented compared to the scientific inquiries into the media systems of other post-Soviet republics. This allows one to dive into the richness and diversity of the emergent field of study. Tendencies and regularities found in the study of Russian media can subsequently be compared and contrasted with the work on other post-Soviet societies in order to see how different media systems evolve in the conditions of regime change and transition.

The composition of the current state-of-the-art in the field of post-Soviet media studies raises the question of possible inclusion of Soviet media studies in such a review. In this respect, the question of *continuity* is both theoretical and political. By introducing the link between Soviet and post-Soviet media studies, we already make a certain theoretical claim, namely the recognition of *path-dependency* between Soviet and post-Soviet[2] media institutions. Indeed, we believe that historical connectivity is crucial for the proper understanding of current developments in Russian media. Thus, we include works on the Soviet media system in our analysis.[3]

The chapter begins by introducing and critically discussing the major works in Soviet and post-Soviet Russian media studies. It reflects upon the major focuses of scientific inquiry into the process of media evolution in a totalitarian society and the role of the media in regime change and democratization. Additionally, the chapter integrates the key conclusions of the international media organizations on current, often dramatic, developments in the Russian media field. The proliferation of the Internet across the post-Soviet region has introduced the question of this new technology's ability to enhance democratization of the former totalitarian regimes. We subsequently examine the topics and conclusions of the emerging field of Russian Internet studies. This chapter then proceeds by assessing shortcomings of existing analyses. We conclude by suggesting that comparative analysis and the accent on the conceptualization may become the most fruitful venues for the future development of the field.

Research on the Soviet Media

Despite the crucial role media played in the domestic and international affairs of the Soviet Union, international analysis of the Soviet media system was limited. *Public Opinion in Soviet Russia* by Inkeles (1950) was the first influential work. However, it was *Four Theories of the Press* (1956) with its chapter on "The Soviet Communist Theory" by Schramm that became recognized as the foundation of Soviet media studies. Otherwise, each period of Soviet history inspired few seminal publications. As such, two early studies in the field dealt with the Stalin period (Inkeles, 1950/1967) and the Khrushchev period (Buzek, 1964). The Brezhnev period inspired books by Hopkins (1970) and Mickiewicz (1981). There is also a range of lesser-known and seldom quoted works on the Soviet period (e.g., International Press Institute, 1959; Lendvai, 1981; Dzirkals, Gustafson, & Johnson, 1982). The most recent work on the media is *Governing Soviet Journalism* by Wolfe (2005). Occasionally, area-specific journals, such as *Slavic Review* and *Soviet Studies* have published articles on the media-related problem. It is interesting to note that many researchers of Soviet media came either from a journalistic background or analytical units outside an academic scope. Those with backgrounds in academia are seldom media scholars by initial training (e.g., Mickiewicz—political science; Inkeles—sociology; Wolfe—history).

Soviet-period research perceived Soviet media as an integrated part of the Soviet system. That system was seen as closed, static, and hierarchical. The most well-known attempt to develop a theory of the Soviet media was by Schramm (1956). The author approached the Soviet system as "a new and dramatic development" of authoritarianism (Siebert, Peterson, & Schramm, 1956, p. 5). The specificity of that system is based upon an ontological view of society that submitted an individual will to the will of a community. Schramm claimed that it was a special type of authoritarianism, influenced by the works of Marx, Lenin, and Stalin. According to Schramm, the Soviet system did not know a separate theory of communication (p. 116). Consequently, the media did not have integrity of their own (p. 122) and did not exist in parallel with other institutions, but formed a unit defined by the state.

Despite making a number of valuable observations and suggestions, the *Soviet Communist theory of the press* was too ideologically charged. That ideological overload became the focal point for the theory's critique. *Last Rights* (1995) is the major systematic critique of *Four Theories* (1956). Written in a different historical period and from a different ideological angle, *Last Rights* provides an in-depth analysis of historical and philosophical inconsistencies of *Four Theories*. It criticizes *Four Theories* as too ideologically driven by Cold War myths in its explanation of Soviet media. The key argument: *Four Theories* failed to present a theory of the Soviet media. Instead, it had provided a description of four applications of the media-in-society theory (Nerone, 1995, p. 18), one of which was Soviet, but had failed to acknowledge that. *Last Rights*, however, does not offer a fully elaborated alternative view, limiting itself to a vision of the Soviet model as a form of state capitalism. In another critique, Nordenstreng (1997) agrees that the authors of *Four Theories* offered a poor response to their own thesis that "the press always takes on the form and coloration of the social and political structures within which it operates" (Siebert et al., 1956, pp. 1–2). Sparks (1998a) sees a major problem in the focus of *Four Theories* on the system of values and beliefs that leads "to a concentration upon what people say about themselves and their beliefs, rather than the concrete realities of their lives and actions" (p. 53). The author also claims that *Four Theories* has "no apparent room for any contingent evolution or change independent of the central value system of the dominant social group" (p. 53). On the contrary, De Smaele (2005) calls for "cautious rehabilitation" of *Four Theories*, since that book "is more often rejected by its criticizers than replaced by alternative models" (p. 7).

Buzek (1964) approached the Soviet media system as a *political institution* that had certain features of the press. In his view, the Soviet press organization had "the same pyramidal structure" based on the same territorial-production principles as that of the Communist party (p. 65). Inkeles (1950/1967) added that it was "a carefully ranked, thoroughly unified system" (p. 188). Dzirkals et al. (1982), however, claimed that the Soviet media did "... differ from one another, not only in general liveliness and readability, but also in such attributes as degree of liberalism or conservatism" (p. 40). Overall, researchers agreed that specialized publications had greater freedom (Buzek, 1964; Dzirkals et al., 1982), while central media were vigorously scrutinized (Dzirkals et al., 1982) and regional and provincial outlets found themselves in the most difficult position (Inkeles, 1950/1967). Inefficiency and a poor image of the Soviet press were related to technological insufficiency of the press industry, shortages of raw materials, and an unwillingness to apply the methods of Western journalism (e.g., Buzek, 1964; Inkeles, 1950/1967; Wolfe, 2005).

Total media control was named as one of the six conditions of totalitarianism introduced by Friedrich and Brzezinski (1956) and applied by the authors in their study of the Soviet Union. Two other researchers of the Soviet media, Inkeles (1950/1967) and Buzek (1964), also agreed that *totality* was the major social definition of those media. Soviet media adjusted their roles to the demands of the party and did this through the fulfillment of propagandist, agitational, organizational, and critical functions coupled with a media-biased, ideological, and partisan nature (Buzek, 1964, p. 55). Schramm (1956) stated that the Soviet media "were conceived of instrumentally" and "… have grown so as to reflect the Soviet official ideology, the Soviet state, and the Soviet 'ideal personality'" (p. 116). Moreover, if requested, Soviet media were capable of changing their coverage "overnight" in accordance with "the new line" (p. 120). Researchers emphasized a preoccupation of Soviet journalists with serving party officials as their prime audience and their ignorance concerning public demands (e.g., Haddix, 1990; Remington, 1988; Mickiewicz, 2000).

Nevertheless, and despite the seemingly meticulous control and supervision (Schramm, 1956, p. 131), most researchers noticed certain dynamism, differentiation, and dysfunction in the Soviet media. In this way, Friedrich and Brzezinski (1956) acknowledged the limits to the totalistic effects of propaganda caused by rumor-mongering, general disillusionment, a vacuum of information and communication around the leadership, and the maintenance of the "islands of separateness" such as family, church, university, and military establishment. Likewise, Inkeles (1950/1967) pointed to the existence of potential counterbalances to the party dominance. He saw such a counterbalance in the Soviet intelligentsia, youth, and technical management. Finally, foreign policy studies considered the *inter-elite conflict* to be the most crucial element of potential dysfunctionality. Researchers tried to find the traces of potential inter-elite conflicts through the analysis of the Soviet media message. That led Rush to introduce the concept of *esoteric communication*, "… hidden messages, which enable factional leaders to communicate quickly, safely, and decisively with the sub-elites whose support they solicit" (Rush, 1959, p. 614). Also Griffith (1970) saw "decipherment of esoteric communication" as the major method of communist communications analysis. The author argued that such a communication strategy was common to all authoritarian societies, whether ideologically or theologically driven. Dzirkals et al. (1982) also addressed the relationship between media controversy on certain subjects and intra-elite dissent. The authors questioned, however, the consistency of esoteric communication throughout all periods of the Soviet regime. They called for a more differentiated approach that would recognize that "in times of stable and unchallenged one-man leadership … the probability of partisan communication should be considered low" while "in times of relaxation or leadership turmoil, the media reveal more about the Soviet system" (Dzirkals et al., 1982, pp. x–xii). Finally, the authors note that despite general predictability of media responses, journalistic initiative was possible. Its success depended on "the ability to exploit safe openings" (Dzirkals et al., 1982, p. 69). For Dzirkals and colleagues (1982), it was primarily self-censorship (and not censorship or other means of control), which kept any serious controversy out of the Soviet media (p. 37). The authors noted a significant difference in the source of self-censorship over the time—if during the Stalin period it was sustained by fear of losing one's life, later it was replaced by fear of jeopardizing a good career.

Reflecting on the nature and the future of the Soviet press, Buzek (1964) argued that inefficiency and "defects and weaknesses" of Soviet media were inherent in the regime type. The essence of Soviet one-party rule came into "direct conflict" and "insoluble contradiction" with the effectiveness of the press. The media were sending "the right message" as long as they were totally supervised and controlled, which simultaneously meant their dullness and ineffectiveness. Any attempts to invigorate them would inevitably reduce effectiveness of their control and challenge the position of the party through the journalistic probe into different problems that society faced. Also Friedrich and Brzezinski (1956) argued that the monopolistic control over information would gradually lead to "a profound distrust of all news" among the general public "that even paramount facts are disbelieved" (p. 171). This in turn would negatively impact any communication between rulers and ruled, creating the "phenomenon of vacuum" eroding the relationship of subordination, and destroying genuine authority of the party (p. 166). The most recent approach to the study of the Soviet media is offered by Wolfe (2005). The author approaches the Soviet press through Foucault's concept of *governmentality*. He underlines both the active role of Soviet journalism and constant attempts by the government to redefine this role and its limits. Although governed by the party, journalists were the "important class of governors" occupying "key positions at the switches and relays" between the party and society.

Researchers of the Soviet media did not see a possibility for systematic cross-regime comparisons between Western societies and the Soviet Union. Neither did they consider Western concepts' applicability in the study of Soviet outlets. From a historical-descriptive point of view, Soviet media studies offer a very rich collection of material. Rather, it is the conceptual side of the research that raises questions. So, for example, it becomes immediately clear that Soviet media studies were as much affected by the ideological considerations of the moment as they were by the desire to establish a viable theoretical framework for study of Soviet media. While critically assessing the theoretical contribution of *Four Theories* (1956), Nerone (1995) views that work, not as a theory in the scientific sense, but as a rationale (p. 17), which on many occasions "mystifies the role of media in society" and uses terminology that promotes "a white/black, good/bad understanding" (p. 23). The question at the heart of many inquiries was not *how the Soviet media work* but rather *how wrong the things are* and *can something be done to improve them*? So, Wortman (1965) criticizes Buzek's work for attempting "to present a system without its history" with the press being almost an artificial creation, which leaps "into life directly from the pages of V. I. Lenin and J. V. Stalin" (pp. 281–282).

During the Soviet period, some Western researchers resorted to a *double* normative prism: first explaining the functioning of the Soviet media through Marxism-Leninism theory and then evaluating the latter through the frame of the liberal-democratic theory. A one-sided emphasis of many works on the dominant role of the party in media affairs suffered from the *repetitiveness* and neglected other factors and impacts. Another issue was overuse of the censorship concept. That led to the image of powerless, suppressed, and passive media. Questions of internal dynamics, change, its timing and directionality (although widely acknowledged), remained poorly addressed. Seldom did researchers allow dynamics to become part of their analysis. Media were approached in terms of their instrumental and utilitarian use by the party. Political and economic crises, dissent, and changes, although discussed, scarcely became integrated into the explanatory framework. Even an esoteric communication approach, while introducing the elements of conflict and contention into the study of Soviet society, failed to acknowledge any active position of the media.

Taken together, these and other issues created a fixed and inflexible approach to media analysis, with the dominance of certain clichés and the stress on greater problems and a bigger picture at the expense of details and nuances. A static picture of Soviet media performance emerged, almost unchanged, uninterrupted, and uncorrupted by social, political, and economic challenges and upheavals. Since only a few works attempted consistent and systematic test of their claims, their validation became problematic. Moreover, *disconnectedness* among the studies did not allow enriching and specifying the picture.

Perestroika

International scholars met *perestroika* with great scientific enthusiasm. It had opened up the country politically and physically: finally researchers could freely travel to conduct their fieldwork, to communicate with people, to organize joint conferences and to have greater access to sources of information inside the formerly closed societies. It resulted in a significant amount of publications (e.g., Mickiewicz, 1988; Remington, 1988; McNair, 1991; Roxburgh, 1987; McReynolds, 1991). The number of articles on the Soviet media in area-specific and general communication journals also increased (e.g., Remington, 1985; Benn, 1987; Gaunt, 1987; Downing, 1988; Goban-Klas, 1989; McNair, 1989).

Researchers noticed considerable transformation in the media role and their position vis-à-vis power center(s) and society. According to many authors, the media stood at the vanguard of the country's democratization due to their active use by Gorbachev and his accomplices who "… raised the mass media to a position alongside the Party as the second factor in the change" (Paasilinna, 1995, pp. 83–84). So, Zhou (1988) registers the change in the media role towards the position of "an observer of life," "a chronicler of the present day," and "a public opinion accumulator" (p. 193). Nevertheless, as Weaver (1993) remarks, although Soviet journalists knew the direction they were headed, they had no roadmap to get there. Among the specific challenges of media democratization, researchers noticed weaknesses in journalistic training (Haddix, 1990), a psychological legacy of self-censorship practices (Paasilinna, 1995), and the lack of differentiation between journalist personal views and official positions (Zhou, 1988). By the same token, although the Soviet media could now be "… comparable in their openness, reliability, depth of information, and entertainment quality to those of most western societies" (McNair, 1991, p. 202), matters of news objectivity and neutrality were not scrutinized (e.g., Zhou, 1988). Nevertheless, there were noticeable changes in news timeliness and factuality, in scope of coverage, and in presentation of dissenting and "moderately negative" opinions (Mickiewicz & Jamison, 1991, p. 151; Zhou, 1988, p. 193).

Overall, researchers positively evaluated democratization, despite disagreements concerning the "primary source" of change: Did media spark the general transition (Mickiewicz, 1988, 1997; Paasilinna, 1995), or did the general reform affect media (McNair, 1991; Zhou, 1988)? Simultaneously, researchers raised a question of continuity in the instrumental use of media (Price, 1996; Paasilinna, 1995) due to the top-down launch of perestroika through the personal initiative of Gorbachev (e.g., Benn, 1992; Haddix, 1990; Price, 1996), which meant that "the level of press openness usually corresponded to either Gorbachev's own sentiments or how he read the political risks" (Gibbs, 1999, pp. 8–9).

Russian Media Studies

The collapse of the Soviet Union provided a new impetus to development of media studies. The field was transformed along with the object of its analysis. It is characterized by greater diversity for research interests and chosen approaches. Several new foci can be distinguished in post-Soviet Russian media studies. These include studies of democratization and economic liberalization, social responsibility and civil society, and professional standards and media-effects studies.

In the early years of the transition, some researchers (Manaev, 1993, 1995; Androunas, 1993) embraced the market as a panacea. Written in the first decade of the Russian independence, their works use the concepts of economic liberalization and private ownership as a way to rescue of the media from the state and political dependency. Other researchers, while understanding the shortcomings of the Russian emerging market, did not see the need to critically approach or adjust market theory (e.g., Mickiewicz, 2000; I. Zassoursky, 2000). However, there were also researchers who expressed doubts about market's ability to solve the problems of media ownership, independence, and democratization (Voltmer, 2000; McNair, 1994, 2000). They argued that the

Russian example demonstrates that there are no perfect, theory-like conditions for market operation divorced from the country's historical context. Likewise, there is also no possibility for an ideal comprehension of the market advantages by yesterday's Soviet citizens and managers. Researchers also noticed that specific conditions (e.g., legal status of a media owner; economic profitability of media; development of advertisement markets; and of small and medium businesses) that enable market and private ownership to become a feasible alternative to the state are still missing. Additionally, pronounced unprofessionalism of managerial arrangements (Owens, 2002) and the lack of Western investors (Voltmer, 2000) reinforce the existing difficulties. Moreover, the Russian intellectual elite saw commercialization, market, and advertising—the crucial elements of media autonomy in liberal societies—as the major threats to media independence (McNair, 1994, 2000).

The situation is further complicated by the lack of effective legal mechanisms, with Russian media law being "a time-bounded monument to the experience of new freedoms and the traumas of transformation" (Price, 2002, p. 36). Media laws exist "in a nascent, uneven legal culture" (Mickiewicz, 2005, p. 361) linked to a general lack of democratic traditions (Ellis, 1999). This leads to: an unclear definition of ownership (Belin, 1997); the rapid succession of decrees and the unpredictable changes in policy (De Smaele, 2002); and to a fierce battle for political control over broadcasting (McNair, 1994; Mickiewicz, 2000).

In the early 1990s, emergence of civil society was treated as an important factor of media democratization (e.g., McNair, 1994; Haddix, 1990). Nevertheless, there was no significant application of social responsibility or civil society as analytical concepts. Some researchers conclude that the weakness of post-Soviet civil society makes this concept insignificant, not only for the media but also for research (e.g., Koltsova, 2000; Juskevits, 2002). On the other hand, the concept of the media's social responsibility regularly appears in the works as a normative conclusion—this is the ideal that post-Soviet media need to strive for (e.g., Y. Zassoursky, 1996; Shaikhitdinova, 2001; Ustimova, 2000).

Methodologically and conceptually, media-effects studies are the most developed and systematically tested approach. These works confirm media importance for political choices. According to some analyses, national television is both the most important source of news for voters and a single predictor of the voting choice for the pro-Kremlin Unity party (White, McAlliter, & Oates, 2002). Oates (2006) introduces the notion of "broadcast" party, arguing that "these ephemeral 'broadcast' parties and candidates increasingly are able to win votes at the cost of more accountable parties and candidates with definable ideologies, platforms and policies" (p. 66). Nevertheless, researchers stop shortly of admitting a far-reaching power of the media. Instead they see "major but quite selective effects" of television on voters (White, Oates, & McAllister, 2005). Studying the process of perception and decoding of television news by Russian audiences, Mickiewicz (2000) notes "an extraordinary degree of media literacy and active engagement with news messages" (p. 103) in the public whom the researcher considers "extraordinarily sophisticated media consumers" (p. 88). Viewers are able "to extract meaning from extremely limited political information on their television" (Mickiewicz, 2008, p. 199) and to challenge stories where "tradeoffs are thoroughly concealed" (Mickiewicz, 2005, p. 355). On the other hand, Oates (2006) stresses a new wave of audience receptiveness to the patriotic image of the nation on television (p. 129).

Analysis into professionalism and media standards attempts to track changes in journalistic norms, values, and practices. While a few researchers (e.g., Svitich, 2000) put forward the argument of radical change in post-Soviet media, others find confirmation of the continuity argument (Voltmer, 2000; Pasti, 2005). Scholars observe that objectivity, impartiality, and factuality are not seen as essential news values. Actuality is often replaced by *otcherk* with in-depth subjective handling of an issue-at-stake (Voltmer, 2000), where "at times the commentary preceded the presentation of facts" (Fossato, 2001, p. 344). At the same time, researchers understand that decades of suppression could lead journalists to understand press freedom "primarily as the freedom to express subjective convictions publicly" (Voltmer, 2000, p. 479) and as the "first bold step" against "the state-dominated message" (Mickiewicz, 2000, pp. 107–108).

Scholars discuss a biased position and compliance of the media with the external political demands and pressures. Journalistic choices of "the obtrusive partisanship" (Mickiewicz & Richter, 1996) or of "the lesser evil" (Oates & Roselle, 2000) in political conflicts confirm both the obscured position of journalists (Belin, 2002) and their continuous adherence to the mobilization function (De Smaele, 2002). Similarly, Wu, Weaver, and Johnson (1996) argue that Russian journalists feel at home with the role of agitator, while De Smaele (2004) calls them "missionaries of ideas" and McNair (2000) "politically committed propagandists."

Researchers also note the significant role of the media in establishment of the post-Soviet party system (White et al., 2002; Oates, 2006), which leads some authors to suggest that the media substitute for parties' historical function (Mickiewicz, 2000). On the other hand, Belin (1997, 2002) argues that there is a remarkable ineffectiveness of Russian media since the authorities and the military ignore their investigations and allegations. Nordenstreng and Pietiläinen (1999) observe the lack of solidarity and common professional culture among journalists, which constrains them from working in a plural society (p. 155) and results in a situation where journalists "pick sides in the oligarchic battles and typically support a party or group of parties at the expense of informing the electorate" (p. 191).

While in his earlier work McNair (1994) expresses optimism upon the arrival of a new generation of journalists "who are less tied to the 'collective genetic memory' of the Soviet past" (p. 131), in his later work he notes less optimistic transformations in the editorial identities of privatized outlets (McNair, 2000). Similarly, Pasti (2005) and Juskevits (2002), while recognizing emergence of new professional subcultures, particularly among the younger generation of journalists, argues in favor of a strong element of continuity that is not affected by generation change.

In the post-Soviet research, the party factor is replaced by the state and oligarchs. McNair (2000) notes that replacement of party bosses by the new media barons was one of the most visible changes (p. 79). However, the appearance of new players did not damage "the inevitability of continuing state involvement in the Russian media" (McNair, 1994, p. 126). In a comparative analysis of the Chechen wars' media coverage, Belin (2002) concludes that lack of elite consensus and weakness of the state and military were the reasons for unrestricted critical coverage during the first war. Once the state regained strength, restrictions were imposed and journalists submitted to them. McNair (1994) sees the first sign of that renewed state control in Yeltsin's decision to ban pro-coup newspapers and in transferring all-union media assets to the jurisdiction of the Russian Federation. Paasilinna (1995) sees a hand of the state in "... differentiated support (favorable prices for paper, subsidies for printing and distribution) for publications pleasing to the authorities" (p. 65). The most recent publications discuss the role of the media with the context of a consolidation or even sacralization of the strong state and presidential power (Fossato, 2006), as well as the return of the Soviet media model (Oates, 2007).

Although following a similar choice of topics in general, national scholars place different stresses on their analyses than to those by their Western colleagues.[4].National researchers see certain peculiarities of Russian marketization in the constant growth, for example, of the political advertising market under conditions of general media unprofitability (Vartanova, 1999; Koltsova, 2001; Pasti, 2005) and in the media's readiness to accommodate economic and political interests simultaneously (see Gulyaev, 1996; Y. Zassoursky, 1997; Korkonosenko, 1997; Svitich, 2000). As for overall adherence to emerging liberal ideas, Vartanova (1999) argues that many journalists saw the market as an equivalent of democracy and *glasnost*. Similarly, I. Zassoursky (2000) states that "the 'market fundamentalism' was as much their [journalists'] creation as of liberal economists." This leads researchers to the development of several new market-related concepts characteristic of the post-Soviet transition (e.g., the concepts of politicized capital and the market of political influence (I. Zassoursky, 1998, 2000, 2004), and of business-political media holdings (Vartanova, 1996, 1997, 1999)).

The idea of all-powerful media attracts significant academic inquiry in Russia. Belief in media power brings Dubin (2000) to claim an emergence of a society of viewers and I. Zassoursky (2000) to argue about media holdings as prototypes of political parties in Russia. On the other hand, the instrumental use of media confirms continuity of Soviet practices of media outlets as ideological institutions (Kolesnik, 1996) and as an extension of the government (Pasti, 2005). According to some researchers, the signs of continuity are particularly visible in the media coverage (I. Zassoursky, 2000; Davletshina, 2002; Melnikov, 2004).

Confusion is seen in matters of professional standards, journalistic ethics, and values (Pasti, 2005; Juskevits, 2002; Koltsova, 2000, 2001). Koltsova (2000) argues, for example, that while admitting a positive perception of objectivity, Russian journalists simultaneously denounce it as a naïve Western ideal (p. 106). Lipman (1998) argues that from 1994 onwards, the position of media grew strangely ambiguous, "the same publication would be both pro-government and in opposition to it." Journalists as such do not: consider the interests of their audiences as paramount (Pasti, 2005); adhere to the ideas of social responsibility (Y. Zassoursky, 1996; also Resnianskaia & Fomicheva, 1999); develop "effective mechanisms of self-defence and self-limitation" Usacheva (2000, p. 125); nor observe the letter of the law (Kolesnik, 1996). Instead, they demonstrate a pragmatic need to serve specific political and economic interests (Melnikov, 2002; also Ustimova, 2000). Registering only limited differences between generations of journalists, Juskevits (2003) concludes that Russian journalists act in accordance with the logic of survival.

Scholars unanimously point to transformation of the dominant factor although disagree in their explanations of change. Koltsova (2001) sees a split of "a relatively unified agent of control (the Party-State) ... into a number of competing actors" (p. 321). Andronas (1993) argues about substitution of the party by the state. Vartanova (1996) and I. Zassoursky (1998) discuss convergence of political and financial elites. In their other works, Vartanova (2001, 2002) and I. Zassoursky (2000) define global economic forces as an emerging factor in media affairs. Among the counter-factors that may guarantee economic and political independence of the media but still fail to do so, researchers cite advertising markets, political opposition, media legislation, NGOs, and civil society at large (Y. Zassoursky, 1996; Richter, 1995; Vartanova, 1996; Usacheva, 2000; Juskevits, 2003; Koltsova, 2000; Lipman, 2005).

The role of the state, although more subtle and indirect, continues to dominate media affairs through control and ownership of broadcasting and printing facilities (Y. Zassoursky, 2000; Andronas, 1993; Vartanova, 1996; Kolesnik, 1996; Koltsova, 2000). Moreover, officials define the media agenda (I. Zassoursky, 2000), which creates a situation of a permanent monologue of power in the media (Boretsky, 1998) and personification of information policy (Melnikov, 2002).

National researchers approach the question of regime change and its impact on the media, although not in a systematic way. Vartanova (2002) notes that the complexity of new pressures and new structures found in the media "provide real competition between the authoritarian past and emerging more democratic and open society." She adds that "it is important to remember that the present Russian media has sustained many features of the 'old' Soviet media order, but in a specific mixture of the national and global, particular and general, European and Asian nature." I. Zassoursky (2000) believes that despite attempts of Putin's government to regain control over media, "the global financial markets cannot be overpowered." In turn, Richter (1995) argues that the task of constructing and strengthening democratic society is more complex and demanding than that "of overturning the communist machine." The author adds: "This goal seems to create the biggest challenge for Russian journalists." Some other researchers also acknowledge the role of the system's collapse in the weakness of the current media institution (Koltsova, 2001; Panfilov, 2000). Contrary to many opinions, Lipman (2005) sees a direct link between recent problems and weaknesses of media freedom and Yeltsin's policies and practices: "Although Yeltsin's government did not directly attack press freedom, the fundamental principles that make it possible ... were compromised during his tenure before they had a chance to take root in the Russian soil. Problematic ownership of media assets, murky business practicers, and institutional weakness all helped to erode the foundations of an independent media" (pp. 321–322).

The development of national media studies in Russia is heterogeneous in its quality, impact, and international academic recognition. There is a relatively small group of researchers whose works are widely published and recognized both inside the country and on an international level (e.g., Vartanova, Y. Zassoursky, I. Zassoursky, Koltsova, Richter). Being primarily members of the Faculty of Journalism, Moscow State University, these researchers have developed strong international connections with other media and post-Soviet schools worldwide. There is also a group of national media scholars who are mainly known as the authors of textbooks on media-related theories and issues (e.g., Grachev, Shaikhitdinova, Korkonosenko, Svitich, Prokhorov, Fedotova, Dzyaloshinsky). Finally, a large number of research groups have developed in different universities across Russia. Their works are regionally concentrated, have narrow circulation, and are practically unknown in broader academic circles outside the country.

There is a noticeable *generational* difference in Russian media research. Junior researchers are more exposed to international contacts and better acquainted with international media theory and analysis. However, as Vartanova (2009) observes, textbooks and courses in media studies are often based on the Soviet-period literature (p. 287). Related is the problem of international literature accessibility. Hardly any classical works in international media studies were known in the Soviet Union. While currently this problem is partially solved, poor knowledge of foreign languages does not allow researchers to become familiar with the original works. Slow and selective translation of such works into Russian leads to the situation when certain classical texts are perceived as present-day analysis.[5] Western scientific tradition appears to the national scientific eye as a consensual entity with insignificant variations, often deprived of its diversity of theoretical schools; differences between qualitative and quantitative analyses; between critical approach and positivism; between cultural studies and political economy, etc. Likewise, Western researchers mistakenly put more emphasis on the differences in approaches they track in post-Soviet national studies, believing that such differences are inspired by the diversity of research schools.

Overall, international and national research into Russian media shows increasing signs that the media change only partially corresponds with the ideal(-istic) expectations of media democratization and liberalization. Puzzled by the fluidity, multi-dimensionality, unpredictability of processes, and by the combination of the old and the new, researchers are inclined to understand transformative processes in terms of change and continuity of varying degrees. We can distinguish between recognition of a considerable, partial, or minimal change, and a reverse wave. Works that recognize considerable change express greater optimism about post-Soviet progress in the establishment of a new order (e.g., I. Zassoursky, 2000; Vartanova, 2002). Those who stress partiality of change are more inclined to see difficulties of transition (e.g., Koltsova, 2000, 2001; Medvedev, 2002; McNair, 1994, 2000; Mickiewicz, 2000). Supporters of the minimal change argument stress the slowness of change and the continuity of old values and practices (e.g., Voltmer, 2000; Foster, 2002; Pasti, 2005; Lipman & McFaul, 2001; Lipman, 2005). More recently, some researchers have identified a reversibility of the change in post-Soviet societies (e.g., Nordenstreng & Pietiläinen, 1999; Oates, 2006; Usacheva, 2000). Yet others argue (e.g., Pasti, 2005; Shaikhitdinova, 2001; Jones, 2002; Davis, Hammond, & Nizamova, 1998) that the simultaneous existence of the old and the new resulted in the logic of survival that cannot easily be identified either with previous journalistic practices or with new ones. Only a few researchers (e.g., Androunas, 1993) argue that post-Soviet media cannot be reformed.

As consolidation of authoritarian rule in Russia continues, we see an even more pronounced shift in *Western* researchers' attention from the issue of democratization to the question of full-scale continuity. Sparks (1998) insisted on the crucial aspect of continuity in an analysis of post-Soviet media systems and did so when it was still commonly assumed that Russia was heading towards Western-style democracy. However, even if more researchers now agree with the role of continuity in their analysis, they continue to approach such media through the application of democratically generated concepts. In this way, continuity becomes the residual category for those phenomena which cannot be properly explained by means of democratic media concepts.

The article by Becker (2004) is, in our opinion, the first significant attempt to approach Russian media developments through a non-democratic theoretical frame. The author compares the post-Soviet situation with similar processes in other authoritarian countries and suggests approaching Russia as a neo-authoritarian system. Even more recently, examining the issues of government interference, harassment of media outlets and the rapid decline in journalistic values of balance, impartiality, and objectivity with the simultaneous increase in self-censorship, Oates (2007) chooses a neo-Soviet model. What makes the system "neo" is "a list of new controls and pressures on journalists, notably market forces as well as a miasma of harassment and violence" (Oates, 2007, p. 1296). At the same time, subsequent research into post-Soviet media is likely to confront the necessity to take into account and explain increasing levels of media and public *de-politicization*.

The complex interplay between media de-politicization and continuous consolidation of state involvement in media affairs has become the center of analysis in a recently published volume on the post-Soviet media (Beumers, Hutchings, & Rulyova, 2009). The editors note the simultaneous de-politicization of media content and audience preferences and increased reliance on governmental sources of information (Beumers et al., 2009, p. 21). The authors connect this fact with the return to "simple information," with the general lack of interest in politics and with a certain "satisfaction with the status quo" (p. 22). Similar seemingly contradictory conclusions are reached by Oates (2006) in her study of Russian audiences, where the researcher notes that many Russian viewers "are content with less information if it means more control" (p. 190). Dunn (2009) argues that de-politicization of Russian television began in 2000 with Putin's ascension to presidential power. Mickiewicz (2008), however, observes different dynamics in the younger generation of college-educated professionals. They support diversity of viewpoint on television and have no nostalgic longing for the earlier Soviet model of broadcasting (p. 205).

At the same time, there is a growing share of scholarly analysis where the question of political impact is moved backstage. National researchers, in particular, focus on other aspects of media change and evolution, such as innovation, modernization, globalization, regionalization, and marketization. As contributions by national scholars to another recently published volume demonstrate, the Russian media studies are experiencing a *diversification* of research interests, focusing on applied research in audience studies, popular culture and entertainment media, market mechanisms, and modernization (e.g., Vartanova, 2009; Fomicheva, 2009; Anikina, 2009).[6] What is also traceable in these recent works, however, is a shift away from the study of the *political factor* in the media activities at the *national* level.[7] It is, of course, too early to claim that a true shift in research priorities has taken place. Moreover, even if such a shift has taken place, no evidence suggests that what we see is the effect of the state authoritarian discourse on the research preferences of Russian scholars. The issues of globalization or glocalization attract academic attention worldwide and there is no reason to assert that this should not be the case in Russia.

These recent publications reflect, in our view, the real state of affairs in the Russian media sphere where sharp de-politicization of the media and the public goes hand in hand with proactive and reactive controls by authoritarian rulers. The observation of these tendencies leads to the suggestion that in the near future, post-Soviet media analysis may develop along two major lines of inquiry. Along one line, researchers will be interested in the analysis of the impact of authoritarian rule on diverse media practices and behavior. Along the other line, researchers will shift away from the question of authoritarianism toward a de-politicized analysis of media issues. In other words, while the former will investigate the broader socio-political framework of media activities, the latter will be more media-centered.

International Organizations and Monitoring Missions

The rift is also noticeable in the focus of analysis between universities' based research groups in Russia and international and national NGOs and research centers which still operate in Russia (e.g., Glasnost Defense Foundation; Media Law & Policy Institute, Carnegie Moscow Centre). All international organizations report a decrease of media freedom in Russia compared to the early years of post-Soviet democratization. These organizations report the excessive use of control mechanisms by the authorities against oppositional and critical outlets. Moreover, not only do local media and media organizations experience considerable difficulties in their work, but several international organizations also have recently reported tensions with the Russian authorities.[8]

Freedom House, which has been monitoring the dynamics of political and media freedom since 1972 and 1980 respectively, has lowered the Russia press freedom score from 40 (partly free) in 1994 to 80 (not free) in 2009. Its rating of the independent media has worsened from 4.25 in 1998 to 6.25 in 2008. Reporters Without Borders ranked Russia's press freedom at 141 out of 173 countries studied in 2008.

Organization for Security and Cooperation in Europe (OSCE) has been monitoring elections in Russia since the early 1990s.[9] Its conclusion on media involvement in campaigns grows gloomier every time. One of its last election reports states: "Since the 2000 presidential election, it is widely considered that administrative restrictions and obstructions have been used to eliminate the most significant and influential media outlets that attempted to offer an editorial line independent from or critical of the presidency or government" (OSCE, 2004). The Committee to Protect Journalists (2005) evaluation of the same campaign said: "Putin summoned national television executives to a meeting in January to discuss editorial plans for the campaign." Investigative journalism, reports on corruption, and war-zone reporting are of primary concern for the international community. According to the CPJ, 17 journalists have been killed in Russia since 2000. On the list of most life-threatening countries, Russia is outranked only by Iraq and Algeria. "This is a sorry record for a great and powerful nation that embarked on democratization after more than 70 years of brutal repression," concludes the CPJ in its most recent report (2009).[10] Accreditation is another area of the authorities' intervention into journalistic work. The Kremlin chooses outlets and individual journalists who are allowed to cover governmental activities.

Fruitful cooperation about the Russian media has developed between national and international scholars and international organizations. Thus in the 1990s, Radio Free Europe/Radio Liberty (RFE/RL) produced a number of reports on the Russian media empires by Fossato (Oxford University) and Kachkaeva (Moscow State University). Their articles investigated the emergence, development, and decline of the most prominent media empires. Several prominent Russia's political scientists and journalists (e.g., Arbatov, Malashenko, Petrov, Ryabov, Shevtsova, Lipman) cooperate on a regular basis with the Carnegie Moscow Centre, one of the few international organizations that continue to operate in Russia. Finally, several Russian NGOs monitor the situation in the country's media sphere. The most prominent among them are the Media Law & Policy Institute and the Glasnost Defense Foundation.

The Internet and Russian Media Studies

For diverse socioeconomic reasons, the arrival and spread of the Internet communication in Russia has been delayed compared to advanced Western economies.[11] On the other hand, and compared to other post-Soviet states (with the exception of the Baltic states), Russia's familiarization with the Internet has developed considerably faster. Saunders (2009) registers striking differences in the levels of online information freedom amongst ex-USSR republics. On one end of the spectrum, Saunders places "*E*-stonia," "a liberal, plural democracy which places higher in media freedom rankings than either Great Britain or Australia" (p. 2). On the other end, Saunders sees Turkmenistan, "a country where media freedom is non-existent and which only began to allow private citizens to access the internet in mid-2008" (p. 2).

According to one analysis, the Internet at least partially takes the place of newspapers as a source of information for the middle class and the elite (Pietiläinen, 2008, p. 383). Still, only 27% of Russians have Internet access.[12] That may also be a reason why academic research into the news and political segment of the Russian Internet is relatively poorly developed compared with research into more traditional mass media.

The early 2000s have seen the boom of news and political websites. To a certain extent, the prominence of the Internet as a (political) news medium coincided with the first governmental attempts to crack down on liberal and oppositional traditional media outlets (the row around the media empires of Berezovsky and Gusinsky). Research at the time that portrayed the Internet as a virtual civil society and free political platform, confirmed the opposition nature of the Internet news resources, and predicted their power to counterbalance official information (see, e.g., Krasnoboka, 2002; Semetko & Krasnoboka, 2003). Those observations and predictions were in line with the conclusions from research in other non-democratic and transitional societies; namely that online media disseminate publicly important information not available otherwise or which content in traditional media is censored and framed by state authorities (e.g., Kalathil & Boas, 2001, 2003; Taubman, 1998; Rodan, 1998; Ott & Rosser, 2000; Hill & Sen, 2000). Moreover, expectations about the Internet's role in the enhancement of democracy have been widely shared by pioneers of Internet research in the West (e.g., Rheingold, 1993; Negroponte, 1995; Livingstone, 1999), whom Norris (2000) called cyber-optimists.

Even before Russia had witnessed the first attempts by its state authorities to consolidate their presence on the Internet and to control over online information flows, international research into the Internet became populated by more pessimistic and realistic works which questioned the ability of the Internet to facilitate democracy (e.g., Davis, 1997; Selnow, 1998; Resnick, 1998; Bimber, 1999; Margolis, Resnick, & Wolfe, 1999). Furthermore, Kalathil and Boas (2001, 2003) introduced the notion of reactive and proactive Internet strategies which, in their view, are used by authoritarian regimes to control information flows online.[13] Indeed, more recent developments in the Russian segment of the Internet confirm the active involvement of the state in proactive and reactive control of online communication. One of the most recent reactive moves by authorities against the blogosphere is the criminal case against a blogger who left in his blog a hatred-generated comment against a policeman.[14] In its latest report on Internet freedom worldwide, Freedom House (2009) lists other instances of violence, criminal investigations, and hacker attacks on opposition and activists' online resources. Some researchers, however, conclude that in contrast to Belarusian-style reactive control of the Internet, which is also widely used in the Central Asia states, Russia is keen to employ more proactive strategies (Saunders, 2009). Also, Fossato, Lloyd, and Verkhovsky (2008) observe that in Russia reactive strategies against online activities have been mainly taken by the local authorities as revenge against activists who criticize them (p. 17) or as an "over-zealous initiative" to impress the central power (p. 53).

Yet the Russian Internet continues to evolve and function. Although the culture of blogging entered Russian cyberspace later than in Western society, its current vitality is remarkable (e.g., Gorny, 2004; Rutten, 2009).[15] Gorny (2004) defines the LiveJournal (the most popular blog-site on the Russian Internet) as "an independent collective medium influencing traditional media and cultural production at large and a significant part of Russian Internet culture" (p. 6). The researcher identifies several key features that differentiate the Russian LiveJournal from the average Western blogging patterns. Russian bloggers are older (adult professionals) and discuss serious topics online. There are also higher levels of inter-blogs connectivity. Some blogs have audiences of hundreds and even thousands and are in a position to influence online and offline media (Gorny, 2004, p. 7). Trying to understand the popularity of blogging in Russia, the Gorny concludes that the architecture of blogs fits well the Russian mentality "that attaches value to friendship and informal networks" (p. 14). Interestingly, the limits of friendship do not exceed the limits of the Russian segment of the Internet: "the Russians communicate almost exclusively with other Russians" (Gorny, 2004, p. 36). Neglecting the logic of global Internet culture, Russian-language blogs help reunite Russians across the world in the virtual Russian environment.

Goroshko and Zhigalina (2009) identify several functions of these blogs. Researchers stress close interconnection between the news published in or withheld from traditional media and the content of the blogs. Moreover, media-related events often become the focus of blog-news. Furthermore, blogs run by the known politicians and policy-makers have the ability to influence public and media agenda-setting (pp. 90–91). The launch of a personal blog by president Medvedev in April 2009 confirmed the last point. His LiveJournal blog immediately became extremely popular with visitors, thanks to its popularization by traditional media.[16]

A simultaneous vitality of Internet information and communication exchange and the intensity of official restrictions create a complex picture of the Internet evolution, bringing researchers to conflicting conclusions. Although there are clear signs of authorities' attempts to control content and interactions, there are currently only a few examples that point towards an aggressive and consistent policy of cracking down on the alternative opinions and positions expressed online (e.g., Oates, 2008; Fossato, 2009; Fossato et al., 2008; Freedom House, 2009).

Researchers, however, have spotted several developments that question wide-spread assumptions and expectations concerning the role of the Internet in Russia's political and civil life (for a more in-depth discussion, see Fossato, 2009). The most crucial among them, in our view, is the closed nature of online public expressions, their lack of mobilizing functions and goals, and disconnectedness from any potential offline civic action. This development has different manifestations. Thus Fossato et al. (2008) conclude that the Russian segment of the Internet performs informative and communicative functions, "but largely among closed clusters of like-minded users who are seldom able or willing to cooperate" (p. 53). Etkind (2006) sees LiveJournal as a kind of online "ghetto" where intellectuals find refuge from the realities of the offline world.[17] Other examples of the online community's remoteness or escape from the offline reality are noted by Rutten (2009) and Sokolova (2009). Analysis of the responses of Russia's literary blogs to a number of political events in recent history, Rutten (2009) cites "the collective silence" of many blogs to the election of Medvedev as the president in 2008. The author explains such silence by a "simple unwillingness to devote energy to a publicly staged event" (Rutten, 2009, p. 27). The issue of "non-involvement" is also noted by Sokolova (2009) in her analysis of online fan clubs. Finally, Fossato (2009) suggests viewing the Internet as an "adaptation tool" to the reality that surrounds the users and over which they have no real influence.

Paradoxically, it seems that even when online sources tend to differ from more traditional ones, the extent of their diversification remains questionable. So, Trakhtenberg (2006) observes that even when some online resources deliberately aim at presenting an alternative to the official discourse reality, they produce the same discursive oppositions of "we–they," "simple people –authorities."

Despite obvious challenges and shortcomings of the role of the Internet in Russian society, many researchers still incline to see the Internet as a crucial communication and information tool in fighting authoritarian tendencies and enhancing democracy (Beumers et al., 2009; I. Zassoursky, 2009; Dunn, 2009). Dunn (2009) believes that the Internet reinforces the creation of "a two-tier information society" where the vast majority of the population uses national television as the main (or sole) source of information, while a small minority has relatively unrestricted access to diverse sources of information via the Internet (pp. 52–53).

At the same time, Fossato (2009) stresses the crucial importance of a given society in adaptation and application of any technology. In Russia, while the Internet still offers relatively unrestricted opportunities for political and civic engagement online, citizens choose to use the Internet for other ends. In the words of Fossato et al. (2008), "the internet route is technically open, but is not much taken" (p. 8). So, Russian audiences continuously choose state-run television as the most trust-worthy source of information (Oates, 2006).

This review of Internet studies would not be complete if we do not mention that the major share of research focuses on the technological and economic aspects of this new medium, as well as the dynamics of the Internet accessibility (e.g., articles in *Perspectives to the Media in Russia: "Western" Interests and Russian Developments,* 2009). As with research into more traditional media, Internet research undergoes a differentiation of the interests and a shift away from the study of state and political factor(s) effects on the media functioning and content.

Current Shortcomings

As could be expected, the collapse of the Soviet Union has resulted in a media change analysis. Few researchers, though, posed the question of whether the *media* change was necessary or inevitable in the first place. Which attributes or components of the old media institution urgently needed to undergo such change? Another relevant question is does media change occur in a particular way. Is there any pattern in media change or is each media change country- or even outlet-specific?

Disconnection between the Soviet and post-Soviet Russian studies is more than evident. Russian media studies position themselves as a newly emerged field rather than as a continuation of the Soviet-period research tradition.[18] When in the early 1990s the sudden collapse of the Soviet Union looked like a radical break with the past—scholarly intentions to create a new field of study seemed to be, if not entirely reasonable, then at least understandable. However, today when empirical data from the region demonstrates stronger signs than expected of *continuity*, the previous break with the Soviet media studies hinders the conceptualization of continuity and empirical testing of the argument. For the same reason, it becomes difficult to evaluate how much the role of the state in media affairs has changed compared to the Soviet period.

Although factors affecting media behavior have diversified in post-Soviet media analysis, the research focus on a single factor still often dominates the inquiries.[19] There are few disputes in the scholarly literature on the relevance and priority of any given factor. Researchers continue to pursue their line of argumentation, seldom interacting with other arguments or offering critical reflections on alternative explanations. In this way, the *historical* disconnection with Soviet media studies is reinforced by the *horizontal* disconnection amongst contemporary works.[20] One example is the notion of press freedom. Until the late 1990s, scholars shared the opinion that press freedom was "the most important achievement and success of the newly born Russian democracy" (Y. Zassoursky, 1996). Although later developments caused concerns about the democratic backsliding, there are few critical reflections in the literature on early 1990s claims of the great democratic transformation and of the irreversibility of democratic change. Without such a discussion, it becomes practically impossible to establish the source of the current decline. Do we really witness a backlash in freedom of the press and democratic change in Russia, or did we *incorrectly* define the earlier stages of transition?

Theoretical diversity in Russian media studies remains low. Liberal or social responsibility democratic theories, or the concepts generated within these theories, as well as the modernization approach continue to be the most commonly used theoretical frameworks. Recent years have seen the (re-)emergence of the neo-authoritarian approach, as well as some claims of Russia's unique path. However, such works are isolated examples. Some interesting concepts have been developed in Soviet media studies yet have never received sufficient scholarly attention. That can be said, for example, about the concepts of media bureaucratisation (Inkeles, 1950/1969; Buzek, 1964), esoteric communication (Rush, 1959; Griffith, 1970), intra-elite communication (Dzirkals et al., 1982), or governmentality (Wolfe, 2005). We believe that their further development and application can enrich not only Soviet media studies but Russian media studies as well.

Studies on the effects of media have made the greatest progress in the post-Soviet domain. These studies are distinguished by their coherent and clear way of argumentation and analysis, as well as by their systematic approach and (comparative) linkage with media effects studies elsewhere. However, the greatest advantage—although also a disadvantage—of this approach is in its ability to focus (exclusively) on the effects of the media, leaving the broader social complexity outside its immediate concern. In other words, media effects studies are able, when necessary, to be media-centered. In this way, researchers can offer certain concrete explanations of media activities, but must stop short from making broader conclusions and claims. Thus, it is still an open question whether all logical explanations are sustained intact as a part of a greater (social) explanatory framework.

Comparative Approach

In our view, the utility of any approach is limited if the works on post-Soviet media continue to be exclusively country-specific. Hallin and Mancini (2004) explain the relevance of comparative analysis in the following way: "Comparative analysis makes it possible to notice things we did not notice and therefore had not conceptualized, and it also forces us to clarify the scope and applicability of the concepts we do employ" (p. 3). Similarly, Becker (2004) argues that "the analytic utility of single-state studies is limited" (p. 143). Wu et al. (1996) agree that comparative studies help "gain a better understanding and a less biased view" (p. 545). A comparative approach sheds a light on the question of the uniqueness or typicality of the Russian media. A systematic comparison between the Russian media system and media systems of other countries also allows for the development of interesting conceptual innovations towards the study of media change. This said, it is worth remembering that post-Soviet societies "present a major challenge to comparative research" (Davis et al., 1998, p. 78).

In two recent publications, Richter (2006, 2008) attempted to analyze certain media developments across *all* post-Soviet states. In his first article, Richter (2006) analyzes reasons for the weak development of self-regulatory mechanisms in post-Soviet media. The author distinguishes several common characteristics which, in his view, hinder the spontaneous evolution of a self-regulatory framework in the post-Soviet media sphere. These are: (a) fusion of legal and ethical definitions of journalism, when ethical norms of journalistic activity get incorporated in national (media) legislation; (b) inefficiency and formality of self-regulatory initiatives that emerge in specific situations and disappear unimplemented with a change of the situation; (c) state control of and state involvement into self-regulatory initiatives of journalists; and (d) top-down initiation of self-regulation by media owners, managers, and state organs. As a result, self-regulatory initiatives that emerge in such a context only reinforce journalists' responsibility before state authorities, simultaneously alienating media and society from each other (Richter, 2006, p. 59). Notably, the scholar reports such developments not only in Russia, Ukraine, or the Central Asian republics, but also in the Baltic states.

In his second article, Richter (2008) looks at media legislation in all 15 post-Soviet states, acknowledging a close link "between the progress of democracy and of the legal framework" in all cases (p. 319). Comparing statutory guarantees of media rights under different post-Soviet media laws, Richter distinguishes four groups of countries. In terms of statutory regulation, the Baltic states, Georgia, Ukraine, and Azerbaijan are regarded as having a high degree of media freedom. Armenia and Moldova have average media freedom. Tajikistan, Uzbekistan, Kyrgyzstan, and Russia have legislative frameworks that are "significantly inferior" to those of the previous two groups. Finally, Belarus, Kazakhstan, and Turkmenistan offer the least guarantee of media freedom (p. 320). Richter admits that the presence or absence of a particular law does not provide a direct guarantee of actual freedom of the media. He notes that the authorities in the post-Soviet countries often resort to what is called "soft censorship,"[21] that is—"the use by the authorities and officials of the means at their disposal to exert direct or indirect pressure on media and journalists in order to restrict the gathering, production and distribution of mass information so as to secure their own political interests and ensure lack of monitoring of their political activities" (p. 314).

In her newly published work, Oates (2008) uses the case studies of media developments in the United States, the UK, and Russia in her analysis of the key areas of political communication. The author notes that despite the seriousness of the challenges that the Western style journalism faces today its problems seem to be rather trivial in comparison with those of the Russian media sphere. Oates (2008) establishes systemic differences between all three systems but acknowledges that the Russian case falls short of practically all major norms, values, and interactions established in Western journalism.

We also see potential fruitfulness in the Russian/post-Soviet versus Central-European media systems comparisons. Starting from the early 1990s, such researchers as Splichal, Jakubowicz, Sparks, Downing, and Gross have been trying to demonstrate, both theoretically and empirically, existing similarities between Central European and post-Soviet societies and their media systems, calling on a more systematic comparative analysis. Their works are often treated as part of general post-Soviet media studies (e.g., De Smaele, 1999, 2005; Becker, 2004). We consider this to be incorrect, however. All these researchers clearly state their specialization in the Central European countries (Poland, Czech Republic, Hungary, Slovakia, Slovenia, Baltic states). Only the disregard of this fact can place them in the same group with researchers of post-Soviet media.

These researchers suggest that the comparison of post-Soviet societies with Central European countries is more productive than direct comparison with western democracies. Focusing on media developments in Russia, Poland, and Hungary, Downing (1996) develops a differentiational approach to the stages of the Soviet regime, comparing Soviet transition in the late 1980s to other transitions from dictatorship and viewing such transition as "the interrelation between the intent to liberalize within one wing of the regime and the pressure from underneath for wider freedoms" (p. 66), where democratization is "the result of a very multi-level, multi-factor interaction" (p. 81). Jakubowicz (2001, 2004) introduces a typology of media change, grouping countries in the region based on their chances of successful transition and looks at factors that trigger or obstruct such change. The author agrees that Central European countries undergo a triple (Offe, 1991), and post-Soviet countries a quadruple (Kuzio, 2001), transformation. Jakubowicz (2004) considers subjective factors (elements of social consciousness and culture) playing equally crucial roles with objective (external, societal) factors (p. 54). The author also points to the importance of the international factor (Western influence) in Central European media change (p. 61). One result of this factor, Jakubowicz notes in media laws which reflect "hybridization and adaptive borrowing from different western models" (p. 63). Jakubowicz (1994) says that neither new political elites nor the former dissidents-turned-power-holders across the region were willing to relax political control over the media, revitalizing on many occasions "… some elements of the same mobilization-transmission model that had been hallmark of the communist system" (pp. 281–282). Jakubowicz (1995) defines media policy in Central European countries as "a strange, internally inconsistent mixture of old and new elements" which combines the well-known problem of Western media with the "old problem of direct government control of the media" (p. 129). No country in the region represents a stable and finished model of transformation, sharing the features of high media politicization and a paternal-didactic style of journalism.

Sparks (2001) strongly rejects any "geographical exceptionalism" with regards to post-Soviet media systems, arguing that the most important distinctions are among regimes with a different degree of fusion between politics and economics. In another work, the author argues for "a particular kind of continuity" in post-communist media systems with some significant differences between press and broadcasting (Sparks, 1998a, p. 70). According to Sparks (1998a), there was a political revolution in Eastern Europe with an "elite" model of power transfer and without any serious popular mobilization (p. 96). Media change in these societies can be best explained through "the conflicting logics of economic and political forces rather than clearly defined values" (p. 180). Sparks argues that social continuity in the elite groups and institutional continuity of large-scale social organizations are the strongest and most striking features of transition (p. 187). On the other hand, there have been systemic changes at the level of politics that resulted in the current political fragmentation, with direct consequences for the media (p. 188). Social continuity is also seen in continued control of the media by the *nomenklatura*. Thus, although these countries have undergone serious political changes that could be called revolution, there is also a marked continuity of social structure. Media in particular continue to perform "as a mechanism for ensuring social continuity in the face of political change" (p. 106). At the same time, "none of the plans for the empowerment of ordinary citizens with regards to broadcasting policy have anywhere been implemented" (Sparks, 2001, p. 25). These can be seen as consequences of the lack of an adequate political culture shared by the main political forces and journalists (Sparks, 1998b, p. 114). Political interference with broadcasting was "a structural consequence of the more general uncertainty about power relations in post-communist societies" (Sparks 1998a, p. 137). By the same token, post-communist countries develop political capitalism where political connections are essential to enter the market and gain economic advantage (Sparks, 1999).

According to Splichal (1994), there is a lack of "any genuine democratic tradition" in Central European societies, which makes their democratization more difficult and may lead to the transformation of "emerging democracies into a new form of authoritarian system" (p. xi). The author finds that the Central European countries "... ended up in imitating West European practices in economy and polity rather than in reexamining the possible contributions of a 'Western model' to the specific situations in East-Central Europe" (p. 30). Splichal warns against quick generalizations across the region, ignoring "disturbing details." He notes that although most of these countries proceed in the same direction and share similar ideas, their democratic revolutions "... originate in different social circumstances, they differ in their acceleration (or delay), and they do not always result in equivalent consequences" (p. 24).

Splichal argues that commercialism, paternalism, and nationalism dominate the post-communist political and media scene.

Downing, Sparks, Jakubowicz, Splichal, and some other comparativists look at the processes of societal transformation and media change. Their views are similar with respect to major findings and conclusions, but differ in focus. The authors conclude that there is no clear-cut recipe in democracy replacing the previous regime in the region's countries. Post-1989/91 Central European and post-Soviet countries are neither democracies (yet) nor authoritarian systems.[22] Instead, they are undergoing a transformation that may take different shapes and speed in different countries, all the while triggering similar processes and phenomena. Along with confirmation of the chances for these countries to develop some kind of democratic society in the future, all authors are clear about the dangers of authoritarianism, vividly demonstrating that there is nothing in post-communist transition that necessitates democracy as its final product. They are also rather pessimistic (or realistic?) about the failure of radical/ideal democratic change in these societies. Overall, these researchers agree upon a set of features and developments characteristic of Central European and post-Soviet transformations. Such a list includes elements of continuity with the previous regime type, fusion of political, economic, and societal dimensions, instability and dynamism of the current processes, politicization, ideological exclusivity, and nationalism, and, imitative or mimicking practices in attempts to introduce a new system.

Conclusions

The rapidity of societal change in Russia and other former Soviet states produced a situation where "...books, articles on Soviet society, and particularly its media and communication systems, are, almost inevitably, hopelessly dated by the time they go to press" (Hogarth, 1992), because the focus of their analysis is a moving target (McNair, 1991). In a later article, McNair (2000) specifies the challenge: "Changes which took a century of capitalist development in Europe or North America have unfolded in Russia in less time than it takes to research, write and see published an academic monograph" (p. 79). Downing (1996) defines the current scholarly problem as "How to freeze flux" (p. 122).

Russian media studies constitute a rich source of unique descriptive data on dynamic transformations in the media. However, currently, it is a collection of disparate works of different quality and scope that can be seen as characteristic of an emerging field of study. Most of the attributes that would define a specialized field of study, such as terminology, commonality of research history, distinctive approaches, methodological, and conceptual consistency, are still missing.[23]

The composition of state-of-the-art inquiries, in our view, can promote consolidation of the field. Such inquiries help draw the boundaries of the field. They also help us to see what we already know about the field and what the next priorities may look like. This chapter attempts to map the field of the Russian media studies, highlighting the most important works and findings as well as discussing major challenges, shortcomings, and potential future steps.

Proper conceptualization of scientific inquiries into the nature of the Russian media seems to be the next *crucial* step towards further development and consolidation of the field. Despite the richness and often exclusivity of empirical data and analysis, the field does not present a coherent picture of the Russian media reality. There are no serious debates on the chosen approaches characteristic to other fields of social sciences (the article by Becker (2004) is one of the most successful exceptions). Apparent consensus reigns over the field. Yet disagreement and debate are urgently needed. They are essential because it makes a big difference in how we address, for example, the most recent wave of state control and repression again the media. Do we approach these developments as a matter of continuity (Sparks), as the emergence of a neo-authoritarian model (Becker), as a further evolution of a (neo-)Soviet model (Oates), or as Russia's unique path (De Smaele)? The choice of one concept over another shapes further research steps. Researchers do not need to be *unanimous* in their definitions of Russian media but need to be *clear* in our definitions.

Despite weaknesses and shortcomings of Soviet media studies, they offered exactly this—clarity of definitions. It is true that such clarity made their works vulnerable for subsequent criticism. However, the same clarity allowed the field to establish itself and expand.

Although the question of regime change has become the central focus of scholarly investigation, researchers are disproportionally preoccupied with the effects and aftermath of regime change. The works that systematically analyze and compare different periods of the Soviet media system are still to be written. Their relevance becomes more important once we realize that the majority of works on the Russian media find a continuous presence of the Soviet system's traces in post-Soviet Russian media. Thus, conclusions reached by many researchers of the Russian media on the *continuous* persistence of certain features and practices of the Soviet-period media confirm the appropriateness of a more systematic approach to Soviet versus post-Soviet media studies. Without this we would fail to identify *which* features and practices remain preserved from the previous media system and which are newly emergent.

Previous attempts to analyze and explain an emerging post-Soviet media system through the prism of democratic liberal theory have yielded contradictory outcomes. In the case of the Russian transition, application of democratic theory offered satisfactory analytical grounds as long the country's democratization did not cast significant doubts. For a while, the explanation of regime and media change through the diminished types of democracy (see Collier & Levitsky, 1997) seemed relevant. Indeed, the primary reason for the uncritical application of concepts generated from democratic (media) theory and the empirical reality of Western democracies is the uncontested assumption that Russia *is* a democracy.[24] Undoubtedly, the question of whether Russia is a democracy goes beyond the direct competence of media studies and into the (interdisciplinary) fields of political science, social change, and sociology. Nevertheless, those discrepancies which arise from the application of democratic concepts in the study of Russian media and which are reported in practically all works should alert scholars about potential pitfalls and shortcomings.

With mounting signs of authoritarian rule's consolidation in Russia, the application of democratic theory becomes highly questionable. The search for a theoretical framework to explain a *partial* transformation of the "old" Soviet media system into a post-Soviet one may become a next step in the development of a coherent approach to Russian media. The major challenge here is that the nature of the transformation and the final shape of the emerging system remain unclear. Suggestions by Becker (2004) to analyze Russia as a neo-authoritarian type or Oates (2007) as a neo-Soviet model should certainly be considered as viable alternatives to the continued application of democratic theory. Even the "unique" model of Russia's transition once suggested by De Smaele (1999) may offer interesting insights into specific features of its media system.

Annual and special reports by international (media) organizations and monitoring groups successfully combine valuable empirical findings with methodological and conceptual innovations. The regularity of these reports has made them an asset for social science research, which heavily relies on them in scholarly analysis. Finally, development of the Internet in Russia allows one to make certain conclusions on whether technological innovations are always beneficial for the country's democratization. Internet-related publications reveal the complexity of interactions between state power, traditional media, technology, and alternative sources of information. They also demonstrate how crucial the current state of society is to identify ways in which new technologies may be adopted in one or another country.

There is a clear lack of a comparative approach in post-Soviet media studies, which on many occasions would be not only suitable but also essential. The systematic conceptualization and comparative approach developed in the Central European media studies offer researchers of post-Soviet media a unique possibility to test and compare results for counties within close geographic, ideological, and cultural proximity. Although only the work of Downing (1996) includes a systematic examination of the Russian case, along with some of Central European countries, different authors consistently refer to post-Soviet societies as examples of often extreme appearances of transitional features. These examples demonstrate systematic similarities between post-Soviet and Central European transformations.

However, there should be reservations about the applicability of generalizations across the region. Nordenstreng and Pietiläinen (1999) correctly stress that "more consideration is needed in applying these models since Russia differs significantly from many other Eastern European countries" (p. 152).

Nevertheless, similarities with post-Soviet media developments found in the Central European comparative analyses lead to two important conclusions. First, the Central European comparisons look more productive than direct comparisons with Western democracies, at least as to premises of transformation processes and media change across the region. Second, such comparisons seriously challenge the validity of the uniqueness claims that presuppose a special type of development and a special conceptualization exclusive to post-Soviet societies and their media.

Notes

1. There is no agreement among researchers on *how* to call this field of media studies and *what* to include within the field. This chapter defines post-Soviet media studies as the field that analyses media developments in the former republics of the Soviet Union (with the exception of the three Baltic states). In this way we draw a distinction not only between post-Soviet media studies and Western media studies but also between post-Soviet media studies and the study of Central European media systems, as well as the study of other non-democratic and transitional systems.

2. Beumers, Hutchings, and Rulyova (2009) reflect on the use of the prefix "post-" as the intention "… to signal that, although the period (or phenomenon) in question supersedes something now defunct, it has yet fully to transcend its predecessor, and persists in bearing its trace" (p.1).

3. This analysis is limited to works published in English or Russian, with the focus on the Soviet Union and Russia. Jukka Pietiläinen of Tampere University has compiled a comprehensive list of (post-) Soviet media works available at http://www.uta.fi/~tijupie/Rusmedialiterature2008.pdf. To the best of our knowledge, only a few publications may be potentially missing from this list.

4. This overview reflects only the most general tendencies in present-day national research into Russian media. It is based on the selection of works by leading Russian media scholars. Another criterion for the selection of the works discussed here is their combination of conceptual arguments with empirical inquiries. A significant amount of media related publications is composed of general theoretical works and textbooks (not discussed in this review).

5. The first Russian translation of the *Four Theories of the Press* appeared in 1998.

6. Out of ten contributions by the Russian authors to this volume only one discusses in a systematic way the potential impacts of the consolidation of authoritarian rule in Russia on the country's media (Khvostunova & Voinova, 2009).

7. The focus on political factor remains pronounced in the studies of *regional* media in Russia (e.g., Resnianskaia, 2009; Smirnov & Dunas, 2009).

8. In addition to the OSCE decision to withdraw from the monitoring of Russia's elections due to imposed (travel) restrictions, the British Council faced a legal row with state authorities and was forced to close its offices in Russia outside Moscow (2008). Furthermore, the Educated Media Foundation (former Internews Russia) was forced to suspend its work in Russia in 2007.

9. In December 2007, the OSCE decided not to monitor parliamentary elections due to restrictions imposed on the work of observers by authorities.

10. Russia is rated as the third out of 20 countries with the highest toll of journalists' death since 1992. According to CPJ data, 50 journalists were killed in Russia between 1992 and 2009. Retrieved May 18, 2009, from http://cpj.org/deadly/index.php. Twenty out of 50 journalists were killed between 2000 and 2009. Retrieved May 21, 2009, from http://www.rsf.org/article.php3?id_article=31127.

11. The Internet statistics retrieved May 22, 2009, from http://www.internetworldstats.com.

12. The exact percentage of the Internet users in Russia slightly varies depending on the source consulted.

13. Reactive strategies are "restricting internet access, filtering content, monitoring online behavior, or even prohibiting internet use entirely" (Kalathil & Boas, 2001, p. i). Proactive strategies are defined by the authors as the guidance of the internet development and promotion of their own "interests and priorities" (p. i).

14. Retrieved May 22, 2009, from http://expert.ru/articles/2008/02/26/terentblog/.

15. According to the Russian search engine Yandex, if in 2005 on average 20 new blogs appeared every hour, in 2006 there were more than 100 new blogs appearing every 60 minutes. Retrieved May 22, 2009, from http://company.yandex.ru/news/2006/0926/.

16. Retrieved May 18, 2009, from http://www.themoscowtimes.com/article/1010/42/376462.htm.

17. Cited in Rutten (2009, p. 26).

18. There has been a certain change in the positioning of post-Soviet media studies. With the consolidation of authoritarian tendencies in Russia media researchers incline to identify more signs of continuity between Soviet and post-Soviet Russian media (see, for example, Oates, 2006; Mickiewicz, 2008). Despite more systematic consideration of similarities between Soviet and post-Soviet media, references to the research and theory of Soviet media remain infrequent.

19. Recent book by Oates (2008) attempts to resolve this shortcoming by looking at several key factors that affect news production.

20. By making this statement we do not mean that researchers fail to *cite* each other works (although this is also the case in many Russian-language publications). Few scholars go *beyond* mere reference to the works of their colleagues and into a dynamic discussion of alternative explanations.

21. Although the author does not mention explicitly whether the practice of soft censorship is used in the Baltic states, the article does not mention any example of soft censorship in those countries.

22. At least that was a conclusion when those works were written, most of which date back to the mid/late 1990s.

23. This becomes particularly visible in the poor bibliographical references of many works, particularly those by scholars in Russia.

24. In the recent years, this assumption has become increasingly contested. Nevertheless, a few media scholars questioned the democratic nature of post-Soviet transformations in Russia in 1991–2001.

References

Androunas, E. (1993). *Soviet media in transition. Structural and economic alternatives.* Westport, CT: Praeger.

Anikina, M. (2009). The youth audience in Russia: Between new and traditional media. In E. Vartanova, H. Nieminen, & M.-M. Salminen (Eds.), *Perspectives to the media in Russia: "Western" interests and Russian developments* (pp. 243–256). Helsinki, Finland: Aleksanteri Institute, University of Helsinki.

Becker, J. (2004). Lessons from Russia. A neo-authoritarian media system. *European Journal of Communication, 19*(2), 139–163.

Belin, L. (1997, November). *Politicization and self-censorship in the Russian media.* Paper presented at the national conference of the American Association for the Advancement of Slavic Studies, Seattle, Washington.

Belin, L. (2002, April). *Russian media policy in the first and second Chechen campaigns.* Paper presented at the Political Studies Association conference, Aberdeen, Scotland, UK.

Benn, D. W. (1987). Glasnost in the Soviet media: Liberalization or public relations? *Journal of Communist Studies, 3*(3), 267–276.

Benn, D. W. (1992). *From glasnost to freedom of speech. Russian openness and international relations.* London: Pinter Publishers.

Beumers, B., Hutchings, S., & Rulyova, N. (Eds.). (2009). *The post-Soviet Russian media. Conflicting signals.* London: Routledge.

Bimber, B. (1999). The internet and citizen communication with government: Does the medium matter? *Political Communication, 16*(4), 409–428.

Boretsky, R. (1998). *Bermuda triangle of television.* Moscow: Ikar.

Buzek, A. (1964). *How the Communist press works?* London: Pall Mall Press.

Collier, D., & Levitsky, S. (1997). Democracy with adjectives. Conceptual innovation in comparative research. *World Politics, 49*(3), 430–451.

Committee to Protect Journalists (CPJ). (2009). *Anatomy of injustice: The unsolved killings of journalists in Russia.* Retrieved September 15, 2009, from http://cpj.org/reports/2009/09/anatomy-injustice-preface-by-kati-marton.php

Davis, G. (1997). Tocqueville revisited. Alexis de Tocqueville and the internet. *Harvard International Journal of Press/Politics, 2*(2), 120–126.

Davis, H., Hammond, P., & Nizamova, L. (1998). Changing identities and practices in post-Soviet journalism. The case of Tatarstan. *European Journal of Communication, 13*(1), 77–97.

Davletshina, N. (2002). President of Russia in the information field of the modern media. *Social Sciences and Modernity, 2*, 59–66.

De Smaele, H. (1999). The applicability of Western media models on the Russian media system. *European Journal of Communication, 14*(2), 173–189.

De Smaele, H. (2002, March). *'In the name of democracy'. The paradox of democracy and press freedom in post-Communist Russia.* Paper presented at the ECPR Joint Sessions, Turin, Italy.

De Smaele, H. (2004). Limited access to information as a means of censorship in post-communist Russia. *Javnost/The Public, 11*(2), 65–82.

De Smaele, H. (2005, November). *Is there a life after death for four theories of the press?* A paper presented at the first European Communication Conference, Amsterdam.

Downing, J. D. H. (1988). Trouble in the backyard: Soviet media reporting on the Afghanistan conflict. *Journal of Communication, 38*(2), 5–32.

Downing, J. D. H. (1996). *Internationalizing media theory. Transition, power, culture. Reflections on media in Russia, Poland and Hungary 1980–95.* London: Sage.

Dubin, B. (2000). From initiative groups towards anonymous media: mass communications in the Russian society. *Pro et Contra, 5*(4), 31–60.

Dunn, J. A. (2009). Where did it all go wrong? Russian television in the Putin era. In B. Beumers, S. Hutchings, & N. Rulyova (Eds.), *The post-Soviet Russian media. Conflicting signals* (pp. 42–55). London: Routledge.

Dzirkals, L., Gustafson, T., & Johnson, R. A. (1982). *The media and intra-elite communication in the USSR.* RAND Report. Retrieved January 28, 2010, from http://www.rand.org/pubs/reports/2006/R2869.pdf

Ellis, F. (1999). *From glasnost to the internet: Russia's new infosphere.* New York: St. Martin's Press.

Fomicheva, I. (2009). The Russian audience in an environment of mass media competition and convergence. In E. Vartanova, H. Nieminen, & M.-M. Salminen (Eds.), *Perspectives to the media in Russia: "Western" interests and Russian developments* (pp. 199–242). Helsinki, Finland: Aleksanteri Institute, University of Helsinki.

Fossato, F. (2001, October). The Russian media: from popularity to distrust. *Current History, 100*(648), 343–348.

Fossato, F. (2006). *Vladimir Putin and the Russian television "family."* CERI: The Russia Papers. Retrieved June 10, 2009, from http://www.ceri-sciencespo.com/publica/cahier_russie/cahier_1.pdf

Fossato, F. (2009). Web as an adaptation tool? *Russian Cyberspace, 1*(1). Retrieved June 10, 2009, from http://www.russian-cyberspace.com/index.php?lng=English

Fossato, F., Lloyd, J., & Verkhovsky, A. (2008). *The web that failed. How opposition politics and independent initiatives are failing on the internet in Russia.* Reuters Institute for the Study of Journalism. Retrieved January 28, 2010, from http://reutersinstitute.politics.ox.ac.uk/fileadmin/documents/Publications/The_Web_that_Failed.pdf

Foster, F. H. (2002). Izvestiia as a mirror of Russian legal reform: press, law, and crisis in the post-Soviet era. In M. E. Price, A. Richter, & P. K. Yu (Eds.), *Russian media law and policy in the Yeltsin decade. Essays and documents* (pp. 60–88). The Hague: Kluwer Law International.

Freedom House (2009). *Freedom on the net. A global assessment of internet and digital media.* Retrieved June 10, 2009, from http://www.freedomhouse.org/template.cfm?page=383&report=79

Friedrich, C. J., & Brzezinski, Z. K. (1956). *Totalitarian dictatorship and autocracy.* Cambridge, MA: Harvard University Press.

Gaunt, P. (1987). Developments in Soviet journalism. *Journalism Quarterly, 64*(2–3), 526–532.

Gibbs, J. (1999). *Gorbachev's glasnost. The Soviet media in the first phase of perestroika.* College Station: Texas A&M University Press.

Goban-Klas, T. (1989). Gorbachev's glasnost: A concept in need of theory and research. *European Journal of Communication, 4*(3), 247–254.

Gorny, E. (2004). Russian LiveJournal: National specifics in the development of a virtual community. Retrieved June 10, 2009, from *Russian-cyberspace.org* website, http://www.ruhr-uni-bochum.de/russ-cyb/library/texts/en/gorny_rlj.pdf

Goroshko, O., & Zhigalina, E. (2009). Quo Vadis? Political interactions in Russian blogosphere. *Russian Cyberspace, 1*(1), 81–100 [in Russian]. Retrieved June 10, 2009, from http://www.russian-cyberspace.com/index.php?lng=English

Griffith, W. E. (1970). On esoteric communications. *Studies in Comparative Communism, 3*(1), 47–54.

Gulyaev, M. (1996). Media as contested power in post-Glasnost Russia. *Post-Soviet Media Law & Policy Newsletter, 29*. Retrieved February 1, 2009, from http://www.vii.org/monroe/issue29/paper.html

Haddix, D. (1990). Glasnost, the media and professionalism in the Soviet Union. *International Communication Gazette, 46*(3), 155–173.

Hallin, D., & Mancini, P. (2004). *Comparing media systems. Three models of media and politics.* Cambridge, UK: Cambridge University Press.

Hill, D., & Sen, K. (2000). The internet in Indonesia's new democracy. *Democratization, 7*(1), 119–136.

Hogarth, D. (1992). Beyond the Cold War: Soviet and American media images. *Canadian Journal of Communication, 17*(4). Retrieved June 10, 2009, from http://www.cjc-online.ca/index.php/journal/article/view/705/611

Hopkins, M. W. (1970). *Mass media in the Soviet Union.* New York: Pegasus.

Inkeles, A. (1950/1967). *Public opinion in Soviet Russia. A study in mass persuasion.* Cambridge, MA: Harvard University Press.

International Press Institute. (1959). *The press in authoritarian countries.* Zurich: International Press Institute, Survey No. 5.

Jakubowicz, K. (1994). Equality for the downtrodden, freedom for the free: changing perspectives on social communication in Central and Eastern Europe. *Media, Culture & Society, 16*(2), 271–293.

Jakubowicz, K. (1995). Media within and without the state: Press freedom in Eastern Europe. *Journal of Communication, 4*(4), 125–139.

Jakubowicz, K. (2001). Rude awakening: Social and media change in Central and Eastern Europe. *Javnost/ThePublic, 8*(4), 59–80.

Jakubowicz, K. (2004). Ideas in our heads. Introduction of PSB as part of media system change in Central and Eastern Europe. *European Journal of Communication, 19*(1), 53–74.

Jones, A. (2002). The Russian press in the post-Soviet era: a case study of Izvestia. *Journalism Studies, 3*(3), 359–375.

Juskevits, S. (2002). Professional roles of Russian journalists at the end of the 1990s. A case study of St. Petersburg Media. Unpublished thesis, University of Tampere. Finland. Retrieved February 1, 2009, from http://tutkielmat.uta.fi/pdf/lisuri00006.pdf

Kalathil, S., & Boas, T. (2001). The internet and state control in authoritarian regimes: China, Cuba, and the Counterrevolution. *First Monday 6*(8). Retrieved June 12, 2009, from http://firstmonday.org/htbin/cgiwrap/bin/ojs/index.php/fm/article/view/876.

Kalathil, S., & Boas, T. (2003). *Open networks, closed regimes: The impact of the internet on authoritarian rule.* Washington, DC: Carnegie Endowment for International Peace.

Khvostunova, O., & Voinova, E. (2009). Media changes in Russia: Threats, challenges and prospects. In E. Vartanova, H. Nieminen, & M.-M. Salminen (Eds.), *Perspectives to the media in Russia: "Western" interests and Russian developments* (pp. 187–198). Helsinki, Finland: Aleksanteri Institute, University of Helsinki.

Kolesnik, S. (1996). Content control on TV in Russia. *Post-Soviet Media Law & Policy Newsletter, 32*. Retrieved February 1, 2009, from http://www.vii.org/monroe/issue32/kolesnik.html

Koltsova, O. (2000). Who and how affects news production in contemporary Russia. *Pro et Contra, 5*(4), 82–108.

Koltsova, O. (2001). News production in contemporary Russia. Practices of power. *European Journal of Communication, 16*(3), 315–335.

Korkonosenko, S. (1997). The "new politicization" of Russian journalism, *The Global Network, 8*, 81–89.

Krasnoboka, N. (2002). "Real journalism goes underground. Internet underground." Phenomenon of online media in the former Soviet Union republics. *International Communication Gazette, 64*(5), 479–500.

Kuzio, T. (2001). Transition in post-communist states: Triple or quadruple? *Politics, 21*(3), 168–177.

Lendvai, P. (1981). *The bureaucracy of truth. How communist governments manage the news*. London: Burnett Books.

Lipman, M. (1998, November). *Political journalism in post-communist Russia*. Paper presented at the conference Russia at the end of the 20th century, Palo Alto, CA: Stanford University.

Lipman, M. (2005). Constrained or irrelevant: The media in Putin's Russia. *Current History, 104*(684), 319–324.

Lipman, M., & McFaul, M. (2001). "Managed democracy" in Russia. Putin and the press. *Harvard International Journal of Press/Politics, 6*(3), 116–127.

Livingstone, S. (1999). New media, new audiences? *New Media and Society, 1*(1), 59–66.

Manaev, O. (1993). Media autonomy, diversity versus unity and the state in transition: The Belorus experience. In O. Manaev & J. Priliuk (Eds.), *Media in transition: from totalitarianism to democracy* (pp. 151–157). Kiev, Russia: ABRIS.

Manaev, O. (1995). Rethinking the social role of the media in a society in transition. *Canadian Journal of Communication, 20*(1). Retrieved February 1, 2009, from http://www.cjc-online.ca/viewissue.php?id=35

Margolis, M., Resnick, D., & Wolfe, J. D. (1999). Party competition on the internet in the United States and Britain. *Harvard International Journal of Press/Politics, 4*(4), 24–47.

McNair, B. (1989). Glasnost, restructuring and the Soviet media. *Media, Culture and Society, 11*(3), 327–350.

McNair, B. (1991). *Glasnost, perestroika and the Soviet media*. London: Routledge.

McNair, B. (1994). Media in post-Soviet Russia: An overview. *European Journal of Communication, 9*(2), 115–135.

McNair, B. (2000). Power, profit, corruption, and lies. The Russian media in the 1990s. In J. Curran & M.-J. Park (Eds.), *De-Westernizing media studies* (pp. 79–94). London: Routledge.

McReynolds, L. (1991). *The news under Russia's old regime: The development of a mass-circulation press*. Princeton, NJ: Princeton University Press.

Melnikov, M. (2002). The major mechanisms of media regulation. Civil and ethical regulation [in Russian]. Retrieved June 15, 2009, from http://www.pressclub.host.ru/ID/eo6.shtml

Melnikov, M. (2004). The state and ethical practices in the media. *Media*

Expert, *4*(8). Retrieved June 15, 2009, from http://www.cjes.ru/publications/?pid=248&lang=rus.

Mickiewicz, E. (1981). *Media and the Russian public.* New York: Praeger.

Mickiewicz, E. (1988). *Split signals. Television and politics in the Soviet Union.* New York: Oxford University Press.

Mickiewicz, E. (1997). *Changing channels: Television and the struggle for power in Russia.* New York: Oxford University Press.

Mickiewicz, E. (2000). Institutional incapacity, the attentive public, and media pluralism in Russia. In R. Gunther & A. Mughan (Eds.), *Democracy and the media. A comparative perspective* (pp. 85–121). Cambridge, UK: Cambridge University Press.

Mickiewicz, E. (2005). Excavating concealed tradeoffs: how Russians watch the news. *Political Communication, 22*(3), 355–380.

Mickiewicz, E. (2008). *Television, power, and the public in Russia.* Cambridge, UK: Cambridge University Press.

Mickiewicz, E., & Jamison, D. (1991). Ethnicity and Soviet television news. *Journal of Communication, 41*(2), 150–161.

Mickiewicz, E., & Richter, A. (1996). Television, campaigning, and elections in the Soviet Union and post-Soviet Russia. In D. Swanson & P. Mancini (Eds.), *Politics, media, and modern democracy: an international study of innovations in electoral campaigning and their consequences* (pp. 107–128). Santa Barbara, CA: Greenwood.

Negroponte, N. (1995). *Being digital.* London: Hodder and Stoughton.

Nerone, J. C. (Ed.). (1995). *Last rights. Revisiting four theories of the press.* Urbana: University of Illinois Press.

Nordenstreng, K. (1997). Beyond the four theories of the press. In J. Servaes & R. Lee (Eds.), *Media and politics in transition: Cultural identity in the age of globalization* (pp. 97–109). Leuven, Belgium: Acco.

Nordenstreng, K., & Pietiläinen, J. (1999). Normative theories of the media: Lessons from Russia. In Y. Zassoursky & E. Vartanova (Eds.), *Media, communications and the open society* (pp. 146–159). Moscow: IKAR.

Norris, P. (2000). *A virtuous circle: Political communication in post-industrial societies.* Cambridge, UK: Cambridge University Press.

Oates, S. (2002, March). *Turning out democracy: Television, voters and parties in Russia, 1993–2000.* Paper presented at the ECPR Joint Sessions conference, Turin, Italy.

Oates, S. (2006). *Television, democracy and elections in Russia.* London: Routledge.

Oates, S. (2007). The neo-Soviet model of the media. *Europe-Asia Studies, 59*(8), 1279–1297.

Oates, S. (2008). *Introduction to media and politics.* London: Sage.

Oates, S., & Roselle, L. (2000). Russian elections and TV news. Comparison of campaign news on state-controlled and commercial television channels. *Harvard International Journal of Press/Politics, 5*(2), 30–51.

Offe, C. (1991). Capitalism by democratic design? Democratic theory facing the triple transition in East Central Europe. *Social Research, 58*(4), 865–881.

Organization for Security and Cooperation in Europe. (2004, June). Final Report on the presidential election in the Russian Federation, 14 March 2004. Retrieved June 15, 2009, from http://www.osce.org/documents/odihr/2004/06/3033_en.pdf

Ott, D., & Rosser, M. (2000). The electronic republic? The role of the internet in promoting democracy in Africa. *Democratization, 7*(1), 137–155.

Owens, B. (2002). The independent press in Russia: integrity and the economics of survival. In Ch. Marsh, & N. Gvosdev (Eds.), *Civil society and the search for justice in Russia* (pp. 105–124). Lanham, MD: Lexington Books.

Paasilinna, R. (1995). *Glasnost and Soviet television. A study of the Soviet mass media and its role in society from 1985–1991*. Helsinki, Finland: YLE, Finnish Broadcasting Co.

Panfilov, O. (2000). Putin and the media — no love lost. *East European Constitutional Review, 9*(1–2). Retrieved June 15, 2009, from http://www.cjes.ru/publications/?pid=49&lang=rus

Pasti, S. (2005). Two generations of contemporary Russian journalists. *European Journal of Communication, 20*(1), 89–115.

Pietiläinen, J. (2008). Media use in Putin's Russia. *Journal of Communist Studies & Transition Politics, 24*(3), 365–385.

Price, M. E. (1996). Book review: Glasnost and Soviet television. *Post-Soviet Media Law & Policy Newsletter*, 33–34. Retrieved February 1, 2009, from http://www.vii.org/monroe/issue33_34/book.html

Price, M. E. (2002). Law, force, and the Russian media. In M. E. Price, A. Richter, & P. K. Yu (Eds.), *Russian media law and policy in the Yeltsin decade. Essays and documents* (pp. 31–46). The Hague: Kluwer Law International.

Remington, T. F. (1985). Politics and professionalism in Soviet journalism. *Slavic Review, 44*(3), 489–503.

Remington, T. F. (1988). *The truth of authority: Ideology and communication in the Soviet Union*. Pittsburgh, PA: University of Pittsburgh Press.

Resnianskaia, L. (2009). Modern trends in the development of the regional press. In E. Vartanova, H. Nieminen, & M.-M. Salminen (Eds.), *Perspectives to the media in Russia: "Western" interests and Russian developments* (pp. 145–160). Helsinki, Finland: Aleksanteri Institute, University of Helsinki.

Resnianskaia, L., & Fomicheva, I. (1999). *Newspaper for entire Russia*. Moscow: MGU.

Resnick, D. (1998). Politics on the internet: The normalization of cyberspace. In C. Toulouse & T. Luke (Eds.), *The politics of cyberspace: A new political science reader* (pp. 48–68). New York: Routledge.

Rheingold, H. (1993). *The virtual community: Homesteading on the electronic frontier*. Reading, MA: Addison-Wesley.

Richter, A. (1995). The Russian press after perestroika. *Canadian Journal of Communication, 20*(1). Retrieved June 15, 2009, from http://www.cjc-online.ca/index.php/journal/article/view/842/748

Richter, A. (2006). Journalistic self-regulation in the post-Soviet states. *Pro et Contra, 10*(4), 50–61 [in Russian]. Retrieved June 10, 2009, from http://www.carnegie.ru/ru/pubs/procontra/vol10num4-05.pdf

Richter, A. (2008). Post-Soviet perspective on censorship and freedom of the media. *International Communication Gazette, 70*(5), 307–324.

Rodan, G. (1998). The internet and political control in Singapore. *Political Science Quarterly, 113*(1), 63–89.

Roxburgh, A. (1987). *Pravda, inside the Soviet news machine*. London: Victor Gollancz.

Rush, M. (1959). Esoteric communication in Soviet politics. *World Politics*, *11*(4), 614–620.

Rutten, E. (2009). More than a poet? Why Russian writers didn't blog on the 2008 elections. *Russian Cyberspace*, *1*(1), 25–30. Retrieved June 10, 2009, from http://www. russian-cyberspace.com/index.php?lng=English

Saunders, R. A. (2009). Wiring the Second World: The geopolitics of information and communications technology in post-totalitarian Eurasia. *Russian Cyberspace*, *1*(1), 1–24. Retrieved June 10, 2009, from http://www.russian-cyberspace.com/index. php?lng=English

Schramm, W. (1956). The Soviet communist theory. In F. Siebert, Th. Peterson, & W. Schramm (Eds.), *Four theories of the press* (pp. 105–146). Urbana: University of Illinois Press.

Selnow, G. W. (1998). *Electronic whistle-stops: The impact of the internet on American Politics*. Westport, CT: Praeger.

Semetko, H. A., & Krasnoboka, N. (2003). The political role of the internet in societies in transition: Russia and Ukraine compared. *Party Politics*, *9*(1), 77–104.

Shaikhitdinova, S. (2001). Our journalism lives according to our rational norms. In S. Shaikhitdinova & Y. Kazakov (Eds.), *On the way towards professionally correct: Russian media-ethos as the territory of search* [in Russian] (pp. 632–641). Moscow: Centre of Applied Ethics.

Siebert, F., Peterson, Th., & Schramm, W. (1956). *Four theories of the press*. Urbana: University of Illinois Press.

Smirnov, S., & Dunas, D. (2009). Competition in regional media markets: Expert assessments of press freedom in Russia. In E. Vartanova, H. Nieminen, & M.-M. Salminen (Eds.), *Perspectives to the media in Russia: "Western" interests and Russian developments* (pp. 171–186). Helsinki, Finland: Aleksanteri Institute, University of Helsinki.

Sokolova, N. (2009). Runet for television fans: The space of/without politics. *Russian Cyberspace*, *1*(1), 71–80 [in Russian]. Retrieved June 10, 2009, from http://www. russian-cyberspace.com/index.php?lng=English

Sparks, C. (with Reading, A.) (1998a). *Communism, capitalism and the mass media*. London: Sage.

Sparks, C. (1998b). Post-communist media in transition. In J. Corner, P. Schlesinger, & R. Silverstone (Eds.), *International media research: A critical survey* (pp. 96–122). New York: Routledge.

Sparks, C. (1999). CME and broadcasting in the former Communist countries. *Javnost/ The Public*, *6*(2), 25–44.

Sparks, C. (2001). Democratizations and the media. A preliminary discussion of experiences in Europe and Asia. *Javnost/The Public*, *8*(4), 7–30.

Svitich, L. (2000). *Phenomenon of journalist* [in Russian]. Moscow: Ikar.

Splichal, S. (1994). *Media beyond Socialism. Theory and practice in East-Central Europe*. Boulder, CO: Westview Press.

Taubman, G. (1998). A not-so World Wide Web: The internet, China, and the challenges to nondemocratic rule. *Political Communication*, *15*(2), 255–272.

Trakhtenberg, A. (2006). Runet as public sphere: The ideal of Habermas and reality. Retrieved June 10, 2009, from Eurasian Network of Political Research website http://www.espi.ru/Content/Conferences/Papers2006/2006razd2/Trakhtenberg. htm

Usacheva, V. (2000). Power and media in Russia: How their relationship has changed? *Pro et Contra*, *5*(4), 109–127.

Ustimova, O. (2000). Socio-political orientations of Russian journalists. *Vestnik Moskovskogo Universiteta*, Series 10, Journalism, *4*, 15–28.

Vartanova, E. (1996). Corporate transformation of the Russian media. *Post-Soviet Media Law & Policy Newsletter*, *32*. Retrieved February 1, 2009, from http://www.vii.org/monroe/issue32/vartanova.html.

Vartanova, E. (1997). The Russian financial elite as media moguls. *Post-Soviet Media Law & Policy Newsletter*, *35*. Retrieved February 1, 2009, from http://www.vii.org/monroe/issue35/vartanova.html

Vartanova, E. (1999, October). *Diversity at media markets in transition: Threats to openness*. Paper presented at the second expert meeting on Media and Open societies. Amsterdam, The Netherlands.

Vartanova, E. (2001). Media structures: changed and unchanged. In K. Nordenstreng, E. Vartanova, & Y. Zassoursky (Eds.), *Russian media challenge* (pp. 21–72). Helsinki, Finland: Kikimora Publications.

Vartanova, E. (2002). A global balancing act: New structures in the Russian Media. *Media Development, 1*. Retrieved June 15, 2009, from http://archive.waccglobal.org/wacc/publications/media_development/archive/2002_1/a_global_balancing_act_new_structures_in_the_russian_media

Vartanova, E. (2009). Russian media: Market and technology as driving forces of change. In E. Vartanova, H. Nieminen, & M.-M. Salminen (Eds.), *Perspectives to the media in Russia: "Western" interests and Russian developments* (pp. 283–301). Helsinki, Finland: Aleksanteri Institute, University of Helsinki.

Voltmer, K. (2000). Constructing political reality in Russia. Izvesitya — between old and new journalistic practices. *European Journal of Communication*, *15*(4), 469–500.

Weaver, H. (1993). *Northern news service. The origin and performance of an arctic news cooperative, 1988–1992*. Unpublished thesis, University of Cambridge. Retrieved June 15, 2009, from http://howard.weaver.org/cambridge/thesis/index.html

White, S., Oates, S., & McAllister, I. (2005). Media effects and Russian elections, 1999–2000. *British Journal of Political Science*, *35*, 191–208.

White, S., McAllister, I., & Oates, S. (2002). Was it Russian public television that won it? *Harvard International Journal of Press/Politics*, *7*(2), 17–33.

Wolfe, T. C. (2005). *Governing Soviet journalism. The press and the socialist person after Stalin*. Bloomington: Indiana University Press.

Wortman, R. (1965). How the communist press works (review). *The Journal of Modern History*, *37*(2), 281–282.

Wu, W., Weaver, D., & Johnson, O. V. (1996). Professional roles of Russian and U.S. journalists: A comparative study. *Journalism and Mass Communication Quarterly*, *73*(3), 534–548.

Zassoursky, I. (1998, January). Are Russian media dangerous for society? The outcome of concentration and politicization of capital. *Russian Journal*. Retrieved February 1, 2009, from http://old.russ.ru/journal/media/98-01-06/zasurs.htm

Zassoursky, I. (2000). The social responsibility of the media as a concept in transition. In J., van Cuilenburg & R. van der Wurff (Eds.), *Media & open societies* (pp. 48–58). Amsterdam: Het Spinhuis.

Zassoursky, I. (2004). *Media and power in Post-Soviet Russia.* Armonk, NY: M.E. Sharpe.

Zassoursky, I. (2009). Free to get rich and fool around. In B. Beumers, S. Hutchings, & N. Rulyova (Eds.), *The post-Soviet Russian media: Conflicting signals* (pp. 29–41). London: Routledge.

Zassoursky, Y. (1996). Freedom and responsibility in the Russian media. *Post-Soviet Media Law & Policy Newsletter, 32.* Retrieved February 1, 2009, from http://www. vii.org/monroe/issue32/zassoursky.html

Zassoursky, Y. (1997). Media and politics in transition: Three models. *Post-Soviet Media Law & Policy Newsletter, 35.* Retrieved February 1, 2009, from http://www. vii.org/monroe/issue35/zassoursky.html

Zhou, H. (1988). Changes in the Soviet concept of news — to what extent and why? *International Communication Gazette, 42*(3), 193–211.

CHAPTER CONTENTS

12 Media Performance, Agenda Building, and Democratization in East Africa

Yusuf Kalyango Jr.

Ohio University

Petya Eckler

University of Iowa

This chapter discusses media performance during the democratization process in the Eastern African countries of Burundi, Kenya, Tanzania, Uganda, and Rwanda, which form a regional union called the East African Community (EAC). The analysis is inspired by over 200 seminal academic studies and expert texts from various disciplines, mostly on East Africa, to assess how these governments influence media performance during their wave of democratization. The chapter examines a range of issues that demonstrate the autocratic means of building a government agenda, such as restrictive press laws, sectarianism, election malpractice, political and ethnic violence, and influence peddling. It shows how this agenda-building approach exercised by the EAC member states undercuts the contributions of the media to the democratization process. The authors demonstrate how the emergence of independent media and religious institutions in some of the EAC member states constitute the most vigilant and influential part of civil society. Further, the argument is that media performance is most successful when its agenda mobilizes citizens to challenge the structures of authoritarian rule by promoting human rights, economic empowerment, and the rule of law.

Introduction

Since the mid-1980s, a wave of democratization has spread to the regimes in Eastern Africa, particularly in Kenya, Tanzania, Uganda, Rwanda, and Burundi. During this wave, new challenges have surfaced in understanding the influence of governments on the general public and on news media performance in transitioning democracies. These challenges deserve exploration by political communication scholars and the attention of global leaders.

This chapter discusses how East African governments influence media performance during their wave of democratization. Media intimidation, suppression of information, and government propaganda still exist in East Africa (Mwenda, 2007; Rubongoya, 2007) and affect more than just the media. In emerging and transitioning democracies, citizens need free and independent media to inform them on how the societal system works, before they can participate in policy debates (Gunther & Mughan, 2000; Miller, 1991). The majority of Africans lead parochial lives with limited political understanding (Bratton, Mattes, & Gyimah-Boadi, 2005; Ocitti, 2006). The media could play a major role by helping citizens evaluate how they are governed. Thus, undue influences by regimes impact not only the media but also the process of public participation.

This chapter demonstrates how the state-owned media in all five countries still remain subjected to undue state influence and coercion, whereas the privately owned outlets remain fiscally dependent due to the undeveloped market economy. Through this domination and control by privileged elites and the government, the East African media have become guardians of state propaganda and by-products of partisan interest groups. Further, the analysis exposes another concern: that media viability, autonomy, and continued existence may potentially be hampered by these countries' legal frameworks and monitoring policies through which press freedoms are hampered. We theorize and speculate that an agenda-building tradition has occurred during this wave of democratization in East Africa and may continue to thrive if the challenges to media performance persist.

Comparative research offers unique learning prospects about the interaction of states within the international order, as mass communication, politics, interstate trade and business foster deep global connections (Joseph, Kesselman, & Krieger, 2000). Only a cross-national perspective can enhance understanding of the imperatives taken for granted within one particular system (Esser & Pfetch, 2004). Therefore, it is important to concurrently assess media performance and democratic governance in the five East African nations because of the nature of the polity and formation of each state. Some of the issues addressed here reflect problems encountered in most other sub-Saharan countries, and therefore this analysis can benefit the study of the larger African community.

The chapter is organized into six sections. The first section provides an overview of each East African country and the region's socioeconomic status and prospects for integration. The second section discusses the agenda-building perspective as a theoretical proposition for governmental influence over media performance. The next section conceptualizes democratization and the rule of law in East Africa. The fourth section reviews the literature about media performance in East Africa and specific cases of the relationship between media and government. The next section integrates media performance with the agenda-building tradition in the entire region. We demonstrate this agenda-building function as a process through which East African governments either construct the propaganda or undercut independent media performance through interference, censorship, and mobilization. We also present prospects for democratic governance and the kind of media performance required to achieve democratization in the region. The final sixth section provides a summary.

Overview of East Africa

East Africa is located on the eastern coast of sub-Saharan Africa. In the 1960s and 1970s, the term referred exclusively to the countries of Uganda, Kenya, and Tanzania, but geographers later incorporated Rwanda, Burundi, and Ethiopia. Politically, the phrase often refers to the East African Community (EAC). The EAC includes Uganda, Kenya, Tanzania, Rwanda, and Burundi and is the focus of this chapter.

EAC Political Integration

In 1967, Kenya, Tanzania, and Uganda formed the Permanent Tripartite Commission for East African Co-operation for regional collaboration (Sircar, 1990). Ten years later, the initiative failed for a lack of political will. In the 1980s, while working to divide the assets and liabilities of the commission, the three member states agreed on another attempt. In 1990, they called for a restoration of the tripartite agreement to strengthen their economic, social, cultural, political, and sustainable development and to foster the common interests of East Africans (Aseka, 2005). The heads of state set the bar high by calling for a peaceful settlement of political and ethnic conflicts among and within member states, a common monetary currency and, ultimately, a political federation.

In 1999, the Treaty for the Establishment of the East African Community was signed at the EAC headquarters in Arusha, Tanzania, and enacted a year later. Since then, the EAC has established it own Legislative Assembly, a common passport, and a new flag. In 2007, Rwanda and Burundi joined. Meanwhile, the debate continued into 2009 about the election of a common president under universal suffrage, who would have executive power over the EAC.

In addition to the EAC membership, each country has a unique political culture and ideology, which sometimes contradict the common political, economic and administrative goals. For example, Rwanda and Burundi have a Francophone legacy, while Kenya, Uganda, and Tanzania have English traditions. In late 2006, the Rwanda government changed its official language from French to English to create closer bonds with its EAC neighbors. Currently, Burundi is still debating this move.

While the creation of the EAC is supported by some scholars (e.g., see Kamanyi, 2006), others argue that it rests upon theoretically sound but practically unachievable premises (Aseka, 2005; Kaiser & Okumu, 2004). According to the critics, a political federation could cause further volatility because of variations in the military, judicial, and economic status of each country. These differences are rooted in the distinct history of each state. Uganda has emerged from a long period of civil conflict under President Milton Obote in the 1960s and 1980s and numerous coup d'états during President Idi Amin in the 1970s. Tanzania held a socialist philosophy under President Julius Nyerere in the 1960s-early 1980s, and joined capitalism under Ali Hassan Mwinyi in the 1980s. Kenya endured a long regime of monocracy and absolutism under

Presidents Jomo Kenyatta in the 1960s and 1970s and Daniel arap Moi in the early 1980s to the late 1990s. Rwanda and Burundi have had similar political and economic challenges since independence in the 1960s and rely heavily on the EAC for support for their efforts to disarm and demobilize rebel forces from neighboring Democratic Republic of Congo.

From early 2006, the member-states have debated regularly to move towards a political federation. The EAC treaty stipulates a union government with central authority and regional autonomy and distinctiveness. This future political federation is not clearly defined, however, because of disagreement about constitutional confederacy and basic justice which would supersede national laws (Kasaija, 2004). Thus far, no institutions have been created within the EAC legislative chambers to address those irreconcilable differences and facilitate the establishment of a political federation. It remains unclear how the EAC will achieve political integration given its members' profound disagreement on constitutionalism.

EAC Socioeconomic Integration

The formation of the EAC has contributed significantly to the establishment of a common economic bloc through the East Africa Customs Union. The creation of a common currency is also an ongoing debate. To foster monetary integration, the central banks had to promote convertibility of their currencies amid low volume of cross-border trade and investment flows (Podpiera & Cihaik, 2005). Economists argue that the progress towards harmonization of monetary and fiscal policy is hampered by disparities in measuring macroeconomic indicators such as inflation (Goldstein & Ndung'u, 2003).

Further, economic disparities themselves impede the harmonization of micro and macroeconomic performance. For instance, by the end of 2007, Burundi was the poorest member state with a purchasing power of less than 500 USD per capita, while Rwanda's was at 609 USD (Lawson, 2008). Tanzania's is less than 780 USD, compared to Kenya's at 1,540 USD, and Uganda's at 1,820 USD. Kenya has the largest economy in the region, although Uganda has experienced faster growth in the past 12 years. In 2007, Kenya's share of the regional GDP declined from 33% to 30%, while Uganda's grew from 32% to 33%. Tanzania's declined from 27% to 26%. Rwanda's and Burundi's share remained at 15% (Lawson, 2008).

Meanwhile, the broader economic environment remains backward and volatile. In terms of doing business and trading across borders in 2008 and early 2009, Tanzania ranked 103rd out of 181 countries, Uganda placed 145th, Kenya was 148th, Rwanda ranked 168th, while Burundi ranked 170th (World Bank, 2008). The concern is that economic disparities and poor social capital in one state could trigger a move of labor forces towards the better economy of another and thus destabilize the region. The uncertainty of this economic integration is further increased by poor fiscal discipline, corruption, and embezzlement (Kasaija, 2004). Corruption by public office holders also stifles East Africa's struggle to eradicate poverty (Transparency International, 2007).

Arguably, economic development is necessary in East Africa for a vibrant and independent media. The more industrialized and economically viable a society is, the greater the diversion of resources from investments and commercial markets to the masses through media advertisements (Przeworski, Alvarez, Cheibub, & Limongi, 2005). Consequently, if the private media and civil society are successful in securing a fair share of revenues from competing business and commercial services, they could restrict dictatorships and demand resource accountability, so that democratic institutions and a middle class are established and the regimes begin to act in general societal interest.

Overview: Kenya

The power center in Kenya is the presidency, and the first president was Jomo Kenyatta. He led the country to independence from Britain in 1963 and ruled until his death in 1978. The successor, Daniel arap Moi, ruled until 2002 through political nepotism, which solidified his influence. He was supported by his own ethnic group, the Kalenjin, and political benefactors, such as Maasai leaders, the Luo, and the Luyia. The Kikuyu people, who lived around the nation's capital, Nairobi, were mostly neglected. Ethnic fragmentation within the power structure intensified regional economic imbalances and the unequal provision of social services, as some ethnic groups used their presidential patronage to exploit government resources in the healthcare and welfare sectors.

In 1991, Kenya started a new era of transition to democratic governance, when Moi's totalitarian regime was pressured by civil society and donor governments to re-introduce multiparty electoral democracy. In December 1992, the country held the first national elections since independence (Klopp, 2001). However, the 1992 and 1997 elections were marred by malpractices, including impropriety in providing opportunities for all presidential contestants and sporadic clashes between supporters of the incumbent and the opposition parties. Moi, the then-incumbent, won both elections amidst the opposition's claims for fraud (Klopp, 2001). In 2002, Kenyans affected a regime change in multiparty national elections by electing Mwai Kibaki as president. This was the first time an incumbent had been democratically unseated by the opposition (Anderson, 2003).

Overview: Tanzania

Tanzania is a union of the mainland Tanganyika and the islands of Zanzibar and Pemba. It has had four presidents since 1961, when Tanganyika received its independence from Britain. The colonial rulers left behind a multiparty tradition, but in 1964 then-president Julius Nyerere established a single-party system (Pratt, 1976). A major event in Nyerere's presidency was the issuing of the Arusha Declaration in 1967, which called for the establishment of social-ism, and a focus on human development and self-reliance (Smith, 1998). In 1975, Nyerere strengthened the legitimacy and supremacy of the party over parliament and the government through constitutionally establishing the Tan-zanyika African National Union (TANU) as a leading institution (Pratt, 1999), which controlled the politics of the mainland throughout his rule. Two years later, TANU transformed into the party Chama cha Mapinduzi (CCM) and continued its domination.

The first multiparty elections occurred in 1985 after Nyerere resigned. They ushered in Ali Hassan Mwinyi, who was reelected in 1990 and retired in 1995. Benjamin Mkapa became the third president, again through multiparty elec-tions, and completed two terms in 2005. The current president is Jakaya Kik-wete, former minister of foreign affairs under Mkapa and chosen by him to head the ruling CCM party. Kikwete won 80% of the national vote despite the decreasing popularity of CCM.

Tanzania now has 12 political parties, but CCM has governed since inde-pendence. Opposition leaders have argued that the country was experiencing a de facto one-party system and a reversal to the consolidation of democracy (Hossain, Killian, Sharma, & Siitonen, 2003). CCM controls government resources and uses them to reward supporters with state posts and loans. All opponents have been destroyed politically through media rhetoric by the sup-porters of the president (Ahluwalia & Zegeye, 2001). This dominance has begun to diminish in the last 15 years due to the work of independent journal-ists and organized critical debates on current affairs talk shows. In the lead up to Jakaya Kikwete's election in December 2005, Tanzanians had continu-ously used the media to voice displeasure with the ruling party over rampant unemployment, corruption, mismanagement of public funds, and the overall economic stagnation. In early 2006, after the presidential elections, the gov-ernment weakened press freedom laws to demobilize and suppress the callers who had been politically vocal.

Overview: Uganda

Uganda has gone through several political changes since the current president, Yoweri Museveni, and his National Resistance Army (NRA) seized power from General Tito Okello Lutwa's government in 1986. Before that (1971–1979), the country was under the military dictatorship and despotic tyranny of President Idi Amin Dada (Rubongoya, 2007), who used the military to instigate vio-lence against real and imagined opponents. During President Milton Obote's reign (1980–1985), the regime continued the militarization of the state as a way of sustaining the president's political fortunes (Kabwegere, 1995). Yet, Obote allowed multiparty politics and rose to power through a rigged general election. The recognition of political contestation and election of leaders under multiparty activities during Obote's regime in the early 1980s were seen as the first wave of democratization.

The second wave of democratic transition in Uganda started during Museveni's leadership. In the late 1980s–1990s, Museveni imposed legal restrictions on multiparty activities to suppress political dissent over his stronghold on the presidency. Parallel to that though, local institutions with elected village councilors were created and parliament was restored, thus allowing for opposing views in parliamentary debates (Joshua, 2001). Although the country has transitioned to multiparty electoral democracy, scholars and international observers have criticized its inconsistencies of governance (Kannyo, 2004; Mugisha, 2004).

One such contradiction occurred in 2005 when Museveni reached the constitutional two-term limit on elected office. He aggressively lobbied the parliament to run a referendum amending the constitution and lifting the presidential term limit (Afako, 2006). The referendum was subsequently supported by voters. This change resumed multiparty competition, while allowing Museveni to run for the presidency again. Another contradiction came as he continued to influence the legislative assembly, which rubberstamps all bills and constitutional changes (Oloka-Onyango, 2004). The president also exercises significant influence over the judiciary and parliament. Yet another democratic incongruity is the excessive participation of the military in civilian governance, as commanders serve in the cabinet, parliament, and other institutions.

Overview: Rwanda

Unlike the EAC founding members Kenya, Tanzania, and Uganda, which trace their colonial past to Britain, Rwanda's goes back to Germany and later Belgium, the latter of which influenced its Francophone background. Rwanda's ethnic composition, politics, history, culture, and economy are quite similar to Burundi's. In both countries, for instance, the colonial rulers treated the minority Tutsi ethnic groups as superior to the Hutus, and politically empowered them to subjugate the Hutu majority (Manirakiza, 2005).

While the 1994 genocide is often seen as a watershed, other smaller-scale clashes have dated back to the 1950s. The culmination of the recurrent ethnic violence came when a plane carrying President Juvenale Habyarimana and Burundi President Cyprien Ntaryamira was shot down in 1994. The Tutsi were blamed (Chalk, 1999; Prunier, 1995), and Hutu civilians, the national army, the militia, and the Presidential Guard were mobilized to kill all Tutsis and moderate Hutus (Schabas, 2000). Local officials orchestrated the genocide through the mass media (Gourevitch, 2000; Prunier, 1995), which disseminated war propaganda and called this extermination a "self-defense response" (Rotberg & Weiss, 1996).

After the genocide, the Tutsi-led Rwanda Patriotic Front (RPF) rebel group, which ousted Habyarimana's army and government, named a Hutu politician, Pasteur Bizimungu, to preside over the government, so the Hutu majority could become part of the "new Rwanda" (Gourevitch, 2000). The RPF leader, Major General Paul Kagame, became vice president and in 2000 assumed the presidency after Bizimungu resigned. The resignation triggered protests from leading Hutu politicians and members of parliament when Bizimungu accused Tutsi legislators of selectively persecuting Hutu politicians. Since then, President Kagame has condemned his opponents for instigating ethnic anxieties and his RPF government has suspended political party activities and forcibly co-opted political opponents into his party. Kagame held the first presidential elections since the genocide in 2003 and received 95% of the votes.

Overview: Burundi

When Burundi gained its independence from Belgium in 1962, the new post-colonial government established a constitutional monarchy, which was over-thrown 4 years later by the military, and a series of one-party regimes followed until 1992. Throughout those 30 years under a Tutsi party called the Union for National Progress (UPRONA), internal conflicts transformed into armed rebellions between the authoritarian Tutsi governments and the militia groups led by the Hutu opposition (Jennings, 2001). Much of the oppression in Burundi was done by the Tutsi minority on the Hutu majority; whereas in Rwanda, the Hutu majority suppressed the Tutsi minority until 1994.

The socioeconomic struggles in the 1990s resulted from political instability from the ethno-political fragmentation (Ould-Abdallah, 2000). The 1990s saw politically motivated executions based on ethnic identity and assassinations of Hutu politicians (Ould-Abdallah, 2000). The assassinations of two Hutu presidents, Melchior Ndadaye in 1993 and Cyprien Ntaryamira in 1994 (the latter was in the plane with Rwandan President Habyarimana), led to mass uprisings, civil unrests, and unlawful detentions (Reyntjens, 2004). The Burundi government answered with violent retaliation (Ould-Abdallah, 2000; Reyntjens, 2006).

President Pierre Buyoya tried in early 2000 to mitigate the escalating ethno-political conflicts by inviting former president of South Africa, Nelson Mandela, to mediate a peace agreement, which resulted in signing the Arusha Peace Accord (Neethling, 2003). Yet, clashes continued in some areas and perpetuated a cycle of violence.

Consequent attempts to democratize Burundi did not yield the stability and peace Buyoya wished for (Neethling, 2003). He adopted a new constitution, which aimed to restore democratic principles, but generated hostility from warring parties who did not participate in drafting it (Gahama, Makoroka, Nditije, Ntahombaye, & Sindayizeruka, 1999). Nevertheless, the country slowly progressed towards reconciliation and stability; local and national elections were held in 2005, the first since 1993.

The above overview demonstrates the various macro-level challenges faced by the EAC and the individual advances and problems of the member states. Despite the vast differences in each county's development, a common theme is the strong governmental control on political life, which maintains a prevalent and often absolute agenda on society, the media, and civic life. This approach is examined through the concept of agenda building in the following section.

Agenda Building as a Government Influence

Most literature on Africa shows that the media provide political leaders with an outlet for their agendas, rather than engage in independent reporting (Hyden, Leslie, & Ogundimu, 2002). This finding relates to the theory of agenda building, which addresses who influences the media's agenda. For some scholars, agenda building is especially appropriate for comparative analysis because "it occurs in every political system from the smallest to the largest, from the simplest to the most complex, while at the same time there are important variations in its form and structure" (Cobb, Ross, & Ross, 1976, p. 127).

This theory is pertinent to media performance and democratization in the EAC because the governments have not only controlled and dominated the discourse on national media for almost four decades, but have also used the media for state propaganda. For instance, after independence in the early 1960s, the new regimes demanded and received favorable coverage from the national media. They appointed ministers of information, whose duties included controlling the media and ensuring that journalists subscribed to their agenda of unity, solidarity, and development (Mamdani, 1996).

While traditional agenda-setting research has focused on how the media influence public opinion, agenda building examines what contingent conditions affect this process (Johnson et al., 1996). Such contingent conditions come from news editors, policy makers, PR practitioners, and the interests of audiences (Sallot, Cameron, & Lariscy, 1997; Sheafer & Weimann, 2005; Walters, Walters, & Gray, 1996). Political actors have also been identified as influencers but in varying degrees (Wanta, Stephenson, Turk, & McCombs, 1989), which has suggested the existence of intervening variables, such as the personality of the politician (Wanta et al., 1989), the nature of the issue and real-world events (Johnson et al., 1996; Walgrave & Van Aelst, 2006). Many Western scholars have placed increasing attention on news sources and real-world events (conflicts or disasters) as key determinants of media agendas (Berkowitz, 1987; Johnson et al., 1996).

Individuals in power, who are also major news sources, build sociopolitical ideas they propagate through the press, and the press imparts them as salient issues to the public (Weaver & Elliot, 1985). In emerging democracies like the EAC member states, government sources influence, and in extreme cases control, both the media messages and the type of issues debated by the public on state-owned media. However, one can argue that media ownership and the rule of law are also intervening factors that shape the selection of issues on media and public agendas. For instance, Kalyango (2008) found that governments in Africa build an agenda based on regional ethno sectarianism to maximize their political power by taking advantage of citizens who are less educated and who lack basic understanding of their political rights.

Three different conceptual models of agenda building have been identified (Cobb et al., 1976). The first model, outside initiative, relates to instances when issues arise at the non-governmental/civic level, reach the public agenda and, finally, the formal government agenda. The second, mobilization model, is said to occur when politicians want to move an issue from their formal agenda to the public, as when newly accepted political doctrines need to be implemented in society. The third model, inside access, is proposed to occur when groups or individuals with close access to the government initiate issues and place them on the formal agenda but without making the issue public. The authors cautioned that these models were conceptual rather than empirical and a different combination of them may appear under various circumstances. The mobilization model is most applicable to East Africa's media performance. The EAC member states have controlled the media since the 1960s and thus have mobilized support for their antidemocratic propaganda and autocratic agenda. These practices have continued during the transitional democratization period.

This discussion has touched on four different agendas presented in the literature primarily from Western media systems: media, public, source, and policy. The first two are typically the focus of agenda-setting research as it relates primarily to the Western media systems (e.g., McCombs & Shaw, 1972). In East Africa however, the agenda-setting function is not the primary vehicle for driving issue salience, because the state-owned media do not autonomously investigate and disseminate new information to the public without having the content filtered by state-appointed gatekeepers in the news organization. Source agenda pertains to how newsmakers try to influence the media, which is studied by agenda-building research (e.g., Johnson et al., 1996). The last type, policy agenda, pertains to how media coverage and public opinion influence political decision making (Cobb et al., 1976).

One of the few agenda-building studies on Africa (Wanta & Kalyango, 2007) examined the role of the four agendas in a political communication process involving 20 African nations, including the five EAC member states. They found support for a source agenda in that President George W. Bush successfully influenced the *New York Times'* coverage of the African nations through his public statements. The study also found a connection between the *New York Times'* media agenda and the U.S. administration's policy agenda when the media used a terrorism news frame. The more coverage a country received linking it to terrorism, the more U.S. foreign aid went to the country to fight terrorism. The authors speculated, however, that the relationship between media and policy on the issue of terrorism could be a result of a particularly strong source agenda, where the president was able to influence both the media and the policy of his administration in the direction of his public statements.

Considering the political culture of the EAC explicated throughout this chapter, the agenda-building effects on the media could be stronger compared to the Western media because of the poorer training of local journalists and the stronger influences of autocratic leaders. In East African societies, many untrained journalists are still learning about the values of democratic governance and thus could be unaware of the influences they are under. East African presidents have long sustained their political legitimacy by exploiting citizens' lack of understanding of their political rights to participatory democracy

(Weiler, 1997). In addition, the proposed interrelatedness and dynamic among the media, public and policy agendas could be stronger than in Western societies because of the larger influence of the governments' policy agenda over the media and the public and the tight control that local leaders exercise on both media and public.

Democratization and Rule of Law

The complexities of the theoretical explication of democratization call for exploring the concept through the lens of the East African experience. We undertake this to make a case for agenda building as a theory that explains how the governments influence the media to report about the democratization process. The transformation of regimes in East Africa from military juntas to civilian dictatorships and, ultimately, to multiparty political systems cannot be fully explained by the conceptualization of democracy from the Western perspective. Therefore, we explore an alternative conceptualization from the East African experience. The first concept is the transition stage. In the EAC, transition refers to the process of dissolving authoritarian regimes into political contestation and thereby enabling citizens and groups to compete for political power and economic resources under some form of an egalitarian system. The second concept is economic and political liberalization. It refers to the enabling of basic rights that protect citizens from arbitrary coercion or censure of their freedoms to associate with groups and other citizens, communicate via mass media, and express individual or collective dissent. It also refers to the endorsement of wealth accumulation and competition in commerce, and the pursuit of modernization through mass appeal. The final concept is the rule of law, which we explicate later in this section. In East Africa, the democratization process has been slow because it threatens the authority and autocracy of the regimes.

Diamond (1999) and Sen (1999) offered differing definitions and conceptualizations of the democratization process. While Sen saw democracy as a universal value, which all nations of the world will ultimately embrace, Diamond emphasized the attaining of successive free, fair, meaningful, and competitive elections before making a judgment about its universality. O'Donnell and Schmitter (1986) and Shin (1994) argued that democratization should be based on gradualism, moderation and compromise. Huntington (1991) conceptualized democracy as a dichotomous variable, with democratic qualities based on fragility of legitimacy, stability of alternation, and sovereignty of the people. Although this is beyond the scope of our chapter, it is important to point out Huntington's observation that sometimes authoritarian regimes that do not democratize can nonetheless become liberalized, more open and competitive, and less repressive.

Freedom House's reports on freedom in the world provide a rough comparative overview of the democratic developments in the five countries, as indicated in Figure 12.1.

Political Rights in the EAC

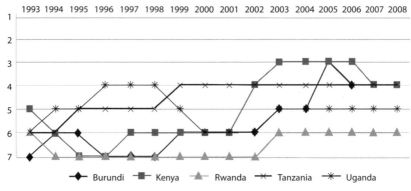

1 = the most free; 7 = the least free

Figure 12.1 Indicators of political rights freedoms in the East African community. Source: Freedom House (2009).

Some African scholars have argued that democratization in sub-Saharan Africa did not start with Huntington's (1991) third wave of democratization between 1974 and 1990. Mamdani (1996) and Kirschke (2000) claimed that democracy had deeper roots, as Africans organized and governed themselves starting with the traditional local chiefs and ending with the administrative political rulers. Democratization in Africa began as a political struggle within and against the nation-state during colonial days (Ocitti, 1999). This resistance was enforced by tribal-clannish factions and other domestic forces, such as labor struggles and peasant groups. They engaged in political violence with the post-colonial dictatorships in the 1960–1980s and fought for freedom and self-determination (Mamdani, 1996).

In East Africa, the struggle for democracy has always been accompanied by violence (Klopp, 2001). Violent political action is particularly common as ethnic groups begin to suspect the ruling clan or political elite of being unrepresentative and lose hope for peaceful redress of grievances (Snyder, 2000). Such disaffection has been evident since colonial days, as social or communal groups were targeted, estranged, and completely excluded from power (Crescenzi, 1999; Klopp, 2001). Mamdani (1996) noted that throughout postcolonial regimes, the informal civil society demanded the rule of law, liberalization, and free expression, thus achieving a degree of normalcy. These forces, which emerged before political parties in East Africa, expressed popular sentiments through violence and thus influenced governments to be more responsible (Kannyo, 2004; Young, 2002).

The rule of law works in conjunction with other concepts of democracy and ensures political rights, instruments of accountability, and civil liberties, and thus leads to equality of all citizens. Hayek (1972) defined the rule of law as a reflection that a government is held accountable for all its actions. This means that societies under the rule of law have sufficient individual liberties and citizens enjoy equal rights, protection, and privileges from the state. For Henderson (2003), an independent judiciary, free media, and an informed and engaged civil society are crucial for achieving the rule of law. According to Mahoney (1999), societies are more likely to be stable democracies and achieve fast economic growth if they enjoy the rule of law. Deutsch (1977) and Mahoney (1999) argued that respect for the rule of law contributes to international order. Weak states adopting the rule of law pacify society during institution-building. The rule of law guarantees that a regime's power and influence are legitimately exercised according to openly disclosed rules and acts enforced on established procedure (Deutsch, 1977). In this chapter, the rule of law is defined as a set of formal rules and principles of democratic governance and the existence of leaders who exercise political authority to safeguard the constitution and to govern by those rules and rights.

Rule of Law in East Africa

In East Africa, state actors and law enforcement agencies refer to the rule of law in these broad terms: constitutionalism, a well-functioning judicial system, and respected or sufficient legal policy (Schmitz, 2006). East African leaders do not address or consider contemporary political events, respect for civil and political rights and other political virtues as tenets of the rule of law (Shivji, 1995). In most cases, their characterization is so lax that it allows contradictory interpretations of the law between the enforcement agencies and the judiciary.

Article 7(2) of the EAC Treaty talks about the rule of law and preservation of human rights, but it is unclear how East African governments enforce it. The challenges for improving the rule of law seem to be affected by the pace and scope of democratization. In light of the growing but contested political federation, Kamanyi (2006) outlined some key necessities for the restoration of the rule of law in the EAC: presumption of innocence, the right not to be imprisoned without trial, equal rights before the law, and independence of the judiciary. However, each EAC member state has faced its own challenges in applying these principles. These are briefly outlined below.

In Uganda for instance, the police regularly detain suspects beyond the constitutional limit of 48 hours (Schmitz, 2006). The Human Rights Watch of 2005 reported that torture had become commonplace. The government has come under increased criticism for the political instability instigated by the Uganda police. Press reports and election observers have said that the police and military have dispersed opposition campaign rallies, beat up and detained followers, and sometimes charged them with treason (Baker, 2004). More than 120 politicians and independent local journalists have been charged with engaging in or supporting terrorism since the Ugandan government passed the

2002 Anti-terrorism Act (Mwenda, 2007). This has impeded civilians from freely engaging in the electoral process.

Tanzania has also suffered episodes of country-wide political violence. In the late 1990s, citizens became agitated by the increased arrest of human rights activists and some journalists on weak charges of being idle and disorderly. The disintegration of civil order and collapse of the rule of law increased political dissatisfaction, violence, and insecurity (Kaiser, 2000a). Press reports alleged that President Benjamin Mkapa's government overlooked the situation when the administration of justice was based on status-quo patronage. The Chama Cha Mapinduzi (CCM) party enjoyed police protection for the atrocities committed in line with their political activities (Kaiser, 2000b). When some CCM bureaucrats faced criminal charges for killings and corruption, they were released for lack of evidence. During the 2001 general elections at the island of Pemba, armed security forces massacred more than 30 opposition demonstrators who demanded new presidential elections. Human rights nongovernmental organizations (NGOs) gathered eyewitness testimonies but the government never pressed charges. During and soon after the past two election cycles in 2000 and 2005, many citizens believed to be antagonistic to the CCM were arrested for several days (Ahluwalia & Zegeye, 2001).

In Kenya, violent outbreaks during the presidential and parliamentary elections of the late 1980s–1990s killed hundreds and displaced thousands (Brown, 2003). Moi's regime (1980s–1990s) held suspects without trial (Steeves, 2006). During the second and third multiparty elections, opposition supporters suffered constant violations of human rights by the Kenya African National Union (KANU; Brown, 2003). Dozens were killed and hundreds arrested during outbreaks of ethnic violence (Brown, 2003). Many of these deaths have remained unsolved, and international human rights advocates attempting to file these cases in the courts have been threatened with deportation. A 2005 annual Human Rights Watch report found widespread use of excessive, unnecessary, and lethal force on civilians by the police during arrest and under detention.

In Rwanda, the ethnic propaganda of the Habyarimana government inspired political violence, while the regime destroyed the judicial infrastructure and killed most moderate judges in 1994 (Werchick, 2003). Lawmakers and the state police were unconcerned or even encouraged the ethnic killings (Mamdani, 1996). In the post-genocide era, the government set up a tribunal to prosecute the offenders, which was supervised by the International Criminal Justice based in The Netherlands. But the Rwandan government's agenda to build the legitimacy of the command justice, an institution meant to promote peace and reconciliation between the Hutu and Tutsi, instead politicized perpetrators as Hutus and victims or survivors as Tutsis. Consequently, in the first decade of the tribunal, Kagame's refusal to prosecute some of the RPF rebel commanders accused of war crimes generated the notion of an ethnocratic regime (Tiemessen, 2004). Since 2000, the Kagame government has used the national media, especially radio and television, to dismiss allegations from the opposition that Tutsi politicians and army receive state-backing to subjugate the majority Hutu peasants.

Since Rwanda and Burundi share a common border and are closely linked ethnically, the ethno-political events in one often influence and precipitate similar reaction in the other (Gahama et al., 1999). The 2000 Arusha Accord, spearheaded by Nelson Mandela, led to the drafting of a new constitution and a 2005 referendum. It established a democratic foundation, while allowing for the development of a multi-party system. The legal system is based on both traditional tribal customs and the German and French models. One of the major challenges is the administration of justice for political prisoners (Reyntjens, 2006). The Tutsi-dominated military and police have detained and imprisoned suspects for being sympathizers of armed rebellion. By late 2006, there were more than 5,500 political and petty crime prisoners still awaiting trial or judicial review (Reyntjens, 2006; Van Eck, 2004).

The examples provided here demonstrate the breakdown of the rule of law within the EAC members due to uncertainties in the state leaders' governance. This governance has been conditioned by ethnic and regional identities, thereby causing injustices and the proliferation of armed insurrections at the expense of the majority of ordinary citizens. Consequently, throughout the 1990s, the governments of Rwanda, Burundi, and Uganda stayed committed to ensuring that they monopolize and cling to power using military control and occupation of key political positions. The governments resorted to intimidation and draconian laws, which suffocated civil society and left its imprint on the consciousness of the people to accept permanent military rule. In the late 1990s, the governments directed their attention to the liberalized mass media, which had started exposing state corruption, social injustice, and state autocracy. Since 1996, the predicaments in Rwanda, Uganda, and Burundi triggered civil disobedience and unrest, which led to rapid delegitimization of their military governments; while in Kenya and Tanzania, civil societies opposed the military states' engagement in politics, inspired by their neighbors.

Media Performance in East Africa

Most communication literature emphasizes that the professional role of the news media is to advance democratic governance and the welfare of society. Recent scholarship in political communication and journalism has also debated the professional values and ideologies of journalists in relation to democratization (Bennett, 2004; McChesney, 2000; Ocitti, 2006). Hughes and Lawson (2004) provided some convincing evidence that the news media are either predominantly an entity of major concentrated commercial interests in the industrialized world or owned and controlled by governments in the developing countries. Accordingly, most literature from the developing nations of

Latin America and Africa shows that media ownership and partisan bias in political news coverage have generated concerns for the legitimacy and independence of the media and have eroded public trust in emerging democracies (Hallin & Papathanassopoulos, 2002; Lawson, 2002).

A major obstacle for the freedom and professionalism of the African press is the conflict between reliance on official sources and the agenda-building practices of these sources and the state agencies behind them (Bourgault, 1995). Evidence from media scholars (McQuail, 1992) and independent observers, such as The Freedom Forum, suggests that the news media rarely resist the framework provided by government officials. The reliance on authoritative and often government-supported sources presents a daunting challenge for the unsophisticated audience, which is ill equipped to critically evaluate political news.

On the other hand, state-owned news media in Africa have been subject to censorship and direct political control for years (Ochs, 1987; Wanyande, 1996). In the dawn of post-colonialism, the media engaged in self-censorship for self-preservation as part of development journalism (Faringer, 1991). Some African states outside the EAC still endorse development journalism, the basic premise of which is that the government must mobilize the news media for nation building to increase political consciousness and further economic development (Faringer, 1991; Nyamnjoh, 2005). Critics see development journalism as another form of governmental PR but proponents call it an opportunity for investigative reporting (Ogan, Fair, & Shah, 1984). In practice, the idea was often used to manipulate the media into accepting and promoting government propaganda. Thus, although development journalism is not synonymous with self-censorship per se, the two often coexist in the same media systems.

Since 1963, the Kenyan governments have curtailed press freedom by requiring the state-owned and privately owned media to embrace nationalism, nation building, and project the head of state as a symbol of the nation (Heath, 1997; Maloba, 1992). President Julius Nyerere of Tanzania also developed a social media policy in the late 1960s, which placed responsibility with the media to strictly preserve traditional African values of collective communism, self-reliance, socialism, sharing, and hard work (Grosswiler, 1997). The limited press freedom in Tanzania and Kenya persisted until the mid-1990s, when the two countries liberalized the communication sector. Meanwhile, various regimes in Uganda until the mid-1990s used intimidation, prosecution, and imposing of an advertisement ban on the privately owned press as a means of curtailing press freedom (Robins, 1997). In the early 1960s, the Rwandan and Burundian governments imposed stiffer regulations on national broadcasting and state newspapers to focus their coverage on educational information about health care delivery, morality, national peace, and food security (Frere, 2007). That was before the early 1990s when the media in both countries were used to fuel sectarianism as a means of dividing the population along ethnic lines.

Performance and use of sources in East Africa are related to the media's professional norms and editorial policies created partly by the type of ownership. Media have been classified as state- or privately owned (Bourgault, 1995; Hyden et al., 2002; Norris, 1997). Except for Kenyan newspapers, all news media in East Africa were initially owned and controlled by the state. This continued until the international community, spearheaded by the International Monetary Fund and the World Bank, pressured these governments in the early 1990s to liberalize the media under the Structural Adjustment Programs (Ocitti, 2006). Through these programs, some of the state-run media organizations turned into publicly owned corporations or were completely privatized. Still, the regimes continued to own and control the most influential outlets in each country, mainly the national television and radio. Consequently, media ownership in East Africa has been central to the agenda-building process (Kalyango, 2008).

Commercial media systems also have their shortcomings. Curran (1991) and Norris (1997) argued that in a capitalist society, the private news media respond to the interests of the marketplace rather than the expectations of the public and government officials. Private ownership in North America has been criticized for encouraging the tabloidization of the news under the pressure of market forces (Esser, 1999; McChesney, 2000).

Not every aspect of the media in East Africa, however, is sanctioned by the government. Some studies have found that a few independent media outlets frequently cover citizen oppression (Hyden et al., 2002) and have consistently taken a strong position to report all aspects of a failed state. The independent media provide political opponents and civic activists a platform to convey their message (Zafliro, 2000). The regime counteracts that by using its influence directly through material inducements or by disseminating favorable messages through the state-owned media (Lush, 1998).

Media in Kenya

Presently, Kenya is considered EAC's regional center for mass communication and international news media. It has allowed the emergence of independent journalistic enterprises, but the regimes since President Moi have continued to intimidate and influence most news media outlets, particularly radio and television (Klopp & Zuern, 2003). The privately owned radio stations, for instance, are licensed to broadcast only in designated zones, while only the state-owned Kenya Broadcasting Corporation (KBC) broadcasts to the entire country. More than 80% of radio frequencies have been assigned arbitrarily to friends of the political establishment (Matende, 2005). In other instances, the judiciary has restricted press freedom by the imposition of heavy fines on journalists and news outlets and through the licensing and accreditation of journalists (Matende, 2005).

A few independent news outlets, such as the *Nation* newspaper, advocated for civil liberties in the 1990s and brought the discussion of nepotism and authoritarianism to the forefront. The relative press freedom in the 1990s provided a considerable outlet for the voicing of political dissatisfaction, but this press coverage was quelled by intimidation and journalists' accreditation in 2000. Accredited journalists must adhere to professional standards set by the government and failure to do so leads to suspension from practice.

The media under the current president, Mwai Kibaki, is less free compared to his predecessors, Moi and Kenyatta. Through his first term in office, Kibaki kept silent when his political party was discussing the Kenya Media Bill in parliament, which sought to regulate reckless and irresponsible journalism. The bill obliged journalists to disclose all sources and be accredited before they can practice, which also required the payment of an annual fee. Hundreds of journalists, diplomats, and members of civil society, such as human rights groups, protested the new media bill. Kibaki was finally forced to reject the repressive clauses in late 2007. This was a critical victory and a good indication that a vibrant civil society with fairly critical independent media can succeed in mobilizing the masses against repression. The civil activism and adversarial press have begun to unravel the presidential monocracy and absolutism in Kenya.

The news media played a major role in recent presidential elections. In 2002, they were critical of the incumbent's candidate pick, while the opposition parties all united behind one opponent, Kibaki. The media were called antidemocrats and protagonists of anti-regime protests by the incumbent party and threatened with imprisonment, which curtailed their independence, and led to self-censorship (Kagwanja, 2003). Eventually, the opposition's candidate Kibaki won with a landslide of 62%. Then, in the next presidential elections in December 2007, the outcome between the incumbent Kibaki and the opposition party was split along ethnicity. Accusations of impropriety followed and violence erupted across Kenya. Most independent broadcast media were temporarily closed. The minister of information banned live broadcasts and threatened independent journalists who criticized the government for the violence, while simultaneously using state-owned media to disseminate non-violence news that promoted the government's agenda.

Media in Tanzania

Press freedom in Tanzania was growing between 2000 and 2005, although access to information was still controlled by public officials such as the police, city or district councilors (Kambenga, 2005). The media in Zanzibar are more limited because of the hostility of the local political leadership. Since independence in 1964, politicians there have continued to suppress newspaper and radio journalists who expose their abuse of power (Ochs, 1987). In a country with more than 100 community and major newspapers in five different languages, including 14 major dailies and 59 weeklies, authorities have continued to suppress each one of them. Despite the existence of some 30 radio stations and 20 commercial TV stations, the electronic media cover no more than a quarter of the country and journalists are subjected to constant harassment (Kambenga, 2005).

The press belonged exclusively to the CCM party and government leadership until the mid-1990s. After the liberalization of the press in 1995, it began to increasingly expose political corruption and misappropriation of public and donor funds. But during President Hassan Mwinyi's era (1985–1995) these reports were regularly suppressed and journalists were coerced by law enforcement agents into retracting damaging stories. Some journalists, especially editors, were under intense pressure to stop criticizing the government and were obliged to mobilize for a collective promotion of the Ujamaa principles, which are similar to development journalism. They refer to the family-based concept of socialism introduced by Nyerere in 1964 as a distributive policy associated with socialist communal livelihood (Shivji, 1995).

Throughout Nyerere's reign, development journalism thrived, since the government forced the press to reflect the spirit of Ujamaa in all coverage. The CCM government warned the independent news media against what they referred to as Western imperialist style of journalism. Tanzania today, under the leadership of President Jakaya Kikwete, allows the oppositional viewpoints of the mostly private media, since it is becoming increasingly difficult to suppress alternative political voices in the new liberalized vibrant media environment.

Election coverage has been especially challenging because of the inherent violence, especially in the semi-autonomous island of Zanzibar (Ahluwalia & Zegeye, 2001). In September 2005, *The Guardian* newspaper in Tanzania reported that more than 30 demonstrators were shot dead at five different campaign rallies within a week. The impact on media performance after these particular incidents was not ascertained, but similar harassment in the 1985 elections led the national media to rely on official state propaganda to serve the agenda of the incumbent CCM party and journalist to exercise self-censorship to remain in good standing with the government (Ogunade, 1986).

Media in Uganda

While the media have played a central role in the fight for human rights, most journalists have also practiced increased self-censorship (Dicklitch & Lwanga, 2003) because of the existing libel and treason laws. The constitution guarantees media freedom but through the years governments have occasionally shut down critical outlets for producing material likely to damage their reputation (Ocitti, 2006).

Before the 2001 elections, more than 100 FM radio stations were registered, and most did not follow the government's election coverage guidelines. Popular FM talk shows, which broadcast live listener calls on a range of subjects, were shut down indefinitely. The ban affected many radio stations, including the four most popular ones: *Central Broadcasting Service, Radio One, K-fm,* and *Radio Simba.* Journalists sent 6,000 signed petitions to the government opposing the ban, but it was lifted only after the elections. Some FM stations run by the president's friends and military personnel operate without a broadcast license. This allows them to evade licensing fees and to avoid being scrutinized by the council that regulates electronic media.

Constitutional changes since the introduction of multiparty politics in 1996 have resulted in the removal of some restrictions on the media. The emergence of press freedom started with the liberalization of the media, which had been controlled by the government since colonial days (Kannyo, 2004). In Tanzania and Uganda, veteran journalists, who used to work for the state-owned media, opened their own newspapers, magazines, and newsletters, which criticized incompetence and corruption in the government and investigated human rights violations (Dicklitch & Lwanga, 2003; Hossain et al., 2003). The same regimes, however, continue to intimidate journalists by charging them with libel, sedition, treason, and defamation whenever they become too critical of the political elite and the establishment (Mwesige, 2004).

Media ownership influenced the coverage of the 2006 presidential and parliamentary elections. State-owned radio and TV stations were used to selectively label opposition politicians as terrorists and thus dissuaded critics from launching a successful campaign. Both the government-owned press, such as *The New Vision,* and the independent media, such as *The Daily Monitor,* however, reported on the violent outbreaks and law abuses during the campaign. *The Daily Monitor* uncovered that the national army, clad in the incumbent's party attire, killed 17 civilians nationwide, all supporting the opposition, a report that was not challenged by the state.

Media in Rwanda

The newcomer in the EAC, Rwanda, is a prominent case study on how the media can be detrimental to democratic values. The media instigated the ethnic cleansing of more than half a million Tutsis and told the Hutu majority how to do it (Frohardt & Temin, 2003; Mamdani, 1996). The news organizations involved heavily were RTLM and ORINFOR, which were owned and controlled by associates of the Hutu President Juvenale Habyarimana and the Rwandan government respectively.

The Rwanda Patriotic Front (RPF), which overthrew Habyarimana's government to end the genocide, faced an enormous challenge to rehabilitate the national media. Major General Paul Kagame, who has presided over Rwanda since the 1994 genocide, has gradually reformed the public and private press (Karnell, 2002). The government secured funds from international agencies such as the IMF, UNESCO, and others to renovate and rebuild newsroom equipment and train young journalists (Karnell, 2002). This local and international training lasted more than a decade. The new generation of reporters has been charged with sensitizing citizens to respect human dignity, peace, reconciliation, tolerance, human rights and the rule of law. Yet, despite all of these positive developments, the Rwandan government had its own agenda.

The Kagame government passed a media law in July 2002, which established the High Press Council to guarantee freedom of the press. This body regulates electronic broadcasting and censors the press under the pretense of preventing a repeat of the 1994 hate speech (Reyntjens, 2004). The first privately owned independent radio station was established in 2004, but all private media face government restrictions and exercise self-censorship (Reyntjens, 2004). Some proprietors of the so-called privately owned press are members of the governing council with close ties to the presidency.

Many critics have been alarmed by the government's harsh restrictions and intimidation whenever Rwandan journalists investigate corruption, authoritarianism and abuse of public office (Franklin & Love, 1998). Seventeen well-known journalists have been incarcerated in the past 10 years, some without trial, on charges and allegations of treason, inciting genocide, and hate speech. Many young journalists have disappeared without a trace. Rwanda lacks a daily independent newspaper. Some topics are forbidden, such as covering the military, justice department, state house, and any tyrannical acts committed by the ruling RPF.

Media in Burundi

The media have been severely hurt by the country's political and economic conditions. The government still controls the one national radio and one TV station. The main media outlets are Radio Television Nationale du Burundi (RTNB), *Le Renouveau* newspaper, and an official weekly *Ubumwe* (Frère, 2007). In 1994, there were 22 newspapers, but by 1999 they dropped to four and another 13 appeared irregularly (Philippart, 2000). The only private and partially independent newspaper is *Ndongozi*, which is owned by the Catholic Church and enjoys some international financial backing. Similar to Rwanda, Uganda, and Tanzania, radio has been the most important source of information for ordinary Burundians. Private radio stations have played an essential role in promoting pluralism (Frère, 2007). Unlike in Rwanda, where radio became the medium of state propaganda, in Burundi newspapers were the weapons of war during political campaigns and responsible for reinforcing ethnic stereotypes (Frère, 2007).

Since the early 1990s, the Press Freedom Index has consistently classified both the Burundian and Rwandan press as not free. The 1992 law which guaranteed freedom of expression and speech also protected institutions like the army and state security from any unauthorized news coverage about personnel (Frère, 2007). The government suspended press freedoms in 1996, and the regime used the media to spread its messages of ethnic sectarianism (Nyankanzi, 1998; Sullivan, 2005). In 1997, a new law banned dissemination of information deemed as propaganda or an embarrassment to state officials and the people of Burundi (Freedom House, 2008). The government argued that such restrictions were necessary to protect the public from messages that would fuel hatred and incite Rwanda-like genocide (Frère, 2007). A more liberal press law was adopted in 2003, which however imposed fines and prison terms of up to 5 years for defamation and attacks on the president. In addition, Article

31 of the 2005 Penal Code–16.9 states that 1 year of imprisonment will be imposed on "anyone who has willfully and publicly imputed a specific fact likely to undermine the honor or the reputation of that person or to expose him to public contempt."

The government continues to harass the media by arresting journalists or closing publications critical of its activities. The National Council of Communication (NCC), which oversaw press freedom and respect for the law, closed two newspapers and suspended the license of a private FM radio due to messages considered extreme and dangerous to national security (Frère, 2007). The press remains under heavy control despite laws that formally guarantee freedom. The 2008 Press Freedom Index compiled by Reporters without Borders (RWB) ranked Burundi 94th and Rwanda 145th out of 173 countries in the world (RWB, 2008). In 2006, Burundi was ranked as Africa's third leading jailer of journalists by the Committee to Protect Journalists (CPJ, 2007).

Agenda Building, Media Performance, and Democratization

The assessment of media performance in the five EAC countries through the concepts of agenda building and democratization is a new approach to understanding the central importance and role of the East African media for democratic governance. Much of the previous mass communication research from East Africa, and consequently much of the literature examined here, is nontheoretical. Thus, the agenda-building perspective is a relatively new theoretical proposition that is currently being advanced (Kalyango, 2009b, 2008; Lancendorfer & Lee, 2003) to explain the conditions through which governments in Africa influence media performance. For instance, Kalyango (2008) determined that audiences exposed to the media in Kenya, Tanzania, and Uganda perceive the state-owned media as the voice of the nation, promoting peace and security, and fostering public debate on good health and economic empowerment. The majority of East Africans also indicated that state leaders use the media to positively infuse their authority directly to the people in order to garner public support on issues concerning nation building, unity, peace, and poverty alleviation.

The East African governments exercise an agenda-building influence on the media through a variety of approaches. The media, in turn, transfer this influence to the public through the uncritical coverage of issues they have received from above. The media could potentially influence public opinion about democratic governance by mobilizing citizens to politically challenge the authoritarian structures. This process, however, is only in its very primitive stages. Still, if such public mobilization were to develop further, it could be bidirectional because as societies become more democratic, they influence the media by lessening restrictions and increasing rights and opportunities. More democratic societies will also exert different agenda-building forces. In the EAC, it would require the media to promote economic and political liberalization, equal rights, free choices, and self-development. We propose that the agenda-building influences on both the state-owned and privately owned media in East Africa fit the overall framework in the following ways, as illustrated in Table 12.1.

We see the agenda-building influence on the media in East Africa as a mixed function. On the one hand, abuse of power and repression of the media are widespread, but on the other, certain positive developments, such as the relaxing of state monopoly of the national media and growing independence of privately owned media, are encouraging. Agenda building is central to the political control of messages and has helped some EAC leaders like President Museveni of Uganda, President Kagame of Rwanda, and President Kibaki of Kenya to sustain their grip on power. Our assessment also suggests that despite the continued political violence and intimidation of the press, these politically inspired actions have not completely curtailed the media's vigilance during elections, political mobilization, and the reinforcement of a participatory society in political discourse, which engenders the EAC's transition to democracy.

Not all of the conceptual models of agenda building reviewed earlier (Cobb et al., 1976) fit the East African context. For instance, the outside initiative,

Table 12.1 Examples of Agenda Building Influences on the East African Media

AGENDA BUILDING (Issues originated by Gov.)	From elites to media	MEDIA PERFORMANCE (Issues delivered by the media)
• Unautocratic president • Government of the people	→	• His Excellency, the people's president • Statesman, liberator, honorable chief • New breed of African leaders
• Independent judiciary • Human rights	→	• Constitutionalism thrives • Affirmative action empowers women • We have equal rights before the law
• Economic development • Free market	→	• State committed to poverty alleviation • Cash market economy empowers citizens • Prices of goods and services are low
• Legitimate regime • Free and fair elections	→	• Regime is democratic and legitimate • We exercise our right to choose leaders • Our visionary regime champions peace
• Public health • Service infrastructure	→	• A healthy nation, productive citizens • Health care delivery is better with this regime • Efficient delivery of public service

Notes: Table 12.1 illustrates the agenda-building influence on the media. In this model, the governments of Burundi, Kenya, Rwanda, Tanzania, and Uganda propagate the messages and discourse listed in the agenda building column on the left. Then the media (particularly state-owned media) deliver those messages using the exact phrases (and many other similar phrases) listed in the media performance column on the right.

under which issues arise at the non-governmental level and then reach the public and finally the government agenda, has not applied to the East African experience of the past two to three decades. NGOs and civil society in general are disempowered by the states, and their mobilization potential is undermined by the governments' administrative and policy control over civil society. Inside access does not fit the East African context either. It is said to occur when groups or individuals with close access to the government initiate agendas and place them on the formal agenda but without making the issue public. This approach has not been common in the region.

The mobilization agenda-building model, however, applies. This model occurs when politicians want to move an issue from their formal agenda to the public through the media. Some of the agenda-building techniques used by East African governments to influence the media include coercion and strict supervision, regulation, such as political censorship and laws banning critical adversarial journalism, financial control, such as heavy taxation, and interference in appointments of media managers and editors. Editors and their journalists who work with state-owned media are state employees. These journalists depend upon the government to provide most of the content they publish and broadcast, which makes state-owned news organizations merely public relations institutions that are dictated by political expediency and manipulation.

Another aspect through which agenda building occurs and thrives in East Africa is the lack of adequate investments and commercialization in the free market economy to demonopolize media ownership. Most of the state-owned and privately owned media, including radio and television studios, have not upgraded to modernized newsrooms with fast Internet services and efficient computers. Further, the inadequate training of journalists has contributed to stagnation in the quality of journalism, which again contributes to the agenda-building process.

A few case studies (e.g., see Kalyango, 2009b) have demonstrated how agenda building thrives in situations where the rule of law is disregarded. East African governments have often constrained journalists' freedoms through archaic media statutes, anti-terrorism statues, and anti-defamation laws, which have been used to intimidate, arrest, and punish journalists for exposing corruption and abuse of public office in state institutions (Kagwanja, 2003; Kalyango, 2009a). Over the past 20 years, the media have become dependent on government mercy and power because of legal requirements to practice journalism with a government-issued license.

The media and religious institutions constitute the most vigilant and influential part of civil society in most of Africa, including the EAC member states. In a democratic society, institutional frameworks such as the independent media (provided the existence of press freedom) help to advocate for the rule of law. The media, however, have in some ways failed to serve as free and independent outlets to propel emerging democracies to consolidation (Kambenga, 2005; Matende, 2005; Ocitti, 2006). Instead, the state-run media and some journalists in the privately owned media have condoned state-inspired political violence, which suits the authoritarian regimes. Based on the examples presented throughout this chapter, media performance and the current governance in the EAC cannot be considered equivalent to those of fully democratic states. Notwithstanding those constraints, the news media in East Africa are still relevant and central to providing the electoral masses with a forum for public debate.

Yet, in East Africa, citizens who lack civic education perceive democracy merely as an elite's struggle for national power. The fact that the media have often been used as a tool for spreading antidemocratic propaganda and supporting an autocratic agenda has contributed to citizens' inability to form basic political attitudes and to their mistrust in democracy (Ochs, 1987). Because of that, politicians who use the media to damage the reputation of other candidates through ethno-sectarian tactics usually win the parliamentary elections (Hughes, 2005). Consequently, we argue that the state-run national media throughout the EAC can also be seen as a threat to the consolidation of democracy because they are used as a political propaganda tool that maintains and reinforces the state's interests and unequal relations of political power.

Political mobilization through both formal education and the mass media is needed to enable the electorate to understand basic tenets of democracy and fundamental human rights upon which to judge the legitimacy of their governments. Media performance is most successful when its agenda mobilizes citizens to challenge the structures of authoritarian rule by promoting human rights, economic empowerment, and the rule of law. In fact, being a populist mobilizer is one of the professional roles that American and international journalists envision for themselves (Weaver, 1998). While views about these roles are hardly universal among journalists, a focus on mobilizing citizens for democratic changes through education and empowerment could develop into a unique feature of African journalists.

One positive indicator of progress toward this goal is that the privately owned media have continuously reported and created public awareness of what constitutes good governance by exposing corruption, abuse of human rights, and state accountability. This has generated numerous mass protests and a sustained civil activism, especially in Kenya and Uganda. There is a good indication that vibrant civil societies in the EAC, with a fairly critical independent media, could play a central role in mobilizing the masses to force regime change through elections. In this respect, civil society and the privately owned independent press continue to change the political landscape toward democratization despite the persistent draconian measures.

The focus on the media's mobilizing power should not be confused with the mobilization model of agenda building conceptualized by Cobb and colleagues (1976). According to that model, mobilization happens from the top down and the media are only used as a mouthpiece and a distribution channel. The model has been a major function for the relationship between the media and the democratization process in the region, as governments have used the media for one-way communication with their constituents to advance the regimes' political agendas but with little regard for feedback and alternative views.

The type of political mobilization we discuss originates from the media, not the government, and spreads to the audience first before it reaches the top to influence public policy. Thus, it is more in line with the outside initiative model by Cobb et al. (1976), which they argue happens mainly in egalitarian societies. The question is whether an egalitarian society needs to exist before this type of agenda building can occur, or whether this new approach to building public agendas can influence the establishment of egalitarian societies in East Africa. This chicken-and-egg question can only be answered through further research and professional involvement of journalists and civic leaders and organizations.

Despite the restrictive press laws still on the books, it has become increasingly difficult for the transitional EAC countries to curtail the emergence of consolidated democracies. These are still transitioning unstable democracies because although the regimes hold regular elections, the rule of law is on the decline, they engage in ethnocratic sectarianism, suppress information, and are partly responsible for the political violence. The conditions for consolidation of democracy are either minimally met or deliberately constrained through totalitarianism (Lindberg, 2006). At the moment, member states are engaged in regime policies and procedures that make some of these democratization gains reversible. For instance, Uganda and Rwanda have recently banned some political parties and ideologies through coercive control and electoral administrative procedures. Kenya and Tanzania have established an unattainably high threshold for the formation of opposition political parties and have restricted some opposition candidates who are admissible under the electoral commission laws. Most damaging to democratic consolidation is the current inability of the political opposition to solicit private funds for campaigns and grassroots mobilization. In addition, the opposition parties are usually denied media access to deliberate their political platform.

One could argue that East Africa's democratization process has come to refer to some spurious aspect of a political culture whereby leaders such as President Yoweri Museveni of Uganda and Rwanda's Paul Kagame scramble to guarantee some aspects of good governance, yet they guard their offices and positions against equal competition and strict accountability. It has also come to refer to a political culture where Tanzania's leader Jakaya Kikwete has created a supra-partisan arrangement that discriminates against opposition parties and privileges the regime's CCM party. East Africa's democratization, to our knowledge, has come to mean a political culture where Kenya's Mwai Kibaki and President Pierre Nkurunziza of Burundi either co-opt political opponents in case they are defeated in an election or eliminate political insiders who disagree with the regime. All these accounts of democratization may explain why those regimes (except in Tanzania) have either reverted to an authoritarian undemocratic mold or resorted to political violence once new actors emerge and mobilize popular upsurge to defeat the incumbents through the electoral process. As we have surmised in the current and previous paragraphs, when a country is in the midst of a political violence outbreak and the rule of law is practically abrogated, agenda-building influences on the media become especially powerful and often morph into outright intimidation and violence towards journalists.

As pointed out earlier, the basic question of whether an appropriate agenda-building model can trigger the development of an egalitarian society or, conversely, such a society must exist before the agenda-building model can develop is a question best answered through further research and professional involvement of journalists and civic leaders. From a research standpoint, the performance of the news media and their impact on citizens to enhance democratic support and to facilitate political participation has not been adequately investigated. The next phase of research should consider how the privately owned and the state-owned media differ in their coverage of critical issues facing the polity of these countries. An examination of the populist mobilizer role among African journalists is also interesting because of the implications of these findings for the profession of journalism in the region and for the processes of democratization and agenda setting. Further, differences in public agendas and attitudes among countries should also be examined as a way to study the effects of media agendas in these same systems. Once enough research about these phenomena is accumulated, mass communication scholars should engage in a higher level of theorizing that advances theoretical development relevant to the region. Presently, such abstract views of the issues in East Africa are hampered by the insufficient theory-driven research from the area.

From a professional standpoint, one approach to improving media performance in these transitioning democracies is through training young journalists to make public officials accountable and to continuously engender applied comparative communication research that can improve the quality of journalism in this and other regions of Africa. For instance, there are only two universities in Uganda that have a journalism and mass communication program. Tanzania has two higher institutions that teach journalism, and Kenya has three. Rwanda has one journalism diploma-granting institution, while Burundi has no known degree-granting school of journalism. Moreover, less than half of all practicing journalists in Uganda, Rwanda, Burundi, and Tanzania have a bachelor's degree. Consequently, a freer press can emerge if it can be supported with adequate training of journalists, a continued commitment to universal formal education for all citizens, a strong independent civil society, and respect for the rule of law.

Conclusion

Much of the previous mass communication research from East Africa, and thus much of the literature examined here, is non-theoretical. The agenda-building perspective is a relatively new theoretical proposition attempting to explain the conditions through which governments in Africa influence media performance. Accordingly, East African governments exercise an agenda-building influence on the media through a variety of methods ranging from restrictive laws and regulations, to intimidation and state patronage. The media, on the other hand, fulfill and impose a variety of government-backed agendas on the public, both consciously and unconsciously. Journalists in state-owned media, for instance, consciously reinforce government propaganda through self-censorship and overall cooperation out of fear of either losing their professional licenses or being arrested. The media also unconsciously propagate the government agendas by not investigating and ascertaining facts, due to lack of professional training that would help them recognize these influences.

Either way, these media outlets deny the public its right to participate in the political life of the country. The public is given biased and insufficient information that does not allow it to make an educated choice or is simply unaware of its rights in the political processes of democratic governance. The lack of a strong and involved citizenry, in turn, supports the status quo of the regimes and their continued abuse of power. The way to break this vicious cycle is through empowering the media to act as a mobilizer of the masses and an educator. This could be achieved by understanding and applying the journalistic responsibilities and professional norms of fairness, skepticism, and balance. East African journalists can resist attempts by elite figures, particularly politicians, who fuel partisan agenda and propagate unsupported claims, by moderating contradictory discourse with impartiality and clarity. These and other media practices, if performed well, would make news a valuable institution for democratic transformation in East Africa. Such an outcome would also benefit the media, as a more relaxed societal structure would also relieve some of the governments' pressures on them.

These societal changes can be sustained in the long term only by injecting revenue from competing markets into struggling East African media to promote the free flow of information, which can lead to the protection of investments, extension of liberalized markets, creation of jobs, and expansion of an informed society. An informed East African public can make rational choices ranging from products to political alternatives. Job creation and increased income also leads to better education and quality of life. A free and independent East African media can endorse and publicize market choices to promote consumption and the use of resources for economic growth, which inadvertently would increase the quality of life and democratization. The better informed, educated, and employed East Africans become, the more likely they are to embrace democratic values.

References

Afako, B. (2006). Uncharted waters: The movement approaches transition in Uganda. Report prepared for DFID, Makerere University, Kampala, Uganda.

Ahluwalia, P., & Zegeye, A. (2001). Multiparty democracy in Tanzania. *African Secu-*

rity Review, 10(3), Article 4. Retrieved March 10, 2006, from http://www.iss.co.za/pubs/asr/10No3/AhluwaliaAndZegeye.html

Anderson, D. M. (2003). Kenya's elections 2002 — dawning of a new era? *African Affairs, 102*, 331–342.

Aseka, E. M. (2005). *Transformational leadership in East Africa: Politics, ideology and community.* Kampala, Uganda: Fountain Books.

Baker, B. (2004). Popular justice and policing from Bush war to democracy: Uganda 1981–2004. *International Journal of the Sociology of Law, 32*(4), 333–348.

Bennett, W. L. (2004). *News: The politics of illusion* (6th ed). New York: Longman.

Berkowitz, D. (1987). TV news sources and news channels: A study in agenda-building. *Journalism Quarterly, 64*, 508–513.

Bourgault, L. (1995). *Mass media in Sub-Saharan Africa.* Bloomington: Indiana University Press.

Bratton, M., Mattes, R., & Gyimah-Boadi, E. (2005). *Public opinion, democracy, and market reform in Africa.* Cambridge, UK: University Press.

Brown, S. (2003). Quiet diplomacy and recurring ethnic clashes in Kenya. In C. L. Sriram. & K. Wermester (Eds.), *From promise to practice: U.N. capacities for the prevention of violent conflict* (pp. 69–100). Boulder, CO: Lynne Rienner.

Chalk, F. (1999). Hate radio in Rwanda. In H. Adelman & A. Suhrke (Eds.), *The path of a genocide: The Rwanda crisis from Uganda to Zaire* (pp. 93–110). New Brunswick, NJ: Transaction.

Cobb, R., Ross, J. K., & Ross, M. H. (1976). Agenda building as a comparative political process. *The American Political Science Review, 70*(1), 126–138.

Committee to Protect Journalists. (2007, February 5). Attacks on the press 2006: Burundi. Retrieved April 15, 2009, from http://cpj.org/2007/02/attacks-on-the-press-2006-burundi.php#more

Crescenzi, M. (1999). Violence and uncertainty in transitions. *Journal of Conflict Resolution, 43*(2), 192–212.

Curran, J. (1991). Rethinking the media as a public sphere. In P. Dahlgren & C. Sparks (Eds.), *Communication and citizenship: Journalism and the public sphere in the new media age* (pp. 27–58). London: Routledge.

Deutsch, E. P. (1977). *An international rule of law.* Charlottesville: University Press of Virginia.

Diamond, L. (1999). *Developing democracy: Toward consolidation.* Baltimore, MD: Johns Hopkins University Press.

Dicklitch, S., & Lwanga, D. (2003). The politics of being non-political: Human rights organizations and the creation of a positive human rights culture in Uganda. *Human Rights Quarterly, 25*(2), 482–509.

Esser, F. (1999). "Tabloidization of news": A comparative analysis of Anglo-American and German press journalism. *European Journal of Communication, 14*(3), 291–324.

Esser, F., & Pfetch, B. (2004). Comparing political communication: Theories, cases, and challenges. *Communication, Society and Politics.* Cambridge, UK: Cambridge University Press.

Faringer, G. L. (1991). *Press freedom in Africa.* New York: Praeger.

Franklin, A., & Love, R. (1998). Whose news? Control of the media in Africa. *Review of African political economy, 78*(25), 545–590.

Freedom House. (2008). Countries at the crossroads. Retrieved April 12, 2009, from http://www.freedomhouse.org/template.cfm?page=251&year=2008

Freedom House. (2009). Freedom in the world comparative and historical data: Country ratings and status, FIW 1973–2009. Retrieved April 20, 2009, from http://www.freedomhouse.org/template.cfm?page=439

Frère, M. S. (2007). *The media and conflicts in Central Africa*. Boulder, CO: Lynne Reinner.

Frohardt, M., & Temin, J. (2003). The use and abuse of media in vulnerable societies. In A. Thompson (Ed.), *The media and the Rwandan genocide* (pp. 3–37). Ottawa, Canada: The International Development Research Center.

Gahama, J., Makoroka, S., Nditije, C., Ntahombaye, P., & Sindayizeruka, O. (1999). Burundi. In A. Adedeji (Eds.), *Comprehending and mastering African conflict: The search for sustainable peace and good governance*. London: Zed Books, in association with African Centre for Development and Strategic Studies.

Goldstein, A., & Ndung'u, N. (2003, March 1). *Regional integration experience in the Eastern African region*. Paper presented at the African Forum for Regionalism on Integration and Co-operation in Sub-Saharan Africa, Cape Town, South Africa.

Gourevitch, P. (2000). *We wish to inform you that tomorrow we will be killed with our families*. New York: St. Martin's Press.

Grosswiler, P. (1997). Changing perceptions of press freedom in Tanzania. In F. Eribo & W. Jong-Ebot (Eds.), *Press freedom and communication in Africa* (pp. 101–120). Trenton, NJ: Africa World Press.

Gunther, R., & Mughan, A. (2000). *Democracy and the media: A comparative perspective*. Cambridge, UK: Cambridge University Press.

Hallin, D. C., & Papathanassopoulos, S. (2002). Political clientelism and the media: Southern Europe and Latin America in comparative perspective. *Media, Culture & Society, 24*(2), 175–195.

Hayek, F. (1972). *The road to serfdom*. Chicago: University of Chicago Press.

Heath, C. W. (1997). Communication and press freedom in Kenya. In F. Eribo & W. Jong-Ebot (Eds.), *Press freedom and communication in Africa* (pp. 29–50). Trenton, NJ: Africa World Press.

Henderson, Sr. K. (2003). *Separation of powers in a constitutional democracy*. Washington, DC: International Foundation for Election Systems.

Hossain, M., Killian, B., Sharma, S., & Siitonen, L. (2003). *Democratization and development co-operation: Finland's democracy assistance to Nepal and Tanzania*. Brighton, UK: Institute of Development Studies.

Hughes, L. (2005). Malice in Maasailand: The historical roots of current political struggles. *African Affairs, 104*(415), 207–224.

Hughes, S., & Lawson, C. (2004). Propaganda and crony capitalism: Partisan bias in Mexican television news. *Latin American Research Review, 39*(3), 81–105.

Huntington, S. (1991). *The third wave: Democratization in the late twentieth century*. Norman: University of Oklahoma Press.

Hyden, G., Leslie, M., & Ogundimu, F. (2002). *Media and democracy in Africa*. New Brunswick, NJ: Transaction Publishers.

Jennings, C. (2001). *Across the Red River: Rwanda, Burundi, and the heart of darkness*. London: Indigo.

Johnson, T., Wanta, W., Boudreau, T., Blank-Libra, J., Schaffer, K., & Turner, S. (1996). Influence dealers: A path analysis model of agenda building during Richard Nixon's war on Drugs. *Journalism & Mass Communication Quarterly, 73*(1), 181–194.

Joseph, W. A., Kesselman, M., & Krieger, J. (2000). *Introduction to third world politics*. Boston, MA: Houghton Mifflin.

Joshua, L. C. (2001). Mainstreaming alternative strategies into structural adjustment: What's really going on between the state, non-governmental actors and donors in Uganda? *Africa Studies Review, 42*(1), 96–115.

Kabwegere, T. (1995). *The politics of state formation and destruction in Uganda.* Kampala, Uganda: Fountain Publishers.

Kagwanja, P. M. (2003). Facing Mount Kenya or facing Mecca? The Mungiki, ethnic violence and the politics of the Moi succession in Kenya, 1987–2002. *African Affairs, 102,* 25–49.

Kaiser, P. (2000a). Elections and conflict management in Africa. *Journal of Asian and African Studies, 34*(4), 461–463.

Kaiser, P. (2000b). Postmodern insurgencies: Political violence, identity formation and peacemaking in comparative perspective. *The Journal of Modern African Studies, 38*(3), 511–549.

Kaiser, P., & Okumu, W. (2004). *Democratic transitions in East Africa.* Hampshire, UK: Ashgate Publishing.

Kalyango, Y. Jr. (2008). *Media performance and democratic rule in East Africa: Agenda setting and agenda building influences on public attitudes* (Unpublished doctoral dissertation). University of Missouri.

Kalyango, Y. Jr. (2009a). Frame building and media framing of the joint counterterrorism efforts: comparing the U.S.-Uganda Efforts. In G. Golan, T. Johnson, & W. Wanta (Eds.), *International media communication in a global age* (pp. 220–240). New York: Routledge.

Kalyango, Y. Jr. (2009b). Political news use and democratic support: A study of Uganda's radio impact. *Journal of Radio and Audio Media, 16*(2), 200–216.

Kamanyi, J. (2006, April). *The East African political federation: Progress, challenges and prospects for constitutional development.* Paper presented at the 10th Annual Sir Udo Udoma Symposium, KCK Study Series, 9, at Makerere University, Kampala, Uganda.

Kambenga, G. (2005, August). *Unionism among Tanzanian media workers.* Paper prresented to the bi-annual general assembly of the Tanzania Union of Journalists and other stakeholders, Addis Ababa, Ethiopia.

Kannyo, E. (2004). Change in Uganda: A new opening? *Journal of Democracy, 15*(2), 125–139.

Karnell, A. P. (2002). Counteracting hate radio in Africa's Great Lakes region: responses and lessons. *Journal of International Communications, 8*(1), 111–137.

Kasaija, P. A. (2004). Regional integration: A political federation of the East African Countries? *African Journal of International Affairs, 7*(2), 21–34.

Kirschke, L. (2000). Informal repression, zero-sum politics and late third wave transitions. *The Journal of Modern African Studies, 38,* 383–405.

Klopp, J. (2001). Ethnic clashes and winning elections: The case of Kenya's electoral despotism. *Canadian Journal of African Studies, 35*(3), 473–517.

Klopp, J. M., & Zuern, E. (2003, September). *The politics of violence in democratization.* Paper presented at the annual conference of the European Consortium for Political Research, Marburg, Germany.

Lancendorfer, K. M., & Lee, B. (2003). Agenda building and the media: A content analysis of the relationship between candidates and the media in the 2002 elections in South Africa. *British Journal of Political Science, 17*(2), 201–219.

Lawson, C. (2002). *Building the fourth estate: Democratization and the rise of a free press in Mexico.* Berkeley: University of California Press.

Lawson, F. E. (2008). 2007 Country performance assessment. *African Development Bank Group, 32,* 1–14.

Lindberg, I. S. (2006). *Democracy and elections in Africa.* Baltimore, MD: Johns Hopkins University Press.

Lush, D. (1998). The role of the African media in the promotion of democracy and human rights. In S. Kayizzi-Mugerwa, A. Olukoshi, & L. Wohlgemuth (Eds.), *Towards a partnership with Africa: Challenges and opportunities* (pp. 42–65). Uppsala, Sweden: Nordic African Institute.

Mahoney, P. G. (1999). The common law and economic growth: Hayek might be right. *Transition, 10*(6), 28–37.

Maloba, W. (1992). The media and Mau Mau: Kenyan nationalism and colonial propaganda. In B. G. Hawk (Ed.), *Africa's media image* (pp. 51–66). Westport, CT: Praeger.

Mamdani, M. (1996). *Citizen and subject: Contemporary Africa and the legacy of late colonialism.* Princeton, NJ: Princeton University Press.

Manirakiza, M. (2005). Nation-building in Burundi. History and its impact on the future. *Trends, (2),* 27–36.

Matende, D. (2005, June). *The state of the news media in Kenya.* Paper presented at the annual meeting of the Kenya Union of Journalists, Nairobi, Kenya.

McChesney, R. (2000). *Rich media, poor democracy: Communication politics in dubious times.* New York: The New Press.

McCombs, M. E., & Shaw, D. L. (1972). The agenda-setting function of mass media. *Public Opinion Quarterly, 36*(2), 176–187.

McQuail, D. (1992). *Media performance: Mass communication and the public interest.* London: Sage.

Miller, W. L. (1991). *Media and voters. The audience, content, and influence of press and television at the 1987 general elections.* Oxford, UK: Clarendon Press.

Mugisha, A. (2004). Museveni's machinations. *Journal of Democracy, 15*(2), 140–144.

Mwenda, A. (2007). Personalizing power in Uganda. *Journal of Democracy, 18*(3), 23–37.

Mwesige, P. G. (2004). Disseminators, advocates, and watchdogs: A profile of Ugandan journalists in the new millennium. *Journalism, 5*(1), 69–96.

Neethling, T. (2003). South Africa's evolving role in peacekeeping: Nation interests and international responsibilities. *Journal of Military and Strategic Studies, 6*(2), 1–21.

Norris, P. (1997). *Politics and the press: The news media and their influences.* New York: Lynne Rienner.

Nyamnjoh, F. (2005). *Africa's media, democracy and the politics of belonging.* London: Zed Books.

Nyankanzi, E. L. (1998). *Genocide: Rwanda and Burundi.* Rochester, VT: Schenkman Books.

Ochs, M. (1987). *The African press.* Cairo: American University in Cairo Press.

Ocitti, J. (1999). *Media and democracy in Africa.* Cambridge, MA: Weatherhead Center for International Affairs.

Ocitti, J. (2006). *Press politics and public policy in Uganda: The role of journalism in democratization.* London: Edwin Mellen Press.

O'Donnell, G., & Schmitter, P. (1986). *Transition from authoritarian rule: Tentative conclusions about uncertain democracies.* Baltimore, MD: Johns Hopkins University Press.

Ogan, C. L., Fair, J. E., & Shah, H. (1984). A little good news: Development news in Third World newspapers. *Communication Yearbook 8,* 628–644.

Ogunade, D. (1986). The mass media systems of Kenya and Tanzania: A comparative analysis. *Africa Media Review, 1*(1), 99–111.

Oloka-Onyango, J. (2004). *Constitutional change and political transition in contemporary Uganda: A socio-legal analysis. Change analysis in Uganda: Supporting implementation of the PEAP.* Study presented to the Department for International Development, Kampala, Uganda.

Ould-Abdallah, A. (2000). *Burundi on the brink, 1993–95: A UN special envoy reflects on preventive diplomacy.* Washington, DC: United States Institute of Peace Press.

Philippart, M. (2000). Media status report: Burundi. Retrieved April 11, 2009, from http://www.gret.org/parma/uk2/ressource/edm/pdf/burundi.pdf

Podpiera, R., & Cihaik, M. (2005). *Bank behavior in developing countries: Evidence from East Africa* (IMF Working Papers). Geneva: International Monetary Fund.

Pratt, C. (1976). The critical phase in Tanzania, 1945–1968: *Nyerere and the emergence of a socialist strategy.* Cambridge, UK: Cambridge University Press.

Pratt, C. (1999). Julius Nyerere: Reflections on the legacy of his socialism. *Canadian Journal of African Studies, 33*(1), 137–189.

Prunier, G. (1995). *The Rwanda crisis: History of a genocide.* New York: Columbia University Press.

Przeworski, A., Alvarez, M., Cheibub, J., & Limongi, F. (2005). *Democracy and development: Political institutions and well-being in the world, 1950–1990.* Cambridge, UK: Cambridge University Press.

Reporters Without Borders. (2008). Press freedom index: Press freedom day by day. Retrieved April 18, 2009, from http://www.rsf.org/article.php3?id_article=29031

Reyntjens, F. (2004). Rwanda, ten years on: From genocide to dictatorship. *African Affairs, 103*(441), 177–191.

Reyntjens, F. (2006). Briefing. Burundi: A peaceful transition after a decade of civil war? *African Affairs, 105,* 117–135.

Robins, M. (1997). Press freedom in Uganda. In F. Eribo & W. Jong-Ebot (Eds.), *Press freedom and communication in Africa* (pp. 121–135). Trenton, NJ: Africa World Press.

Rotberg, R., & Weiss, T. (1996). *From massacres to genocide.* Cambridge. MA: The World Peace Foundation.

Rubongoya, J. (2007). *Regime hegemony in Museveni's Uganda: Pax Musevenica.* New York: Palgrave MacMillan.

Sallot, L. M., Cameron, G. T., & Lariscy, R. A. (1997). Professional standards in public relations: A survey of educators. *Public Relations Review, 23*(3), 197–216.

Schabas, W. A. (2000). Hate speech in Rwanda: The road to genocide. *McGill Law Journal, 46,* 141–171.

Schmitz, H. P. (2006). *Transnational mobilization and domestic regime change: Africa in comparative perspective* (International Political Economy series). New York: Palgrave Macmillan.

Sen, A. (1999). Democracy as a universal value. *Journal of Democracy, 10*(3), 3–17.

Sheafer, T., & Weimann, G. (2005). Agenda building, agenda setting, priming, individual voting intentions, and the aggregate results: An analysis of four Israeli elections. *Journal of Communication, 55,* 347–365.

Shin, D. C. (1994). On the third wave of democratization: A synthesis and evaluation of recent theory and research. *World Politics, 47*(1), 135–170.

Shivji, I. (1995). The rule of law and Ujamaa in the ideological formation of Tanzania. *Social and Legal Studies, 4*(2), 147–174.

Sircar, P. (1990). *Development through integration: Lessons from East Africa.* New Delhi, India: South Asia Books.

Smith, M. K. (1998). Julius Nyerere, lifelong learning and informal education (Infed). Retrieved April 20, 2009, from http://www.infed.org/thinkers/et-nye.htm

Snyder, J. (2000). *From voting to violence: Democratization and nationalist conflict.* New York: W.W. Norton.

Steeves, J. (2006). Presidential succession in Kenya: The transition from Moi to Kibaki. *Commonwealth and Comparative Politics, 44*(2), 211–233.

Sullivan, D. (2005). The missing pillars: a look at the failure of peace in Burundi through the lens of Arend Lijphart's consociational theory. *The Journal of Modern African Studies 43*(1), 75–95.

Tiemessen, A. E. (2004). After Arusha: Gacaca justice in post-genocide Rwanda. *African Studies Quarterly, 8*(1), 57–76.

Transparency International. (2007). Report on the transparency international global corruption barometer 2007. *Policy and Research Development,* 1-24.

Van Eck, J. (2004). Challenges to a durable peace in Burundi. *Situation Report.* Pretoria, South Africa: Institute for Security Studies.

Walgrave, S., & Van Aelst, P. (2006). The contingency of the mass media's political agenda setting power: Toward a preliminary theory. *Journal of Communication, 56,* 88–109.

Walters, T. N., Walters, L. M., & Gray, R. (1996). Agenda building in the 1992 presidential campaign. *Public Relations Review, 22*(1), 9–25.

Wanta, W., & Kalyango, Y., Jr. (2007). Terrorism and Africa: A study of agenda building in the United States. *International Journal of Public Opinion Research, 19*(4), 434–450.

Wanta, W., Stephenson, M. A., Turk, J. V., & McCombs, M. E. (1989). How president's State of Union Talk influenced news media agendas. *Journalism Quarterly, 66*(3), 537–541.

Wanyande, P. (1996). Mass media-state relations in post-colonial Kenya. *Africa Media Review, 9*(3), 54–76.

Weaver, D. H. (1998) *The global journalist: news people around the world.* Cresskill, NJ: Hampton Press.

Weaver, D., & Elliot, S. (1985). Who sets the agenda for the media? A study of local agenda building. *Journalism Quarterly, 62,* 87–94.

Weiler, J. (1997). Legitimacy and democracy of union governance. In G. Edwards & A. Pijpers (Eds.), *The politics of European treaty reform* (pp. 249–287). London: Pinter Publications.

Werchick, L. (2003). Prospects for justice in Rwanda's citizen tribunals. *Human Rights Brief, 8*(3), 3–15.

World Bank. (2008). *Business planet: Mapping the business environment.* World Bank Economic Indicators. Retrieved April 30, 2009, from http://rru.worldbank.org/businessplanet/

Young, C. (2002). Deciphering disorder in Africa: Is identity the key? *World Politics,* *54*(4), 532–557.

Zafliro, J. (2000). Broadcasting reform and democratization in Botswana. *Africa Today, 47,* 7–25.

CHAPTER CONTENTS

13 Facing a Bloody Past
Discourses and Practices of Transitional Justice

Fadoua Loudiy

Slippery Rock University

Countries with bloody pasts attempting to reinvent their national ethos have found hope in the idea of transitional justice. The restorative practices of reconciliation, reparation programs, and memorialization are the typical means by which countries attempt to address issues of responsibility and accountability. Using a variety of national experiences, this chapter distinguishes between restorative and retributive genres, with focus on how restorative discourses and practices inform the forensic rhetoric of transitional justice. It also sheds light on the political and ethical limitations of non-retributive approaches to justice and the challenges of achieving any kind of justice in cases of large-scale atrocities. In sum, this chapter provides an overview of and a rhetorical framework for engaging in scholarship about transitional justice.

We were haunted by this idea of disappearing forever, vanishing into thin air, reduced to a mound of earth without being officially declared dead. Lost and never found. Lost and never buried. (Benjelloun, 2006, p. 49)

The metaphor of transitional justice has emerged only recently but practices and discourses that are implied in this approach to intra-national conflict have a long tradition. Jon Elster (2004), author of *Closing the Books: Transitional Justice in Historical Perspective*, notes that neither the idea nor the practice of transitional justice is new, as they go back to at least the Athenians in the early development of deliberative democracy. Interestingly enough, more and more nations are choosing to face their traumatic pasts and address issues of responsibility and accountability primarily through the restorative practices of truth commissions, reparation programs, and memorialization, eschewing retribution, which suggests that justice can also be served in non-legalistic ways even in situations of mass atrocity. At the heart of these approaches are public discourses and rhetorical practices that seek to do justice to victims through variously open negotiations of the legacy of a horrific past, with the hope than in so doing a new national ethos will emerge and prevent these atrocities from repetition.

Most scholarly discussions of transitional justice focus primarily on legalistic and psychological aspects of such lived experiences. While some scholars in communication studies such as Erik Doxtader (2003), John Hatch (2003, 2008), Bradford Vivian (2006, 2009), Mark McPhail (2002, 2004, 2009), Lane Bruner (2005), Stephen H. Browne (1995), Barbie Zelizer (2000), and others highlight the rhetorical dimensions of transitional justice, they amplify democratization and constitution building, or the deliberative aspect of the political process; public and visual memory, and the epideictic rhetoric at the heart of commemorative activities; or issues of grace, atonement, and redemption, which epitomize the theological undertones of discourses of reconciliation. All of these accounts make significant contributions, but largely ignored is the forensic dimension of transitional justice, and associated ethical tensions and implications. Forensic rhetoric concerns discourses and practices that seek to render justice, whether they occur in a courtroom, tribunal, or other public domains, including the media. The emphasis in this genre is praise and blame, moral and ethical judgment and, assigning responsibilities. Aristotle articulated this species of rhetoric around issues of wrongs, judgment, and justice/injustice, which are indeed the focal point of all experiences of transitional justice. Emphasis on the forensic needs to be considered within the realm of civic rhetoric, public discourse, and political actions that are guided by citizens' active involvements with the city or polity they live in. A polis without a concern for justice is not a just city. While a philosophical discussion of the ideal of justice is beyond the scope of this chapter, it is nevertheless important to point to how judgment and responsibility constitute the basis of justice in political and institutional contexts.

French philosopher Paul Ricoeur (2000) considers judgment to be the most important role of justice; it establishes a just distance between the perpetrator and the victim of the crime. Judgment for Ricoeur (2000) consists in "separating spheres of activity, in delimiting the claims of the one from those of the other, and finally in correcting unjust distributions, when the activity of one party encroaches on the field of exercise of other parties. In this respect, the act of judging certainly consists in separating" (p. 130). The horizon of the act of separating between wrongdoer and victim is social peace, which according to Ricoeur (2000), "has to do with mutual recognition" (p. 131). To seek justice is to recognize (identify) both perpetrator and victim: the perpetrator as the person guilty of an act that disrupted social peace and friendship and inflicted pain and injustice onto another or others, one who should take responsibility for the act and its consequences; and the victim as a subject whose rights have been infringed upon and should be repaired. The disruption of social harmony and friendship that results from unjust and violent actions cannot be ignored; doing so only fuels more disruptions born out of a desire for vengeance and anger. Justice is thus the attempt to restore the balance of rights within society by assigning responsibilities and repairing harm through mutual recognition. Of course it is easier to agree on what constitutes injustice than what constitutes justice or just action, especially in cases of genocide and mass atrocities. Recognizing this challenge is important; still, for a new moral order to emerge under such conditions, and a genuine political transition to take place, it is imperative that attempts be made to genuinely remedy the harm that has been inflicted on innocent citizens and achieve at least a modicum of justice.

How does the rhetoric of transitional justice serve as the remedy to injustice and impunity? How do retribution and reconciliation, for instance, contribute to moving from suffering, grief and enmity to achieving a sense of peace after national trauma? In taking up these questions, I first provide an overview of the field of transitional justice, then discuss the different paradigms of transitional justice with focus on three species of restorative transitional justice: (a) truth and reconciliation commissions, (b) reparations, and (c) memorialization. What insights can be gained by investigating how these practices operate and inform the forensic rhetoric of transitional justice? To begin, we must recognize that restorative practices associated with such an approach to justice stands in contradistinction to retribution and legal practices of accountability, which tend to gloss the political and ethical consequences they produce in the societies where they take place. I address some of the reasons and consequences for the shift of emphasis after a brief review of the history of the idea of transitional justice.

Transitional Justice: A Historical and Conceptual Framework

> Vengeance and forgiveness are marks along the spectrum of human responses to atrocity. Yet they stand in opposition: to forgive is to let go of vengeance; to avenge is to resist forgiving. Perhaps justice itself "partakes of both revenge and forgiveness." (Minow, 1998, p. 21)

As the quotation from legal scholar Martha Minow suggests, responses to the many instances of genocide and other atrocities committed by human beings against fellow human beings during the 20th century have ranged from the most noble to the most vindictive. The ideal of justice might be found in the continuum between these two poles. The massacre of the Armenian population by the Turks is assumed to be historically the first genocide of the 20th century, but the magnitude of the Holocaust caught the world's collective consciousness as "the emblematic limit case of human rights abuse" (Schaffer & Smith, 2004, p. 20). The Holocaust has marked humanity's memory because of the incommensurability of its horror as well as the failure of world leaders and citizens to take responsibility for the fate of the victims. This sense of guilt and responsibility, bewilderment at the "banality of evil," coupled with the massive archival and mnemonic work done to remember that which should never have happened—innocent children, men, and women being killed in the most atrocious and inhumane way so that there are little or no remains, no traces left—launched a conversation about evil, responsibility, guilt, memory, and forgiveness that continues fervently today. This discourse constitutes a fallible but necessary attempt to come to terms and comprehend that which is beyond comprehension but still demands accountability and justice.

For experts, this event and the end of World War II constitute the beginning of what is commonly referred to as the first wave of transitional justice in modern history. The establishment of the Nuremberg Military Tribunal and other tribunals set up to prosecute Nazi collaborators in Israel, France, and other European countries are the most significant consequences of this trend (Huntington, 1993). The second wave took transitional justice and democratization to the southern part of Europe, with countries such as Greece, Portugal, and Spain undergoing major political shifts in the mid to late 1970s. While these experiences have first been geographically limited to Western Europe, their impact has been felt worldwide. In addition, the flourishing of human rights discourse worldwide and end of the Cold War gave a boost to these political phenomena and contributed to a domino effect of transitional initiatives in Latin America and Eastern Europe, beginning in the mid-1980s. By the end of the century, the African and Asian continents were no longer immune to these upheavals as citizens in countries like South Africa, Burundi, Morocco in Africa, and the Philippines and Sri Lanka in Asia began to call for accountability and justice for crimes committed by states against their own people and for a change in political practices and institutions to safeguard against similar future massacres. These developments point to the emergence of a new global moral barometer evident in the international institutionalization of human rights discourses and practices (Barkan, 2000), an ongoing effort with setbacks as well as accomplishments. With this paradigm shift came an implicit universal understanding that democratic forms of governance are the most conducive to the actualization of these ideals, leading to calls for democratization in several parts of the globe.

These political upheavals have prompted the development of democratization studies as a field of study. For Guillermo O'Donnell and Phillippe Schmitter (1994), two political scientists who are credited with inaugurating the field of democratization studies, a transition is the period that marks "the interval between one political regime and another" (p. 6). Typically, transitional justice implies a transition from an authoritarian or repressive political regime to a more democratic arrangement or, in some cases, from a state of war to an enduring peace, or more generally from a violence, terror, and repression to a more dialogic state of affairs characteristic of deliberative democracy where inclusion of citizens' voices is integral to the political game (Hayner, 2002; Elster 2004; Smith, 2008). It is in this critical transitional period that new practices of rendering justice are formed. Because justice plays a central role in the political and moral foundation of any society, understanding the relative success or failure of these practices can provide insight into how the political future of any particular national community will likely unfold.

I should note, before going much further, that there is an additional approach to transitional justice that I do not discuss here: distributive justice, where the focus is more on the structural and institutional circumstances that led to the crime(s) or political violence. In this approach, to deal with the past and prevent it from happening again, one has to look at the material conditions that allowed the abuses to happen in the first place and to change them. Some observers who are critical of the South African experience of transitional justice point out that this is the approach that needed to be followed because the restorative approach did nothing to change the political and socioeconomic makeup of the country. The so-called distributive approach is often neglected because of its lack of popularity, difficulty of execution, and effective demand that the root structures of a society be revolutionized. But it also brings to the forefront of discussion the real conditions and costs for those who survive atrocity, which also highlights the variety of ethical and political practices, historical and national contexts, and particular cases that coalesce in determining retributive, distributive or restorative approaches, or some hybrid thereof, that is most appropriate.

Some nations, like Germany after the fall of Nazism, chose to prosecute the guilty and compensate victims, a combination of retribution (making perpetrators accountable through the judicial system) and restoration (repairing some of the harm done to victims through monetary compensation). Others like the Spanish after the death of Franco in the mid-1970s, chose collective amnesia (the pact of oblivion) and focused on the future (democratization) to the detriment of accountability and justice. Transitional justice, in post-Franco Spain, was a transition with neither punitive nor reparatory justice. Still, other countries like Argentina and Chile, decided that both retributive and restorative approaches to transitional justice with official trials, amnesty laws, and truth commissions were necessary to settle past accounts and build a better political future. Justice in these and other Latin American countries was meaningful only to the extent that those proven to be part of the killing squads were held accountable for their criminal actions. More recently, countries like South Africa and Morocco chose to forgo prosecutions and deal with their criminal political past primarily through truth commissions and reparation programs, which may signal a new shift in favor of restorative processes. This shift needs further examination, especially since it is not always clear why a country chooses a particular path to achieve transitional justice. Oftentimes, it is a negotiated deal between the outgoing regime and incoming government or, in some cases, the result of international pressure, like in Germany and Yugoslavia, or simply a matter to be determined by those in power. Be that as it may, the differences between retributive and restorative genres are especially important to ponder.

Retributive Justice

Retributive justice connotes punishment or penalizing of the person found guilty of the crime and is based on the principle of an eye-for-an-eye. The focus of the entire retributive process is on the criminal act itself and the presumed perpetrator of the crime who needs to pay for breaking the law; victims are rarely involved, except for monetary damages. The argument is favor of retribution is based on justice and accountability, which first begins with forensic truth. While the exposition and recording of truth are of utmost importance in a transition, there is disagreement among scholars about what constitutes the best course of action to expose or ascertain the truth and manage it. Mark Osiel (1999) argues that, in the aftermath of mass atrocities committed by a brutal state, it is best to take the retributive approach and address issues of truth in criminal trials where such an exposition can also have a pedagogical purpose. "This is because," he argues, "such trials, when effective as public spectacle, stimulate public discussion in ways that foster the liberal virtues of toleration, moderation, and civil respect" (p. 2). Public prosecution of those responsible can open up a space for a conversation about the moral and political foundations of the nation, thus contributing to the emergence and fostering of the deliberative space necessary for the flourishing of a democracy. Public trials can thus constitute an opportunity for reassessing and reasserting the moral foundation of a nation. In other words:

> [b]y highlighting official brutality and public complicity, these trials often make people willing to reassess their foundational beliefs and constitutive commitments, as few events in political life can do. [...] They are "moments of truth," in several senses. Specifically, they present moments of transformative opportunity on the lives of individuals and societies. (Osiel, 1999, p. 2)

Public trials can become the *Event* that marks the transition of a nation from a past of violence to a future free of violence and injustice, and where questions about public memory and national identity are engaged. Osiel (1999) refers to such public prosecutions as "refounding myths" of a nation, as they mark "a decisive break from their own pasts, celebrating the courage and imagination of those who effected this rupture" (p. 4). It is perhaps difficult for the victims or their families to accept that a genuine transition is in effect if those responsible for suffering have not accounted for their actions and paid a debt to society. Juan E. Mendez (1997), a legal scholar who has written extensively on transitional justice in Latin America and a proponent of prosecutions in situations of crimes against humanity, readily recognizes that the prosecutions are a tough choice to make and need to "be thoroughly justified in moral terms" (p. 274). He insists that retribution should not be equated with vengeance but as the natural consequence of actions that society recognizes as unlawful. He states that "An enlightened theory of punishment, therefore, puts the victim at the center of the need to redress wrongs: societies punish because they wish to signify to the victim that his or her plight will not go unheeded" (p. 275). In other words, to not punish the person or people responsible for the victim's plight is to fail the victims and society as well.

The argument for prosecution has to do with power, impunity and accountability, and the need to signify a genuine rupture with a past that needs to be known, evaluated, and judged according to universally established rules of justice. Turning the page on a bloody past without establishing the record in terms of individual and institutional responsibilities for crimes against humanity can be risky for a "re-born" nation, as it sets a bad precedent of impunity for a newly established government and may leave victims with a bad aftertaste of justice not being served. Mendez (1997) also notes that:

> both the need to consolidate a shaky democracy and the need to stop the fighting in a conflict situation undoubtedly condition the possibilities of redressing past wrongs, placing limits on what a policy of accountability can achieve. Those urgent demands, however, by no means diminish the objectives of truth and justice. On the contrary, it is increasingly recognized that making state criminals accountable says something about the democracy they are trying to establish, and that preserving memory and settling human rights accounts can be part of the formula for a lasting peace, as opposed to a lull in the fighting. (p. 257)

Prosecutions constitute an opportunity to distinguish collective from individual guilt by preventing or removing "the stigma of historic misdeeds from the innocent members of communities that are collectively blamed for the atrocities committed on other communities" (Mendez, 1997, p. 276).

Despite its merits, criminal law is no longer a first choice for transitioning societies primarily because it is not easy for new leaders to make the case for retribution in the midst of political shuffling and embryonic institutions. It is a difficult decision that poses political as well as ethical challenges for societies trying to turn the page on a traumatic past. The political price for trials is not always clear, but, of course, neither is the moral price for resisting justice. In addition, retribution rarely allows for the moral complexities of tragic situations to emerge and instead regards most criminal instances in rigid, black and white terms—that is, as perpetrator and victim. With this categorization set up as its foundation, criminal law makes the pursuit of reconciliation difficult and sometimes impossible. While criminal law puts the burden on the wrongdoer alone, the interactive process of reconciliation demands that both parties (victim and wrongdoer) engage one another and find common ground to move beyond the hatred, anger, and pain. For Wole Soyinka (1999), this common ground should be framed as "a need for a purgation of the past, the creation of a new sense of being ... after the collapse of a discredited and criminal order" (p. 19). This new sense of being and harmony, which may have never existed in that society previously, cannot easily be achieved within an exclusive legalistic framework, especially when it is difficult to assign blame and responsibility due to bureaucratic or logistical obstacles, or because bringing people to courts will unleash a new wave of violence, anger, and vindictiveness. Rwanda, Yugoslavia, and Iraq come to mind as primary exemplars of such vindictiveness, as many observers and citizens were dubious that justice was served through trials, or whether it was simply revenge, or a political ploy to close the can of worms that transitions tend to open. The fear of further violence creating a vicious cycle of revenge is often cited as a justification, and sometimes pretext, for avoiding retribution for perpetrators. The Spanish experience is a good example of this, as I discuss further on.

Retributive justice, in short, presupposes "that even [...] massive horrors can and should be treated as punishable criminal offenses perpetrated by identifiable individuals," and that fairness can never be achieved otherwise (Minow, 1998, p. 26). Fairness rarely results, as Minow (1998) argues: "the Nuremberg and Tokyo trials were condemned by many as travesties of justice, the spoils of the victors of war, and the selective prosecution of individuals for acts more properly attributable to governments themselves" (p. 27). If these trials were meant to set the tone and be a warning for would-be murderous regimes to deter future mass atrocities and genocides, they failed. In Rwanda, where genocide claimed the lives of 800,000 people, several flaws within the court were found. These included the lack of legal representation for several defendants and the public execution of at least 22 people, despite calls from several international organizations and the Pope to halt the executions. It was perceived as another round of ethnic revenge, rather than an attempt to serve justice for the victims of the genocide (Minow, 1998, p. 124). Still, Mendez (1997) argues that deterrence should never be the motivation for retribution or the sole argument in favor of prosecution: "Societies can only hope that punishment will deter the transgressor as well as other potential offenders, but can never assume deterrence" (p. 275). Retribution, then, is an attractive option for societies seeking to establish a clean break with a shameful past by recognizing the injustice and suffering incurred by victims and making those found responsible accountable for their criminal actions. But this path can also create societal and political tensions and make the restoration of societal bond and trust a challenging task.

Restorative Justice

Restorative justice is an approach where all parties to the criminal event are involved: perpetrators and victim/survivors.[1] The rationale here is that perpetrators and victims are part of the same community and the outcome of any justice served must involve all. More important than the crime committed and the law broken are the consequences of the criminal act(s) on victims. We should keep in mind that restorative approaches to crime emerged first in small scale individual contexts, where bringing the offender and the victim together to face each other and seek apology, gaining forgiveness (respectfully) and ultimately reconciliation, seemed a better alternative than retributive justice in some cases, especially within small communities where there is a threat that retributive justice will bring more harm than good to the community as a whole. Through symbolic gestures such as apology and financial incentives such as monetary compensations, restorative justice typically provides for repairing the relationship between the person(s) who committed the harmful acts and those who were affected directly by it:

> Restorative justice emphasizes the humanity of both offenders and victims. It seeks repair of social connections and peace rather than retribution against the offenders. Building connections and enhancing communication between perpetrators and those they victimized, and forging ties across the community, takes precedence over punishment or law enforcement. (Minow, 1998, p. 92)

In short, the restorative approach is less procedural and more relational and dialogic than its retributive counterpart. In addition, as Hugo Van Der Merwe (2009) argues, it is "a more inclusive process, involving participation by both victim and perpetrator" (p. 119).

Inclusiveness and dialogism may explain why the restorative approach has become the dominant trend in dealing with mass intra-national human rights violations, when traditional approaches to justice do not seem like a realistic option either because of logistic issues or the fear that retribution would seem too much like vengeance or victors' justice. In addition, jurists and scholars have long agonized about the difficulty of establishing responsibilities in large-scale crimes. The dynamics of collective decision-making are so complex that it is difficult to assign responsibility for crimes, and pointing a finger at ostensibly responsible individuals becomes a very thorny issue. Instead, the state typically assigns institutional responsibility to commissions whose members are appointed by the President, Monarch or other ruling authority. One of the logistical and legal challenges faced by many courts after the fall of a discredited and murderous regime is that no viable state exists to assign responsibility or investigate the alleged violations. The prosecutions are then moved elsewhere, as witnessed in the Nuremberg trials, the International Tribunal for the former Yugoslavia, and other instances.

The restorative genre of transitional justice as a means for dealing with the aftermath of large-scale political violence in recent years merits more intensive critical scrutiny because countries emerging from decades of conflict and political violence have turned to such approaches not so much because of moral or ethical imperatives, or the need to establish political and legal legitimacy, but as an expedient way to settle accounts. Truth-seeking and reconciliation commissions, forums for redress and compensations, and the development of venues for remembrance of past victims are not as costly, nor as politically risky, as legal prosecutions. If restorative justice can be an acceptable and working forum for seeking justice in small scale offenses where parties involved are easily identified and show clear willingness to be part of the project, can the same be said about mass violations where neither victims nor perpetrators are willing participants, where the state that oversees the process is implicated in the atrocities, and where the outcome largely determines the future of society as a whole?

In order to establish their legitimacy and institute a clear rupture with past practices, transitional states have indeed embraced truth commissions as a politically safe and socially acceptable means of coming to terms with their past. There is an ethical as well as political dimension to these undertakings implicit in the phrase *transitional justice*. The transition is the goal of these efforts as the new leaders and society want to start fresh and build a better political future, free of the demons of the past. Still, transitions cannot happen without addressing the ethical, unethical, and perhaps quasi-ethical features of the past; that is, serving justice for those innocent citizens who had been arbitrarily jailed, tortured, disappeared, or murdered. There are exceptions, of course, like Spain, a nation that made a wild bid to turn the page and never look back at its violent past; but even the Spanish experience has recently shown that an indigested past will always come back to haunt its people. The Spanish people are now on a quest to make sense of their Francoist past and amends with its victims because, clearly, despite the political success of their transition, issues of justice are still looming in Spanish collective memory (Aguilar, 2001).

The process of burying a bloody past is not simply one of moving on but also developing strategies that can adequately serve justice and rebuild a national political identity based on trust and a sense of belonging. Reforms that seek to redistribute shares of political power more equally within the system and establish safeguards to prevent political abuse and corruption are part of the democratization (and consolidation) package. The connection between transitional justice processes and democratization has clearly been established and is important, but a full explication of this relationship is beyond the scope of this writing.[2] Still, it is worth restating that the rhetoric of transitional justice has borrowed much from the liberal ideals of democracy and human rights discourse. While this heritage does exist, one should not necessarily assume that countries that develop truth and reconciliation commission, and adopt juridical and rhetorical practices to deal with past political violence, automatically transition to democracy. In fact, some scholars such as Carothers point out that only a small percentage of countries that are called transitional do in fact become democratic. Instead of relying on these processes as a sign or an index of democratization, perhaps the pertinent question to ask is how do rhetorical practices of transitional justice such as truth commissions, reparation programs, and memorialization contribute to the larger and more challenging task of transforming the political culture of a country from a rule of violence and terror to the rule of law, a just law? What do these practices accomplish for citizens and nations emerging from violence and victimization?

There is no recipe or blueprint to follow in any given case of transitional justice. But it is safe to say that restorative transitional processes seek to serve some kind of justice after the end of a violent political era, an era marked by authoritarian rule and civil strife, and they do so by (a) devising means to repair damages incurred by victims, and (b) making sure that similar abuses and violence do not happen again. Through civic engagement with the past and the drive to build a just society where citizens are free from coercion, fear and violence, a societal and political transformation takes place ipso facto. Historical and contemporary experiences of transitional justice show that the rhetoric of transitional justice seeks to reintroduce the idea of the just within the polis and within civic discourse, at the very least. Citizens who are the driving force behind experiences of transitional justice are rhetors who present arguments to advance the idea of the just by pointing out injustices in their country and in humanity generally. Thus it seems clear that, while discourses and practices of transitional justice do not always guarantee a genuine or lasting democratization, or justice for that matter, they are necessarily transformative for the societies in which they take place.

The national experiences noted thus far reveal that transitional justice incorporates a variety of trends and practices that seek answers to questions such as those posed by Priscilla Hayner (2002):

> What should be done with a recent history full of victims, perpetrators, secretly buried bodies, pervasive fear, and official denial? Should this past be exhumed, preserved, acknowledged, apologized for? How can a nation of enemies be reunited, former opponents reconciled, in the context of such a violent history and often bitter, festering wounds? What should be done with hundreds or thousands of perpetrators still walking free? And how can a new government prevent such atrocities from being repeated in the future? (p. 4)

In the attempt to address these daunting questions, I elaborate in the following pages on the three major non-legalistic trends that have emerged in response to widespread violence perpetrated by individuals acting in the name of the state. The first is the establishment and recording of truth and, sometimes, mending of rifts and enmity, through what has come to be known as truth and reconciliation commissions. Here victims and perpetrators come to narrate and confront their common past and, sometimes, attempt to reconcile. The second is the development of initiatives aimed at dealing with and repairing the physical, financial as well as the psychological harm suffered by victims and their families, a process referred to as reparations. Third is the creation of programs for memorialization purposes, such as the building of museums, the establishment of commemorative ceremonies and other such events and spaces to document and remember the past. Beyond the political capital these processes provide the incoming or continuing leaders, I am interested in how the rhetoric of truth, justice, and memory invoked during transitions shape the past, and most importantly, contribute to the development of a new ethical sensibility within a polity that is facing its own state's violence against its own people.

Truth Commissions, Reconciliation, and the Problem of Forgiveness

> [t]he only ground they share is that of recognition of a need for a purgation of the past, the creation of a new sense of being, but they do serve us as two extreme options for the initiation of such a process after the collapse of a discredited and criminal order. (Soyinka, 1999, p. 19)

In recent years, truth commissions (also called truth and reconciliation commissions or TRCs) have emerged as a new instrument in efforts to address crimes committed by a state against its own people. As previously suggested, the restorative approach has become popular because of logistical, political, and ethical issues that might arise from retribution. TRCs have gained momentum because transitional states face the moral imperative to address the injustices done to victims and their families by officials acting in the name of the state; addressing the past is also a political necessity for the new leaders to establish their legitimacy and institute a clear rupture with past politics. Hayner (2002) defines truth commissions as:

> [B]odies that share the following characteristics: (1) truth commissions focus on the past; (2) they investigate a pattern of abuses over a period of time, rather than a specific event; (3) a truth commission is a temporary body, typically in operation for six months to two years, and completing its work with the submission of a report; and (4) these commissions are officially sanctioned, authorized, or empowered by the state. (p. 14)

Truth commissions conduct investigations and collect testimonies for the purpose of compiling a story about the past, a narrative of survivors, perpetrators and, sometimes, bystanders. But one would be naïve to believe that such narrative has only historical value. The work of TRCs has implications for the past but also for the present and the future of the community because by opening up the past for review and judgment, issues of accountability and impunity are addressed. In the exposition of facts about the past, responsibilities are assigned and wrongdoers identified, so these commissions have forensic value as well. It is a rhetorical effort to make sense of the past and assign meaning to the nation's collective narrative. Uncovering what happened in a country's bloody past is necessary, but not sufficient. Of equal importance is the necessity to "*disseminate* the truth about past atrocities" (Crocker, 2006, p. 3; emphasis added).

The emphasis on dissemination of information about the past is important to consider. In most countries with a history of political violence, while the repressive practices of the state are usually widely known, very few people dare to speak publicly about them. As Hannah Arendt (1958) argues, fear is one the first consequences of the rule of terror in a totalitarian, and by extension, authoritarian state. Fear is a strong political ally of the state that is terrorizing its people and serves to silence and keep most citizens in line. The fear that a friend or a family member could be the next victim of arbitrary repression and violence serves as a strong motivation for silence. While most people are typically aware that some of their fellow citizens or neighbors are being arbitrarily detained, tortured, and executed, the gritty details escape their knowledge because of the secrecy that is central to such political formations. Lack of information and dissemination contributes to citizens being kept in a state of continuous fear because no one knows for sure what happens and why, and even those who do have some knowledge or understanding of what is going on can only speak in muffled voices. Thus, after the fall of a criminal regime, it becomes crucial that information about the past be widely disseminated; by making the "hard facts" public, "the moral significance of individual account-ability, the identity of individual perpetrators is brought to light" (Crocker, 2006, p. 3). Listening to victims' testimonies during public hearings is only the first stage in acknowledging their story; publicizing it provides greater acknowledgment and serves to symbolically repair the harm and humiliation that victims endured. But testimonies and public hearings have other objectives beyond appeasing victims by providing them with a forum to share their bleak stories. Mark Freeman (2006) argues that the fact that victims are the main focus of truth commissions does not mean that "a truth commission is always self-consciously victim-centered (because some are not), nor does it mean that a truth commission is concerned only with victims (because they are not)" (p. 17). Besides the ethical horizon of redeeming victims and recognizing the injustice they have been subjected to, truth commissions have a political value. As a significant part of truth commissions, public hearings provide legitimacy to the entire restorative process. By showcasing victims and their stories dur-ing public hearings, national and international audiences are invited to see for themselves that silencing victims is no longer accepted and that some form of justice is being served. Public hearings showcase a "society in transition" and are meant to be an indicator of change and transformation because they nec-essarily suggest an affinity with the South African experience of transitional justice, one that many regimes try to emulate, as I will discuss.

The purpose of TRCs, then, is two-fold. First, they seek to reconstruct a nar-rative of the past, primarily from the victims' perspective. This reconstruction is embedded in a historical (educational) horizon, but, as previously suggested, also serves a political goal. By knowing what happened, it may be possible institutionally to prevent it from happening again by putting in place reforms that safeguard against horrific practices reproducing themselves. Second, and just as important, TRCs provide the victims with a voice. Suddenly, after many years of repression, having an official and safe forum to speak and share their past with their fellow citizens does grant citizen status again and welcomes citizens/survivors back into the political community. The forum to speak sig-nifies that their voices matter within the polis, that their suffering matters, that what happened to them was wrong, and that something should come out of their brave act of narrating their suffering. The information gathered during the hearings of the commissions typically serves as the basis for determining eligibility for reparations and for determining the type and amount of repa-ration necessary in each case. More importantly, truth commissions provide victims and society with hope, which might be faint and myopic, but after years of silence, violence, and horror, to be able to participate in public life in itself constitutes a hopeful moment, if one believes one will help bring about significant change as transitional practices promise.

The best contemporary illustration of the pursuit of such lofty goals and hope is, almost unanimously, to be found in the South African experience of truth and reconciliation, prompting some observers to refer to it as the African Athens. The creation of the South African Truth and Reconciliation Commission in the mid-1990s did indeed popularize the idea of truth commissions and political reconciliation as legitimate and appropriate means to address past violence and oppression. But, as intimated in the introduction, transitional justice did not begin with South Africa, as it can be traced (in the West at least) to the Greeks (Elster, 2004). Millennia ago, like South Africa and many contemporary national communities, the Athenians had to find ways to come together as citizens of the same polis after two political transitions, resulting from civil war (Elster, 2004, p. 3). Athenian citizens were faced with civil strife several times and had to devise means to deal with the aftermath of these difficult moments in their history. Andrew Wolpert (2002) argues that amnesty and reconciliation were at the center of Athens' recovery, deemed the best course of action due to the urgent political need to restore peace and harmony within the polis. But reconciliation for the Athenians did not mean that people forgot the violence that preceded the amnesty, nor the betrayal of some of their fellow citizens. They did not simply start a new page of their history. These events served as an opportunity to think and deliberate about the causes, consequences of and means to address political disruptions that cause harm to the polis. This historian's discussion of the Athenian experience of reconciliation after the War of the Thirty suggests that reconciliation is not only an ancient approach to conflict resolution but also one that cannot be explained in purely political terms. Wolpert (2002) notes:

> Historians have advanced many explanations for the success of the reconciliation: the terms of the agreement, the political condition of the Greek world, the social and economic problems of Athens. They have shown that revenge and retribution were not viable options, but the Athenians could have simply dismissed pragmatic considerations in order to obtain private satisfaction for past grievances. Causal explanations present the reconciliation as a *fait accompli*, as if there were only one possible outcome to the civil war. But as Corcyra shows, pragmatic considerations do not always lead a people to choose the course of action that best serves its interests. (p. xii)

Although political considerations—or negotiated deals—certainly contribute to the making or re-making of a nation, as the Athenian situation has shown, moral and ethical considerations do as well, or, in any case, should. The quest for truth within a national context foreshadows a rhetorical process that is ethically charged because the outcome has consequences for the past, the present, and the future for generations to come. Although truth and reconciliation have pragmatic consequences with respect to the way a nation or community reinvents itself after a period of violence, mistrust and injustice, they are fundamentally rhetorical metaphors with serious ethical implications. For a national community whose sociopolitical identity and sense of morality have been shattered by violence and injustice, establishing and listening to the truth and finding the words to come together as part of the same nation are indeed important goals. But so is ethical judgment, as public discourse about the atrocities establishes a new teleological orientation, one marked most significantly by the metaphor of reconciliation.

The process of burying the past in such circumstances is not simply one of moving on but also developing strategies that can adequately serve justice and rebuild a national political identity based on trust and a sense of belonging. Hence the rhetorical significance of the reconciliation metaphor, which has captured the imagination of global citizens and scholars alike, especially in relation to the South African experience. The leadership of Archbishop Desmond Tutu and Nelson Mandela in South Africa has provided legitimacy and confirmation to the practice of reconciliation. Although the term has several possible referents, it should be clear that, in the context of this discussion, reconciliation is an attempt to move beyond enmity and reach a modicum of normalcy in socio-political relationships. One cannot expect that victims/survivors and perpetrators will become friends or convivial colleagues, or even speak to each other if they happen to meet in the street, but hope typically is that reconciliation can achieve a minimal level of civility that is conducive to peaceful political cohabitation. The question remains: How is reconciliation achieved? Or, as Marc Howard Ross (2004) asks: "How do we know it when we see it?" (p. 198). The potential of reconciliation lies in its rhetorical power. Doxtader (2003) argues that reconciliation is a rhetorical exercise in recollecting the past for the purpose of making the future; it is very much a call for rhetoric that parties engaged in conflict use to move beyond the violence of the past: "With a middle voice, reconciliation both enacts and opens the potential for rhetorical invention. It is a constitutive faith in the work of those words that strive to open, make and sustain a beginning" (Ross, p. 268). Reconciliation is an attempt to transform an event into something that is acceptable to the parties involved; it is a rhetorical framing of the past for the purpose of a present that moves beyond the violence and enmity of the past. In short, reconciliation serves to re-join the community and construct a narrative about the past that parties to the conflict accept as part of their common legacy.

As rhetorical praxis, the mission of reconciliation is to struggle to communicate even when speechless because at that very moment, the "saying" matters more than the "said" (in the sense articulated by Levinas). One trusts that the saying of the words, not only their referents, have the power or force to change enmity into trust. Trust in these circumstances, and thus the significance of the words spoken, can only be achieved through forgiveness, which is often considered either a condition for, or an outcome of, reconciliation. As Elder (1998) argues:

> When collectivities are involved, the issue of forgiveness becomes much more complicated than in the one-to-one model of an injured person and a wrongdoer sharing a moral community. The increased complexity of the

situation need not lead us to abandon efforts to encourage "forgiveness" or the attitudes that accompany forgiveness. If, ultimately, one is interested in processes of reconciliation, the study of forgiveness as a potential contributor to reconciliation becomes of prime importance. (p. 161)

Tutu thinks of forgiveness as a necessity, even a pre-requisite for peace and reconciliation. If people recognize their guilt and confess it, which is indeed the hope of every TRC, then victims should be able to forgive them—but not be asked to forget. When a person says that he or she forgives someone, one assumes that a wrong has been committed, but that the wronged person no longer holds grudges against that perpetrator of the wrong. Joanna North (1998) argues that forgiveness should not mean forgetting and that an appropriate conception of forgiveness does not:

> require that we forgo punishment altogether or that we should, in forgiving, attempt to annul the existence of the wrong done. Forgiveness does not remove the fact or the event of wrongdoing but instead relies upon the recognition of wrong having been committed in order for the process of forgiveness to be made possible. (p. 17)

To forgive is neither to forget nor to accept the consequences of another's wrongdoing but to put distance between the act, the fault, and the actor, the doer of the act. Still, determining responsibility and seeking forgiveness should be just the beginning of the work of reconciliation, not its end. As Doxtader (2003) argues:

> Reconciliation is not the end of violence but a demonstration of how the threat of endless violence can instill a mutual desire for dialogue between enemies, it is not a revolutionary promise but the appearance of a present in which to make the time and space for invention; ... it is not forgiveness but the occasion for deliberation about what can and ought to be forgiven; it is not the achievement of peace but the creation of a commons in which to address the substantive question of what living in peace actually means. (p. 284)

It follows, then, that to reconcile is not necessarily to forgive, but to engage in a conversation about the event that led to the conflict in the first place; it is the attempt to find common ground to create the possibility for a non-violent present and potentially achieve forgiveness.

Reconciliation presupposes that public discourse about atrocities has developed, that those damaged or wronged have found an idiom (be it religious, nationalist, or ethical) to express these damages and wrongs, and that their expression is heard and acknowledged by those responsible, and by other witnesses however far removed they may be from the original acts. Reconciliation suggests a kind of absolution. But forgiveness is not absolution, nor does it necessarily lead to reconciliation. So what does an act of forgiveness entail? Jacques Derrida's insights on this truly remarkable phenomenon are notewor- thy. In his essay on forgiveness, Derrida (2001) asks:

> In order for there to be forgiveness, must one not on the contrary forgive both the fault and the guilty as such, where the one and the other remain as irreversible as the evil, as evil itself, and being capable of repeating itself, unforgivably, without transformation, without amelioration, without repentance or promise? Must one not maintain that an act of forgiveness worthy of its name, if there ever is such a thing, must forgive the unforgiv- able, and without condition? (p. 39)

Derrida's question is a rhetorical one—an act of forgiveness exists only to the extent that it forgives that which cannot be forgiven, or at least conceived as such. Forgiveness is an unconditional act not to be used strategically or politi- cally. It is a gift that does not ask for exchange, reward, or reciprocity:

> Each time forgiveness is at the service of a finality, be it noble and spiri- tual (atonement or redemption, reconciliation, salvation), each time that it aims to re-establish a normality (social, national, political, psychological) by a work of mourning, by some therapy or ecology of memory, then the "forgiveness" is not pure—nor is its concept. (Derrida, 2001, p. 32)

When persons or groups use forgiveness to normalize relations or to reconcile, as Tutu argues (1999), the act of forgiveness loses its essence because it is no longer the end but the means to an end. Derrida (2001) argues against the use of forgiveness in the context of a nation attempting to deal with a traumatic past: "Forgiveness does not, it should never amount to a therapy of reconcili- ation" (p. 41). If reconciliation requires a mediator or a mediating institution, forgiveness does not. Still, it is primarily the perpetrator and the victim who are involved in an instance of forgiveness and, for Derrida (2001) "as soon as a third party intervenes, one can again speak of amnesty, reconciliation, repara- tion, etc., but certainly not of pure forgiveness in the strict sense" (p. 42). For authentic forgiveness to take place, it must occur between the people who are directly concerned. No state or institution has the right to grant forgiveness in the name of a victim (especially one who cannot speak for himself or herself). Hannah Arendt (1958) goes further and argues that forgiveness "unexpect- edly, unconditioned by the act which provoked it and therefore freeing from its consequences both the one who forgives and the one who is forgiven" (p. 241). This is not to say that the quest for justice and the act of forgiveness are mutu- ally exclusive; they simply belong to different registers. That said, the South African example needs to be considered an exception, not the rule, and the particulars of that case—regaining control of the nation, conditions of nego- tiation, etc. that allowed the oppressed not to punish the oppressors—should perhaps be more fully considered.

Reconciliation and retribution also belong to different registers—one practice cannot be substituted for the other, or translated into one another, but in some instances they are intimately connected. As I hope to have shown thus far, national political reconciliation is a project to re-invent the community after a bloody past and create a space of dialogue and deliberation that is free from violence and coercion and includes all political actors—victims, perpetrators, and bystanders. Reconciliation as such is a rhetorical and civic effort to find words to frame the past and negotiate the terms of the transition into the future. Along these lines, John Hatch (2003) argues that reconciliation should be conceived within a "tragicomic framing" that does indeed include symbolic acts such as apology and forgiveness (p. 753). To reconcile is then to take atrocities seriously and assign blame, but also to transform tragedy into comedy such that the focus is on the offense rather than the offenders or offended. This switch of focus produces the opposite of what a retributive framework is likely to produce, as previously indicated. For Kirt Wilson (2004), the model that Hatch (2003) refers to does nothing to address the real problem that led to the crisis and violence in the first place.

For instance, if South Africa is the model to emulate for reconciliation, one has first to acknowledge that reconciliation did nothing much in changing the structural injustices that were present during the Apartheid government. Searching for truth and bringing victims and perpetrators together to practice reconciliation might have ended the bloodshed and squelched the enmity and hatred, but these practices have not affected the political and socioeconomic make-up of the country, as White South Africans did not lose the privileges bestowed upon them during Apartheid, and the masses of Black South Africans still live in poverty and despair. Mark McPhail (2004) argues that, while Hatch's call for reconciliation could contribute to a genuine dialogue about race in the United States, "it [reconciliation] will require coming to grips with the past in order to construct a new vision for the future" (p. 398). For McPhail (2004), this engagement with the past must include a collective effort of atonement and apology from Whites, in the case of both South Africa and the United States.

Although such a collective apology does not seem to be forthcoming, reconciliation still may occur if there is a moral or theological drive on the part of the antagonists to change the present and build a harmonious and interdependent future. Moreover, reconciliation demands an acknowledgment of unjust and criminal actions and expressions of remorse for the horrific consequences of those actions on innocent people. Reconciliation is not justice but an acknowledgment of injustice; this is why issues of apology, atonement and forgiveness are almost always invoked. As an acknowledgment of guilt and expression of remorse, apologies are a pre-requisite for reconciliation; otherwise how would a victim accept to reconcile with her victimizer? Reconciliation cannot be authentic if the victims do not have a feeling that some kind of justice has been served, not necessarily retributive justice but justice nevertheless—we might call it symbolic justice. Symbolic justice, then, should be at the heart of reconciliation and begins with the unveiling of the truth that takes place during public hearings. For example, in Morocco, where a process of equity and reconciliation was recently launched by the same state that committed the crimes against its citizens, the idea of reconciliation appears devoid of any substance or meaning for some victims, a cipher to be filled by whatever the dominant order wants the public to believe. Victims are not sure who they are supposed to reconcile with as no one has come forward to tell the truth about the state's involvement in criminal activity during what is commonly referred to by survivors of Hassan II as the "Years of Lead" (Smith & Loudiy, 2005). Unlike what we have seen in South Africa, no one in Hassan II's regime has ever stepped forward or taken responsibility for his murderous acts, let alone asked for forgiveness. Thus far, the equity and reconciliation process in Morocco has produced a truth commission for victims to relate their ordeal, with clear instructions not to name any perpetrator. Several Moroccan victims I spoke with have suggested that, for them, reconciliation as it has been framed by the state's commission is meaningless because no one has even acknowledged wrongdoing.

I will offer a personal example here, as several members of my family were unjustly persecuted for their political beliefs during the Years of Lead in Morocco. My grandmother lost her 25-year-old daughter (my aunt, Saida Menebhi) because of the state's criminal action. Who is my grandmother supposed to reconcile with if no one has ever come forward to take responsibility for her loss and grief? My father was imprisoned for 10 years for a political opinion when I was 1 month old. Who is he supposed to reconcile with for the loss of those years, or his wife or daughter? Ostensibly we and thousands of other Moroccan families are supposed to reconcile with an abstract entity, as the final report of the commission encourages; there is no mention of any name. We are supposed to reconcile with "security forces" or "the authorities," or even more generally, with "history." In fact, the commission's report proffers an understanding of reconciliation as an idea that does not involve victims and perpetrators at all. According to the report, the process of reconciliation of Moroccans with their history began in the early 1990s with the implementation of institutional reforms and the promotion of human rights and is an ongoing process. But clearly, this process has not involved perpetrators who have been provided with both anonymity and impunity. Many victims and Moroccan human rights advocates are justly calling this a farce, a ploy to provide the state with renewed legitimacy and squash any effort to secure accountability. Surely, it is not an effort geared toward genuine reconciliation. In this particular case, reconciliation is connected to the issue of cheap grace and will not happen without perpetrators joining in the effort, either voluntarily or involuntarily. Reconciliation needs to be framed in terms of an exchange, and the terms of the exchange must be clearly articulated. In South Africa, for example, the gain for perpetrators was quite attractive: amnesty. It was an opportunity for perpetrators to express genuine remorse and take responsibility for their actions, or buy off one's freedom and clear one's conscience of guilt and responsibility. In either case, perpetrators had the courage to show their faces and accept the shame and stigma associated with their actions.

As a political process, TRCs have limitations, and that is why, as previously suggested, victims often do expect more from these experiences that they can possibly deliver (Hayner, 2002). When victims or their families expect a sense of closure as an outcome of testifying and sometimes meeting with those who committed crimes against them or their family members, this goal can rarely be achieved. If the act of testifying and remembering the past can, in the long run, bring a sense of closure, it probably does not do so in the immediate aftermath of a public testimony where the witness (victim) must recall his or her torturous experience. Surely, the act of testifying and reliving the ordeal of being tortured, or witnessing one's sister or daughter being raped, tortured, or murdered must be an excruciating experience. Still, the hope is that the pain that such an experience brings about is somewhat matched by feelings of acknowledgment and relief that the duty of memory has been accomplished. In terms of bringing the nation closer to a genuine political transition or democracy, TRCs can both contribute and hinder such a goal.

Truth commissions do contribute to democratization by exposing some truths about the past, providing victims with a political voice, acknowledgment of the wrongs they have been subjected to, and establishing responsibilities. All of these contributions are positive achievements for a nation that desires to reinvent itself. Nevertheless, truth commissions alone are never sufficient to move a society beyond a past of violence amidst calls for justice. They constitute only the first step in engaging the past, one part of the puzzle. It is in their investigative work that the next step for serving justice is discovered: reparations. The issue of reparations is a rhetorical battle about (a) what constitutes a legitimate claim for reparations or, in other words, who is a worthy recipient of reparation; (b) how to assess the worth of human suffering and loss, and, once all of these issues have been settled; (3) what is the appropriate type of reparation required for the particular case: apology, restitution, or monetary compensation?

The Rhetoric of Reparations, Restitutions, and Compensations

What is cost no one is telling.
Can't subtract what might have been.
Can't add up to a sum we understand.
Can't subdivide what once was seen

Can carve a tombstone for the dead,
memorialize with flowers and crosses,
exhume a body, clear a name,
issue receipts for wrongs and losses.

But can't repair, and can't restore,
an uncut arm, unbruised genital,
untroubled sleep, unscarred face,
unweeping mother, children, faith
or wide unwatching private space.

(Ingrid De Kok, 2006, p. 139)

Demands for reparations have become common, and so have public apologies for past injustices. As one scholar has noted, claims for restitution or compensation for past injustice have reached epidemic proportions (Thompson, 2002). We should keep in mind that there is a difference between reparation and restitution. Barkan (2000) notes that "restitution traverses the legal boundaries between actual restitution, reparation, compensation, and even apologies for wrongdoing and acquires cultural and political significance" (p. xix). Some see in this new phenomenon the emergence of a new global morality, others the festering of a culture of victimhood (Barkan, 2000). While this trend is recent, the experiences it attempts to address are not; political and historical injustices are as old as humanity itself. What has changed is the increasing legitimacy and righteousness of these claims, especially in the aftermath of World War II and the legacy of the Nuremberg trials. As a case in point, Barkan (2000) argues that

> In this context [post-Cold War] public awareness of crimes against humanity committed by governments is increasingly translated into a political force. The abhorrence of such violations of such human rights has even become an acceptable motive for national and international intervention in "domestic" politics and a rationale for war waged by regional and international organizations. [...] opposition to genocide, support for human rights, and the fear of being implicated in crimes against humanity (even by inaction) have become practical, not even lofty, ideals. (p. xi)

Victims/survivors have become more assertive about their right to restitution and compensation, and it also seems that perpetrators no longer resist the call for reparations from their victims, due to feelings of guilt, perhaps shame and, most likely, the stigma associated with being a perpetrator of violence. With this increasing legitimacy of the human rights discourse within the international political community, and its acceptance by public opinion as a legitimate framework for dealing with injustice, reparations have become linked to political morality and justice. These ideas of justice and morality are actually at the heart of discussions about reparations, and can be traced back to the Enlightenment ideals of liberty, equality, and the pursuit of happiness, which, Barkan (2000) argues, have "become the predominant global ideology" (p. 310). I reference Barkan at some length here because he engages in an important discussion about the postmodern critique of enlightenment principles (and the modernist project) as they relate to today's politics. He explains how, despite their widespread critique in academic circles over the last few decades, these Enlightenment ideals have heavily impacted political claims for justice worldwide, so it is true that any discourse about restitution or reparation for lost of life and liberties under a tyrannical regime would simply be impossible otherwise. Still, he argues that "demands for political and economic justice, which go beyond the traditional liberal principles, inform [a] neo-Enlightenment that increasingly includes compensation for past deprivations and historical injustices" (pp. 311–312). In short, Enlightenment ideals alone cannot explain the redress or reparations movement; especially in the face of the incoherence that characterizes global responses to reparation claims.

For instance, many nations, like Japan and Turkey, still refuse to accept their responsibility in past genocide and other mass human rights violations. Although it has acknowledged the facts of the Nanking massacre in China, for example, and expressed regret for the consequences of the "incident" and "deeply reproaches itself," Japan has yet to present an official apology to China (Brooks, 1999, p. 109). Similarly, Turkey continues to refer to the politically motivated killing of two million Armenians as the unfortunate consequence of civil war during the reign of the Ottoman Empire and still resists calls for acknowledgment of the Armenian genocide. It would be a moral victory for victims and descendants of the Nanking massacre and the Armenian genocide, to mention just these two, if their proper names were used in reference to them, and if they received public apologies from leaders of Japan and Turkey, respectively. Their claims for reparations are symbolic; giving the massacre of thousands of people its proper name and apologizing for the harm inflicted on victims will not bring back the dead but simply honor their memory.

Given the previous discussion of the supremacy of the human rights discourse in global politics, one would infer that Turkey and Japan, two democratic countries with excellent relationships with their Western counterparts, would be either pressed to give in to these moral demands (as respectable national actors in the international community), or become political pariahs. But other issues complicate this, including geopolitical concerns. For instance, U. S. Senate Resolution 106 is a bill that sought to have the Armenian genocide publicly recognized by the President of the United States, but it was shelved in 2007 because of concerns that such a rhetorical act might alienate our Turkish allies during challenging times. Ultimately, the United States (in the person of its leader) surrendered to purely strategic needs and did not sign the bill, so as not to embarrass our allies in the war against terror. These historical examples are a testament to the power of rhetorical acts such as apologies; their utterance literally changes the moral landscape for victims and perpetrators, which explains the Turkish and Japanese resistance. As Nicholas Tavuchis nicely puts it: "Apology speaks to something larger than any particular offense and works its magic by a kind of speech that cannot be contained or understood merely in terms of expediency or the desire to achieve reconciliation" (quoted in Minow, 1998, p. 91).

In the context of pervasive violence that shatters people's lives and strips them from their most basic rights, it is perhaps difficult to grasp what is truly meant by reparations, or to come up with anything that can repair such loss and mitigate the pain. Reparations clearly have a symbolic aspect but there must also be a tangible gain for victims who lost loved ones and whose livelihood was compromised as a result of state violence and criminal acts. Ingrid De Kok, a South African poet whose powerful phrases introduce this section, sees reparations as "The action of restoring something to a proper or former state; spiritual restoration; the action of making amends for a wrong or loss; compensation for war damage by a defeated state" (2006, p. 139, italics in original). This definition suggests, first, that reparations are about restoration. Restoration can include restitution (of lost property, for example), compensation or indemnification (a lump sum of money to help with medical expenses or scholarship funds), and apology (a symbolic gesture). It is also about making good again. And it is often the result of defeat, political or moral.

Alfred Brophy's (2008) discussion of reparations about the impact of slavery on the African American community in the United States clearly highlights these nuances. Brophy (2008) distinguished two types of reparations: Backward-looking and forward-looking. Backward-looking reparations include efforts that seek to evaluate the damage that occurred in the past and repair it though financial means such as restitution of lost property or wages, payment of medical expenses for physical or psychological harm, as well as public apologies or calls for forgiveness. Forward-looking efforts, on the other hand, focus more on the future as their goal is to improve the livelihood of those impacted by past harm as well as consider and implement institutional reforms to ensure that similar violations never happen again. Building better houses and schools, offering scholarships and other such measures seek to augment the quality of life of those who were victimized by previous circumstances. Reparations, in this case, are equated with the improvement of victims' future lives, injustices of the past can be expunged, and perpetrators are able to atone for past deeds.

The most significant reparations package in modern history is without doubt the compensatory efforts towards German Jews after the fall of Nazi Germany, which have been widely documented because, as previously suggested, postwar trials established the legal precedent and historical foundation for an international legal system that not only recognized and defined genocide and human rights but also established a framework for dealing with the consequences of what is now commonly referred to as crimes against humanity. While it was clear that no money can ever resurrect the deceased nor make up for the suffering of millions of innocent people, the Jewish population had lost so much (in terms of human life as well as financial assets) because of Nazi persecution that compensatory efforts were necessary to "make good" again (Kritz, 1995, p. 47). In a speech meant for German and international audiences, Chancellor Konrad Adenauer, who is credited with starting the reparation program for victims of Nazi Germany, explained the necessity for repairing the harm incurred by Jews:

> unspeakable crimes were perpetrated in the name of the German people which impose upon them the obligation to make moral and material amends, both with regard to the material damage which Jews have suffered and with regard to Jewish property for which they are no longer individual claimants. (Kritz, 1995, p. 48)

These reparations were not only a political necessity but also a moral obligation for Germany to regain its status of a respectable nation in the world. To clear their conscience and their name, Germans developed two types of reparation programs: Restitution and indemnification. In addition, persons who had been stripped of their citizenship or professional degrees because of political motives were rehabilitated (Kritz, 1995, p. 48). In terms of indemnification, under the Federal Restitution Law, the Federal Compensation Law, and the Luxembourg Agreement with Israel, Germany provided victims of the Holocaust with over 80 DM billion and some claims for reparations are still pending. Thus, some observers note that although these billions can never match the suffering of the Jews during the Holocaust, the scope of reparations they benefited from has "facilitated demands for reparations by other groups that have suffered tragic histories" (Torpey, 2006, p. 41).

In the United States, calls for reparations come from many directions, but most vocal are members of the African American community asking for an apology and compensation (backward- and forward-looking) for the suffering and trauma their forefathers and mothers were subjected to as slaves, a traumatic experience that, they argue, continues to have an impact on them and their children despite the passing of time. These efforts have thus far been met with silence and even rejection. President Clinton refused to apologize to African Americans for historical injustices suffered because of slavery and Jim Crow laws, a refusal that Brooks (1999) attributes to the lack of strong internal support (p. 6). This stance is in sharp contrast to the most recent case of reparations in U. S. history, resulting from the internment of entire communities of Japanese Americans after Japan's bombing of Pearl Harbor. It appears that, despite some internal noise, this case has been settled with an official apology from President Reagan (and the passing of the Civil Liberties Act of 1988) to families affected by the internment, along with a sum of $20,000 per person to compensate for incurred damages and harm (Minow, 1998, p. 100). It is not clear then what accounts for the seemingly double-standard applied to these claims for reparations for historical injustices against entire communities based on their ethnicity or race. Perhaps in the case of the United States, apologizing and compensating for the internment of people of Japanese decent was a much smaller project than addressing the long overdue demands of atonement, apology, and reparations from the African American community.

In other contexts, claims for reparations have been more modest. Minow

(1998) discusses victims in South Africa asking for a proper burial for their relatives, a death certificate, or removal of bullets from private parts, which suggests that these survivors have no illusion about the potential for "external repair" (p. 106). A primary difference between the redress movement in the United States and other places like South Africa, Morocco, or even Rwanda, is that reparatory efforts have not been the genuine result of civil society efforts. I do not want to suggest that civil society has not been vocal or efficacious in these countries but simply that despite all of their efforts and good will, victims' organizations in Morocco, for example, have not been involved or consulted in the decision-making process of developing the reparatory plans. It has been a top down process and, in some instances, a process with so many requirements and arbitrary deadlines (for victims) that one wonders if it is genuine—victims must offer empirical proof that they have been victimized. In the case of the Moroccan Justice and Reconciliation Commission (referred to in Morocco as l'Instance de l'Equite et la Reconciliation, or IER), victims were given 2 or 3 months to apply for reparations claims from the state and if they did not do so within that window of opportunity, they did not qualify, which was criticized both locally and internationally but never reversed. Further, the state (in the person of the king) has not officially apologized for its decades of repression and violence against its people, which makes victims and observers question the authenticity of the entire process of reconciliation. This case makes it clear that symbolic reparations such as official apologies and expressions of remorse and regret (to survivors and their families) are just as important, if not more important, than material compensation. Wole Soyinka (1999) points out: "And even as justice is not served by punishing the accused before the establishment of guilt, neither is it served by discharging the guilty without evidence of mitigation—or remorse" (p. 3). Money can fix physical damages, but it cannot erase the trauma and loss suffered by victims, nor can it restore trust in state institutions and officials. That would require that perpetrators acting in the name of these institutions account for their actions, at the very least. In addition, when reparations are not part of a larger project of institutional reforms that seek to safeguard against repetition of abuses, they do not advance the bigger goal of changing the political culture. With respect to Morocco, Abdeslam Maghraoui (2003) points out that the country "is no closer today to a decisive democratic breakthrough than it was four decades ago" (p. 73). This statement was made after two kings ordered the disbursement of considerable amounts of money to some victims.

The rhetoric of reparations highlights the moral and political necessity that states be held accountable for criminal actions against their own citizens. After all, states that aspire to be democratic should be for and by the people, so when trust between a state and its citizens becomes frail, it needs to be addressed in some legitimate forum. In some cases of transitional justice, like in South Africa and Morocco, that state-citizen bond was never there to begin with, so it is not a matter of fixing a weak link but developing trust in government institutions and agents of the state, and nurturing that trust through symbolic gestures. Reparations can be part of the effort to repair political relationships and ensure that measures are put in place to safeguard against such happenings in the future. Crocker (2006) argues: "To reckon fully with past wrongs, an emerging democracy must identify the causes of past abuses and take steps to reform the law and basic institutions to reduce the possibility that such violations will be repeated" (p. 3). Thus institutional reforms must to be part of reparatory or compensatory efforts. If backward-looking reparations serve to acknowledge that harm was done and offer some symbolic and material compensation for it, forward-looking types of reparation have a broader horizon as they seek to prevent recurrence of similar experiences and enshrine the memory of those who perished. In both cases, the burden of proof is upon victims, who are expected to make a public case to explain how they have been wrongly and unjustly victimized and why and how their injustice needs to be rectified. Whether their case is heard and heeded is a rhetorical process that is negotiated between victims, perpetrators, public opinion, and the political leadership. It is clear, as Slyomovics (2009) insists, that victims' narratives of suffering are often used as a measure for determining the hierarchy of victimhood or victimization and the type and amount of reparations that the victims' suffering (and story) warrants. The outcome of reparations contributes to and is inseparable from other practices of transitional justice, such as reconciliation and memorialization (and even the political process of democratic transition). It is important to stress, as Minow (1998) does, that "[s]ocial and religious meanings rather than economic values lie at the heart of reparations" (p. 110).

It is, however, dangerous to assume or expect that reparations are the end of the road for transitional justice. To expect victims to forgive and forget after symbolic gestures of apology and repentance or monetary compensation is tantamount to buying them off to clear one's conscience and wipe out the guilt. In some experiences of transitional justice and historical injustice, some victims refuse to accept compensations either because they consider it to be blood money or because there is no other rhetorical or symbolic effort to acknowledge their suffering and make amends. The money is not accompanied by expressions of regret and remorse and public attempt to "make good again." Some victims and their families in Morocco, for example, have put uncompromising conditions on the entire process of reparations before they can accept any financial reparations, such as the state revealing the whole truth about the fate of their loved ones who have disappeared or been murdered. Otherwise, they see it as soiling the memory of the deceased. Along these lines, the International Center for Transitional Justice (2008) warns:

> Reparations that are not linked to prosecutions or truth-telling may be perceived as "blood money"—an attempt to buy the silence or acquiescence of victims. Similarly, reforming institutions without any attempt to satisfy victims' legitimate expectations of justice, truth and reparation, is not only ineffective from the standpoint of accountability, but unlikely to succeed in its own terms. (p. 2)

This has been the main criticism directed at the Moroccan program of reparations. Its sole focus has been on monetary compensations at the expense of other forms, such as public apologies, vetting (instead of promotion) of state officials known to have participated in torture and disappearing of political dissidents, and a more sustained effort to account for the fate of the disappeared. In other words, it seems that the Moroccan state has favored counting money as a form of reparation at the expense of accounting for victims, assigning blame, and taking responsibility for past violent actions that harmed thousands of Moroccan citizens. In addition, as Minow (1998) argues:

> The core idea behind reparations stems from the compensatory theory of justice. Injuries can and must be compensated. Wrongdoers should pay victims for losses. Afterwards, the slate can be wiped clean. Or at least a kind of justice has been done. [...] Extending this idea to victims of mass violence substitutes money or other material benefits—such as insurance, or scholarships—for the devastation inflicted by wrongful incarcerations, or tortures, or murders. This means crossing over differing lexicons of value. (p. 104)

Serving some kind of justice should be the moral horizon of reparations and when that horizon is lost, reparations become all about counting; it is indeed blood money.

Reparations that seek to "make good" again can contribute to the dialogue between victims/survivors and perpetrators, a collective act of accounting that begins with the truth commission. Barkan (2000) points out that "[t]his interaction between perpetrator and victim is a new form of political negotiation that enables the rewriting of memory and historical identity in ways that both can share" (p. xviii). In other words, one can suggest that reparations in the context of mass violence subverts the relationship between perpetrators and victims/survivors not necessarily because of the financial exchange, but because they constitute in themselves an acknowledgment of responsibility and an effort at being accountable for one's actions. As an effort towards accountability, reparations programs can greatly contribute towards democratization by setting the tone for future regimes and restoring trust in political life but they can only do so if they include a symbolic component: acknowledgment of responsibility and apology.

For instance, Brooks (1999) argues that for many Holocaust survivors and their descendants, as well as Japanese Americans who were interned and racially stigmatized in the aftermath of Pearl Harbor, there is a real fear that the past might be revisited upon them or their children. That is why apologies, as a rhetorical affirmation of guilt and remorse, are so important for these victims and the society they dream to build for future generations. For them, apologies and compensations act as a deterrent for the future, as a promise that their children will not suffer like they did. In addition, Brooks (1999) notes that "Remorse improves the national spirit and health. It raises the moral threshold of a society" (p. 3). Another important ethical implication of reparations is that they greatly contribute to efforts to preserve the memory of victims and survivors of political injustices. As such, the following section opens up discussion about practices of memorization within transitional justice.

Between Remembrance and Oblivion: The Praxis of Memory

> Memory breathes revenge as often as it breathes reconciliation, and the hope of reaching catharsis through liberated memories might turn out to be an illusion. (Margalit, 2004, p. 5)

Memorialization is one of the hallmarks of the 20th century. The fear that no trace will be left of those who perished in wars, genocide, civil wars, and other catastrophes, or that their memory will be distorted, has led to a compulsive drive to remember and record all details of life. The explosion of devices, artifacts, practices, and places that seek to record and memorialize involve many media—the Internet, films, cameras, recorders, biographies, books museums, commemorative events, and witnessing. Maurice Halbwachs' claim in the early 1900s that memory is a social phenomenon and that remembering is a collective process opened up the field of memory studies to many disciplines, resulting in an important body of scholarship that focuses on issues of identity, collective/public memory and nationalism (1992). Conversely, the field of rhetorical studies has discovered new life in the concept of memory, first with scholarship that focused on historical narratives, and, more recently, public memory (White, 1975; Ricoeur, 1984; Phillips, 2004). The connection between memory and rhetoric has shifted with the understanding that memory not only serves as the foundation for the construction of historical narratives but greatly contributes to shaping national symbols and identities. In an essay published in the *Quarterly Journal of Speech* almost 15 years ago, Stephen H. Browne (1995) sheds light on this:

> As a form of cultural practice, public memorializing outsteps established genres, eludes intent and improvises on both material and symbolic resources.... such memorializing is a textual practice; to speak of it at all is to put into play an interpretive procedure. However varied those procedures, they collectively stress a sense of the text as a site of symbolic action, a place of cultural performance, the meaning of which is defined by its public and persuasive functions. (p. 237)

In addition, Carol Blair (2006) has noted that memory is "a phenomenon of community," which highlights the importance of memory for the study of communication. Memory has epistemological value, manifest in public expressions in museums, commemorations, history manuals, and other places, thus making it a powerful political instrument, open to all kinds of appropriations and misappropriations.

Scholars have investigated the use and abuses of public memory during critical national times such as the national policy of collective amnesia in Spain after the death of Franco (*El Pacto del Olvido*), Germany during the Nazi regime, and then again afterwards (the passionate efforts of survivors not to forget what happened in Auschwitz and other concentration camps). The aftermath of dramatic events such as the ones mentioned here constitutes a "rhetorical interruption" for communities impacted; it also inaugurates civic deliberation about what constitutes a people or a nation (Loudiy, 2008, p. 58). Blair (2006, p. 53) notes that, in addition to being political, public memory is also an "emotionally invested phenomenon," because of the powerful linkages between remembrance, language/culture and identity. Surely, for survivors of the Holocaust in Europe, Apartheid in South Africa, the Years of Lead in Morocco, and other atrocities, recalling experiences of torture, rape, loss of loved ones, and other forms of inhumanity is certainly an emotionally charged experience. Without falling into psychologism, it is fair to say that remembrance is necessarily and dynamically affective, not simply cognitive. Happy and peaceful feelings emerge with happy memories. Violent or traumatic memories evoke a plethora of disturbing emotions such as sadness, fear, hate, shame, horror, and guilt. The events remembered belong to a different time frame but the emotions associated with those events are very much present-lived and become enacted in the now. Public memory is a collective embodiment of past events and the motor for practices that have implications for the present and the future.

Experiences of transitional justice problematize the praxis of memory precisely because the decisions that people make about both remembering and disremembering during times of crisis impacts the society they are attempting to rebuild *and* the historical narrative they are writing. Much has been said recently about the role of political amnesia and forgetting in the construction of national identity, and interestingly enough, Lane Bruner (2005) argues that strategic forgetfulness is what rhetoricians call public memory. He explains: "Every articulation necessarily highlights some features at the expense of others; it is simply that some articulations tend to repress more potentially significant political issues than others (thus some articulations are more ethical than others)" (p. 316). In other words, what is (deliberately) forgotten is sometimes more important than what is remembered. In addition, Bradford Vivian (2009), who readily concedes that "forgetting has had a bad reputation," notes that "the notion that forgetting need not amount to amnesia, erasure, or loss of memory—that it may, as an available trope or public deliberation, constitute a principled and judicious response to the past—remains conspicuously unorthodox" (p. 91). Vivian's review of recent works in ethics, phenomenology, and anthropology suggests that the practice of forgetting needs to be further investigated to "affirm its positive contributions to public life, ethics, and decision making" (p. 91). Achieving an ethico-political balance between excessive remembrance and amnesia isn't easy, to be sure. Some nations have fallen prey to the totality of erasure (amnesia), hoping to start anew without disturbing shadows from the past, and others have made of remembrance their national pastime. For example, after the fall of Nazism in Germany, the stigma associated with being part of such brutal events prompted Germans to want to quickly forget and turn the page. But, it soon became clear that in the effort to forget one cannot help but remember, as Vivian (2009) points out: "asking others to forget something ironically draws attention to, and brings to mind or memory, that very thing" (p. 102). German attempts to delete a very unpleasant period of their history were futile, although German national amnesia lasted 20 years. But teachers and parents could not lie (by omission) to future generations; to do so was to negate that the Holocaust ever happened, which would have been adding insult to injury to Jewish people. When amnesia is prescribed as a national policy, like the "pact of oblivion" in Spain after the civil war, it might work in the short term but is bound to fail: those who suffered cannot forget; they can suppress their memories, but they do not forget, and the past comes back to haunt them. As Minow (1998) points out: "Some countries simply forget the past and attempt to induce a national amnesia in its people. Of course that is bound to fail—the victims do not, indeed cannot, forget. And their unanswered calls for retribution develop into hate and invariably that hate is directed collectively at the group from which the perpetrators came" (p. ix).

If some countries have worked hard to expose and publicize the horrors of their past and establish responsibilities of perpetrators of the atrocities (South Africa might be a good example here), Spain has done just the opposite after the death of Franco in the early 1970s. Spain can be seen either as an anomaly in terms of its policy of national amnesia or a model to emulate since over 30 years after the death of Franco the country seems to have joined the club of democratized nations with a vibrant and mostly peaceful citizenry. Still, the pact of oblivion appears to have been broken as there are growing calls for the re-opening of that page in Spanish history to set the record straight, identify and bury the dead, and establish truth about the past. This new development in Spanish affairs verifies, as Madeleine Davis (2005) notes, the fact:

> that Spaniards [did not] genuinely forgot the past but that a collective decision was made, for political purposes, to place a particular construction on that past, to suppress or de-emphasize those memories felt to be likely to endanger the stability and consensus, and to foreground those likely to promote "reconciliation". (p. 867)

To stress the importance of public memory and remembrance is not to suggest that individual memories or trauma alone should dictate decisions relating to an entire nation, but to emphasize that a society cannot build a meaningful existence without a historical collective consciousness, made up of shared individual narratives about the past.

Obviously, there is always a danger that public memory can be abused and manipulated for political ends, as noted earlier and as many scholars have warned, including Ricoeur (2004). Negotiating these tensions and excesses can be challenging for a nation in the midst of moral chaos, feelings of victimization, fear, and guilt. Indeed, how does a nation achieve what Ricoeur (2000) calls a "just memory?" In the cacophony of public memories that emerge in such times, as emphasized previously, the testimony is to be understood at an ethical as well as pragmatic level; witnesses contribute to a praxis of memory. Following Ricoeur, then, testimony distinguishes the moral witness as a citizen with a burden or obligation (or a promise) to tell the story of his/her and others' ordeal. In doing so, the moral witness records this struggle in the annals of humanity's history, and ultimately reconciles official history and memory (the vernacular type of history). As we have seen, truth commissions greatly contribute to a praxis of memory. In the aftermath of national violence, the narratives of witnesses serve as a powerful opportunity for deliberation not just about past actions (responsibility, accountability, and justice) but also about possibilities for the future of a people and the inauguration of a new collective identity. As Phillips (2004) notes: "to speak of public memory as the memory of publics is to speak of more than individuals remembering the same thing. It is to speak of a remembrance together, indeed, of remembrance together as a crucial aspect of our togetherness, our existence as a public" (p. 5). Correlatively, Barbie Zelizer (2000) argues that visual memory (especially photographs) has been instrumental in securing the public memory of the Holocaust, but she also suggests that the contemporary obsession with remembering past atrocities is in fact an effort at forgetting them (p. 202). She makes the argument that, as a manifestation of visual memory, photography has contributed to the normalization of atrocity. It replaces doing something to stop the atrocity, with the act of witnessing itself—that is, looking at the picture (p. 212). As such, the act of bearing witness is in danger of becoming hollow and devoid of meaning in contemporary societies. Zelizer says, "Bearing witness, then, might have turned into an act carved out of the shadows of habituation, a mere outline for the call for substantive action it seems to have played at the end of World War II" (p. 213). Still, bearing witness to a horrific event, living to tell the story of what has been witnessed, or turning horrors that have no sense into sensible objects through visual means, do not necessarily constitute what I am referring to as moral witnessing. Testimonies do indeed provide an opportunity, as Hayner (2002) argues, for a nation to remember in order to forget (p. xi). And Zelizer (2000) is correct that the extraordinary can be made mundane through visual and other rhetorical means. But such forgetting or normalization is neither the end of rhetorical attempts to achieve transitional justice nor the ethical basis for it. Without such rhetorical acts, those who perished in concentration camps during the Holocaust, at the hands of the Apartheid regime, in the Rwandan, Armenian, and Cambodian genocides, at the hands the state during Morocco's Years of Lead, and in many other places, either disappear entirely or become merely an anonymous number on a tombstone, a name without any meaning, as if they were never part of the living. That is the most terrible injustice, as it compounds the horror of their deaths.

Conclusion

Minow (1998) warns: "There are no tidy endings following mass atrocity" (p. 102), because no response to the horrors of genocide and other violations of life is ever adequate enough. There are, in fact, no endings. Transitional justice is thus an ongoing, agonizing process that is continually enacted and re-enacted, tested, and challenged. Still, there has to be a response. Opening a new page without engaging the past in an authentic way, where one knows who one is reconciling with, and those responsible are held accountable through symbolic forms of justice at the very least, there is still no guarantee of peace and harmony. While the rhetoric of transitional justice initiates a difficult conversation about what human beings are capable of and what kind of world we want our children to live in, and even though there are no guarantees, the conversation and associated analyses, judgments, and recommendations are indispensable.

Not all experiences of transitional justice are created equal, and the jury is still out on what the perfect recipe for a transition is. Transitions represent an important moment in the history of a nation, they constitute a rhetorical opportunity for rethinking the ethos of a given society. Such has been the case in the past with ancient Athens, Germany, Spain, and the United States, and such is the case today with many countries such as Yugoslavia, Morocco, and Iraq. Coming to terms with the past is an agonizing process where irreconcilable versions of "what happened" and "what should happen" vie for recognition and legitimacy. More importantly, it is a time for mutual recognition, as Ricoeur (2000) would argue. To recognize each other as citizens of the same nation entails judgment and addressing the harm done by violent actions.

The rhetoric of transitional justice provides a framework for thinking about how best to address the aftermath of atrocity, the forensic categories it recommends allow for judgment to take shape. When engaged with the goal of making good again and establishing trust and friendship in the community, these practices can modestly contribute to serving justice, albeit a symbolic justice. As previously suggested, without the focus on justice, humanity loses its moral compass. Soyinka (1999) states: "Justice assigns responsibility, and few will deny that justice is an essential ingredient of social cohesion—indeed, I have asserted elsewhere that justice constitutes 'the first condition of humanity'" (p. 3). Justice, in the sense I have attempted to advance here may be counterfactual, and some may argue never attainable, still, it is the horizon that should guide and drive the types of transitions discussed in this paper. Since the goal of a restorative perspective is to establish a just distance between wrongdoers and victims and make judgments about political actors, the discourses and practices it entails need to be considered within the horizon of forensic rhetoric, just like retributive justice. However, despite its forensic telos, restorative justice often falls short of contributing to a genuine transition, especially when carried out as a politically expedient and safe alternative to retribution, as the Moroccan case suggests. But, of course, these two approaches need not to be mutually exclusive and can be engaged in tandem, as the Chilean experience has recently shown, many years after the end of the Pinochet regime.

As citizens of the world, and scholars of communication, ethics, and rhetoric, we would do well to be attentive to these phenomena and the modes of communication they engender to further contribute rhetorical accounts and interpretations of such lived experiences. Ronald C. Arnett (2005) argues that communication does not always originate with us but, often, with history: " ... the historical moment speaks. It is our response that furthers the conversation. History is marked by public points of memory ... calling us from the routine of everyday life into response" (p. 5). The historical moment that emerges after mass atrocity compels all of us and must be engaged. It is not always clear what such engagement would entail, or what the end product would look like. But certainty is not a feature of life generally and that is why the focus on rhetoric is so important. The rhetorical practices of restorative justice, such as truth and reconciliation commissions, reparations, and memorialization, sketch a transformation of the society and political culture in which they take place, a collective transformation that enhances the ethical sensibilities of humanity generally.

Notes

1. The term used to describe people who have been victimized by a criminal state has been problematized because many so-called victims have rejected the label of victim, preferring to be referred to as "survivor." Hence, I will be using the two terms interchangeably to refer to citizens who have been at the receiving end of political violence and repression.
2. According to Huntington (1993), about 30 countries have "shifted from authoritarianism to democracy, and at least a score of other countries were affected by the democratic wave" (p. 5).

References

Aguilar, P. (2001). Justice, politics and memory in the Spanish transition. In A. B. De Brito, C. Gonzalez-Enriquez, & P. Aguilar (Eds.), *The politics of memory: Transitional justice in democratizing societies* (pp. 92–118). New York: Oxford University Press.

Arendt, H. (1958). *The human condition*. Chicago: University of Chicago Press.

Arnett, R. C. (2005). *Dialogic confession: Bonhoeffer's rhetoric of responsibility*. Carbondale: Southern Illinois University Press.

Barkan, E. (2000). *The guilt of nations: Restitution and negotiating historical injustices*. Baltimore, MD: Johns Hopkins University Press.

Benjelloun, T. (2006). *This blinding absence of light*. New York: Penguin.

Blair, C. (2001). Communication as collective memory. In G. J. Shepherd, J. St. John, & T. Striphas (Eds.) *Communication as ... perspectives on theory* (pp. 51–59). Thousand Oaks, CA: Sage.

Booth, W. J. (2006). *Communities of memory: On witness, identity, and justice*. Ithaca, NY: Cornell University Press.

Brooks, R. L. (1999). The age of apology. In R. L. Brooks (Ed.), *When sorry isn't enough: The controversy over apologies and reparations for human justice* (pp. 3–11). New York: New York University Press.

Brophy, A. L. (2008). *Reparations: Pros and cons.* Cambridge, UK: Oxford University Press.

Browne, S. H. (1995). Reading, rhetoric and the texture of public memory. *Quarterly Journal of Speech, 81*(2), 237–265.

Bruner, L. A. (2005). Rhetorical theory and the critique of national identity construction. *National Identities, 7*(3), 309–327.

Carothers, T. (2002). The end of the transition paradigm. *Journal of Democracy, 13*(1), 5–21.

Cobban, H. (2007). *Amnesty after atrocity? Healing nations after genocide and war crimes.* Vancouver, B.C.: Paradigm.

Crocker, D. A. (2006, November). *Truth commissions, transitional justice, and civil society.* Paper presented at the Symposium on Reconciliation, University of Wisconsin, Madison.

Davis, M. (2005). Is Spain recovering its memory? Breaking the Pacto del Olvido. *Human Rights Quarterly, 27*(3), 858–880.

De Gruchy, J. W. (2002). *Reconciliation: Restoring justice.* London: SCM Press.

De Kok, I. J. (2006). *Seasonal fires: Selected and new poems.* New York: Seven Stories.

Derrida, J. (2001). *Cosmopolitanism and forgiveness.* New York: Routledge.

Doxtader, E. (2003). Reconciliation—A rhetorical concept/ion. *Quarterly Journal of Speech, 89*(4), 267–292.

Elder, J. W. (1998). Expanding our options: The challenge of forgiveness. In R. D. Enright & J. North (Eds.), *Exploring forgiveness* (pp. 150–165). Madison: University of Wisconsin Press.

Elster, J. (2004). *Closing the books: Transitional justice in historical perspective.* Cambridge, UK: Cambridge University Press.

Freeman, M. (2006). *Truth commissions and procedural fairness.* Cambridge, UK: Cambridge University Press.

Halbwachs, M. (1992). *On collective memory* (L. A. Coser, Trans.). Chicago: University of Chicago Press.

Hatch, J. (2003). Reconciliation: Building a bridge from complicity to coherence in the rhetoric of race relations. *Rhetoric & Public Affairs, 6*(4), 737–764.

Hatch, J. (2008). *Race and reconciliation: Redressing wounds of injustice.* Lanham, MD: Lexington Books.

Hayner, P. B. (2002). *Unspeakable truths: Facing the challenge of truth commissions.* New York: Routledge.

Huntington, S. (1993). *The third wave: Democratization in the twentieth century.* Norman: University of Oklahoma Press.

Hutton, P. H. (1993). *History as an art of memory.* Hanover, CT: University Press of New England.

International Center for Transitional Justice. (2008). What is transitional justice? Retrieved March 7, 2010, from http://www.ictj.org/static/TJApproaches/WhatisTJ/ICTJ/Whatis TJ_pa2008_.pdf

Kritz, N. J. (Ed.). (1995). *Transitional justice: How emerging democracies reckon with former regimes: Country studies.* Washington, DC: United States Institute of Peace.

Loudiy, F. (2008). Narrative identity and public memory in Morocco. In M. Cook &

A.M. Holba (Eds.), *Philosophies of communication: Implications for everyday life* (pp. 57–77). New York: Peter Lang.

Maghraoui, A. M. (2003). Depoliticization in Morocco. In L. Diamond, M. F. Plattner, & D. Brumberg (Eds.), *Islam and Democracy in the Middle East* (pp. 67–75). Baltimore, MD: Johns Hopkins University Press.

Margalit, A. (2004). *The ethics of memory.* Cambridge, MA: Harvard University Press.

May, L. (1996). *Sharing responsibility.* Chicago: University of Chicago Press.

McPhail, M. L. (2002). *The rhetoric of racism revisited: Reparations or separation?* Lanham, MD: Rowman and Littlefield.

McPhail, M. L. (2004). A question of character: Re(-)signing the racial contract. *Rhetoric and Public Affairs, 7*(3), 391–405.

McPhail, M. L. (2009). The politics of complicity revisited: Race, rhetoric, and the (im) possibility of reconciliation. *Rhetoric and Public Affairs, 12*(1), 107–162.

Mendez, J. E. (1997). Accountability for past abuses. *Human Rights Quarterly, 19*(2), 255–282.

Minow, M. (1998). *Between vengeance and forgiveness: Facing history after genocide and mass violence.* Boston: Beacon.

Nora, P. (1996). *Realms of memory: Conflicts and divisions.* New York: Columbia University Press.

North, J. (1998). *Exploring forgiveness.* Madison: University of Wisconsin Press.

O'Donnell G., & Schmitter, P. C. (1993). *Transitions from authoritarian rule: Tentative conclusions about uncertain democracies.* Baltimore, MD: Johns Hopkins University Press.

Osiel, M. (1999). *Mass atrocity, collective memory and the law.* New Brunswick, NJ: Transaction Publishers.

Phillips, K. R. (2004). Introduction. In K. R. Phillips (Ed.), *Framing public memory* (pp. 1–14). Tuscaloosa: The University of Alabama Press.

Ricoeur, P. (1984). *Time and narrative* (Vol. 1, K. McLaughin & D. Pellauer, Trans.). Chicago: University of Chicago Press.

Ricoeur, P. (2000). *The just* (D. Pellauer, Trans.). Chicago: University of Chicago Press.

Ricoeur, P. (2004). *Memory, history, forgetting* (K. Blamey & D. Pellauer, Trans.). Chicago: University of Chicago Press.

Ross, M. H. (2004). Ritual and the politics of reconciliation. In Y. Bar-Siman-Tov (Ed.), *From conflict resolution to reconciliation* (pp. 197–224). Oxford, UK: Oxford University Press.

Schaffer, K., & Smith, S. (2004). *Human rights and narrated lives: The ethics of recognition.* New York: Palgrave Macmillan.

Slyomovics, S. (2009). Reparations in Morocco: The symbolic Dirham. In B. R. Johnston & S. Slyomovics (Eds.), *Waging war, making peace: Reparations and human rights* (pp. 95–114). Walnut Creek, CA: Left Coast Press.

Smith, A. R. (2008). Dialogue in agony: The problem of communication in authoritarian regimes. *Communication Theory, 18*(1), 160–185.

Smith, A. R., & Loudiy, F. (2005). Testing the red lines: On the liberalization of speech in Morocco. *Human Rights Quarterly, 27*(3), 1069–1119.

Soyinka, W. (1999). *The burden of memory, the muse of forgiveness.* New York: Oxford University Press.

Thompson, J. (2002). *Taking responsibility for the past: Reparation and historical injustice.* Cambridge, UK: Polity Press.

Torpey, J. (2006). *Making whole what has been smashed: On reparations politics.* Cambridge, MA: Harvard University Press.

Tutu, D. M. (1999). *No future without forgiveness.* New York: Image.

White, H. (1975). *Metahistory: The historical imagination in Nineteenth-Century Europe.* Baltimore, MD: Johns Hopkins University Press.

Wilson, K. H. (2004). Is there interest in reconciliation? *Rhetoric and Public Affairs, 7*(3), 367–377.

Wolpert, A. (2002). *Remembering defeat. Civil war and civic memory in Ancient Athens.* Baltimore, MD: Johns Hopkins University Press.

Van Der Merwe, H. (2009). Delivering justice during transition: Research challenges. In H. Van Der Merwe, V. Baxter, & A. R. Chapman (Eds.), *Assessing the impact of transitional justice: Challenges for empirical research* (pp. 115–142). Washington, DC: United States Institute of Peace.

Vivian, B. (2006). Neoliberal epideictic: Rhetorical form and commemorative politics on September 11, 2002. *Quarterly Journal of Speech, 92*(1), 1–26.

Vivian, B. (2009). On the language of forgetting. *Quarterly Journal of Speech, 95*(1), 89–104.

Zelizer, B. (2000). *Remembering to forget: Holocaust memory through the camera's eye.* Chicago: University of Chicago Press.

14 *Commentary*
On Expectations and Transition
Seeing Things on Their Own Terms

Barbie Zelizer

University of Pennsylvania

Expectations are a peculiar kind of endeavor. We examine a phenomenon, interpret what we find with what we hope are systematic, grounded, and detached assumptions, and then try to fit those findings to our expectations. What we expect and anticipate, however, is often not what we find. Yet nowhere in our research endeavors do we make place for unrequited expectation.

Perhaps nowhere is expectation as pronounced as when dealing with transitions. Defined as a movement from one state to another, transitions signal interim conditions, and we invoke them with considerable degrees of investment about what we hope to see at the other end of their unfolding. A transition implies beginning and end points, an identifiable sequencing of action in between, and some notion of real change between the two. In transitioning between two points, however, a slew of questions rise to the fore: What happens when transitions do not unfold in a clear-cut fashion? How do we determine a transition's beginning and end points? Does the pre-transition circumstance ever fall entirely away? How do we know at which point to recognize the new circumstance coming aboard? And what happens to our expectations when things do not transpire as we anticipate?

These reviews of four areas of communication literature demonstrate beyond all doubt that our scholarly expectations of transition—of media systems in a variety of transitional contexts—are lacking, because transition rarely unfolds in the way we might think. More important, they suggest that underlying our expectations of change are prescriptive and invested assumptions that may be blinding us to the evidence on the ground. Specifically, primarily Western expectations that transitions necessarily engender more projects similar to "ourselves" have failed to address the situated nature of communication in non-Western environments. These reviews—of the Arab cyberspace, of Russian media studies, of East African media performance, and of transitional justice in multiple places around the globe—remind us of the critical role yet to be played in negotiating from anew the expectations associated with our scholarship. They suggest—elegantly, insightfully, and critically—a need to harvest existing scholarly thought by re-orienting it in directions that are simultaneously broad and narrow—broad because there is need to pinpoint the multiple situated contexts in which communication occurs, narrow because the local setting and its associated contingencies have not disappeared in this era of globalization but have rather given rise to new forms of collectivity and communicative practice.

In "The New Arab Cyberscape: Redefining Boundaries and Reconstructing Public Spheres," Sahar Khamis and Vít Šisler use the mediascape in the Arab world to challenge Habermasian notions of the public sphere. When seen through the Arab cyberscape, multiple aspects of Habermas' views on the public sphere fall short: he presumes universality for what remain situated and limited claims; he expects a foregrounding of politics over religion as motivating impulses for the public sphere; he insists on clear dichotomies between public and private; he envisions communicative over strategic action; his notions of who counts remain exclusionary. Drawing from the central role that the Internet plays in forming Arab public opinion, Khamis and Šisler argue that a public sphere different from that envisioned by Habermas, orchestrated through the platform of digital audiovisual media, has emerged as instrumental in encouraging critical reflection in the Arab world. Accommodating political video games released by the Hezbollah and propagandistic jihadi videos alongside liberal video blogs protesting political, social, and religious issues, their cyberscape is bursting with debate, contradiction, passion, and strategic interest and particularly draws in a group silenced or otherwise marginalized in more traditional public spaces in the Arab world—youth. They link its continued vitality, however, to three challenges—of democratization, dialogue, and diaspora: On the first count, they show that the Arab media scene displays transformation that has not necessarily led to democratization. Even new media, which escape the clientelism and instrumentalism that characterize other media in the region, still face restrictions and impediments to freedom of expression, such as potential maltreatment or the threat of legal punishment. Given the undemocratic and non-liberal nature of the larger political systems and the essentially unstable and contingent nature of networked societies, it is then no surprise that the Internet empowers liberal and democratic voices alongside authoritarian and ideological ones. On the second count, though the content of new media exhibits tendencies of undermining and enhancing tolerance and dialogue simultaneously, Khamis and äisler correctly note that without extending across the range of platforms and media outlets, the potential for true dialogue remains limited. On the third count, the Internet's stature as a transnational medium enhances its capacity to draw diasporic communities, which is itself built on contradictory notions of pluralism and segmentation, on the one hand, and unity and cohesion, on the other. Noting that the Internet can thus unify and integrate, separate, and marginalize, or create a hybrid combination of the two, they argue that the Arab cyberspace in effect gives birth to cultural divergence, which challenges the connection between globalization, Westernization and secularization. By redefining local cultural and religious identities within a global context, it creates hybrid public spheres both locally and globally.

On all three counts, then, transition produces no either/or dichotomies or obvious before and after moments. Khamis and Šisler tellingly reflect on what they call "two bipolar extremes of optimism" which overestimate the role of new media in inducing change and deliberative democracy and underestimate its role in accelerating political reform and catalyzing democratization. In much the same way that such reform can stimulate civic society and democratization it can stimulate its opposite too. The multiple overlaps—between local and global, traditional and modern, religious and political—that take on myriad forms and the contradictory impulses which the new media environment houses—gender inclusiveness, Islamization, transnationalism—suggest too a need to complicate our conceptual prisms so as to accommodate the complicated phenomena under examination. These givens suggest important patterns for other situated uses of new media. For instance, does the rise of pan-Arabism and the interwoven nature of Arab and Muslim public spheres suggest a new substitute principle for the nation-state? Do they augur alternative modes of organizing collectivity? Are there particular conditions under which the contradictions of the Arab cyberspace might work differently?

In "Between the Rejected Past and Uncertain Future: Russian Media Studies at a Crossroads," Natalya Krasnoboka reviews the state of the field of Russian media studies. She critically notes that though the transition from totalitarian to democratic societies rests on media involvement, we do not yet have a full picture of post-totalitarian regimes and their media. In large part, this has to do with the difficulties in establishing a workable continuity between Soviet and post-Soviet media periods and how media institutions work in each. While many Western researchers erroneously conceived of the Soviet media through a liberal-democratic frame that simplified its workings and overemphasized the centrality of censorship, Krasnoboka contends that when perestroika arrived, researchers' interest piqued, but scholars remained disagreed about how to interpret the media practices that ensued: was it reform, writ broadly, or the media themselves? Though post Soviet Russian media studies tackled the study of democratization and economic liberalization, social responsibility and civil society, and professionalism and media effects, on each count researchers found themselves interpreting the evidence from both sides of the continuum. For example, though some embraced the market, others decried the capacity of the market to effect change without historical context; similarly, while many targeted social responsibility and the ascent of civil society as interwoven conditions of the post Soviet Russian media, others saw neither coming to fruition. Slowed down by a lack of access to international literature, Russian researchers employed various facets of democratic theory to try and explain what was happening on the ground. Krasnoboka pointedly posits that it was only by recently coming to terms with the status of Russia as a neo-authoritarian system—and its associated decline in journalistic values, increase in self-censorship and increase in government interference—that Russian scholars have finally situated the post Soviet Russian media in a space crafted by its own terms, rather than refracted through a Western prism.

Such terms in Krasnoboka's eyes offer a picture not quite consonant with the overly optimistic expectations that prevailed in the West as to which kind of transitions would—and could—occur in post Soviet Russia. In its more muted instantiation, political impact has moved backstage, as the depoliticization of the media and the public has taken place simultaneous to the reinstatement of proactive and reactive authoritarian controls. Krasnoboka persuasively and skillfully demonstrates that the collapse of the Soviet Union has rendered no clear answer to the question of media change in a transitory political regime. As she says (here, slightly paraphrased), was change necessary or inevitable? Which attributes or components of the old media institution needed to undergo change? Does change occur in a particular way? Is there any pattern to media change? Furthermore, the role of the Internet and its contradictory attributes of a relatively closed nature of online expression, a lack of mobilizing functions, and a disconnectedness from offline civic action all render questionable the degree to which the Internet might significantly alter the trajectory of the mediated environment. As Khamis and äisler noted about Arab cyberspace, the post Soviet mediated environment has no obvious before and after points, and it does not follow a linear progression from authoritarian to democratic regime.

Like Khamis and äisler, Krasnoboka underscores how narrow has been the Western prism for understanding the complex unfolding of media systems in diverse national settings. At issue is whether or not the originary premises of much existing research were incorrect. As Krasnoboka succinctly observes in her discussion of press freedom, "did we really witness a backlash in freedom of the press and democratic change in Russia, or did we incorrectly define the earlier stages of transition?" In other words, the analysis of what has happened to the media in their transitional moments has been crafted, often erroneously, through the prism of those who could not read what was happening on the ground.

Yusuf Kalyango Jr. and Petya Eckler discuss media performance in autocratic political systems in "Media Performance, Agenda Building, and Democratization in East Africa." In an environment that includes media intimidation, information suppression, and government propaganda, they ask how can the media be better used to encourage democratization. With such attempts undercut by restrictive press laws, election malpractice, and political and ethnic violence, they argue that the media can and should sidestep these obstructions and mobilize citizens in small but instrumental increments. Equally important, their actions need to be recognized as critical in transitional democracies, even if they stop short of full democratic practice.

Kalyango and Eckler offer a comprehensive tracking of the complicated setting inhabited by East African media. Surveying the media of five East African nations, they show how each draws equally from autocratic and democratic political traditions, creating an institutional environment that lacks clarity, certainty, predictability, and stability. At which point the media face increases or decreases in authoritarian controls remains erratic, and this forces the media to employ an often contradictory blend of practices associated with both modes of regime, acting as guardians of state propaganda and partisan interest groups at the same time as they mobilize public debate. This zig-zagging relationship with press freedom, which emerges and retreats seemingly without rhyme or reason, raises the fundamental question: How can the media be better used to mobilize the public if press freedom remains a moving target?

To answer that question, Kalyango and Eckler advance the notion of agenda building. Given strong governmental control on political life in each of the East African nations they survey, they argue that the East African governments set agendas for the media which the media then transfer as uncritical coverage to the public, but they wonder as to the potential for the media to set agendas on their own. To recognize that potential, they break the democratizing process into three stages—transition, economic and political liberalization, and the rule of law. Noting that the transformation of East African regimes from military juntas to civilian dictatorships cannot be fully explained by Western concepts of democracy, they suggest that this bottom-up, step-by-step view of the democratizing process creates a potentially more active space for the media to engage citizenry within the various stages. They argue for recognition of an interim state—with possibly less repression, more liberalization, more competition, and more transparency—even if it stops short of achieving full democracy. For instance, fostering public debate on health and nutrition, human rights, or economic empowerment are all part of democratizing because public engagement helps to create a civil society, even if such topics skirt some of the fundamental political issues that are stopped cold by governmental radar. Through the prism of agenda building, Kalyango and Eckler suggest revamping assessments from afar of transitional democracies that have not sufficiently made sense of their on-ground conditions. Though East African media would not qualify as the media of fully democratic states, they are still a critical force in providing a forum for public debate in a context in which such debate is sorely needed.

At issue here is the telling focus on bits and pieces of the process of democratization rather than the Western embrace of democracy, writ large. Have Western notions of democracy sufficiently understood the necessary blend of democratizing practices in mixed and transitional regimes? Has the rush for the full scope of democratic practice sideswiped recognition of the steps that often unfold gradually and critically yet still stop short of reaching that goal? Such questions underscore not only the difficulties in understanding ground conditions other than one's own but show that we need to refine our theories when our analytical sites are not as clear-cut as we want them to be.

Fadoua Loudiy discusses the vagaries of transitional justice in "Facing a Bloody Past: Discourses and Practices of Transitional Justice." Focusing on countries with bloody pasts which attempt to reinvent their national ethos and find hope in the idea of transitional justice, she addresses how restorative discourses and practices shape the rhetoric of transitional justice and how political and ethical limitations of non-retributive approaches to justice determine the challenges implicit in achieving justice following large-scale atrocities.

Loudiy offers a compelling discussion of the development of the notion of transitional justice, which finds its origins among the Athenians in the early days of deliberative democracy. Positing it as a choice of restorative practices over retributive ones, Loudiy targets the forensic, non-legalistic dimensions of transitional justice and its associated ethical tensions, arguing that it constitutes a fertile way of addressing justice in the transition from repressive to more democratic regimes, from war to peace, and from terror to deliberative democracy. Addressing its contemporary development in multiple locations, she notes multiple waves of transitional justice that have disseminated it increasingly around the globe in recent times: it first emerged in the 1940s as a response to the Holocaust, producing the Nuremburg Military Tribunal and other tribunals to prosecute Nazi collaborators in Israel, France, and across Europe; it then spread to southern Europe, when countries like Greece, Portugal, and Spain used it to address their liberalization of formerly authoritarian regimes during the 1970s; it arose with the spread of human rights and end of the Cold War in Latin America and eastern Europe by the end of the 1980s; and most recently it emerged in Africa and Asia where large-scale massacres pushed the call for accountability.

In that justice is a system that grows from lived experience in an environment, the question of how to invoke justice when the environment is itself transitional does not have one pat resolution. Thus, different modes of transitional justice have been used in different countries: Argentina and Chile, for instance, combined trials with amnesty laws and truth commissions, while South Africa opted only for truth commissions and reparation programs instead of prosecution. Recognizing that transitional justice travels a difficult road that must account for the contradictions in coming to terms with a bloody past while repairing the relationships wrought asunder by that past, Loudiy pushes for engaging with the past in a relational and dialogical fashion, suggesting solutions whose porousness and flexibility offer different ways of tackling it. She sees three stages as relevant to crafting a new ethical sensibility through transitional justice—truth and reconciliation commissions, discussions over reparations, and memorialization practices. Not all work in any one situation, but rather draw in multiple ways upon each other.

One aspect of transitional justice that Loudiy raises is its reliance on potential rather than certainty. We aren't certain that we get where we want with transitional justice. In that regard, its uncertain outcomes introduce noise into the system. Lacking conventional types of endings, transitional justice instead constitutes an ongoing process that is "continually enacted and re-enacted, tested and challenged."

As with Khamis and Šisler, Krasnoboka, and Kalyango and Eckler, Loudiy suggests the need to let go of expectations of full democracy. As she correctly notes, only a portion of transitional regimes ever turn democratic. In her words: "instead of relying on these processes as a sign or index of democratization, perhaps the pertinent question to ask is how do rhetorical practices of transitional justice ... contribute to the larger and more challenging task of transforming the political culture of a country from a rule of violence and terror to the rule of law." And in tamping down a smaller set of expectations—rule of law, mechanisms of forgiveness, a sense of moving forward—she reminds us of the basic truth that necessarily transformative does not mean necessarily democratic. In this regard, transitional justice needs to be seen as an end in its own right, not as a means to an end of democracy. More broadly, she notes correctly the need to recognize the path and process as equal in importance to the aspired end result.

So what do we do with our expectations?

These chapters raise questions about some of the basic concepts by which we think about societies in transition, and particularly the role of their media as an integral part of that process. What does transition look like when the end of the transition in question is not clear, assured, or certain? How can we better appreciate transitional states for what they provide, even if they do not produce circumstances aligned with our expectations?

All of these authors call for comparative research, and such research is no doubt part of the future horizon by which we can better account for the variations in practice and aspiration that are suggested by transitional societies and their media. But comparative research is only part of the solution. We need to hinge our expectations on the grounded circumstances prevalent in transitional societies and let them lead us in reconceptualizing the boundaries and limits of where they in effect go, rather than uphold a situation in which we lead them in conforming to our notions of where we think they should go. The circumstances around the world that need further elaboration in this regard are vast: Afghanistan and Iraq are two that come to mind, but they only tip the iceberg in terms of societies in transition that deserve a proximate examination consonant with their own terms of existence.

Equally important, all of these chapters call on us to amend our intellectual assessments—about the viability of democracy in multiple contexts, about the linearity of change, about the centrality and pacing of progression, about the relevance and value of uncertainty, messiness, contradiction, tentativeness, and noise in the contexts which we strive to understand. They call for the development of more context-sensitive and bottom-up elaborations of the notions we profess to share across time and space. As Loudiy notes about transition, writ broadly: it "represents an important moment in a country's history, a rhetorical opportunity for rethinking what a society should be about ... that challenges its people to both preserve their traditions and envision news forms of living." Transitions offer societies a chance to reinstate trust, to reshape boundaries of belonging and to embark on some future course.

Phrased another way, these reviews of different transitional societies and their media all suggest two interrelated points: The first is that things may be incomplete in transitional situations but that is because they are by definition transitional. That lack of completeness and its often associated contradictions in situ call on us to recognize the new forms of living that they generate regardless of whether or not they reach the aims we expect of them, such as Western notions of democratization. It may be that democratization is not as relevant to our examination of them as we have tended to make it. The second is that we need to do a better job of recognizing them on their own terms, generating critical value within their societies just by virtue of their unfolding. The message of these chapters is clear: We need theory that better attends to situational variation, noise, messiness, tentativeness, and contradiction not as obstructions to research expectations but as critically formative data for understanding systems as the complicated phenomena they inevitably turn out to be.

About the Editor

Charles T. Salmon earned his Ph.D. in Mass Communication from the University of Minnesota and nine years later became the first recipient of a named professorship in the College of Communication Arts and Sciences at Michigan State University. Today, he holds the Ellis N. Brandt Chair and is Past Dean of the College, while also holding the position of Professor at the Interdisciplinary Center, Israel.

Professor Salmon has been a Rockefeller Scholar in Residence at Bellagio, Italy, a Fulbright Scholar at Tel Aviv University, a Visiting Professor at the Norwegian School of Management, an Arthur W. Page Legacy Scholar, a recipient of the Pathfinder Award for Outstanding Research in Public Relations, and a Visiting Scientist at the U.S. Centers for Disease Control and Prevention.

His research on public communication, public opinion, and public health has appeared in such journals as: *Archives of Internal Medicine, American Behavioral Scientist, Bioethics, Health Education and Behavior, International Journal of Public Opinion Research, Journal of Acquired Immune Deficiency Syndromes, Journal of Communication, Journal of Health Communication, Public Health Reports*, and *Public Opinion Quarterly*.

His books include *Information Campaigns: Balancing Social Values and Social Change* and *Public Opinion and the Communication of Consent* (with Theodore Glasser). He has served on more than 50 doctoral committees and headed a Task Force on the Status and Future of Doctoral Education in Mass Communication.

About the Associate Editors

Cindy Gallois (Ph.D., University of Florida) is Professor in the Faculty of Social and Behavioural Sciences at the University of Queensland. She is a Fellow of the Academy of the Social Sciences in Australia, International Communication Association, Society of Experimental Social Psychology, and International Academy of Intercultural Relations. Her research interests encompass intergroup communication in health, intercultural, and organisational contexts, with major emphasis on communication accommodation. She has published more than 150 books, chapters, and articles; her research has been funded continuously by external agencies since 1987. She serves on the editorial boards of most major journals in her fields, and is past President of ICA, International Association for Language and Social Psychology, and Society of Australasian Social Psychologists. She has been supervisor for 39 successful PhD students.

Christina Holtz-Bacha (Ph.D., University of Muenster) is Professor of Communication at the University of Erlangen-Nürrnberg, Germany. Prior to her current position she taught at universities in Mainz, Bochum, and Munich. She was a Visiting Scholar at the University of Minnesota and a Research Fellow at the Joan Shorenstein Center on the Press, Politics and Public Policy at the John F. Kennedy School of Government, Harvard University. She is Co-Editor of the German journal *Publizistik* and has served as Chair of the Political Communication Division of ICA. She has published widely in the area of political communication and media policy. Among her most recent publications is the two-volume *Encyclopedia of Political Communication*, co-edited with Lynda L. Kaid.

Guillermo Mastrini (Ph.D., University of Buenos Aires) is Professor of Communication at the University of Buenos Aires and the National University of Quilmes. He is the former Head of the Department of Communication Studies (University of Buenos Aires) and President of the Argentine Federation of Social Communication Schools. He is in charge of the courses "Communication Planning and Policies" and "Information Economy" at the University of Buenos Aires. His publications include: *Globalization and Monopolies in Latin America's Media* (Globalización y monopolios en la comunicación en América Latina, Biblos, 1999), *Much Ado About Laws: Economy and Politics of Communication in Argentina* (Mucho ruido, pocas leyes. Economía y políticas de comunicación en la Argentina, La Crujía, 2005), *Journalists and Tycoons* (Periodistas y Magnates, Prometeo, 2006), and *The Owners of Speech* (Los dueños de la palabra, Prometeo, 2009).

Onuora Nwuneli (Ph.D., University of Wisconsin-Madison) is Professor of Communication at Nnamdi Azikiwe University, Awka Nigeria. He specializes in communication for social change and population and health communication. Formerly he was Head of the Department of Mass Communication at the University of Lagos, UNESCO Chief Technical Advisor in Population Communication at the Kenya Institute of Mass Communication, Population Communication Specialist to the Government of Botswana, Consultant to UNICEF (Nigeria and Ghana) in Polio Communication, and Consultant to UNFPA (Nigeria) in Census Population Communication. He has edited *Communication and Human Needs in Africa, Mass Communication in Nigeria* and *The Development and Growth of the Film Industry in Nigeria* (with Alfred Opubor).

Joseph B. Walther (Ph.D., University of Arizona) is Professor of Communication and of Telecommunication, Information Studies & Media at Michigan State University. His research focuses on computer-mediated communication in personal relationships, groups, organizational, and educational settings, in which he has published several original theories and empirical studies. He has held appointments in Psychology, Information Science, and Education in the United States and England. He has been an officer in the Academy of Management and the International Communication Association. He has been recognized twice with the National Communication Association's Woolbert Research Award for articles that offered new conceptualizations of communication phenomena that have influenced thinking in the discipline for more than 10 years.

Xinshu Zhao (Ph.D., University of Wisconsin-Madison) is Dean of the School of Communication at Hong Kong Baptist University. In 2006, he was named one of the Top 100 Chinese public intellectuals, voted by Internet users inside and outside of China. He is author of *Plight of Elections: A Critique of the World's Election Systems and Constitutional Reforms*, as well as articles on intercultural communication and mass communication. He has served as Director of the Center for Research in Journalism and Mass Communication at the University of North Carolina, Chapel Hill. His degrees are from Fudan University, Stanford University, and the University of Wisconsin-Madison.

About the Contributors

Silke Adam (Ph.D., University of Hohenheim) is Assistant Professor in the Institute of Communication and Media Studies at the University of Bern. In her research, she focuses on comparative political communication, media impact, European integration and identity, and empirical research methods. She is a former recipient of the Robert M. Worcester Prize, awarded by the World Association for Public Opinion Research, the annual article award of the German National Association of Communication Science, and the Dr. Alois-Mock Foundation Science Award.

Natalya N. Bazarova (Ph.D. Cornell University) is Assistant Professor in the Department of Communication at Cornell University. Her primary research interests lie at the intersection of interpersonal communication, social cognition, and technology. Some of her recent work has focused on how people assign attributions to communication behaviors, and, in return, how their attributions shape subsequent communication and interpersonal dynamics in computer-mediated social interaction. Her other research interests include small group behavior and decision-making, cross-cultural communication, and interpersonal relationships. She has received several best paper awards from national and international communication conferences for her work.

Susanna Dilliplane (M.A., University of Pennsylvania) is a doctoral candidate at the Annenberg School for Communication, University of Pennsylvania. Her primary research focus is political communication and its effects on political attitudes, knowledge, and behaviors, with a particular interest in the implications of expanded news and information choices.

Anthony Dudo (M.A., University of Delaware) is a doctoral candidate at the University of Wisconsin-Madison in the School of Journalism and Mass Communication. His research examines the intersection of science, media, and the public. He is particularly interested in media representations of science, health, and environmental issues; scientists' public communication activities and interactions with journalists; and the effects of informational and entertainment media on the public uptake of science. Some of his recent work has investigated factors influencing scientists' likelihood to interact with journalists, the effect of television entertainment programs on public perceptions of science, and media coverage of stem cell research, avian influenza, and nanotechnology.

Petya Eckler (Ph.D., University of Missouri) is Assistant Professor in the School of Journalism and Mass Communication at the University of Iowa with research interests in health communication, new media, international communicatio, and advertising. Her health-related work covers tobacco control and cessation, arthritis, cancer, and doctor-patient communication. Her research on new media and advertising focuses on electronic word-of-mouth communication, such as consumer reviews and viral advertising. Her international work includes surveys of international journalists, comparative content analyses, and experimental studies of international public health messages.

Cindy Gallois (Ph.D., University of Florida) is Professor in the Faculty of Social and Behavioural Sciences at the University of Queensland. She is a Fellow of the Academy of the Social Sciences in Australia, International Communication Association, Society of Experimental Social Psychology, and International Academy of Intercultural Relations. Her research interests encompass intergroup communication in health, intercultural, and organisational contexts, with major emphasis on communication accommodation. She has published more than 150 books, chapters, and articles; her research has been funded continuously by external agencies since 1987. She serves on the editorial boards of most major journals in her fields, and is past President of ICA, International Association for Language and Social Psychology, and Society of Australasian Social Psychologists. She has been supervisor for 39 successful PhD students.

Nurit Guttman (Ph.D., Rutgers University) is Head of the Herzog Institute of Media, Politics and Society in the Faculty of Social Sciences, and a faculty member in the Department of Communication at Tel Aviv University. Her research focuses on participatory approaches to social marketing, dissemination of rights information, citizen involvement in policy issues, and entertainment television for social change. Her areas of emphasis are health, road safety and the environment. She is a former recipient of the Distinguished Researcher Award from Tel Aviv University and a current member of Israel's National Council of Health Promotion. She is the author of *Public Health Communication Interventions: Values and Ethical Dilemmas.*

Ingunn Hagen (Ph.D., University of Bergen) is Professor in the Department of Psychology at the Norwegian University of Science and Technology, Trondheim. Her research includes audience reception studies, political communication, consumption of popular culture, and children, media and commercialization. She is on the editorial board of journals such as *Participation and European Journal of Cultural Studies.* Professor Hagen's authored and edited books include: *Mediegenerasjonen. Barn og unge i det nye medieland-skapet* (*The Media Generation. Children and Young People in the New Media Landscape*, with Thomas Wold); *Medias Publikum: Frå mottakar til brukar?* (*Media Audiences. From Receiver to User?*); and *Consuming Audiences: Production and Reception in Media Research*, edited with Janet Wasko. She has published articles in a number of books and journals, in English as well as Norwegian.

Jeffrey T. Hancock (Ph.D., Dalhousie University) is Director of Graduate Studies and Associate Professor in the Department of Communication at Cornell University. He is also Co-Director of Cognitive Science and a member of the Faculty of Computing and Information Science. His work is concerned with how communication technologies affect the way we understand and relate to one another, with a particular emphasis on deception. His research is supported by funding from the National Science Foundation.

Matthew J. Hornsey (Ph.D., University of Queensland) is Associate Professor in the School of Psychology at the University of Queensland. Since graduating in 1999, he has published more than 60 papers on topics related to group processes, intergroup relations, and intergroup communication. His research primarily focuses on the tension between individual and group will, and the conditions under which people are willing and able to challenge the status quo. He is on the editorial boards of 6 journals and has received 16 grants, 6 of which are from the Australian Research Council. He is currently Associate Dean for Research in the Faculty of Social and Behavioural Sciences.

Yusuf Kalyango, Jr. (Ph.D., University of Missouri) is Director of the Institute for International Journalism in the E. W. Scripps School of Journalism at Ohio University. His research focuses on comparative political communication, media and democratization, and international crises, for which he has won three AEJMC and ICA awards. He is a former correspondent for CNN International's *Inside Africa*, and recipient of more than ten international journalism awards from three continents. He teaches broadcast news, international journalism, international media systems, and a graduate seminar in media and politics. He is currently working on his first academic book, *African Media and Democratization*, which is a survey-based study covering ten Eastern and Southern African countries.

Sahar Khamis (Ph.D., University of Manchester) is Assistant Professor in the Department of Communication at the University of Maryland, College Park. She is the former Head of the Mass Communication Department in Qatar University and an expert on Arab and Middle Eastern media. She is co-author (with Mohammed el-Nawawy) of *Islam Dot Com: Contemporary Islamic*

Discourses in Cyberspace, and author of chapters in *Women and Media in the Middle East: Power Through Self-Expression* and *New Media and the New Middle East*. She has published in English and Arabic academic journals and is a member of several editorial boards.

Natalya Krasnoboka (M.A., University of Amsterdam) is a doctoral candidate at the University of Antwerp, Belgium. In 2009, she was a Visiting Fellow at the Davis Center for Russian and Eurasian Studies, Harvard University. Her research interests include: effects of social and political change on media institutions in post-Soviet societies; and comparative analysis of media systems in non-democratic societies.

Timothy R. Levine (Ph.D., Michigan State University) is Professor of Communication at Michigan State University. Levine's research interests are diverse and include deception and deception detection, persuasion, communication in personal relationships, cross-cultural communication, measurement validation, and statistical conclusions validity. Levine has previously published over 100 articles and chapters on these topics. His research on deception is currently funded by the National Science Foundation.

Fadoua Loudiy (Ph.D., Duquesne University) is a faculty member in the Department of Communication at Slippery Rock University. Her research focuses on the rhetoric of transitional justice and democratization in the Middle East and North Africa, communication ethics, intercultural and international communication, and the philosophy of Paul Ricoeur. In 2006–2007, Dr. Loudiy was the recipient of a fellowship from the Center for Interpretive & Qualitative Research (CIQR), at Duquesne University. She is co-author of "Testing the Red Lines: On the Liberalization of Speech in Morocco," in *Human Rights Quarterly*, and author of "Narrative Identity and Public Memory in Morocco," in *Philosophies of Communication: Implications for Everyday Experience*. She is co-author, with Andrew R. Smith, of *Sanctifying Speech as a Rule of Law: Rhetorics of Authority and Resistance in Morocco* (in press).

Michaela Maier (Ph.D., Friedrich Schiller University of Jena) is Professor at the Institute for Communication Psychology, Media Pedagogics and Speech at the University of Koblenz-Landau, Germany. Her research focuses on political communication with a specific interest in the reception and effects of campaign communication. She has written or edited several books such as *Campaigning in Europe — Campaigning for Europe* (with Jens Tenscher); *Schröder vs Merkel. Perception and Effect of the Televised Debate 2005 in East and West Germany* (with Markus Maurer, Carsten Reinemann and Jürgen Maier), and *Audience-Response-Measurement in the Social Sciences* (with Jürgen Maier, Markus Maurer, Carsten Reinemann, and Vincent Meyer).

Robin Mansell (Ph.D., Simon Fraser University) is Professor of New Media and the Internet in the Department of Media and Communications, London School of Economics and Political Science, where she also has served as Head of the Department and Director of Graduate Studies. Her research focuses on the social, political, and economic aspects of older and newer communication technologies and on their policy and regulatory implications. She is author or editor of numerous books including *The Information Society — Critical Studies in Sociology*, and author of more than 100 articles focusing both on the political economy and sociology of media and communication. She is a former president of the International Association for Media and Communication Research.

Ronald E. Rice (Ph.D., Stanford University) is the Arthur N. Rupe Chair in the Social Effects of Mass Communication in the Department of Communication, and Co-Director of the Carsey-Wolf Center for Film, Television, and New Media, at the University of California, Santa Barbara. Dr. Rice has held the positions of President of ICA, Fulbright Scholar in Finland, and Visiting Professor in Singapore. He has co-authored, edited, or co-edited: *Organizations and Unusual Routines: A Systems Analysis of Dysfunctional Feedback Processes*; *Media Ownership: Research and Regulation*; *The Internet and Health Care: Theory, Research and Practice*; *Social Consequences of Internet Use: Access, Involvement and Interaction*; *The Internet and Health Communication; Accessing and Browsing Information and Communication*; *Public Communication Campaigns*; *Research Methods and the New Media*; *Managing Organizational Innovation*; and *The New Media: Communication, Research and Technology*.

Dietram A. Scheufele (Ph.D., University of Wisconsin-Madison) is the John E. Ross Chaired Professor and Director of Graduate Studies in the Department of Life Sciences Communication at the University of Wisconsin-Madison, and Co-Principal Investigator of the Center for Nanotechnology in Society at Arizona State University. Scheufele's current work deals with the intersection of science, politics, and society and has been recognized with the Robert M. Worcester Award and the Naomi C. Turner Prize from the World Association for Public Opinion Research, the Young Scholar Award for outstanding early career research from the International Communication Association, the Young Faculty Teaching Excellence Award from the College of Agriculture and Life Sciences at Cornell University, and the Pound Research Award from the College of Agricultural & Life Sciences at the University of Wisconsin-Madison.

Vít Šisler (M.A., Charles University) is a doctoral candidate at Charles University in Prague, where he is finishing his thesis on new media, the Internet, and production of contemporary Islamic knowledge. In 2008–2009, he was a visiting Fulbright Scholar at the Buffett Center for International and

Comparative Studies at Northwestern University. He is founder and editor-in-chief of Digital Islam, a compound research project on Islam, the Middle East and digital media (digitalislam.eu).

Barbie Zelizer (Ph.D., University of Pennsylvania) is Professor and Raymond Williams Chair of Communication and Director of the Scholars Program in Culture and Communication in the Annenberg School for Communication at the University of Pennsylvania. Her work focuses on the cultural dimensions of journalism, with a specific interest in journalistic authority, collective memory, and journalistic images in times of crisis and war. She is co-editor and founder of the journal, *Journalism: Theory, Practice, and Criticism*, and has served on numerous editorial boards. Currently the President of the International Communication Association, Dr. Zelizer has been a Guggenheim Fellow, a Research Fellow at the Freedom Forum Media Studies Center, a Fellow at Harvard University's Joan Shorenstein Center on the Press, Politics, and Public Policy, and a Fulbright Senior Scholar.

Author Index

Forest, P, 182
Forester, J., 172, 173, 175
Forsyth, D. R., 76
Fossato, F., 325, 326, 333, 334, 335
Foster, F. H., 329
Foucault, M., 22
Fox, S., 22
Fraenkel, E., 240
Frank, M. G., 47, 50
Franklin, A., 375
Fransen, M. L., 97, 123
Franz, M., 240
Frasca, G., 300, 301
Fraser, N., 284, 304, 305, 307
Freedman, P., 240, 241
Freedom House, 333, 334, 375
Freeman, M., 403
Freimuth, V. S., 123
Frère, M. S., 370, 375, 376
Frey, S., 146
Friedman, S. M., 52
Friedrich, C. J., 320, 321
Friesen, W. V., 45
Frohardt, M., 374
Fuchs, D., 217, 221, 222
Fung, A., 169, 170, 171, 174, 178, 184,
    185, 186, 204, 205, 206
Funkhouser, G. R., 150

G
Gable, S., 4
Gaborit, N, 205
Gabriel, O. W., 216, 219, 222, 227, 228,
    230, 231, 233
Gahama, J., 362, 369
Gaither, C., 24
Galasinski, D., 79
Gallois, C., 133
Galtung, J., 231
Gamson, W. A., 240, 266
Gandy, O., 22, 23
Gans, H. J., 156
Gantwerk, H., 205
Gaskell, G., 152
Gastil, J., 151, 170, 171, 173, 178, 179,
    184, 185, 191, 204, 205, 241
Gaudet, H., 160
Gaunt, P., 322
Geldart, A., 145
Genz, A., 219, 226
Gerber, M. M., 8
Gerbner, G., 150, 157
Gergen, K., 4
Gerhards, J., 239, 240

Gerhrard, J., 266
Gharbeia, A., 297
Gher, L. A., 285, 286
Giammanco, C. A., 76
Gibbs, J. L., 77, 323
Gilbert, D. T., 54
Gilens, M., 224, 225, 227
Ginsburg, G., 67
Gitlin, T., 156
Gladarev, B., 29
Glasser, T. L., 176
Global Deception Research Team, The,
    46, 55
Glotz, P., 5
Goban-Klas, T., 322
Godbold, L. C., 123
Goffman, E., 11, 157
Goggin, G., 3
Goldberg, J. H., 115
Goldenberg, J. L., 94, 95, 96, 98, 99, 108,
    111, 112, 115, 123, 124, 135
Goldstein, A., 358
Goldstein, K., 240
Goode, L., 274, 280, 285, 287
Goodin, R. E., 171
Goorha, S., 80
Goplen, J., 123
Gopnik, A., 74
Gorny, E., 333
Goroshko, O., 333
Gorss, J., 152, 267
Gourevitch, P., 361
Grabe, M. E., 222, 225, 230, 233
Graber, D. A., 225, 233, 240
Gräf, B., 290
Graner, J., 216
Granhag, P. A., 47, 52, 57, 59
Gray, R., 363
Green, N., 6, 11, 17, 18, 20
Greenberg, J. L., 95, 96, 97, 113, 114
Greenberg, J., 94, 95, 96, 97, 98, 99, 108,
    109, 114, 116, 121, 122, 123, 124
Green-Pedersen, C., 226
Greger, V., 216
Gregory, O., 152
Grice, H. P., 71, 79
Griffin, R. J., 64
Griffith, W. E., 320, 336
Grinter, R. E., 8, 12, 14, 18
Gronbeck, B. E., 219
Gross, E., 4
Gross, K., 64, 78
Gross, L., 150, 157
Grosswiler, P., 370

Subject Index

Page numbers in italic refer to figures or tables.